W9-CCL-263

ECLECTIC EDUCATIONAL SERIES.

M^CGUFFEY'S®

THIRD

ECLECTIC READER.

REVISED EDITION.

McGuffey Editions and Colophon are Trademarks of

JOHN WILEY & SONS, INC.
NEW YORK · CHICHESTER · WEINHEIM · BRISBANE · SINGAPORE · TORONTO

PREFACE.

THE long-continued popularity of McGUFFEY'S READERS is sufficient evidence of the positive merits of the books. The aim of this revision has been to preserve unimpaired the distinctive features of the series, and at the same time to present the matter in a new dress, with new type, new illustrations, and with a considerable amount of new matter.

Spelling exercises are continued through the first half of the THIRD READER. These exercises, with those furnished in the two lower books, are exhaustive of the words employed in the reading lessons. Words are not repeated in the vocabularies.

In the latter half of the book, definitions are introduced. It is hoped that the teacher will extend this defining exercise to all the words of the lesson liable to be misunderstood. The child should define the word in his own language sufficiently to show that he has a mastery of the word in its use.

Drills in articulation and emphasis should be given with every lesson. The essentials of good reading are not to be taught by one or two lessons. Constant drill on good exercises, with frequent exhibitions of the correct method from the teacher, will be found more effectual than any form prescribed in type.

If the pupils are not familiar with the diacritical marks, they should be carefully taught; such instruction constitutes an excellent drill on articulation, and enables the pupils to use the dictionary with intelligence.

Copyright, 1879, by VAN ANTWERP, BRAGG & Co.
Copyright, 1896, by AMERICAN BOOK COMPANY.
Copyright, 1907 and 1920, by H. H. VAIL.

M'G. 3D 8O REV.

EP 308

CONTENTS

iv CONTENTS.

INTRODUCTION.

ARTICULATION.

A distinct articulation can only be gained by constant and careful practice of the elementary sounds.

Whenever a word is imperfectly enunciated, the teacher should call attention to the *sounds* composing the spoken word.

If the pupil fails to sound any element correctly, as in the case of lisping, the fault can be overcome by calling attention to the correct position of the organs of speech, and insisting upon exact execution. Except in case of malformation of these organs, every pupil should sound each element correctly before such drill should cease.

TABLE OF VOCALS.

LONG SOUNDS.

ā,	as in	āte.	ẽ,	as in	ẽrr.
â,	"	eâre.	ī,	"	īçe.
ä,	"	ärm.	ō,	"	ōde.
ȧ,	"	lȧst.	ū,	"	tūne.
a̤,	"	a̤ll.	û,	"	bûrn.
ē,	"	ēve.	ōō,	"	fōōl.

SHORT SOUNDS.

ă, as in ăm.		ŏ, as in ŏdd.
ĕ, " ĕlm.		ŭ, " ŭp.
ĭ, " ĭn.		o͝o, " lo͝ok.

DIPHTHONGS.

oi, as in oil. | ou, as in out.

TABLE OF SUBVOCALS.

b, as in bĭb.	v, as in vălve.
d, " dĭd.	th, " thĭs.
g, " ḡĭḡ.	z, " zĭn̠e.
j, " jŭḡ.	z, " ăzure.
n, " nīne.	r, " râre.
m, " māim.	w, " wē.
ng, " hăng.	y, " yĕt.

l, as in lŭll.

TABLE OF ASPIRATES.

f, as in fīfe.	t, as in tärt.
h, " hĭm.	sh, " shē.
k, " eāke.	ch, " chăt.
p, " pīpe.	th, " thĭck.
s, " sāme.	wh, " whȳ.

NOTE.—The above forty-five sounds are those most employed in the English language. Some of these sounds are represented by other letters, as shown in the following table.

TABLE OF SUBSTITUTES.

ạ,	for	ŏ,	as in	whạt.	y̆,	for	ĭ,	as in	my̆th.
ê,	"	â,	"	thêre.	ᴇ,	"	k,	"	ᴇăn.
ẹ,	"	ā̆,	"	fẹint.	ç,	"	s,	"	çīte.
ï,	"	ē,	"	polïçe.	çh,	"	sh,	"	çhāiṣe.
ĩ,	"	ẽ,	"	sĩr.	ᴇh,	"	ᴋ,	"	ᴇhāos.
ȯ,	"	ŭ,	"	sȯn.	ġ,	"	j,	"	ġĕm.
ọ,	"	o͞o,	"	tọ.	ṋ,	"	ng,	"	ĭṋk.
o̤,	"	o̯o,	"	wo̤lf.	ṣ,	"	z,	"	ăṣ.
ô,	"	ạ,	"	fôrk.	s,	"	sh,	"	s̤ure.
õ,	"	û,	"	wõrk.	x̱,	"	g̱z,	"	ĕx̱ăᴇt.
ụ,	"	o͞o,	"	fụll.	gh,	"	f,	"	läugh.
u̱,	"	o͞o,	"	ru̱de.	ph,	"	f,	"	phlŏx.
ȳ,	"	ī,	"	flȳ.	qu,	"	k,	"	pïque.

qu, for kw, as in quĭt.

EXERCISES IN ARTICULATION.

The following exercises may be used for drill after the tables are fully understood. Pronounce the word first; then, the sound indicated.

EXERCISE I.

ā—āte,	fāte.		ē—mē,	shē.
ă—ăt,	hăt.		ĕ—mĕt,	wĕll.
â—câre,	snâre.		ẽ—hẽr,	jẽrk.
ä—ärm,	bärn.		ī—īçe,	kīte.
ȧ—ȧsk,	pȧst.		ĭ—ĭn,	bĭt.
a̤—a̤ll,	qua̤rt.		ī—sīr,	fīrm.

EXERCISE II.

ō—gō,	ōde.		ô—nôr,	môrn.
ŏ—hŏt,	plŏt.		ū—ūse,	tūne.
o̤—do̤,	mo̤ve.		ŭ—ŭs,	tŭb.
ȯ—sȯn,	dȯne.		ṳ—pṳt,	pṳll.
o̤—wo̤lf,	wo̤man.		û—bûrn,	ûrġe.

EXERCISE III.

o͞o—fo͞ol,	mo͞on.		b—bābe,	Bīble.
o͝o—ġo͝od,	fo͝ot.		d—dĭd,	dăndy.
oi—oil,	boil.		f—ĭf,	fīfe.
oy—toy,	joy.		ġ—ġăġ,	ġīġ.
ou—out,	loud.		h—hĭt,	how.
ow—now,	owl.		j—jāy,	lärġe.

EXERCISE IV.

k	—kīte,	eăn.	s —săuçe.	rīçe.
l	—lăd,	pĭll.	t —tăt,	tōtal.
m	—mä'am,	mŭm.	v —văn,	lóve.
n	—ĭn,	nīne.	w —wĭn,	wīde.
p	—ăpple,	pīpe.	y —yĕs,	yọu.
r	—râre,	rōar.	z —sīze,	wĭṣe.

EXERCISE V.

Bl	—blāde,	blĕd.	Dw—dwĕll,	dwạrf.
Br	—brăd,	brīde.	Fl —flăt,	flee.
Bs	—rŏbṣ,	fĭbṣ.	Fr —frāme,	frȳ.
Ch	—chăt,	rĭch.	Fs —mŭffs,	läughs.
Dl	—lādle,	săddle.	Gl —ḡlăd,	ḡlīde.
Dr	—drăb,	drōne.	Gr —ḡreāt,	ḡrōw.
Ds	—rĭdṣ,	bŭdṣ.	Kn —knee,	knōw.

EXERCISE VI.

Pl	—plāte,	plŏt.	Sq —squạt,	squĭrm.
Pr	—prāy,	prōne.	St —stănd,	stōne.
Sh	—shăll,	çhāiṣe.	Sw —swạrm,	swĭm.
Sl	—slăp,	slōw.	Th —thĭck,	thĭn.
Sm	—smärt,	smīte.	Th —thīne,	wĭth.
Sn	—snâre,	snōw.	Tw —twīçe,	twĕnty
Sp	—spĭn,	spoil.	Wh—whĕn,	whĭch

EMPHASIS.

NOTE.--If the pupil has received proper oral instruction, he has been taught to *understand* what he has read, and has already acquired the *habit* of emphasizing words. He is now prepared for a more formal introduction to the SUBJECT of emphasis, and for more particular attention to its first PRINCIPLES. This lesson, and the examples given, should be repeatedly practiced.

In reading and in talking, we always speak some words with more force than others. We do this, because the meaning of what we say depends most upon these words.

If I wish to know whether it is George or his brother who is sick, I speak the words *George* and *brother* with more force than the other words. I say, Is it *George* or his *brother* who is sick?

This greater force with which we speak the words is called EMPHASIS.

The words upon which emphasis is put, are sometimes printed in slanting letters, called *Italics,** and sometimes in CAPITALS.

The words printed in Italics in the following questions and answers, should be read with more force than the other words, that is, with emphasis.

Did *you* ride to town yesterday? No, my *brother* did.

Did you *ride* to town yesterday? No, I *walked.*

Italics are also used for other purposes, though most frequently for emphasis.

Did you ride to *town* yesterday? No, I went into the *country*.

Did you ride to town *yesterday?* No, I went *the day before.*

Have you seen *James* or *John* lately? I have seen *James,* but not *John.*

Did you say there were *four* eggs in the nest, or *three?* There were only *three* eggs, not *four.*

Were the eggs *white* or *blue?* The eggs were *white,* not *blue.*

Had the boy a *hat* on his head, or a *cap?* He had a *cap* on, not a *hat.*

PUNCTUATION.

☞ PUNCTUATION should be thoroughly studied by the pupil, in order that he may become perfectly familiar with the marks and pauses found in the reading lessons of this volume.

MARKS AND PAUSES.

These marks are used to point off written or printed matter into sentences and parts of sentences, and thus to assist the reader in obtaining the meaning of the writer. They seldom indicate the length of the pause to be made; this must be determined by the sense.

A **Hyphen** (-) is used between syllables in a word divided at the end of a line; as, " be-cause," "ques-tion," page 10, and between the parts of a compound word; as,

Rocking-chair, good-by.

The **Comma** (,), **Semicolon** (;), and **Colon** (:) mark grammatical divisions in a sentence; as,

> God is good; for he gives us all things.
> Be wise to-day, my child: 't is madness to defer.

A **Period** (.) is placed at the end of a sentence; as,

> God is love. Life is short.

Or is used after an abbreviation; as,

> Dr. Murphy. Jan. 10, 1879.

An **Interrogation Point** (?) denotes a question; as,

> Has he come? Who are you?

An **Exclamation Point** (!) denotes strong feeling; as,

> O Absalom! my son! my son!

The **Dash** (—) is used where there is a sudden break or pause in a sentence; as,

The truth has power—such is God's will—to make us better.

Quotation Marks (" ") denote the words of another; as,

> God said, "Let there be light."

An **Apostrophe** (') denotes that a letter or letters are left out; as,

> O'er, for over; 't is, for it is.

And is also used to show ownership; as,

> The man's hat. Helen's book.

THIRD READER.

LESSON I.

| ēi'ther | trĭe'kle | făn'çied | mûr'mur | re flĕet'ed |
| ḡlŏss'y | ĕn'tered | shĕp'herd | chĕst'nuts | eom mánd' |

THE SHEPHERD BOY.

1. Little Roy led his sheep down to pasture,
   And his cows, by the side of the brook;

(13)

But his cows never drank any water,
   And his sheep never needed a crook.

2. For the pasture was gay as a garden,
   And it glowed with a flowery red;
But the meadows had never a grass blade,
   And the brooklet—it slept in its bed:

3. And it lay without sparkle or murmur,
   Nor reflected the blue of the skies;
But the music was made by the shepherd,
   And the sparkle was all in his eyes.

4. Oh, he sang like a bird in the summer!
   And, if sometimes you fancied a bleat,
That, too, was the voice of the shepherd,
   And not of the lambs at his feet.

5. And the glossy brown cows were so gentle
   That they moved at the touch of his hand
O'er the wonderful, rosy-red meadow,
   And they stood at the word of command.

6. So he led all his sheep to the pasture,
   And his cows, by the side of the brook;
Though it rained, yet the rain never pattered
   O'er the beautiful way that they took.

7. And it was n't in Fairyland either,
   But a house in the midst of the town,
Where Roy, as he looked from the window,
   Saw the silvery drops trickle down.

8. For his pasture was only a table,
      With its cover so flowery fair,
   And his brooklet was just a green ribbon,
      That his sister had lost from her hair.

9. And his cows were but glossy horse-chestnuts,
      That had grown on his grandfather's tree;
   And his sheep only snowy-white pebbles,
      He had brought from the shore of the sea.

10. And at length when the shepherd was weary,
       And had taken his milk and his bread,
    And his mother had kissed him and tucked him,
       And had bid him " good night " in his bed;

11. Then there entered his big brother Walter,
       While the shepherd was soundly asleep,
    And he cut up the cows into baskets,
       And to jackstones turned all of the sheep.

Emily S. Oakey.

LESSON II.

eoŭn'try	ḡrōveṣ	loṣ'ing	sūḡ'ar	freez'eṣ

JOHNNY'S FIRST SNOWSTORM.

1. Johnny Reed was a little boy who never had seen a snowstorm till he was six years old. Before this, he had lived in a warm country, where the sun shines down on beautiful

orange groves, and fields always sweet with flowers.

2. But now he had come to visit his grandmother, who lived where the snow falls in winter. Johnny was standing at the window when the snow came down.

3. "O mamma!" he cried, joyfully, "do come quick, and see these little white birds flying down from heaven."

4. "They are not birds, Johnny," said mamma, smiling.

5. "Then maybe the little angels are losing their feathers! Oh! do tell me what it is; is it sugar? Let me taste it," said

Johnny. But when he tasted it, he gave a little jump—it was so cold.

6. "That is only snow, Johnny," said his mother.

7. "What is snow, mother?"

8. "The snowflakes, Johnny, are little drops of water that fall from the clouds. But the air through which they pass is so cold it freezes them, and they come down turned into snow."

9. As she said this, she brought out an old black hat from the closet. "See, Johnny! I have caught a snowflake on this hat. Look quick through this glass, and you will see how beautiful it is."

10. Johnny looked through the glass. There lay the pure, feathery snowflake like a lovely little star.

11. "Twinkle, twinkle, little star!" he cried in delight. "Oh! please show me more snow-flakes, mother."

12. So his mother caught several more, and they were all beautiful.

13. The next day Johnny had a fine play in the snow, and when he came in, he said, "I love snow; and I think snowballs are a great deal prettier than oranges."

LESSON III.

daugh'ter   quĕnch   wrēathş   bŭt'ter   thîrst'y

LET IT RAIN.

Rose. See how it rains! Oh dear, dear, dear! how dull it is! Must I stay in doors all day?

Father. Why, Rose, are you sorry that you had any bread and butter for breakfast, this morning?

Rose. Why, father, what a question! I should be sorry, indeed, if I could not get any.

Father. Are you sorry, my daughter, when you see the flowers and the trees growing in the garden?

Rose. Sorry? No, indeed. Just now, I wished very much to go out and see them, —they look so pretty.

Father. Well, are you sorry when you see the horses, cows, or sheep drinking at the brook to quench their thirst?

Rose. Why, father, you must think I am a cruel girl, to wish that the poor horses that work so hard, the beautiful cows that give so much nice milk, and the pretty lambs should always be thirsty.

Father. Do you not think they would die, if they had no water to drink?

Rose. Yes, sir, I am sure they would. How shocking to think of such a thing!

Father. I thought little Rose was sorry it rained. Do you think the trees and flowers would grow, if they never had any water on them?

Rose. No, indeed, father, they would be dried up by the sun. Then we should not have any pretty flowers to look at, and to make wreaths of for mother.

Father. I thought you were sorry it rained. Rose, what is our bread made of?

Rose. It is made of flour, and the flour is made from wheat, which is ground in the mill.

Father. Yes, Rose, and it was rain that helped to make the wheat grow, and it was water that turned the mill to grind the wheat. I thought little Rose was sorry it rained.

Rose. I did not think of all these things, father. I am truly very glad to see the rain falling.

LESSON IV.

ăn'ḡer	eăs'tle	foun dā'tion	răt'tling	tow'er
dis māy'	sō'fä	ĭn'ter ĕst ed	păs'sion	pīle
mĭm'ie	nŏd'ded	ex elāimed'	ạl rĕad'y	spĭlled

CASTLE-BUILDING.

1. "O pussy!" cried Herbert, in a voice of anger and dismay, as the blockhouse he was building fell in sudden ruin. The playful cat had rubbed against his mimic castle,

and tower and wall went rattling down upon the floor.

2. Herbert took up one of the blocks and threw it fiercely at pussy. Happily, it passed over her and did no harm. His hand was reaching for another block, when his little sister Hetty sprang toward the cat, and caught her up.

3. "No, no, no!" said she, "you sha'n't hurt pussy! She did n't mean to do it!"

4. Herbert's passion was over quickly, and, sitting down upon the floor, he covered his face with his hands, and began to cry.

5. "What a baby!" said Joe, his elder brother, who was reading on the sofa. "Crying over spilled milk does no good. Build it up again."

6. "No, I wo n't," said Herbert, and he went on crying.

7. "What's all the trouble here?" exclaimed papa, as he opened the door and came in.

8. "Pussy just rubbed against Herbert's castle, and it fell down," answered Hetty. "But she did n't mean to do it; she did n't know it would fall, did she, papa?"

9. "Why, no! And is that all the trouble?"

10. "Herbert!" his papa called, and held out his hands. "Come." The little boy got up from the floor, and came slowly, his eyes full of tears, and stood by his father.

11. "There is a better way than this, my boy," said papa. "If you had taken that way, your heart would have been light already. I should have heard you singing over your blocks instead of crying. Shall I show you that way?"

12. Herbert nodded his head, and papa sat down on the floor by the pile of blocks, with his little son by his side, and began to lay the foundation for a new castle.

LESSON V.

strĭng	pā′per	ĕa′ḡer ly	dăshed	eāse
erăsh	dĭsh′eṣ	re tôrt′ed	sĕn′tençe	trāy

CASTLE-BUILDING.

(CONCLUDED.)

1. Soon, Herbert was as much interested in castle-building as he had been a little while before. He began to sing over his work. All his trouble was gone.

2. "This is a great deal better than crying, is n't it?" said papa.

3. "Crying for what?" asked Herbert, forgetting his grief of a few minutes before.

4. "Because pussy knocked your castle over."

5. "Oh!" A shadow flitted across his face, but was gone in a moment, and he went on building as eagerly as ever.

6. "I told him not to cry over spilled milk," said Joe, looking down from his place on the sofa.

7. "I wonder if you did n't cry when your kite string broke," retorted Herbert.

8. "Losing a kite is quite another thing," answered Joe, a little dashed. "The kite was gone forever; but your blocks were as good as before, and you had only to build again."

9. "I do n't see," said papa, "that crying was of any more use in your case than in Herbert's. Sticks and paper are easily found, and you had only to go to work and make another kite." Joe looked down at his book, and went on reading. By this time the castle was finished.

10. "It is ever so much nicer than the one

pussy knocked down," said Hetty. And so thought Herbert, as he looked at it proudly from all sides.

11. "If pussy knocks that down, I'll—"

12. "Build it up again," said papa, finishing the sentence for his little boy.

13. "But, papa, pussy must not knock my castles down. I can't have it," spoke out Herbert, knitting his forehead.

14. "You must watch her, then. Little boys, as well as grown up people, have to be often on their guard. If you go into the street, you have to look out for the carriages, so as not to be run over, and you have to keep out of people's way.

15. "In the house, if you go about heedlessly, you will be very apt to run against some one. I have seen a careless child dash suddenly into a room just as a servant was leaving it with a tray of dishes in her hands. A crash followed."

16. "It was I, was n't it?" said Hetty.

17. "Yes, I believe it was, and I hope it will never happen again."

18. Papa now left the room, saying, "I do n't want any more of this crying over spilled milk, as Joe says. If your castles get knocked down, build them up again."

LESSON VI.

teâr	dāi′ly	hŏn′or	tȯngueş	sus pĭ′cion
ĕn′vy	fōrçed	prŏmpt	ma lĭ′cioŭs	to-mŏr′row

LEND A HAND.

I.

Lend a hand to one another
In the daily toil of life;
When we meet a weaker brother,
Let us help him in the strife.
There is none so rich but may,
In his turn, be forced to borrow;
And the poor man's lot to-day
May become our own to-morrow.

2.

Lend a hand to one another:
When malicious tongues have thrown
Dark suspicion on your brother,
Be not prompt to cast a stone.
There is none so good but may
Run adrift in shame and sorrow.
And the good man of to-day
May become the bad to-morrow.

3.

Lend a hand to one another:
In the race for Honor's crown;
Should it fall upon your brother.
Let not envy tear it down.
Lend a hand to all, we pray,
In their sunshine or their sorrow;
And the prize they've won to-day
May become our own to-morrow

LESSON VII.

fa̱lse′ly	at tĕnd′	trṵ′ant	eŏn′duet	thêre′fŏre
ḡuïlt′y	hāste	rĕḡ′u lar	strŭḡ′gled	ĭḡ′no rant

THE TRUANT.

1. James Brown was ten years old when his parents sent him to school. It was not far from his home, and therefore they sent him by himself.

2. But, instead of going to school, he was in the habit of playing truant. He would go into the fields, or spend his time with idle boys.

3. But this was not all. When he went home, he would falsely tell his mother that he had been to school, and had said his lessons very well.

4. One fine morning, his mother told James to make haste home from school, for she wished, after he had come back, to take him to his aunt's.

5. But, instead of minding her, he went off to the water, where there were some boats. There he met plenty of idle boys.

6. Some of these boys found that James

had money, which his aunt had given him; and he was led by them to hire a boat, and to go with them upon the water.

7. Little did James think of the danger into which he was running. Soon the wind began to blow, and none of them knew how to manage the boat.

8. For some time, they struggled against the wind and the tide. At last, they became so tired that they could row no longer.

9. A large wave upset the boat, and they were all thrown into the water. Think of James Brown, the truant, at this time!

10. He was far from home, known by no one. His parents were ignorant of his danger.

He was struggling in the water, on the point of being drowned.

11. Some men, however, saw the boys, and went out to them in a boat. They reached them just in time to save them from a watery grave.

12. They were taken into a house, where their clothes were dried. After a while, they were sent home to their parents.

13. James was very sorry for his conduct, and he was never known to be guilty of the same thing again.

14. He became regular at school, learned to attend to his books, and, above all, to obey his parents perfectly.

LESSON VIII.

stroke   bĕg'gar   strēaks   need'fŭl   eoun'sel

THE WHITE KITTEN.

1. My little white kitten 's asleep on my knee;
    As white as the snow or the lilies is she;
       She wakes up with a pur
       When I stroke her soft fur:
    Was there ever another white kitten like her?

2. My little white kitten now wants to go out
   And frolic, with no one to watch her about;
     "Little kitten," I say,
     "Just an hour you may stay,
   And be careful in choosing your places to play."

3. But night has come down, when I hear a loud "mew;"
   I open the door, and my kitten comes through;
     My white kitten! ah me!
     Can it really be she—
   This ill-looking, beggar-like cat that I see?

4. What ugly, gray streaks on her side and her back!
   Her nose, once as pink as a rosebud, is black!
     Oh, I very well know,
     Though she does not say so,
   She has been where white kittens ought never to go.

5. If little good children intend to do right,
　　If little white kittens would keep themselves white,
　　　　It is needful that they
　　　　Should this counsel obey,
　　And be careful in choosing their places to play.

LESSON IX.

pre fēr′	trăp′per	fôr′ward	ma tē′ri al	dis tûrb′ing
dŭmb	chiēf′ly	gnąw′ing	A mĕr′ĭ eȧ	eąu′tioŭs ly
heīght	pûr′pȯse	tīght′er	re mīnd′ed	frē′quent ly
ob tāin′	eū′ri oŭs	in hū′man	in elūd′ing	eon strŭet′ed

THE BEAVER.

1. The beaver is found chiefly in North America. It is about three and a half feet long, including the flat, paddle-shaped tail, which is a foot in length.

2. The long, shining hair on the back is chestnut-colored, while the fine, soft fur that lies next the skin, is grayish brown.

3. Beavers build themselves most curious huts to live in, and quite frequently a great number of these huts are placed close together, like the buildings in a town.

4. They always build their huts on the banks of rivers or lakes, for they swim much

more easily than they walk, and prefer moving about in the water.

5. When they build on the bank of a running stream, they make a dam across the stream for the purpose of keeping the water at the height they wish.

6. These dams are made chiefly of mud, and stones, and the branches of trees. They are sometimes six or seven hundred feet in length, and are so constructed that they look more like the work of man than of little dumb beasts.

7. Their huts are made of the same material as the dams, and are round in shape. The walls are very thick, and the roofs are finished off with a thick layer of mud, sticks, and leaves.

8. They commence building their houses late in the summer, but do not get them finished before the early frosts. The freezing makes them tighter and stronger.

9. They obtain the wood for their dams and huts by gnawing through the branches of trees, and even through the trunks of small ones, with their sharp front teeth. They peel off the bark, and lay it up in store for winter food.

10. The fur of the beaver is highly prized. The men who hunt these animals are called trappers.

11. A gentleman once saw five young beavers playing. They would leap on the trunk of a tree that lay near a beaver dam, and would push one another off into the water.

12. He crept forward very cautiously, and was about to fire on the little creatures; but their amusing tricks reminded him so much of some little children he knew at home, that he thought it would be inhuman to kill them. So he left them without even disturbing their play.

3, 3.

LESSON X.

sign	märks	pär′çels	vĕn′ture	in quīre′
chȧlk	rụl′ing	drạw′ing	pĭe′tureṣ	eon fūṣed′

THE YOUNG TEACHER.

1. Charles Rose lived in the country with his father, who taught him to read and to write.

2. Mr. Rose told his son that, when his morning lessons were over, he might amuse himself for one hour as he pleased.

3. There was a river near by. On its bank stood the hut of a poor fisherman, who lived by selling fish.

4. His careful wife kept her wheel going early and late. They both worked very hard to keep themselves above want.

5. But they were greatly troubled lest their only son should never learn to read and to write. They could not teach him themselves, and they were too poor to send him to school.

6. Charles called at the hut of this fisherman one day, to inquire about his dog, which was missing.

7. He found the little boy, whose name was Joe, sitting by the table, on which he was making marks with a piece of chalk.

Charles asked him whether he was drawing pictures.

8. "No, I am trying to write," said little Joe, "but I know only two words. Those I saw upon a sign, and I am trying to write them."

9. "If I could only learn to read and write," said he, "I should be the happiest boy in the world."

10. "Then I will make you happy," said Charles. "I am only a little boy, but I can teach you that.

11. "My father gives me an hour every day for myself. Now, if you will try to learn, you shall soon know how to read and to write."

12. Both Joe and his mother were ready to fall on their knees to thank Charles. They told him it was what they wished above all things.

13. So, on the next day when the hour came, Charles put his book in his pocket, and went to teach Joe. Joe learned very fast, and Charles soon began to teach him how to write.

14. Some time after, a gentleman called on Mr. Rose, and asked him if he knew where Charles was. Mr. Rose said that he was taking a walk, he supposed.

15. "I am afraid," said the gentleman, "that he does not always amuse himself thus. I often see him go to the house of the fisherman. I fear he goes out in their boat."

16. Mr. Rose was much troubled. He had told Charles that he must never venture

on the river, and he thought he could trust him.

17. The moment the gentleman left, Mr. Rose went in search of his son. He went to the river, and walked up and down, in hope of seeing the boat.

18. Not seeing it, he grew uneasy. He thought Charles must have gone a long way off. Unwilling to leave without learning something of him, he went to the hut.

19. He put his head in at the window, which was open. There a pleasant sight met his eyes.

20. Charles was at the table, ruling a copybook. Joe was reading to him, while his mother was spinning in the corner.

21. Charles was a little confused. He feared his father might not be pleased; but he had no need to be uneasy, for his father was delighted.

22. The next day, his father took him to town, and gave him books for himself and Joe, with writing paper, pens, and ink.

23. Charles was the happiest boy in the world when he came home. He ran to Joe, his hands filled with parcels, and his heart beating with joy.

LESSON XI.

ī′ron (ī′urn)

eȳe′ lĭdṣ

fōrġe

in tĕnse′

elĭṇ′ker ty

shrĭṇk

lā′bor

hăm′mer

THE BLACKSMITH.

1. Clink, clink, clinkerty clink!
   We begin to hammer at morning's blink,
       And hammer away
       Till the busy day,
   Like us, aweary, to rest shall sink.

2. Clink, clink, clinkerty clink!
   From labor and care we never will shrink;
       But our fires we'll blow
       Till our forges glow
   With light intense, while our eyelids wink.

3. Clink, clink, clinkerty clink!
   The chain we'll forge with many a link.
      We'll work each form
      While the iron is warm,
   With strokes as fast as we can think.

4. Clink, clink, clinkerty clink!
   Our faces may be as black as ink,
      But our hearts are true
      As man ever knew,
   And kindly of all we shall ever think.

LESSON XII.

shŏŏk	grāv'el	in vīt'ed	as sure'	eon tĭn'ūed
plănts	bôr'derṣ	en joyed'	mĕd'dle	ad mīr'ing

A WALK IN THE GARDEN.

1. Frank was one day walking with his mother, when they came to a pretty garden. Frank looked in, and saw that it had clean gravel walks, and beds of beautiful flowers all in bloom.

2. He called to his mother, and said, "Mother, come and look at this pretty garden. I wish I might open the gate, and walk in."

3. The gardener, being near, heard what Frank said, and kindly invited him and his mother to come into the garden.

4. Frank's mother thanked the man. Turning to her son, she said, "Frank, if I take you to walk in this garden, you must take care not to meddle with anything in it."

5. Frank walked along the neat gravel paths, and looked at everything, but touched nothing that he saw.

6. He did not tread on any of the borders, and was careful that his clothes should not brush the tops of the flowers, lest he might break them.

7. The gardener was much pleased with Frank, because he was so careful not to do mischief. He showed him the seeds, and told him the names of many of the flowers and plants.

8. While Frank was admiring the beauty of a flower, a boy came to the gate, and finding it locked, he shook it hard. But it would not open. Then he said, " Let me in; let me in; will you not let me in this garden ? "

9. "No, indeed," said the gardener, "I will not let you in, I assure you; for when I let you in yesterday, you meddled with my flowers, and pulled some of my rare fruit. I do not choose to let a boy into my garden who meddles with the plants."

10. The boy looked ashamed, and when he found that the gardener would not let him in, he went slowly away.

11. Frank saw and felt how much happier a boy may be by not meddling with what does not belong to him.

12. He and his mother then continued their walk in the garden, and enjoyed the day very much. Before they left, the gardener gave each of them some pretty flowers.

LESSON XIII.

wolf	grĭēved	sleeve	nẽigh'borṣ	ẽar'nest
ăx'eṣ	elŭbṣ	ôr'der	sĭn̄'ġle	de stroy'

THE WOLF.

1. A boy was once taking care of some sheep, not far from a forest. Near by was a village, and he was told to call for help if there was any danger.

2. One day, in order to have some fun, he cried out, with all his might, "The wolf is coming! the wolf is coming!"

3. The men came running with clubs and axes to destroy the wolf. As they saw nothing they went home again, and left John laughing in his sleeve.

4. As he had had so much fun this time, John cried out again, the next day, "The wolf! the wolf!"

5. The men came again, but not so many as the first time. Again they saw no trace of the wolf; so they shook their heads, and went back.

6. On the third day, the wolf came in earnest. John cried in dismay, "Help! help!

the wolf! the wolf!" But not a single man came to help him.

7. The wolf broke into the flock, and killed

a great many sheep. Among them was a beautiful lamb, which belonged to John.

8. Then he felt very sorry that he had deceived his friends and neighbors, and grieved over the loss of his pet lamb.

> The truth itself is not believed,
> From one who often has deceived.

LESSON XIV.

mĕl′o dy   un nō′tĭçed   mŏd′est   eon tĕnt′   Grā′çie

THE LITTLE BIRD'S SONG.

1. A little bird, with feathers brown,
    Sat singing on a tree;
   The song was very soft and low,
    But sweet as it could be.

2. The people who were passing by,
    Looked up to see the bird

That made the sweetest melody
   That ever they had heard.

3. But all the bright eyes looked in vain;
      Birdie was very small,
   And with his modest, dark-brown coat,
      He made no show at all.

4. "Why, father," little Gracie said,
      "Where can the birdie be?
   If I could sing a song like that,
      I'd sit where folks could see."

5. "I hope my little girl will learn
      A lesson from the bird,
   And try to do what good she can,
      Not to be seen or heard.

6. "This birdie is content to sit
      Unnoticed on the way,
   And sweetly sing his Maker's praise
      From dawn to close of day.

7. "So live, my child, all through your life,
      That, be it short or long,
   Though others may forget your looks,
      They'll not forget your song."

LESSON XV.

| lēast | thạw | slīd'ing | plŭnġed | nāt'ured ly |
| băde | seăt'ter | pre tĕnd' | ex plōr'ing | dĭs o bē'di ent |

HARRY AND ANNIE.

1. Harry and Annie lived a mile from town, but they went there to school every day. It was a pleasant walk down the lane, and through the meadow by the pond.

2. I hardly know whether they liked it better in summer or in winter. They used to pretend that they were travelers exploring a new country, and would scatter leaves on

the road that they might find their way back again.

3. When the ice was thick and firm, they went across the pond. But their mother did not like to have them do this unless some one was with them.

4. "Do n't go across the pond to-day, children," she said, as she kissed them and bade them good-by one morning; "it is beginning to thaw."

5. "All right, mother," said Harry, not very good-naturedly, for he was very fond of running and sliding on the ice. When they came to the pond, the ice looked hard and safe.

6. "There," said he to his sister, "I knew it had n't thawed any. Mother is always afraid we shall be drowned. Come along, we will have a good time sliding. The school bell will not ring for an hour at least."

7. "But you promised mother," said Annie.

8. "No, I did n't. I only said 'All right,' and it *is* all right."

9. "I did n't say anything; so I can do as I like," said Annie.

10. So they stepped on the ice, and started to go across the pond. They had not gone

far before the ice gave way, and they fell into the water.

11. A man who was at work near the shore, heard the screams of the children, and plunged into the water to save them. Harry managed to get to the shore without any help, but poor Annie was nearly drowned before the man could reach her.

12. Harry went home almost frozen, and told his mother how disobedient he had been. He remembered the lesson learned that day as long as he lived.

LESSON XVI.

wīfe	ḡreet	bëard	wõrmş	prâyerş
fäith	ḡrōve	erŭsts	chûrch	fûr'nished

BIRD FRIENDS.

1. I once knew a man who was rich in his love for birds, and in their love for him. He lived in the midst of a grove full of all kinds of trees. He had no wife or children in his home.

2. He was an old man with gray beard, blue and kind eyes, and a voice that the

birds loved; and this was the way he made them his friends.

3. While he was at work with a rake on his nice walks in the grove, the birds came

close to him to pick up the worms in the fresh earth he dug up. At first, they kept a rod or two from him, but they soon found he was a kind man, and would not hurt them, but liked to have them near him.

3. 4.

4. They knew this by his kind eyes and voice, which tell what is in the heart. So, day by day their faith in his love grew in them.

5. They came close to the rake. They would hop on top of it, to be first at the worm. They would turn up their eyes into his when he spoke to them, as if they said, "He is a kind man; he loves us; we need not fear him."

6. All the birds of the grove were soon his fast friends. They were on the watch for him, and would fly down from the green tree tops to greet him with their chirp.

7. When he had no work on the walks to do with his rake or his hoe, he took crusts of bread with him, and dropped the crumbs on the ground. Down they would dart on his head and feet to catch them as they fell from his hand.

8 He showed me how they loved him. He put a crust of bread in his mouth, with one end of it out of his lips. Down they came like bees at a flower, and flew off with it crumb by crumb.

9. When they thought he slept too long in the morning, they would fly in and sit

on the bedpost, and call him up with their chirp.

10. They went with him to church, and while he said his prayers and sang his hymns in it, they sat in the trees, and sang their praises to the same good God who cares for them as he does for us.

11. Thus the love and trust of birds were a joy to him all his life long; and such love and trust no boy or girl can fail to win with the same kind heart, voice, and eye that he had.

Adapted from Elihu Burritt.

LESSON XVII.

WHAT THE MINUTES SAY.

1. We are but minutes — little things!
   Each one furnished with sixty wings,
   With which we fly on our unseen track,
   And not a minute ever comes back.

2. We are but minutes; use us well,
   For how we are used we must one day tell.
   Who uses minutes, has hours to use;
   Who loses minutes, whole years must lose.

LESSON XVIII.

dīed	wǫm'an	eon vǐnçed'	a māzed'	wrōte
pǐt'y	mis tāke'	re wạrd'ed	ḡrāte'fụl	chĕck

dis trĕss'

hĕ§ i tā'tion

hŭ§'band

mu §ǐ'cian

wĭd'ow

as sǐst'ançe

THE WIDOW AND THE MERCHANT.

1. A merchant, who was very fond of music, was asked by a poor widow to give her some assistance. Her husband, who was a musician, had died, and left her very poor indeed.

2. The merchant saw that the widow and her daughter, who was with her, were in great

distress. He looked with pity into their pale faces, and was convinced by their conduct that their sad story was true.

3. "How much do you want, my good woman?" said the merchant.

4. "Five dollars will save us," said the poor widow, with some hesitation.

5. The merchant sat down at his desk, took a piece of paper, wrote a few lines on it, and gave it to the widow with the words, "Take it to the bank you see on the other side of the street."

6. The grateful widow and her daughter, without stopping to read the note, hastened to the bank. The banker at once counted out fifty dollars instead of five, and passed them to the widow.

7. She was amazed when she saw so much money. "Sir, there is a mistake here," she said. "You have given me fifty dollars, and I asked for only five."

8. The banker looked at the note once more, and said, "The check calls for fifty dollars."

9. "It is a mistake—indeed it is," said the widow.

10. The banker then asked her to wait

a few minutes, while he went to see the merchant who gave her the note.

11. "Yes," said the merchant, when he had heard the banker's story, "I did make a mistake. I wrote fifty instead of five hundred. Give the poor widow five hundred dollars, for such honesty is poorly rewarded with even that sum."

LESSON XIX.

wīreṣ	trāde	bär′ḡain	săd′ness	prĭṣ′on erṣ
wạr	Frĕnch	a piēçe′	nŭm′ber	re ṣŏlved′

THE BIRDS SET FREE.

1. A man was walking one day through a large city. On a street corner he saw a boy with a number of small birds for sale, in a cage.

2. He looked with sadness upon the little prisoners flying about the cage, peeping through the wires, beating them with their wings, and trying to get out.

3. He stood for some time looking at the birds. At last he said to the boy, "How much do you ask for your birds?"

4. "Fifty cents apiece, sir," said the boy. "I do not mean how much apiece," said the man, "but how much for all of them? I want to buy them *all*."

5. The boy began to count, and found they came to five dollars. "There is your money,"

said the man. The boy took it, well pleased with his morning's trade.

6. No sooner was the bargain settled than the man opened the cage door, and let all the birds fly away.

7. The boy, in great surprise, cried, "What did you do that for, sir? You have lost all your birds."

8. "I will tell you why I did it," said the man. "I was shut up three years in a French prison, as a prisoner of war, and I am resolved never to see anything in prison which I can make free."

LESSON XX.

down'y   fĩrm'ly   stāid   pĕt'als̟   erīme

A MOMENT TOO LATE.

1. A moment too late, my beautiful bird,
     A moment too late are you now;
   The wind has your soft, downy nest disturbed—
     The nest that you hung on the bough.

2. A moment too late; that string in your bill,
     Would have fastened it firmly and strong;
   But see, there it goes, rolling over the hill!
     Oh, you staid a moment too long.

3. A moment, one moment too late, busy bee;
     The honey has dropped from the flower:
   No use to creep under the petals and see;
     It stood ready to drop for an hour.

4. A moment too late; had you sped on your wing,
     The honey would not have been gone;

Now you see what a very, a very sad thing
'T is to stay a moment too long.

5. Little girl, never be a moment too late,
   It will soon end in trouble or crime;
Better be an hour early, and stand and wait,
   Than a moment behind the time.

6. If the bird and the bee, little boy, were too late,
   Remember, as you play along
On your way to school, with pencil and slate,
   Never stay a moment too long.

LESSON XXI.

Wĕst In'diē̱ş	a dôrn'	ap prōach'	mō'tion	at tăched'
su̱g̱'ar plŭm	eŏt'ton	ĭn'stĭṉet	ŏb'jeet	de fĕnd'ing
nĕc'es sa ry	răp'id	brĭl'liant	fī'beṟş	se vēre'ly

HUMMING BIRDS.

1. The most beautiful humming birds are found in the West Indies and South America. The crest of the tiny head of one of these shines like a sparkling crown of colored light.

2. The shades of color that adorn its breast, are equally brilliant. As the bird

flits from one object to another, it looks more like a bright flash of sunlight than it does like a living being.

3. But, you ask, why are they called humming birds? It is because they make a soft, humming noise by the rapid motion of their wings—a motion so rapid, that as they fly you can only see that they have wings.

4. One day when walking in the woods, I found the nest of one of the smallest humming birds. It was about half the size of a very small hen's egg, and

was attached to a twig no thicker than a steel knitting needle.

5. It seemed to have been made of cotton fibers, and was covered with the softest bits of leaf and bark. It had two eggs in it, quite white, and each about as large as a small sugarplum.

6. When you approach the spot where one of these birds has built its nest, it is necessary to be careful. The mother bird will dart at you and try to peck your eyes. Its sharp beak may hurt your eyes most severely, and even destroy the sight.

7. The poor little thing knows no other way of defending its young, and instinct teaches it that you might carry off its nest if you could find it.

LESSON XXII.

de çīde′	bŭe′kled	moun′tain	shĕl′ter	pär′ty
dis pūte′	sue çeed′	fōr′çi bly	măn′tle	ȯv′en

THE WIND AND THE SUN.

A FABLE.

1. A dispute once arose between the Wind and the Sun, as to which was the stronger.

2. To decide the matter, they agreed to try their power on a traveler. That party which should first strip him of his cloak, was to win the day.

3. The Wind began. He blew a cutting blast, which tore up the mountain oaks by their roots, and made the whole forest look like a wreck.

4. But the traveler, though at first he could scarcely keep his cloak on his back, ran under a hill for shelter, and buckled his mantle about him more closely.

5. The Wind having thus tried his utmost power in vain, the Sun began.

6. Bursting through a thick cloud, he darted his sultry beams so forcibly upon the traveler's head, that the poor fellow was almost melted.

7. "This," said he, "is past all bearing. It is so hot, that one might as well be in an oven."

8. So he quickly threw off his cloak, and went into the shade of a tree to cool himself.

9. This fable teaches us, that gentle means will often succeed where forcible ones will **fail.**

LESSON XXIII.

sĭnk′ing   strēam′let   sweet′ness   eow′slĭp

SUNSET.

Now the sun is sinking
 In the golden west;
Birds and bees and children
 All have gone to rest;

And the merry streamlet,
  As it runs along,
With a voice of sweetness
  Sings its evening song.

2.

Cowslip, daisy, violet,
  In their little beds,
All among the grasses
  Hide their heavy heads;
There they'll all, sweet darlings,
  Lie in the happy dreams.
Till the rosy morning
  Wakes them with its beams.

LESSON XXIV.

o pĭn'ion	pĭ ȧn'o	eōarse	bāthe	sweep

BEAUTIFUL HANDS.

1. "O Miss Roberts! what coarse-looking hands Mary Jessup has!" said Daisy Marvin, as she walked home from school with her teacher.

2. "In my opinion, Daisy, Mary's hands are the prettiest in the class."

3. "Why, Miss Roberts, they are as red and hard as they can be. How they would look if she were to try to play on a piano!" exclaimed Daisy.

4. Miss Roberts took Daisy's hands in hers, and said, "Your hands are very soft and white, Daisy—just the hands to look beautiful on a piano; yet they lack one beauty that Mary's hands have. Shall I tell you what the difference is?"

5. "Yes, please, Miss Roberts."

6. "Well, Daisy, Mary's hands are always busy. They wash dishes; they make fires; they hang out clothes, and help to wash them, too; they sweep, and dust, and sew; they are always trying to help her poor, hard-working mother.

7. "Besides, they wash and dress the children; they mend their toys and dress their dolls; yet, they find time to bathe the head of the little girl who is so sick in the next house to theirs.

8. "They are full of good deeds to every living thing. I have seen them patting the tired horse and the lame dog in the street.

They are always ready to help those who need help."

9. "I shall never think Mary's hands are ugly any more, Miss Roberts."

10. "I am glad to hear you say that, Daisy; and I must tell you that they are beautiful because they do their work gladly and cheerfully."

11. "O Miss Roberts! I feel so ashamed of myself, and so sorry," said Daisy, looking into her teacher's face with tearful eyes.

12. " Then, my dear, show your sorrow by deeds of kindness. The good alone are really beautiful."

LESSON XXV.

a void′	pre vĕnt′	for g̅ĭve′	rĭṣe	g̅uĭde
dūr′ing	pout′ing	pro tĕe′tion	slăm	măn′ner
pee′vish	howl′ing	săt′is fīed	trŭst	ăn̦′g̅ry

THINGS TO REMEMBER.

1. When you rise in the morning, remember who kept you from danger during the hight. Remember who watched over you while you slept, and whose sun shines around you, and gives you the sweet light of day.

2. Let God have the thanks of your heart, for his kindness and his care; and pray for his protection during the wakeful hours of day.

3. Remember that God made all creatures to be happy, and will do nothing that may prevent their being so, without good reason for it.

4. When you are at the table, do not eat in a greedy manner, like a pig. Eat quietly,

3. 5

and do not reach forth your hand for the food, but ask some one to help you.

5. Do not become peevish and pout, because you do not get a part of everything. Be satisfied with what is given you.

6. Avoid a pouting face, angry looks, and angry words. Do not slam the doors. Go quietly up and down stairs; and never make a loud noise about the house.

7. Be kind and gentle in your manners; not like the howling winter storm, but like the bright summer morning.

8. Do always as your parents bid you. Obey them with a ready mind, and with a pleasant face.

9. Never do anything that you would be afraid or ashamed that your parents should know. Remember, if no one else sees you, God does, from whom you can not hide even your most secret thought.

10. At night, before you go to sleep, think whether you have done anything that was wrong during the day, and pray to God to forgive you. If any one has done you wrong, forgive him in your heart.

11. If you have not learned something useful, or been in some way useful, during

the past day, think that it is a day lost, and be very sorry for it.

12. Trust in the Lord, and He will guide you in the way of good men. The path of the just is as the shining light that shineth more and more unto the perfect day.

13. We must do all the good we can to all men, for this is well pleasing in the sight of God. He delights to see his children walk in love, and do good one to another.

LESSON XXVI.

ex ăet′ly	fōld′ing	cheeṣe	chăm′ber	răt′tling
pro trṳd′ed	fōre′pawṣ	ḡāzed	doubt	re lēased′
per plĕxed′	lăt′tĭçe	queer	eō′zy	stâir′eāse

THREE LITTLE MICE.

1. I will tell you the story of three little **mice**,
　　If you will keep still and listen to me,
　Who live in a cage that is cozy and nice,
　　And are just as cunning as cunning can be.
　They look very wise, with their pretty red eyes,
　　That seem just exactly like little round beads;
　They are white as the snow, and stand up in a **row**
　　Whenever we do not attend to their needs;—

2. Stand up in a row in a comical way,—
    Now folding their forepaws as if saying,
        "please;"
    Now rattling the lattice, as much as to say,
        "We shall not stay here without more bread
        and cheese."
    They are not at all shy, as you'll find, if you try
    To make them run up in their chamber to bed;
    If they don't want to go, why, they won't go —
        ah! no,
        Though you tap with your finger each queer
        little head.

3. One day as I stood by the side of the cage,
    Through the bars there protruded a funny,
        round tail;

Just for mischief I caught it, and soon, in a rage,
　Its owner set up a most pitiful wail.
He looked in dismay,—there was something to
　　pay,—
But what was the matter he could not make out;
What was holding him so, when he wanted to go
　To see what his brothers upstairs were about?

4. But soon from the chamber the others rushed
　　down,
　Impatient to learn what the trouble might be;
I have not a doubt that each brow wore a frown,
　Only frowns on their brows are not easy to see.
For a moment they gazed, perplexed and amazed;
　Then began both together to—gnaw off the tail!
So, quick I released him,—do you think that it
　　pleased him?
　And up the small staircase they fled like a gale.

Julia C. R. Dorr.

LESSON XXVII.

Ed'ward	re çēive'	wrĕtch'ed	thou'ṣand	ḡrăt'i tūde
re pēat'	lăn̲'ḡuaġe	shĭv'er ing	Gēr'man	ŭn der stŏŏd'

THE NEW YEAR.

1. One pleasant New-year morning, Edward rose, and washed and dressed himself

in haste. He wanted to be first to wish a happy New Year.

2. He looked in every room, and shouted the words of welcome. He ran into the

street, to repeat them to those he might meet.

3. When he came back, his father gave him two bright, new silver dollars.

4. His face lighted up as he took them. He had wished for a long time to buy some pretty books that he had seen at the bookstore.

5. He left the house with a light heart, intending to buy the books.

6. As he ran down the street, he saw a poor German family, the father, mother, and three children shivering with cold.

7. "I wish you a happy New Year," said Edward, as he was gayly passing on. The man shook his head.

8. "You do not belong to this country," said Edward. The man again shook his head, for he could not understand or speak our language.

9. But he pointed to his mouth, and to the children, as if to say, "These little ones have had nothing to eat for a long time."

10. Edward quickly understood that these poor people were in distress. He took out his dollars, and gave one to the man, and the other to his wife.

11. How their eyes sparkled with gratitude! They said something in their language, which doubtless meant, "We thank you a thousand times, and will remember you in our prayers."

12. When Edward came home, his father asked what books he had bought. He hung his head a moment, but quickly looked up.

13. "I have bought no books," said he, "I gave my money to some poor people, who seemed to be very hungry and wretched.

14. "I think I can wait for my books till next New Year. Oh, if you had seen how glad they were to receive the money!"

15. "My dear boy," said his father, "here is a whole bundle of books. I give them to you, more as a reward for your goodness of heart than as a New-year gift.

16. "I saw you give the money to the poor German family. It was no small sum for a little boy to give cheerfully.

17. "Be thus ever ready to help the poor, and wretched, and distressed; and every year of your life will be to you a happy New Year."

LESSON XXVIII.

| stŏck | spĭr′it | hŭm′ble | glōōm′y | sŭn′dī al |
| fŏl′ly | stee′ple | stū′pid | bōast′ing | mŏd′es ty |

THE CLOCK AND THE SUNDIAL.
A FABLE.

1. One gloomy day, the clock on a church steeple, looking down on a sundial, said,

"How stupid it is in you to stand there all the while like a stock!

2. "You never tell the hour till a bright sun looks forth from the sky, and gives you leave. I go merrily round, day and night, in summer and winter the same, without asking his leave.

3. "I tell the people the time to rise, to go to dinner, and to come to church.

4. "Hark! I am going to strike now; one, two, three, four. There it is for you. How silly you look! You can say nothing."

5. The sun, at that moment, broke forth from behind a cloud, and showed, by the sundial, that the clock was half an hour behind the right time.

6. The boasting clock now held his tongue, and the dial only smiled at his folly.

7. MORAL.—Humble modesty is more often right than a proud and boasting spirit.

LESSON XXIX.

pŭn′ish   ăc′tionṣ   wĭck′ed   fạlse′hōŏd   wāke′fụl

REMEMBER.

1. Remember, child, remember,
   That God is in the sky;
   That He looks down on all we do,
   With an ever-wakeful eye.

2. Remember, oh remember,
   That, all the day and night,
   He sees our thoughts and actions
   With an ever-watchful sight.

3. Remember, child, remember,
    That God is good and true;
 That He wishes us to always be
    Like Him in all we do.

4. Remember that He ever hates
    A falsehood or a lie;
 Remember He will punish, too,
    The wicked, by and by.

5. Remember, oh remember,
    That He is like a friend,
 And wishes us to holy be,
    And happy, in the end.

6. Remember, child, remember,
    To pray to Him in heaven;
 And if you have been doing wrong,
    Oh, ask to be forgiven.

7. Be sorry, in your little prayer,
    And whisper in his ear;
 Ask his forgiveness and his love.
    And He will surely hear.

8. Remember, child, remember,
    That you love, with all your might,

The God who watches o'er us,
　　And gives us each delight;
Who guards us ever through the day,
　　And saves us in the night.

LESSON XXX.

| dēal | strāight | eoŭr′aġe | re prōach′ | eow′ard ïçe |
| dĕpth | ĕf′fŏrt | eow′ard | de ṣẽrved′ | sehōōl′mātes |

COURAGE AND COWARDICE.

1. Robert and Henry were going home from school, when, on turning a corner, Robert cried out, "A fight! let us go and see!"

2. "No," said Henry; "let us go quietly home and not meddle with this quarrel. We have nothing to do with it, and may get into mischief."

3. "You are a coward, and afraid to go," said Robert, and off he ran. Henry went straight home, and in the afternoon went to school, as usual.

4. But Robert had told all the boys that Henry was a coward, and they laughed at him a great deal.

5. Henry had learned, however, that true courage is shown most in bearing reproach when not deserved, and that he ought to be afraid of nothing but doing wrong.

6. A few days after, Robert was bathing with some schoolmates, and got out of his depth. He struggled, and screamed for help, but all in vain.

7. The boys who had called Henry a coward, got out of the water as fast as they could, but they did not even try to help him.

8. Robert was fast sinking, when Henry threw off his clothes, and sprang into the water. He reached Robert just as he was sinking the last time.

9. By great effort, and with much danger to himself, he brought Robert to the shore, and thus saved his life.

10. Robert and his schoolmates were ashamed at having called Henry a coward. They owned that he had more courage than any of them.

11. Never be afraid to do good, but always fear to do evil.

LESSON XXXI.

ēast′ern	de lĭv′er ançe	weight	fā′vor ĭte	elĕv′er
sāil′or	e nôr′moŭs	eōurt	quạn′ti ty	sŭb′jeet
ex pĕnse′	ĕl′e phant	strōked	ma çhïne′	lēan′ing
ō′pen ing	dĭf′fi eul ty	rĭṣ′en	re lieved′	ĕmp′ty

WEIGHING AN ELEPHANT.

1. "An eastern king," said Teddy's mother, "had been saved from some great danger. To show his gratitude for deliverance, he vowed he would give to the poor the weight of his favorite elephant in silver."

2. "Oh! what a great quantity that would be," cried Lily, opening her eyes very wide. "But how *could* you weigh an elephant?"

asked Teddy, who was a quiet, thoughtful boy.

3. "There was the difficulty," said his mother. "The wise and learned men of the court stroked their long beards, and talked the matter over, but no one found out how to weigh the elephant.

4. "At last, a poor old sailor found safe and simple means by which to weigh the enormous beast. The thousands and thousands of pieces of silver were counted out to the people; and crowds of the poor were relieved by the clever thought of the sailor."

5. "O mamma," said Lily, "do tell us what it was!"

6. "Stop, stop!" said Teddy. "I want to think for myself—think hard—and find out how an elephant's weight could be known, with little trouble and expense."

7. "I am well pleased," said his mother, "that my little boy should set his mind to work on the subject. If he can find out the sailor's secret before night, he shall have that orange for his pains."

8. The boy thought hard and long. Lily laughed at her brother's grave looks, as he sat leaning his head on his hands. Often

she teased him with the question, "Can you
weigh an elephant, Teddy?"

9. At last, while eating his supper, Teddy
suddenly cried out, "I have it now!"

10. "Do you think so?" asked his mother.

11. "How would you do it," asked Lily.

12. "First, I would have a big boat brought very close to the shore, and would have planks laid across, so that the elephant could walk right into it."

13. "Oh, such a great, heavy beast would make it sink low in the water," said Lily.

14. "Of course it would," said her brother. "Then I would mark on the outside of the boat the exact height to which the water had risen all around it while the elephant was inside. Then he should march on shore, leaving the boat quite empty."

15. "But I don't see the use of all this," said Lily.

16. "Don't you?" cried Teddy, in surprise. "Why, I should then bring the heaps of silver, and throw them into the boat till their weight would sink it to the mark made by the elephant. That would show that the weight of each was the same."

17. "How funny!" cried Lily; "you would make a weighing machine of the boat?"

18. "That is my plan," said Teddy.

19. "That was the sailor's plan," said his mother. "You have earned the orange, my boy;" and she gave it to him with a smile.

Adapted from A. L. O. E.

3, 6.

LESSON XXXII.

răṉks	glō′ry	ar rāyed′	wĕap′onṣ	lĭv′ing
elăd	är′mor	vĭe′to ry	eŏn′test	băt′tle
blôod	en lĭst′	mŭs′tered	lŏng′ing	war′rior

THE SOLDIER.

1. A soldier! a soldier! I 'm longing to be:
The name and the life of a soldier for me!
I would not be living at ease and at play;
True honor and glory I 'd win in my day.

2. A soldier! a soldier! in armor arrayed;
My weapons in hand, of no contest afraid;
I 'd ever be ready to strike the first blow,
And to fight my way through the ranks of the foe.

3. But then, let me tell you, no blood would I shed,
No victory seek o'er the dying and dead;
A far braver soldier than this would I be;
A warrior of Truth, in the ranks of the free.

4. A soldier! a soldier! Oh, then, let me be!
My friends, I invite you, enlist now with me.
Truth's bands shall be mustered, love's foes shall
    give way!
Let 's up, and be clad in our battle array!

J. G. Adams.

LESSON XXXIII.

thĭck'et	härsh'ly	wräth	whĕnçe	răm'bling
prọv'ing	tō'ward	ĕeh'o	mŏck'ing	ăṇ'ḡri ly
fōōl'ish	a broạd'	erŏss	Bī'ble	ĭn'stant ly

THE ECHO.

1. As Robert was one day rambling about, he happened to cry out, "Ho, ho!" He instantly heard coming back from a hill near by, the same words, "Ho, ho!"

2. In great surprise, he said with a loud voice, "Who are you?" Upon this, the same words came back, "Who are you?"

3. Robert now cried out harshly, "You must be a very foolish fellow." "Foolish fellow!" came back from the hill.

4. Robert became angry, and with loud and fierce words went toward the spot whence the sounds came. The words all came back to him in the same angry tone.

5. He then went into the thicket, and looked for the boy who, as he thought, was mocking him; but he could find nobody anywhere.

6. When he went home, he told his moth-

er that some boy had hid himself in the wood, for the purpose of mocking him.

7. "Robert," said his mother, "you are angry with yourself alone. You heard nothing but your own words."

8. "Why, mother, how can that be?" said Robert. "Did you never hear an echo?" asked his mother. "An echo, dear mother? No, ma'am. What is it?"

9. "I will tell you," said his mother. "You know, when you play with your ball,

and throw it against the side of a house, it bounds back to you." "Yes, mother," said he, "and I catch it again."

10. "Well," said his mother, "if I were in the open air, by the side of a hill or a large barn, and should speak very loud, my voice would be sent back, so that I could hear again the very words which I spoke.

11. "That, my son, is an echo. When you thought some one was mocking you, it was only the hill before you, echoing, or sending back, your own voice.

12. "The bad boy, as you thought it was, spoke no more angrily than yourself. If you had spoken kindly, you would have heard a kind reply.

13. "Had you spoken in a low, sweet, gentle tone, the voice that came back would have been as low, sweet, and gentle as your own.

14. "The Bible says, 'A soft answer turneth away wrath.' Remember this when you are at play with your schoolmates.

15. "If any of them should be offended, and speak in a loud, angry tone, remember the echo, and let your words be soft and kind.

16. "When you come home from school, and find your little brother cross and peevish, speak mildly to him. You will soon see a smile on his lips, and find that his tones will become mild and sweet.

17. "Whether you are in the fields or in the woods, at school or at play, at home or abroad, remember,

> The good and the kind,
> By kindness their love ever proving,
> Will dwell with the pure and the loving."

LESSON XXXIV.

fāint	eol lĕet′	re frĕsh′	līn′ing	hăp′pi ness
fēast	seär′let	ŏf′fered	līft′ing	straw′ber rieṣ

GEORGE'S FEAST.

1. George's mother was very poor. Instead of having bright, blazing fires in winter, she had nothing to burn but dry sticks, which George picked up from under the trees and hedges.

2. One fine day in July, she sent George to the woods, which were about two miles from the village in which she lived. He

was to stay there all day, to get as much wood as he could collect.

3. It was a bright, sunny day, and George worked very hard; so that by the time the

sun was high, he was hot, and wished for a cool place where he might rest and eat his dinner.

4. While he hunted about the bank, he saw among the moss some fine, wild strawberries, which were a bright scarlet with ripeness.

5. "How good these will be with my bread and butter!" thought George; and lining his little cap with leaves, he set to work eagerly to gather all he could find, and then seated himself by the brook.

6. It was a pleasant place, and George felt happy and contented. He thought how much his mother would like to see him there, and to be there herself, instead of in her dark, close room in the village.

7. George thought of all this, and just as he was lifting the first strawberry to his mouth, he said to himself, "How much mother would like these;" and he stopped, and put the strawberry back again.

8. "Shall I save them for her?" said he, thinking how much they would refresh her, yet still looking at them with a longing eye.

9. "I will eat half, and take the other half to her," said he at last; and he divided them into two heaps. But each heap looked so small, that he put them together again.

10. "I will only taste one," thought he; but, as he again lifted it to his mouth, he saw that he had taken the finest, and he put it back. "I will keep them all for her,"

said he, and he covered them up nicely, till he should go home.

11. When the sun was beginning to sink, George set out for home. How happy he felt, then, that he had all his strawberries for his sick mother. The nearer he came to his home, the less he wished to taste them.

12. Just as he had thrown down his wood, he heard his mother's faint voice calling him from the next room. "Is that you, George? I am glad you have come, for I am thirsty, and am longing for some tea."

13. George ran in to her, and joyfully offered his wild strawberries. "And you saved them for your sick mother, did you?" said she, laying her hand fondly on his head, while the tears stood in her eyes. "God will bless you for all this, my child."

14. Could the eating of the strawberries have given George half the happiness he felt at this moment?

LESSON XXXV.

hăl′low	ā měn′	temp tā′tion	ḡrā′ cioŭs
kĭng′dòm	for ḡĭve′	trans ḡrĕs′sionş	sup plīed′
pōr′tion	boun′ty	wēak′ness	hĕlp′less
dẹign	sŏl′emn	eom păs′sion	plūm′áḡe
re vēre′	se eūre′	for ĕv′er	pär′donş

THE LORD'S PRAYER.

1. Our Father in heaven,
    We hallow thy name;
  May thy kingdom holy
    On earth be the same;
  Oh, give to us daily
    Our portion of bread;
  It is from thy bounty,
    That all must be fed.

2. Forgive our transgressions,
    And teach us to know
  The humble compassion
    That pardons each foe;
  Keep us from temptation,
    From weakness and sin,
  And thine be the glory
    Forever! Amen!

AN EVENING PRAYER.

1.

Before I close my eyes in sleep,
  Lord, hear my evening prayer,
And deign a helpless child to keep,
  With thy protecting care.

2.

Though young in years, I have been taught
  Thy name to love and fear;
Of thee to think with solemn thought;
  Thy goodness to revere.

3.

That goodness gives each simple flower
  Its scent and beauty, too;
And feeds it in night's darkest hour
  With heaven's refreshing dew.

4.

The little birds that sing all day
  In many a leafy wood,
By thee are clothed in plumage gay,
  By thee supplied with food.

5.

And when at night they cease to sing,
  By thee protected still,
Their young ones sleep beneath their wing,
  Secure from every ill.

6.

Thus mayst thou guard with gracious arm
  The bed whereon I lie,
And keep a child from every harm
  By thine own watchful eye.

Bernard Barton

LESSON XXXVI.

pos sĕs′sion	tôr′ment	sug̅ g̣ĕst′ed	ob ̣sẽrved′
săt is făe′tion	thiĕf	anx ī′e ty	fī′nal ly
bur′y ing (bĕr′-)	eŏn′scioŭs	erĭt′ie al	brĕath′less
ex pē′ri ençed	re spŏnse′	ĕv′i dent	ĭn ter fẽred′

FINDING THE OWNER.

1. " It 's mine," said Fred, showing a white-handled pocketknife, with every blade per-fect and shining. "Just what I 've always

wanted." And he turned the prize over and over with evident satisfaction.

2. "I guess I know who owns it," said Tom, looking at it with a critical eye.

3. "I guess you do n't," was the quick response. "It is n't Mr. Raymond's," said Fred, shooting wide of the mark.

4. "I know that; Mr. Raymond's is twice as large," observed Tom, going on with his drawing lesson.

5. Do you suppose Fred took any comfort in that knife? Not a bit of comfort did he take. He was conscious all the time of having something in his possession that did

not belong to him; and Tom's suspicion interfered sadly with his enjoyment.

6. Finally, it became such a torment to him, that he had serious thoughts of burning it, or burying it, or giving it away; but a better plan suggested itself.

7. "Tom," said he, one day at recess, "did n't you say you thought you knew who owned that knife I found?"

8. "Yes, I did; it looked like Doctor Perry's." And Tom ran off to his play, without giving the knife another thought.

9. Dr. Perry's! Why, Fred would have time to go to the doctor's office before recess closed: so he started in haste, and found the old gentleman getting ready to visit a patient. "Is this yours?" cried Fred, in breathless haste, holding up the cause of a week's anxiety.

10. "It was," said the doctor; "but I lost it the other day."

11. "I found it," said Fred, "and have felt like a thief ever since. Here, take it; I 've got to run."

12. "Hold on!" said the doctor. "I 've got a new one, and you are quite welcome to this."

13. "Am I? May I? Oh! thank you!"
And with what a different feeling he kept it
from that which he had experienced for a week!

LESSON XXXVII.

im mē′di ate ly	en eoun′tered
ehăr′ae ter	pre pâred′
squēal	pŏl′i çy
snăpped	prowl′ing
shŭnned	doŭ′ble
quĭllṣ	ĭn′seet
tĕr′ri bly	de vour
erĕv′iç eṣ	es eāpe

främe′wõrk   nīght′mâre   dis ḡŭst′ing   quạd′rụ ped

BATS.

1. Bats are very strange little animals,
having hair like mice, and wings like birds.
During the day, they live in crevices of rocks,
in caves, and in other dark places.

2. At night, they go forth in search of
food; and, no doubt, you have seen them fly-

ing about, catching such insects as happen to be out rather late at night.

3. The wings of a bat have no quills. They are only thin pieces of skin stretched upon a framework of bones. Besides this, it may be said that while he is a quadruped, he can rise into the air and fly from place to place like a bird.

4. There is a funny fable about the bat, founded upon this double character of beast and bird, which I will tell you.

5. An owl was once prowling about, when he came across a bat. So he caught him in his claws, and was about to devour him. Upon this, the bat began to squeal terribly; and he said to the owl, " Pray, what do you take me for, that you use me thus? "

6. " Why, you are a bird, to be sure," said the owl, "and I am fond of birds. I love dearly to break their little bones."

7. " Well," said the bat, "I thought there was some mistake. I am no bird. Do n't you see, Mr. Owl, that I have no feathers, and that I am covered with hair like a mouse? "

8. " Sure enough," said the owl, in great surprise; "I see it now. Really, I took you

for a bird, but it appears you are only a kind of mouse. I ate a mouse last night, and it gave me the nightmare. I can't bear mice! Bah! it makes me sick to think of it." So the owl let the bat go.

9. The very next night, the bat encountered another danger. He was snapped up by puss, who took him for a mouse, and immediately prepared to eat him.

10. "I beg you to stop one moment," said the bat. "Pray, Miss Puss, what do you suppose I am?" "A mouse, to be sure!" said the cat. "Not at all," said the bat, spreading his long wings.

11. "Sure enough," said the cat: "you seem to be a bird, though your feathers are

3, 7.

not very fine. I eat birds sometimes, but I am tired of them just now, having lately devoured four young robins; so you may go. But, bird or mouse, it will be your best policy to keep out of my way hereafter."

12. The meaning of this fable is, that a person playing a double part may sometimes escape danger; but he is always, like the bat, a creature that is disgusting to everybody, and shunned by all.

S. G. Goodrich—Adapted.

LESSON XXXVIII.

tĭnts	shēaveṣ	fīre′flīeṣ	chĭm′ney	tĭn′kle
lạwnṣ	whīrl	bŭt′ter eŭp	lōw′ing	lánçe

A SUMMER DAY.

1. This is the way the morning dawns:
    Rosy tints on flowers and trees,
    Winds that wake the birds and bees,
    Dewdrops on the fields and lawns—
    This is the way the morning dawns.

2. This is the way the sun comes up:
    Gold on brook and glossy leaves,

Mist that melts above the sheaves,
Vine, and rose, and buttercup—
This is the way the sun comes up.

3. This is the way the river flows:
   Here a whirl, and there a dance;
   Slowly now, then, like a lance,
Swiftly to the sea it goes—
This is the way the river flows.

4. This is the way the rain comes down:
   Tinkle, tinkle, drop by drop,
   Over roof and chimney top;
   Boughs that bend, and skies that frown—
   This is the way the rain comes down.

5. This is the way the birdie sings:
   "Baby birdies in the nest,
   You I surely love the best;
   Over you I fold my wings"—
   This is the way the birdie sings.

6. This is the way the daylight dies:
   Cows are lowing in the lane,
   Fireflies wink on hill and plain;
   Yellow, red, and purple skies—
   This is the way the daylight dies.

George Cooper.

LESSON XXXIX.

çhăn de liĕr′	Pĭ′ṣa	Lòn′dòn	Fĕr′g̃u son
pōr′traits	I′ṣaae	in vĕn′tion	Găl i lē′o
pĕn′du lŭm	ĕn′g̃ĭne	whāle′bōne	lĕe′tureṣ
lō eo mō′tĭve	mŏt′to	Eng′land (ĭn′gland)	tēa′kĕt tle
dis eòv′ered	swāy′ing	dis eoŭr′aġed	im prọved′

I WILL THINK OF IT.

1. "I will think of it." It is easy to say this; but do you know what great things have come from thinking?

2. We can not see our thoughts, or hear, or taste, or feel them; and yet what mighty power they have!

3. Sir Isaac Newton was seated in his garden on a summer's evening, when he saw an apple fall from a tree. He began to *think*, and, in trying to find out why the apple fell, discovered how the earth, sun, moon, and stars are kept in their places.

4. A boy named James Watt sat quietly by the fireside, watching the lid of the tea-kettle as it moved up and down. He began to *think;* he wanted to find out why the steam in the kettle moved the heavy lid.

5. From that time he went on thinking, and thinking; and when he became a man, he improved the steam engine so much that it could, with the greatest ease, do the work of many horses.

6. When you see a steamboat, a steam mill, or a locomotive, remember that it would never have been built if it had not been for the hard thinking of some one.

7. A man named Galileo was once standing in the cathedral of Pisa, when he saw a chandelier swaying to and fro.

8. This set him *thinking*, and it led to the invention of the pendulum.

9. James Ferguson was a poor Scotch shepherd boy. Once, seeing the inside of a watch, he was filled with wonder. "Why should I not make a watch?" thought he.

10. But how was he to get the materials out of which to make the wheels and the mainspring? He soon found how to get them: he made the mainspring out of a piece of whalebone. He then made a wooden clock which kept good time.

11. He began, also, to copy pictures with a pen, and portraits with oil colors. In a few years, while still a small boy, he earned money enough to support his father.

12. When he became a man, he went to London to live. Some of the wisest men in England, and the king himself, used to attend his lectures. His motto was, "I will think of it;" and he made his thoughts useful to himself and the world.

13. Boys, when you have a difficult lesson to learn, don't feel discouraged, and ask some one to help you before helping yourselves. Think, and by thinking you will learn how to think to some purpose.

LESSON XL.

CHARLIE AND ROB.

1. "Don't you hate splitting wood?" asked Charlie, as he sat down on a log to hinder Rob for a while.

2. "No, I rather like it. When I get hold of a tough old fellow, I say, 'See here, now, you think you're the stronger, and are going to beat me; so I'll split you up into kindling wood.'"

3. "Pshaw!" said Charlie, laughing; "and it's only a stick of wood."

4. "Yes; but you see I pretend it's a lesson, or a tough job of any kind, and it's nice to conquer it."

5. "I don't want to conquer such things; I don't care what becomes of them. I wish I were a man, and a rich one."

6. "Well, Charlie, if you live long enough you'll be a man, without wishing for it; and as for the rich part, I mean to be that myself."

7. "You do. How do you expect to get your money? By sawing wood?"

8. "May be—some of it; that's as good a

way as any, so long as it lasts. I do n't care
how I get rich, you know, so that it's in an
honest and useful way."

9. "I'd like to sleep over the next ten
years, and wake up to find myself a young
man with a splendid education and plenty of
money."

10. "Humph! I am not sleepy—a night at a time is enough for me. I mean to work the next ten years. You see there are things that you've got to *work* out—you can't *sleep* them out."

11. "I hate work," said Charlie, "that is, such work as sawing and splitting wood, and doing chores. I'd like to do some big work, like being a clerk in a bank or something of that sort."

12. "Wood has to be sawed and split before it can be burned," said Rob. "I don't know but I'll be a clerk in a bank some time; I'm working towards it. I'm keeping father's accounts for him."

13. How Charlie laughed! "I should think that was a long way from being a bank clerk. I suppose your father sells two tables and six chairs, some days, does n't he?"

14. "Sometimes more than that, and sometimes not so much," said Rob, in perfect good humor.

15. "I did n't say I was a bank clerk now. I said I was working towards it. Am I not nearer it by keeping a little bit of a book than I should be if I did n't keep any book at all?"

16. "Not a whit — such things *happen*," said Charlie, as he started to go.

17. Now, which of these boys, do you think, grew up to be a rich and useful man, and which of them joined a party of tramps before he was thirty years old?

DEFINITIONS.—1. Hĭn′der, *interrupt, prevent from working.* 4. Cŏn̤′quer, *overcome, master.* 9. Splĕn′did, *very fine, complete.* Ed u ēā′tion, *acquired knowledge.* 11. Chōre̤ş, *the light work about a house or yard.*

LESSON XLI.

RAY AND HIS KITE.

1. Ray was thought to be an odd boy. You will think him so, too, when you have read this story.

2. Ray liked well enough to play with the boys at school; yet he liked better to be alone under the shade of some tree, reading a fairy tale or dreaming daydreams. But there was one sport that he liked as well as his companions; that was kiteflying.

3. One day when he was flying his kite, he said to himself, "I wonder if anybody ever tried to fly a kite at night. It seems

to me it would be nice.   But then, if it
were very dark, the kite could not be seen.
What if I should fasten a light to it, though?
That would make
it show.   I'll try it
this very night."

4. As soon as it
was dark, without

saying a word to
anybody, he took
his kite and lan-
tern, and went to
a large, open lot,
about a quarter of
a mile from his
home.   "Well,"
thought he, "this
is queer.   How

lonely and still it seems without any other
boys around!   But I am going to fly my
kite, anyway."

5. So he tied the lantern, which was made
of tin punched full of small holes, to the tail
of his kite.   Then he pitched the kite, and,

after several attempts, succeeded in making it rise. Up it went, higher and higher, as Ray let out the string. When the string was all unwound, he tied it to a fence; and then he stood and gazed at his kite as it floated high up in the air.

6. While Ray was enjoying his sport, some people who were out on the street in the village, saw a strange light in the sky. They gathered in groups to watch it. Now it was still for a few seconds, then it seemed to be jumping up and down; then it made long sweeps back and forth through the air.

7. "What can it be?" said one person. "How strange!" said another. "It can not be a comet; for comets have tails," said a third. "Perhaps it's a big firefly," said another.

8. At last some of the men determined to find out what this strange light was— whether it was a hobgoblin dancing in the air, or something dropped from the sky. So off they started to get as near it as they could.

9. While this was taking place, Ray, who had got tired of standing, was seated in a fence corner, behind a tree. He could see

the men as they approached; but they did not see him.

10. When they were directly under the light, and saw what it was, they looked at each other, laughing, and said, "This is some boy's trick; and it has fooled us nicely. Let us keep the secret, and have our share of the joke."

11. Then they laughed again, and went back to the village; and some of the simple people there have not yet found out what that strange light was.

12. When the men had gone, Ray thought it was time for him to go ; so he wound up his string, picked up his kite and lantern, and went home. His mother had been wondering what had become of him.

13. When she heard what he had been doing, she hardly knew whether to laugh or scold; but I think she laughed, and told him that it was time for him to go to bed.

DEFINITIONS.—2. Dāy'drēamṣ, *vain fancies.* Com păn'-ionṣ, *playmates, friends.* 5. At tĕmpts', *trials, efforts.* 6. Grọups, *several together, small assemblages.* Sweeps, *rapid movements in the line of a curve.* 7. Cŏm'et, *a brilliant heavenly body with a long, fiery tail.* 8. De tēr'mĭned, *concluded, resolved.* Hŏb'gŏb lin, *an ugly fairy or imp.*

LESSON XLII.

BEWARE OF THE FIRST DRINK.

1. "Uncle Philip, as the day is fine, will you take a walk with us this morning?"

2. "Yes, boys. Let me get my hat and cane, and we will take a ramble. I will tell you a story as we go. Do you know poor old Tom Smith?"

3. "Know him! Why, Uncle Philip, everybody knows him. He is such a shocking drunkard, and swears so horribly."

4. "Well, I have known him ever since we were boys together. There was not a more decent, well-behaved boy among us. After he left school, his father died, and he was put into a store in the city. There, he fell into bad company.

5. "Instead of spending his evenings in reading, he would go to the theater and to balls. He soon learned to play cards, and of course to play for money. He lost more than he could pay.

6. "He wrote to his poor mother, and told her his losses. She sent him money to pay his debts, and told him to come home.

7. "He did come home. After all, he might still have been useful and happy, for his friends were willing to forgive the past. For a time, things went on well. He married a lovely woman, gave up his bad habits, and was doing well.

8. "But one thing, boys, ruined him forever. In the city, he had learned to take strong drink, and he said to me once, that when a man begins to drink, he never knows where it will end. 'Therefore,' said Tom, 'beware of the first drink!'

9. "It was not long before he began to follow his old habit. He knew the danger, but it seemed as if he could not resist his desire to drink. His poor mother soon died of grief and shame. His lovely wife followed her to the grave.

10. "He lost the respect of all, went on from bad to worse, and has long been a perfect sot. Last night, I had a letter from the city, stating that Tom Smith had been found guilty of stealing, and sent to the state prison for ten years.

11. "There I suppose he will die, for he is now old. It is dreadful to think to what an end he has come. I could not but think,

as I read the letter, of what he said to me years ago, 'Beware of the first drink!'

12. "Ah, my dear boys, when old Uncle Philip is gone, remember that he told you

the story of Tom Smith, and said to you, 'Beware of the first drink!' The man who does this will never be a drunkard."

DEFINITIONS.—3. Hŏr'ri bly, *in a dreadful manner, terribly.* 4. Dē'çent, *modest, respectable.* 9. Re ṣĭst', *withstand, overcome.* 10. Sŏt, *an habitual drunkard.* Guĭlt'y, *justly chargeable with a crime.*

3, 8.

LESSON XLIII.

SPEAK GENTLY.

1. Speak gently; it is better far
   To rule by love than fear:
   Speak gently; let no harsh words mar
   The good we might do here.

2. Speak gently to the little child;
   Its love be sure to gain;
   Teach it in accents soft and mild;
   It may not long remain.

3. Speak gently to the aged one;
   Grieve not the careworn heart:
   The sands of life are nearly run;
   Let such in peace depart.

4. Speak gently, kindly, to the poor;
   Let no harsh tone be heard;
   They have enough they must endure,
   Without an unkind word.

5. Speak gently to the erring; know
   They must have toiled in vain;
   Perhaps unkindness made them so;
   Oh, win them back again.

6. Speak gently: 't is a little thing
   Dropped in the heart's deep well;
   The good, the joy, which it may bring,
   Eternity shall tell.

   George Washington Langford.

DEFINITIONS.—1. Mär, *injure, hurt.* 2. Ae'çents, *language, tones.* 4. En düre', *bear, suffer.* 5. Err'ing (ẽr'-), *sinning.* 6. E tẽr'ni ty, *the endless hereafter, the future.*

LESSON XLIV.

THE SEVEN STICKS.

1. A man had seven sons, who were always quarreling. They left their studies and work, to quarrel among themselves. Some bad men were looking forward to the death of their father, to cheat them out of their property by making them quarrel about it.

2. The good old man, one day, called his sons around him. He laid before them seven sticks, which were bound together. He said, "I will pay a hundred dollars to the one who can break this bundle."

3. Each one strained every nerve to break the bundle. After a long but vain trial, they all said that it could not be done.

4. "And yet, my boys," said the father, "nothing is easier to do." He then untied the bundle, and broke the sticks, one by one, with perfect ease.

5. "Ah!" said his sons, "it is easy enough to do it so; anybody could do it in that way."

6. Their father replied, "As it is with these sticks, so is it with you, my sons. So

long as you hold fast together and aid each other, you will prosper, and none can injure you.

7. "But if the bond of union be broken, it will happen to you just as it has to these sticks, which lie here broken on the ground."

> Home, city, country, all are prosperous found,
> When by the powerful link of union bound.

DEFINITIONS.—1. Chēat, *deceive, wrong.* Prŏp′er ty, *that which one owns—whether land, goods, or money.* 2. Bŭn′dle, *a number of things bound together.* 3. Nĕrve, *sinew, muscle.* 6. Prŏs′per, *succeed, do well.* 7. Un′ion (ūn′yun), *the state of being joined or united.*

LESSON XLV.

THE MOUNTAIN SISTER.

1. The home of little Jeannette is far away, high up among the mountains. Let us call her our mountain sister.

2. There are many things you would like to hear about her, but I can only tell you now how she goes with her father and brother, in the autumn, to help gather nuts for the long winter.

3. A little way down the mountain side is a chestnut wood.   Did you ever see a chestnut tree?   In the spring its branches are covered with bunches of

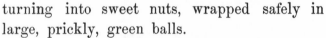

creamy flowers, like long tassels.   All the hot summer these are turning into sweet nuts, wrapped safely in large, prickly, green balls.

4. But when the frost of autumn comes, these prickly balls turn brown, and crack open.   Then you may see inside one, two, three, and even four, sweet, brown nuts.

5. When her father says, one night at supper time, "I think there will be a frost to-night," Jeannette knows very well what to do. She dances away early in the evening to her little bed, made in a box built up against the wall.

6. Soon she falls asleep to dream about

the chestnut wood, and the little brook that springs from rock to rock down under the tall, dark trees. She wakes with the first daylight, and is out of bed in a minute, when she hears her father's cheerful call, "Come, children; it is time to be off."

7. Their dinner is ready in a large basket. The donkey stands before the door with great bags for the nuts hanging at each side. They go merrily over the crisp, white frost to the chestnut trees. How the frost has opened the burs! It has done half their work for them already.

8. How they laugh and sing, and shout to each other as they fill their baskets! The sun looks down through the yellow leaves; the rocks give them mossy seats; the birds and squirrels wonder what these strange people are doing in their woods.

9. Jeannette really helps, though she is only a little girl; and her father says at night, that his Jane is a dear, good child. This makes her very happy. She thinks about it at night, when she says her prayers. Then she goes to sleep to dream of the merry autumn days.

10. Such is our little mountain sister, and

here is a picture of her far-away home. The mountain life is ever a fresh and happy one.

DEFINITIONS.—3. Chĕst'nut (chĕs'nut), *a tree valuable for its timber and its fruit.* Tăs'sels̬, *hanging ornaments, such as are used on curtains.* Wrăpped (răpt), *completely covered up, inclosed.* Prĭck'ly, *covered with sharp points.* 7. Crĭsp, *brittle, sparkling.* Bûrṣ, *the rough coverings of seeds or nuts.*

LESSON XLVI.

HARRY AND THE GUIDEPOST.

1. The night was dark, the sun was hid
     Beneath the mountain gray,
   And not a single star appeared
     To shoot a silver ray.

2. Across the heath the owlet flew,
     And screamed along the blast;
   And onward, with a quickened step,
     Benighted Harry passed.

3. Now, in thickest darkness plunged,
     He groped his way to find;
   And now, he thought he saw beyond,
     A form of horrid kind.

4. In deadly white it upward rose,
     Of cloak and mantle bare,
   And held its naked arms across,
     To catch him by the hair.

5. Poor Harry felt his blood run cold,
     At what before him stood;
   But then, thought he, no harm, I'm sure,
     Can happen to the good.

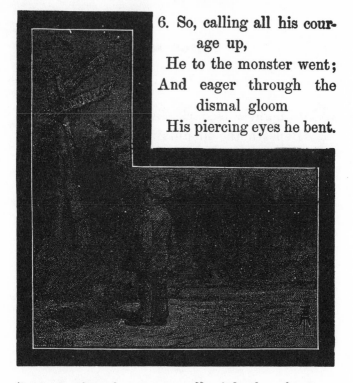

6. So, calling all his cour-
   age up,
   He to the monster went;
   And eager through the
   dismal gloom
   His piercing eyes he bent.

7. And when he came well nigh the ghost
   That gave him such affright,
   He clapped his hands upon his side,
   And loudly laughed outright.

8. For 't was a friendly guidepost stood,
   His wandering steps to guide;
   And thus he found that to the good,
   No evil could betide.

9. Ah well, thought he, one thing I've learned,
    Nor shall I soon forget;
Whatever frightens me again,
    I'll march straight up to it.

10. And when I hear an idle tale,
    Of monster or of ghost,
I'll tell of this, my lonely walk,
    And one tall, white guidepost.

DEFINITIONS.—2. Hēath, *a place overgrown with shrubs.* Be nīght′ed, *overtaken by the night.* 3. Grōped, *felt his way in the dark.* Hŏr′rid, *hideous, frightful.* 6. Mŏn′ster, *a thing of unnatural size and shape.* Dĭṣ′mal, *dark, cheerless.* Piĕr′çing, *sharp, penetrating.* 7. Ghōst (gōst), *a frightful object in white, an apparition.* 8. Guīde′pōst, *a post and sign set up at the forks of a road to direct travelers.* Be tīde′, *befall, happen.* 10. I′dle, *of no account, foolish.*

LESSON XLVII.

THE MONEY AMY DIDN'T EARN.

1. Amy was a dear little girl, but she was too apt to waste time in getting ready to do her tasks, instead of doing them at once as she ought.

2. In the village in which she lived, Mr. Thornton kept a store where he sold fruit of all kinds, including berries in their season. One day he said to Amy, whose parents were quite poor, "Would you like to earn some money?"

3. "Oh, yes," replied she, "for I want some new shoes, and papa has no money to buy them with."

4. "Well, Amy," said Mr. Thornton, "I noticed some fine, ripe blackberries in Mr. Green's pasture to-day, and he said that anybody was welcome to them. I will pay you thirteen cents a quart for all you will pick for me."

5. Amy was delighted at the thought of earning some money; so she ran home to get a basket, intending to go immediately to pick the berries.

6. Then she thought she would like to know how much money she would get if she picked five quarts. With the help of her slate and pencil, she found out that she would get sixty-five cents.

7. "But supposing I should pick a dozen quarts," thought she, "how much should I earn then?" "Dear me," she said, after fig-

uring a while, "I should earn a dollar and fifty-six cents."

8. Amy then found out what Mr. Thornton would pay her for fifty, a hundred, and two hundred quarts. It took her some time to

do this, and then it was so near dinner time that she had to stay at home until afternoon.

9. As soon as dinner was over, she took

her basket and hurried to the pasture. Some boys had been there before dinner, and all the ripe berries were picked. She could not find enough to fill a quart measure.

10. As Amy went home, she thought of what her teacher had often told her—"Do your task at once; then think about it," for "one doer is worth a hundred dreamers."

DEFINITIONS.—1. Tȧsks, *work which one has to do.* 2. Sēa'ṣon, *proper time of the year.* 4. Quȧrt, *the fourth part of a gallon.* 7. Fĭḡ'ur ing, *computing, calculating.* 9. Hŭr'-ried, *went rapidly.* Mĕaṣ'ure, *vessel.*

LESSON XLVIII.

WHO MADE THE STARS?

1. "Mother, who made the stars, which light
　　The beautiful blue sky?
　Who made the moon, so clear and bright,
　　That rises up so high?"

2. "'T was God, my child, the Glorious One,
　　He formed them by his power;
　He made alike the brilliant sun,
　　And every leaf and flower.

3. " He made your little feet to walk;
   Your sparkling eyes to see;
   Your busy, prattling tongue to talk,
   And limbs so light and free.

4 " He paints each fragrant flower that blows,
   With loveliness and bloom;
   He gives the violet and the rose
   Their beauty and perfume.

5. " Our various wants his hands supply;
   He guides us every hour;
   We're kept beneath his watchful eye,
   And guarded by his power.

6. " Then let your little heart, my love,
   Its grateful homage pay
   To that kind Friend, who, from above,
   Thus guides you every day.

7. " In all the changing scenes of time,
   On Him our hopes depend;
   In every age, in every clime,
   Our Father and our Friend."

DEFINITIONS.—2. Glō'ri oŭs, *excellent, exalted.* 3. Prăt'-
tling, *talking lightly like a child.* 4. Blōwṣ, *blossoms.* Per-
fūme', *delightful odor.* 5. Vā'ri oŭs, *many and different.* 6.
Hŏm'aġe, *respect.* 7. Sçēneṣ, *events.* Clīme, *climate, region.*

LESSON XLIX.

DEEDS OF KINDNESS.

1. One day, as two little boys were walking along the road, they overtook a woman carrying a large basket of apples.

2. The boys thought the woman looked very pale and tired; so they said, "Are you going to town? If you are, we will carry your basket."

3. "Thank you," replied the woman, "you are very kind: you see I am weak and ill." Then she told them that she was a widow, and had a lame son to support.

4. She lived in a cottage three miles away, and was now going to market to sell the apples which grew on the only tree in her little garden. She wanted the money to pay her rent.

5. "We are going the same way you are," said the boys. "Let us have the basket;" and they took hold of it, one on each side, and trudged along with merry hearts.

6. The poor widow looked glad, and said that she hoped their mother would not be angry with them. "Oh, no," they replied;

"our mother has taught us to be kind to everybody, and to be useful in any way that we can."

7. She then offered to give them a few of the ripest apples for their trouble. "No,

thank you," said they; "we do not want any pay for what we have done."

8. When the widow got home, she told her lame son what had happened on the road,

3. 9.

and they were both made happier that day by the kindness of the two boys.

9. The other day, I saw a little girl stop and pick up a piece of orange peel, which she threw into the gutter. "I wish the boys would not throw orange peel on the sidewalk," said she. "Some one may tread upon it, and fall."

10. "That is right, my dear," I said. "It is a little thing for you to do what you have done, but it shows that you have a thoughtful mind and a feeling heart."

11. Perhaps some may say that these are *little* things. So they are; but we must not wait for occasions to do great things. We must begin with little labors of love.

DEFINITIONS.—3. Wĭd'ow, *a woman whose husband is dead.* 5. Trŭdġed, *walked.* 9. Gŭt'ter, *the lower ground or channel along the side of a road.* Trĕad, *step.* 11. Oe eā'şionş, *chances, opportunities.*

LESSON L.

THE ALARM CLOCK.

1. A lady, who found it not easy to wake in the morning as early as she wished,

bought an **alarm** clock. These clocks are so made as to strike with a loud whirring noise. at any hour the owner pleases to set them.

2. The lady placed her clock at the head of the bed, and at the right time she found herself roused by the long, rattling sound.

3. She arose at once, and felt better all day for her early rising. This lasted for some weeks. The alarm clock faithfully did its duty, and was plainly heard so long as it was obeyed.

4. But, after a time, the lady grew tired of early rising. When she was waked by the noise, she merely turned over in bed, and slept again.

5. In a few days, the clock ceased to rouse her from her sleep. It spoke just as loudly as ever; but she did not hear it, because she had been in the habit of not obeying it.

6. Finding that she might as well be without it, she resolved that when she heard the sound she would jump up.

7. Just so it is with conscience. If we will obey its voice, even in the most trifling things, we can always hear it, clear and strong.

8. But if we allow ourselves to do what we have some fears may not be quite right, we shall grow more and more sleepy, until the voice of conscience has no longer power to wake us.

DEFINITIONS.—1. A lärm', *a sudden sound calculated to awaken persons from sleep.* Whĭr'ring, *buzzing.* 2. Roușed, *waked.* Răt'tling, *giving quick, sharp noises in rapid succession.* 3. Fāith'fụl ly, *in an exact and proper manner.* Dū'ty, *the right conduct or action.* 4. Mēre'ly, *simply.* 7. Cŏn'sciençe (kŏn'shens), *that within us which tells what is right and what is wrong, reason.* Trī'fling, *of little importance or value.* 8. Al low', *permit, suffer.*

LESSON LI.

SPRING.

1. The alder by the river
    Shakes out her powdery curls;
  The willow buds in silver
    For little boys and girls.

2. The little birds fly over,
    And oh, how sweet they sing!
  To tell the happy children
    That once again 't is Spring.

3. The gay green grass comes creeping
    So soft beneath their feet;
  The frogs begin to ripple
    A music clear and sweet.

4. And buttercups are coming,
    And scarlet columbine,
  And in the sunny meadows
    The dandelions shine.

5. And just as many daisies
    As their soft hands can hold,
  The little ones may gather,
    All fair in white and gold.

6. Here blows the warm red clover,
    There peeps the violet blue;
  Oh, happy little children!
    God made them all for you.

  Celia Thaxter.

DEFINITIONS.—1. Al′der (al′-), *a tree which grows in moist land.* 3. Rĭp′ple, *to cause little waves of sound.*

LESSON LII.

TRUE COURAGE.

One cold winter's day, three boys were passing by a schoolhouse. The oldest was a bad boy, always in trouble himself, and trying to get others into trouble. The youngest, whose name was George, was a very good boy.

George wished to do right, but was very much wanting in courage. The other boys were named Henry and James. As they walked along, they talked as follows:

Henry. What fun it would be to throw a snowball against the schoolroom door, and make the teacher and scholars all jump!

James. *You* would jump, if you should. If the teacher did not catch you and whip you, he would tell your father, and you would get a whipping then; and that would make you jump higher than the scholars, I think.

Henry. Why, we would get so far off, before the teacher could come to the door, that he could not tell who we are. Here is a snowball just as hard as ice, and George would as soon throw it against the door as not.

James. Give it to him, and see. He would not dare to throw it.

Henry. Do you think George is a coward? You do not know him as well as I do.

Here, George, take this snowball, and show James that you are not such a coward as he thinks you are.

George. I am not afraid to throw it; **but** I do not want to. I do not see that it

will do any good, or that there will be any
fun in it.

James. There! I told you he would not
dare to throw it.

Henry. Why, George, are you turning coward? I thought you did not fear anything.
Come, save your credit, and throw it. I
know you are not afraid.

George. Well, I am not afraid to throw.
Give me the snowball. I would as soon
throw it as not.

Whack! went the snowball against the
door; and the boys took to their heels.
Henry was laughing as heartily as he could,
to think what a fool he had made of George.

George had a whipping for his folly, as
he ought to have had. He was such a
coward, that he was afraid of being called a
coward. He did not dare refuse to do as
Henry told him, for fear that he would be
laughed at.

If he had been really a brave boy, he
would have said, "Henry, do you suppose
that I am so foolish as to throw that snowball, just because you want to have me?
You may throw your own snowballs, if you
please!"

Henry would, perhaps, have laughed at him, and called him a coward.

But George would have said, "Do you think that I care for your laughing? I do not think it right to throw the snowball. I will not do that which I think to be wrong, if the whole town should join with you in laughing."

This would have been real courage. Henry would have seen, at once, that it would do no good to laugh at a boy who had so bold a heart. You must have this fearless spirit, or you will get into trouble, and will be, and ought to be, disliked by all.

DEFINITIONS.—Sehŏl'arṣ, *children at school.* Whĭp'ping, *punishment.* Dâre, *have courage.* Crĕd'it, *reputation.* Heärt'i-ly, *freely, merrily.* Re füṣe', *decline.* Fēar'less, *bold, brave.* Dis līked', *not loved.*

LESSON LIII.

THE OLD CLOCK.

1. In the old, old hall the old clock stands,
And round and round move the steady hands;
With its tick, tick, tick, both night and day,
While seconds and minutes pass away.

2. At the old, old clock oft wonders Nell,
   For she can't make out what it has to tell;

She has ne'er yet read, in prose or rhyme,
That it marks the silent course of time.

3. When I was a child, as Nell is now,
   And long ere Time had wrinkled my brow,
   The old, old clock both by night and by day
   Said,—"Tick, tick, tick!" Time passes away.

DEFINITIONS.—2. Prōṣe, *the common language of men in talking or writing,* Rhȳme (rīme), *verse, poetry.* 3. Wrĭṉ'kled (rĭṉ'kld), *having creases or folds in the skin.* Brow, *the forehead.*

LESSON LIV.

THE WAVES.

1. "Where are we to go?" said the little waves to the great, deep sea.

"Go, my darlings, to the yellow sands: you will find work to do there."

2. "I want to play," said one little wave; "I want to see who can jump the highest."

"No; come on, come on," said an earnest wave; "mother must be right. I want to work."

3. "Oh, I dare not go," said another; "look at those great, black rocks close to the sands; I dare not go there, for they will tear me to pieces."

4. "Take my hand, sister," said the earnest wave; "let us go on together. How glorious it is to do some work."

5. "Shall we ever go back to mother?"

"Yes, when our work is done."

6. So one and all hurried on. Even the little wave that wanted to play, pressed on, and thought that work might be fun after all. The timid ones did not like to be left

behind, and they became earnest as they got nearer the sands.

7. After all, it was fun, pressing on one after another—jumping, laughing, running on to the broad, shining sands.

8. First, they came in their course to a great sand castle. Splash, splash! they all

went over it, and down it came. "Oh, what fun!" they cried.

9. "Mother told me to bring these sea-weeds; I will find a pretty place for them," said one—and she ran a long way over the sands, and left them among the pebbles. The pebbles cried, "We are glad you are come. We wanted washing."

10. "Mother sent these shells; I don't know where to put them," said a little fretful wave. "Lay them one by one on the sand, and do not break them," said the eldest wave.

11. And the little one went about its work, and learned to be quiet and gentle, for fear of breaking the shells.

12. "Where is my work?" said a great, full-grown wave. "This is mere play. The little ones can do this and laugh over it. Mother said there was work for *me*." And he came down upon some large rocks.

13. Over the rocks and into a pool he went, and he heard the fishes say, "The sea is coming. Thank you, great sea; you always send a big wave when a storm is nigh. Thank you, kind wave; we are all ready for you now."

14. Then the waves all went back over the wet sands, slowly and carelessly, for they were tired.

15. "All my shells are safe," said one.

16. And, "My seaweeds are left behind," said another.

17. "I washed all of the pebbles," said a third.

18. "And I—I only broke on a rock, and splashed into a pool," said the one that was so eager to work. "I have done no good, mother—no work at all."

19. "Hush!" said the sea. And they heard a child that was walking on the shore, say, "O mother, the sea has been here! Look, how nice and clean the sand is, and how clear the water is in that pool."

20. Then the sea said, "Hark!" and far away they heard the deep moaning of the coming storm

21. "Come, my darlings," said she; "you have done your work, now let the storm do its work."

DEFINITIONS.—6. Prĕssèd, *pushed, followed closely.* Tĭm′id, *wanting courage, not bold.* 10. Frĕt′fụl, *cross, peevish.* Eld′est, *first, foremost.* 20. Mōan′ing, *making a low, dull sound, muttering*

LESSON LV.

DON'T KILL THE BIRDS.

1. Don't kill the birds!
     the little birds,
   That sing about
       your door
   Soon as the joyous
         Spring has come,
   And chilling storms are o'er.

2. The little birds! how sweet they sing!
       Oh, let them joyous live;
     And do not seek to take the life
       Which you can never give.

3. Don't kill the birds! the pretty birds,
       That play among the trees;

For earth would be a cheerless place,
    If it were not for these.

4. The little birds! how fond they play!
    Do not disturb their sport;
But let them warble forth their songs,
    Till winter cuts them short.

5. Don't kill the birds! the happy birds,
    That bless the field and grove;
So innocent to look upon,
    They claim our warmest love.

6. The happy birds, the tuneful birds,
    How pleasant 't is to see!
No spot can be a cheerless place
    Where'er their presence be.

DEFINITIONS.—4. Dis tûrb', *interfere with.* War'ble, *to trill, to carol.* 5. In'no çent, *pure, harmless.* 6. Tūne'fŭl, *musical, melodious.* Prĕṣ'ençe, *state of being at hand, existence.*

LESSON LVI.

WHEN TO SAY NO.

1. Though "No" is a very little word, it is not always easy to say it; and the not doing so, often causes trouble.

2. When we are asked to stay away from school, and spend in idleness or mischief the time which ought to be spent in study, we should at once say "No."

3. When we are urged to loiter on our way to school, and thus be late, and interrupt our teacher and the school, we should say "No." When some schoolmate wishes us to whisper or play in the schoolroom, we should say "No."

4. When we are tempted to use angry or wicked words, we should remember that the eye of God is always upon us, and should say "No."

5. When we have done anything wrong, and are tempted to conceal it by falsehood, we should say "No, we can not tell a lie; it is wicked and cowardly."

6. If we are asked to do anything which we know to be wrong, we should not fear to say "No."

7. If we thus learn to say "No," we shall avoid much trouble, and be always safe.

DEFINITIONS.—1. Caus'es, *makes.* 2. I'dle ness, *a doing nothing, laziness.* 3. Urged, *asked repeatedly.* Loi'ter, *linger, delay.* In ter rŭpt', *disturb, hinder.* 4. Tĕmpt'ed, *led by evil circumstances.* 5. Con çĕal', *hide.* Fạlse'hŏŏd, *untruth.*

3, 10.

LESSON LVII.

WHICH LOVED BEST?

"I love you, mother," said little John;
Then, forgetting work, his cap went on,
And he was off to the garden swing,
Leaving his mother the wood to bring.

2. "I love you, mother," said rosy Nell;
   "I love you better than tongue can tell;"

Then she teased and pouted full half the day,
Till her mother rejoiced when she went to play.

3. "I love you, mother," said little Fan;
"To-day I'll help you all I can;
How glad I am that school does n't keep!"
So she rocked the baby till it fell asleep.

4. Then, stepping softly, she took the broom,
And swept the floor, and dusted the room;
Busy and happy all day was she,
Helpful and cheerful as child could be.

5. "I love you, mother," again they said—
Three little children going to bed;
How do you think that mother guessed
Which of them really loved her best?

Joy Allison.

LESSON LVIII.

JOHN CARPENTER.

1. John Carpenter did not like to buy toys that somebody else had made. He liked the fun of making them himself. The thought that they were his own work delighted him.

2. Tom Austin, one of his playmates, thought a toy was worth nothing unless it cost a great deal of money. He never tried to make anything, but bought all his toys.

3. "Come and look at my horse," said he, one day. "It cost a dollar, and it is such a beauty! Come and see it."

4. John was soon admiring his friend's

horse; and he was examining it carefully, to see how it was made. The same evening he began to make one for himself.

5. He went into the wood shed, and picked

out two pieces of wood—one for the head of his horse, the other for the body. It took him two or three days to shape them to his satisfaction.

6. His father gave him a bit of red leather for a bridle, and a few brass nails, and his mother found a bit of old fur with which he made a mane and tail for his horse.

7. But what about the wheels? This puzzled him. At last he thought he would go to a turner's shop, and see if he could not get some round pieces of wood which might suit his purpose.

8. He found a large number of such pieces among the shavings on the floor, and asked permission to take a few of them. The turner asked him what he wanted them for, and he told him about his horse.

9. "Oh," said the man, laughing, "if you wish it, I will make some wheels for your horse. But mind, when it is finished, you must let me see it."

10. John promised to do so, and he soon ran home with the wheels in his pocket. The next evening, he went to the turner's shop with his horse all complete, and was told that he was an ingenious little fellow.

11. Proud of this compliment, he ran to his friend Tom, crying, "Now then, Tom, here is my horse,—look!"

12. "Well, that is a funny horse," said Tom; "where did you buy it?" "I didn't buy it," replied John; I made it."

13. "You made it yourself! Oh, well, it's a good horse for you to make. But it is not so good as mine. Mine cost a dollar, and yours didn't cost anything."

14. "It was real fun to make it, though," said John, and away he ran with his horse rolling after him.

15. Do you want to know what became of John? Well, I will tell you. He studied hard in school, and was called the best scholar in his class. When he left school, he went to work in a machine shop. He is now a master workman, and will soon have a shop of his own.

DEFINITIONS.—4. Ad mīr'ing, *looking at with pleasure.* Ex ăm'in ing, *looking at every point.* 6. Lĕath'er, *the skin of an animal prepared for use.* 7. Pŭz'zled, *perplexed, caused trouble.* Tûrn'er, *one who shapes wooden or metal articles by means of a lathe.* 8. Shāv'ingṣ, *the thin ribbons of wood which a carpenter makes in planing.* Per mĭs'sion, *privilege, consent.* 10. Com plēte', *finished.* In ġēn'ioŭs, *skillful.* 11. Cŏm'pliment, *praise, approbation.*

LESSON LIX.

PERSEVERE.

1. The fisher who draws in his net too soon,
    Won't have any fish to sell;
  The child who shuts up his book too soon,
    Won't learn any lessons well.

2 If you would have your learning stay,
    Be patient,—do n't learn too fast:
  The man who travels a mile each day,
    May get round the world at last.

LESSON LX.

THE CONTENTED BOY.

Mr. Lenox was one morning riding by himself. He got off from his horse to look at something on the roadside. The horse broke away from him, and ran off. Mr. Lenox ran after him, but soon found that he could not catch him.

A little boy at work in a field near the road, heard the horse. As soon as he saw him running from his master, the boy ran very quickly to the middle of the road, and, catching the horse by the bridle, stopped him till Mr. Lenox came up.

Mr. Lenox. Thank you, my good boy, you have caught my horse very nicely. What shall I give you for your trouble?

Boy. I want nothing, sir.

Mr. L. You want nothing? So much the better for you. Few men can say as much. But what were you doing in the field?

B. I was rooting up weeds, and tending the sheep that were feeding on turnips.

Mr. L. Do you like to work?

B. Yes, sir, very well, this fine weather.

Mr. L. But would you not rather play?

B. This is not hard work. It is almost as good as play.

Mr. L. Who set you to work?

B. My father, sir.

Mr. L. What is your name?

B. Peter Hurdle, sir.

Mr. L. How old are you?

B. Eight years old, next June.

Mr. L. How long have you been here?

B. Ever since six o'clock this morning.

Mr. L. Are you not hungry?

B. Yes, sir, but I shall go to dinner soon.

Mr. L. If you had a dime now, what would you do with it?

B. I do n't know, sir. I never had so much.

Mr. L. Have you no playthings?

B. Playthings? What are they?

Mr. L. Such things as ninepins, marbles, tops, and wooden horses.

B. No, sir. Tom and I play at football in winter, and I have a jumping rope. I had a hoop, but it is broken.

Mr. L. Do you want nothing else?

B. I have hardly time to play with what I have. I have to drive the cows, and to run on errands, and to ride the horses to the fields, and that is as good as play.

Mr. L. You could get apples and cakes, if you had money, you know.

B. I can have apples at home. As for cake, I do not want that. My mother makes me a pie now and then, which is as good.

Mr. L. Would you not like a knife to cut sticks?

B. I have one. Here it is. Brother Tom gave it to me.

Mr. L. Your shoes are full of holes. Don't you want a new pair?

B. I have a better pair for Sundays.

Mr. L. But these let in water.

B. I do not mind that, sir.

Mr. L. Your hat is all torn, too.

B. I have a better one at home.

Mr. L. What do you do when it rains?

B. If it rains very hard when I am in the field, I get under a tree for shelter.

Mr. L. What do you do, if you are hungry before it is time to go home?

B. I sometimes eat a raw turnip.

Mr. L. But if there is none?

B. Then I do as well as I can without. I work on, and never think of it.

Mr. L. Why, my little fellow, I am glad to see that you are so contented. Were you ever at school?

B. No, sir. But father means to send me next winter.

Mr. L. You will want books then.

B. Yes, sir; each boy has a Spelling Book, a Reader, and a Testament.

Mr. L. Then I will give them to you. Tell your father so, and that it is because you are an obliging, contented little boy.

B. I will, sir. Thank you.

Mr. L. Good by, Peter.

B. Good morning, sir.

Dr. John Aiken.

DEFINITIONS.—Rōōt'ing, *pulling up by the roots.* Tĕnd'ing, *watching, attending.* Tûr'nip, *a vegetable.* Wĕath'er, *state of the atmosphere.* Er'rands, *messages.* Rạw, *not cooked.* Tĕs'ta-ment, *the last twenty-seven books of the Bible.*

LESSON LXI.

LITTLE GUSTAVA.

1. Little Gustava sits in the sun,
   Safe in the porch, and the little drops run
   From the icicles under the eaves so fast,
   For the bright spring sun shines warm at last,
       And glad is little Gustava.

2. She wears a quaint little scarlet cap,
   And a little green bowl she holds in her lap,
   Filled with bread and milk to the brim,
   And a wreath of marigolds round the rim:
       "Ha! ha!" laughs little Gustava.

3. Up comes her little gray, coaxing cat,
   With her little pink nose, and she mews, "What's
       that?"
   Gustava feeds her,—she begs for more,
   And a little brown hen walks in at the door:
       "Good day!" cries little Gustava.

4. She scatters crumbs for the little brown hen,
   There comes a rush and a flutter, and then
   Down fly her little white doves so sweet,
   With their snowy wings and their crimson feet:
       "Welcome!" cries little Gustava.

5. So dainty and eager they pick up the crumbs.
   But who is this through the doorway comes?

Little Scotch terrier, little dog Rags,
Looks in her face, and his funny tail wags:
  "Ha! ha!" laughs little Gustava.

6. "You want some breakfast, too?" and down
  She sets her bowl on the brick floor brown,
  And little dog Rags drinks up her milk,
  While she strokes his shaggy locks, like silk:
      "Dear Rags!" says little Gustava.

7. Waiting without stood sparrow and crow,
  Cooling their feet in the melting snow.

"Won't you come in, good folk?" she cried,
But they were too bashful, and staid outside,
   Though "Pray come in!" cried Gustava.

8. So the last she threw them, and knelt on the mat,
With doves, and biddy, and dog, and cat.
And her mother came to the open house door:
"Dear little daughter, I bring you some more,
   My merry little Gustava."

9. Kitty and terrier, biddy and doves,
All things harmless Gustava loves,
The shy, kind creatures 't is joy to feed,
And, oh! her breakfast is sweet indeed
   To happy little Gustava!

        Celia Thaxter.

DEFINITIONS.—1. Gus tä′vȧ, *a girl's name.* I′çi eleṣ, *water frozen in long. needle-like shapes.* Eaveṣ (ēvz), *the lower edges of a roof.* 2. Quāint, *odd.* Măr′i ḡōld, *a yellow flower.* 8. Knĕlt, *bent on her knees.* Bĭd′dy, *chicken.*

LESSON LXII.

THE INSOLENT BOY.

1. James Selton was one of the most insolent boys in the village where he lived. He would rarely pass people in the street without being guilty of some sort of abuse.

2. If a person were well dressed he would cry out, "Dandy!" If a person's clothes were dirty or torn, he would throw stones at him, and annoy him in every way.

3. One afternoon, just as the school was dismissed, a stranger passed through the village. His dress was plain and somewhat old, but neat and clean. He carried a cane in his hand, on the end of which was a bundle, and he wore a broad-brimmed hat.

4. No sooner did James see the stranger, than he winked to his playmates, and said, "Now for some fun!" He then silently went toward the stranger from behind, and, knocking off his hat, ran away.

5. The man turned and saw him, but James was out of hearing before he could speak. The stranger put on his hat, and went on his way. Again did James approach; but this time, the man caught him by the arm, and held him fast.

6. However, he contented himself with looking James a moment in the face, and then pushed him from him. No sooner did the naughty boy find himself free again, than he began to pelt the stranger with dirt and stones.

7. But he was much frightened when the "rowdy," as he foolishly called the man, was struck on the head by a brick, and badly hurt. All the boys now ran away, and James skulked across the fields to his home.

8. As he drew near the house, his sister Caroline came out to meet him, holding up

a beautiful gold chain and some new books for him to see.

9. She told James, as fast. as she could talk, that their uncle, who had been away several years, had come home, and was now in the house; that he had brought beautiful presents for the whole family, that he had left his carriage at the tavern, a mile or two off, and walked on foot, so as to surprise his brother, their father.

10. She said, that while he was coming through the village, some wicked boys threw stones at him, and hit him just over the eye, and that mother had bound up the wound. "But what makes you look so pale?" asked Caroline, changing her tone.

11. The guilty boy told her that nothing was the matter with him; and running into the house, he went upstairs into his chamber. Soon after, he heard his father calling him to come down. Trembling from head to foot, he obeyed. When he reached the parlor door, he stood, fearing to enter.

12. His mother said, "James, why do you not come in? You are not usually so bashful. See this beautiful watch, which your uncle has brought for you."

3, 11.

13. What a sense of shame did James now feel! Little Caroline seized his arm, and pulled him into the room. But he hung down his head, and covered his face with his hands.

14. His uncle went up to him, and kindly taking away his hands, said, "James, will you not bid me welcome?" But quickly starting back, he cried, "Brother, this is not your son. It is the boy who so shamefully insulted me in the street!"

15. With surprise and grief did the good father and mother learn this. His uncle was ready to forgive him, and forget the injury. But his father would never permit James to have the gold watch, nor the beautiful books, which his uncle had brought for him.

16. The rest of the children were loaded with presents. James was obliged to content himself with seeing them happy. He never forgot this lesson so long as he lived. It cured him entirely of his low and insolent manners.

DEFINITIONS.—1. In'so lent, *rude, insulting.* Râre'ly, *hardly ever.* A būse', *ill usage.* 2. Dăn'dy, *a fop.* 3. Dismĭssed', *let out.* 6. Naugh'ty (nạ'ty), *bad, wicked.* 7.

Row'dy, *a low fellow, who engages in fights.* Skŭlked, *went in a sneaking manner.* 9. Uṇ'ele, *the brother of one's father or mother.* Tăv'ern, *a small hotel.* 14. Shāme'fụl ly, *disgracefully.* In sŭlt'ed, *treated with abuse.* 15. In'ju ry, *harm done.* 16. En tīre'ly, *altogether.*

LESSON LXIII.

WE ARE SEVEN.

1. I met a little cottage girl:
     She was eight years old, she said;
   Her hair was thick with many a curl,
     That clustered round her head.

2. She had a rustic, woodland air,
     And she was wildly clad:
   Her eyes were fair, and very fair;—
     Her beauty made me glad.

3. "Sisters and brothers, little maid,
     How many may you be?"
   "How many? Seven in all," she said,
     And, wondering, looked at me.

4. "And where are they? I pray you tell."
     She answered, "Seven are we;
   And two of us at Conway dwell,
     And two are gone to sea.

5. "Two of us in the churchyard lie,
　　My sister and my brother;
　And, in the churchyard cottage, I
　　Dwell near them with my mother."

6. "You say that two at Conway dwell,
　　And two are gone to sea,
　Yet ye are seven! I pray you tell,
　　Sweet maid, how this may be."

7. Then did the little maid reply,
   "Seven boys and girls are we;
   Two of us in the churchyard lie,
   Beneath the churchyard tree."

8. "You run about, my little maid,
   Your limbs, they are alive;
   If two are in the churchyard laid,
   Then ye are only five."

9. "Their graves are green, they may be seen,"
   The little maid replied,
   "Twelve steps or more from mother's door,
   And they are side by side.

10. "My stockings there I often knit,
    My kerchief there I hem;
    And there upon the ground I sit,
    And sing a song to them.

11. "And often after sunset, sir,
    When it is light and fair,
    I take my little porringer,
    And eat my supper there.

12. "The first that died was sister Jane;
    In bed she moaning lay,

Till God released her from her pain;
    And then she went away.

13. "So in the churchyard she was laid;
    And, when the grass was dry,
Together round her grave we played,
    My brother John and I.

14. "And when the ground was white with snow,
    And I could run and slide,
My brother John was forced to go,
    And he lies by her side."

15. "How many are you, then?" said I,
    "If they two are in heaven?"
Quick was the little maid's reply,
    "O master! we are seven."

16. "But they are dead; those two are dead!
    Their spirits are in heaven!"
'T was throwing words away: for still
    The little maid would have her will,
    And said, "Nay, we are seven."

William Wordsworth.

DEFINITIONS.—1. Clŭs'tered, *hung in bunches.* 2. Rŭs'tie, *country-like.* 10. Kēr'chĭef, *handkerchief.* 11. Pŏr'rin ġer, *a small dish for soup or porridge.* 12. Re lēased , *freed, relieved.*

LESSON LXIV.

MARY'S DIME.

1. There! I have drawn the chairs into the right corners, and dusted the room nicely. How cold papa and mamma will be when they return from their long ride! It is not time to toast the bread yet, and I am tired of reading.

2. What shall I do? Somehow, I can't help thinking about the pale face of that little beggar girl all the time. I can see the glad light filling her eyes, just as plain as I did when I laid the dime in her little dirty hand.

3. How much I had thought of that dime, too! Grandpa gave it to me a whole month ago, and I had kept it ever since in my red box upstairs; but those sugar apples looked so beautiful, and were so cheap—only a dime apiece—that I made up my mind to have one.

4. I can see her—the beggar girl, I mean—as she stood there in front of the store, in her old hood and faded dress, looking at the candies laid all in a row. I wonder

what made me say, "Little girl, what do you
want?"

5. How she stared at me, just as if nobody
had spoken kindly to her before. I guess

she thought I was sorry for her, for she said,
so earnestly and sorrowfully, "I was thinking how good one of those gingerbread rolls
would taste. I have n't had anything to eat
to-day."

6. Now, I thought to myself, "Mary Williams, you have had a good breakfast and a good dinner this day, and this poor girl has not had a mouthful. You can give her your dime; she needs it a great deal more than you do."

7. I could not resist that little girl's sorrowful, hungry look—so I dropped the dime right into her hand, and, without waiting for her to speak, walked straight away. I'm so glad I gave her the dime, if I did have to go without the apple lying there in the window, and looking just like a real one.

DEFINITIONS.—1. Tōast, *to scorch until brown by the heat of a fire.* 3. Chĕap, *low in price.* A pieçe', *each.* 4. Hŏŏd, *a soft covering for the head.* Fād'ed, *having lost freshness of color.* 5. Stâred, *looked earnestly.* Sŏr'row ful ly, *full of sadness.* Gĭn'ger brĕad, *a kind of sweet cake flavored with ginger.*

LESSON LXV.

MARY DOW.

1. "Come in, little stranger," I said,
   As she tapped at my half-open door;
   While the blanket, pinned over her head,
   Just reached to the basket she bore.

2. A look full of innocence fell
   From her modest and pretty blue eye,
As she said, "I have matches to sell,
   And hope you are willing to buy.

3. "A penny a bunch is the price,
   I think you'll not find it too much;
They are tied up so even and nice,
   And ready to light with a touch."

4. I asked, "What's your name, little girl?"
   "'T is Mary," said she, "Mary Dow;"

And carelessly tossed off a curl,
　That played on her delicate brow.

5. "My father was lost on the deep;
　　The ship never got to the shore;
And mother is sad, and will weep,
　To hear the wind blow and sea roar.

6. "She sits there at home, without food,
　　Beside our poor, sick Willy's bed;
She paid all her money for wood,
　And so I sell matches for bread.

7. "I'd go to the yard and get chips,
　　But then it would make me too sad
To see the men building the ships,
　And think they had made one so bad.

8. "But God, I am sure, who can take
　　Such fatherly care of a bird,
Will never forget nor forsake
　The children who trust in his word.

9. "And now, if I only can sell
　　The matches I brought out to-day,
I think I shall do very well,
　And we shall rejoice at the pay."

10. "Fly home, little bird," then I thought,
"Fly home, full of joy, to your nest;"
For I took all the matches she brought,
And Mary may tell you the rest.

DEFINITIONS.—1. Blăn'ket, *a square of loosely woven woolen cloth.* 2. Mătch'eş, *small splints of wood, one end of which has been dipped in a preparation which will take fire by rubbing.* 3. Pĕn'ny, *cent.* 4. Dĕl'i eate, *soft and fair.* 8. For sāke', *leave, reject.*

LESSON LXVI.

THE LITTLE LOAF.

1. Once when there was a famine, a rich baker sent for twenty of the poorest children in the town, and said to them, "In this basket there is a loaf for each of you. Take it, and come back to me every day at this hour till God sends us better times."

2. The hungry children gathered eagerly about the basket, and quarreled for the bread, because each wished to have the largest loaf. At last they went away without even thanking the good gentleman.

3. But Gretchen, a poorly-dressed little girl, did not quarrel or struggle with the rest,

but remained standing modestly in the distance. When the ill-behaved girls had left, she took the smallest loaf, which alone was left in the basket, kissed the gentleman's hand, and went home.

4. The next day the children were as ill-behaved as before, and poor, timid Gretchen received a loaf scarcely half the size of the one she got the first day. When she came home, and her mother cut the loaf open, many new, shining pieces of silver fell out of it.

5. Her mother was very much alarmed, and said, "Take the money back to the good gentleman at once, for it must have got into the dough by accident. Be quick, Gretchen! be quick!"

6. But when the little girl gave the rich man her mother's message, he said, "No, no, my child, it was no mistake. I had the silver pieces put into the smallest loaf to reward you. Always be as contented, peaceable, and grateful as you now are. Go home now, and tell your mother that the money is your own."

DEFINITIONS.—1. Făm'ĭne, *a general scarcity of food.* Lōaf, *a molded mass of regular shape* (as of bread or cake). 3. Grĕtch'en, *a girl's name—the shortened form, or pet name, for Marguerite.* Re māined', *staid.* Dĭs'tançe, *place which is far off.* Ill-be hāved', *rude, having bad manners.* 5. Ae'çĭdent, *mistake.* 6. Mĕs'saġe, *word sent, communication.* Pēaçe'able, *quiet, gentle.*

LESSON LXVII.

SUSIE AND ROVER.

1. "Mamma," said Susie Dean, one summer's morning, "may I go to the woods, and pick berries?"

2. "Yes," replied Mrs. Dean, "but you must take Rover with you."

3. Susie brought her little basket, and her mother put up a nice lunch for her. She tied down the cover, and fastened a tin cup to it.

4. The little girl called Rover—a great Newfoundland dog—and gave him a tin pail to carry. "If I bring it home full, mamma," she said, "won't you make some berry cakes for tea?"

5. Away she tripped, singing as she went down the lane and across the pasture. When she got to the woods, she put her dinner basket down beside a tree, and began to pick berries.

6. Rover ran about, chasing a squirrel or a rabbit now and then, but never straying far from Susie.

7. The tin pail was not a very small one. By the time it was two thirds full, Susie began to feel hungry, and thought she would eat her lunch.

8. Rover came and took his place at her side as soon as she began to eat. Did she not give him some of the lunch? No, she was in a selfish mood, and did no such thing.

9. "There, Rover, run away! there's a good dog," she said; but Rover staid near her, watching her steadily with his clear brown eyes.

10. The meat he wanted so much, was soon eaten up; and all he got of the nice dinner, was a small crust of gingerbread that Susie threw away.

11. After dinner, Susie played a while by

the brook. She threw sticks into the water, and Rover swam in and brought them back. Then she began to pick berries again.

12. She did not enjoy the afternoon as she did the morning. The sunshine was as bright, the berries were as sweet and plentiful, and she was neither tired nor hungry.

13. But good, faithful Rover was hungry, and she had not given him even one piece of meat. She tried to forget how selfish she had been; but she could not do so, and quite early she started for home.

14. When she was nearly out of the woods, a rustling in the underbrush attracted her attention. "I wonder if that is a bird or a squirrel," said she to herself. "If I can catch it, how glad I shall be!"

15. She tried to make her way quietly through the underbrush; but what was her terror when she saw a large snake coiled up before her, prepared for a spring!

16. She was so much frightened that she could not move; but brave Rover saw the snake, and, springing forward, seized it by the neck and killed it.

17. When the faithful dog came and rubbed his head against her hand, Susie put her

3, 12.

arms around his neck, and burst into tears. "O Rover," she cried, "you dear, good dog! How sorry I am that I was so selfish!"

18. Rover understood the tone of her voice, if he did not understand her words, and capered about in great glee, barking all the time. You may be sure that he had a plentiful supper that evening.

19. Susie never forgot the lesson of that day. She soon learned to be on her guard against a selfish spirit, and became a happier and more lovable little girl.

Mrs. M. O. Johnson—Adapted.

DEFINITIONS.—8. Sĕlf'ish, *thinking and caring only for one's self.* Mōod, *state of mind.* 9. Stĕad'i ly, *constantly.* 12. Plĕn'ti fụl, *abundant.* Nēi'ther, *not the one or the other.* 14. Un'der brŭsh, *shrubs or small bushes in a forest.* Attrăet'ed, *drew.* At tĕn'tion, *earnest thought.* 15. Tĕr'ror, *fright, fear.* 18. Cā'pered, *frisked.*

LESSON LXVIII.

THE VIOLET.

1. Down in a green and shady bed,
    A modest violet grew;
Its stalk was bent, it hung its head,
    As if to hide from view.

2. And yet it was a lovely flower,
    Its colors bright and fair;
It might have graced a rosy bower
    Instead of hiding there.

3. Yet there it was content to bloom,
    In modest tints arrayed,
And there it spread its sweet perfume,
    Within the silent shade.

4. Then let me to the valley go,
    This pretty flower to see;
That I may also learn to grow
    In sweet humility.

Jane Taylor.

LESSON LXIX.

NO CROWN FOR ME.

1. "Will you come with us, Susan?" cried several little girls to a schoolmate. "We are going to the woods; do come, too."

2. "I should like to go with you very much," replied Susan, with a sigh; "but I can not finish the task grandmother set me to do."

3. "How tiresome it must be to stay at home to work on a holiday!" said one of the girls, with a toss of her head. "Susan's grandmother is too strict."

4. Susan heard this remark, and, as she bent her head over her task, she wiped away a tear, and thought of the pleasant afternoon the girls would spend gathering wild flowers in the woods.

5. Soon she said to herself, "What harm can there be in moving the mark grandmother put in the stocking? The woods must be very beautiful to-day, and how I should like to be in them!"

6. "Grandmother," said she, a few minutes afterwards, "I am ready, now." "What, so

soon, Susan?" Her grandmother took the work, and looked at it very closely.

7. "True, Susan," said she, laying great stress on each word; "true, I count twenty turns from the mark; and, as you have never deceived me, you may go and amuse yourself as you like the rest of the day."

8. Susan's cheeks were scarlet, and she did not say, "Thank you." As she left the cottage, she walked slowly away, not singing as usual.

9. "Why, here is Susan!" the girls cried, when she joined their company; "but what is the matter? Why have you left your dear, old grandmother?" they tauntingly added.

10. "There is nothing the matter." As Susan repeated these words, she felt that she was trying to deceive herself. She had acted a lie. At the same time she remembered her grandmother's words, "You have never deceived me."

11. "Yes, I have deceived her," said she to herself. "If she knew all, she would never trust me again."

12. When the little party had reached an open space in the woods, her companions ran about enjoying themselves; but Susan sat on

the grass, wishing she were at home confessing her fault.

13. After a while Rose cried out, "Let us make a crown of violets, and put it on the head of the best girl here."

14. "It will be easy enough to make the crown, but not so easy to decide who is to wear it," said Julia.

15. "Why, Susan is to wear it, of course," said Rose: "is she not said to be the best girl in school, and the most obedient at home?"

16. "Yes, yes; the crown shall be for Su-

san," cried the other girls, and they began to make the crown. It was soon finished.

17. "Now, Susan," said Rose, "put it on in a very dignified way, for you are to be our queen."

18. As these words were spoken, the crown was placed on her head. In a moment she snatched it off, and threw it on the ground, saying, "No crown for me; I do not deserve it."

19. The girls looked at her with surprise. "I have deceived my grandmother," said she, while tears flowed down her cheeks. "I altered the mark she put in the stocking, that I might join you in the woods."

20. "Do you call that wicked?" asked one of the girls.

"I am quite sure it is; and I have been miserable all the time I have been here."

21. Susan now ran home, and as soon as she got there she said, with a beating heart, "O grandmother! I deserve to be punished, for I altered the mark you put in the stocking. Do forgive me; I am very sorry and unhappy."

22. "Susan," said her grandmother, "I knew it all the time; but I let you go out, hoping

that your own conscience would **tell** you of your sin. I am so glad that you have confessed your fault and your sorrow."

23. "When shall I be your own little girl again?" "Now," was the quick reply, and Susan's grandmother kissed her forehead.

DEFINITIONS.—3. Tīre′sŏme, *tedious, wearisome.* 7. Strĕss, *force, emphasis.* 9. Cŏm′pa ny, *a number of persons together.* Täunt′ing ly, *in a disagreeable, reproachful manner.* 12. Con-fĕss′ing, *telling of, acknowledging.* Fa̤ult, *wrongdoing, sin.* 17. Dĭḡ′ni fīed, *respectful, stately.* 19. Al′tered (a̤l′-), *changed.* 20. Mĭş′er a ble, *wretched, very unhappy.* 23. Fŏre′head (fŏr′ed), *the front part of the head above the eyes.*

LESSON LXX.

YOUNG SOLDIERS.

1. Oh, were you ne'er a schoolboy,
    And did you never train,
 And feel that swelling of the heart
    You ne'er can feel again?

2. Did you never meet, far down the street,
    With plumes and banners gay,
 While the kettle, for the kettledrum,
    Played your march, march away?

3. It seems to me but yesterday,
   Nor scarce so long ago,
Since all our school their muskets took,
   To charge the fearful foe.

4. Our muskets were of cedar wood,
   With ramrods bright and new;
With bayonets forever set,
   And painted barrels, too.

5. We charged upon a flock of geese,
   And put them all to flight—
Except one sturdy gander
   That thought to show us fight.

6. But, ah! we knew a thing or two;
    Our captain wheeled the van;
We routed him, we scouted him,
    Nor lost a single man!

7. Our captain was as brave a lad
    As e'er commission bore;
And brightly shone his new tin sword;
    A paper cap he wore.

8. He led us up the steep hillside,
    Against the western wind,
While the cockerel plume that decked his
        head
    Streamed bravely out behind.

9. We shouldered arms, we carried arms,
    We charged the bayonet;
And woe unto the mullein stalk
    That in our course we met!

10. At two o'clock the roll we called,
  And till the close of day,
With fearless hearts, though tired limbs,
  We fought the mimic fray,—
Till the supper bell, from out the dell,
  Bade us march, march away.

DEFINITIONS.—2. Kĕt'tle drŭm, *a drum made of a copper vessel shaped like a kettle.* 3. Mŭs'ket, *a kind of gun.* 4. Cē'dar, *a very durable kind of wood.* Bāy'o net, *a sharp piece of steel on the end of a gun.* Băr'rel, *the long metal tube forming part of a gun.* 5. Stûr'dy, *stubborn, bold.* 6. Văn, *the front.* Rout'ed, *put to flight.* Scout'ed, *made fun of.* 7. Com mĭs'sion, *a writing to show power.* 8. Cŏck'er el, *a young chicken-cock.* 9. Chärġed, *made an onset.* Mŭl'lein, *a tall plant that grows in neglected fields.* 10. Frāy, *fight, contest.*

LESSON LXXI.

HOW WILLIE GOT OUT OF THE SHAFT.

1. Willie's aunt sent him for a birthday present a little writing book. There was a place in the book for a pencil. Willie thought a great deal of this little book, and always kept it in his pocket.

2. One day, his mother was very busy, and he called his dog, and said, "Come, Caper, let us have a play."

3. When Willie's mother missed him, she went to the door and looked out, and could not see him anywhere; but she knew that Caper was with him, and thought they would come back before long.

4. She waited an hour, and still they did not come. When she came to the gate by the road, she met Mr. Lee, and told him how long Willie had been gone. Mr. Lee thought he must have gone to sleep under the trees. So they went to all the trees under which Willie was in the habit of playing, but he was nowhere to be found.

5. By this time the sun had gone down. The news that Willie was lost soon spread over the neighborhood, and all the men and women turned out to hunt. They hunted all night.

6. The next morning the neighbors were gathered round, and all were trying to think what to do next, when Caper came bounding into the room. There was a string tied round his neck, and a bit of paper tied to it.

7. Willie's father, Mr. Lee, took the paper, and saw that it was a letter from Willie. He read it aloud. It said, "O father! come to me. I am in the big hole in the pasture."

8. Everybody ran at once to the far corner of the pasture; and there was Willie, alive and well, in the shaft. Oh, how glad he was when his father caught him in his arms, and lifted him out!

9. Now I will tell you how Willie came to be in the shaft. He and Caper went to the pasture field, and came to the edge of the shaft and sat down. In bending over

to see how deep it was, he lost his balance, and fell in. He tried very hard to get out, but could not.

10. When the good little dog saw that his master was in the shaft, he would not leave him, but ran round and round, reaching down and trying to pull him out. But while Caper was pulling Willie by the coat sleeves, a piece of sod gave way under his feet, and he fell in too.

11. Willie called for his father and mother as loud as he could call; but he was so far away from the house that no one could hear him.

12. He cried and called till it was dark, and then he lay down on the ground, and Caper lay down close beside him. It was not long before Willie cried himself to sleep.

13. When he awoke it was morning, and he began to think of a way to get out. The little writing book that his aunt had given him, was in his pocket. He took it out, and, after a good deal of trouble, wrote the letter to his father.

14. Then he tore the leaf out, and took a string out of his pocket, and tied it round Caper's neck, and tied the letter to the

string. Then he lifted the dog up, and helped him out, and said to him, "Go home, Caper, go home!" The little dog scampered away, and was soon at home.

DEFINITIONS.—1. Bĭrth'dāy, *the same day of the month in which a person was born, in each succeeding year.* 5. Nẹigh'- bor hŏod, *the surrounding region which lies nearest, vicinity.* Wom'en (wĭm'en), *plural of woman.* 8. Shȧft, *a deep hole made in the earth, usually for mining purposes.* 14. Seăm'- pered, *ran briskly.*

LESSON LXXII.

THE PERT CHICKEN.

1. There was once a pretty chicken;
   But his friends were very few,
For he thought that there was nothing
   In the world but what he knew:
So he always, in the farmyard,
   Had a very forward way,
Telling all the hens and turkeys
   What they ought to do and say.
"Mrs. Goose," he said, "I wonder
   That your goslings you should let
Go out paddling in the water;
   It will kill them to get wet."

2. "I wish, my old Aunt Dorking,"
    He began to her, one day,
  "That you would n't sit all summer
    In your nest upon the hay.
  Wo n't you come out to the meadow,
    Where the grass with seeds is filled?"
  "If I should," said Mrs. Dorking,
    "Then my eggs would all get chilled."
  "No, they wo n't," replied the chicken,
    "And no matter if they do;
  Eggs are really good for nothing;
    What's an egg to me or you?"

3. "What's an egg!" said Mrs. Dorking,
    "Can it be you do not know

You yourself were in an eggshell
    Just one little month ago?
And, if kind wings had not warmed you,
    You would not be out to-day,
Telling hens, and geese, and turkeys,
    What they ought to do and say!

4. " To be very wise, and show it,
    Is a pleasant thing, no doubt;
But, when young folks talk to old folks,
    They should know what they 're about."

Marian Douglas.

DEFINITIONS.—1. Färm'yärd, *the inclosed ground attached to a barn and other farm buildings.* Fôr'ward, *bold, confident.* Tûr'key, *a large domestic fowl.* Gŏṣ'lingṣ, *young geese.* Păd'-dling, *beating the water with the feet, swimming.* 2. Dôr'king, *a species of chicken.*

LESSON LXXIII.

INDIAN CORN.

1. Few plants are more useful to man than Indian corn, or maize. No grain, except rice, is used to so great an extent as an article of food. In some countries corn is almost the only food eaten by the people.

2. Do you know why it is called Indian corn? It is because the American Indians were the first corn growers. Columbus found this grain widely cultivated by them when he discovered the New World. They pounded it in rude, stone bowls, and thus made a coarse flour, which they mixed with water and baked.

3. Indian corn is now the leading crop in the United States. In whatever part of this land we live, we see corn growing every year in its proper season. Yet how few can tell the most simple and important facts about its planting and its growth!

4. Corn, to do well, must have a rich soil and a warm climate. It is a tender plant, and is easily injured by cold weather. The seed corn does not sprout, but rots, if the ground is cold and wet.

5. To prepare land properly for planting corn, the soil is made fine by plowing, and furrows are run across the field four feet apart each way. At every point where these furrows cross, the farmer drops from four to seven grains of seed corn. These are then covered with about two inches of earth, and thus form "hills" of corn.

6. In favorable weather, the tender blades push through the ground in ten days or two weeks; then the stalks mount up rapidly, and the long, streamer-like leaves unfold gracefully from day to day. Corn must be carefully cultivated while the plants are small. After they begin to shade the ground, they need but little hoeing or plowing.

7. The moisture and earthy matter, drawn through the roots, become sap. This passes through the stalk, and enters the leaves. There a great change takes place, which results in the starting of the ears and the growth of the grain.

8. The maize plant bears two kinds of flowers,—male and female. The two are widely separated. The male flowers are on the tassel; the fine silk threads which surround the ear, and peep out from the end of the husks, are the female flowers.

9. Each grain on the cob is the starting-point for a thread of silk; and, unless the thread receives some particle of the dust which falls from the tassel flowers, the kernel with which it is connected will not grow.

10. The many uses of Indian corn and its products are worthy of note. The green

stalks and leaves make excellent fodder for cattle. The ripe grain is used all over the earth as food for horses, pigs, and poultry. Nothing is better for fattening stock.

11. Green corn, or "roasting ears," hulled corn and hominy, New England hasty pudding, and succotash are favorite dishes with many persons. Then there are parched corn and pop corn—the delight of long winter evenings.

12. Cornstarch is an important article of commerce. Sirup and sugar are made from the juice of the stalk, and oil and alcohol from the ripened grain. Corn husks are largely used for filling mat-

tresses, and are braided into mats, baskets, and other useful articles.

13. Thus it will be seen how varied are the uses of Indian corn. And besides being so useful, the plant is very beautiful. The sight of a large cornfield in the latter part of summer, with all its green banners waving and its tasseled plumes nodding, is one to admire, and not to be forgotten.

DEFINITIONS.—1. Ar'ti ele, *a particular one of various things.* 2. Cŭl'ti vāt ed, *grown.* 3. Im pôr'tant, *of much value.* 5. Fŭr'row, *a trench made by a plow.* 6. Fā'vor a ble, *that which is kindly, propitious.* Strēam'er, *a long, narrow flag.* 7. Mois'-ture, *wet, dampness.* Re ṣŭlts', *comes out, ends.* 8. Sĕp'a rat ed, *apart, not connected.* 9. Pär'ti ele, *a very small portion.* 10. Ex'çel lent, *good, superior.* Fŏd'der, *such food for animals as hay, straw, and vegetables.* Pōul'try, *barnyard fowls.* Sŭe'eo-tăsh, *corn and beans boiled together.* 12. Cŏm'merçe, *trade.* Al'eo hol, *distilled liquor.* Măt'tress eṣ, *beds stuffed with hair, straw, or other soft material.* Brāid'ed, *woven or twisted together.*

LESSON LXXIV.

THE SNOWBIRD'S SONG.

1. The ground was all covered with snow one day,
   And two little sisters were busy at play,
   When a snowbird was sitting close by on a tree,
   And merrily singing his chick-a-de-dee.

2. He had not been singing that tune very long
   Ere Emily heard him, so loud was his song:
   "O sister, look out of the window!" said she;
   "Here's a dear little bird singing chick-a-de-dee.

3. "Poor fellow! he walks in the snow and the sleet,
   And has neither stockings nor shoes on his feet:
   I wonder what makes him so full of his glee;
   He's all the time singing his chick-a-de-dee.

4. "If I were a barefooted snowbird, I know,
   I would not stay out in the cold and the snow;
   I pity him so! oh, how cold he must be!
   And yet he keeps singing his chick-a-de-dee.

5. "O mother; do get him some stockings, and shoes,
And a nice little frock, and a hat if he choose:
I wish he'd come into the parlor, and see
How warm we would make him, poor chick-a-de-
    dee!"

6. The bird had flown down for some sweet crumbs of
    bread,
And heard every word little Emily said:
"What a figure I'd make in that dress," thought he,
And laughed as he warbled his chick-a-de-dee.

7. "I am grateful," said he, "for the wish you express,
But have no occasion for such a fine dress;
I rather remain with my little limbs free,
Than to hobble about, singing chick-a-de-dee.

8. "There is One, my dear child, though I can not
    tell who,
Has clothed me already, and warm enough, too.
Good morning! Oh, who are so happy as we?"
And away he flew, singing his chick-a-de-dee.

                              F. C. Woodworth.

DEFINITIONS.—1. Chĭck'-a-dē-dee, *an imitation of the notes of the snowbird.* 6. Fĭg'ūre, *shape, appearance.* 7. Ex prĕss', *nake known, declare.* Hŏb'ble, *to walk with a hitch or hop.*

LESSON LXXV.

MOUNTAINS.

1. The Himalayas are the highest mountains on our globe. They are in Asia, and separate India from Thibet. They extend in a continuous line for more than a thousand miles.

2. If you ever ascend one of these mountains from the plain below, you will have to cross an unhealthy border, twenty miles in width. It is, in fact, a swamp caused by the waters overflowing the river banks.

3. The soil of this swampy border is covered with trees and shrubs, where the tiger, the elephant, and other animals find secure retreat. Beyond this border, you will reach smiling valleys and noble forests.

4. As you advance onward and upward, you will get among bolder and more rugged scenes. The sides of the mountains are very steep, sometimes well wooded to quite a height, but sometimes quite barren.

5. In crossing a river you must be content with three ropes for a bridge. You will find the streets of the towns to be simply stairs

cut out of the rock, and see the houses rising in tiers.

6. The pathways into Thibet, among these mountains, are mere tracks by the side of

foaming torrents. Often, as you advance, you will find every trace of the path swept away by the falling of rocks and earth from above.

7. Sometimes you will find posts driven into the mountain side, upon which branches of trees and earth are spread. This forms a trembling foothold for the traveler.

8. In the Andes, in South America, the sure-footed mule is used to carry travelers. Quite often a chasm must be crossed that is many feet wide and hundreds of feet deep. The mule will leap across this chasm, but not until it is sure it can make a safe jump.

9. "One day," says a traveler, "I went by the worst pass over the Andes Mountains. The path for seventy yards was very narrow, and at one point it was washed entirely away. On one side the rock brushed my shoulder, and on the other side my foot over-hung the precipice."

10. The guide told this man, after he was safely over the pass, that, to his knowledge, four hundred mules had fallen over that precipice, and in many instances travelers had lost their lives at that terrible spot.

DEFINITIONS. — 1. Hĭm ä′la ya, *also written* Him mä′lẹh. Thĭb′et (Tĭb-), *a country of central Asia.* 2. As çĕnd′, *go up, climb.* Swạmp, *low, wet ground.* 3. Re trēat′, *place of safety.* 4. Ad vànçe′, *go forward.* Rŭg̃′g̃ed, *rough.* Băr′ren, *without trees or shrubs, unproductive.* 5. Tiẽrṣ, *rows one above another.*

7. Fŏŏt'hŏld, *that on which one may tread.* 8. An'dēṣ, *next to the highest range of mountains in the world.* Chăṣm (kăzm), *a deep opening in the earth, or cleft in the rocks.* 9. Prĕç'i pïçe, *a very steep and dangerous descent.* 10. Knŏwl'-edġe (nŏl'ej), *that which is known.*

LESSON LXXVI.

A CHILD'S HYMN.

1. God make my life a little light,
     Within the world to glow;
   A little flame that burneth bright
     Wherever I may go.

2. God make my life a little flower,
     That giveth joy to all,
   Content to bloom in native bower,
     Although its place be small.

3. God make my life a little song,
     That comforteth the sad;
   That helpeth others to be strong,
     And makes the singer glad.

4. God make my life a little hymn
     Of tenderness and praise;
   Of faith—that never waxeth dim
     In all His wondrous ways.

LESSON LXXVII.

HOLDING THE FORT.

1. While Genie was walking slowly down street one day, she heard an odd rapping on the pavement behind her. Looking round, she saw Rob Grey hobbling on crutches.

2. "Why, what is the matter?" cried Genie. "I haven't seen you for a week, and now you are walking in that way."

3. "I shall have to walk in this way as much as a week longer, Genie. I sprained my ankle by stopping too quick—no, not too quick, either, for there was something in my way."

"What was it?" asked Genie.

4. "One of the Commandments," replied Rob. "You remember how that lecturer talked to us about 'holding the fort'? Well, I thought I should like to do it; but it's a pretty long war, you know—all a lifetime, and no vacations—furloughs, I think they call them."

5. "If there was nothing to fight, we should not need to be soldiers," said Genie.

6. "Well, I thought I would try; but the

first day, when we came out of the school-house, Jack Lee snatched my books out of my hand, and threw them into the mud.

7. "I started after him as fast as I could run. I meant to throw him where he had

thrown the books, when, all of a sudden, I thought of the Commandment about returning good for evil.

8. "I stopped short—so short, that, some-

how, my foot twisted under me. So, you see, it was one of the Commandments."

9. "If one must stumble at them, it is a good thing to fall on the right side," said Genie, with a wise nod of her head.

10. "The whole thing puzzles me, and makes me feel—well, like giving it up," said Rob. "It might have served me right when I was chasing Jack; but when I thought of the Commandment, I really tried to do the right thing."

11. "You did do it, Rob," said Genie. "You 'held the fort' that time. Why, don't you see—you are only a wounded soldier."

12. "I never thought of that," said Rob. "If I believe that way—" He began to whistle, and limped off to school without finishing the sentence. But Genie knew, by the way he behaved that day, that he had made up his mind to *hold the fort*.

DEFINITIONS.—1. Pāve′ment, *a walk covered with brick or other hard material.* Crŭtch′eş, *long sticks with crosspieces at the top, to aid lame persons in walking.* 3. Sprāined, *injured by wrenching or twisting.* 4. Com mánd′ments, *holy laws recorded in the Bible.* Lĕe′tur er, *a public speaker.* Va eā′tion, *the time between two school terms.* Fûr′lough (fûr′lo), *a soldier's leave of absence.* 11. Wound′ed (wōōnd′ed), *hurt, injured.* 12. Be hāved′, *acted.*

LESSON LXXVIII.

THE LITTLE PEOPLE.

1. A dreary place would be this earth,
    Were there no little people in it;
The song of life would lose its mirth,
    Were there no children to begin it;

2. No little forms, like buds to grow,
    And make the admiring heart surrender;
No little hands on breast and brow,
    To keep the thrilling love chords tender.

3. The sterner souls would grow more stern,
    Unfeeling nature more inhuman,
And man to utter coldness turn,
    And woman would be less than woman.

4. Life's song, indeed, would lose its charm,
    Were there no babies to begin it;
A doleful place this world would be,
    Were there no little people in it.

John G. Whittier.

DEFINITIONS —1. Drēar'y, *cheerless.* 2. Sur rĕn'der, *give up, yield.* Lȯve ehôrd͜s, *ties of affection.* 3. Stĕrn, *severe, harsh.* Ut'ter, *complete.* 4. Dōle'ful, *gloomy, sad.*

LESSON LXXIX.

GOOD NIGHT.

1. The sun is hidden from our sight,
   The birds are sleeping sound;
   'T is time to say to all, "Good night!"
   And give a kiss all round.

2. Good night, my father, mother, dear!
   Now kiss your little son;
   Good night, my friends, both far and near!
   Good night to every one.

3. Good night, ye merry, merry birds!
   Sleep well till morning light;
   Perhaps, if you could sing in words,
   You would have said, "Good night!"

4. To all my pretty flowers, good night!
   You blossom while I sleep;
   And all the stars, that shine so bright,
   With you their watches keep.

5. The moon is lighting up the skies,
   The stars are sparkling there;
   'T is time to shut our weary eyes,
   And say our evening prayer.

Mrs. Follen.

P9-CQN-649

$36.55

PO 73590

5-30-01

DISCARDED

Brooks - Cork Library

Shelton State

Community College

DATE DUE

DEMCO, INC. 38-2931

What is Cognitive Science?

Edited by

Ernest Lepore and Zenon Pylyshyn

Rutgers University

Brooks - Cork Library
Shelton State
Community College

BLACKWELL *Publishers*

Copyright © Blackwell Publishers Ltd 1999

First published 1999

2 4 6 8 10 9 7 5 3 1

Blackwell Publishers Inc.
350 Main Street
Malden, Massachusetts 02148
USA

Blackwell Publishers Ltd
108 Cowley Road
Oxford OX4 1JF
UK

All rights reserved. Except for the quotation of short passages for the purposes of criticism
and review, no part of this publication may be reproduced, stored in a retrieval system, or
transmitted, in any form or by any means, electronic, mechanical, photocopying, recording
or otherwise, without the prior permission of the publisher.

Except in the United States of America, this book is sold subject to the condition that it
shall not, by way of trade or otherwise, be lent, resold, hired out, or otherwise circulated
without the publisher's prior consent in any form of binding or cover other than that in
which it is published and without a similar condition including this condition being
imposed on the subsequent purchaser.

Library of Congress Cataloging-in-Publication Data

What is cognitive science? / edited by Ernest Lepore and Zenon Pylyshyn.
    p.   cm.
   includes bibliographical references and index.
   ISBN 0–631–20493–8 (hardback : alk. paper).—ISBN 0–631–20494–6
(pbk. : alk. paper)
   1. Cognitive science. 2. Cognition. I. LePore, Ernest. 1950–
II. Pylyshyn, Zenon W., 1937–
BF311.W48 1999
153—dc21
                                 98–47772
                                     CIP

British Library Cataloguing in Publication Data

A CIP catalogue record for this book is available from the British Library.

Typeset in 10½ on 12½ pt Galliard
by SetSystems, Saffron Walden, Essex
Printed in Great Britain by
MPG Books Ltd, Bodmin, Cornwall

This book is printed on acid-free paper.

Contents

Preface

Background: RuCCS

Since these essays arose from talks given at the Rutgers Center for Cognitive Science, it is appropriate to begin by introducing that institution. Rutgers University's Center for Cognitive Science (RuCCS) was established on the New Brunswick, New Jersey, campus in October 1991. A primary goal of the Center is to foster research concerned with understanding the nature of certain symbolic processes that are constitutive of intelligent performance. We recognize that the approach in cognitive science, by contrast with the approach taken by other investigators interested in similar issues, is essentially computational; the capacity for intelligence is viewed in this discipline as arising from the processing of representations. The general goal, therefore, is to understand such cognitive capacities as perception, language acquisition and processing, planning, problem solving, reasoning, learning, and the acquisition, representation, and use of knowledge, in terms of the computational processes that underwrite these capacities, as well as their instantiation in silicon hardware or biological tissue. The pursuit is essentially multidisciplinary and involves techniques and knowledge drawn from experimental psychology, computer science, neuroscience, philosophy, linguistics, mathematics, and engineering.

The multidisciplinary nature of the research goes much deeper in cognitive science than in many other interdisciplinary fields. A typical cognitive science research project, say in visual perception, involves substantive contributions from psychological and/or psychobiological experiments, from the application of principles of physical optics, techniques from mathematics and logic, and considerations of representational formalism and cognitive architecture that are sometimes the subject of study in the philosophy of mind and philosophical logic. Finally, such research typically leads to the implementation of a model in the form of a computer program, which may then be examined empirically by applying it to real digitized images. Similarly, the study of how natural language is understood by humans, and how it might be processed by a computer, may involve considerations that are equally widely dispersed across academic disciplines – including physical acoustics, psychophysics, linguistics, psycholinguistics, the study of discourse processes (which involves issues of reasoning, planning, and knowledge representation, frequently studied in artificial intelligence), as well as issues of semantics such as are studied in philosophy of language and philosophy of mind.

Because both the content and the techniques used in such investigations come from such a wide diversity of sources, it is difficult to anticipate which of the contributing disciplines will provide the critical insight for some particular research problem. For this reason the Center provides facilities to enable researchers to interact fully and freely with each other as well as with other external researchers and industrial laboratories.

In its first seven years of existence, RuCCS built up an impressive faculty and an interdisciplinary training program in Cognitive Science, recently re-cognized by an NMRA training grant from the National Institutes of Health. Part of the training that both undergraduate and graduate students receive consists in the experience of hearing and meeting well-known researchers and faculty members who provide models of both teacher and researcher.

Because Rutgers is situated in an area rich in both academic and industrial research, there are always well-known scholars passing through the area. We have taken that opportunity to enlist them in a number of different lecture series during the academic years 1996–8. Our best-attended series, known as "What is Cognitive Science?", was held over lunch every Thursday and drew primarily on Rutgers Cognitive Science faculty. Then there was a series entitled "Human and Machine Vision" which was co-sponsored with several Rutgers academic departments and research laboratories engaged in vision research. Vision is a particularly active area of research both at Rutgers and at nearby universities and industrial research laboratories. The series was able to draw on prominent vision researchers from the seven or so major research universities and some dozen industrial laboratories conducting research in vision. Finally, there was our Distinguished Speakers Colloquium series which met only about once a month but featured distinguished speakers drawn from many disciplines that contribute to the cognitive science enterprise (particularly psychology, linguistics, computer science, and philosophy). These lecture series presented such an array of talent that we felt we should expose a larger audience than our own students to some of this material. And so the idea for this book was born.

What's in this Book?

Between these covers we present a selection of essays based on lectures given under the auspices of the Rutgers Center for Cognitive Science. They provide a sample of cognitive science material of the introductory pedagogical sort, as well as a sampling of the leading technical work being carried out by researchers in what are considered to be different traditional contributing disciplines. In their apprenticeship to cognitive science research, students benefit from both kinds of material – from overviews and from more challenging technical specialty topics. The talks themselves fell naturally into three categories: introductory overview talks, talks about vision, and talks about language. Although neuroscience was underrepresented in the talks held during the first few years of the center's existence (an imbalance that is being redressed this year), we are fortunate in being close to the Newark campus of Rutgers University, which has provided a number of distinguished speakers. Consequently, neuroscience and learning provide our fourth category of talks.

Needless to say, this collection is not an exhaustive, nor even a representative, sample of the work in cognitive science, or even of the talks heard by students during the past few years. But we felt that these particular talks were of sufficient breadth and pedagogical merit that they deserved to be shared with students who were not fortunate enough to have been present for them – including our present and past students, as well as those from other institutions. We hope this collection will inspire some readers to consider Cognitive Science as a research career choice and will provide others with interesting reading about topics that define cognitive science, at least as it is practiced at the Center for Cognitive Science at Rutgers, New Brunswick.

Acknowledgments

The editors wish to thank the people who made both the lecture series and the book possible. First and foremost we thank Trish Anderson, the assistant director for administration of the Center, who did much of the work in organizing the series and in helping to host the speakers. We are also indebted to Sven Dickinson for organizing the vision series, to Jacob Feldman for organizing the RuCCS colloquium series, and to Brian Scholl who helped us to organize and edit the papers in this volume. We would like to thank Carol Esso, Jean van Altena, and Mary Dortch for their efforts, particularly during the final stages of putting this book together. Finally, we would like to recognize the encouragement and help provided by the university itself, primarily through the Faculty of Arts and Science and its ever-supportive dean, Richard Foley.

Ernest Lepore and Zenon Pylyshyn
New Brunswick, NJ

1

What's in Your Mind?

Zenon W. Pylyshyn

1   Introduction

Neuropsychologists have an advantage on us dry cognitive scientists: They always have impressive color slides of PET or MRI or fMRI images showing the exact location of whatever they wish to discuss – the soul or the locus of sinful thoughts or the center of consciousness. If one were to go by popular science articles on the brain, one would have to conclude that we know where everything is located in the brain, and therefore we know everything about it except *how* it manages to do things like think. But I chose the title deliberately, because I believe that what we do here at the Center for Cognitive Science is precisely that we study what is in the mind. Let me explain.

The term "mind" has been associated with psychology at least as far back as William James, who defined psychology as the "Science of Mental Life." Yet in the past 50 years it has fallen into disfavor. But there is good reason to believe that this was a mistake and that psychology really is about the mind, and in particular that explanations of behavior must take into account what is in the mind. The question of what's in the mind should be answered in psychology in the same way that the parallel question is answered in physics. There, a question such as what's in this table or what's in the sun is answered by looking for properties, entities, and causal laws which explain the important regularities that define that particular science.

This essay is based in part on a lecture in the "What is Cognitive Science?" series held at the Rutgers Center for Cognitive Science in the fall of 1996.

The trouble with saying that answers to psychological questions should be provided by looking for properties and laws that explain important regularities in the science is that we do not know in advance of the development of the science exactly what will count as relevant regularities. This is a point that often escapes the social sciences. Physics does not consider it a failure if it can't explain why some parts of the table are dustier than others, why some parts are rougher, why some parts are warped, or why the wood will eventually rot because of bacteria and other microorganisms that infest it. It simply turns out that those are not the regularities that physics is equipped to answer. It doesn't even have categories like corner or rough or smooth or rotting in its laws. That's why there are other sciences, like microbiology perhaps, which address regularities based on such categories.

Notice that we do not demand that the terms that occur in the answer to the question "What's in this table?" be ones that we have any prior understanding of or expectations about, or even that they be things that we can see or feel or taste or otherwise have any sensory contact with. In psychology we always feel that we can set two kinds of agendas in advance. One is that we can say what the relevant data will be. For example, we say that psychology is in the business of predicting behavior. If this were true, much of our work would already be done, since there is already a way of predicting such behavior as that when people fall off the top of a building they accelerate at roughly 10 meters per second for every second of flight. But that's not psychology, you say! Exactly! But what exactly does count as psychology? The second, and closely related agenda that we often feel we can set in advance is specifying what the vocabulary or the categories will be in the science as it develops – as well as what sorts of things it will be able to explain. Is it to be concerned primarily with, say, voluntary behavior? That already presupposes that the category "voluntary" will be recognized and will play a role in the science of mind. Also "voluntary" is far from being a neutral term, since it assumes that we know what it is for some behavior to be voluntary. Moreover, it assumes that this is the type of behavior that cognitive science will be concerned to explain. It turns out that categories such as "voluntary" and "conscious" are very likely ones that we may have to give up as the science of mind develops a scientific base. Similarly, it has been widely assumed that psychology should be concerned with explaining "learning." But can we stipulate that in advance? Do we know what kinds of changes in behavior constitute learning, in the sense relevant to psychology (e.g., is the growth of hair and fingernails a type of "learning" and if not, why not?) and whether these changes will fall to psychology or biology or some other science to explain?

1.1 What is special about intelligent behavior?

The most remarkable property of human behavior involving intelligence (as well as similar behavior of certain other species), is that, in order to capture what is systematic about it, it is necessary to recognize equivalence classes of causal events that cannot be characterized using the terms of existing natural sciences. The anthropologist Kenneth Pike once made the astute observation that human behavior cannot be understood in terms of objective physical properties of the world, which he called *etic* properties, but only in terms of the way in which the world is perceived or represented in the mind, which he called *emic*, or internalized, properties. When viewed in terms of objectively defined classes of stimuli and responses, human behavior appears to be essentially stimulus-independent, and the attempt to cast it in terms of objectively defined stimulus properties runs up against either obvious counter-examples or self-contradictions (see, e.g., Chomsky's review of Skinner's attempt to do just that in his behaviorist analysis of language). On the other hand, when cast in terms of such constructs as beliefs and desires, and when reasoning is allowed as part of the process intervening between stimuli, representations, and actions, the picture becomes much more coherent (though still highly incomplete).

Consider typical folk-psychology explanations of ordinary behavior. Such explanations say, for example, that people do things because of what they know or believe and because of what they want, or more precisely because of their goals and utilities. Although such a general claim should be obvious, it has in fact been widely denied throughout the history of the field. The trouble with denying this truism is that without it you cannot explain the simplest piece of behavior, such as, for example, why there are people in the audience here today. You and I and your granny know that the reason there are people here is that they have been led to believe that there would be a talk given at this particular time in this room. Moreover, this is not a rough and approximate way of talking; it's really and truly the case. The way you know that it is truly the case is to consider what would have happened if the antecedent conditions in my explanation for why you are here had not been true – i.e., if you did not have the beliefs I said you had. For example, if you did not know that the talk was to be in this room, or did not know the time of the talk, or if you had some reason to discount the announcement that there would be a talk given here – for example, if you found out that I had not arrived in time, or if you had been led to believe through any of an indefinite number of ways, that the announcement you received was in error or that it was all a practical joke or that the building had to be evacuated because of a bomb scare, and so on and on without limit – and if I had reason to believe that *you* would not be here, then I too would not be here.

How often do you get such reliable predictions in scientific psychology? Notice that you only get such predictions if the explanatory vocabulary contains at least some of the terms of folk psychology – at least terms like "believes," along with terms for the contents of beliefs like "meeting," "talk," or even "practical joke" or "bomb scare." Moreover, you only get the predictions to come out if the beliefs and the meanings of sentences that people hear can enter into a certain kind of process, a process which we generically refer to as *inference*, wherein new beliefs are established that were not part of the original stimulus information, or, to put it differently, consequences are somehow drawn from the initial beliefs, goals, and data provided to the individual. It's absolutely clear that you cannot get by in cognitive psychology without, at the very minimum, having some way of dealing with this basic fact. Not even the most radical behaviorist fails to accept this fact, even though the polemics very often deny it.

So, for instance, while denying that meanings and knowledge and goals are relevant to the prediction of behavior, behaviorists still make use of the fact that they can predict people's behavior by putting up a poster containing sentences whose meaning is, for example, that if a person shows up at a certain time to take part in an experiment, that person will be paid a certain sum of money or will receive credit toward a course requirement. Notice that the experimenter implicitly accepts that the form of words on the poster, or its physical layout, is not what is relevant to predicting the reader's behavior; what matters is that the poster contains sentences with a certain meaning for the intended readership, and that in the proper context, rational people would come to have certain beliefs after reading those sentences, and that those beliefs together with the readers' goals and utilities would lead them to act in a certain way.[1]

1.2   Meaning and causality

The point of the subject-soliciting poster example is this: The relevant equivalence class of stimuli needed to predict behavior is the class of *synonymous sentences*, or the class of sentences that *mean* the same thing or at least underwrite the same belief. But this equivalence class contains an unbounded number of stimuli, and what the members of this class have in common cannot be specified physically – being "synonymous" is what is called a semantic property. What distinguishes one science from another is the class of events or properties that they appeal to. Geology talks about mountains and rivers; economics talks about value and supply and demand; meteorology talks about precipitation and storms and the jet stream, and so on. In each case the things being discussed are physical things, but the categories are not the ones that physics recognizes – and they differ from science to science. Psychology needs to speak of how we perceive a stimulus, what we believe and what we want – or, more generally, how we *represent* the world (see below).

Now if you accept this – and it would be irrational not to – then you are led immediately to ask how it is possible for a biological entity made of protoplasm and governed by natural laws to have such a property. And that's where the trouble begins, for this is a highly non-trivial problem for a number of reasons. Here is a glimpse of one such reason. In every science, when you have an explanation of the form "Y occurs because of X," then anything that fills the slot X is a causal property; hence any property mentioned in that statement must on each occasion have a real physical existence (assuming, as most of us do, that only physical things can serve as causes). But what about the explanation that you came to this room at this time because you believed there would be a talk given here? It is intrinsic to the explanation that it mention a talk. Yet the explanation would continue to be true whether or not there was in fact a talk. All that is required is that you *believed* that. But that makes belief a strange sort of property, a property characterized in terms of something that need not exist!

It is a true explanation of why King Arthur's knights did certain things in the Middle Ages that they were in search of the Holy Grail, or that other people did certain things because they were searching for the pot of gold at the end of the rainbow. And those explanations hold whether or not there is such a thing as a Holy Grail or a pot of gold at the end of the rainbow. The same is true of people who do things in order to win someone's love or to gain tenure. Depending on what the beliefs are about, people act differently, though nonetheless appropriately to the content of their beliefs. Beliefs about different things count as different beliefs. And this is true whether or not what the beliefs are about exists in the world, or whether it is even physically possible for it to exist (e.g., ghosts). How, then, can the content of belief enter into the causation or the explanation of behavior?

Needless to say, this is a venerable old puzzle, one that was first brought to the attention of psychologists by Franz Brentano, and one which is still hotly debated by philosophers. But it is fair to say that within the research community that identifies with cognitive science and artificial intelligence, there is a hypothesis that has become so deeply entrenched that it is simply taken for granted. The hypothesis is this. What makes it possible for systems – computers or intelligent organisms – to behave in a way that is correctly characterized in terms of what they represent (say, beliefs and goals) is that the representations are *encoded* in a system of physically instantiated symbolic codes. And it is because of the physical form that these codes take on each occasion that the system behaves the way it does, through the unfolding of natural laws over the physical codes.

Stated in this bald way, this may sound like an esoteric and philosophical doctrine. But there is one thing that makes this story more than a little plausible, and that's the fact that it is clearly and literally true of computers. It explains why a computer can be correctly described as behaving in a certain way because of what it represents (e.g., it contains knowledge about medical symptoms and their etiology and is told what symptoms a person has, so it infers a diagnosis and suggests medications). Without getting into the more controversial aspects of the claim that this is the correct way to describe what the computer is doing, it is at least an existence proof that it is possible to have a system which is both clearly governed by physical laws, and at the same time whose behavior can be given a coherent account in terms of what it represents.

1.3 Symbols, codes, and computing

There is good reason why computers can be described as processing knowledge. The reason was discovered at around the same time as the idea of computing itself was developed. This discovery came, perhaps surprisingly, from the development of mathematics and logic in the first half of the twentieth century. A number of far-reaching mathematical ideas came together in the 1930s, associated with names like Hilbert, Kurt Gödel, Betrand Russell (with Alfred North Whitehead), Alan Turing, Alonzo Church, and other logicians. The discovery was this: Reasoning about meaningful things – about things in the world or in the imagination – could be carried out by a process that itself knew nothing of the world or of meanings, did not know what its "thoughts" were about!

To illustrate this fundamental idea, consider what is involved when you go from a set of beliefs to a new belief. Suppose you know (somehow) that John is married either to Mary or to Susan. Then suppose you discover that John is in fact not married to Susan. You can then conclude that he must be married to Mary. We can represent this by equations such as the following, which involve (in this case) two special terms, called Logical Terms, "*or*" and "*not*."

(1)   Married (John, Mary) *or* Married (John, Susan)

and the equation or "statement"

(2)   *not* (Married (John, Susan))

From these two statements you can conclude,

(3)   Married (John, Mary)

But notice that (3) follows from (1) and (2) *regardless* of what is in the parts of the equation not occupied by the terms *or* or *not* so that you could write down the equations without mentioning marriage or John or Mary or, for that matter, anything having to do with the world. Try replacing these expressions with the meaningless letters P and Q. The inference still holds:

(1') P *or* Q
(2')   *not* Q

Therefore,

(3') **P**

The idea that logical inference can be carried out by a process of examining meaningless symbols leads directly to the foundational assumption of cognitive science, which is that thought is a species of computing. This is because the sort of "meaningless" manipulation of symbols just described is just what computers are good at. So if the idea is correct, maybe computing is what the brain does to produce intelligent behavior. The bridge from formal symbol manipulation to computing was completed in 1936 by the mathematician Kurt Gödel who showed that anything that could be described in terms of manipulations of symbols could be carried out by a very simple machine (later called a Turing machine), which became the defining property of reasoning and later of intelligent action.

2   The Tri-level Hypothesis

The behavior of complex systems can often be described at different levels. Sometimes this may be just a convenience in talking about them (e.g., we can describe a car at various levels of specificity). But sometimes this is essential, because the system really has different levels of organization. For example, there appears to be a level of organization at which the laws of economics, like Gresham's law or the law of supply and demand, hold. These are genuine, principled levels at which certain organizing principles apply. If we could describe only the movement of currency and goods, we would have no hope of discovering principles of economics, because the principles hold regardless of what physical form "money" and "goods" take. We all know now that transfers of funds can take place by the most exotic means, including codes sent over a digital network, and that goods and services can also take the most surprising forms; yet the principles of economics and the laws of contractual obligation hold irrespective of the forms that goods, services, payments, and contractual transactions take.

When it comes to trying to understand cognition, the current view in cognitive science is that there are at least three distinct levels at which intelligent systems are organized (this is the so-called tri-level hypothesis discussed at length in my 1984 book – see note 3):

1   The biological or physical level
2   The symbolic or syntactic level
3   The knowledge or semantic level

What this proposal amounts to is the claim that there are different generalizations that exist at each of these levels. There are patterns of behavior that

Figure 1.1 Electromechanical calculator. How do you explain different aspects of its behavior?

can only be explained by appeal to biology – for example, why people's reactions slow down when they drink alcohol, why they get irritated when deprived of sleep, why their memories worsen with age, why certain behaviors change at puberty, and so on. We have already seen that some patterns of behavior can be explained only by appeal to what people want and what they believe (we will see in the next section that the semantic levels also takes in a wider range of behaviors than just rational decisions, since many of the organizing principles of perception, memory, and other aspects of cognition also require that we refer to how aspects of the world are represented – which makes intelligent behavior special in being "representation-governed"). The new twist in the tri-level picture is the idea that the knowledge level is implemented through a system of codes, more or less as we discussed in the previous section.

The idea that different phenomena may require that we appeal to principles at different levels is already familiar to us, since it is routine in computing. For example, a computer may implement an economic model. If it fails to make the correct prediction of a certain change in the economy, we explain that by reference to economic factors, not to properties of the computer program itself, or to the electronics of the computer. But there are cases when we might indeed explain the model's behavior by reference to the program itself – for example, if the program had a bug in it. Similarly there are situations (e.g., a power failure) such that we would explain the behavior by appealing to the electronics. The situation is also clear in the case of a calculator, such as the one shown in figure 1.1.

Various questions can be asked about the calculator's behavior:

1 Why is the calculator's printing faint and irregular? Why are parts of numbers missing in the LED display?
2 Why does it take longer to calculate large numbers than small ones?
3 Why does it take longer to calculate (and display) trigonometrical functions (such as sine and cosine) than sums?
4 Why does it take longer to calculate the logarithms of large numbers than

of small numbers, whereas it takes the same length of time to add large numbers as to add small numbers?

5 Why is it especially fast at calculating the logarithm of 1?
6 Why is it that when one of the keys (labeled $\sqrt{}$) is pressed after a number is entered, the calculator prints what appears to be the square root of that number? How does it know what the square root is?
7 How does the calculator know the logarithm of the number I punch in?
8 When the answer to an arithmetic problem is too long to fit in the display window, why does the form of the answer change and some of the digits get left off?
9 Why is it that even when the answer fits in the window, some of the right-hand digits in the answer are different from what I get when doing it by hand? (It is sometimes off by 1).

It is clear that different *kinds* of answers apply to these questions.[2] Some require an answer stated in terms that refer to electrical and mechanical things – they require physical-level explanations (e.g., question 1). Others require symbol-level explanations – for example, they require that one describe the "method" or algorithm used by the calculator (e.g., questions 2–7 require such a description), including (for question 5) whether some of the answers are pre-computed and stored. Others require something in between the symbol level and the physical level; they require that we describe the machine's *architecture* – which is to say, we must describe things such as the *size of the storage registers* it uses. Notice that the size (in terms of number of bits, or bytes) is not a physical property, since the answer would apply to calculators that were physically quite different (you could ask about the register size of your PC, which works quite differently from the calculator). Questions 8 and 9 concern what are called "rounding errors," and the answer would need to address how individual numbers are represented and what principle applies when the capacity of a register is exceeded. The principle may well reside in the design of the architecture of the calculator, and not in the program it uses in a particular case.

Several of the questions are actually about the relation between the calculator and the world of abstract mathematics. Saying that the calculator computes the *sine* or *logarithm* function is to say more than just what algorithm it uses. It is to claim that the algorithm in question actually computes representations of numbers that correspond to certain mathematically defined abstract functions. Showing that this is the case can be a difficult task. Mathematicians are sometimes concerned to prove mathematically that a certain program will *always* generate outputs that are consistent with a certain mathematically defined function (even though it can only be tested on some finite subset of inputs). This is the computer science task of proving the correctness of programs – a difficult and challenging problem in theoretical computer science. In order to do this, the theorist needs to describe the computer's operation in terms of the mathematical function it was designed to compute.

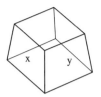

Figure 1.2 Reversing wire figure, showing "coupling" of perceived properties.

In other words, for purposes of proving correctness, the machine must be described in terms of the things it represents (abstract mathematical objects) – this is the semantic level of description.

2.1 Representation-governed behavior

The idea, sketched above, that certain behavioral regularities can be attributed to different representations (some of which are called "beliefs" because they enter into rational inferences) and to symbol-manipulating processes operating over these representations, is a fundamental assumption of cognitive science. This idea is an instance of what is a fundamental claim about intelligent systems: Intelligent systems (including animals and computers) are governed by *representations*. To explain the simplest fact about the behavior of most "higher" organisms, we must say how some aspect of the world is represented – and this applies even where the behavior does not appear to involve reasoning or rational decision making. For example, it is a remarkable fact about perception that you can only state the generalizations or laws of perceptual organization in terms of how patterns are perceived, not in terms of their physical properties. Here are some examples that should make this clear.

Consider the "laws" of color mixing. When yellow light is mixed with red light, the resulting light appears orange. Is this a law about how different wavelengths are perceived? The answer is no. There is an unlimited variety of ways of producing yellow light (by filtering white light to allow only wavelengths of 580 nm or by mixing light of other wavelengths such as 530 nm and 650 nm). Similarly, there is an unlimited variety of ways of producing red light. But *regardless of how each light is produced*, mixing the two lights produces a light that *looks* orange – providing only that one of the lights *looks* yellow and the other *looks* red! How some aspect of a percept looks depends not on objective properties of the display, but on how parts of the display appear. Another way to say this is that how something is seen depends on how different aspects of it are seen or are *represented* by the perceiver. In figure 1.2 above, how the object is seen depends on how you see its parts. If you see edge X as part of the nearest face, then you will also see edge Y as part of the nearest face and the vertex where these two meet as the upper corner nearest you. In that case you are also likely to see the face bounded by X and Y as

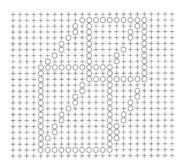

Figure 1.3 An alternative way to present the cube figure.

being the same size as the other faces – that is, you are likely to see the figure as a cube. But if you see the face formed by X and Y as the bottom of a figure (seen from above) then that face is likely to be seen as larger than the top face – so the figure looks like a cut-off pyramid.

This sort of "coupling" between how parts of a figure are perceived is an extremely general phenomenon. The organizing principle cannot be stated over the geometrical properties of the figure, only over its *perceived* properties – or, in our terms, over how parts are *represented* by the mind. The principles take the form, "If X is *represented as* (e.g., being closer, or being yellow, or . . .), then Y will be *represented as* . . . ." It is important to realize that such principles apply *no matter how the parts came to be represented the way they are* – exactly as was the case in the color-mixing example. There is an unlimited variety of ways of producing the perception of a certain edge or vertex. For example, it can be produced by drawing a line, or by selecting a set of pixel points from among an array and making them distinct, as in figure 1.3 where the subset of points defining the figure are distinct because of the shapes of the elements. And the subset can also be made distinct by jiggling the relevant elements while the other elements remain stationary, or by showing the array in stereo with the subset in a different depth plane, or by moving a narrow slit back and forth over the figure 1.3 so that only a slit is visible at any instant but the figure is still seen as lying behind the screen with the slit, and so on. Once again, it matters not how the information is presented. What matters is how it is *seen* or *represented*. This feature of intelligent processing, wherein *what is relevant to principles of operation is how something is represented*, is the main reason why we believe that intelligent processing is computational. In computation, it is how something is encoded – its symbolic form – that determines how the process runs. The computer does not "know" anything about the outside world: All it knows are the symbolic codes or data structures with which it deals.

2.2   What kind of computer is the mind?

If you buy the story I have been sketching, then you are ready to accept the general conclusion that the mind is a type of computer – a story that is getting to be easier and easier to accept in this day and age, when "Artificial Intelligence" is much discussed. But that still leaves a gaping hole in the cognitive science project: To specify what *kind* of computer the mind is. Notice that we are not claiming that the mind runs like your PC or MAC. Whatever kind of computer it is, it is clearly not *that* kind of computer. There is reason to believe that it does not always execute one instruction after another, that it does not store information by encoding it in terms of a binary pattern of bits, that it retrieves it by specifying the address where it is stored, and so on. What it does share with PCs and with all known forms of general-purpose computers is that it manipulates symbolic codes. There is much that needs to be said about even this claim, but such a discussion is beyond the scope of this essay.[3] But the project of understanding the nature of mind cannot get off the ground unless we take seriously the task of specifying, at least in general outline, what kind of computer the mind is. The reason why this is so central a task is itself revealing, and I will devote the rest of this chapter to spelling out the answer to the question, Why do we need to know what kind of computer the mind is?

The reason we need to understand what kind of computer the mind is, is that merely simulating intelligent functions – however interesting and difficult it may be – is not enough for the purpose of *explaining* human intelligence. That's because it is often possible to produce some piece of intelligent behavior in a manner totally different from how it is produced by the human mind. A good example of this is arithmetic. Computers can (and do, routinely) carry out arithmetic operations in a completely different way from the way you were taught in school – because it is faster and more convenient for them to use their special-purpose operations (e.g., using binary arithmetic, shift operations, and so on). The basic operations available to the computer (as well as the way it encodes, stores, and retrieves information) constitute what computer scientists call its functional or computational *architecture*. If we wanted to model how you and I do certain kinds of arithmetical problems, we would need to first find out what the computational architecture of the mind is (what we call its *cognitive architecture* – determining which is the most fundamental problem in all of cognitive science). The cognitive architecture is what determines what the mind can do and the way it can do it. It places strong constraints on any theory of cognitive functioning.

When we carry out some mental operation (say, solve some problem), we use two kinds of resources. One thing we use is what we know – what we have been told or what we have found out by reading or talking to people or by drawing inferences from what we already know to new knowledge. The second resource we use is our *cognitive capacity*: the capabilities that our brain

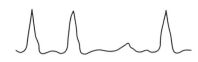

Figure 1.4   A typical pattern produced by an unknown box.

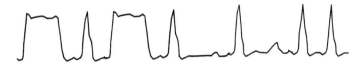

Figure 1.5   An exception to the typical pattern that ocurs in the special context show.

affords us. Much of this capacity is probably innate, but some of it may be acquired through maturation, practice, or other mechanisms we still do not understand. But this cognitive capacity is what we have because of our cognitive architecture, because of the kind of mind we have. The combination of what we know and what our capacities are is what determines what we do.

3   Cognitive Capacity

The idea of cognitive capacity, or cognitive architecture (I use the terms interchangeably), is a straightforward application of an idea from computer science. Because of this, it merits some examples to make it more concrete. What I will do is provide some very simple-minded examples to illustrate the following point: Merely predicting behavior is not good enough for purposes of explanation. We must also separate two major determinants of behavioral regularities: knowledge to highlight the distinction between a structurally defined capacity and a "mere" regularity) to one that is more relevant to a problem in cognitive science that has preoccupied me over the years. First the simple made-up example.

Suppose you were to find a mysterious box with unknown contents that was carrying out some function (also initially unknown) in its normal environment. Suppose further that the box had some conspicuous wires coming out of it that looked to be providing its normal behavioral "output." If we attach the wires to a recorder, we find that the box generates a variety of patterns of electrical activity in the course of its normal functioning. Among the patterns it generates are some single and some double spikes, as shown in figure 1.4.

As we examine the behavior of the box more carefully, we find that while the pattern of single and double spikes is usually as shown above, there are occasional exceptions in which the single spike precedes the double one. Such exceptions, however, occur in a predictable context. We find that the reverse pattern to that of figure 1.4 occurs only when it is preceded by two special long–short blip pairs, as in figure 1.5.

Let us assume that this pattern is quite reliable (we observe it over a long period of time). The question is: What does this pattern tell us about the nature of the box? Suppose you were to develop a theory of how the box works – say, by constructing a computer model that simulates its function. It would be very easy to do so, since the behavioral repertoire is quite simple. But what would we know about the nature of the box from such a model? Or, put another way, What does the behavioral regularity tell us about how the box works?

The answer is *nothing*. In this case, knowing the pattern of behavior tells us very close to nothing about how the box works. That's because we have observed only in its "typical" context or its "ecological niche," so cannot be aware that its capacity is far greater than is shown in that sample. I can reveal to you (because I made up the example!) that the box exhibits the pattern it does because of what the electrical patterns *represent*, not because of how the box is constructed. I can now tell you that the box is a device that transmits English words in International Morse Code (IMC). In IMC a single spike represents the letter *e*, a double spike represents the letter *i*, and the double long–short pattern represents the letter *c*. Thus the pattern we have observed arises entirely from a spelling rule in English: namely, "*i* before *e* except after *c*"! We can determine that the regularity in question does not arise from the architecture of the device even without knowing how it is constructed by simply observing that in different situations (not different wiring or a different physical arrangement) the behavior would be quite different. For example, if we got it to transmit words in German or French, the regularity would disappear. Observing this sort of change in behavior without changing the system's physical structure is one of the main methodological tools we have for distinguishing architectural from representational determinants of behavioral patterns. We will see more of this methodological tool below, where the informational alteration of behavioral regularities is called *cognitive penetration*.

The message of the above example (and other examples I will present below) is that when you encounter a systematic pattern of behavior (what I have called a "regularity" or a "generalization"), you need to ask *why* that generalization holds: Is it because of the way the mind is, or is it because of what we *know* or how we represent the world – because of the architecture or because of properties of what is represented.

Here is another example. Understanding natural language is one of humans' unique and most important and fluent skills. There have been many studies showing complex, sophisticated computations performed in the course of understanding a sentence. Some of the operations we perform on parts of a sentence (such as looking up a string of characters in a mental dictionary, or "lexicon," to check on what concept it corresponds to and what grammatical form it might take) may reveal properties of the cognitive architecture. But some don't. Take, for example, the pair of sentences below and ask yourself who the italicized pronouns refer to in each case. Then ask whether the answer reveals something about the architecture of the language-understanding system or whether it reveals something about what the listener knows about the world.

(1) John gave the book to Fred because *he* finished reading it.
(2) John gave the book to Fred because *he* wanted to read it.

In this case we would expect the explanation of why the pronoun refers to different people in the two sentences to appeal to one's knowledge of what books are for and where things end up when they are given. Only factors like this would explain why in particular cases the pronouns are assigned different referents in the two sentences and why the reference assignment could be easily changed in a logically coherent way by altering the belief context. (For example, suppose we knew that John was trying to encourage Fred to learn to read and had promised Fred the book as a reward if Fred finished reading all of it; or if we knew that John was blind and that Fred would often read to him. In such cases we might well assign the pronouns differently in these sentences.) In other words, the cognitive penetrability of the observed regularity marks it as being knowledge-dependent and as involving reasoning – even if one is not aware of such reasoning taking place. It is within the cognitive capacity of the organism to assign a different referent to the pronoun, with the new assignment being explicable in terms of the principles that explained the original assignment – namely, in terms of an inference from general background beliefs. The difference between the cases would be attributed to a difference in the state of knowledge or belief, not to a difference in their capacity or cognitive architecture.

Let's look at a somewhat different case that is of special interest to us as psychologists or students of cognitive functioning. It is known, through countless experiments, that when people imagine certain situations, they tend to exhibit many patterns of behavior (particularly of timing) that are similar to those that would be observed if they witnessed the corresponding situation. For example, it takes longer to "see" details in a "small" mental image than in a "large" image; it takes longer to imagine solving a construction problem (such as the task of folding a piece of paper to form a given figure) if it would have taken you a large number of steps to solve it in real life; and so on. As noted above, in order to decide whether this is due to the architecture or to the represented world, we need to ask why each of these regularities holds.

Take, for example, the case of "mental color mixing" at which many people excel. Suppose I ask you to imagine a transparent yellow disk and a transparent red disk, and then to imagine that the two disks are slowly moved together until they overlap (as in the color-mixing example mentioned earlier). What color do you see now where they overlap? People differ in their abilities to imagine color mixing. But no matter what color you see the overlapping disks to be, or whether you even experience any color mixing at all, the question of interest to us is *why*: Is the color you see in this example a result of the nature

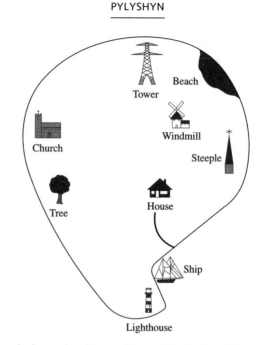

Figure 1.6 Map to be learned and imaged in one's "mind's eye" to study mental scanning.

or structure of your mind, or is it a result of what you know or remember about how colors mix? In this case it seems clear enough that what determines the solution you get is not some intrinsic property of your mind or brain – its cognitive architecture – but your memory or knowledge of how things work in the world and in perception. Of course, being able to remember such laws or past experiences *is* a property of your mind, but the actual way that colors mix (in contrast with what happens in vision, where the laws of color mixture really are immutable properties of the visual system) is very likely not, since you can make the overlapping pair of filters have any color you want it to have.

Here is another similar example of using a mental image – only this one represents a real experimental finding that has received a great deal of attention in the psychological literature on mental imagery. It has been shown over and over that it takes you longer to "see" a feature in an image if that feature is further away from one you have just examined. So, for example, if you are asked to imagine a dog and inspect its nose and then to "see" what its tail looks like, it will take you longer than if you were asked to first inspect its hind legs. Here is an actual experiment carried out by Steven Kosslyn.[4] Subjects were asked to memorize a map such as the one in figure 1.6.

They were then asked to imagine the map and to focus their attention on one place – say the "church." Then the experimenter said the name of a second place (say, "beach" or "ship") and subjects were asked to press a button as soon as they could "see" the second named place on their image of the map. What Kosslyn (and many others) found is that the further away the second place is from the place on which subjects initially focused, the longer it takes to "see" the second place in their "mind's eye." From this, most researchers have concluded that larger map distances are represented by greater distances, in some mental space. In other words the conclusion is that mental images have spatial properties – they have *magnitudes*. This is a strong conclusion about cognitive architecture. It says, in effect, that the symbolic code idea we have discussed earlier does not apply to mental images. In a symbolic encoding two places can be represented as being further away just the way we do it in language; by saying the places are *x* meters (or whatever) from one another. But the representation of larger distances is not itself in any sense *larger*. The question, then, is: Is this conclusion about architecture warranted? Does the difference in time in this case reveal a property of the architecture or a property of what is represented. This exactly parallels the situation in the code-box example, where we asked whether a particular regularity revealed a property of the architecture or a property of what was being represented. In that case the fact that the regularity shown in figures 1.4 and 1.5 goes away if the box transmits words in another language suggests that it is not. What about the image-scanning case? Is it like the code-box case or the imagined color-mixing case, or does the time pattern indicate something about the architecture, as generally assumed? To answer this question, we need to determine whether the pattern arises from a fixed capacity of the image-encoding system or whether it can be changed by changing the task or the beliefs people hold about how things work in the world.

This is a question to be settled by careful experiment. But there is already informal reason to suspect that the time course of scanning is not a property of the cognitive architecture. Do the following test on yourself. Imagine that there are lights at each of the places on the imagined map. Now imagine that a light goes on at, say, the beach. Now imagine that this light goes off and one comes on at the lighthouse. Did you need to scan your attention to see this happen and to see the lit-up lighthouse in your "mind's eye"? We did this experiment by showing subjects a real map with lights at the target locations. We allowed them to turn lights on and off. Whenever a light was turned on at one location, it was simultaneously extinguished at other locations. Then we asked subjects to imagine the map and to indicate (by pressing a button) when a light was on and they could see the illuminated place. The time between button presses was recorded and correlated to the distances between illuminated places on the map. As expected, the result was that there was no relation between distance on the imagined map and time. You might think: Of course there was no time increase with increasing distance, because I was not imagining that I was scanning that distance. That's just the point: You can imagine scanning the imagined map if you want to, or you can imagine just hopping from place to place on the imaginary map. If you imagine scanning, you can imagine scanning quickly or slowly at a constant speed or at some variable speed. You can in fact, do whatever you wish, since it is *your image* and *your imagining*, so you can make it do whatever you like over time! If the marchitecture restricts the operations you can perform (which it may well do), this does not show up in the experimental data on timing that are widely cited as showing that images are laid out in space. Thus it appears that the time pattern of mental scanning is like the pattern of blips observed in the code-box example. In both cases, while the pattern *could* have been due to the architecture of the relevant system, the evidence we discussed suggests that it is not. Rather, it is due to a correctly encoded pattern in the represented domain. In the code-box case this pattern is due to the spelling of English words, and in the image-scanning case it arises from the fact that subjects know what happens when you scan a picture with your eyes, and they make the same thing happen in their imagining – probably because this is what they assume the experimenter meant when he or she asked them to "scan" their image.

The empirical test of whether the pattern in such cases (including the mental color-mixing example cited earlier) is due to the architecture or to the representation is to ask whether the pattern can be systematically and rationally altered by changing beliefs about the task. That was the point of our experiment, which showed that this is indeed what happens. This shows that the pattern is what we call "cognitively penetrable" and allows us to conclude that it does not arise from a property of the cognitive architecture.

4   Unconscious Processes

What goes on in mental imagery, as well as what goes on in understanding linguistic utterances such as those discussed earlier, looks to be largely some kind of reasoning – drawing conclusions from what you know. But the nature of this reasoning is entirely opaque to your conscious experience. This is a universal finding: Most of what we need to hypothesize in order to explain how the mind works is *not* available to introspection, and what is available to introspection is usually not what is relevant – it's not what is doing the work. Recall our earlier example of assigning a referent to a pronoun in two sentences. This case clearly illustrates that the pronoun assignment depends on reasoning and on drawing inferences from facts that you know about the world, about social interactions, and perhaps even about the characters John and Fred if the sentences have occurred in a story. But you normally have no awareness whatsoever of there being any inferences involved in your under-standing the sentences. There is rarely any consciousness of processing sentences. Yet it is known that complex grammatical analyses are involved. You need to uncover what is called the "thematic" or "logical" structure of the sentence – to discern who did what to whom. And this involves an extremely complex process known as "parsing," which entails a large number of rules of grammar, some specific to English, some relevant to all languages, and some idiosyncratic to a particular (discourse or story) context or to particular individuals. But you have no awareness of any of these.

We should view it as a major discovery of twentieth-century cognitive science that most of what goes on when we act intelligently is not available to conscious inspection. And since what goes on is reasoning, we have every reason to believe that it takes place in a system of symbols – that's the only way we know of doing it without hiding a homunculus inside the machine.

4.1 How can we know how it works inside?

Where do these observations leave a *science* of mind (e.g. cognitive science)? If you can't rely on introspection of your conscious experience to tell you what's going on in your mind, and if you can't rely on looking inside the skull using biological techniques to tell you what psychological processes are taking place, then how in the world *can* you tell? Of course, you can observe the organism in various ways in the laboratory. But if you are observing only the visible behavior – the input–output behavior – then can you distinguish among theories that produce the same input–output behavior? If the answer is no, then we are in trouble, because science is not interested in merely predicting input–output behavior. It is interested in the question: *how does it work?* And to say how it works is to do much more than predict what output it will produce, given a particular input.[5] At the very least, it is to specify the form in which representations are encoded and to give the algorithm by which the input–output function is computed in detail. But how can we do this if we do not have access to the program, if we cannot look inside the black box but are confined to examining only the organism's observable behavior?

This is a serious question and has been debated from time to time by both philosophers and psychologists. Yet strangely enough, experimental psychologists have been proposing and verifying detailed theories of how information is processed for the past 35 years. How can they do that? Here is the issue. If you say that all you have to go by is input–output behavior, you are making the methodological mistake underlying the ideology of behaviorism. You are not only assuming that all you have is a record of observed behavior, but also that any record of behavior is like any other record of behavior. Recall that we noted earlier that even the strict behaviorist must put up posters to solicit subjects, and when he does that, he assumes that it is the meaning of the sentences on the poster that is relevant to whether subjects will show up. Similarly, if the investigator is gathering data in an experiment and the subject says something like "Oops, I meant to hit the button on the right but hit the one on the left by mistake," no scientist, no matter how ideologically pure, will write down as part of the record, along with the list of buttons that were pressed, "Response 12: S uttered 'Oops, I meant . . .'" Rather, the scientist will do something like mark the response as an error, delete the erroneous response, start the trial over, or reject the subject's data. Why? Because some responses are taken to be the pure outputs of the system being studied, and some are taken to be statements about what the subject thought. A linguist gathers data by recording sentences in the language and examining patterns of co-occurences (e.g., what types of phrases go with what other types, and so on). But he or she also asks native speakers of the language such questions as whether a particular sentence (call it A) is a grammatically acceptable sentence, whether it is ambiguous, whether it means the same as another sentence B, or whether the meaning of sentence A is related to the meaning of sentence B as sentence D is related to sentence C (e.g., "John hit the ball" is to "The ball was hit by John" as "The dog chased the cat" is to "The cat was chased by the dog"; and "John hit the ball" is to "Who hit the ball?" or to "What did John hit?" as other related pairs of sentences you can easily think up. The linguist takes the answers to such questions to be not merely a sample of the language but as the speakers' judgements about the test sentences – as truthful claims *about* sentences. There is a world of difference between sentences that form the data-base of observations and sentences that constitute expert judgments about these sentences.

So here is one possible way to do better than merely trying to reproduce the input–output behavior that is observed in a laboratory. Ask the subject to tell you what he is trying to do, or what he is doing, or what he knows at various times during the process. This method (which of course applies only to more deliberate, conscious, and relatively slow processes, such as solving crossword puzzles or playing chess) has been used a great deal and is referred to as "protocol analysis." Protocol analysis is an instance of a more general class of methods for gathering evidence of intermediate states in the process. If your theory says that a certain input–output (I–O) behavior is the result of a certain program, then a way to test this is to ask what intermediate stages the program goes through – what partial solutions it has at various stages – and to compare this with the intermediate stages that a subject goes through. Such intermediate-state evidence can often be obtained by asking subjects to "think out loud" while solving a problem. But there are many other, more subtle ways of getting such data. For example, one can use eyetracking equipment to record what a subject is looking at (say, while doing an arithmetic problem or while reading). Such evidence tells you whether the subject is "looking ahead" or examining the problem in some unusual order. Scientists Alan Newell and Herbert Simon have used the protocol-analysis technique to great advantage in formulating and testing computational theories of problem-solving processes. More and more clever intermediate-state evidence has been accumulated by creative investigators.

Intermediate-state evidence, however, is not always available, especially for rapid and highly fluent processes such as visual perception. And it is sometimes misleading, since subjects can (and do) report what they think they were doing rather than what they actually were doing. But no technique is perfect by itself, and science always relies on converging evidence from many sources

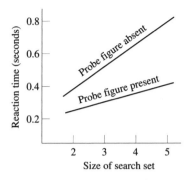

Figure 1.7 The graph on the left illustrates the results expected if search for the probe target was serial and self-terminating. The one on the right, which was actually found by Sternberg (1966), is what you would expect if the search was serial and exhaustive (did not stop when the target was found).

to increase the confidence level of its conclusions. Fortunately the arsenal of techniques for obtaining evidence of what process is being carried out is limited only by the creativity of the scientists, and every month new techniques and analysis tools appear in publications.

A major source of evidence in cognitive science is what I have called "relative complexity evidence." A major example of this entails the use of reaction times. If you vary some property of the task in a systematic way and observe an equally systematic change in the time taken to produce a response, you may be able to exclude one type of model and provide support for another. Probably the most frequently cited example of the use of this method is a study by Sternberg (1966). Sternberg did the following experiment. He asked subjects to memorize a small set of items – say, the letters G, A, F, and T (called the search set) – and then showed them one letter (called the probe) on a screen. Subjects had to press one button as fast as they could if the probe was a member of the memorized set and another button if it was not. The question Sternberg was asking is: How does a subject look up items in short-term memory? He found that it took longer to decide that the probe was not a member of the memorized set than to decide that it was. But that in itself tells us very little. What tells us much more is to examine how the reaction time increases as the size of the search set increases and to look at this function for positive cases (where the probe was a member of the search set) and for negative cases (where the probe was not a member of the search set). Figure 1.7 shows what Sternberg found (the graph and the numbers here are for illustrative purposes).

The relevant properties of these data are that the time it takes to find the probe in the search set increases linearly as the size of the set increases. This suggests that a serial search through the items in memory is taking place – *despite the fact that it seems to the subject to involve no processing and no search at all!* It looks from the figure as if each additional item adds about 0.07

seconds to the reaction time (i.e., the search time, or slope of the curve, is 70 milliseconds per item). But perhaps even more surprising is the comparison of the slopes of the case where the probe item is actually in the memory set with the case where it is not. We would expect the slope to be about twice as great when the probe is not in the memory set. Why? Because to establish that the item is not found in the memory set the subject must continue to search until the end of the list is reached. In that case, then on average twice as many items would have to be examined. For example, if the search set has four items and the probe is in the set, then on average (with the correct item being located in random positions in the set) it will be successfully located after two comparisons. But if it is not in the set, the subject will have to search through to the end to discover that, resulting in four comparisons. But Sterberg found that the slopes in the two cases were the same (as shown in the graph on the right in figure 1.7). So these results suggest that locating an item in a set that is stored in what is called short-term memory is accomplished by a *serial exhaustive search algorithm*. Although the facts are slightly more complicated than this, and disagreements still persist, this example illustrates the use of the what might be called *relative complexity methodology* to decide among different possible processes all of which could produce the same input–output behavior. In this case measurements of the relative time it takes for different task parameters helps to decide whether the lookup of the probe happens in parallel or serial, whether the search is exhaustive or self-terminating, and so on. Just knowing that people can tell whether a probe was a member of the search set is itself not very interesting, since any of a large number of possible processes could accomplish that.

Notice that we call this example an instance of the relative complexity methodology, because we are not actually interested in the amount of time it takes (since that depends on a lot of things, many of which, like the strength and mass of the fingers used to hit the button, have nothing to do with the information processing itself). Rather, time is simply being used as a measure of how many steps it takes. We assume that the more steps it takes, the longer will be the reaction time. But there are other ways to measure relative complexity. For example, if more errors are found under one condition than another, this could also be because the more error-prone condition requires more steps (on the assumption that there is more opportunity for an error to occur). Other more subtle measures are also possible and depend upon a more detailed mathematical model of the process. For example, subjects can decrease their response time by sacrificing accuracy. But this sacrifice, called the speed–accuracy trade-off, can itself have a different pattern depending on how difficult the response is (as opposed to how difficult the memory search is), and this can be analyzed mathematically to tell you whether a decrease in speed is due to more time being spent on the search or on the decision as to which response button to press. This is the beginning of a "stage analysis," which is a more refined way of breaking down the process into different stages, and for which some extremely refined techniques are available.

It is also possible to obtain evidence both for stages and for which of several possible processes are actually being used by the subject, by finding certain measurable properties that we have independent evidence to believe are correlated with different operations, or stages. For example, there are certain patterns in human brain waves (or EEGs) that are known to be correlated with detecting and recognizing a stimulus, as opposed to preparing to make a response. One of the more interesting of these so-called *event-related potential* patterns is known as the P300 pattern (because it consist of positive spikes occurring about 300 milliseconds after a stimulus). There is reason to believe that the duration of the P300 pattern may tell us how much time is spent recognizing the stimulus, even when the actual overt response takes longer and is affected by different variables. This technique has been used to investigate whether certain manipulations of the stimulus (say, making it dimmer or noisier or a rarer type – e.g., an infrequent word) that are known to slow down reaction time also slow down recognition time, or whether the slowdown occurs in the response-selection stage. Similarly, *galvanic skin response* (or "lie detector" response) can be used to show that a stimulus has been registered, even if the subject is unaware of it, and so on. There is no limit to the kinds of evidence that can be brought to bear on deciding what process is being used to derive a response. In each case the method depends on an assumption about what the measurement is actually related to in the information processing, just as we assumed that reaction time was related to number of operations. But the step from observation to theory always depends on such methodological assumptions, which have to be justified independently – and this is true in every science. In other words, there is nothing special about finding out how the process inside the black box works – even without opening it up and looking inside. It's the same as finding out what makes water change from liquid to solid at low temperatures. You don't do it by "looking inside." The secret, as elsewhere in science, is just to be clever!

4.2 What, then, is really in your mind?

The answer to the question "What's in your mind?" is that, although we don't know in any detail, we think that it will turn out to be symbolic expressions, and that thinking is some form of operation over these symbolic codes. The symbolic codes are likely to be quite different from any contemporary calculus or language (e.g., the symbols would have to be able to encode procedures as well as facts), and the operations over these symbols are likely to be very different from those encountered in contemporary computer languages, in probably being richer and possibly making use of apparatus that evolved for other purposes – like perception. But so far, nobody has been able to come up with anything that feels more natural – that looks like the objects of experience – and that is able to do the job. Moreover, whenever people have tried to propose radically different schemes – for example, ones that *look* like the nervous system – it has turned out to be the case that the *looking-like* was very superficial, and that in order to be able to reason, we still need to invent another layer of organization corresponding to some language-like combinatorial symbol system.

Of course, this all sounds strange and unnatural. But think of how unnatural the idea of a heliocentric planetary system, with planets kept in place by invisible forces acting at a distance, must have sounded to the Aristotelians of the seventeeth century, and how unnatural is the scientific answer to the question "What is in this table?" (i.e., almost entirely empty space with a variety of unobservable forces acting on unobservable particles and electromagnetic wave patterns). That's the way it is in science: Things are rarely what they seem. But over time, we all learn to live with the strangeness, and it usually becomes the mundane orthodoxy of the next generation.

Notes

1 In this connection I recommend a paper by Bill Brewer (1974), in which he examines the vast literature on classical and operand conditioning of adult human subjects and finds in each case that the pattern of responses is best explained in terms of what the subject is led to *believe* about the outcomes of different voluntary actions.

2 Here is an exercise you might perform for yourself. Suppose we are interested in how a person, as opposed to an electromechanical device, does arithmetic. Can you think of some empirical observations – along the lines of those implied by the questions above – that you could make that would help decide how the person carried out the arithmetic? For example, measuring the time taken to perform the task when the inputs are varied in certain systematic ways has been one of the main sources of evidence in cognitive science. Would some of the patterns of behavior tell you more about the biological level than about the computation carried out by the mind (the way it does in this example for certain of the observations listed in questions 1 and 2)? After you have thought about this for a while, you might look at the section "How can we know how it works inside?"

3 See, however, the extended discussion of these issues in Pylyshyn 1984 and Fodor and Pylyshyn 1988.

4 See the original study described in Kosslyn et al. 1978 as well as the subsequent discussion in Pylyshyn 1981.

5 A theory that accounts only for the input–output behavior observed in a laboratory is said to be "weakly equivalent" to the subject being modeled. A theory that claims to tell you by what means (i.e., by what algorithm or program) the input–output behavior is generated is said to be "strongly equivalent" to the subject being modeled. Pylyshyn 1984 is mostly about what it takes to be a strongly equivalent theory.

References

Brewer, W. F. (1974) There is no convincing evidence for operand or classical conditioning in adult humans. In W. B. Weiner and D. S. Palermo (eds), *Cognition and the Symbolic Processes*, Hillsdale, NJ: Erlbaum 324–48.

Fodor, J. A. and Pylyshyn, Z. W. (1988) Connectionism and cognitive architecture: a critical analysis. *Cognition* 28, 3–71.

Kosslyn, S. M., Ball, T. M. and Reiser, B. J. (1978) Visual images preserve metric spatial information: evidence from studies of image scanning. *Journal of Experimental Psychology: Human Perception and Performance* 4, 46–60.

Pylyshyn, Z. W. (1981) The imagery debate: analogue media versus tacit knowledge. *Psychological Review* 88, 16–45.

—— (1984) *Computation and Cognition: Toward a Foundation for Cognitive Science*, Cambridge, MA: MIT Press.

Sternberg, S. (1966) High speed scanning in human memory. *Science* 153, 652–4.

2

Explaining the Infant's Object Concept: Beyond the Perception/Cognition Dichotomy

Brian J. Scholl and Alan M. Leslie

1 Introduction

Some of the most exciting research in recent cognitive science has involved the demonstration that young infants possess a remarkable array of discriminative abilities. Infants a few months old have been shown to have a substantial amount of "initial knowledge" about objects, in domains such as physics and arithmetic (for recent reviews and overviews, see Baillargeon 1995; Carey 1995; Spelke 1994; Spelke et al. 1995a; Spelke et al. 1995c). In this chapter we will be concerned with what such results tell us about the structure of the infant's mind – in other words, with what the phrase "initial knowledge" means in terms of the underlying cognitive architecture. For the duration of this chapter, we will adopt Spelke's phrase "initial knowledge" without scare-quotes, having recognized that it is precisely the meaning of this phrase which is at issue.

Traditional discussions have often addressed the nature of initial knowledge in terms of an implicit dichotomy between "perception" and "cognition" (e.g., Bogartz et al. 1997; Kellman 1988; Leslie 1988; Spelke 1988a, 1988b). From within such a dichotomy, "perception" has often been found wanting as an explanation, resulting in more "conceptual" theories which attribute to the infant various *thoughts, theories, principles*, and *beliefs* about objects. Such views are highlighted by the idea that this initial knowledge is the core which develops into and interacts with other, later-acquired beliefs in the relevant domains. At one extreme, many researchers "doubt . . . that mechanisms for apprehending objects can be distinguished from mechanisms of thought in any sense" (Spelke 1998b: 220). We will refer to this as the *maximally central* view of the infant's object concept. At the other extreme, deflationary accounts of initial knowledge explicitly reject the maximally central view and attempt to defend modified perceptual explanations (e.g., Bogartz et al. 1997; Melkman and Rabinovitch 1998). These deflationary accounts have their origin in the traditional empiricist accounts of the origin of the object concept, whereby infants initially interact with the world via fleeting sensations, which they gradually organize into more structured entities. We will refer to theories which attempt to explain initial knowledge by appeal only to sensation as *maximally sensory* theories.

We will argue that neither the maximally central view nor the maximally sensory view is correct, and that the dichotomy between "perceptual" and "cognitive" explanations is of dubious value. The mechanisms and processes which drive infants' discriminative abilities may best be characterized as neither "perceptual" nor "conceptual," but somewhere in between. We agree with several traditional arguments that maximally sensory views cannot adequately explain the object concept. At the same time, these arguments (discussed below) do not entail a maximally central account, since there do exist mental mechanisms which are not captured by the dichotomy – for example, mechanisms of object-based visuospatial attention.

In this chapter we will explore the prospects for explaining parts of the infant's object concept by appeal to such mechanisms. Object-based mechanisms of visuospatial attention enjoy many of the crucial properties which serve to rule out maximally sensory explanations, yet are not maximally central. We will suggest that the initial knowledge comprising the infant's object concept is best characterized in terms of this *attentional interface* between perception and cognition.[1] The attentional mechanisms at this interface may be able to account for the infants' abilities without appeal to beliefs or principles about object *types* (i.e., without appeal to general explicit beliefs about objects), but only to reactions to specific object *tokens*, via mechanisms whose existence has been motivated independently of the cognitive development literature. In this vein, we hope to draw together two literatures which have been developed completely independently: developmental research on the infant's "object concept" and research on the nature of object-based visuospatial attention in adults (see also Leslie et al. 1998).

In the next section we discuss the results of experiments with infants, which comprise the *explananda* for the different competing accounts. We discuss the general design of the relevant experiments and describe in detail some examples of initial knowledge in the domains of physics and arithmetic. We then turn to the explanation of these data. In section 3 we identify several arguments which have been taken to favor maximally central explanations over maximally sensory explanations, and we discuss the resulting appeals to high-level thought and cognition. We then argue in section 4 that these arguments rest on a dubious dichotomy. We appeal to object-based mechanisms of visuospatial attention as an example of mental mechanisms that possess the crucial properties lacked by maximally sensory accounts but that are not maximally central. The conclusion of this section will be a modest claim of possibility: that there is an alternative to both maximally sensory and maximally central accounts which rules out a strategy of arguing for one by arguing against the other.

An account of the infant's object concept which is neither maximally sensory nor maximally central may well be possible. But could such mechanisms actually explain any of the infancy data? We address this question in section 5, by discussing our "object-indexing" framework – a theory of the infant's object concept which is motivated by mechanisms at the attentional interface between perception and cognition. We discuss some related theories of the object concept in section 6 (including other recent "deflationary" explanations of the object concept and appeals to *sortal* concepts), and we offer some concluding thoughts in section 7. Throughout we use notions such as "knowledge" without prejudging the issue of what property of infant cognitive architecture is implicated.

2 Spatiotemporally-based Initial Knowledge in Infancy

2.1 Spatiotemporal vs contact-mechanical properties

What is the appropriate scope for a theory of the infant's object concept – that is, for an account of what infants know about objects, where and when they must exist, and how they interact with each other? On the one hand, there has been an enormous amount of research in recent years on many kinds of initial knowledge about objects, and it might seem a priori implausible that a single theory could account for everything. On the other hand, it seems unfair for a theory to arbitrarily pick and choose its *explananda*. One wants to specify the domain of an explanation in some non-arbitrary way, which characterizes the domain as a natural kind. For the purpose of this chapter, we will draw a distinction between those parts of object knowledge which are based on *contact mechanics* and those which are not.

Some of the initial knowledge which infants seem to enjoy concerns how objects can physically interact with each other. Baillargeon, Spelke and Wasserman (1985), for instance, investigated infants' knowledge of object *solidity* and argued that infants are sensitive to the constraint that objects cannot occupy the same place at the same time and thus cannot pass through each other. Other examples of such "contact-mechanical" knowledge include Spelke's studies of *solidity and persistence* (e.g., Spelke et al. 1992), Leslie's studies of *physical causality* (e.g., Leslie 1984; Leslie and Keeble 1987), and Baillargeon's studies of *support* and *collision* phenomena (summarized in Baillargeon 1995).

At the same time, many other parts of the object concept do not seem to focus on the physical interactions of objects. Other studies ask under what conditions infants apprehend the existence of an object in the first place, under what conditions object representations will persist, and how objects are enumerated. (We discuss several examples of this type below.) We do not intend our discussion in this chapter to speak to knowledge of contact-mechanical constraints, but only to this latter type of knowledge, of what we might call *"spatiotemporal" constraints*. We believe that there may be a basic architectural distinction between those types of initial knowledge based on contact-mechanical constraints and those based on spatiotemporal constraints. We suggest that these two types of initial knowledge may be subserved by specific, distinct mechanisms. In any case, we address only the spatiotemporal types of initial knowledge in this chapter.

This discussion thus complements Leslie's (1994) notion of *ToBy* – the "theory of body" mechanism – which is a more specialized (and perhaps modular) piece of core architecture on which later developing knowledge can bootstrap (cf. Leslie 1986, 1988). Motivated by the fact that infants of certain ages seem to have initial knowledge about properties such as *solidity, substance* and *causality* (e.g., Leslie and Keeble 1987; Spelke et al. 1992), but not *inertia* or *gravity* (e.g., Kim and Spelke 1992; Spelke et al. 1992: experiments 4 and 5; Spelke et al. 1994; cf. Needham and Baillargeon 1993), Leslie has suggested that we might think of ToBy as an embodiment of contact-mechanical knowledge – that is, knowledge of the ways in which solid objects can (and cannot) interact with each other. See Leslie 1994 for details.

Having established the scope of our discussion, we now review the general design of the looking-time experiments which frequently characterize infant research in this area and then discuss three demonstrations of initial "spatio-temporal" knowledge which employ these methods.

2.2 Looking-time methods of assessing infant knowledge

Demonstration of initial knowledge in infancy often relies on analyzing infants' *looking times*. The amount of time infants spend looking at a stimulus display decreases with repeated presentations. Several experimental paradigms based on this fact have been employed, in order to determine the character of cognitive abilities in infancy.

A canonical example works as follows. When you present an infant with a stimulus, she will typically visually orient herself to it and focus attention on it, but then eventually look away. Repeat this event, until the infant's looking times have decreased by some specified amount. The infant is now *habituated* to (or *familiarized* with) the event. At this point, introduce some change in the stimulus event and present it as before. If the infant detects the difference and interprets it as a fundamentally novel stimulus, then she will *dishabituate* (or "recover" looking time), and her looking time will jump back up by some measurable amount. We might say that she is "surprised", so long as we leave open what this means in terms of the infant's cognitive architecture. If she fails to detect the difference (or if she does not interpret it is a significant difference), then her looking time will stay near the familiarized level, since she is just seeing another instance of the same familiar stimulus.

The trick, then, is to design test events and control events such that infants will look longer at those test events which violate some principle (e.g., of physics or arithmetic) than at control events which incorporate similar perceptual differences without violating the principle. By designing ingenious controls, one can work toward a precise characterization of the properties on the basis of which the infants recover looking times. If this property seems characterizable only in terms of some principle or law, then researchers can conclude that the infant has a mechanism with knowledge of that principle.

Again, though, the nature of this knowledge is exactly what is at issue here. This becomes especially clear when the results of such experiments are phrased in terms of "surprise": "The infant was *surprised* by the 'impossible' event." Some writers (e.g., Bogartz et al. 1997) have taken issue with such descriptions, arguing that infants in such experiments do not demonstrate *bona fide* surprise, but merely look longer at the relevant test stimuli. As with "initial knowledge," however, we suggest that the meaning of such phrases is exactly what is at issue.

2.3   Example 1: spatiotemporal continuity

Consider the following physical principle: *Objects cannot jump in and out of existence. If an object moves from point A to point B, it must do so by traversing a continuous path through space.* Do infants employ this principle, as we do, when perceiving and reasoning about the physical world? Spelke and her colleagues (Spelke and Kestenbaum 1986; Spelke et al. 1995b) have demonstrated that indeed they do, based on the stimuli of Moore, Borton, and Darby (1978).

They tested four-month-old infants on displays involving an object which traveled from left to right (and back again), passing behind two occluders (see figure 2.1). In the "continuous" condition the object appeared in between the two occluders; in the "discontinuous" condition the object did not appear between the two occluders: it disappeared behind the first and then reappeared (after an appropriate delay) from behind the second, without ever traversing the intervening space. Infants were habituated to one of these events and were subsequently presented with a test event, consisting of the same object motions but without the occluders. In the one-object test event, a single object moved from left to right (and back again), simulating the motion of the continuous event. Likewise, the two-event test event simulated the discontinuous event.

Looking times for these test events were compared with each other and with control groups who saw only the test events, with no previous habituation. Infants habituated to the "continuous" event tended to look longer at

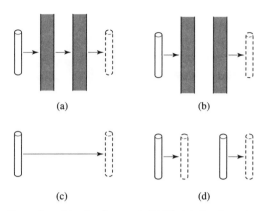

Figure 2.1. Stimuli employed by Spelke et al. 1995: (a) the "continuous" familiarization event; (b) the "discontinuous" familiarization event; (c) the one-object test event; (d) the two-object test event. See text for details. (Adapted from Spelke et al. 1995: 119.)

the two-object test event, while infants habituated to the "discontinuous" event tended to look longer at the one-object test event. In other words, infants generalized more from the continuous event to the single-object test and from the discontinuous event to the two-object test. In general: "Although preferences for the two-object display did not differ consistently from control levels over the . . . experiments, the trends in the data . . . suggest that infants perceived a single object in the continuous event and two objects in the discontinuous event" (Spelke et al. 1995: 136). Spelke and her colleagues (see also Spelke 1998a) take these results as reflecting initial knowledge of the principle of spatiotemporal continuity.[2]

2.4   Example 2: arithmetic

Karen Wynn (1992) has reported similar experiments, suggesting that infants may possess initial knowledge of numerical principles, including the arithmetical laws which define addition and subtraction. Two of the conditions of from her experiment are presented in figure 2.2[3]

In her "1 + 1 = 1 or 2" condition, five-month-old infants viewed a single doll resting on a small stage. A screen then rose up to cover part of the stage, obscuring the doll. While the screen was up, a hand appeared with a second doll, moved behind the screen, and left empty-handed. The screen then dropped, revealing either one or two dolls. Wynn measured infants' looking times to this final tableau and found longer looking time for the single-object case compared to the two-object case, suggesting that the infants "expected" there to be two objects.

A separate "2 − 1 = 1 or 2" condition was run to be sure that infants weren't simply responding preferentially to fewer items. When two objects appear initially and a hand removes one from behind a screen, leaving either

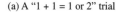

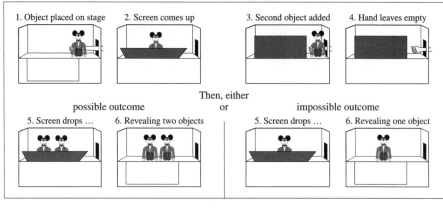

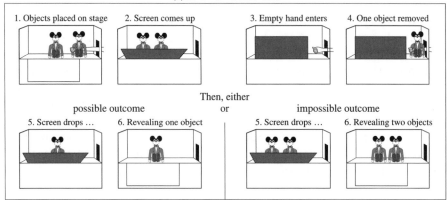

Figure 2.2. Stimuli employed by Wynn (1992): (a) the "1 + 1 = 1 or 2" condition; (b) the "2 − 1 = 1 or 2" condition. See text for details. (Adapted from Wynn 1992: 749.)

one or two objects, infants looked longer at the two-object display. These results suggested to Wynn that either (a) infants are able to "compute the numerical results of these arithmetical operations" (Wynn 1992: 750) or (b) they simply know that arithmetical operations *change* quantities of items – that addition leads to more items and subtraction to fewer items. To test these hypotheses, she ran another, "1 + 1 = 2 or 3" condition (not pictured), in which the result was either two or three objects. Infants looked longer at the three-item final tableaux, suggesting to Wynn that they are indeed doing arithmetic.

Simon, Hespos, and Rochat (1995) replicated Wynn's results, but added an interesting twist. Using "Ernie" and "Elmo" dolls as stimuli, their experiment included not only conditions with *arithmetical violations* (e.g., Ernie + Ernie = Ernie, as in Wynn 1992) but also conditions with *identity violations* (e.g., Ernie + Ernie = Ernie + Elmo) and conditions with *both* types of violations (e.g., Ernie + Ernie = Elmo). Following Wynn (1992), the experiments tested both addition (1 + 1 = 1 or 2) and subtraction (2 − 1 = 1 or 2). (A control condition verified that the infants could indeed distinguish the two dolls.)

Simon et al. (1995) measured the duration of the infants' first gazes at the different outcomes and found a tendency to look longer at arithmetical violations (compared to final tableaux with the "correct" arithmetical answer), but no tendency to look longer at identity violations (compared to the final tableaux containing the "correct" dolls). These results suggest that infants expected there to be the correct number of objects in the final tableau, but didn't care about the identities of those objects, even if they had somehow (magically) changed during the period of occlusion. This experiment thus supported Wynn's contention that young infants possess initial knowledge of at least some principles of arithmetic.[4]

2.5   Example 3: spatiotemporal and property-based criteria for object apprehension

Xu and Carey (1996) have recently explored more carefully when (and on what basis) infants apprehend the existence of an object behind a screen. In a typical experiment, infants were familiarized with events in which two objects were taken from and then replaced behind a screen. (One object was always removed and replaced from the left side of the screen, while the other was always removed and replaced from the right side of the screen.) During their removal and replacement, the two objects were either in view simultaneously (in what we will call the *spatial condition* – see figure 2.3) or only sequentially (in what we'll call the *property condition* – see figure 2.4) The two objects (e.g., a yellow duck and a white truck) typically differed both in their perceptual properties (i.e., size, shape, color) and in their categorical kind. Following this familiarization phase was a test phase, in which the screen was removed to reveal either one or both of the previously seen objects (see figures 2.3 and 2.4).

Ten-month-old infants in the spatial condition tended to look longer at final tableaux containing only a single object, but they showed no preference for one or two test objects in the final tableaux of the property condition. Twelve-month-old infants, by contrast, showed a preference for one test object in both the spatial and the temporal conditions.[5]

We can interpret these results as follows. Ten-month-old infants expected there to be two objects in the final tableau of the spatial condition (and thus looked relatively longer at a single test object), but had no such expectation in the property condition. In other words, infants appeared to use *spatio-temporal* information (i.e., the simultaneous presence of both objects) as a basis on which to form an expectation for two objects, but declined to use *property/kind* information (i.e., the difference in the identities and visible properties of the two objects) as such a basis, in situations where no spatio-

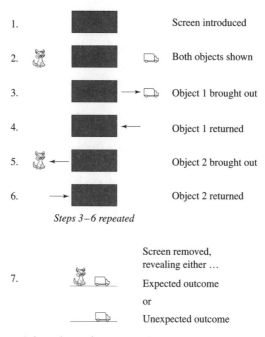

1.   Screen introduced

2.   Both objects shown

3.   Object 1 brought out

4.   Object 1 returned

5.   Object 2 brought out

6.   Object 2 returned

        Steps 3–6 repeated

                                    Screen removed,
                                    revealing either ...

7.   Expected outcome

                                    or

                                    Unexpected outcome

Figure 2.3. The *spatial* condition from Xu and Carey 1996. See text for details. (Adapted from Xu and Carey 1996: 125.)

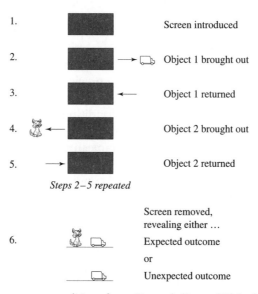

1.   Screen introduced

2.   Object 1 brought out

3.   Object 1 returned

4.   Object 2 brought out

5.   Object 2 returned

        Steps 2–5 repeated

                                    Screen removed,
                                    revealing either ...

6.   Expected outcome

                                    or

                                    Unexpected outcome

Figure 2.4. The *property* condition from Xu and Carey 1996. See text for details. (Adapted from Xu and Carey 1996: 126.)

temporal information was available. The results of this experiment and others "are consistent with the strong claim that the property differences between the two objects had no effect at all on the [ten-month-old] baby's looking time patterns" (Xu and Carey 1996: 136). This is in marked contrast, of course, to our mature perceptions of such events: adults (and 12 months-olds) will readily form an expectation for two objects behind the screen, not only when the two objects are simultaneously revealed, but also if two sequentially revealed items differ in their visible properties.[6]

In sum, these studies have demonstrated that infants possess the ability to discriminate stimuli in looking-time experiments in ways which respect various physical and arithmetical principles – in particular, those principles which seem to be based on spatiotemporal factors rather than contact-mechanical factors. Xu and Carey (1996) conclude from their experiments that 10-month-old infants possess the capacity to infer the existence of an object behind a screen on the basis of earlier spatiotemporal information, but not property/kind information, while 12-month-olds can use both sorts of information when inferring the existence of occluded objects. Wynn concludes from her "arithmetic" experiments that infants are able to "compute the numerical results of . . . arithmetical operations" (1992: 750) and that "The existence of these arithmetical abilities so early in infancy suggests that humans innately possess the capacity to perform simple arithmetical calculations" (ibid.). And Spelke concludes from the continuity experiments that "Infants appear to apprehend the identity of objects by analyzing the apparent continuity or discontinuity of paths of motion, in accord with the principle that objects move on spatio-temporally continuous paths" (Spelke 1988a: 179).

3 'Conceptual' vs "Perceptual" Accounts of the Object Concept

Having reviewed some examples of the sorts of experiments which motivate claims of initial knowledge about objects, we now turn to the issue of exactly how this initial knowledge is embedded in the cognitive architecture. Previous discussions of the nature of infants' discriminative abilities in these domains have tended to focus on a distinction between "perceptual" explanations and "cognitive" or "conceptual" explanations (e.g., Bogartz et al. 1997; Kellman 1988; Leslie 1988; Spelke 1988a, 1988b). Spelke, for instance, discussed (in a paper titled "Where perceiving ends and thinking begins") why "perceptual" explanations are inappropriate:

> [They] assume that objects are *perceived*: that humans come to know about an object's unity, boundaries, and the persistence in ways like those by which we come to know about its brightness, color, or distance. I suggest, in contrast, that objects are *conceived*: Humans come to know about an object's unity,

boundaries, and persistence in ways like those by which we come to know about its material composition or its market value. (Spelke 1988b: 198)

From within such a dichotomy between perceptual (or what we have been calling maximally sensory) explanations and conceptual (what we call maximally central) explanations, any arguments against one of these options can be taken as support for the other. And since nearly all of the relevant discussions proceeded by providing arguments that the maximally sensory explanations could not be correct, their conclusion is that the correct explanations must appeal to maximally central cognition: high-level thoughts, theories, and beliefs about objects. Below we review three examples of such arguments, based on (a) the necessity for discrete object representations, (b) the necessity for representations which are not tied to retinal images, and (c) the fact that in some cases perceptual systems seem to violate the very constraints which comprise initial knowledge in infancy.

3.1   The object-individuation argument

The first reason for thinking that parts of the infant's object concept cannot be explained in maximally sensory terms is that perceptual systems are thought to be intrinsically *continuous* in nature, and so do not map distinct objects to distinct representations.

> Perceptual systems do not package the worlds into units. The organization of the perceived world into units may be a central task of human systems of thought. . . . The parsing of the world into things may point to the essence of thought and to its essential distinction from perception. Perceptual systems bring knowledge of an unbroken surface layout. (Spelke 1988b: 229)

Perception, in other words, does not individuate discrete *objects*, whereas infants "are predisposed to interpret physical world as composed of discrete, individual entities when perceiving spatial layouts" (Wynn 1992: 750). And again: "[T]he ability to apprehend physical objects appears to be inextricably tied to the ability to reason about the world. Infants appear to understand physical events in terms of a set of principles that guide . . . the organization of the perceived world into units" (Spelke 1988b: 198). "*Thought*, in contrast, breaks this continuous layout into units – into objects and events – and finds relations between these units" (Leslie 1988: 201). Since perception doesn't represent discrete objects, and "thought" does, the correct explanations must appeal to the latter.

3.2   The occlusion argument

A second factor which militates against maximally sensory explanations is that perceptual representations are thought to be intrinsically *fleeting* in nature, active only when the corresponding objects in the world are actually visible on the retinae. For example, the sorts of discriminative abilities described above (involving objects traveling behind occluders) must be due to a mechanism which, unlike "perception", "organizes events in ways that extend beyond the immediately perceivable world in space and time" (Spelke 1988a: 180). "[T]he mechanism appears to carry infants beyond the world of immediate perception, allowing them to make sense of events in which objects are completely hidden" (ibid., 172). Contemporary writers still give credence to this argument. Wellman and Gelman (in press) note that these sorts of experiments are "designed to tap *conceptions* about objects, not just object *perception*, in that [they assess] infants' expectations about unseen events – the object's unwitnessed path of movement behind the screen" (our emphases), and Bertenthal notes in a recent review that "these abstract representations about the motions of objects are accessible to infants as explicit knowledge. . . . The principle evidence for this knowledge derives from occlusion studies in which inferences are required because the entire event is not visible" (1996: 450). The mechanisms responsible must therefore "carry infants beyond the world of immediate perception" (Spelke 1988a: 172). When this issue is approached from a dichotomy between perception and cognition, this argument favors the latter: since perceptual representations only exist while their objects are visible, while "conceptual" representations are free to persist indefinitely, the correct explanations must be maximally central in nature and appeal to the latter.

(This concern with occlusion, of course, has always been a part of research on the infant's object concept. Piaget (1954), for instance, held that an important aspect of a "true" object concept was an ability to represent the locations of objects which were fully hidden from view.)

3.3   The "Pulfrich pendulum" argument

A third sort of argument against perceptual explanations consists in showing that perceptual systems sometimes violate the very constraints they would have to explain. Leslie (1988) proffered this sort of argument against perceptual explanations of the contact-mechanical principle of "solidity", by which infants seem to have initial knowledge of the principle that objects cannot occupy the same place at the same time and thus cannot pass through each other (e.g., Baillargeon et al. 1985). To rule out a perceptual explanation of this type of initial knowledge, Leslie identified a type of evidence which would be conclusive:

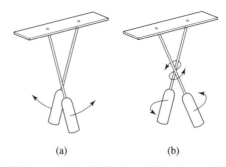

Figure 2.5. The "Pulfrich pendulum" illusion: (a) what really happens; (b) what is perceived. See text for details. (Adapted from Leslie 1988: 198.)

> Much better would be evidence that input systems are actually quite happy with the idea of one object passing through another. . . . The following kind of evidence is needed: a robust and clearly describable illusion in which one solid rigid object is seen to pass through another solid rigid object; the illusion arises from the visual system's attempt to resolve an incongruity; and it occurs despite the continuous availability of perceptual information that conflicts with the resolving (illusory) percept. (Leslie 1988: 196–7)

It turns out that this type of evidence actually exists, in the form of the *Pulfrich double pendulum illusion* (see figure 2.5).

Wilson and Robinson (1986) constructed a display in which two pendulums (sand-filled detergent bottles attached to rigid metal rods) swing back and forth in parallel but in opposite phase, one slightly behind the other. This event is entirely ordinary, unless viewed in dim light (by both eyes), while wearing a neutral density filter over one eye. Such a filter reduces the luminance for one eye, resulting in slightly slower processing. This leads to a percept in which a pendulum's perceived depth varies with its location and direction of motion. A single pendulum is thus seen as swinging in an ellipse, while two pendulums swinging in opposite phase are seen as following intersecting ellipses (Wilson and Robinson 1986; see figure 2.5). Leslie (unpublished) replicated this effect and subsequently verified that subjects receive "the clear perception of the rigid solid rods passing through each other. Most observers were able to find an angle of view where even the pendulum bottles appear to pass through one another despite their large size and marked surface texture" (Leslie 1988: 199).

The fact that perceptual systems are "willing" to construct this sort of percept suggests that they are not the architectural locus of the solidity constraint, which is being blatantly violated. The intended conclusion of this demonstration is that perceptual systems cannot be responsible for infants' initial knowledge of the solidity constraint, since they themselves appear to violate this constraint in constructing the percept of the Pulfrich pendulum. Again, the implication is that the responsible mechanisms must actually be maximally central.

3.4   The maximally central view of the infant's object concept

The impact of these sorts of arguments against perceptual explanations is apparent today in the popularity of explaining these facets of the infant's object concept by appeal to innate *knowledge* and the like. Once more, though, it is precisely the nature of this knowledge which we are discussing. "Initial knowledge" is not a technical term, and there is nothing inherently objectionable or controversial about suggesting (for example) that "the infant's mechanism for apprehending objects is a mechanism of thought: an initial theory of the physical world" (Spelke 1988a: 181). However, many interpretations of looking-time data are obviously intended to be maximally central in nature. Baillargeon, for example, attributes to Leslie and Spelke the view that "infants are born . . . with substantive beliefs about objects" (1995: 184; also 1994: 133); and recall Spelke's suggestion that our initial knowledge comprising the object concept is acquired "in ways like those by which we come to know about [an object's] material composition or its market value" (Spelke 1988b: 198). (See also Gopnik and Meltzoff 1997: ch. 4 for another explicitly maximally central theory of the infant's object concept.)

In sum, several traditional arguments have suggested that perceptual systems cannot be responsible for initial knowledge in infancy, and in the context of the perception/cognition dichotomy this militates in favor of "cognition" and "thought". We are in general agreement with these arguments and take our task to be an explication of exactly what "thought" amounts to in this context. We disagree, however, that the mechanisms responsible must therefore be maximally central and cannot "be distinguished from thought in any sense." In our view, the foundation of spatiotemporally-based initial knowledge lies in neither maximally sensory nor maximally central mechanisms, but rather at the attentional interface between these levels.

4   Beyond the Perception/Cognition Dichotomy: Object-based Mechanisms of Visuospatial Attention

The arguments reviewed in the previous section require that the mechanisms responsible for the infants' discriminative abilities to be able to "parse" the visual world into discrete objects, employing representations which survive occlusion. Maximally central mechanisms certainly meet these requirements. We are struck, however, by the fact that there exist independently motivated mechanisms of object-based visuospatial attention which also meet these constraints, but which appear to be neither fully "perceptual" nor fully "conceptual" in nature. In short, we may have been misled by this artificial dichotomy between "perception" and "thought" into thinking that the answer must lie fully at one extreme or the other.

Below, we describe recent object-based conceptions of visuospatial attention, focusing on two theories which will be especially relevant for our purposes: object file theory and the FINST theory of visual indexing.

4.1   The shift to object-based conceptions of visuospatial attention

Attention imposes a limit on our capacity to process visual information, but it is not clear at the outset what the correct *units* are for characterizing the limitation. It was traditionally argued or assumed that attention simply restricts various types of visual processing to certain spatial areas of the visual field – for example, in the popular *spotlight* models of visual attention (e.g., Eriksen and Hoffman 1972; Posner et al. 1980) or the *zoom-lens* metaphor of Eriksen and St James (1986). It has recently been demonstrated, however, that there must also be an *object-based* component to visual attention, in which attentional limitations are characterized in terms of the number of preattentively defined discrete *objects* which can be processed simultaneously.

There now exist several demonstrations of object-based effects in visuospatial attention. These include:

- Demonstrations that it is possible to pay attention to distinct objects or "object schemas" while ignoring other stimuli (comprising different objects) which happen to be spatially superimposed or to overlap (e.g., Neisser and Becklen 1975; Rock and Gutman 1981)

- Experimental demonstrations that it is easier to attend to multiple parts of a single object than to multiple parts of two distinct objects, even when the "parts" in question reside in identical spatial locations, and when the difference is defined only by perceptual set (e.g., Baylis and Driver 1993; Duncan 1984)

- Experimental demonstrations that attention automatically spreads more readily from one part of an object to another part of the same object, versus another part of a different object – again, even when the "parts" in question are spatially identical (e.g., Egly et al. 1994)

- Experimental demonstrations that attentional phenomena such as *inhibition of return* and the *negative priming effect* adhere to objects rather than (or in addition to) locations (e.g., Tipper et al. 1990; Tipper et al. 1991)

- Corroborating neuropsychological evidence that the phenomenon of *unilateral spatial neglect* operates (at least in some cases) in object-centered rather than scene-centered coordinates, so that patients neglect halves of multiple objects at different locations in the visual field, rather than half of the visual field as a whole (e.g., Behrmann and Tipper 1994; Driver and Halligan 1991)

- Additional corroborating neuropsychological evidence from *Balint syndrome*, in which patients exhibit *simultanagnosia*, the inability to perceive more than one object at a time (for a review, see Rafal 1997)

For reviews of the recent turn to object-based conceptions of visuospatial attention, see Egeth and Yantis 1997 and Kanwisher and Driver 1992.

Several recent theories have been concerned with how visual objects are individuated, accessed, and used as the basis for memory retrieval. These theories include Kahneman and Treisman's *object file* theory (Kahneman and Treisman 1984; Kahneman et al. 1992), Pylyshyn's *FINST* theory of visual indexing (Pylyshyn 1989, 1994), Yantis's *attentional priority tags* (Yantis and Johnson 1990; Yantis and Jones 1991), the notion of *object tokens* (Chun and Cavanagh 1997; Kanwisher 1987), and Wolfe's theory of *preattentive object files* (Wolfe and Bennett 1997).

To get the flavor of these theories, and how they enjoy the relevant properties which rule out "perceptual" accounts of the infant's object concept, we will now describe two of these theories in some detail. (These will be central to our theory of *Object Indexing*, presented in section 5.)

4.2   The FINST theory of visual indexing

Pylyshyn's theory of *visual indexing* (e.g., Pylyshyn 1989, 1994) complements other theories of object-based attention by postulating a mechanism whereby preattentive object-based individuation, tracking, and access are realized. In order to detect even simple geometrical properties among the elements of a visual scene (e.g., being collinear or being "inside"), Pylyshyn argues that the visual system must be able to simultaneously reference – or "index" – multiple objects. Similarly, although focal attention may scan until it finds objects, it cannot orient directly to a particular object which has not already been indexed. These considerations suggest a need for multiple loci of "attention".

A more concrete demonstration of these requirements is the *multiple-object tracking* (MOT) paradigm. In the standard MOT task (Pylyshyn and Storm 1988; Yantis 1992), subjects must track a number of independently and unpredictably moving identical items in a field of identical distractors. In the original experiment, Pylyshyn and Storm (1988) introduced the MOT paradigm as a direct test of the visual-indexing theory. Subjects in their first experiment viewed a display initially consisting of a field of identical white items. A certain subset of the items were then flashed several times to mark their status as targets. All the items then began moving independently and unpredictably about the screen, constrained only so that they could not pass too near each other, and could not move off the display. At various times during this motion, one of the items was flashed, and subjects pressed keys to indicate whether the flash had been at the location of a target, a non-target, or neither. (See figure 2.6 for a schematic representation of this basic MOT

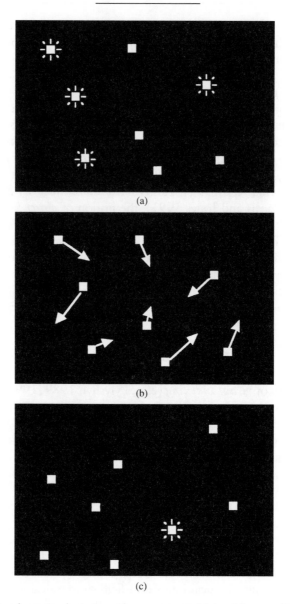

Figure 2.6. A schematic depiction of a generic multiple-object tracking task (not to scale). A number of items are presented, and a subset of them is flashed several times to indicate their status as targets. All the items then begin moving randomly and unpredictably about the screen. At one or more predetermined intervals, the motion stops, and one of the items is flashed again to indicate its status as the probe. Subjects are to decide if the probe item is one of the target items and respond appropriately.

task.) Since all items were identical during the motion interval, subjects could succeed only by picking out the targets when they were initially flashed and then tracking them through the motion interval. Subjects were successful (never than 85.6 percent accurate) in these experiments when tracking up to five targets in a field of ten identical independently and unpredictably moving items.[7]

All these considerations suggest the need for multiple loci of attention, which can serve to independently "index" and track a number of salient items. The FINST model of visuospatial attention provides just such a mechanism. Pylyshyn's model is based on *visual indexes* which can be independently assigned to various items in the visual field, and which serve as a means of *access* to those items for the higher-level processes that allocate focal attention. In this regard, they function rather like pointers in a computer data structure: they reference certain items in the visual field (identifying them *as* distinct objects) without themselves revealing any properties of those objects.

Pylyshyn initially called these indexes *FINST's*, for FINgers of INSTantiation, due to the fact that physical fingers work in an analogous way: "Even if you do not know anything at all about what is located at the places that your fingers are touching, you are still in a position to determine such things as whether the object that finger number 1 is touching is to the left of or above the object that finger number 2 is touching. . . . [T]he access that the finger contact gives makes it inherently possible to track a *particular* token, that is, to keep referring to what is, in virtue of its historical trace, the *same* object" (Pylyshyn 1989: 68).

Visual indexes can be assigned to objects in the visual field regardless of their spatial contiguity (by contrast with spotlight models), with the following restriction: the architecture of the visual system provides only about *four* indexes. Furthermore, the indexes are *sticky*: if an indexed item in the visual field moves, the index moves with it. The visual indexes confer a processing priority on the indexed items, insofar as they allow focal attention to be shifted to indexed (and possibly moving) items without first searching for them by scanning the intervening space. (Note that the visual-indexing theory thus complements, rather than competes with, theories that posit a single locus of focal attention; cf. Pylyshyn and Storm 1988: 180). Attention is typically thought to improve various sorts of low-level visual processing, speeding response times to attended objects or areas (e.g., Downing and Pinker 1985; Posner et al. 1980). Similarly, visual indexes confer a processing advantage on the indexed items, since they can be immediately accessed by higher-level processes without a serial search. Intriligator (1997: experiment 2) and Sears and Pylyshyn (in press) explored these issues in the context of multiple-object tracking, demonstrating that this type of processing advantage is target-specific; in particular, it doesn't hold for non-targets – even those located within the convex polygon bounded by the moving targets. Thus, it must be the items *themselves* which are being indexed and tracked in the MOT task, not the region of space in which they're located.

Of particular relevance here is the recent demonstration that visual indexes survive occlusion. Scholl and Pylyshyn (in press) used the standard MOT task but had different conditions where occluders were (visually or functionally) present on the screen. Subjects were able to track items even when the items were briefly (but completely) occluded at various times during their motion, suggesting that occlusion is taken into account when computing enduring perceptual objecthood (see also section 4.4.2). Unimpaired performance required the presence of accretion and deletion cues along fixed contours at the occluding boundaries. Performance was significantly impaired when items were present in the visual field at the same times and to the same degrees as in the occlusion conditions, but disappeared and reappeared in ways which did not implicate the presence of occluding surfaces (e.g., by imploding and exploding into and out of existence, instead of accreting and deleting along a fixed contour). (See figure 2.7 for a schematic depiction of these types of conditions.) This suggests that the visual-indexing system is making allowances for occlusion *qua* occlusion and is not merely robust in the face of any modest interruptions in spatiotemporal continuity.

Several additional experimental paradigms have been used to adduce support for the visual-indexing framework, including evidence from *subitizing* (Trick and Pylyshyn 1993, 1994), *visual search* (Burkell and Pylyshyn 1997), and the *line-motion illusion* (Schmidt, et al. 1998). For concise reviews of this experimental support, see Pylyshyn 1994 and Pylyshyn et al. 1994.

4.3   Object files

Like Pylyshyn's visual-indexing theory, Kahneman and Treisman's *object file* theory attempts to describe the nature of object-based representations of visual attention. We assume, as do Kahneman and Treisman, that visual indexes and object files are both parts of a single indexing system. Kahneman et al. suggests that "We might think of [a visual 'FINST' index] as the initial spatiotemporal label that is entered in the object file and that is used to address it. . . . [A] FINST might be the initial phase of a simple object file before any features have been attached to it" (1992: 216).

One traditional model of visual experience contends, roughly, that visual stimuli are identified as objects when their visual projections activate semantic representations in long-term memory (LTM). Visual experience, then, consists in shifting patterns of this type of LTM activation. Kahneman et al. (1992) call this the "display-board model of the mind", and note that it has a number of serious shortcomings. It appears to be the case, for instance, that objects can be perceived and tracked through space even when they remain unidentified. Furthermore, when objects are initially misidentified, and later correctly recognized, there is still never any doubt that the object involved was the same object. "Two identical red squares in successive fields may be perceived as distinct objects if the spatial/temporal gap between them cannot be bridged, but the transformation of frog into prince is seen as a change in a single visual object" (Kahneman et al. 1992: 179). Identification *of* a particular object, in other words, is distinct from identification *as* an object in the first place.

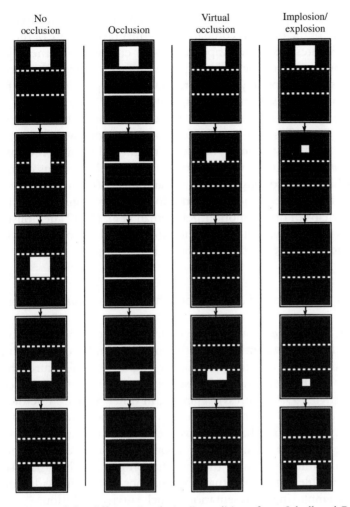

Figure 2.7. Some of the different "occlusion" conditions from Scholl and Pylyshyn, in press. The inherently dynamic nature of the occlusion conditions makes them difficult to represent in a static medium, but here we present some of them as sequences of static "snapshot" diagrams. In each condition, an item travels downward through five sequential frames of motion, interacting with a hypothetical occluder position (not to scale). Solid boundaries represent visible occluders, while dashed boundaries represent invisible occluders (presented to aid comprehension). (Adapted from Scholl and Pylyshyn in press.)

Kahneman and Treisman have argued that an intermediate level of representation is needed to mediate this latter task. In their theoretical framework, this role is played by object files. According to their theory, attending to an object in the visual field causes a temporary representation called an object file to be created. This object file stores information about the object's properties (including its color, shape, and current location), and this information is continually updated when the world changes. Object files are allocated and maintained primarily on the basis of spatiotemporal factors, however. Each time an object's spatiotemporal properties change (e.g., in item motion or apparent motion), the new state of the object is compared with the previous state of the object file. If these two states are spatiotemporally similar enough, then the object is seen as continuous, and the object file is updated appropriately. If the two states are sufficiently spatiotemporally dissimilar, however, the previous object file decays, and a new object file is opened to represent the "new" object.

Kahneman et al. (1992) describe three operations which are involved in managing object files: (a) a *correspondence* operation, which determines for each object whether it is novel, or whether it moved from a previous location; (b) a *reviewing* operation, which retrieves an object's previous characteristics, some of which may no longer be visible; and finally (c) an *impletion* operation which uses both current and reviewed information to construct a phenomenal percept, perhaps of object motion. Kahneman et al. (1992) demonstrated that object files survive real and apparent motion, and Scholl and Pylyshyn (in press) suggest that they also survive occluded motion.

4.4   Object-based attention and the anti-perceptual arguments

These and other object-based mechanisms of visuospatial attention are not thought to be entirely continuous with "thought" and "cognition" in general, but rather to occupy a distinct part of the cognitive architecture which serves as an interface between early visuospatial processing and cognition (Julesz 1990; Pylyshyn 1999, in press). They lie, in other words, in neither extreme of the "perception"/"cognition" dichotomy, but somewhere in the middle. And although these mechanisms have been motivated and developed completely independently from concerns about the infant's object concept, they seem, at a minimum, to enjoy those crucial properties which have sometimes been taken to rule out "perceptual" explanations, such as individuating distinct objects and employing representations which survive occlusion.

4.4.1   *Attending to the object-individuation argument*

The first argument that we discussed concerned the requirement that the mechanisms responsible employ discrete representations of individual objects – in contrast to the intrinsically continuous nature of perception. Object-based mechanisms of visuospatial attention meet this constraint. As their very name indicates, these mechanisms are designed to represent discrete objects. Indeed, the object-based attention literature was originally motivated by just this sort of distinction, between continuous spatial representations and discrete object-based representations.

Similarly, both the object file and the visual indexing frameworks were designed explicitly for indexing discrete objects, in an attempt to explain exactly how and when discrete objects are represented by mechanisms of visuospatial attention. The existence of such mechanisms casts doubt on the inference from the necessity of discrete representations to the necessity of appealing to maximally central thought to explain the infant's competence. It may be true that "thought," unlike "perception," "packages the world into units," but so do mechanisms of object-based visuospatial attention, which reflect parts of cognitive architecture which are not maximally central.

4.4.2   Attending to the occlusion argument

The second argument concerned the need for representations which could survive total occlusion – in contrast to the fleeting, retinally bound nature of perceptual representations. While persistence in the absence of retinal stimulation is perhaps not a necessary feature of object-based representations, it is a feature of both the object-file and the visual-indexing theories. This is most explicit in the case of visual indexing, as discussed above. Moreover, Scholl and Pylyshyn (in press) argued that their results also had to be interpreted in the object file framework as involving object files persisting through occlusion, and Treisman has confirmed that no upper bound has been experimentally determined concerning how long object files can persist during a cessation of retinal input (personal communication, 1997).

In fact, the persistence of representations through occlusion may be a general theme of attentional processing. There are several reasons to think that allowances for occlusion *should* characterize early visual processing, based on the fact that occlusion permeates visual experience. As Nakayama and his colleagues have noted:

> [O]cclusion varies greatly, depending on seemingly arbitrary factors – the relative positions of the distant surface, the closer surface, the viewing eye. Yet, various aspects of visual perception remain remarkably unimpaired. Because animals, including ourselves, seem to see so well under such conditions and since this fact of occlusion is always with us, it would seem that many problems associated with occlusion would have been solved by visual systems throughout the course of evolution. (Nakayama and Shimojo 1990, quoted in Nakayama et al. 1995: 62)

These sorts of general considerations have been borne out by Scholl and Pylyshyn's (in press) experiments, and also by several recent, related demonstrations. Many of these experiments involve static stimuli in the context of visual search (e.g., Davis and Driver 1994; Enns and Rensink 1998; He and Nakayama 1994), but similar results have been reported in other paradigms involving dynamic stimuli (Shimojo and Nakayama, 1990; Tipper et al. 1990; Yantis 1995). We will not discuss these studies here for lack of space, but the general lesson of these experiments is that "preattentive processes do more than simply register and group together elementary properties of the two-dimensional image – they are also capable of determining properties of the corresponding three-dimensional scene" (Enns and Rensink 1991: 346). Compare this to Spelke et al. (1995c) on the relevant occlusion constraint in cognitive development: "[I]nfants' perception of objects depends on analyses of the arrangements and motions of surfaces in the three-dimensional visual layout, not on analyses of the arrangements and motions of the elements in any two-dimensional retinal projection of the layout. . . . [This] suggest[s] that the processes underlying object perception occur relatively late in visual analysis" (p. 168). Spelke and her colleagues are explicitly assuming that properties of the 3-D scene are computed only in *late* visual processes, whereas the evidence cited above demonstrates that such computation is performed in early, preattentive processing.

In sum, some preattentive and attentive mechanisms do recognize occlusion, and make allowances for it. In such situations, perceptual objecthood is continuously maintained throughout an item's trajectory via some internal representation – such as a visual index or an object file – even though the object may frequently disappear completely from the visual field.

4.4.3   Attending to the "Pulfrich pendulum" argument

The point of the third argument was that in some cases "perceptual" systems seem to violate the very constraints that they are being asked to explain. Above, we offered the example of the "Pulfrich pendulum," in which the visual system constructs a percept which seems to violate the contact-mechanical "solidity constraint," about which infants seem to enjoy initial knowledge. The point we wish to stress is that no case has been found in which the attentional system violates the spatiotemporal constraints with which this chapter is concerned, as opposed to contact-mechanical constraints (see section 2.1).

We believe that there may be a fundamental, architecturally real distinction between the spatiotemporal and contact-mechanical types of initial knowledge, and that the former may be explained by appeal to mechanisms analogous to object-based mechanisms of visuospatial attention (see section 5). According to the logic of the "Pulfrich pendulum" argument, we should thus be unable to demonstrate violations of the relevant spatiotemporal principles in the operation of the attentional mechanisms themselves. And indeed, there do not seem to be cases like this in which the attentional systems interpret dynamic scenes in ways which violate basic laws of spatiotemporal continuity, object individuation, and arithmetic. (This is despite the fact that certain contact-mechanical constraints are interchangeable with certain spatiotemporal constraints, such as solidity and continuity; see Spelke et al. 1992). Nor should this seem surprising, since the hypothesized purposes of many attentional mechanisms are exactly analogous to spatiotemporally-based initial knowledge. To foreshadow our discussion in secion 5, consider:

- *Spatiotemporal continuity*

    Infants seem to have initial knowledge concerning the principle that objects must trace spatiotemporally continuous paths through space, while mechanisms such as visual indexes are designed in the first instance to represent visuospatial objects as they trace spatiotemporal paths through space. Thus, when a tracked item in the visual indexing framework disappears from the visual field, the index which was tracking it becomes de-assigned (unless the disappearance is accounted for by an occluding surface, just as in the infancy research).

- *Subitizing*

  Infants seem to have initial knowledge concerning basic arithmetic operations, so long as the cardinality of the operands is less than about five. This is exactly the limit which has been independently motivated in the visual indexing framework, and indeed one of the primary sources of experimental support for visual indexing comes from studies of the ability of adults to *subitize*, or rapidly determine the cardinality of sets with fewer than five items (Trick and Pylyshyn 1993, 1994).

- *The primacy of spatiotemporally-based object individuation*

  Infants seem to have initial knowledge of how to individuate objects based on spatiotemporal information, which is exactly what mechanisms such as visual indexes and object files are designed to do – to account for the individuation and tracking objects, regardless of their (perhaps tenuous) properties. Indeed, the performance of 10-month-olds in Xu and Carey's (1996) experiments exactly mirrors the motivation for mechanisms such as object files.

(We return to these three analogous aspect in more detail below, in section 5.) While it could be that phenomena analogous to the "Pulfrich pendulum" could yet be observed in the case of spatiotemporal constraints, we are not aware of any at present, and we predict that no such violations will be found.

To summarize where we have come: The nature of initial "spatiotemporal" knowledge of the object concept has sometimes been addressed in terms a dichotomy between perception and cognition, and, given this framework, there are several arguments which militate in favor of cognition. The resulting explanations of initial knowledge have sometimes attributed to infants various beliefs and theories which supply the relevant principles about how objects must behave. Such maximally central explanations are not mandated by the traditional arguments, however, since, as we have seen, other mechanisms which are neither maximally central nor maximally sensory find the traditional anti-perceptual arguments entirely congenial. (In the years since the traditional anti-perceptual arguments were first formulated, Spelke has continued to develop her ground-breaking views about the object concept, and seems now to agree, at least, that these two literatures have been developed in similar ways. In recent writings, she keeps the door open to the relevance of the attentional interface, but she does not develop these connections; cf. Spelke et al. 1995a: sect. 8.5.2.) All this suggests that it would be interesting to pursue a theory of the object concept which was modeled after such attentional mechanisms, rather than after maximally central aspects of objects such as their "market value."[8]

5   Object-Indexing Theory

Leslie et al. (1998) introduced the *object-indexing* theory as an attempt to embody the analogous aspects of the cognitive development and visual attention research programs in a concrete framework. This is not the place to mount a detailed defense of the framework, but having emphasized the potential importance of an attentionally-based theory in principle, we hope to sketch a plausible theory in which the insights from the object-based attention literature are put to good use.

The key notion in the object-indexing framework is the "sticky" index. Like Pylyshyn's visual indexes, an object index is an internal representation that is inherently abstract: an index picks out and keeps track of an object by location, without representing any of the object's properties. Once pointing to an object, however, the object can be accessed rapidly, and properties and featural information can be associated with, or "bound," to an index. An object index functions in the way that a pointer in a computer program might reference a data structure in the computer's memory: it references data without itself revealing any of the data.

To a first approximation, object indexes can do many of the things that pointing fingers can do. Both object indexes and fingers can point to, and thus individuate, items based on spatiotemporal criteria (e.g., independent motion, the existence of a spatial gap between the items) and can track the continuing identity of an object as it moves about the world. Both object indexes and fingers can also serve to enumerate the number of objects in the world – at least up to the number of available indexes or fingers. At the same time, neither object indexes nor fingers can by themselves reveal an object's color, luminance, composition, or global shape.

As a mechanism of selective attention, the object-indexing system is resource-limited, and has only a small number of available indexes. Following Pylyshyn's visual-indexing experiments, we predict that there are not more than *four* object indexes, and that this number serves as an effective compromise between focusing resources and being able to compute relations between distinct objects. We hypothesize the following properties of object-index assignment (compare Spelke et al. 1995a: sect. 8.2.4):

1   Indexes are assigned primarily *by* location, but not *to* locations. Rather, indexes are assigned to objects in locations.
2   A distinct object can attract only a single index. Multiple indexes cannot be assigned to identical objects.
3   Multiple spatially-separated areas of the visual field may in some cases be assigned a single index if there is no spatiotemporal information (e.g., relative motion) to distinguish them. (Thus, groups with common motion may be assigned a single index.)
4   Once assigned, an index sticks to its object even as the object moves

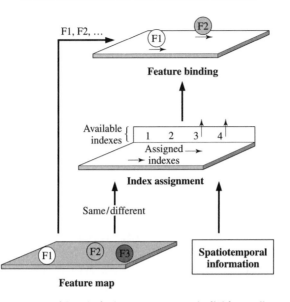

F1, F2, ...

F2

F1

Feature binding

Available indexes

| 1 | 2 | 3 | 4 |

Assigned → indexes

Index assignment

Same/different

F1   F2   F3

Spatiotemporal information

Feature map

Figure 2.8. The mature object-indexing system can individuate (i.e., assign indexes) either by location or by feature. The binding of featural information (e.g., F1, F2) to an index (denoted by an arrow) occurs after the index has been assigned, if it occurs at all. Although feature binding is not required for individuation, it is required for identification of objects. We assume that there is only a limited number of available indexes. See text for discussion. (Adapted from Leslie et al. 1998: 15.)

through several different locations. Indexes may follow objects behind occluders, in which case they point to "somewhere behind the occluder."
5   When all available indexes are already assigned to objects, a new object can be indexed only by first de-assigning one of the active indexes, flushing its bound features, and reassigning it to the new object. In this case, the previously indexed object is no longer represented within the object-indexing system.

Property information may later drive object indexing, but we assume that this will occur only if spatiotemporal information is absent or ambiguous, and that this process matures only later in development.[9] Featural information, when present, is stored on our model in a *feature map* which simply registers the *presence* of a feature (cf. Treisman and Gelade 1980). Crucially, featural information at this stage is registered without any indication of *where* the feature is in the visual field (or what object it is bound to), but only its presence or absence. The appearance of a red cross and a green circle may thus not be distinct on this level from the appearance of a green cross and a red circle, since the same features are present in each case.[10] See figure 2.8 for a summary of this model.

The architectural distinction between indexing and feature binding under-writes a functional distinction between spatiotemporally-driven object *individ-*

uation and featurally-driven object *identification*. In processes of visuospatial attention, the former task is accomplished separately and perhaps earlier in online processing than the latter task (cf. Johnston and Pashler 1990; Pylyshyn 1989; Quinlan 1998; Sagi and Julesz 1985; Tanaka and Shimojo 1996). In cognitive development, the former task seems to be accomplished separately and perhaps earlier in maturational development (cf. Bower 1974; Xu and Carey 1996).

It is tempting to put all this in terms of another traditional distinction, between the processing of "what" and "where" – between the processing of which objects are present (regardless of their locations) and where there exist objects (regardless of their identities). Featural and locational information are thought to be processed, largely independently, by distinct anatomical "streams" in the brain (e.g. Maunsell 1995; Sagi and Julesz 1985; Underleider and Mishkin 1984). Talking about "what" versus "where" in functional terms is a useful way to characterize our theory of the object concept, but we remain agnostic on the relation of these ideas to the actual relevant neuroanatomical pathways, (a) since it is unclear how these neural circuits map onto the object-based attentional mechanisms, and (b) because the nature of the domains of these circuits has recently become less clear (e.g., Goodale 1995; see also Bertenthal 1996).

Why might it make sense to divide up the effort in this way and to give priority to the processing of spatiotemporal information? One reason may simply be *learnability*. Some objects undergo radical featural changes (and may also merely *seem* to do so) while still retaining their identity. Without a reliable guide to which objects engage in such behavior, it may behoove infants to remain agnostic about object identities as determined by featural properties (see also Simon 1997):

> It might serve the human baby well to use spatiotemporal information to individuate objects, and then slowly learn about the more specific kinds of individuals, and for each, which properties change over time and which do not. . . . The infant must learn which properties stay constant for various categories of objects. In order to learn this, however, the infant must have some way of individuating objects and tracing them through time. The spatiotemporal criteria for object fulfill this need. (Xu and Carey 1996: 114, 150)

5.1   What object indexing is not: sensations, principles, types, and tokens

Most properties of object indexing are modeled on ideas which were completely independently motivated (e.g., the indexing model, the "stickiness" of the indexes, the properties of index assignment, the priority of spatiotemporal information, the limit on the number of available indexes, and the feature-binding model). Such a framework differs in several important respects from both maximally sensory and maximally central theories of the object concept.

In the traditional empiricist view, infants first encounter objects in the world only in terms of continuous, fleeting sensations and only slowly associate these sensations, resulting in bundles of features. Object indexing turns this on its head and suggests that featural information may often be *ignored* for some purposes early in life and that the core of the object concept may rather be a kind of mental pointing at a "this" or "that." In any case, the indexing framework accepts the traditional arguments against maximally sensory views and assumes that the mechanisms responsible must involve discrete object representations which persist through occlusion. Object indexing is thus opposed to "perceptual" accounts of the object concept, and we take pains in section 6.3 to dissociate our framework from contemporary "perceptual" empiricist, and otherwise deflationary theories (e.g., Bogartz el al. 1997; Munakata et al. 1997).

We take object indexing to be continuous with the projects of other researchers such as Carey, Spelke, and Wynn, who have advanced claims of initial knowledge in infancy. The goal of object indexing is to explain what this "initial knowledge" amounts to, albeit in novel architectural terms. Object indexing does stand opposed, however, to maximally central views of the object concept (see section 3.4) and tries to steer a course between the maximally sensory and central extremes.

One salient difference between object indexing and maximally central views lies in the fact that any initial knowledge afforded by object indexing would not be in the form of general principles in the way suggested by analogies to scientific theories (Gopnik and Meltzoff 1997). Several writers have suggested that we think of initial knowledge in infancy in terms of a scientific theory, or an innately driven "core theory," consisting of general principles (e.g., Gopnik and Meltzoff, 1997). The object-indexing mechanisms, by contrast, may be seen as involving "principles" only in the sense that there are mechanisms of attention that *implement* object principles, without explicitly representing them. The operation of these mechanisms may indeed conform to certain intelligible physical or numerical principles, but such principles need not be explicitly represented anywhere, any more than "Objects are rigid!" is explicitly stored in the visual system (which treats them as such; e.g., Ullman 1979). See Pylyshyn, in press, for a general discussion of this distinction.

One way to clarify this is via a distinction between "types" and "tokens".[11] (This terminology is intended only to highlight a crucial distinction involving the *generality* of object representations. In particular, talk of object "types" in this context has nothing to do with specific *kinds* of objects – e.g., *animals* or *artifacts*.) *Type*-based statements about objects will explicitly quantify over "objects" in general – for example, the statements that "Objects trace spatio-temporally continuous paths through space" or that "Moving objects that disappear behind other surfaces with occlusion cues continue to exist behind those surfaces." *Token*-based statements about objects, by contrast, concern only the behaviors and states of affairs of *particular*, individual objects – for example, the statement that "*That* object is currently somewhere behind that screen."

Object-indexing mechanisms account for infants' abilities without appeal to beliefs or principles about object *types*, but only to reactions to specific object *tokens*. In maximally central accounts, the initial knowledge is thought to take the form of principles concerning object types in general. Infants, for example, know that "Objects must trace spatiotemporally continuous paths through space" – an explicit statement about objects in general. The object-indexing mechanisms, by contrast, may be such that they eventually result in beliefs about individual object tokens (i.e., *that* object must be behind the screen; *that* object must have disappeared; *this* object must be different from that object which I saw a moment ago) without appealing to object types in general. In other words, the relevant conclusions about particular objects fall out of the design of the system and may conform to the relevant principles without ever explicitly representing them (cf. Kellman 1988).

Could object indexing account for the results of the infancy experiments which fueled the attributions of spatiotemporally-based initial knowledge? In the following sections we return briefly to the three experimental demonstrations of initial knowledge originally discussed in section 2, and we interpret them in the context of object indexing.

5.2   Indexing and spatiotemporal continuity

In the first example, Spelke and her colleagues (Spelke and Kestenbaum 1986; Spelke et al. 1995b) demonstrated that infants had initial knowledge of the principle that "Objects must trace spatiotemporally continuous paths through space" by examining their looking times while they observed objects moving behind occluders (see section 2.3 and figure 2.1).

The results of these experiments can readily be explained within the object-indexing framework. The single item in the first moments of the familiarization displays (figure 2.1a and b) attracts a single index, which stays attached as it moves along behind occluders (analogous to visual indexes tracking objects behind occluders; Scholl and Pylyshyn, in press). In the "continuous" condition (figure 2.1a), occlusion cues signal the indexing system that the object is behind an occluder. When the item reappears, the single object index reacquires and continues to track it. The event is thus apprehended using only a single index, and infants therefore expect only a single object. The one-object probe (figure 2.1c) also employs only a single object index, so has little novelty. With the two-object probe (figure 2.1d), however, increased attention is allocated in the form of a new index, and infants look longer.

In the "discontinuous" condition (figure 2.1b), the first index does not reacquire the object at the screen's occluding boundary and cannot jump the gap. When an object then appears from the far side of the other occluder, a new index must be assigned. This event requires two object indexes and is thus apprehended as involving two distinct objects. The two-object test event (figure 2.1d) will then require the same number of indexes and has little novelty. In the one-object test event (figure 2.1c), however, increased attention is allocated to search for the "missing" object corresponding to the original index (which is still pointing "somewhere"), and infants look longer.

Spelke concludes from the continuity experiments that "Infants appear to apprehend the identity of objects by analyzing the apparent continuity or discontinuity of paths of motion, in accord with the principle that objects move on spatio-temporally continuous paths" (Spelke 1988a: 179). This is entirely true in the object-indexing framework, but the "in accord with" part becomes crucial: maintenance of spatiotemporal continuity is part of the *modus operandi* of the indexing system (operating over object *tokens*), rather than an explicitly represented principle (about objects as *types*).

5.3   Indexing and arithmetic

The second example of spatiotemporally-based initial knowledge we discussed above was Wynn's (1992) demonstration that five-month-old infants can "compute the numerical results of . . . arithmetical operations" (p. 750) (see section 2.4 and figure 2.2). Object-indexing theory can explain these results by appealing to the fact that the indexing system can track the numerosity of objects in a scene simply by assigning indexes – rather than by counting to determine a cardinal value.

Infants' looking times in Wynn's "1 + 1 = 1 or 2" condition are explained as follows. The original item draws an object index, which continues to point to "somewhere behind the screen" when the object is occluded. The new item then appears in a location remote from the screen, attracting a new index. When it too disappears behind the screen, the system has two indexes both pointing to "somewhere behind the screen". These two active indexes translate into an attentional expectation for two objects when the screen is lowered. If only a single object remains on the stage, then one active index is left objectless, and increased attention is allocated in a "search" for the missing object. This increased attentional allocation yields longer looking times.

Similarly, in the "2 − 1 = 1 or 2" case: two indexes are assigned initially to the visible and distinct pair of objects and then point to "somewhere behind the screen" when they are occluded. When the single object is removed, one of the active indexes reacquires it and tracks if off the stage. The lone remaining active index reacquires an object as soon as the screen is lowered, but a new index must be assigned in the anomalous case, because there is an extra (i.e., non-indexed) object present behind the occluder. Attention is allocated to effect this index assignment, which yields longer looking. The same type of explanation holds in the "1 + 1 = 2 or 3" case. Wynn is correct that the "precise result" is being computed, but this may be affected implicitly by index assignment, not explicitly by representing cardinal values. Again, the patterns of looking times in these experiments may simply reflect the *modus operandi* of the object-indexing system, rather than knowledge of general, explicitly represented arithmetical principles.

Object indexing also provides a straightforward account of the upper limit on infants' numerical abilities. On the account just sketched, the infant will only be able to track precise numerosities if they remain in the range of available indexes. We assume – in line with the FINST and object-file theories – that there exist no more than about four object indexes. That there should be *some* limit follows from the fact that indexing is a resource-limited mechanism of selective attention. The *particular* limit of about four derives empirically from studies of visual indexing and its relation to subitizing (Pylyshyn 1994; Trick and Pylyshyn 1993, 1994).

Finally, object indexing explains the otherwise non-intuitive result of Simon et al. (1995). Simon et al. (1995) found that five-month-old infants in Wynn's paradigm have expectations regarding the numerosity of occluded objects, but do not seem to have any expectations about the properties or identities of those objects. Again, this is to be expected if the indexes are assigned and accessed by location, without feature binding. The assigned indexes are "feature blind" and serve only to *individuate* the objects. The different properties of the objects in Simon et al.'s (1995) experiment are not "visible" to the infant's object-indexing system.

In sum, using the object-indexing framework to account for the "arithmetic" results seems quite natural. Indexing theory can account for the numerosity tracking, the apparent upper bound on infants' numerical competence, and the lack of anomalous-property effects, all without appeal to explicitly represented arithmetical principles or cardinal values.

5.4   Indexing and object individuation

The third example discussed above was Xu and Carey's (1996) demonstration that 10-month-old infants will infer the existence of two occluded objects on the basis of spatiotemporal information (i.e., seeing both objects simultaneously in different locations), but not on the basis of property/kind information (e.g., seeing a duck and a ball sequentially), whereas 12-month-old infants will infer objecthood on the basis of both sorts of information (see section 2.5 and figures 2.3 and 2.4). In the object-indexing framework, these results exemplify the development of feature binding.

The 10-month-old's performance can be explained by feature-blind object indexing. In the spatial condition, the infant sees two objects in different locations simultaneously at the beginning of the familiarization phase, which results in the assignment of two object indexes. These indexes continue to point to "somewhere behind the screen," occasionally reacquiring one of the objects as it returns to view momentarily. These two active indexes translate into an attentional expectation for two objects, so that when only a single test object is revealed behind the screen, increased attention is allocated in a search for the missing object. Again, this increased attentional allocation engenders longer looking times. In the property condition, a single index is initially assigned when the single object – say, a duck – first emerges from behind the occluder. When the duck returns behind the screen, the index tracks it and ends up pointing to "somewhere behind the screen". When an object – say, a ball – then appears from behind the other side of the screen, the "feature-blind" index has no information contradicting the assumption that this is the originally indexed object, so the object reacquires the old index, rather than attracting a new index. At the end of the familiarization period, the indexing system thus has only a single index active and doesn't track the existence of the second object, despite its distinct property/kind information.

By 12 months, however, featural differences can now drive index assignment in this type of situation, where spatiotemporal information is ambiguous (see figure 2.8). The presence of novel features on the feature map now indicates to the system that the current object is distinct from the earlier object. Perhaps the development from feature-blind to feature-driven indexing reflects increased integration of "what" and "where" systems in the brain (Leslie et al. 1998).

Recent studies have suggested that feature binding may still be fragile at 12 months (Tremoulet 1998). These results indicate that there is also an important distinction between *individuation* by feature (which appears to develop earlier) and *identification* by feature (which appears to develop later). For details of these experiments, see Tremoulet 1998; for discussion, see Leslie et al. 1998.

Again, it should not be surprising that the object-indexing framework can address these results, since it is modeled on mechanisms from the visuospatial attention literature which are specifically posited to do just the sorts of things that infants seem to be doing in these experiments. In developing the object-file framework, for instance, Treisman and her colleagues were motivated by the necessity (a) to individuate objects solely on the basis of spatiotemporal information when there is no featural information available, and (b) to maintain a continuing representation of objecthood on the basis of spatiotemporal factors, even when featural information is in flux. Thus, again: "Two identical red squares in successive fields may be perceived as distinct objects if the spatial/temporal gap between them cannot be bridged, but the transformation of frog into prince is seen as a change in a single visual object" (Kahneman et al. 1992: 179). Ten-month-old infants in Xu and Carey's (1996) experiment responded precisely in accord with these motivations: (a) they cognized two objects when they saw the objects appear simultaneously, while (b) they did not cognize the existence of two objects when two featurally dissimilar objects were presented sequentially.

In the preceding pages, we have attempted to motivate the idea that the object-indexing framework provides a useful way to think about some spatiotemporal aspects of the infant's object concept. In the following section, we highlight some of the challenges that the theory faces.

5.5   Challenges for object indexing

Work on visuospatial attention and cognitive development has uncovered surprisingly parallel phenomena concerning the relationship between spatio-temporal individuation and featural identification of objects. This suggests that similar mechanisms may be at work in both cases. At this stage, however, we present the object-indexing model primarily as a framework to guide research in both fields and to emphasize the theoretical importance of several open questions. We have left it an open question as to the precise relationship between object indexes and the analogous entities from visuospatial attention such as visual indexes and object files (see Leslie et al. 1998). While it may be that these are merely analogous mechanisms and ideas, it is also possible that the FINST and object-file frameworks are continuous with object indexing (Scholl 1997). At least in this strong form, the proposal faces several challenges, which we identify below.

- *Reconciling time scales*

  The crucial events in looking-time experiments with infants typically take on the order of tens of seconds. The experiments of Wynn (1992) and Xu and Carey (1996), for instance, typically involve objects which are occluded for several seconds at a time. The time scales at work in the attention experiments, by contrast, are often on the order of tens or hundreds of milliseconds (e.g., the latency between spatiotemporal individuation and featural identification, or the "reviewing" process for object files). Further work is necessary to determine if these time scales can be reconciled. For instance, it would be worthwhile to determine exactly how long an object file stays "open" when its object goes behind a screen and doesn't emerge. Object files are thought to remain active for "at least 600–700 ms, and perhaps much longer" (Kahneman et al. 1992: 208), but an upper bound on the persistence of object files has yet to be determined (Treisman, personal communication, 1997).

- *Cognitive penetrability*

  Since object indexing is thought to be driven by parts of cognitive architecture which are not maximally central, we might predict that only limited kinds of information influence indexing. We might predict, in other words, that at least in some cases, object indexing will be *cognitively impenetrable* (Pylyshyn 1980, 1984). Some contact-mechanical judgments about objects' behavior do seem to be cognitively penetrable. In Baillargeon's "drawbridge" experiments (Baillargeon et al. 1985), for instance, infants look longer at a drawbridge which impossibly rotates "through" a solid object, but this pattern of looking does not occur if infants are given evidence that the object is compressible and not rigid (Baillargeon 1987). Do such cases exist for the spatiotemporal aspect of the infants' object concept? We are not aware of any. Indeed, it may be that the spatiotemporal individuation versus property-based identification distinction marks an architectural distinction in terms of "top-down influences", including cognitive penetrability (e.g., Heller 1997; Scholl 1999).

- *Cross-modality*

  An interesting challenge to the object-indexing framework comes from cross-modal aspects of the object concept (see Spelke 1988b). Some contact-mechanical aspects of the object concept, at least, do seem to be cross-modally sensitive (e.g., Streri and Spelke 1988; Streri et al. 1993), and the same may hold for spatiotemporal aspects (cf. Starkey et al. 1990; Wynn 1996). In general: "Objects do not appear to be apprehended by separate visual and haptic mechanisms but by a single mechanism that operates on representations arising either through vision or through touch" (Spelke 1988a: 175). The apparent conflict lies in the fact that mechanisms of object-based attention have primarily been proposed to function over only a *visual* domain and to be somewhat distinct from other modalities. Of course, nothing precludes similar mechanisms existing in other modalities: it has often been noted that visual and auditory processing, for instance, share several surprisingly similar mechanisms (e.g., Julesz 1980). In addition, although it is the visual aspects of Pylyshyn's visual-indexing framework that have received the most experimental attention, visual indexes are primarily intended to be part of a visuo-*spatial* system, and Pylyshyn's model explicitly includes a proprioceptive component (Pylyshyn 1989). It is possible that object indexing operates in a single cross-model space, but this is not a necessary aspect of our model.

- *Other spatiotemporal* explananda?

  We have aimed the object-indexing framework only at those *non*-contact-mechanical, "spatiotemporal" aspects of the infant's object concept, and have discussed how it might address several relevant experiments. Are there other "spatiotemporal" aspects of the object concept which resist explanation via object indexing? Certainly there are many other sorts of spatiotemporally-based initial knowledge which we have not examined in this chapter, but at first blush many of them seem like excellent candidates for an explanation in terms of object indexing. One such example is Kellman and Spelke's demonstrations that infants will use common motion to infer the *unity* of dynamic partially occluded objects, but at the same time (and unlike adults) they will not use static featural information to infer the existence of two separate objects (Kellman and Spelke 1983; Kellman et al. 1986; see also Johnson and Aslin 1995, 1996). Another example is inferring object unity from successive dynamic displays (van de Walle and Spelke 1996). Are there any examples which do not seem to fall within the domain of object indexing – perhaps involving sensitivity to objects' *heights* (e.g., Baillargeon and Graber 1987; Baillargeon and DeVos 1991)? (Are properties like "height" spatiotemporal or featural in nature?)

• *Language and the object concept*

One final potential challenge to the object-indexing framework may be a link to *language learning*. Xu and Carey 1996 (experiments 4 and 5) reported some provocative preliminary evidence suggesting that infants will individuate objects on the basis of property/kind information only when they know the words which name those objects. Of course, as Xu and Carey note, one cannot infer any causal relation from this pattern. Nevertheless, "The correspondence in time of the two developments – the ability to use the differences between a ball and a bottle to individuate objects and the ability to comprehend nouns such as 'ball' and 'bottle' – raises the question of the relation between the two achievements" (Xu and Carey 1996: 145). Object indexing, as presented, contains no explicit (much less necessary) link to language learning, and thus could only account for this type of result by appeal to *ad hoc* additions to the theory. On the other hand, the same might be said for many other explanations of the object concept, which has traditionally been thought to be functionally divorced from the language acquisition. Spelke, for instance, has suggested in the past that "language plays no important role in the spontaneous elaboration of physical knowledge" (Spelke 1988a: 181). It may be that noticing an object kind is a prelude to learning a verbal label for it. A mature object-indexing system may in turn be required before a given object can be noticed.

5.6   Summary

Despite – and because of – these challenges, we believe that object indexing provides a refreshing way to think about spatiotemporal aspects of the infant's object concept. We have tried with the object-indexing framework to bring together two literatures which have previously been developed independently. The surprising parallels between recent results in cognitive developmental psychology and the study of object-based visuospatial attention suggest that the two areas of inquiry may have something to do with each other, and we have tried to flesh out this intuition in our framework. While our theory is intended at present simply as a framework to guide research into these analogies, we have tried to present a plausible story of how such a theory could actually begin to address some of the experiments which have been used to characterize the infant's object concept.

It seems to be the case, as Spelke suggests, that we come into our initial knowledge of the object concept in ways quite different from how we come to know about an object's properties (e.g., its color and form), but it may also be the case that we acquire initial knowledge about objects in ways quite different from "those by which we come to know about its material composition or its market value" (Spelke 1988b: 198). Our earliest knowledge of objecthood may involve not undifferentiated arrays of sensations (as in maximally sensory views), and not explicitly represented principles about object types (as in maximally central views), but rather a kind of inherently abstract mental "pointing" at a "this" or a "that."

In any case, the object-indexing framework is an example of a theory which attempts to escape the traditional bounds of the perception/cognition dichotomy, to a more motivated middle ground, at the attentional interface.

6   Related Theories

In this section we briefly relate both the perception/cognition dichotomy and the object-indexing framework to several other recent, related accounts of the infant's object concept.

6.1   Simon's "non-numerical" account of numerical competence

Simon (1997) has offered an account of Wynn's "arithmetic" experiments (see section 2.4) which in some respects the object-indexing framework finds congenial. Simon argues that the patterns of looking times in Wynn's experiments do not require any specifically numerical abilities, but only domain-general abilities which are being co-opted for a purpose for which they were not specifically designed. These abilities include (1) "the ability to remember and compare items from a previously viewed collection," (2) the ability "to make discriminations between collections of up to four objects," (3) "the ability to form representations that generalize over some or all of the perceptual details of the actual items involved," and (4) the ability to notice the disappearance of an occluded object (Simon 1997: 361). Simon argues that these sorts of general abilities are sufficient to account for Wynn's results, and in particular, that no additional ability to compute ordinal relationships is needed. Simon's strategy is to catalog this minimal set of necessary abilities and then to cite evidence that each ability exists. (Simon, in press, also presents a straightforward computational model of this pattern of abilities and uses the model to emulate the results of the infants in Simon et al. 1995.)

Like object indexing, Simon's account appears to be neither maximally central nor maximally sensory in nature. There are, however, a number of salient differences between our approaches. First, Simon's theory is intended to account only for the results concerning initial knowledge of number and arithmetic, whereas object indexing addresses all spatiotemporally-based initial knowledge. Even within the domain of number, however, our approaches differ on several counts. While Simon does mention mechanisms like FINSTs and object files, his theory is based primarily on an analysis of the *abilities* required to give rise to the relevant patterns of looking times, without proposing specific mechanisms. Object indexing, by contrast, is focused directly on the *mechanisms* of cognitive architecture responsible and thus draws together all these otherwise unrelated abilities into a single coherent explanation. For example, Simon appeals to the abilities to subitize and to generalize over perceptual features, whereas we appeal to a specific architectural system which explains these abilities (viz, the visual-indexing system; see section 4.2). Simon has clearly recognized the analogies between the visual attention and cognitive development literatures, however, and it may be possible to read our theory as an architectural explanation of the abilities present in Simon's theory. Again, however, the scope of our indexing theory is greater and is not restricted to the domain of number and arithmetic – only one of the types of initial knowledge addressed by object indexing.

6.2   Sortal concepts and the object-first hypothesis

Xu and Carey (1996) have offered a theory of the infant's object concept based on the notion of *sortal concepts* (e.g., Hirsch 1982; Wiggins 1980; Xu 1997). A sortal, to a first approximation, is a concept that provides criteria for determining object individuation and identification. As an example, Xu and Carey (1996) ask us to consider the question "How many are there in a deck of cards?" This question has no well-defined answer, since it doesn't specify what is to be individuated and counted (cards? suits? particles of matter?). As this example suggests, sortal concepts are typically lexicalized as count-nouns, at least in those languages which employ a count-noun/mass-noun distinction.

Xu and Carey (1996) explain their results (see section 2.5) by appeal to the notion of sortal concepts, along with the "*object-first*" *hypothesis*. Xu and Carey argue that infants employ the sortal concept BOUNDED PHYSICAL OBJECT before they represent any other more specific sortals.[12] This explains why 10-month-olds expect two objects behind the final screen only when given appropriate spatiotemporal information – because that is the only type of information embodied in their only sortal concept. By 12 months, in contrast, other sortal concepts (e.g., BOTTLE, TRUCK) have begun to develop (along with *language*; see section 5.5), so that the older infant is able to use these additional sortals to succeed in property/kind conditions, where the spatiotemporal information is ambiguous.

We're intrigued by this proposal, because BOUNDED PHYSICAL OBJECT is just the sort of necessarily abstract representation afforded by object indexing. However, we are not yet sure that this idea is best explained by appeal to sortal concepts. One way to characterize our preference here is in terms of *falsifiability*. Consider what the two theories could have said if the relevant experiments had come out the other way for the 10-month-olds – success in property condition (figure 2.4), but failure in spatiotemporal condition (figure 2.3). The sortal framework could have accounted for this pattern of results just as easily – Xu and Carey could simply posit an "*object-last*" *hypothesis* instead of an object-first hypothesis. Object indexing, by contrast, motivated independently by object-based mechanisms of visuospatial attention, has no such recourse. In other words, object indexing *must* predict the Xu and Carey (1996) results, whereas the sortals framework can easily be accommodated to fit nearly any pattern of results. This is an explanatory advantage of the object-indexing account.

6.3   Contemporary empiricist accounts of the object concept

There is always a temptation to group all non-maximally central views of the object concept together, as deflationary tendencies, toward the maximally sensory extreme. However, we also reject the other extreme and have proposed that the appropriate explanation lies at the attentional interface between perception and cognition. In an effort to clarify the distinction between empiricist sensory views and the attentional/indexing view, we briefly discuss two examples of other recent non-maximally central theories.

Bogartz et al. (1997) explicitly reject maximally central explanations of the object concept and argue that the relevant patterns of infant looking times can be explained by appeal to "perceptual processing", adopting the other extreme: "We assume that young infants cannot reason, draw inferences, or have beliefs" (p. 411). Bogartz and his colleagues replicated a study by Baillargeon and Graber (1987) which they suggest had previously been interpreted in maximally central terms. Baillargeon and Graber's study, which we have not discussed, involved sensitivity to the *height* of an occluded object. Infants were habituated to both a "short" and a "tall" toy rabbit passing behind a tall solid screen and were then tested with a screen which had a high "window" cut out of its center. Infants dishabituated to a "tall" rabbit which did not appear through this high "window" while passing behind the screen, but did not dishabituate to a "short" rabbit which did not appear in the same high "window" while passing behind the same screen. These results were interpreted in terms of initial knowledge of spatiotemporal continuity and how it interacts with the *heights* of objects. (See also Baillargeon & DeVos 1991 and section 5.5 of this chapter.) Bogartz et al. (1997) replicated this experiment using a more complex experimental design and statistical analysis (involving regression rather than the analysis of variance), and concluded: "The results show unambiguously that the possibility of the rabbit not showing up in the window played no role in the looking times of these infants" (p. 418). They take this demonstration to support what they call their "perceptual processing" view of the infant's object concept. (See Bogartz and Shinskey 1998, 1999 for recent applications of this view to other experiments.)

Bogartz and his colleagues enthusiastically adopt the dichotomy between "perception" and "cognition", noting the potential "over-interpretation" involved in maximally central, "cognitive" interpretations and opposing this with a "perceptual" story. While we agree with their careful treatment of maximally central views, we find "perceptual" approaches to be inadequate as well, for all the reasons discussed above in section 3.

We find it hard to discern what exactly Bogartz et al. mean by "perception" and how the distinction between "perception" and "cognition" is to be drawn. All they tell us is that "Perceptual processing consists of analysis of the immediate representations of events, the construction in associative memory of transformations of these immediate representations, abstraction of their forms, and the comparison of immediate perceptual representations to the representations stored in memory" (p. 411). They then offer the "modifiable videotape" metaphor: "The young infant is primarily engaged in making 'videotapes' of events in the world and storing these tapes for access and updating. When new events are perceived, they are compared with the closest tape in the library. If there is a match, nothing new is entered into the library. If there is a discrepancy, either a new tape is created or the old tape is modified to include the new representation as a permissible variation" (p. 411 n.). Without a serious account of the nature of these representations, the proposal is largely empty. For example, in order to avoid circularity, Bogartz et al. need to characterize "representations of events" that are "immediate" independently of characterizing "perceptual processing." In any case, how could perceptual processes possibly do *all* these things? Unfortunately, aside from a single allusion to visual mental imagery, Bogartz et al. do not provide a single reference to work on perception or vision supporting the claim that perceptual systems have these abilities. It remains to be seen whether their notion of "perceptual processing" can be made concrete enough to be useful or falsifiable and whether their operations of "transformation," "abstraction," and "comparison" can really be distinguished from "cognition." In contrast to these proposals, object-indexing theory makes a set of specific empirical claims about how spatiotemporally-based initial knowledge is embodied in infants and adults at the attentional interface between perception and cognition.[13] (These comments, however, do not impugn the novel methodology employed by Bogartz et al. 1997, which we view as a tremendous improvement over traditional methods.)

Munakata et al. (1997) also reject maximally central explanations of the object concept and favor instead an approach based on parallel distributed processing. Munakata et al. focus on the question of why certain types of initial knowledge manifest themselves in some tasks but not in others. In particular, they focus on the fact that looking-time measures seem to reveal accurate representations of the locations of occluded objects, while reaching measures seem to indicate that infants do not possess such representations (e.g., the "A-not-B error": Piaget 1954). They suggest that a maximally central view of the object concept (what they call a "principle-based approach") is not necessary to explain this pattern of results, since they can be adequately modeled in a connectionist network. Munakata and her colleagues have attempted to model infants' looking and reaching behaviors in a computer simulation by employing two sets of output units. To account for the delay between looking and reaching competence, they simply delayed training on one set of outputs and used a reduced learning rate. They call this set of outputs "reaching" and thus model the developmental sequence. The relevant 'knowledge' isn't simply present or absent, but rather exists to different *degrees* in different systems: "the ability to represent occluded objects depends on the connections among relevant neurons and . . . the ability is acquired through a process of strengthening these connections" (p. 689). The idea is basically that a "weak" internal representation in the network may suffice to guide looking, but may not be strong enough to drive reaching.

These are interesting ideas, though we think the connectionist modeling plays little useful role in the explanation. Suppose the infant had been organized so that initial knowledge was revealed by reaching behaviors *before* being revealed by looking times. This would imply a very different architectural arrangement in the infant, but the Munakata et al. model could accommodate this simply by changing the label on the delayed set of outputs from "reaching" to "looking"!

Object-indexing theory does not yet address the issue of why reaching behaviors show delayed initial knowledge relative to looking times. Bertenthal (1996) has argued for the relevance to infancy of a distinction between "perception for action" and "perception for cognition", a distinction motivated independently by findings with adults (e.g., Goodale 1995). One possibility is that these distinct systems employ different indexing mechanisms. In any case, both object indexing and Munakata's approach agree that the infant's object concept is not maximally central.

7   Concluding Thoughts

In this chapter we have focused on the mechanisms of cognitive architecture which underwrite and explain parts of the infant's object concept. Our project is continuous with those of other researchers such as Carey, Spelke, and Wynn, who have demonstrated a wide array of initial knowledge in infancy. The interesting question is what this initial knowledge amounts to in terms of the underlying cognitive architecture. Traditionally, these issues have been viewed in terms of a sharp dichotomy between "perception" and "cognition." Some theorists have rejected explanations involving "initial knowledge", and have attempted to explain the discriminative abilities of infants solely in terms of low-level perceptual systems. Other researchers have argued that "perception" lacks several crucial properties (e.g., object-directedness and the ability to survive occlusion), and that the responsible mechanisms must therefore be mechanisms of maximally central thought.

We reject these extreme approaches and instead have explored the idea that the origins of the object concept lie at the attentional interface between perception and cognition. In an attempt to further motivate this type of explanation beyond mere possibility, we have offered our *object-indexing* framework as a potential incarnation of this type of explanation and have discussed several other sorts of competing theories. In so doing, we have highlighted the facts that the range of possible architectural interpretations of this exciting research is wider than is sometimes thought and that there are intriguing parallels between research on the infant's object concept and research in the nature of object-based visuospatial attention in adults. We welcome the vigorous debate that is clearly beginning about the underlying cognitive mechanisms, since for us this is the point of the whole endeavor.

Notes

Portions of this chapter were presented by Scholl at the 1997 Annual Meeting of the Society for Philosophy and Psychology, New York, 5 May 1997. We are grateful to the following people for stimulating conversation and for helpful comments and criticism on earlier (in some cases much earlier) drafts: Richard Bogartz, Susan Carey, Jonathan Cohen, Jacob Feldman, Jerry Fodor, Ron Mallon, Amy Needham, Thomas Papathomas, Zenon Pylyshyn, Richard Samuels, Elizabeth Spelke, Stephen Stich, Anne Treisman, Polly Tremoulet, Jonathan Weinberg, and Fei Xu. We also wish to thank the members of the Princeton–Rutgers–NYU Object Group for extremely helpful discussion of these issues.

1 On visuospatial attention as the interface between perception and cognition, see Julesz 1990 and Pylyshyn 1999, in press.
2 Parts of these experiments were previously reported by Spelke and Kestenbaum (1986), who used slightly different test events. For another modified replication, see Xu and Carey 1996: experiment 1).
3 Several earlier studies demonstrated numerical competence in infants, particularly the ability to detect correspondences between sets of items. These studies demonstrated that infants can reliably detect differences between sets of two and three items (e.g., Antell and Keating 1983; Starkey and Cooper 1980; Starkey et al. 1990; Strauss and Curtis 1981) and sometimes between sets of three and four items (e.g., Starkey and Cooper 1980; Von Loosbroek and Smitsman 1990).
4 Simon et al. (1995) were actually pursuing a deflationary account of Wynn's experiments, in which infants were responding not to arithmetical violations *per se*, but only to the associated physical violations (i.e., of the principle that objects can't jump in and out of existence). Their results, however, failed to support or disconfirm this hypothesis. More recently, Simon (1997, 1998) has offered another "non-numerical" account of these results, which we discuss in section 6.1.
5 The data were actually more complicated than this. In all conditions there was a baseline preference for looking at two objects (compared to one), so that "success" in these experiments consisted of overcoming this baseline preference. In the experiment described above, for instance, ten-month-old infants looked longer at a final tableau containing two objects in both the *baseline* and the *property* conditions, but looked equally long at one and two test objects in the *spatial* condition (thus overcoming the baseline preference and looking relatively longer at one test object). See Xu and Carey 1996 for details.

6 Xu and Carey (1996) interpret their results in terms of *sortal concepts*, and more particularly as support for the *object-first hypothesis*, wherein infants employ the sortal concept BOUNDED PHYSICAL OBJECT before they employ any more specific sortal concepts. We discuss this proposal in section 6.2.

7 Pylyshyn and Storm ruled out a class of alternative explanations for this result in which a single spotlight of attention sequentially and repeatedly visits each item in turn: even at the fastest reported scan velocities (around 250°/sec), a simulated attentional spotlight, augmented with several location-prediction and guessing heuristics, was unable to approach the actual performance of human subjects. See Pylyshyn and Storm 1988 for the details of this simulation.

8 Another analogous aspect of the infancy experiments and the object-based attentional research lies in the role of *novelty*. Recall that in the looking-time measures, the test phase checks to see if a novel event is interpreted by the infant as a fundamentally new event. The longer looking times, in other words, correspond to perceived novelty. This bears a striking resemblance to another recent trend in the study of visuospatial attention, emphasized by Steven Yantis. Yantis has argued that visual attention is automatically captured by the appearance of *new visual objects* (Yantis 1993, 1995). Abrupt onsets, for example, capture attention, "not because they are accompanied by a luminance increment, but because they mark the appearance of a new perceptual object" (Yantis 1993: 157). In different contexts (e.g., the reappearance of an object from behind an occluder), the same luminance increment will not be interpreted as a new visual object, and so will not exogenously attract visual attention. Yantis explains this in terms of the underlying responses of the object-file system.

9 When featural information does begin to play a role in object indexing, it may do so in two importantly distinct ways: *individuation by feature* and *identification by feature*. These are distinct processes in principle and also appear to be dissociable experimentally, with feature-driven individuation maturing earlier (for some features) than feature-driven identification (Tremoulet 1998).

10 Cf. Wolfe and Bennett 1997 for an intermediate step in this type of process.

11 We are extremely grateful to Susan Carey for helping us to see object indexing in these terms.

12 Xu and Carey (1996) do not claim that the BOUNDED PHYSICAL OBJECT sortal is lexicalized for the infant, or indeed in the language at all, but they do claim that it is psychologically real for the infant (n. 1). For critical discussion of the notion of a PHYSICAL OBJECT sortal, see Xu 1997 and commentaries by Ayers (1997), Hirsch (1997), and Wiggins (1997).

13 In a similar vein, Melkman and Rabinovitch (1998) suggest that the results of Spelke et al. (1995b) can be explained by appeal only to "sensory or perceptual understanding" (p. 258). However, they do not say what they mean by this, and, like Bogartz et al. (1997), they do not provide a single reference to the vision or perception literature to substantiate their dubious claims about the abilities of "vision" and "perception."

References

Antell, S. and Keating, D. (1983) Perception of numerical invariance in neonates. *Child Development* 54, 695–701.

Ayers, M. (1997) Is *physical object* a sortal concept? A reply to Xu. *Mind and Language* 12, 393–405.

Baillargeon, R. (1987) Young infants' reasoning about the physical and spatial properties of a hidden object. *Cognitive Development* 2, 179–200.

—— (1994) How do infants learn about the physical world? *Current Directions in Psychological Science* 3, 133–40.

—— (1995) Physical reasoning in infancy. In M. S. Gazzaniga (ed.), *The Cognitive Neurosciences*, Cambridge, MA: MIT Press, 181–204.

Baillargeon, R. and DeVos, J. (1991) Object permanence in young infants: further evidence. *Child Development* 62, 1227–46.

Baillargeon, R. and Graber, M. (1987) Where is the rabbit? 5.5-month-old infants' representation of the height of a hidden object. *Cognitive Development* 2, 375–92.

Baillargeon, R., Spelke, E. and Wasserman, S. (1985) Object permanence in 5-month-old infants. *Cognition* 20, 191–208.

Baylis, G. and Driver, J. (1993) Visual attention and objects: evidence for hierarchical coding of location. *Journal of Experimental Psychology: Human Perception and Performance* 19, 451–70.

Behrmann, M. and Tipper, S. (1994) Object-based visual attention: evidence from unilateral neglect. In C. Umilta and M. Moscovitch (eds), *Attention and performance 15: Conscious and Nonconscious Processing and Cognitive Functioning*, Cambridge, MA: MIT Press, 351–75.

Bertenthal, B. (1996) Origins and early development of perception, action, and representation. *Annual Review of Psychology* 47, 431–59.

Bogartz, R. and Shinskey, J. (1998) On perception of a partially occluded object in 6-month olds. *Cognitive Development* 13, 141–63.

—— (1999) Object permanence in five-and-a-half-month-old infants? Manuscript in preparation.

Bogartz, R., Shinskey, J. and Speaker, C. (1997) Interpreting infant looking: the event set × event set design. *Developmental Psychology* 33, 408–22.

Bower, T. (1974) *Development in Infancy*. San Francisco: W. H. Freeman.

Burkell, J. and Pylyshyn, Z. W. (1997) Searching through selected subsets of visual displays: a test of the FINST indexing hypothesis. *Spatial Vision* 11, 225–58.

Carey, S. (1995) Continuity and discontinuity in cognitive development. In E. Smith and D. Osherson (eds), *Thinking*, Vol. 3 of *An Invitation to Cognitive Science*, 2nd edn, Cambridge, MA: MIT Press, 101–30.

Chun, M. and Cavanagh, P. (1997) Seeing two as one: linking apparent motion and repetition blindness. *Psychological Science* 8, 74–9.

Davis, G. and Driver, J. (1994) Parallel detection of Kanizsa subjective figures in the human visual system. *Nature* 371, 791–3.

Downing, C. and Pinker, S. (1985) The spatial structure of visual attention. In M. Posner and O. S. M. Marin (eds), *Attention and Performance II*, London: Erlbaum, 171–87.

Driver, J. and Halligan, P. (1991) Can visual neglect operate in object-centered coordinates? An affirmative single case study. *Cognitive Neuropsychology* 8, 475–94.

Duncan, J. (1984) Selective attention and the organization of visual information. *Journal of Experimental Psychology: General* 113, 501–17.

Egeth, H. E. and Yantis, (1997) Visual attention: control, representation, and time course. *Annual Review of Psychology* 48, 269–97.

Egly, R., Driver, J. and Rafal, R. (1994) Shifting visual attention between objects and locations: evidence for normal and parietal lesion subjects. *Journal of Experimental Psychology: General* 123, 161–77.

Enns, J. and Rensink, R. (1991) Preattentive recovery of three-dimensional orientation from line drawings. *Psychological Review* 98, 335–51.

—— (1998) Early completion of occluded objects. *Vision Research* 38, 2489–505.

Eriksen, C. W. and Hoffman, J. E. (1972) Temporal and spatial characteristics of selective encoding from visual displays. *Perception and Psychophysics* 12, 201–4.

Eriksen, C. W. and St James, J. D. (1986) Visual attention within and around the field of focal attention: a zoom lens model. *Perception and Psychophysics* 40, 225–40.

Goodale, M. (1995) The cortical organization of visual perception and visuo-motor control. In S. Kosslyn and D. Osherson (eds), *Visual Cognition*, Vol. 2 of *An Invitation to Cognitive Science*, 2nd edn, Cambridge, MA: MIT Press, 167–214.

Gopnik, A. and Meltzoff, A. (1997) *Words, Thoughts, and Theories*, Cambridge, MA: MIT Press.

He, Z. and Nakayama, K. (1994) Perceiving textures: beyond filtering. *Vision Research* 34, 151–62.

Heller, M. (1997) Gaps in perception. *Perception* 26, 1481–4.

Hirsch, E. (1982) *The Concept of Identity*, New York: Oxford University Press.

—— (1997) Basic objects: a reply to Xu. *Mind and Language* 12, 406–12.

Intriligator, J. M. (1997) The spatial resolution of visual attention. Unpublished Ph.D. diss. Harvard University.

Johnson, A. and Aslin, R. (1995) Perception of object unity in 2-month-old infants. *Developmental Psychology* 31, 739–45.

—— (1996) Perception of object unity in young infants: the roles of motion, depth, and orientation. *Cognitive Development* 11, 161–80.

Johnston, J. and Pashler, H. (1990) Close binding of identity and location in visual feature perception. *Journal of Experimental Psychology: Human Perception and Performance* 16, 843–56.

Julesz, B. (1980) Spatial frequency channels in one-, two-, and three-dimensional vision: variations on an auditory theme by Bekesy. In C. Harris (ed.), *Visual Coding and Adaptability*, Hillsdale, NJ: Erlbaum, 263–316.

—— (1990) Early vision is bottom-up, except for focal attention. In *Cold Spring Harbor Symposia on Quantitative Biology – The Brain*, vol. 55, New York: Cold Spring Harbor Laboratory Press, 973–8.

Kahneman, D. and Treisman, A. (1984) Changing views of attention and automaticity. In R. Parasuraman and D. R. Davies (eds), *Varieties of Attention*, New York: Academic Press, 29–61.

Kahneman, D., Treisman, A. and Gibbs, B. J. (1992) The reviewing of the object files: object-specific integration of information. *Cognitive Psychology* 24, 174–219.

Kanwisher, N. (1987) Repetition blindness: type recognition without token individuation. *Cognition* 27 117–43.

Kanwisher, N. and Driver, J. (1992) Objects, attributes, and visual attention: which, what, and where. *Current Directions in Psychological Science* 1, 26–31.

Kellman, P. (1988) Theories of perception and research in perceptual development. In A. Yonas (ed.), *Perceptual Development in Infancy*, Vol. 20 of the *Minnesota Symposium on Child Psychology*, Hillsdale, NJ: Erlbaum, 267–81.

Kellman, P. and Spelke, E. (1983) Perception of partly occluded objects in infancy. *Cognitive Psychology* 15, 483–524.

Kellman, P., Spelke, E. and Short, K. (1986) Infant perception of object unity from translatory motion in depth and vertical translation, *Child Development* 57, 72–86.

Kim, I. and Spelke, E. (1992). Infants' sensitivity to effects of gravity on object motion. *Journal of Experimental Psychology: Human Perception and Performance* 18, 385–93.

Leslie, A. M. (1984) Spatiotemporal continuity and the perception of causality in infants. *Perception* 13, 287–305.

—— (1986) Getting development off the ground: modularity and the infants' perception of causality. In P. van Geert (ed.), *Theory Building in Development*, Amsterdam: North Holland, 405–37.

—— (1988) The necessity of illusion: perception and thought in infancy. In L. Weiskrantz (ed.), *Thought without Language*, Oxford: Oxford Science Publications, 185–210.

—— (1994) ToMM, ToBy, and agency: core architecture and domain specificity. In L. A. Hirschfield and S. A. Gelman (eds), *Mapping the Mind: Domain Specificity in Cognition and Culture*, Cambridge: Cambridge University Press, 119–48.

Leslie, A. M. and Keeble, S. (1987) Do six-month-old infants perceive causality? *Cognition* 25, 265–88.

Leslie, A. M., Xu, F., Tremoulet, P. and Scholl, B. J. (1998) Indexing and the object concept: developing "what" and "where" systems. *Trends in Cognitive Sciences* 2(1) 10–18.

Maunsell, J. (1995) The brain's visual world: representation of visual targets in cerebral cortex. *Science* 270, 764–8.

Melkman, R. and Rabinovitch, L. (1998) Children's perception of continuous and discontinuous movement. *Developmental Psychology* 34, 258–63.

Moore, M., Borton, R. and Darby, B. (1978) Visual tracking in young infants: evidence for object identity or object permanence? *Journal of Experimental Child Psychology* 25, 183–98.

Munakata, Y., McClelland, J. L., Johnson, M. H. and Siegler, R. S. (1997) Rethinking infant knowledge: toward an adaptive process account of successes and failures in object permanence tasks. *Psychological Review* 104, 686–713.

Nakayama, K. and Shimojo, S. (1990) Toward a neural understanding of visual surface representation. In *Cold Spring Harbor Symposia on Quantitative Biology – The Brain*, vol. 55, New York: Cold Spring Harbor Laboratory Press, 911–24.

Nakayama, K., He, Z. and Shimojo, S. (1995) Visual surface representation: a critical link between lower-level and higher-level vision. In S. M. Kosslyn and D. Osherson (eds), *Visual Cognition*, Vol. 2 of *An Invitation to Cognitive Science*, 2nd edn, Cambridge, MA: MIT Press, 1–70.

Needham, A. and Baillargeon, R. (1993) Intuitions about support in 4.5-month-old infants. *Cognition* 47, 121–48.

Neisser, U. and Becklen, R. (1975) Selective looking: attending to visually specified events. *Cognitive Psychology* 7, 480–94.

Piaget, J. (1954) *The Construction of Reality in the Child*. New York: Basic Books.

Posner, M., Snyder, C. and Davidson, B. (1980) Attention and the detection of signals. *Journal of Experimental Psychology: General* 109, 160–74.

Pylyshyn, Z. W. (1980) Computation and cognition: issues in the foundations of cognitive science. *Behavioral and Brain Sciences*, 3 111–69.

—— (1984) *Computation and Cognition: Towards a Foundation for Cognitive Science*, Cambridge, MA: MIT Press.

—— (1989) The role of location indexes in spatial perception: a sketch of the FINST spatial index model. *Cognition* 32, 65–97.

—— (1994) Some primitive mechanisms of spatial attention. *Cognition* 50, 363–84.

—— (in press) Is vision continuous with cognition? The case for impenetrability of visual perception. *Behavioral and Brain Sciences*.

—— (1999) *Seeing: An Essay on Vision and Mind*. Manuscript in preparation.

Pylyshyn, Z. W. and Storm, R. W. (1988). Tracking multiple independent targets: evidence for a parallel tracking mechanism. *Spatial Vision* 3, 179–97.

Pylyshyn, Z. W., Burkell, J., Fisher, B., Sears, C., Schmidt, W. and Trick, L. (1994) Multiple parallel access in visual attention. *Canadian Journal of Experimental Psychology* 48, 260–83.

Quinlan, P. T. (1998) The recovery of identity and relative position from visual input: further evidence for the independence of processing of what and where. *Perception and Psychophysics*, 60, 303–18.

Rafal, R. D. (1997) Balint syndrome. In T. Feinberg and M. Farah (eds), *Behavioral Neurology and Neuropsychology*, New York: McGraw-Hill, 337–56.

Rock, I. and Gutman, D. (1981) The effect of inattention and form perception. *Journal of Experimental Psychology: Human Perception and Performance* 7, 275–85.

Sagi, D. and Julesz, B. (1985) Detection versus discrimination of visual orientation. *Perception* 14, 619–28.

Schmidt, W. C., Fisher, B. D. and Pylyshyn, Z. W. (1998) Multiple-location access in vision: evidence from illusory line motion. *Journal of Experimental Psychology: Human Perception and Performance* 24, 505–25.

Scholl, B. J. (1997) Cognitive development and cognitive architecture: two senses of "surprise". Paper read at the 23rd annual meeting of the Society for Philosophy and Psychology, New York, May 97.

—— (1999) Varieties of "top-down processing" in perception. Manuscript in preparation.

Scholl, B. J. and Pylyshyn, Z. W. (in press) Tracking multiple items through occlusion: clues to visual objecthood. *Cognitive Psychology*.

Sears, C. R. and Pylyshyn, Z. W. (in press) Multiple object tracking and attentional processing. *Canadian Journal of Experimental Psychology*.

Shimojo, S. and Nakayama, K. (1990) Amodal presence of partially occluded surfaces determines apparent motion. *Perception* 19, 285–99.

Simon, T. J. (1997) Reconceptualizing the origins of number knowledge: a "non-numerical" account. *Cognitive Development* 12, 349–72.

—— (1998). Computational evidence for the foundations of numerical competence. *Developmental Science* 1, 71–8.

Simon, T., Hespos, S. and Rochat, P. (1995) Do infants understand simple arithmetic? A replication of Wynn 1992. *Cognitive Development* 10, 253–69.

Spelke, E. (1988a) The origins of physical knowledge. In L. Weiskrantz (ed.), *Thought without Language*, Oxford: Oxford Science Publications, 168–84.

—— (1988b) Where perceiving ends and thinking begins: the apprehension of objects in infancy. In A. Yonas (ed.), *Perceptual Development in Infancy*, Hillsdale, NJ: Erlbaum, 197–234.

—— (1994) Initial knowledge: six suggestions. *Cognition* 50, 431–45.

Spelke, E. and Kestenbaum, R. (1986) Les origines du concept d'objet. *Psychologie française* 31, 67–72.

Spelke, E., Breinlinger, K., Macomber, J. and Jacobson, K. (1992) Origins of knowledge. *Psychological Review* 99, 605–32.

Spelke, E., Katz, G., Purcell, S., Erlich, S. and Breinlinger, K. (1994) Early knowledge of object motion: continuity and inertia. *Cognition* 51, 131–76.

Spelke, E., Gutheil, G. and Van de Walle, G. (1995a) The developement of object perception. In S. Kosslyn and D. Osherson (eds), *Visual Cognition*, vol. 2 of *An Invitation of Cognitive Science*, 2nd edn, Cambridge, MA: MIT Press, 297–330.

Spelke, E., Kestenbaum, R., Simons, D. J. and Wein, D. (1995b) Spatiotemporal continuity, smoothness of motion and object identity in infancy. *British Journal of Developmental Psychology* 13, 113–42.

Spelke, E., Vishton, P. and Von Hofsten, C. (1995c) Object perception, object-directed action, and physical knowledge in infancy. In M. S. Gazzaniga (ed.), *The Cognitive Neurosciences*, Cambridge, MA: MIT Press, 165–79.

Starkey, P. and Cooper, R. (1980) Perception of numbers by human infants. *Science* 210, 1033–5.

Starkey, P., Spelke, E. and Gelman, R. (1990) Numerical abstraction by human infants. *Cognition* 36, 97–128.

Strauss, M. and Curtis, R. (1981) Infant perception of numerosity, *Child Development* 52, 1146–53.

Streri, A. and Spelke, E. (1988) Haptic perception of objects in infancy. *Cognitive Psychology* 20, 1–23.

Streri, A., Spelke, E. and Rameix, E. (1993) Modality-specific and amodal aspects of object perception in infancy: the case of active touch. *Cognition* 47, 251–79.

Tanaka, Y. and Shimojo, S. (1996). Location vs. feature: reaction time reveals dissociation between two visual functions. *Vision Research* 36, 2125–40.

Tipper, S., Brehaut, J. and Driver, J. (1990) Selection of moving and static object for the control of spatially directed action. *Journal of Experimental Psychology: Human Perception and Performance* 16, 492–504.

Tipper, S. P., Driver, J. and Weaver, B. (1991) Object-centered inhibition of return of visual attention. *Quarterly Journal of Experimental Psychology* 43A, 289–98.

Treisman, A. and Gelade, G. (1980) A feature-integration theory of attention. *Cognitive Psychology* 12, 97–136.

Tremoulet, P. (1998) Individuation and identification of physical objects: evidence from human infants. Rutgers University Center for Cognitive Science Technical Report no. 41.

Trick L. and Pylyshyn, Z. W. (1993) What enumeration studies can show us about spatial attention: evidence for limited-capacity preattentive processing. *Journal of Experimental Psychology: Human Perception and Performance* 19, 331–51.

—— (1994) Why are small and large numbers enumerated differently? A limited-capacity preattentive stage in vision. *Psychological Review* 101, 80–102.

Ullman, S. (1979) The interpretation of structure from motion. *Proceedings of the Royal Society of London* B203, 405–26.

Ungerleider, L. and Mishkin, M. (1984) Two cortical visual systems. In D. Ingle, M. Goodale and R. Mansfield (eds), *Analysis of Visual Behavior*, Cambridge, MA: MIT Press, 549–86.

van de Walle, G. and Spelke, E. (1996) Spatiotemporal integration and object perception in infancy: perceiving unity vs. form. *Child Development* 67, 2621–40.

van Loosbroek, E. and Smitsman, A. (1990) Visual perception of numerosity in infancy. *Developmental Psychology* 26, 916–22.

Wellman, H. and Gelman, S. (in press) Knowledge acquisition in foundational domains. In D. Kuhn and R. Siegler (eds), *Cognition, Perception, and Language*, Vol. 2 of the *Handbook of Child Psychology*, 5th edn, New York: Wiley.

Wiggins, D. (1980) *Sameness and Substance*. Oxford: Blackwell.

—— (1997) Sortal concepts: a reply to Xu. *Mind and Language* 12, 413–21.

Wilson, J. and Robinson, J. (1986) The impossibly twisted Pulfrich pendulum. *Perception* 15, 503–4.

Wolfe, J. M. and Bennett, S. C. (1997) Preattentive object files: shapeless bundles of basic features. *Vision Research* 37, 25–43.

Wynn, K. (1992) Addition and subtraction by human infants. *Nature* 358, 749–50.

—— (1996) Infants' individuation and enumeration of actions. *Psychological Science* 7, 164–9.

Xu, F. (1997) From Lot's wife to a pillar of salt: evidence that physical object is a sortal concept. *Mind and Language* 12, 365–92.

Xu, F. and Carey, S. (1996) Infants' metaphysics: the case of numerical identity. *Cognitive Psychology* 30, 111–53.

Yantis, S. (1992) Multielement visual tracking: attention and perceptual organization. *Cognitive Psychology* 24, 295–340.

—— (1993) Stimulus-driven attentional capture. *Currect Directions in Psychological Science* 2, 156–61.

—— (1995) Perceived continuity of occluded visual objects. *Psychological Science* 6, 182–6.

Yantis, S. and Johnson, D. (1990) Mechanisms of attentional priority. *Journal of Experimental Psychology: Human Perception and Performance* 16, 812–25.

Yantis, S. and Jones, E. (1991) Mechanisms of attentional selection: temporally-modulated priority tags. *Perception and Psychophysics* 50, 166–78.

3

Rethinking Rationality:
From Bleak Implications to Darwinian Modules

Richard Samuels, Stephen Stich, and Patrice D. Tremoulet

1 Introduction

There is a venerable philosophical tradition that views human beings as intrinsically rational, though even the most ardent defender of this view would admit that under certain circumstances people's decisions and thought processes can be very irrational indeed. When people are extremely tired, or drunk, or in the grip of rage, they sometimes reason and act in ways that no account of rationality would condone. About 30 years ago, Amos Tversky, Daniel Kahneman, and a number of other psychologists began reporting findings suggesting much deeper problems with the traditional idea that human beings are intrinsically rational animals. What these studies demonstrated is that even under quite ordinary circumstances where fatigue, drugs and strong emotions are not factors, people reason and make judgments in ways that systematically violate familiar canons of rationality on a wide array of problems. Those first surprising studies sparked the growth of a major research tradition whose impact has been felt in economics, political theory, medicine, and other areas far removed from cognitive science. In section 2, we will sketch a few of the better-known experimental findings in this area. We've chosen these particular findings because they will play a role at a later stage of the paper. For readers who would like a deeper, more systematic account of the fascinating and disquieting research on reasoning and judgment, there are now several excellent texts and anthologies available (Nisbett and Ross 1980; Kahneman et al. 1982; Baron 1988; Piatelli-Palmarini 1994; Dawes 1988; Sutherland 1994).

Though there is little doubt that most of the experimental results reported in the literature are robust and can be readily replicated, there is considerable debate over what these experiments indicate about the intrinsic rationality of ordinary people. One widely discussed interpretation of the results claims that they have "bleak implications" for the rationality of the man and woman in the street. What the studies show, according to this interpretation, is that ordinary people lack the underlying *competence* to handle a wide array of reasoning tasks, and thus that they must exploit a collection of simple *heuristics* which often lead to seriously counter-normative conclusions. Advocates of this interpretation would, of course, acknowledge that there are some people who have mastered the correct rules or procedures for handling some of these problems. But, they maintain, this knowledge is hard to acquire and hard to use. It is not the sort of knowledge that the human mind acquires readily or spontaneously in normal environments, and even those who have it often do not use it unless they make a special effort. In section 3, we will elaborate on this interpretation and explain the technical notion of competence that it invokes.

The pessimistic interpretation of the experimental findings has been challenged in a number of ways. One of the most recent and intriguing of these challenges comes from the emerging interdisciplinary field of evolutionary psychology. Evolutionary psychologists defend a highly *modular* conception of mental architecture, which views the mind as composed of a large number of special-purpose information-processing organs, or "modules," that have been shaped by natural selection to handle the sorts of recurrent information-processing problems that confronted our hunter-gatherer forebears. Since good performance on a variety of reasoning tasks would likely have served our Pleistocene ancestors in good stead, evolutionary psychologists hypothesize that we should have evolved mental modules for handling these tasks well. However, they also maintain that the modules should be well adapted to the sorts of information that was available in the pre-human and early human environment. Thus, they hypothesize, when information is presented in the right way, performance on reasoning tasks should improve dramatically. In section 4 we will offer a more detailed sketch of the richly modular picture of the mind advanced by evolutionary psychologists and of the notion of a mental module that plays a fundamental role in that picture. We will also take a brief look at the sorts of arguments offered by evolutionary psychologists for their contention that the mind is massively modular. Then, in section 5, we will consider several recent studies that appear to confirm the evolutionary psychologists' prediction: When information is presented in ways that would have been important in our evolutionary history, performance on reasoning tasks soars. While the arguments and the experimental evidence offered by evolutionary psychologists are tantalizing, they hardly constitute a conclusive case for the evolutionary psychologists' theory about the mind and its origins. But a detailed critique of that theory would be beyond the scope of this essay. Rather, what we propose to do in our final section is to ask a hypothetical question: If the evolutionary psychologists' account turns out to be on the

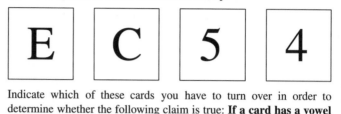

Here are four cards. Each of them has a letter on one side and a number on the other side. Two of these cards are shown with the letter side up, and two with the number side up.

Indicate which of these cards you have to turn over in order to determine whether the following claim is true: **If a card has a vowel on one side, then it has an odd number on the other side.**

Figure 3.1

right track, what implications would this have for questions about the nature and the extent of human rationality or irrationality?

2 Exploring Human Reasoning and Judgment: Four Examples

2.1   The Selection Task

In 1966, Peter Wason reported the first experiments using a cluster of reasoning problems that came to be called the *Selection Task*. A recent textbook on reasoning has described that task as "the most intensively researched single problem in the history of the psychology of reasoning" (Evans et al. 1993: 99). A typical example of a Selection Task problem is shown in figure 3.1.

What Wason and numerous other investigators have found is that subjects typically do very poorly on questions like this. Most subjects respond, correctly, that the E card must be turned over, but many also judge that the 5 card must be turned over, despite the fact that the 5 card could not falsify the claim no matter what is on the other side. Also, a large majority of subjects judge that the 4 card need *not* be turned over, though without turning it over there is no way of knowing whether it has a vowel on the other side. And, of course, if it does have a vowel on the other side then the claim is not true. It is not the case that subjects do poorly on all selection task problems, however. A wide range of variations on the basic pattern have been tried, and on some versions of the problem a much larger percentage of subjects answer correctly. These results form a bewildering pattern, since there is no obvious feature or cluster of features that separates versions on which subjects do well from those on which they do poorly. As we will see in section 5, some evolutionary psychologists have argued that these results can be explained if we focus on the sorts of mental mechanisms that would have been crucial for reasoning about social exchange (or "reciprocal altruism") in the environment of our hominid forebears. The versions of the selection task we're good at, these theorists maintain, are just the ones that those mechanisms would have been designed to handle. But, as we will also see in section 5, this explanation is hardly uncontroversial.

2.2 The conjunction fallacy

Ronald Reagan was elected President of the United States in November 1980. The following month, Amos Tversky and Daniel Kahneman administered a questionnaire to 93 subjects who had had no formal training in statistics. The instructions on the questionnaire were as follows:

> In this questionnaire you are asked to evaluate the probability of various events that may occur during 1981. Each problem includes four possible events. Your task is to rank order these events by probability, using 1 for the most probable event, 2 for the second, 3 for the third and 4 for the least probable event.

Here is one of the questions presented to the subjects:

> Please rank order the following events by their probability of occurrence in 1981:
> (a) Reagan will cut federal support to local government.
> (b) Reagan will provide federal support for unwed mothers.
> (c) Reagan will increase the defense budget by less than 5%.
> (d) Reagan will provide federal support for unwed mothers and cut federal support to local governments.

The unsettling outcome was that 68 percent of the subjects rated (d) as more probable than (b), despite the fact that (d) could not happen unless (b) did (Tversky and Kahneman 1982). In another experiment, which has since become quite famous, Tversky and Kahneman (1982) presented subjects with the following task:

> Linda is 31 years old, single, outspoken, and very bright. She majored in philosophy. As a student, she was deeply concerned with issues of discrimination and social justice, and also participated in anti-nuclear demonstrations.
>
> Please rank the following statements by their probability, using 1 for the most probable and 8 for the least probable.
> (a) Linda is a teacher in elementary school.
> (b) Linda works in a bookstore and takes Yoga classes.
> (c) Linda is active in the feminist movement.
> (d) Linda is a psychiatric social worker.
> (e) Linda is a member of the League of Women Voters.

(f)   Linda is a bank teller.
(g)   Linda is an insurance sales person.
(h)   Linda is a bank teller and is active in the feminist movement.

In a group of naive subjects with no background in probability and statistics, 89 percent judged that statement (h) was more probable than statement (f). When the same question was presented to statistically sophisticated subjects – graduate students in the decision science program of the Stanford Business School – 85 percent made the same judgement! Results of this sort, in which subjects judge that a compound event or state of affairs is more probable than one of the components of the compound, have been found repeatedly since Kahneman and Tversky's pioneering studies.

2.3   Base-rate neglect

On the familiar Bayesian account, the probability of a hypothesis on a given body of evidence depends, in part, on the prior probability of the hypothesis. However, in a series of elegant experiments, Kahneman and Tversky (1973) showed that subjects often seriously undervalue the importance of prior probabilities. One of these experiments presented half of the subjects with the following "cover story."

> A panel of psychologists have interviewed and administered personality tests to 30 engineers and 70 lawyers, all successful in their respective fields. On the basis of this information, thumbnail descriptions of the 30 engineers and 70 lawyers have been written. You will find on your forms five descriptions, chosen at random from the 100 available descriptions. For each description, please indicate your probability that the person described is an engineer, on a scale from 0 to 100.

The other half of the subjects were presented with the same text, except the "base rates" were reversed. They were told that the personality tests had been administered to 70 engineers and 30 lawyers. Some of the descriptions that were provided were designed to be compatible with the subjects' stereotypes of engineers, though not with their stereotypes of lawyers. Others were designed to fit the lawyer stereotype, but not the engineer stereotype. And one was intended to be quite neutral, giving subjects no information at all that would be of use in making their decision. Here are two examples, the first intended to sound like an engineer, the second intended to sound neutral:

> Jack is a 45-year-old man. He is married and has four children. He is generally conservative, careful and ambitious. He shows no interest in political and social issues and spends most of his free time on his many hobbies which include home carpentry, sailing, and mathematical puzzles.

Dick is a 30-year-old man. He is married with no children. A man of high ability and high motivation, he promises to be quite successful in his field. He is well liked by his colleagues.

As expected, subjects in both groups thought that the probability that Jack is an engineer is quite high. Moreover, in what seems to be a clear violation of Bayesian principles, the difference in cover stories between the two groups of subjects had almost no effect at all. The neglect of base-rate information was even more striking in the case of Dick. That description was constructed to be totally uninformative with regard to Dick's profession. Thus the only useful information that subjects had was the base-rate information provided in the cover story. But that information was entirely ignored. The median probability estimate in both groups of subjects was 50 percent. Kahneman and Tversky's subjects were not, however, completely insensitive to base-rate information. Following the five descriptions on their form, subjects found the following "null" description:

> Suppose now that you are given no information whatsoever about an individual chosen at random from the sample.
> The probability that this man is one of the 30 engineers [or, for the other group of subjects: one of the 70 engineers] in the sample of 100 is —— %.

In this case subjects relied entirely on the base-rate; the median estimate was 30 percent for the first group of subjects and 70 percent for the second. In their discussion of these experiments, Nisbett and Ross offer this interpretation.

> The implication of this contrast between the "no information" and "totally nondiagnostic information" conditions seems clear. When *no* specific evidence about the target case is provided, prior probabilities are utilized appropriately; when *worthless* specific evidence is given, prior probabilities may be largely ignored, and people respond as if there were no basis for assuming differences in relative likelihoods. People's grasp of the relevance of base-rate information must be very weak if they could be distracted from using it by exposure to useless target case information. (Nisbett and Ross 1980: 145–6)

Before leaving the topic of base-rate neglect, we want to offer one further example illustrating the way in which the phenomenon might well have serious practical consequences. Here is a problem that Casscells et al. (1978) presented to a group of faculty, staff, and fourth-year students at Harvard Medical School.

> If a test to detect a disease whose prevalence is $1/1000$ has a false positive rate of 5%, what is the chance that a person found to have a positive result actually has the disease, assuming that you know nothing about the person's symptoms or signs? —— %

Under the most plausible interpretation of the problem, the correct Bayesian answer is 2 percent. But only 18 percent of the Harvard audience gave an answer close to 2 percent. Forty-five percent of this distinguished group completely ignored the base-rate information and said that the answer was 95 percent.

2.4   Overconfidence

One of the most extensively investigated and most worrisome clusters of phenomena explored by psychologists interested in reasoning and judgment involves the degree of confidence that people have in their responses to factual questions – questions like:

> In each of the following pairs, which city has more inhabitants?
>
> (a)   Las Vegas   (b)   Miami
> (a)   Sydney   (b)   Melbourne
> (a)   Hyderabad   (b)   Islamabad
> (a)   Bonn   (b)   Heidelberg
>
> In each of the following pairs, which historical event happened first?
>
> (a)   Signing of the Magna Carta   (b)   Birth of Mohammed
> (a)   Death of Napoleon   (b)   Louisiana Purchase
> (a)   Lincoln's assassination   (b)   Birth of Queen Victoria

After each answer subjects are also asked:

> How confident are you that your answer is correct?
> 50%   60%   70%   80%   90%   100%

In an experiment using relatively hard questions it is typical to find that for the cases in which subjects say they are 100 percent confident, only about 80 percent of their answers are correct; for cases in which they say that they are 90 percent confident, only about 70 percent of their answers are correct; and for cases in which they say that they are 80 percent confident, only about 60 percent of their answers are correct. This tendency to overconfidence seems to be very robust. Warning subjects that people are often overconfident has no significant effect, nor does offering them money (or bottles of French champagne) as a reward for accuracy. Moreover, the phenomenon has been demonstrated in a wide variety of subject populations, including undergraduates, graduate students, physicians, and even CIA analysts. (For a survey of the literature see Lichtenstein et al. 1982.)

3   Bleak Implications: Shortcomings in Reasoning Competence

The experimental results we've been recounting and the many related results reported in the extensive literature in this area are, we think, intrinsically disquieting. They are even more alarming if, as has occasionally been demonstrated, the same patterns of reasoning and judgment are to be found outside the laboratory. None of us want our illnesses to be diagnosed by physicians who ignore well-confirmed information about base rates. Nor do we want our public officials to be advised by CIA analysts who are systematically overconfident. The experimental results themselves do not entail any conclusions about the nature or the normative status of the cognitive mechanisms that underlie people's reasoning and judgment. But a number of writers have urged that these results lend considerable support to a pessimistic hypothesis about those mechanisms, a hypothesis which may be even more disquieting than the results themselves. On this view, the examples of faulty reasoning and judgment that we've sketched are not mere *performance errors*. Rather, they indicate that most people's underlying *reasoning competence* is irrational or at least normatively problematic. In order to explain this view more clearly, we'll have to back up a bit and explain the rather technical distinction between competence and performance on which it is based.

The competence/performance distinction, as we will characterize it, was first introduced into cognitive science by Chomsky, who used it in his account of the explanatory strategy of theories in linguistics (Chomsky 1965: ch. 1; 1975; 1980). In testing linguistic theories, an important source of data are the "intuitions" or unreflective judgments, that speakers of a language make about the grammaticality of sentences and about various linguistic properties (e.g., Is the sentence ambiguous?) and relations (e.g., Is this phrase the subject of that verb?). To explain these intuitions, and also to explain how speakers go about producing and understanding sentences of their language in ordinary speech, Chomsky and his followers proposed what has become one of the most important hypotheses about the mind in the history of cognitive science. What this hypothesis claims is that a speaker of a language has an internally represented grammar of that language – an integrated set of generative rules and principles that entail an infinite number of claims about the language. For each of the infinite number of sentences in the speaker's language, the internally represented grammar entails that it is grammatical; for each ambiguous sentence in the speaker's language, the grammar entails that it is ambiguous, etc. When speakers make the judgments that we call "linguistic intuitions," the information in the internally represented grammar is typically accessed and relied upon, though neither the process nor the internally represented grammar are accessible to consciousness. Since the internally represented grammar plays a central role in the production of linguistic intuitions, those intuitions can serve as an important source of data for linguists trying to specify what the rules and principles of the internally represented grammar are.

A speaker's intuitions are now, however, an infallible source of information about the grammar of the speaker's language, because the grammar cannot produce linguistic intuitions by itself. The production of intuitions is a complex process in which the internally represented grammar must interact with a variety of other cognitive mechanisms, including those subserving perception, motivation, attention, short-term memory, and perhaps a host of others. In certain circumstances, the activity of any one of these mechanisms may result in a person offering a judgment about a sentence which does not accord with what the grammar actually entails about that sentence. The attention mechanism offers a clear example of this phenomenon. It is very likely the case that the grammar internally represented in typical English speakers entails that an infinite number of sentences of the form:

A told B that p, and B told C that q, and C told D that r, and . . .

are grammatical in the speaker's language. However, if the present authors were asked to judge the grammaticality of a sentence containing a few hundred of these conjuncts, or perhaps even a few dozen, there is a good chance that our judgments would not reflect what our grammars entail, since in cases like this our attention easily wanders. Short-term memory provides a more interesting example of the way in which a grammatical judgment may fail to reflect the information actually contained in the grammar. There is considerable evidence indicating that the short-term memory mechanism has difficulty handling center-embedded structures. Thus it may well be the case that our internally represented grammars entail that the following sentence is grammatical:

What what what he wanted cost would buy in Germany was amazing.

though our intuitions suggest, indeed shout, that it is not.

Now in the jargon that Chomsky introduced, the rules and principles of a speaker's internalized grammar constitute the speaker's *linguistic competence*; the judgments a speaker makes about sentences, along with the sentences the speaker actually produces, are part of the speaker's *linguistic performance*. Moreover, as we have just seen, some of the sentences a speaker produces and some of the judgments the speaker makes about sentences will not accurately reflect the speaker's linguistic competence. In these cases, the speaker is making a *performance error*.

There are some obvious analogies between the phenomena studied in linguistics and those studied by cognitive scientists interested in reasoning. In both cases there is spontaneous and largely unconscious processing of an open-ended class of inputs; people are able to understand endlessly many sentences and to draw inferences from endlessly many premises. Also, in both cases, people are able to make spontaneous intuitive judgments about an effectively infinite class of cases – judgments about grammaticality, ambiguity, etc. in the case of linguistics, and judgments about validity, probability, etc. in the case of reasoning. Given these analogies, it is plausible to explore the idea that the mechanism underlying our ability to reason is similar to the mechanism underlying our capacity to process language. And if Chomsky is right about language, then the analogous hypothesis about reasoning would claim that people have an internally represented integrated set of rules and principles of reasoning – a "psycho-logic" as it has been called – which is usually accessed and relied upon when people draw inferences or make judgments about them. As in the case of language, we would expect that neither the processes involved nor the principles of the internally represented psycho-logic are readily accessible to consciousness. We should also expect that people's inferences and judgments would not be an infallible guide to what the underlying psycho-logic actually entails about the validity or plausibility of a given inference. For here, as in the case of language, the internally represented rules and principles must interact with lots of other cognitive mechanisms – including attention, motivation, short-term memory, and many others. The activity of these mechanisms can give rise to *performance errors* – inferences or judgments that do not reflect the psycho-logic which constitutes a person's *reasoning competence*.

There is, however, an important difference between reasoning and language, even if we assume that a Chomsky-style account of the underlying mechanism is correct in both cases. For in the case of language, it makes no clear sense to offer a normative assessment of a normal person's competence. The rules and principles that constitute a French speaker's linguistic competence are significantly different from the rules and principles that underlie language processing in a Chinese speaker. But if we were asked which system was better or which one was correct, we would have no idea what was being asked. Thus, on the language side of the analogy, there are performance errors, but there is no such thing as a competence error or a normatively problematic competence. If two otherwise normal people have different linguistic competences, then they simply speak different languages or different dialects. On the reasoning side of the analogy, things look very different. It is not clear whether there are significant individual and group differences in the rules and principles underlying people's performance on reasoning tasks, as there so clearly are in the rules and principles underlying people's linguistic performance. But if there are significant interpersonal differences in reasoning competence, it surely *appears* to make sense to ask whether one system of rules and principles is better than another.[1] If Adam's psycho-logic ignores base rates, endorses the conjunction fallacy, and approves of affirming the consequent, while Bertha's does not, then, in these respects at least, it seems natural to say that Bertha's reasoning competence is better than Adam's. And even if all normal humans share the same psycho-logic, it still makes sense to ask how rational it is. If everyone's psycho-logic contains rules that get the wrong answer on certain versions of the selection task, then we might well conclude that there is a normative shortcoming that we all share.

We are now, finally, in a position to explain the pessimistic hypothesis that some authors have urged to account for the sort of experimental results sketched in section 2. According to this hypothesis, the errors that subjects make in these experiments are very different from the sorts of reasoning errors that people make when their memory is overextended or when their attention wanders. They are also different from the errors people make when they are tired or drunk or blind with rage. These are all examples of *performance errors* – errors that people make when they infer in ways that are *not* sanctioned by their own psycho-logic. But the sorts of errors described in section 2 are *competence errors*. In these cases people *are* reasoning and judging in ways that accord with their psycho-logic. The subjects in these experiments do not use the right rules because they do not have access to them; they are not part of the subjects' internally represented reasoning competence. What they have instead is a collection of simpler rules, or "heuristics," that may often get the right answer, though it is also the case that often they do not. So, according to this bleak hypothesis, the subjects make mistakes because their psycho-logic is normatively defective; their internalized rules of reasoning are less than fully rational. It is not at all clear that Kahneman and Tversky would endorse this interpretation of the experimental results, though a number of other leading researchers clearly do.[2] According to Slovic, Fischhoff, and Lichtenstein, for example, "It appears that people lack the correct programs for many important judgmental tasks. . . . We have not had the opportunity to evolve an intellect capable of dealing conceptually with uncertainty" (1976: 174).

Suppose it is in fact the case that many of the errors made in reasoning experiments are competence errors. This is not a flattering explanation, certainly, and it goes a long way toward undermining the traditional claim that man is a rational animal. But just how pessimistic a conclusion would it be? In part, the answer depends on how hard it would be to improve people's performance, and that in turn depends on how hard it is to improve reasoning competence. Very little is known about this at present.[3] By invoking evolution as an explanation of our defective competence, however, Slovic, Fischhoff, and Lichtenstein certainly do not encourage much optimism, since characteristics and limitations attributable to evolution are often innate, and innate limitations are not easy to overcome. The analogy with language points in much the same direction. For if Chomsky is right about language, then though it is obviously the case that people who speak different languages have internalized different grammars, the class of grammars that humans can internalize and incorporate into their language-processing mechanism is severely restricted, and a significant part of an adult's linguistic competence is innate. If reasoning competence is similar to language competence, then it may well be the case that many improvements are simply not psychologically possible, because our minds are not designed to reason well on these sorts of problems. This deeply pessimistic interpretation of the experimental results has been endorsed by a number of well-known authors, including Stephen J. Gould, who makes the point with his characteristic panache.

I am particularly fond of [the Linda] example, because I know that the [conjunction] is least probable, yet a little homunculus in my head continues to jump up and down, shouting at me – "but she can't just be a bank teller; read the description." . . . Why do we consistently make this simple logical error? Tversky and Kahneman argue, correctly I think, that our minds are not built (for whatever reason) to work by the rules of probability. (1992: 469)

It is important to be clear about what it means to claim that improving our reasoning competence may be "psychologically impossible." In the case of language, people clearly do learn to use artificial languages like BASIC and LISP, which violate many of the constraints that a Chomskian would claim that all natural (or "psychologically possible") languages must satisfy. However, people do not acquire and use BASIC in the way they acquire English or Arabic. Special effort and training is needed to learn it, and those who have mastered it only use it in special circumstances. No one "speaks" BASIC or uses it in the way that natural languages are used. Similarly, with special effort, it may be possible to learn rules of reasoning that violate some of the constraints on "natural" or "psychologically possible" rules and to use those rules in special circumstances. But in confronting the myriad inferential challenges of everyday life, a person who had mastered a non-natural (but normatively superior) rule would typically use a less demanding and more natural "heuristic" rule. This is the point that Gould makes so vividly by conjuring up a little homunculus jumping up and down in his head, and it might explain the otherwise surprising fact that graduate students in a prestigious decision science program are no better than the rest of us at avoiding the conjunction fallacy.

As we noted in the introduction, there have been many attempts to challenge the pessimistic interpretation of the experimental findings on reasoning. In the two sections to follow we will focus on one of the boldest and most intriguing of these, the challenge from evolutionary psychology. If evolutionary psychologists are right, the rules and principles of reasoning available to ordinary people are much better than the "bleak implications" hypothesis would lead us to expect.

4   The Challenge from Evolutionary Psychology

In explaining the challenge from evolutionary psychology, the first order of business is to say what evolutionary psychology is, and that is not an easy task since this interdisciplinary field is too new to have developed any precise and widely agreed upon body of doctrines. There are, however, two basic ideas that are clearly central to evolutionary psychology. The first is that the mind consists of a large number of special-purpose systems – often called "modules," or "mental organs." The second is that these systems, like other systems in the body, have been shaped by natural selection to perform specific functions or to solve information-processing problems that were important in the environment in which our hominid ancestors evolved. In this section, we propose to proceed as follows. First, in section 4.1, we'll take a brief look at some of the ways in which the notion of a "module" has been used in cognitive science and focus on the sorts of modules that evolutionary psychologists typically have in mind. In section 4.2, we will contrast the massively modular account of the mind favored by evolutionary psychologists with another widely discussed conception of the mind according to which modules play only a peripheral role. In section 4.3, we will consider an example of the sort of theoretical considerations that evolutionary psychologists have offered in support of their contention that the mind consists of large numbers of modules – and perhaps nothing else. Finally, in section 4.4, we will give a very brief sketch of the evolutionary psychology research strategy.

4.1   What is a mental module?

Though the term "module" has gained considerable currency in contemporary cognitive science, different theorists appear to use it in importantly different ways. In this section we will outline some of these uses, with the intention of getting a clearer picture of what evolutionary psychologists mean – and what they don't mean – by "module." The notions of modularity discussed in this section by no means exhaust the ways in which the term is used in contemporary cognitive science. For a more comprehensive review see Segal 1996.

When speaking of modules, cognitive scientists are typically referring to mental structures or components of the mind that can be invoked in order to explain various cognitive capacities. Moreover, it is ordinarily assumed that modules are domain-specific (or functionally specific), as opposed to domain-general. Very roughly, this means that modules are dedicated to solving restricted classes of problems in unique domains. For instance, the claim that there is a vision module implies that there are mental structures which are brought into play in the domain of visual processing and are not recruited in dealing with other cognitive tasks. Later in this section we will discuss the notion of domain specificity in greater detail. For the moment, however, we want to focus on the fact the the term "module" is used to refer to two fundamentally different sorts of mental structures. (i) Sometimes it is used to refer to systems of mental representations. (ii) On other occasions the term "module" is used in order to talk about computational mechanisms. We will call modules of the first sort *Chomskian modules* and modules of the second sort *computational modules*.

4.1.1 *Chomskian modules*

A Chomskian module is a domain-specific body of mentally represented knowledge or information that accounts for a cognitive capacity. As the name suggests, the notion of a Chomskian module can be traced to Chomsky's work in linguistics. As we saw in section 3, Chomsky claims that our linguistic competence consists in the possession of an internally represented grammar of our natural language. This grammar is a paradigm example of what we mean when speaking of Chomskian modules. But, of course, Chomsky is not the only theorist who posits the existence of what we are calling Chomskian modules. For instance, developmental psychologists such as Susan Carey and Elizabeth Spelke have argued that young children have domain-specific, mentally represented theories – systems of principles – for physics, psychology, and mathematics (Carey and Spelke 1994). Theory-like structures of the sort posited by Carey and Spelke are an important kind of Chomskian module. However, if we assume that a theory is a *truth-evaluable* system of representations – that is, one in which it makes sense to ask whether the representations are true or false – then not all Chomskian modules must be theories. There can also be Chomskian modules that consist entirely of non-truth-evaluable systems of representations. There may, for example, be Chomskian modules that encode domain-specific knowledge of how to perform certain tasks – for example, how to play chess, how to do deductive reasoning, or how to detect cheaters in social exchange settings.

As we have already noted, a domain-specific mental structure is one that is dedicated to solving problems in a restricted domain. In the case of Chomskian modules, it is ordinarily assumed that they are dedicated in this way for a specific reason: the content of the representations that constitute a given Chomskian module represent only properties and objects that belong to a specific domain. So, for example, if physics is a domain, then a Chomskian module for physics will contain only information about physical properties and physical objects. Similarly, if geometry constitutes a domain, then a Chomskian module for geometry will contain only information about geometrical properties and objects.

There are many problems with trying to characterize the notion of a Chomskian module in more precise terms. Clearly we do not want to treat just any domain-specific collection of mental representations as a Chomskian module, since this would render the notion theoretically uninteresting. We do not, for example, want to treat a child's beliefs about toy dinosaurs as a module. Consequently, it is necessary to impose additional constraints, in order to develop a useful notion of a Chomskian module. Two commonly invoked constraints are (i) innateness and (ii) restrictions on information flow. So, for example, according to Chomsky, Universal Grammar in an innate system of mental representations, and most of the information that is contained in the Universal Grammar is not accessible to consciousness. (See Segal 1996 for an elaboration of these points.) We don't propose to pursue the issue of constraints any further, however, since, as will soon become clear, when evolutionary psychologists speak of modules, they are usually concerned with a rather different kind of module – a computational module.

4.1.2   Computational modules

Computational modules are a species of computational device. As a first pass, we can characterize them as domain-specific, computational devices. A number of points of elaboration and clarification are in order, however. First, computational modules are ordinarily assumed to be classical computers – that is, symbol- (or representation-) manipulating devices which receive representations as inputs and manipulate them according to formally specifiable rules in order to generate representations (or actions) as outputs. (For detailed discussions of the notion of classical computation see Haugeland 1985 and Pylyshyn 1984.) Classical computers of this sort contrast sharply with certain sorts of connectionist computational systems, which cannot plausibly be viewed as symbol-manipulating devices.[4]

Second, it is ordinarily assumed that computational modules are dedicated to solving problems in a specific domain because they are only capable of carrying out computations on a restricted range of inputs – namely, representations of the properties and objects found in a particular domain (Fodor 1983: 103). So, for instance, if phonology constitutes a domain, then a phonology computational module will only provide analyses of inputs which are about phonological objects and properties. Similarly, if arithmetic is a domain, then an arithmetic computational module will only provide solutions to arithmetical problems.

Third, computational modules are usually assumed to be relatively autonomous components of the mind. Though they receive input from, and send output to, other cognitive processes or structures, they perform their own internal information processing unperturbed by external systems. For example, David Marr claims that the various computational modules on which parts of the visual process are implemented "are as nearly independent of each other as the overall task allows" (Marr 1982: 102).

Fourth, we want to emphasize the fact that computational modules are a very different kind of mental structure from Chomskian modules. Chomskian modules are *systems of representations*. By contrast, computational modules are processing devices – they *manipulate* representations. However, computational modules can coexist with Chomskian modules. Indeed, it may be that Chomskian modules, being bodies of information, are often manipulated by computational modules. Thus, for example, a parser might be conceived of as a computational module that deploys the contents of a Chomskian module devoted to linguistic information in order to generate syntactic and semantic representations of physical sentence-forms (Segal 1996: 144). Moreover, some Chomskian modules may be accessible only to a single computational module. When a Chomskian module and a computational module are linked in this way, it is natural to think of the two as a unit, which we might call a *Chomskian/computational module*. But it is also important to note that the existence of Chomskian modules does not entail the existence of computational modules, since it is possible for a mind to contain Chomskian modules while not containing any computational modules. For example, while humans may possess domain-specific systems of knowledge for physics or geometry, it does not follow that we possess domain-specific computational mechanisms for processing information about physical objects or geometrical properties. Rather, it may be that such domain-specific knowledge is utilized by domain-general reasoning systems.

A final point worth making is that the notion of a computational module has been elaborated in a variety of different ways in the cognitive science literature. Most notably, Fodor (1983) developed a conception of modules as domain-specific, computational mechanisms that are also (1) informationally encapsulated, (2) mandatory, (3) fast, (4) shallow, (5) neurally localized, (6) susceptible to characteristic breakdown, and (7) largely inaccessible to other processes.[5] Although the full-fledged Fodorian notion of a module has been highly influential in cognitive science (Garfield 1987), evolutionary psychologists have not typically adopted his conception of modules. In his recent book *Mindblindness*, for example, Simon Baron-Cohen explicitly denies that the modules involved in his theory of "mind reading"[6] need to be informationally encapsulated or have shallow outputs (1994: 515).

4.1.3 Darwinian modules

What, then, do evolutionary psychologists typically mean by the term "module"? The answer, unfortunately, is far from clear, since evolutionary psychologists don't attempt to provide any precise characterization of modularity and rarely bother to distinguish between the various notions of module that we have set out in this section. Nevertheless, from what they do say about modularity, we think it is possible to piece together an account of what we propose to call a *Darwinian module*, which can be viewed as a sort of prototype of the evolutionary psychologists' notion of modularity. Darwinian modules have a cluster of features, and when evolutionary psychologists talk about modules, they generally have in mind something that has most or all of the features in the cluster.

The first feature of Darwinian modules is that they are domain-specific. According to Cosmides and Tooby, who are perhaps the best-known proponents of evolutionary psychology, our minds consist primarily of "a constellation of specialized mechanisms that have domain-specific procedures, operate over domain-specific representations, or both" (Cosmides and Tooby 1994: 94).

Second, Darwinian modules are computational mechanisms. On the colorful account offered by Tooby and Cosmides, "our cognitive architecture resembles a confederation of hundreds or thousands of functionally dedicated computers (often called modules)" (Tooby and Cosmides 1995: p. xiii). Thus Darwinian modules are not Chomskian modules but, rather, a species of computational module. However, evolutionary psychologists also assume that many Darwinian modules utilize domain-specific systems of knowledge (i.e., Chomskian modules) when doing computations or solving problems, and that in some cases this domain-specific knowledge is accessible only to a single Darwinian module. Thus some Darwinian modules are a kind of Chomskian/ computational module. The "theory of mind" module posited by a number of recent theorists may provide an example. This module is typically assumed to employ innate, domain-specific knowledge about psychological states when predicting the behavior of agents, and much of that information may not be available to other systems in the mind.

A third feature of Darwinian modules is that they are innate cognitive structures whose characteristic properties are largely or wholly determined by genetic factors. In addition, evolutionary psychologists make the stronger claim that the many Darwinian modules which predominate in our cognitive architecture are the products of natural selection. They are, according to Tooby and Cosmides, "kinds invented by natural selection during the species" evolutionary history to produce adaptive ends in the species' natural environment' (Tooby and Cosmides 1995: p. xiii; see also Cosmides and Tooby 1992). Thus, not only do evolutionary psychologists commit themselves to the claim that modules are innate, they also commit themselves to a theory about how modules came to be innate – namely, via natural selection. Though Darwinian modules need not enhance reproductive fitness in modern environments, they exist because they did enhance fitness in the environment of our Pleistocene ancestors. Or, to make much the same point in the jargon favored by evolutionary psychologists, though Darwinian modules need not now be adaptive, they are *adaptations*. This account of the origins of these modules is, of course, the reason that we have chosen to call them "Darwinian," and as we shall see in section 4.4 the fact that Darwinian modules are adaptations plays an important role in structuring the research program that evolutionary psychologists pursue.

Finally, evolutionary psychologists often insist that Darwinian modules are universal features of the human mind, and thus that we should expect to find that all (normally functioning) human beings possess the same specific set of modules. According to evolutionary psychologists, then, not only has natural selection designed the human mind so that it is rich in innate, domain-specific, computational mechanisms; it has also given us all more or less the same design. (For an interesting critique of this claim, see Griffiths 1997: ch. 5.)

To sum up, a (prototypical) Darwinian module is an innate, naturally selected, functionally specific, and universal computational mechanism which may have access (perhaps even unique access) to a domain-specific system of knowledge of the sort we've been calling a Chomskian module.

4.2 Peripheral versus massive modularity

Until recently, even staunch proponents of modularity typically restricted themselves to the claim that the mind is modular at its periphery.[7] So, for example, although the discussion of modularity as it is currently framed in cognitive science derives largely from Jerry Fodor's arguments in *The Modularity of Mind* (1983), Fodor insists that much of our cognition is subserved by non-modular systems. According to Fodor, only input systems (those responsible for perception and language processing) and output systems (those responsible for action) are plausible candidates for modularity. By contrast, "central systems" (those systems responsible for reasoning and belief fixation) are likely to be non-modular. As Dan Sperber has observed:

> Although this was probably not intended and has not been much noticed, "modularity of mind" was a paradoxical title, for, according to Fodor, modularity is to be found only at the periphery of the mind. . . . In its center and bulk, Fodor's mind is decidedly nonmodular. Conceptual processes – that is, thought proper – are presented as a holistic lump lacking joints at which to carve. (Sperber 1994: 39)

Evolutionary psychologists reject the claim that the mind is only peripherally modular in favor of the view that the mind is largely or even entirely composed of Darwinian modules. We will call this thesis the Massive Modularity Hypothesis (MMH). Tooby and Cosmides elaborate on the Massive Modularity Hypothesis as follows:

> [O]ur cognitive architecture resembles a confederation of hundreds or thousands of functionally dedicated computers (often called modules) designed to solve adaptive problems endemic to our hunter-gatherer ancestors. Each of these devices has its own agenda and imposes its own exotic organization on different fragments of the world. There are specialized systems for grammar induction, for face recognition, for dead reckoning, for construing objects and for recognizing emotions from the face. There are mechanisms to detect animacy, eye direction, and cheating. There is a "theory of mind" module . . . a variety of social inference modules . . . and a multitude of other elegant machines. (Tooby and Cosmides 1995: p. xiv)

According to the MMH, "central capacities too can be divided into domain-specific modules" (Jackendoff 1992: 70). So, for example, the linguist and cognitive neuroscientist Steven Pinker has suggested that not only are there modules for perception, language, and action, but there may also be modules for many tasks traditionally classified as central processes, including

> Intuitive mechanics: knowledge of the motions, forces, and deformations that objects undergo. . . . Intuitive biology: understanding how plants and animals work. . . . Intuitive psychology: predicting other people's behavior from their

beliefs and desires. . . . Self-concept: gathering and organizing information about one's value to other people, and packaging it for others. (Pinker 1994: 420)

According to this view, then, "the human mind . . . [is] . . . not a general-purpose computer but a collection of instincts adapted for solving evolutionary significant problems – the mind as a Swiss Army knife" (Pinker 1994).[8]

4.3   Arguments for massive modularity

Is the Massive Modularity Hypothesis correct? Does the human mind consist largely or even entirely of Darwinian modules? This question is fast becoming one of the central issues in contemporary cognitive science. Broadly speaking, the arguments in favor of MMH can be divided into two kinds, which we'll call "theoretical" and "empirical." Arguments of the first sort rely heavily on quite general theoretical claims about the nature of evolution, cognition, and computation, while those of the second sort focus on experimental results which, it is argued, support the MMH view of the mind. While a systematic review of the arguments that have been offered in support of the MMH would be beyond the scope of this essay, we think it is important for the reader to have some feel for what these arguments look like. Thus, in this section we'll present a brief sketch of one of the theoretical arguments offered by Cosmides and Tooby and suggest one way in which the argument might be criticized.[9] In section 5, we'll consider some of the empirical results about reasoning that have been interpreted as supporting the MMH.

Cosmides and Tooby's argument focuses on the notion of an *adaptive problem*, which can be defined as an evolutionary recurrent problem whose solution promoted reproduction, however long or indirect the chain by which it did so (Cosmides and Tooby 1994: 87). For example, in order to reproduce, an organism must be able to find a mate. Thus finding a mate is an adaptive problem. Similarly, in order to reproduce, one must avoid being eaten by predators before one mates. Thus predator avoidance is also an adaptive problem. According to Cosmides and Tooby, once we appreciate both the way in which natural selection operates and the specific adaptive problems that human beings faced in the Pleistocene era, we will see that there are good reasons for thinking that the mind contains a number of distinct, modular mechanisms. In developing the argument, Cosmides and Tooby first attempt to justify the claim that when it comes to solving adaptive problems, selection pressures can be expected to produce highly *specialized* cognitive mechanisms – that is, modules.

[D]ifferent adaptive problems often require different solutions and different solutions can, in most cases, be implemented only by different, functionally distinct mechanisms. Speed, reliability and efficiency can be engineered into specialized mechanisms because there is no need to engineer a compromise between different task demands. (Cosmides and Tooby 1994: 89)

By contrast, "a jack of all trades is necessarily a master of none, because generality can be achieved only by sacrificing effectiveness" (ibid.). In other words, while a specialized mechanism can be fast, reliable, and efficient, because it is dedicated to solving a specific adaptive problem, a general mechanism that solves many adaptive problems with competing task demands will attain generality only at the expense of sacrificing these virtues. Consequently:

(1) 'As a rule, when two adaptive problems have solutions that are incompatible or simply different, a single solution will be inferior to two specialized solutions' (ibid.).

Notice that the above quotation is not specifically about *cognitive* mechanisms. Rather, it is supposed to apply generally to all solutions to adaptive problems. Nevertheless, according to Cosmides and Tooby, what applies generally to solutions to adaptive problems also applies to the specific case of cognitive mechanisms for solving adaptive problems. Thus, they claim, we have good reason to expect task-specific or domain-specific cognitive mechanisms to be superior solutions to adaptive problems than domain-general systems. Moreover, since natural selection can be expected to favor superior solutions to adaptive problems over inferior ones, Cosmides and Tooby conclude that when it comes to solving adaptive problems:

(2) 'domain-specific cognitive mechanisms . . . can be expected to systematically outperform (and hence preclude or replace) more general mechanisms' (ibid.).

So far, then, we have seen that Cosmides and Tooby argue for the claim that selection pressures can be expected to produce domain-specific cognitive mechanisms – modules – for solving adaptive problems. But this alone is not sufficient to support the claim that the mind contains a *large number* of modules. It must also be the case that our ancestors were confronted by a large number of adaptive problems that could be solved only by cognitive mechanisms. Accordingly, Cosmides and Tooby insist that

(3) 'Simply to survive and reproduce, our Pleistocene ancestors had to be good at solving an enormously broad array of adaptive problems – problems that would defeat any modern artificial intelligence system. A small sampling include foraging for food, navigating, selecting a mate, parenting, engaging in social exchange, dealing with aggressive threat, avoiding predators, avoiding pathogenic

contamination, avoiding naturally occurring plant toxins, avoiding incest and so on' (ibid., 90).

Yet, if this is true, and if it is also true that when it comes to solving adaptive problems, domain-specific cognitive mechanisms can be expected to preclude or replace more general cognitive mechanisms, then it would seem to follow that:

> (4)   The human mind can be expected to include a large number of distinct, domain-specific mechanisms.

And this, of course, is just what the Massive Modularity Hypothesis requires.

This argument is not supposed to be a deductive proof that the mind is massively modular. Rather, it is offered as a plausibility argument. It is supposed to provide us with plausible grounds to expect the mind to contain many modules (ibid., 89). Nonetheless, if the conclusion of the argument is interpreted as claiming that the mind contains lots of *prototypical Darwinian* modules, then we suspect that the argument claims more than it is entitled to. For even if we grant that natural selection has contrived to provide the human mind with many specialized solutions to adaptive problems, it does not follow that these specialized solutions will be prototypical Darwinian modules. Rather than containing a large number of specialized computational devices, it might instead be the case that the mind contains lots of innate, domain-specific items of knowledge, and that these are employed in order to solve various adaptive problems. Thus, rather than exploiting Darwinian modules, our minds might contain lots of innate, *Chomskian* modules. And it is perfectly consistent with the claim that we possess Chomskian modules for solving adaptive problems that the information contained within such modules is utilized only by *domain-general* and hence nonmodular computational devices. Moreover, the claim that natural selection prefers certain kinds of adaptive specializations to others – namely, Darwinian computational modules to Chomskian modules – surely does not follow from the general claim that specialized solutions (of some kind) typically outperform more general ones. So instead of producing Darwinian modules as solutions to adaptive problems, natural selection might instead have provided specialized solutions in the form of innate, domain-specific knowledge that it utilized by a domain-general computational mechanism. In order to make it plausible that the mind contains large numbers of Darwinian modules, one must argue for the claim that natural selection can be expected to prefer domain-specific *computational* devices over domain-specific *bodies of information* as solutions to adaptive problems. And, at present, it is far from clear that anyone knows how such an argument would go.

4.4 The research program of evolutionary psychology

A central goal of evolutionary psychology is to construct and test hypotheses about the Darwinian modules which, the theory maintains, make up much of the human mind. In pursuit of this goal, research may proceed in two quite different stages. The first, which we'll call *evolutionary analysis*, has as its goal the generation of plausible hypotheses about Darwinian modules. An evolutionary analysis tries to determine as much as possible about recurrent information-processing problems that our forebears would have confronted in what is often called *the environment of evolutionary adaptation* or EEA – the environment in which *Homo sapiens* evolved. The focus, of course, is on *adaptive* problems whose successful solution would have directly or indirectly contributed to reproductive success. In some cases these adaptive problems were posed by physical features of the EEA; in other cases they were posed by biological features; and in still other cases they were posed by the social environment in which our forebears were embedded. Since so many factors are involved in determining the sorts of recurrent information-processing problems that our ancestors confronted in the EEA, this sort of evolutionary analysis is a highly interdisciplinary exercise. Clues can be found in many different sort of investigations, from the study of the Pleistocene climate to the study of the social organization in the few remaining hunter-gatherer cultures. Once a recurrent adaptive problem has been characterized, the theorist may hypothesize that there is a module which would have done a good job at solving that problem in the EEA.

An important part of the effort to characterize these recurrent information-processing problems is the specifications of the sorts of constraints that a mechanism solving the problem could take for granted. If, for example, the important data needed to solve the problem was almost always presented in a specific format, then the mechanism need not be able to handle data presented in other ways. It could "assume" that the data would be presented in the typical format. Similarly, if it was important to be able to detect people or objects with a certain property that is not readily observable, and if in the EEA that property was highly correlated with some other property that is easier to detect, the system could simply assume that people or objects with the detectable property also had the one that was hard to observe.

It is important to keep in mind that evolutionary analyses can be used only as a way of *suggesting plausible hypotheses* about mental modules. By themselves, evolutionary analyses provide no assurance that these hypotheses are true. The fact that it would have enhanced our ancestors' fitness if they had developed a module that solved a certain problem is no guarantee that they *did* develop such a module, since there are many reasons why natural selection and the other processes that drive evolution may fail to produce a mechanism that would enhance fitness (Stich 1990: ch. 3).

Once an evolutionary analysis has succeeded in suggesting a plausible hypothesis, the next stage in the evolutionary psychology research strategy is to *test* the hypothesis by looking for evidence that contemporary humans actually have a module with the properties in question. Here, as earlier, the project is highly interdisciplinary. Evidence can come from experimental studies of reasoning in normal humans (Cosmides 1989; Cosmides and Tooby 1992, 1996; Gigerenzer 1991; Gigerenzer and Hug 1992), from developmental studies focused on the emergence of cognitive skills (Carey and Spelke 1994; Leslie 1994; Gelman and Brenneman 1994), or from the study of cognitive deficits in various abnormal populations (Baron-Cohen 1995). Important evidence can also be gleaned from studies in cognitive anthropology (Barkow 1992; Hutchins 1980), history, and even from such surprising areas as the comparative study of legal traditions (Wilson and Daly 1992). When evidence from a number of these areas points in the same direction, an increasingly strong case can be made for the existence of a module suggested by evolutionary analysis.

5   Evolutionary Psychology Applied to Reasoning: Theory and Results

In this section we will consider two lines of research on human reasoning in which the two-stage strategy described in the previous section has been pursued. Though the interpretation of the studies we will sketch is the subject of considerable controversy, a number of authors have suggested that they show there is something deeply mistaken about the "bleak" hypothesis set out in section 3. That hypothesis claims that people lack normatively appropriate rules or principles for reasoning about problems like those set out in section 2. But when we look at variations on these problems that may make them closer to the sort of recurrent problems our forebears would have confronted in the EEA, performance improves dramatically. And this, it is argued, is evidence for the existence of at least two normatively sophisticated Darwinian modules, one designed to deal with probabilistic reasoning when information is presented in a relative frequency format, the other designed to deal with reasoning about cheating in social exchange setttings.

5.1   The frequentist hypothesis

The experiments reviewed in sections 2.2–2.4 indicate that in many cases people are quite bad at reasoning about probabilities, and the pessimistic interpretation of these results claims that people use simple ("fast and dirty") heuristics in dealing with these problems because their cognitive systems have no access to more appropriate principles for reasoning about probabilities. But, in a series of recent, very provocative papers, Gigerenzer (1994: Gigerenzer and Hoffrage 1995) and Cosmides and Tooby (1996) argue that from an evolutionary point of view this would be a surprising and paradoxical result. "As long as chance has been loose in the world," Cosmides and Tooby note, "animals have had to make judgments under uncertainty" (1996: 14). Thus making judgments when confronted with probabilistic information posed adaptive problems for all sorts of organisms, including our hominid ancestors, and "if an adaptive problem has endured for a long enough period and is important enough, then mechanisms of considerable complexity can evolve to solve it" (ibid.). But, as we saw in the previous section, "one should expect a mesh between the design of our cognitive mechanisms, the structure of the adaptive problems they evolved to solve, and the typical environments that they were designed to operate in – that is, the one that they evolved in" (ibid.). So, in launching their evolutionary analysis, Cosmides and Tooby's first step is to ask: "what kinds of probabilistic information would have been available to any inductive reasoning mechanisms that we might have evolved?" (ibid., 15).

In the modern world we are confronted with statistical information presented in many ways: weather forecasts tell us the probability of rain tomorrow, sports pages list batting averages, and widely publicized studies tell us how much the risk of cancer of the colon is reduced in people over 50 if they have a diet high in fiber. But information about the probability of single events (like rain tomorrow) and information expressed in percentage terms would have been rare or unavailable in the EEA.

> What *was* available in the environment in which we evolved was the encountered frequencies of actual events – for example, that we were successful 5 times out of the last 20 times we hunted in the north canyon. Our hominid ancestors were immersed in a rich flow of observable frequencies that could be used to improve decision-making, given procedures that could take advantage of them. So if we have adaptations for inductive reasoning, they should take frequency information as input. (ibid., 15–16)

After a cognitive system has registered information about relative frequencies, it might convert this information to some other format. If, for example, the system has noted that 5 out of the last 20 north canyon hunts were successful, it might infer and store the conclusion that there is a 0.25 chance that a north canyon hunt will be successful. However, Cosmides and Tooby argue, "there are advantages to storing and operating on frequentist representations because they preserve important information that would be lost by conversion to single-event probability. For example, . . . the number of events that the judgment was based on would be lost in conversion. When the n disappears, the index of reliability of the information disappears as well" (ibid., 16).

These and other considerations regarding the environment in which our cognitive systems evolved lead Cosmides and Tooby to hypothesize that our ancestors "evolved mechanism that took frequencies as input, maintained such

information as frequentist representations, and used these frequentist representations as a database for effective inductive reasoning."[10] Since evolutionary
psychologists expect the mind to contain many specialized modules, Cosmides
and Tooby are prepared to find other modules involved in inductive reasoning
that work in other ways.

> We are not hypothesizing that every cognitive mechanism involving statistical
> induction necessarily operates on frequentist principles, only that at least one of
> them does, and that this makes frequentist principles an important feature of
> how humans intuitively engage the statistical dimension of the world. (ibid., 17)

But, while their evolutionary analysis does not preclude the existence of
inductive mechanisms that are not focused on frequencies, it does suggest that
when a mechanism that operates on frequentist principles is engaged, it will
do a good job, and thus the probabilistic inferences it makes will generally be
normatively appropriate ones. This, of course, is in stark contrast to the bleak
implications hypothesis, which claims that people simply do not have access to
normatively appropriate strategies in this area.

From their hypothesis, Cosmides and Tooby derive a number of predictions:

(1)   Inductive reasoning performance will differ depending on whether subjects
      are asked to judge a frequency or the probability of a single event.
(2)   Performance on frequentist versions of problems will be superior to
      nonfrequentist versions.
(3)   The more subjects can be mobilized to form a frequentist representation,
      the better performance will be.
(4)   . . . Performance on frequentist problems will satisfy some of the constraints
      that a calculus of probability specifies, such as Bayes's rule. This would
      occur because some inductive reasoning mechanisms in our cognitive
      architecture embody aspects of a calculus of probability. (ibid., 17)

To test these predictions, Cosmides and Tooby ran an array of experiments
designed around the medical diagnosis problem which Casscells et al. used to
demonstrate that even very sophisticated subjects ignore information about
base rates. In their first experiment Cosmides and Tooby replicated the results
of Casscells et al. using exactly the same wording that we reported in section
2.4. Of the 25 Stanford University undergradates who were subjects in this
experiment, only 3 (= 12 percent) gave the normatively appropriate bayesian
answer of "2 percent", while 14 subjects (= 56 percent) answered "95
percent".[11] As we noted in 2.3, the Harvard Medical School subjects in the
original Casscells et al. study did slightly better; 18 percent of those subjects
gave answers close to "2 percent" and 45 percent answered "95 percent."

In another experiment, Cosmides and Tooby gave 50 Stanford students a
similar problem in which relative frequencies rather than percentages and
single-event probabilities were emphasized. The "frequentist" version of the
problem read as follows:

1 out of every 1000 Americans has disease X. A test has been developed to detect when a person has disease X. Every time the test is given to a person who has the disease, the test comes out positive. But sometimes the test also comes out positive when it is given to a person who is completely healthy. Specifically, out of every 1000 people who are perfectly healthy, 50 of them test positive for the disease.

Imagine that we have assembled a random sample of 1000 Americans. They were selected by lottery. Those who conducted the lottery had no information about the health status of any of these people.

Given the information above:

on average,

How many people who test positive for the disease will *actually* have the disease? —— out of —— .[12]

On this problem the results were dramatically different: 38 of the 50 subjects (= 76 percent) gave the correct Bayesian answer.[13]

A series of further experiments systematically explored the differences between the problem used by Casscells et al. and the problems on which subjects perform well, in an effort to determine which factors had the largest effect. Although a number of different factors affect performance, two predominate. "Asking for the answer as a frequency produces the largest effect, following closely by presenting the problem information as frequencies" (ibid., 58). The most important conclusion that Cosmides and Tooby want to draw from these experiments is that "frequentist representations activate mechanisms that produce bayesian reasoning, and that this is what accounts for the very high level of Bayesian performance elicited by the pure frequentist problems that we tested" (ibid., 59).

As further support for this conclusion, Cosmides and Tooby cite several striking results reported by other investigators. In one study, Fiedler (1988), following up on some intriguing findings of Tversky and Kahneman (1983), showed that the percentage of subjects who commit the conjunction fallacy can be radically reduced if the problem is cast in frequentist terms. In the "feminist bank teller" example, Fiedler contrasted the wording reported in section 2.2 with a problem that read as follows:

Linda is 31 years old, single, outspoken, and very bright. She majored in philsophy. As a student, she was deeply concerned with issues of discrimination and social justice, and also participated in anti-nuclear demonstrations.

There are 200 people who fit the description above. How many of them are:

bank tellers?

bank tellers and active in the feminist movement?

. . .

In Fiedler's replication using the original formulation of the problem, 91 percent of subjects judged the feminist bank teller option to be more probable than the bank teller option. However, in the frequentist version only 22 percent of subjects judged that there would be more feminist bank tellers than bank tellers. In yet another experiment, Hertwig and Gigerenzer (1994; reported in Gigerenzer 1994) told subjects that there were 200 women fitting the "Linda" description, and asked them to estimate the number who were bank tellers, feminist bank tellers, and feminists. Only 13 percent committed the conjunction fallacy.

Studies on overconfidence have also been marshaled in support of the frequentist hypothesis. In one of these Gigerenzer, Hoffrage, and Kleinbölting (1991) reported that the sort of overconfidence described in section 2.4 can be made to "disappear" by having subjects answer questions formulated in terms of frequencies. Gigerenzer and his colleages gave subjects lists of 50 questions similar to those described in section 2.4, except that in addition to being asked to rate their confidence after each response (which, in effect, asks them to judge the probability of that single event), subjects were, at the end, also asked a question about the frequency of correct responses: "How many of these 50 questions do you think you got right?" In two experiments, the average overconfidence was about 15 percent, when single-event confidences were compared with actual relative frequencies of correct answers, replicating the sorts of findings we sketched in section 2.4. However, comparing the subjects' "estimated frequencies with actual frequencies of correct answers made 'overconfidence' *disappear*. . . . Estimated frequencies were practically identical with actual frequencies, with even a small tendency towards underestimation. The 'cognitive illusion' was gone" (Gigerenzer 1991: 89).

Both the experimental studies we have been reviewing and the conclusions that Gigerenzer, Cosmides, and Tooby want to draw from them have provoked a fair measure of criticism. For our purposes, perhaps the most troublesome criticisms are those demonstrating that various normatively problematic patterns of reasoning arise even when a problem is stated in terms of frequencies. In their detailed study of the conjunction fallacy, for example, Tversky and Kahneman (1983) reported an experiment in which subjects were asked to estimate both the number of "seven-letter words of the form '-----n-' in four pages of text" and the number of "seven-letter words of the form '----ing' in four pages of text." The median estimate for words ending in "ing" was about three times *higher* than for words with "n" in the next-to-last position. As Kahneman and Tversky (1996) note, this appears to be a clear counter-example to Gigerenzer's claim that the conjunction fallacy disappears in judgments of frequency.

As another challenge to the claim that frequency representations eliminate base-rate neglect, Kahneman and Tversky cite a study by Gluck and Bower (1988). In that study subjects were required to learn to diagnose whether a patient had a rare disease (25 percent) or a common disease (75 percent) on the basis of 250 trials in which they were presented with patterns of four symptoms. After each presentation subjects guessed which disease the patient had, and were given immediate feedback indicating whether their guess was right or wrong. Though subjects encountered the common disease three times more often than the rare disease, they largely ignored this base-rate information and acted as if the two diseases were equally likely.

There is also a substantial body of work demonstrating that antecedent expectations can lead people to report illusory correlations when they are shown data about a sequence of cases. In one well-known and very disquieting study, Chapman and Chapman (1967, 1969) showed subjects a series of cards each of which was said to reproduce a drawing of a person made by a psychiatric patient. Each card also gave the diagnosis for that patient. Subjects reported seeing "intuitively expected" correlations (e.g., drawings with peculiar eyes and diagnoses of paranoia) even when there was no such correlation in the data they were shown. In another widely discussed study, Gilovich, Vallone, and Tversky (1985) showed that people "see" a positive correlation between the outcome of successive shots in basketball (thus giving rise to the illusion of a "hot hand") even when there is no such correlation in the data.

In our view, what these criticisms show is that the version of the frequentist hypothesis suggested by Gigerenzer, Cosmides, and Tooby is too simplistic. It is not the case that all frequentist representations activate mechanisms that produce good bayesian reasoning; nor is it the case that presenting data in a sequential format from which frequency distribution can readily be extracted always activates mechanisms that do a good job at detecting correlations. More experimental work is needed to determine what additional factors are required to trigger good bayesian reasoning and good correlation detection. And more subtle evolutionary analyses are needed to throw light on why these more complex triggers evolved. But despite the polemical fireworks there is actually a fair amount of agreement between the evolutionary psychologists and their critics. Both sides agree that people *do* have mental mechanisms which can do a good job at bayesian reasoning, and that presenting problems in a way that makes frequency information salient can play an important role in activating these mechanisms. Both sides also agree that people have other mental mechanisms that exploit quite different reasoning strategies, though there is little agreement on how to characterize these non-bayesian strategies, what factors trigger them, or why they evolved. The bottom line, we think, is that the experiments demonstrating that people sometimes do an excellent job of bayesian reasoning go a long way toward refuting the gloomy hypothesis sketched in section 3. Gould's claim that "our minds are not built . . . to work by the rules of probability" is much too pessimistic. Our cognitive systems clearly do have access to reasoning strategies that accord with the rules of probability, though it is also clear that we don't always use them. We also think that the evidence reviewed in this section is compatible with the hypothesis that good probabilistic reasoning, when it occurs, is subserved by one or more Darwinian modules, though of course the evidence is compatible with lots of alternative hypotheses as well.

In its crackdown against drunk drivers, Massachusetts law enforcement officials are revoking liquor licenses left and right. You are a bouncer in a Boston bar, and you'll lose your job unless you enforce the following law:

"If a person is drinking beer, then he must be over 20 years old."

The cards below have information about four people sitting at a table in your bar. Each card represents one person. One side of the card tells what a person is drinking and the other side of the card tells that person's age. Indicate only those card(s) you definitely need to turn over to see if any of these people are breaking the law.

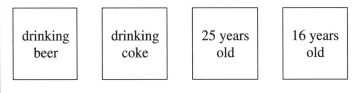

Figure 3.2

5.2 The cheater detection hypothesis

In section 2 we reproduced one version of Wason's four-card selection task on which most subjects perform very poorly, and we noted that, while subjects do equally poorly on many other versions of the selection task, there are some versions on which performance improves dramatically. An example from Griggs and Cox (1982) is shown in figure 3.2. From a logical point of view, this problem is structurally identical to the problem in section 2.1, but the *content* of the problems clearly has a major effect on how well people perform. About 75 percent of college student subjects get the right answer on this version of the selection task, while only 25 percent get the right answer on the other version. Though there have been dozens of studies exploring this "content effect" in the selection task, the results have been, and continue to be, rather puzzling, since there is no obvious property or set of properties shared by those versions of the task on which people perform well. However, in several recent and widely discussed papers, Cosmides and Tooby have argued that an evolutionary analysis enables us to see a surprising pattern in these otherwise bewildering results (Cosmides 1989; Cosmides and Tooby 1992).

The starting point of their evolutionary analysis is the observation that in the environment in which our ancestors evolved (and in the modern world as well) it is often the case that unrelated individuals can engage in "non-zero-sum" exchanges, in which the benefits to the recipient (measured in terms of reproductive fitness) are significantly greater than the costs to the donor. In a hunter-gatherer society, for example, it will sometimes happen that one hunter has been lucky on a particular day and has an abundance of food, while another hunter has been unlucky and is near starvation. If the successful hunter gives some of his meat to the unsuccessful hunter rather than gorging on it himself, this may have a small negative effect on the donor's fitness, since the extra bit of body fat that he might add could prove useful in the future, but the benefit to the recipient will be much greater. Still, there is *some* cost to the donor; he would be slightly better off if he didn't help unrelated individuals. Despite this, it is clear that people sometimes do help non-kin, and there is evidence to suggest that non-human primates (and even vampire bats) do so as well. On first blush, this sort of "altriusm" seems to pose an evolutionary puzzle, since if a gene which made an organism *less* likely to help unrelated individuals appeared in a population, those with the gene would be slightly *more* fit, and thus the gene would gradually spread through the population.

A solution to this puzzle was proposed by Robert Trivers (1971), who noted that, while one-way altriusm might be a bad idea from an evolutioniary point of view, *reciprocal altriusm* is quite a different matter. If a pair of hunters (be they humans or bats) can each count on the other to help when one has an abundance of food and the other has none, then they may both be better off in the long run. Thus organisms with a gene or a suite of genes that inclines them to engage in reciprocal exchanges with non-kin (or "social exchanges" as they are sometimes called) would be more fit than members of the same species without those genes. But, of course, reciprocal exchange arrangements are vulnerable to cheating. In the business of maximizing fitness, individuals will do best if they are regularly offered and accept help when they need it, but never reciprocate when others need help. This suggests that if stable social exchange arrangements are to exist, the organisms involved must have cognitive mechanisms that enable them to detect cheaters and to avoid helping them in the future. And since humans apparently are capable of entering into stable social exchange relations, this evolutionary analysis leads Cosmides and Tooby to hypothesize that we have one or more Darwinian modules whose job it is to recognize reciprocal exchange arrangements and to detect cheaters who accept the benefits in such arrangements but do not pay the costs. In short, the evolutionary analysis leads Cosmides and Tooby to hypothesize the existence of one or more cheater detection modules. We call this *the cheater detection hypothesis*.

If this is right, then we should be able to find some evidence for the existence of these modules in the thinking of contemporary humans. It is here that the selection task enters the picture. For, according to Cosmides and Tooby, some versions of the selection task engage the mental module(s) which were designed to detect cheaters in social exchange situations. And since these mental modules can be expected to do their job efficiently and accurately, people do well on those versions of the selection task. Other versions of the task do not trigger the social exchange and cheater detection modules. Since we have no mental modules that were designed to deal with these problems, people find them much harder, and their performance is much worse. The bouncer-in-the-Boston-bar problem presented earlier is an example of a selection task that triggers the cheater detection mechanism. The problem involving vowels and odd numbers presented in section 2 is an example of a selection task that does not trigger the cheater detection module.

In support of their theory, Cosmides and Tooby assemble an impressive body of evidence. To begin, they note that the cheater detection hypothesis claims that social exchanges, or "social contracts," will trigger good performance on selection tasks, and this enables us to see a clear pattern in the otherwise confusing experimental literature that had grown up before their hypothesis was formulated.

> When we began this research in 1983, the literature on the Wason selection task was full of reports of a wide variety of content effects, and there was no satisfying theory or empirical generalization that could account for these effects. When we categorized these content effects according to whether they conformed to social contracts, a striking pattern emerged. Robust and replicable content effects were found only for rules that related terms that are recognizable as benefits and cost/requirements in the format of a standard social contract. . . . No thematic rule that was not a social contract had ever produced a content effect that was both robust and replicable. . . . All told, for non-social contract thematic problems, 3 experiments had produced a substantial content effect, 2 had produced a weak content effect, and 14 had produced no content effect at all. The few effects that were found did not replicate. In contrast, 16 out of 16 experiments that fit the criteria for standard social contracts . . . elicited substantial content effects. (Cosmides and Tooby 1992: 183)

Since the formulation of the cheater detection hypothesis, a number of additional experiments have been designed to test the hypothesis and rule out alternatives. Among the most persuasive of these are a series of experiments by Gigerenzer and Hug (1992). In one set of experiments, these authors set out to show that, contrary to an earlier proposal by Cosmides and Tooby, *merely* perceiving a rule as a social contract was not enough to engage the cognitive mechanism that leads to good performance in the selection task, and that cueing for the possibility of *cheating* was required. To do this, they created two quite different context stories for social contract rules. One of the stories required subjects to attend to the possibility of cheating, while in the other story cheating was not relevant. Among the social contract rules they used was the following, which, they note, is widely known among hikers in the Alps:

> (i) If someone stays overnight in the cabin, then that person must bring along a bundle of wood from the valley.

The first context story, which the investigators call the "cheating version," explained:

There is a cabin at high altitude in the Swiss Alps, which serves hikers as an overnight shelter. Since it is cold and firewood is not otherwise available at that altitude, the rule is that each hiker who stays overnight has to carry along his/her own share of wood. There are rumors that the rule is not always followed. The subjects were cued into the perspective of a guard who checks whether any one of four hikers has violated the rule. The four hikers were represented by four cards that read "stays overnight in the cabin," "carried no wood," "carried wood," and "does not stay overnight in the cabin."

The other context story, the "no cheating version,"

cued subjects into the perspective of a member of the German Alpine Association who visits the Swiss cabin and tries to discover how the local Swiss Alpine Club runs this cabin. He observes people bringing wood to the cabin, and a friend suggests the familiar overnight rule as an explanation. The context story also mentions an alternative explanation: rather than the hikers, the members of the Swiss Alpine Club, who do not stay overnight, might carry the wood. The task of the subject was to check four persons (the same four cards) in order to find out whether anyone had violated the overnight rule suggested by the friend. (Gigerenzer and Hug 1992: 142–3)

The cheater detection hypothesis predicts that subjects will do better on the cheating version than on the no cheating version, and that prediction was confirmed. In the cheating version, 89 percent of the subjects got the right answer, while in the no cheating version, only 53 percent responded correctly.

    In another set of experiments, Gigerenzer and Hug showed that when social contract rules make cheating on both sides possible, cueing subjects into the perspective of one party or the other can have a dramatic effect on performance in selection task problems. One of the rules they used that allows the possibility of bilateral cheating was:

(ii)   If an employee works on the weekend, then that person gets a day off during the week.

Here again, two different context stories were constructed, one of which was designed to get subjects to take the perspective of the employee, while the other was designed to get subjects to take the perspective of the employer.

The employee version stated that working on the weekend is a benefit for the employer, because the firm can make use of its machines and be more flexible. Working on the weekend, on the other hand is a cost for the employee. The context story was about an employee who had never worked on the weekend before, but who is considering working on Saturdays from time to time, since having a day off during the week is a benefit that outweighs the costs of working on Saturday. There are rumors that the rule has been violated before. The subject's task was to check information about four colleagues to see whether the rule has been violated. The four cards read: "worked on the weekend," "did not get a day off," "did not work on the weekend," "did get a day off."

In the employer version, the same rationale was given. The subject was cued into the perspective of the employer, who suspects that the rule has been violated before. The subjects' task was the same as in the other perspective [viz., to check information about four employees to see whether the rule has been violated]. (Gigerenzer & Hug 1992: 154)

In these experiments about 75 percent of the subjects cued to the employee's perspective chose the first two cards ("worked on the weekend" and "did not get a day off"), while less than 5 percent chose the other two cards. The results for subjects cued to the employer's perspective were radically different. Over 60 percent of subjects selected the last two cards ("did not work on the weekend" and "did get a day off"), while less than 10 percent selected the first two.

The evolutionary analysis that motivates the cheater detection hypothesis maintains that the capacity to engage in social exchange could not have evolved unless the individuals involved had some mechanism for detecting cheaters. There would, however, be no need for our hominid forebears to have developed a mechanism for detecting "pure altruists" who help others but do not expect help in return. If there were individuals like that, it might of course be useful to recognize them, so that they could be more readily exploited. However, altruists of this sort would incur fitness costs with no compensating benefits, and thus an evolutionary analysis suggests that they would have been selected against. Since altruists would be rare or non-existent, there would be no selection pressure for an altruist detection mechanism. These considerations led Cosmides and Tooby to predict that people will be much better at detecting cheaters in a selection task than at detecting altruists. To test the prediction, they designed three pairs of problems. In each pair the two stories are quite similar, though in one version subjects must look for cheaters, while in the other they must look for altruists. In one pair, both problems begin with the following text:

You are an anthropologist studying the Kaluame, a Polynesian people who live in small, warring bands on Maku Island in the Pacific. You are interested in how Kaluame "big men" – chieftains – wield power.

'Big Kiku' is a Kaluame big man who is known for his ruthlessness. As a sign of loyalty, he makes his own "subjects" put a tattoo on their face. Members of other Kaluame bands never have facial tattoos. Big Kiku has made so many enemies in other Kaluame bands, that being caught in another village with a facial tattoo is, quite literally, the kiss of death.

Four men from different bands stumble into Big Kiku's village starving and desperate. They have been kicked out of their respective villages for various misdeeds, and have come to Big Kiku because they need food badly. Big Kiku offers each of them the following deal:

'If you get a tattoo on your face, then I'll give you cassava root.'

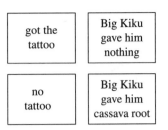

Figure 3.3

Cassava root is a very sustaining food which Big Kiku's people cultivate. The four men are very hungry, so they agree to Big Kiku's deal. Big Kiku says that the tattoos must be in place tonight, but that the cassava root will not be available until the following morning.

At this point the two problems diverge. The *cheater version* continues:

You learn that Big Kiku hates some of these men for betraying him to his enemies. You suspect he will cheat and betray some of them. Thus, this is a perfect opportunity for you to see first hand how Big Kiku wields his power.

The cards below have information about the fates of the four men. Each card represents one man. One side of a card tells whether or not the man went through with the facial tattoo that evening and the other side of the card tells whether or not Big Kiku gave that man cassava root the next day.

Did Big Kiku get away with cheating any of these four men? Indicate only those card(s) you definitely need to turn over to see if Big Kiku has broken his word to any of these four men.

The *altruist version* continues:

You learn that Big Kiku hates some of these men for betraying him to his enemies. You suspect he will cheat and betray some of them. However, you have also heard that Big Kiku sometimes, quite unexpectedly, shows great generosity towards others – that he is sometimes quite altruistic. Thus, this is a perfect opportunity for you to see first hand how Big Kiku wields his power.

The cards below have information about the fates of the four men. Each card represents one man. One side of a card tells whether or not the man went through with the facial tattoo that evening and the other side of the card tells whether or not Big Kiku gave that man cassava root the next day.

Did Big Kiku behave altruistically towards any of these four men? Indicate only those card(s) you definitely need to turn over to see if Big Kiku has behaved altruistically towards any of these four men.

The four cards, which were identical in both versions, are shown in figure 3.3. In the version of the problem that requires subjects to detect cheaters, Cosmides (1989) had found that 74 percent of subjects get the correct answer. In the version that requires subjects to detect altruists, however, only 28 percent answered correctly (Cosmides and Tooby 1992: 193–7).

These experiments, along with a number of others reviewed by Cosmides and Tooby (1992) are all compatible with the hypothesis that we have one or more Darwinian modules designed to deal with social exchanges and detect cheaters. However, this hypothesis is, to put it mildly, very controversial. Many authors have proposed alternative hypotheses to explain the data, and in some cases they have supported these hypotheses with additional experimental evidence. One of the most widely discussed of these alternatives is the *pragmatic reasoning schemas* approach defended by Cheng, Holyoak, and their colleagues (Cheng and Holyoak 1985, 1989; Cheng et al. 1986). On this account, reasoning is explained by the activation of domain-specific sets of rules (called "schemas") which are acquired during the lifetime of the individual through general inductive mechanisms. These rules subserve people's reasonings about permission, obligation, and other deontic concepts that may be used in their culture. Rules for reasoning about social exchanges are just one kind of reasoning schema. One virtue of this theory is that it provides an explanation for the fact that people perform well on problems like the "bar bouncer" task which are not assimilated comfortably to the model of reciprocal social exchange. However, as Cummins (1996) argues, there is little evidence for the claim that schemas involved in reasoning about permission and obligation are learned, and a fair amount of evidence suggesting that capacity to engage in deontic reasoning emerges relatively early in childhood. This, along with a number of other lines of evidence, leads Cummins to propose an intriguing hypothesis that integrates ideas from both the social exchange theory and the pragmatic reasoning schemas theory. On Cummins's hypothesis, reasoning about "permissions, obligations, prohibitions, promises, threats and warnings" (1996: 166) is subserved by an innate, domain-specific module devoted exclusively to deontic contents. This reasoning module "evolved for the very important purpose of solving problems that frequently arise within a dominance hierarchy – the social structure that characterizes most mammalian and avian species" (ibid.). A core component of the deontic reasoning module, Cummins maintains, is a mechanism whose job is violation detection. "[T]o reason effectively about deontic concepts, it is necessary to recognize what constitutes a violation, respond to it appropriately (which often depends on the respective status of the parties involved), and appreciate the necessity of adopting a violation-detection strategy whenever a deontic situation is encountered" (ibid.). Still other hypotheses to account for the content effects in selection tasks have been proposed by Oaksford and Chater (1994), Manktelow and Over (1995), and Sperber, Cara, and Girotto (1995).

This is not the place to review all these theories; nor would we venture a judgment – even a tentative one – on which theory is most promising. These are busy and exciting times for those studying human reasoning, and there is obviously much that remains to be discovered. What we believe we can safely conclude from the studies recounted in this section is that the hypothesis that much of human reasoning is subserved by a cluster of domain-specific Darwinian modules deserves to be taken very seriously. Whether or not it ultimately proves to be correct, the highly modular picture of the mechanisms underlying reasoning has generated a great deal of impressive research and will continue to do so for the foreseeable future. Thus we would do well to begin exploring what the implications would be for various claims about human rationality *if* the Massive Modularity Hypothesis turns out to be correct. In the final section of this paper we will begin this exploration by asking what implication the Massive Modularity Hypothesis might have for the "bleak implications" interpretations of some of the experimental studies of reasoning.

6 Massive Modularity, Bleak Implications, and the Panglossian Interpretation

One possible response to the Massive Modularity Hypothesis – we'll call it the *Panglossian interpretation* – maintains that if the MMH turns out to be correct, it would make the bleak implications interpretation of the experimental studies of rationality completely untenable. According to the bleak implications interpretation, the sorts of experimental results surveyed in section 2 reflect shortcomings in human reasoning *competence*. People deal with the problems in those experiments by exploiting various normatively problematic heuristics, and they do this because they have nothing better available. They "lack the correct programs for many important judgmental tasks,"[14] because, as Gould maintained, "our minds are not built . . . to work by the rules of probability" (Gould 1992: 469). But, according to the Panglossian this is simply the wrong interpretation. If the Massive Modularity Hypothesis is correct, then the mind contains "a multitude of . . . elegant machines" (Tooby and Cosmides 1995: p. xiv). There are Darwinian modules that reason in *normatively appropriate* ways about probability, cheating, and threats and also about dead reckoning, intuitive mechanics, intuitive biology, and intuitive psychology, and no doubt a host of others as well. So humans *do* have access to the correct programs for important judgmental tasks; our minds include Darwinian modules that *are* built to "work by the rules of probability"; and humans are "good intuitive statisticians after all." The errors reported in the experimental literature, if indeed they really are errors,[15] are merely *performance* errors, and the bleak implications interpretation must be rejected.

We are not at all sure that anyone actually advocates this very strong version of the Panglossian interpretation, though we suspect that a fair number of people would endorse a more hedged and cautious version.[16] We don't believe that anything very close to the strong version of the Panglossian interpretation can be defended, though we think there is a great deal to be learned by exploring why the Panglossian interpretation fails.

One fairly straightforward objection to the Panglossian interpretation begins with the observations that the experimental literature on human reasoning has documented many quite different sorts of problems on which subjects perform poorly. Those reviewed in section 2 are a small and highly selective sample. If the Panglossian interpretation is correct, then people must have Darwinian modules capable of handling in normatively appropriate ways *all* of the problems on which subjects perform poorly, though for one reason or another the performance of experimental subjects does not reflect their underlying competence. That is, of course, a very strong claim, much stronger than currently available evidence will support. Nor is there any plausible evolutionary argument for the claim that natural selection would have provided us with Darwinian modules for handling *all* these cases. So the Panglossian interpretation rests on a bold speculation with relatively little empirical or theoretical support. But even if we put this concern off to the side and concentrate on those cases where there is some evidence for the existence of a Darwinian module, there are serious problems with the Panglossian idea that all errors are performance errors.

To bring these problems into focus, let us start by considering Kahneman and Tverky's seven-letter-word problem, discussed in section 5.1. In that problem subjects were not asked about the probability of a particular event. Rather, they were asked to estimate the *frequency* of words of the form "----ing" and words of the form "-----n-" in four pages of text. Yet, despite being asked to estimate frequencies, most subjects said that the number of "----ing" words would be greater than the number of "-----n-" words. If, as advocates of the MMH have argued, we have one or more Darwinian modules that do a good job of probabilistic reasoning when problems are couched in terms of frequencies, what sort of explanation can be offered for the error that these subjects make? One plausible hypothesis is that, rather than using their probabilistic reasoning module(s), subjects are relying on what Kahneman and Tversky call an "availability heuristic." They are searching memory for examples of words of the form "----ing" and also for words of the form "-----n-", and because of the way in which our memory for such facts is organized, they are coming up with far more of the former than of the latter. But now let us ask *why* subjects (or their cognitive systems) are dealing with the problem in this way. Why *aren't* they using a probabilistic reasoning module which, presumably, would not produce responses that violate the conjunction rule? For an advocate of the MMH, perhaps the most natural hypothesis is that there is a mechanism in the mind (or maybe more than one) whose job it is to determine which of the many reasoning modules and heuristics that are available in a massive modular mind get called on to deal with a given problem, and that this mechanism, which we'll call *the allocation mechanism*, is routing the problem to the wrong component of the reasoning system. If that's right, and if we further suppose that this misallocation is the result of persisting and systematic features of the allocation mechanism, then it seems natural to conclude that the allocation mechanism itself is normatively problematic. It produces errors in reasoning by sending problems to the wrong place.

If this speculation is correct – if certain errors in reasoning are generated by a normatively problematic allocation mechanism – then it seems odd to say that the resulting errors are "performance errors." For, unlike performance errors that result from fatigue or alcohol or emotional stress, this is not a case in which factors arising outside the reasoning system interfere with the normal functioning of the system and cause it to operate in a way that it does not usually operate. In dealing with cases like the seven-letter-word problem, the allocation mechanism works just the way it normally does. The reasoning error is produced because what it normally does is send problems like these to the wrong place. Nor does this look much like the sort of performance errors that are produced in language processing as the result of limited short-term memory. There is no resource that runs out in these cases of misallocation, no parameter that is exceeded. The subject gets the wrong answer because the principles governing the operation of the allocation system are themselves normatively defective. There is (we have been assuming) a Darwinian module capable of doing a good job on the problem, and the allocation mechanism fails to send it there. At this point, a defender of the Panglossian interpretation might insist that since the correct rules for handling these cases of faulty reasoning are available in the subject's mind, the errors are not the product of a defective competence, and thus allocation errors must be just *another kind* of performance error. This argument assumes that there are only two kinds of cognitive errors – performance errors and competence errors – and that anything which doesn't count as one sort of error must be an instance of the other sort. But that is not an assumption we see any reason to accept. Since misallocation errors are not comfortably viewed either as competence errors or as performance errors, we are inclined to think that one lesson to be learned from examples like this is that in a massively modular mind the performance error/competence error distinction does not exhaust the possibilities.

Let us turn now to the original version of the feminist bank teller problem (section 2.2) and the original version of the Casscells et al. "Harvard Medical School" problem (section 2.3). In both cases subjects perform poorly. How might an advocate of the MMH explain this poor performance? One possibility is that these are further examples of allocation errors, and that there is a reasoning module that would have solved them correctly had they been routed there. But there is also a very different possibility that needs to be explored. Darwinian modules are designed by natural selection to handle recurrent information-processing problems. To enable a module to handle problems efficiently, one strategy that natural selection might exploit is to design the module in such a way that it can deal successfully with a problem only if the problem is presented in an appropriate format or in an appropriate system of representation. Thus, for example, Gigerenzer argues that since frequentist formats were the only ones to play a major role in the EEA, we would expect the mental module(s) that handle probabilistic reasoning to be designed to "expect" that format and to be unable to solve the problems successfully if they are presented in some other format. If Gigerenzer is right, then the module(s) subserving good bayesian reasoning simply cannot solve problems posed in terms of single-event probabilities. But in that case, subjects' errors in the original version of the Harvard Medical School problem and the feminist bank teller problem cannot be treated as allocation errors, since the allocation system hasn't sent them to the wrong place. It has no good place to send them. In ordinary subjects there is no module or component of the reasoning system that has the right algorithms for dealing with the problem as posed.

If these speculations are right, then it might be tempting to conclude that the errors are competence errors, and thus that the bleak implications interpretation has gained a foothold even within a massively modular picture of the mind. But, while the matter may be largely terminological, we are not entirely comfortable with the conclusion that these errors are competence errors. For while it is true that the hypothesized Darwinian module(s) don't contain algorithms that can deal with the problem as *posed*, it is also the case that the modules do contain algorithms for dealing with *reformulated* versions of the problems. Thus it may be possible to improve people's performance on these problems without modifying their competence or enriching the reasoning algorithms that the mind makes available. For we may be able to teach them to restate the problems, to put them into a format that their Darwinian modules are designed to process. Since the distinction between those errors that can be avoided by reformulation and those that cannot is potentially a very important one, we think the avoidable errors merit a category of their own. We'll call them *formulation errors.*

One central claim made by the Panglossian interpretation is that all the errors reported in the experimental literature are merely performance errors. But we've now seen two quite different reasons to be suspicious of that claim. If the MMH is correct, then some reasoning errors are likely to be misallocation errors, while others may be formulation errors. On our view, the right conclusion to draw from the MMH is not that all errors are performance errors, but rather that there are a number of importantly different kinds of errors that can't be comfortably characterized as either performance errors or competence errors. If the MMH is right, then the assumption that all reasoning errors are either performance errors or competence errors will have to be abandoned.

The other central claim made by the Panglossian interpretation is that the mind is well stocked with Darwinian modules that reason in normatively appropriate ways. In the remaining pages of this chapter we want to consider some of the problems that confront this aspect of the Panglossian interpretation. A first problem is settling on what might be called a *general normative theory of reasoning* – a theory which specifies the standards by which any inference mechanism or reasoning strategy should be evaluated. In the philosophical literature there is a great deal of debate about the attractions of competing general normative theories.[17] Some theorists defend "reliabilist" accounts in which attaining true beliefs plays a central role. Others advocate accounts on which attaining more pragmatic goals like health and happiness are central. Still others urge that reasoning strategies should be evaluated by appeal to our reflective intuitions about what is and is not rational. This is not the place to review the arguments for and against these general normative theories. Rather, we will assume, as we have throughout this chapter, that some version of reliabilism is correct, and that truth is central to the evaluation of inferential mechanisms. Other things being equal, one inferential mechanism is better than another if it does a better job at getting the right answer. But even if we assume that reliabilism is the correct general normative theory of reasoning, the domain specificity of Darwinian modules poses a cluster of new and quite unique problems that traditional epistemology has not yet explored.

Consider, for example, the module that subserves reasoning about social contracts. We can assume that this module does a relatively good job at answering questions about cheating and contract violation. But there are also indefinitely many problems – elementary arithmetic problems, for example, or "theory of mind" problems about what people would believe or decide to do in various circumstances – for which the social contract module does not produce the right answer; indeed, it produces no answer at all. But surely it would be perverse to criticize the social contract module on the grounds that it can't solve mathematical problems. This would be a bit like criticizing a toaster on the grounds that it cannot be used as a typewriter. To evaluate a toaster, we must attend to its performance on an appropriate range of tasks, and clearly typing is not one of them. Similarly, to evaluate the social contract module, we must attend to its performance on an appropriate range of tasks, and solving mathematical problems is not one of them. The moral to be drawn here seems fairly obvious: Normative evaluations of domain-specific modules must be relativized to a specific domain or a specific range of problems. But this immediately raises a new puzzle: If normative evaluations of domain-specific modules must be relativized to a domain, which domain should it be?

One suggestion is that the right domain is what Sperber (1994) calls the *actual domain*. The actual domain for a given reasoning module is "all the information in the organism's environment that (once processed by perceptual modules, and possibly by other conceptual modules) satisfies the module's input conditions" (p. 52). By "input conditions" Sperber means those conditions that must be satisfied in order that the module be able to process a given item of information. So, for example, if a module requires that a problem be stated in a particular format, then any information not stated in that format fails to satisfy the module's input conditions.

A quite different suggestion is that the domain relevant to the evaluation of domain-specific modules is what Sperber calls the *proper domain*, which he characterizes as "all the information that it is the module's biological function to process" (ibid.). The proper domain is the information that the module was designed to process by natural selection. In recent years, many philosophers of biology have come to regard the notion of a biological function as a particularly slippery one.[18] For current purposes we can rely on the following very rough characterization. The biological functions of a system are the activities or effects of the system in virtue of which it has remained a stable feature of an enduring species.

In some cases the actual domain of a Darwinian module may coincide with its proper domain. But it is also likely that in many cases the two domains will not be identical. For example, it is plausible to suppose that the proper domain of the folk-psychology module includes only the kind of information about the mental states of human beings and the behavior caused by those states that would have been useful to our Pleistocene forebears. But it is very likely that the module also processes information about lots of other things, including the activities of non-human animals, cartoon characters, and even mindless physical objects like trees and heavenly bodies. If this is right, then a normative evaluation of the module relativized to its proper domain is likely to be much more favorable than a normative evaluation relativized to its actual domain. We suspect that those Panglossian-inclined theorists who describe Darwinian modules as "elegant machines" are tacitly assuming that normative evaluation should be relativized to the proper domain, while those who offer a bleaker assessment of human rationality are tacitly relativizing their evaluations to the actual domain, which, in the modern world, contains a vast array of information-processing challenges that are quite different from anything that our Pleistocene ancestors had to confront.

So which domain should we use to evaluate the module, the proper domain or the actual one? Which domain is the *right* one? We don't think there is any principled way of answering this question. Rather, we maintain, normative claims about Darwinian modules or the algorithms they embody make no clear sense until they are explicitly or implicitly relativized to a domain. Moreover, the choice confronting us is actually much more complex than we have suggested so far. For both actual domains and proper domains are best viewed not as single options but as families of options. There are different ways of explicating both the notion of a proper domain and the notion of an actual domain, and these differences will make a difference, in some cases a major difference, to the outcome of relativized normative assessments. Nor should it be assumed that actual domains and proper domains are the only two families of options that might be considered. Normative assessments can serve many different purposes, and for some of these it may be appropriate to relativize to a domain which is neither actual nor proper.

Our conclusion is that neither the Panglossian interpretation nor the bleak implications interpretation offers a satisfactory response to the Massive Modularity Hypothesis. If it is indeed the case that our minds contain a large number of Darwinian modules, and that the modules subserve most of our everyday reasoning, then many of the categories and distinctions that philosophers and cognitive scientists have used to describe and assess cognition will have to be reworked or abandoned. If the Massive Modularity Hypothesis is correct, we will have to rethink what we mean by "rationality."

Notes

Earlier versions of some of this material served as the basis of lectures at the City University of New York Graduate Center, Canterbury University in Christchurch, New Zealand, Rutgers University, and at the Fifth International Colloquium on Cognitive Science in San Sebastian, Spain. We are grateful for the many helpful comments and criticisms that were offered on these occasions. Special thanks are due to Kent Bach, Michael Bishop, Margaret Boden, Derek Browne, L. Jonathan Cohen, Jack Copeland, Stephen Downes, Mary France Egan, Richard Foley, Gerd Gigerenzer, Daniel Kahneman, Ernie Lepore, Brian McLaughlin, Brian Scholl, and Ernest Sosa.

1 Though at least one philosopher has argued that this appearance is deceptive. In an important and widely debated article, Cohen (1981) offers an account of what it is for reasoning rules to be normatively correct, and his account entails that a normal person's reasoning competence *must* be normatively correct. So on Cohen's view normal people can and do make lots of performance errors in both reasoning and language, but there is no such thing as a competence error in either domain. However, a number of critics, including one of the current authors, have argued that Cohen's account of what it is for reasoning rules to be correct *is* mistaken (Stich 1990: ch. 4). For Cohen's reply see Cohen 1986, and for a well-informed assessment of the debate, see Stein 1996.

2 In a frequently cited passage, Kahneman and Tversky write: "In making predictions and judgments under uncertainty, people do not appear to follow the calculus of chance or the statistical theory of prediction. Instead, they rely on a limited number of heuristics which sometimes yield reasonable judgments and sometimes lead to severe and systematic errors" (1973: 237). But this does not commit them to the claim that people do not follow the calculus of chance or the statistical theory of prediction because these are not part of their cognitive competence, and in a more recent paper they acknowledge that in *some* cases people *are* guided by the normatively appropriate rules (Kahneman and Tversky 1996: 587). So presumably they do not think that people are simply ignorant of the appropriate rules, only that they often do not exploit them when they should.

3 For some pioneering empirical explorations of this issue, see Nisbett et al. 1987; Lehman et al. 1988; Lehman and Nisbett 1990.

4 Though we can't pursue the issue here, we see no reason why the notion of a connectionist computational module – i.e., a domain-specific, connectionist computational system – might not turn out to be a theoretically interesting notion. See Tanenhaus et al. 1987 for an early attempt to develop connectionist modules of this sort.

5 Here are brief explanations of the characteristics that Fodor ascribes to modules:

  1 Informational encapsulation: A module has little or no access to information that is not contained in its own proprietary data base. This should not be confused with the sort of limited access characteristic of a Chomskian/ computational module, where the proprietary information to which a computational module has access is not available to *other* components in the system.

  2 Mandatoriness: One cannot control whether or not a module applies to a given input.

   3 Speed: By comparison to nonmodular systems, modules process information very swiftly.

   4 Shallow output: Modules provide only a preliminary characterization of input.

   5 Neural localization: Modular mechanisms are associated with fixed neural architecture.

   6 Susceptibility to characteristic breakdown: Since modules are associated with fixed neural architecture, they exhibit characteristic breakdown patterns (Fodor 1986: 15).

   7 Lack of access of other processes to its intermediate representations: Other systems have limited access to what is going on inside a module.

6 This is his theory of how people attribute mental states to each other and use them to predict behavior.

7 See Gardner 1983 for an early attempt to develop a more fully modular account of the mind.

8 For some additional discussion of the Massive Modularity Hypothesis, see Pinker 1997: 27–8.

9 For other theoretical arguments in support of the claim that the mind is massively modular, see Marr 1982: 102, Cosmides and Tooby 1987, 1992, 1994; Pinker 1994, 1997; and Sperber 1994. For some arguments *against* the MMH, see Fodor 1983: part 4; Karmiloff-Smith 1992: ch. 1; Quartz and Seinowski 1994. For a more systematic review of the debate, see Samuels, in press.

10 Cosmides and Tooby call "the hypothesis that our inductive reasoning mechanisms were designed to operate on and to output frequency representations" *the frequentist hypothesis* (1996: 21), and they give credit to Gerd Gigerenzer for first formulating the hypothesis. See, e.g., Gigerenzer 1994: 142.

11 Cosmides and Tooby use "bayesian" with a small "b" to characterize any cognitive procedure that reliably produces answers that satisfy Bayes's rule.

12 This is the text used in Cosmides and Tooby's (1996) experiments E2-C1 and E3-C2.

13 In yet another version of the problem, Cosmides and Tooby explored whether an even greater percentage would give the correct bayesian answer if subjects were forced "to actively construct a concrete, visual frequentist representation of the information in the problem" (ibid., 34). On that version of the problem, 92 percent of subjects gave the correct bayesian response.

14 Slovic et al. 1976: 174.

15 Gigerenzer (1991, 1994; Gigerenzer and Murray 1987) argues that in many cases the putative errors are not really errors at all, and that those who think they are errors are relying on mistaken or overly simplistic normative theories of reasoning. Gigerenzer's challenge raises many interesting and important issues about the nature of rationality and the assessment of reasoning. A detailed discussion of these issues would take us far beyond the bounds of the current chapter.

16 See, e.g., Pinker 1997: 345.

17 See, e.g., Goldman 1986 and Stich 1990.

18 See, e.g., Godfrey-Smith 1994; Neander 1991; Plantinga 1993.

References

Barkow, J. (1992) Beneath new culture is old psychology: gossip and social stratification. In Barkow et al. 1992, 627–7.

Barkow, J., Cosmides, L. and Tooby, J. (eds) (1992) *The Adapted Mind: Evolutionary Psychology and the Generation of Culture*, Oxford: Oxford University Press.

Baron, J. (1988) *Thinking and Deciding*, Cambridge University Press.

Baron-Cohen, S. (1994) How to build a baby that can read minds: cognitive mechanisms in mindreading. *Cahiers de psychologie* 13(5), 513–52.

—— (1995) *Mindblindness: An Essay on Autism and Theory of Mind*, Cambridge, MA: MIT Press.

Carey, S. and Spelke, E. (1994) Domain-specific knowledge and conceptual change. In Hirschfeld and Gelman (1994), 169–200.

Carruthers, P. and Smith, P. (eds), (1996) *Theories of Theories of Mind*. Cambridge: Cambridge University Press.

Casscells, W., Schoenberger, A. and Grayboys, T. (1978) Interpretation by physicians of clinical laboratory results. *New England Journal of Medicine* 299, 999–1000.

Chapman, L. and Chapman, J. (1967) Genesis of popular but erroneous diagnostic observations. *Journal of Abnormal Psychology* 72, 193–204.

—— (1969) Illusory correlation as an obstacle to the use of valid psychodiagnostic signs. *Journal of Abnormal Psychology* 74, 271–80.

Cheng, P. and Holyoak, K. (1985) Pragmatic reasoning schemas. *Cognitive Psychology* 17, 391–416.

—— (1989) On the natural selection of reasoning theories. *Cognition* 33, 285–313.

Cheng, P., Holyoak, K., Nisbett, R. and Oliver, L. (1986) Pragmatic versus syntactic approaches to training deductive reasoning. *Cognitive Psychology* 18, 293–328.

Chomsky, N. (1965) *Aspects of the Theory of Syntax*, Cambridge, MA: MIT Press.

—— (1975) *Reflections of Language*, New York: Pantheon Books.

—— (1980) *Rules and Representations*, New York: Columbia University Press.

Cohen, L. (1981) Can human irrationality be experimentally demonstrated? *Behavioral and Brain Sciences* 4, 317–70.

—— (1986) *The Dialogue of Reason*, Oxford: Clarendon Press.

Cosmides, L. (1989) The logic of social exchange: has natural selection shaped how humans reason? Studies with Wason selection task. *Cognition* 31, 187–276.

Cosmides, L. and Tooby, J. (1987) From evolution to behavior: evolutionary psychology as the missing link. In J. Dupré (ed.), *The Latest on the Best: Essays on Evolution and Optimality*, Cambridge, MA: MIT Press.

—— (1992) Cognitive adaptations for social exchange. In Barkow et al. (1992), 163–228.

—— (1994) Origins of domain specificity: the evolution of functional organization. In Hirschfeld and Gelman (1994), 85–116.

—— (1996) Are humans good intuitive statisticians after all? Rethinking some conclusions from the literature on judgment under uncertainty. *Cognition* 58(1), 1–73.

Cummins, D. (1996) Evidence for the innateness of deontic reasoning. *Mind and Language* 11, 160–90.

Dawes, R. (1988) *Rational Choice in an Uncertain World*, Orlando, FL: Harcourt Brace Jovanovich.

Evans, J. St B. T., Newstead, S. E. and Byrne, R. M. J. (1993) *Human Reasoning: The Psychology of Deduction*, Hove: Lawrence Erlbaum Associates Ltd.

Fiedler, K. (1988) The dependence of the conjunction fallacy on subtle linguistic factors. *Psychological Research* 50, 123–9.

Fodor, J. (1983) *The Modularity of Mind*, Cambridge, MA: MIT Press.

—— (1986) The modularity of mind. In Pylyshyn and Demopoulos (1986), 3–18.

Gallistel, C. (1990) *The Organization of Learning*, Cambridge, MA: MIT Press.

Gardner, H. (1983). *Frames of Mind: The Theory of Multiple Intelligences*, New York: Basic Books.

Garfield, J. (ed.) (1987) *Modularity in Knowledge Representation and Natural-Language Understanding*, Cambridge, MA: MIT Press.

Gelman, S. and Brenneman, K. (1994) First principles can support both universal and culture-specific learning about number and music. In Hirschfeld and Gelman (1994), 369–87.

Gigerenzer, G. (1991) How to make cognitive illusions disappear: beyond "heuristics and biases." *European Review of Social Psychology* 2, 83–115.

—— (1994) Why the distinction between single-event probabilities and frequencies is important for psychology (and vice versa). In G. Wright and P. Ayton (eds), *Subjective Probability*, New York: John Wiley, 129–61.

Gigerenzer, G. and Hoffrage, U. (1995) How to improve Bayesian reasoning without instruction: frequency formats. *Psychological Review* 102, 684–704.

Gigerenzer, G. and Hug, K. (1992) Domain-specific reasoning: social contracts, cheating and perspective change. *Cognition* 43, 127–71.

Gigerenzer, G. and Murray, D. (1987) *Cognition as Intuitive Statistics*, Hillsdale, NJ: Erlbaum.

Gigerenzer, G., Hoffrage, U. and Kleinbölting, H. (1991) Probabilistic mental models: a Brunswikean theory of confidence. *Psychological Review* 98, 506–28.

Gilovich, T., Vallone, B. and Tversky, A. (1985) The hot hand in basketball: on the misconception of random sequences. *Cognitive Psychology* 17, 295–314.

Gluck, M. and Bower, G. (1988) From conditioning to category learning: an adaptive network model. *Journal of Experimental Psychology: General* 117, 227–47.

Godfrey-Smith, P. (1994) A modern history theory functions. *Nous* 28, 344-62.

Goldman, A. (1986) *Epistemology and Cognition*, Cambridge, MA: Harvard University Press.

Gould, S. (1992) *Bully for Brontosaurus: Further Reflections in Natural History*, London: Penguin Books.

Griffiths, P. (1997) *What Emotions Really Are*, Chicago: University of Chicago Press.

Griggs, R. and Cox, J. (1982) The elusive thematic-materials effect in Wason's selection task. *British Journal of Psychology* 73, 407–20.

Haugeland, J. (1985) *Artificial Intelligence: The Very Idea*, Cambridge, MA: MIT Press.

Hertwig, R. and Gigerenzer, G. (1994) The chain of reasoning in the conjunction task. Unpublished manuscript.

Hirschfeld, L. and Gelman, S. (eds) (1994) *Mapping the Mind*, Cambridge: Cambridge University Press.

Hutchins, E. (1980) *Culture and Inference: A Trobriand Case Study*, Cambridge, MA: Harvard University Press.

Jackendoff, R. (1992). Is there a faculty of social cognition? In R. Jackendoff, *Languages of the Mind*, Cambridge, MA: MIT Press, 69–81.

Kahneman, D. and Tversky, A. (1973) On the psychology of prediction. *Psychological Review* 80, 237–51; rep. in Kahneman et al. (1982), 48–68.

—— (1996) On the reality of cognitive illusions. *Psychological Review* 103, 582–91.

Kahneman, D., Slovic, P. and Tversky, A. (eds) (1982) *Judgment under Uncertainty: Heuristics and Biases*, Cambridge: Cambridge University Press.

Karmiloff-Smith, A. (1992) *Beyond Modularity: A Developmental Perspective on Cognitive Science*, Cambridge, MA: MIT Press.

Lehman, D. and Nisbett, R. (1990) A longitudinal study of the effects of undergraduate education on reasoning. *Developmental Psychology* 26, 952–60.

Lehman, D., Lempert, R. and Nisbett, R. (1988) The effects of graduate education on reasoning: formal discipline and thinking about everyday life events. *American Psychologist* 43, 431–43.

Leslie, A. (1994) ToMM, ToBY, and agency: core architecture and domain specificity. In Hirschfeld and Gelman (1994), 119–48.

Lichenstein, S., Fischoff, B. and Phillips, L. (1992) Calibration of probabilities: the state of the art to 1980. In Kahneman et al. (1982), 306–34.

Manktelow, K. and Over, D. (1995) Deontic reasoning. In S. Newstead and J. St B. Evans (eds) *Perspectives on Thinking and Reasoning*, Hillsdale, NJ: Erlbaum, 91–114.

Marr, D. (1982) *Vision*, San Francisco: W. H. Freeman.

Neander, K. (1991) The teleological notion of "function." *Australasian Journal of Philosophy* 59, 454–68.

Nisbett, R. and Ross, L. (1980) *Human Inference: Strategies and Shortcomings of Social Judgment*, Englewood Cliffs, NJ: Prentice-Hall.

Nisbett, R., Fong, G., Lehman, D. and Cheng, P. (1987) Teaching reasoning. *Science* 238, 625–31.

Oaksford, M. and Chater, (1994) A rational analysis of the selection task as optimal data selection. *Psychological Review* 101, 608–31.

Piattelli-Palmarini, M. (1994) *Inevitable Illusions: How Mistakes of Reason Rule Our Minds.* New York: John Wiley & Sons.

Pinker, S. (1994) *The Language Instinct*, New York: William Morrow and Co.

—— (1997) *How the Mind Works*, New York: W. W. Norton.

Plantinga, A. (1993) *Warrant and Proper Function*, Oxford: Oxford University Press.

Pylyshyn, Z. (1984) *Computation and Cognition*, Cambridge, MA: MIT Press.

Pylyshyn, Z. and Demopoulos, W. (eds), (1986) *Meaning and Cognitive Structure: Issues in the Computational Theory of Mind*, Norwood, Ablex.

Quartz, S. and Sejnowski, T. (1994) Beyond modularity: neural constructivist principles in development. *Behavioral and Brain Sciences* 17, 725–6.

Samuels, R. (1998) Evolutionary psychology and the massive modularity hypothesis. *British Journal for the Philosophy of Science* 49, 575–602.

Segal, G. (1996) The modularity of theory of mind. In Carruthers and Smith (1995), 141–57.

Slovic, P., Fischhoff, B. and Lichtenstein, S. (1976) Cognitive processes and societal risk taking. In J. S. Carol and J. W. Payne (eds) *Cognition and Social Behavior*, Hillsdale, NJ: Erlbaum, 165–84.

Sperber, D. (1994) The modularity of thought and epidemiology of representations. In Hirschfeld and Gelman (1994), 39–67.

Sperber, D., Cara, F. and Girotto, W. (1995) Relevance theory explains the selection task. *Cognition* 57(1) 31–95.

Stein, E. (1996) *Without Good Reason*, Oxford: Clarendon Press.

Stich, S. (1990) *The Fragmentatiuon of Reason*, Cambridge, MA: MIT Press.

Sutherland, S. (1994) *Irrationality: Why We Don't Think Straight!*, New Brunswick, NJ: Rutgers University Press.

Tanenhaus, M., Dell, G. and Carlson, G. (1987) Context effects and lexical processing: a connectionist approach to modularity. In Garfield (1987), 83–108.

Tooby, J. and Cosmides, L. (1995) Foreword to Baron-Cohen (1995), pp. xi–xviii.

Trivers, R. (1971) The evolution of reciprocal altruism. *Quarterly Review of Biology* 46, 35–56.

Tversky, A. and Kahneman, D. (1981) Judgments of and by representativeness. In Kahneman et al. (1982), 84–98.

—— (1983) Extensional versus intuitive reasoning: the conjunction fallacy in probability judgment. *Psychological Review* 90, 293–315.

Wason, P. (1966) Reasoning. In B. Foss (ed.), *New Horizons in Psychology*, Harmondsworth: Penguin, 135–51.

Wilson, M. and Daly, M. (1992) The man who mistook his wife for a chattel. In Barkow et al. (1992), 289–322.

4

New Foundations for Perception

Michael Leyton

1 Introduction

In this chapter, we shall argue that current approaches to defining and investigating perception are founded on ideas that necessarily prevent these approaches from discovering the basic regularities governing the perceptual system. We shall develop a substantially different approach and show how this approach actually produces these basic regularities.

Perception has been defined in a number of fundamentally different ways, yielding theoretical frameworks based on fundamentally different constructs and empirical methodologies aimed at fundamentally different goals. For example, at one extreme, the Gestalt school and its contemporary followers regard perception essentially as a process of *grouping* the separate retinal stimuli together – a process that the perceptual system carries out by applying general criteria for obtaining the most economical organization of the stimulus array. Such criteria include "proximity" and "similarity"; that is, it is argued that the perceptual system groups together stimuli that are proximal and similar to each other. Consequently, the Gestalt school takes grouping as the fundamental construct and investigates issues related to the perceptual system's application of grouping criteria.

In contrast, consider the framework of computational vision. Throughout this paper, the term *computational* vision will refer not to *computer* vision, but to the *computational analysis* of vision. Computational vision (e.g., Marr 1982) regards perception as a system of rules aimed at the extraction of specific environmental information from specific features in the stimulus array. Therefore, computational vision is founded on an investigation of how specific environmental structures produce certain features in the retinal image. This investigation is then used by the researcher as a basis on which to discover the rules by which the perceptual system can use the image features to recover the environmental structures.

It is worth noting that the framework of the Gestalt school, in the particular, restricted way we described it above, differs from the framework of computational vision, in that the Gestalt school does not carry out an analysis of environmental structure. Furthermore, it believes that perceptual rules are aimed essentially at grouping and regards these rules as acting in a *general-purpose* capacity – that is, independently of whatever alternative environmental substructures might be responsible for the retinal features to be grouped.

In addition to the frameworks of the Gestalt school and computational vision, there are various other frameworks. For example, the framework of Gibson (1950) was a profoundly important precursor of computational vision, in that it placed crucial emphasis on grounding perceptual research on the analysis of environmental structure. However, researchers in computational vision (e.g., Marr 1982) argued that Gibson's system was deficient, in that it denied the need for actual computation. Gibson's framework and the frameworks of several other schools can be understood either as incomplete versions or as hybrids of the two systems described above – that of the Gestalt school and that of computational vision. As an example of a hybrid system, certain researchers in computational vision (e.g., Poggio et al. 1985) have argued that, at an intermediate level, perception carries out a "regularization" procedure – a process that is strongly reminiscent of the economy-of-organization process within the Gestalt approach. Thus, within a single framework, one might find a mixture of the two systems – that of the Gestalt school and that of computational vision.

Our purpose here is to argue that the various existing frameworks for understanding perception are fundamentally incorrect and actually obscure what is going on in perception. Research elaborated within these frameworks cannot, we argue, arrive at the underlying regularities of the perceptual system. Our intention is to provide a new framework that, we will argue, leads to a system of deep and surprising regularities.

2   The Fundamental Constructs

Any research framework is based on certain fundamental constructs. For example, as we shall see later, when we examine computational vision in detail, a fundamental construct of that framework – a construct taken from Gibsonian psychology – is that of *environmental surface*. Any rule used by the perceptual system is regarded as explained when a researcher shows how this rule yields, to the perceptual system, information about *surfaces in the environment*. The construct of surface therefore has an ultimate explanatory role. One can therefore say that surface is a fundamental construct of computational vision. Similarly, as noted above, the notion of *grouping* is a fundamental construct in the Gestalt framework.

We shall argue that, by choosing the notion of surface or grouping as a fundamental construct, the current frameworks prevent themselves from arriving at a genuine understanding of perception. These constructs should be regarded as secondary ones, derivable within a system that is grounded on still deeper and more important constructs. If, as is presently the case, one regards surface and grouping as "axiomatic" – that is, as nonderivable – then one obscures their derivation, and this has serious consequences, because, as we shall see, the derivation is the very one that is responsible for identifying the regularities of the perceptual system.

From where should more basic constructs come? We argue that all current frameworks for investigating perception fail to make use of this profound point: Perception is, fundamentally, a form of *memory*. The retinal array is *memory* of events in the environment. As memory, the retinal array is ultimately the same type of thing as any memory store within the brain. In particular,

A theory of perception must be grounded on a theory of memory

This is the fundamental idea to be explicated in this essay. In particular, we propose that, before one begins an analysis of perception, one must first develop a theory of memory. This proposal will determine the structure of the essay. Our theory of memory will be presented over the next six sections, and it is only then that we will be able to develop our theory of perception.

In order to introduce our theory of memory, we ask the reader to imagine now a situation in which one is walking along a road and one comes across a squashed aluminum can on the sidewalk. The fact that one sees the can as having been squashed means that one has interpreted it as memory of an event in the past – a squashing event. Furthermore, although one did not actually witness the past event, one is able to *infer* the event, given only the present condition of the can. In fact, one does so by examining certain of the present features of the can and explaining how those features were caused – that is, by explaining them as having been caused by a squashing process.

This situation contains all the crucial ingredients of the definition of memory that we will propose. First there is an *observer* that will interpret something as memory – that is, as holding information about the past. Second, the "thing" that will be interpreted as holding information about the past is always a *physical object*. For example, it could be a squashed aluminum can in the external environment of the observer or a piece of neuronal material that, within the observer, stores a memory of some past event. Third, the physical object must exist in the *present* of the observer – otherwise it cannot be used. Finally, the past, about which the object is interpreted as holding information, is the hypothesized past of the object itself. Most crucially, the object is converted into memory when the observer examines the present condition of the object and *causally explains* how certain features of this condition came about. Thus, our definition of memory is founded on the notion of *causal explanation*.

We can summarize the above points as follows:

> DEFINITION OF MEMORY: *A memory is a physical object that is in the present of some observer and that has features that the observer causally explains.*

In Leyton 1992, we examine this definition with respect to what it can tell us about cognition generally – an issue we will not pursue here. What is crucial here is to be certain that the definition works as a definition of *retinal memory*. We do this by observing that the definition implies that a *stimulus* can be memory, thus:

> For the observer, a stimulus is a state of a receptor. This means that the stimulus is a *physical object*, the receptor, at the moment of stimulation – that is, in the *present* of the observer. The visual system *causally explains* the state of the receptor by hypothesizing an external environment that determined the receptor's current state. Thus a stimulus fulfills all the conditions in the above definition of memory.

More rigorously, the retina is a physical object that has a state that is determined by a sequence of two *causal interactions*: Light, coming from a source, has causally interacted with the environment and then gone on to causally interact with the retina. In order to *see* the environment, the visual system must examine the retinal state and undo this history backwards in time. When the visual system has traced the history back through the earlier of the two causal interactions, it will have inferred the structure of the environment that interacted with the light. Thus, *seeing* involves the retracing of the causal history of the state of the physical object we call the retina.

Researchers in computational vision often speak of the retinal image as being *caused* by factors in the environment. For example, Marr (1982:41) lists four causal factors which are responsible for the properties of the image and regards the task of the visual system as sorting out those causal factors. What, therefore, is the difference between the view we shall elaborate here and that of contemporary computational vision?

The difference is this: Although there is some mention of causality in current theorizing, *causality plays no theoretical role*. For example, the construct of causality is actually omitted in describing the structure of the environment, because the structure, as described, is essentially a *geometric arrangement*. Ultimately, there is no actual *analysis* of causality, or any sense that an analysis of causality is required as a basis for a theory of perception. In the end, computational vision hypothesizes perceptual rules for inferring specific environmental factors without using the fact that what brings these factors together, and therefore allows their recovery, is the phenomenon of causality.

By contrast, the system we shall build here makes causality the central theoretical construct. Furthermore, since we are interested in how causality can be inferred – that is, how it can leave memory – our system is founded on an analysis of the relation between causality and memory. Most crucially, the perceptual rules we advance are not rules for the inference of *specific environmental factors*, as in contemporary computational vision, but rules for the inference of *causality generally*.

Before we begin to develop our theoretical system, we should note that the fact that this essay involves a critique of contemporary computational vision should not be taken to mean that we are opposed to the existence of any form of computational vision – that is, to the existence of a *computational analysis of vision*. Quite the contrary. Our intention here is to build a new form of computational vision – a computational analysis that is elaborated from foundations that are profoundly different from the foundations of contemporary computational vision. We shall see that, whereas the contemporary framework is built on an analysis of the environment, ours is built on an analysis of computation itself. This is because, ultimately, ours is built on an analysis of the very substance manipulated in a computation – namely, memory.

3 The History-Recovery Problem

To begin: In sections 3–8, we give a theory of how an object can be converted into memory, and in section 9 onwards, we apply this theory to understand how the retina can become memory – that is, how it is that one can *see*.

In order that a situation fulfill our definition of memory, one of the conditions that must be met can be described as follows: An individual observes a single state, which we will call the *present moment*. A certain structural ingredient of that moment allows the individual to "run time backwards" and recapitulate the processes that led to that moment. That is, the individual is able to recover history from x, where x is *atemporal and completely contained within the present*. We shall say that the individual is solving the *history-recovery problem*, which we will also call the *process-recovery problem*. In Leyton 1992 we argued that the history-recovery problem is basic to cognition generally – for example, to linguistics. However, the present chapter is devoted entirely to perception.

Now the recovered history consists of events that are of course prior to the present – for example, the squashing that was responsible for the current condition of the aluminum can. Thus, by definition, the recovered past – the actual squashing – can no longer be observed. That is, since actual observations can be made only in the present, the past is always inaccessible. This inacces-

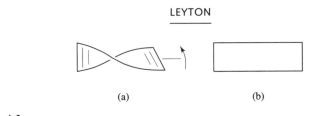

(a)   (b)

Figure 4.1

sibility forces a fundamental requirement on the ability to recover the past. We shall now turn to this requirement.

4   Process Directionality

Because the past is inaccessible, one can quite validly hypothesize any possible history. This is because there is no way of actually going back into the past to test a historical hypothesis. One therefore needs some consistent way of eliminating the arbitrariness – that is, of guaranteeing a unique choice of history. We shall say that one requires a means of guaranteeing *unique recoverability*.

The requirement of unique recoverability forces processes in the past to be psychologically represented in a particular way. To understand this means of representing processes, let us consider an alternative means of representation that does not allow unique recoverability.

Barr (1984) has developed representations of a number of common deformations – for example, twisting, bending, tapering, scaling. Consider his representation of *twisting*. Although this representation is expressed mathematically, it can be described intuitively as follows: Turn one end of the object with respect to the other.

For the process-recovery problem – that is, the problem of recovering history – there is a crucial difficulty with Barr's representation. Consider the object shown in figure 4.1a. Now twist it so that the right-hand end of the object is rotated by 90° in the direction shown by the arrow, while the left-hand end is held fixed. The result is shown in figure 4.1b. However, people presented with figure 4.1b. are unlikely to regard the latter as a twisted shape. Nevertheless, the progression from figure 4.1a to 4.1b was obtained by a twist in Barr's sense.

The problem is that deformation is psychologically a *unidirectional* phenomenon: it goes from straight objects to non-straight objects, not the reverse. But Barr's representation of twisting can be used in both directions.

The unidirectional nature of deformation can be understood as conforming to a principle of *prototypicality* due to Rosch (1975, 1978). Rosch found that non-prototypical objects are seen in terms of prototypical ones, but that the reverse tends not to occur. For example, off-red is seen in terms of red, diagonal orientations in terms of the vertical (or horizontal), the number 99 in terms of 100. However, the reverse relationships are not conceived: for example, red is not seen in terms of off-red. Now, returning to figure 4.1, we find that deformation also has this structure. That is, although one sees figure 4.1a as a twisted version of figure 4.1b, one does not see figure 4.1b as a twisted version of figure 4.1a.

We shall now see that, in order to carry out the recovery of process history, the mind requires a unidirectional definition of processes. To illustrate: If processes were to be understood as bi-directional, then figures 4.1a and 4.1b could both be understood as the starting state for the other. Suppose, then, that one wanted to recover the history of figure 4.1a. Then, one could hypothesize figure 4.1b in its past. But, due to bi-directionality, figure 4.1b could itself contain figure 4.1a in its past. However, this would mean that figure 4.1a could have both figure 4.1b and figure 4.1a in its past. Thus, one could regard figure 4.1a as originating from figure 4.1b or from figure 4.1a. The choice would be arbitrary. That is, bi-directionality prevents one from having *unique recoverability*.

5   The Fundamental Proposals

Having identified a basic requirement that a process-recovery system must satisfy, we shall now state our two fundamental proposals for the solution of the process-recovery problem. Our entire argument will be an elaboration of these proposals.

It is first necessary to note explicitly that the recovery of a process is possible only if it leaves a *memory*. While many types of processes leave memory, there are many types of processes that do not. In fact, there are many types of processes whose effect is to actually wipe out memory – for example, removing a stain. Observe that in these latter cases the processes cannot be recovered by an examination of their results. Only processes that leave memory can be recovered. This notion will soon be prolifically illustrated.

On a concrete level, there are many forms of memory that can be left on objects: scars on the surface of the moon, chips on vases, graffiti on subway trains, etc. However, we will claim that a single *abstract* property characterizes *all* perceptual situations of memory. This property is *asymmetry*. That is:

> *Asymmetry is the memory that processes leave on objects.*

Furthermore, we will also claim the following:

> *Symmetry is the abcense of process memory.*

The claim about asymmetry we will call the *Asymmetry Principle*, the claim about symmetry the *Symmetry Principle*. They will be stated more precisely at the end of this section.

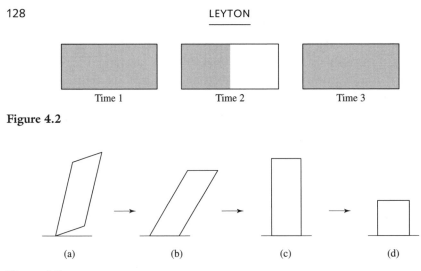

Figure 4.2

Figure 4.3

We shall now illustrate these two proposals in detail. Consider first a situation that is much discussed in physics: a tank of gas. Suppose that a tank of gas stands on a table in a room. Suppose also that the gas has settled to equilibrium – that is, that the gas is uniform through the tank, as shown at TIME 1 in figure 4.2. Uniformity is an example of symmetry. In the case being considered, every position in the tank is equivalent – that is, symmetric – to every other position. In particular, the gas configuration is reflectionally symmetric about the middle vertical line. Now use some means, such as a magnet, to cause the gas to move to the left side of the tank, as shown in TIME 2 in figure 4.2. The gas has become *asymmetrically* arranged. If a person came into the room at this point and saw the gas compressed into the left side like this, he or she would conclude that the gas had undergone movement to the left side. Thus, even though the person did not see the movement, the asymmetry acts as a *memory* of the movement.

Now let the gas settle again to equilibrium – that is, to uniformity throughout the tank, as shown at TIME 3. Suppose that, at this point, a person, who has not yet been in the room, now walks into the room. He or she would not jump to the conclusion that anything had happened to the gas. This is because, in returning to the symmetrical state, the gas has wiped out any memory of the event that previously occurred. That is, if one has symmetry in the present, one cannot deduce a past that is any different from it.

Now let us go to another illustration. The following phenomenon comes from a series of five psychological experiments that we described in Leyton 1986b. In those experiments we found that, when human subjects are presented with only a parallelogram oriented in the picture plane as shown in figure 4.3a they see the parallelogram in terms of a non-rotated one shown in figure 4.3b, which they then see in terms of the rectangle shown in figure 4.3c, which they then see in terms of the square shown in figure 4.3d. That is, given *only* the first shape, that shown on the far left of figure 4.3, their minds go through the entire sequence of shapes shown in the figure. It must be emphasized that the sequence is generated not by the experimenter, but by the subjects.

Examining this sequence, it seems that what the subjects are doing here is providing a process explanation for the first shape: that is, the shape in figure 4.3a is understood as having been obtained by rotating that in figure 4.3b off its horizontal base. This latter shape is understood, in turn, as having been obtained by skewing the rectangle in figure 4.3c. And the rectangle, in turn, is understood as having been obtained by stretching the square in figure 4.3d.

What is crucial to observe here is that the process history, backwards in time (from left to right), is given by successive symmetrization. In fact, if one compares any successive pair of shapes, the left-hand member of the pair has a single asymmetry that the right-hand member does not have. For example, the second parallelogram has unequal angles, whereas the rectangle, to the right of it, does not. Again, the rectangle has unequal sides, whereas the square, to the right of it, does not. On this view, it is an *asymmetry* at any stage that indicates that some process has acted; that is, each asymmetry is a *memory* of a prior event. By removing each asymmetry, one is able to go backwards through the events – that is, successively recover the past.

These examples enable us to understand how an asymmetry in the present can act as a memory of a process. The asymmetry is a memory of the process that *created* the asymmetry. That is, at some point in the past, the asymmetry did not exist; that is, there was symmetry, and the process replaced the symmetry with the current asymmetry. Realizing this allows us to state the Asymmetry Principle more precisely:

ASYMMETRY PRINCIPLE: *An asymmetry in the present is understood as having originated from a past symmetry.*

Now observe, in the sequence of shapes in figure 4.3, that once a symmetry has been gained – for example, equal angles, as in the rectangle – it is retained throughout the rest of the sequence, backwards in time; thus the equal angles gained in the rectangle are retained by the square. This means that, where a symmetry exists, it is assumed to have existed at all prior points. We saw that the tank of gas also illustrates this phenomenon. When the gas is uniform, as at TIME 3 in figure 4.2, a person entering the room for the first time will not hypothesize any past configuration that is different from what he or she sees. That is, a symmetry in the present is not a memory of anything other than itself. One can state this concept as follows:

SYMMETRY PRINCIPLE: *A symmetry in the present is understood as having always existed.*

An investigation of these two principles will be the subject of the entire chapter. We shall argue that they are the fundamental rules of perception.

Finally, we note that we will sometimes use the term "shape" and "asymmetry" interchangeably. This is because we regard the shape of an object as the collection of its asymmetries. Thus, when we propose that the asymmetries within an object constitute the ingredient from which history is extracted, we are proposing that it is the object's shape that allows the extraction of history.

6   Conforming to the Unidirectionality Requirement

Recall now that, because the past states – that is, the goal of the process-recovery problem – are inaccessible, one must have some means of insuring their uniqueness. Recall also that this implies that recoverable processes must be represented unidirectionally.

It is therefore necessary to check that the Asymmetry and Symmetry Principles do indeed allow unique recoverability and define processes unidirectionally. In fact, it is easy to see that they do, as follows.

We need first a definition of *symmetry*. Basic to the standard mathematical definition of symmetry is this: *Symmetry is indistinguishability*. For example, human faces are usually regarded as symmetric because the left side tends to be indistinguishable from the right side. Notice that, in this case, the indistinguishability can be defined only because one uses a reflection transformation to map the left side of the face onto the right side. Thus indistinguishability often exists by virtue of a transformation. Conversely: *Asymmetry is distinguishability*. For example, some faces are actually asymmetric because, for example, the left eyelid droops more than the right.

With these basic definitions of symmetry and asymmetry, let us return to the successive reference phenomenon shown in figure 4.3. Consider the first parallelogram (a). This shape has three crucial distinguishabilities:

(D1)   Its orientation is distinguishable from the gravitational orientation.
(D2)   Its vertices have two distinguishable sizes.
(D3)   Its sides have two distinguishable lengths.

Now observe that, in moving from this parallelogram to the next one, the first distinguishability is removed. Next observe that, in moving from the second parallelogram to the rectangle, the distinguishability between the vertex sizes is removed; that is, all vertex sizes become indistinguishable. Finally, observe that, in moving from the rectangle to the square, the distinguishability between the side lengths is removed; that is, all side lengths become equal.

Thus each successive symmetrization is the removal of a distinguishability. Note that the above illustrates the Asymmetry Principle, which claims that situations in which distinguishabilities can be found point to situations in which the distinguishabilities do not exist. It also illustrates the Symmetry Principle, which claims that an indistinguishability can be a memory of only itself; that is, at any point in the sequence of figure 4.3, a recovered indistinguishability remains for the rest of the sequence.

Now let us turn to the issue of unique recoverability. Observe that, for each situation with a distinguishability, one can define a unique situation which removes that distinguishability. Thus the Asymmetry Principle, which states that, from a situation with distinguishability, one recovers a situation which removes the distinguishability, allows unique recoverability. So does the Symmetry Principle, because, quite simply, it says that from a situation with indistinguishabilities, one recovers only the same.

We can now see that the two principles constrain processes to be defined unidirectionally: a process moved from symmetry to asymmetry, but not vice versa. This can be seen by looking at both principles. According to the Asymmetry Principle, a process moves from a past symmetry to a present asymmetry. If the reverse could happen, then a process could move from a past asymmetry to a present symmetry. However, the Symmetry Principle forbids this. It says that a symmetry in the present corresponds to the same symmetry in the past – that is, the absence of a process. Thus processes can go only from symmetries to asymmetries. Therefore, using the Asymmetry and Symmetry Principles *together* forces processes to conform to the unidirectionality requirement.

Apparent Counter-Example   At first it might appear to the reader that there is an apparent counterexample to the above principles: an object that is symmetric in the present, but which one *remembers* or *knows* or *assumes* to have been asymmetric in the past. As an example, one can, in the present, come across a straight rod that one knows to have been not straight in the past.

Close examination reveals, however, that, when described correctly, this type of apparent counterexample actually *conforms* to our memory principles. To understand how it does, we need a concept that will be introduced in section 8, at which time we will return to this problem and solve it.

Thermodynamics   The reader might think that we are simply reinventing the second law of thermodynamics. This is not the case. Consider the following example. A circular ring which is slanted with respect to the viewer will project as an ellipse on the viewer's retina. Nevertheless, the viewer will assume that the environmental shape is a circle. That is, the asymmetric shape, the ellipse, in the image, will be assumed to have come from a symmetric shape, a circle, in the environment. This is a use of the Asymmetry Principle, an asymmetry being traced back to a symmetry. However, it has nothing to do with thermodynamics, but is a simple consequence of projective geometry. This example will be discussed in detail later on, along with many examples that also have nothing to do with thermodynamics.

7   The Second System Principle

The Asymmetry Principle states that an asymmetry in the present is explained by a process that introduced that asymmetry from a previous symmetry. By *process*, we mean a *sequence of states* of the system undergoing the transition from past to present.

On this definition of process, the Asymmetry Principle makes no mention of the notion of *causality*: that is, what actually made the system undergo this change. We introduce the notion of causality via this next principle:

> SECOND SYSTEM PRINCIPLE: *Increased asymmetry over time can occur in a system only if the system has a causal interaction with a second system.*

It is crucial to understand that the Asymmetry Principle and the Second System Principle are completely independent principles. In order to understand this, let us see what the two principles would infer from an asymmetry in the present.

Observe that, on its own, the Second System Principle concludes absolutely nothing from an asymmetry in the present. It can form a conclusion only if it knows that the asymmetry originated from a symmetry. However, if it does not know whether the asymmetry originated in this way, then it can conclude nothing. In particular, it cannot say anything about events prior to the present. Thus, we can say that given even the *entire* present, the Second System Principle cannot conclude anything from it.

By contrast, the Asymmetry Principle, on its own, does produce a conclusion from an asymmetry in the present. It says that the asymmetry originated from a symmetry in the past. That is, the Asymmetry Principle makes a fundamental statement about the structure of the preceding history. Thus we can say that, given *only* the present, the Asymmetry Principle can conclude something about every single asymmetry in the present.

The Second System Principle can perform its job only after the Asymmetry Principle has been used. That is, once the Asymmetry Principle has established that there was a transition from symmetry to asymmetry over time, the Second System Principle can be brought in to infer something from this new piece of information: namely, that there must have been a causal interaction with a second system.

Besides the fact that the Second System Principle is subordinate to the Asymmetry Principle, we should observe that there is a clear division of labor between the two principles. The Asymmetry Principle deduces change in the structure of a system over time. However, it does not concern causality. By contrast, the Second System Principle does concern causality. But at a cost: it cannot deduce change in the structure of a system.

8   Recovery from Several States

In the examples of process recovery that we have examined so far, the information available in the present moment has been a *single state of a process*. For example, consider the situation in which, given a parallelogram, the mind infers a rectangle. The parallelogram is the *only* state that is presented. The inferred past state, the rectangle, is not contained within the present. Thus we shall say that the past is *external* to the present, and the type of inference used will be called *external inference*.

In some situations, however, the record left in the present moment is that of more than one state. For example, a scratch that has been left on a surface is a record of a sequence of states. Each of the points comprising the scratch is a result that was produced at a different time. Since the present contains the entire scratch, it contains records of a entire trace of past states. Most crucially, the past states are *represented within the present*. Thus, from the present – that is, the scratch – one infers past states that have records *within* the present. We shall therefore call this type of inference *internal inference*.

What rules does one apply to be able to carry out internal inference? The answer is that one applies the basic rules we proposed above. Therefore consider the scratch. Any two points on the scratch are distinguishable by *position*. Thus, by the Asymmetry Principle, which states that a distinguishability is seen as having arisen from an indistinguishability, the two points must have come from a situation in which they were not distinguishable by position; that is, there was only a single position: i.e., only one point. Applying the argument to all pairs of points on the scratch, one concludes that the whole trajectory of distinguishable points must have been generated from only one point, the starting point (see Leyton 1992: ch. 6 for the full inference procedure).

The example of a scratch illustrates that, with internal inference, the Asymmetry Principle is applied to the asymmetries *between* states – for example, the differences between the positions of the points along the scratch. By contrast, with external inference, the Asymmetry Principle is applied to asymmetries *within* a state. That is:

External inference concerns **intra**-state asymmetries.

Internal inference concerns **inter**-state asymmetries.

A more complex example of internal inference is the situation in which a doctor puts on a screen two X-rays of a tumor, one taken a month ago and one taken that day. The problem he is concerned with is that of inferring the history going from one state to the other. In this situation, the present contains records of more than one state of the object, the tumor, and the doctor is therefore concerned with inferring the *internal* history – that is, the history in which the past state (the tumor a month ago) has a record internal to the present. Because the history is internal, the doctor will solve this inference problem by applying the Asymmetry Principle to the *inter*-state asymmetries: that is, to the differences *between* the two states. Using our memory principles, a complete solution to this "doctor's problem" is derived in Leyton 1992: ch. 2.

Let us now return to the class of apparent counterexamples that were raised in section 6 against our memory principles. The counterexamples have this form: One comes across a symmetric object in the present that one remembers to have been asymmetric in the past; for example, one comes across a straight rod that one remembers as having been non-straight at some time in the past.

To see that such counterexamples are not in fact counterexamples at all, one must first ask oneself *what the present contains*. It is crucially important to observe that the present contains not only the current state of the object, but a memory of the past state of the object; for example, in the case of the rod, the present contains not only the current shape of the rod but also the *memory* of the past shape of the rod. This means that the present contains *records of two states of the object* – one coming from the observer's perceptual system, the other coming from the observer's memory structure. Even though these two records come from two different sources, the fact still remains that the observer has, within the present, the records of two states. However, if the present contains records of two states, then the situation is an example of *internal inference*. Thus the situation is formally like that where a doctor is looking at two X-rays of a tumor taken a month apart. Since the inference involved is *internal*, the Asymmetry Principle is therefore applied to the *inter*-state asymmetries, reducing them backward in time. That is, this situation conforms once again to our theory of memory.

If the reader wishes to understand these issues in greater depth, several hundred pages in Leyton 1992 are devoted to an analysis of internal inference, demonstrating in detail that it conforms to our four memory principles.

9   Perception

We have, in the previous sections, elaborated our basic rules for the use of objects as memory. We shall now argue that these rules constitute the fundamental rules of perception.

According to contemporary computational vision, the central problem of perception is this: The visual system is able to see the world using remarkably little information. The only information that is available is the two-dimensional array of stimuli on the retina. Yet, given this array, the perceptual system is able to create a three-dimensional representation of the environment.

Our purpose now is to offer a new set of foundations for the theory of perception and, in particular, for the computational analysis of perception. We

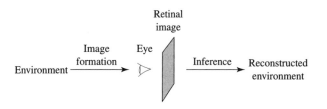

Figure 4.4

will argue that the theory of perception should be founded on the notion of *causality* and its relation to *memory*.

In sections 10–20, we shall go through several of the main principles and results of contemporary computational vision and show that they can be understood more deeply if they are subsumed under our general theory of causal inference. In fact, we shall argue that the main ideas and theoretical results of computational vision are simply instantiations of the general principles which we have elaborated for the recovery of process history. Since these general principles are based on the concept of *symmetry*, this will allow us to show that *all computational vision can be reduced purely to symmetry principles*. That is, we shall argue that the principles that best exhibit the computational regularities of the perceptual system are principles based on the notion of symmetry and its use in causal inference.

10 Contemporary Computational Vision

Let us first examine two of the basic aspects of contemporary computational vision: (1) the image-formation methodology and (2) the view that perception is the recovery of surfaces.

10.1   The image-formation methodology

In order to understand how the environmental structure can be recovered from the retinal image, it is currently believed that one should investigate how the image is related to the environment. Consider figure 4.4. It shows the following sequence of events from left to right. At the far left, one has the environment. This is projected onto the retina in the middle, represented here by a plane. All that the mind has available is the image on this plane. From this image, the mind tries to reconstruct the structure of the environment. That is, the mind tries to produce a reconstructed version of the environment, shown on the far right.

There are two stages involved in going from the far left to the far right in figure 4.4. The first is the projection of the environment onto the retinal image. This stage is generally called *image formation*. The second is that in which the mind *infers* the structure of the environment from the image. This stage is called the *inference stage*.

A basic principle of computational vision is that, in order to understand how the mind *infers* the structure of the environment from the image – that is, accomplishes the second stage – one should first understand what has happened in the first stage, the image formation. In fact, a basic claim in computational vision is that, in order to solve any problem concerning perception, the researcher must go through the following three-stage research program:

Stage 1:   Develop a theory of the environment independent of the observer.
Stage 2:   Develop a theory of how the environment is projected onto the observer's retina to create the image.
Stage 3:   Develop a theory of how the observer-independent environment can be recovered from the image.

Researchers who use this program will be said to be conform to the *image-formation methodology*.

10.2   Perception as the recovery of surfaces

An important idea in computational vision, one inherited from Gibson (1950), is that the primary goal of perception is the recovery of *surfaces* in the environment. It is argued that this is the case because, on the human level, environmental structure is primarily a structure of surfaces.

Surface structure is often referred to as *shape*: that is, the shape of objects and the spaces between them. Thus the primary role of perception is the recovery of environmental shape from the retinal image.

It is also argued that environmental shape is recovered from a variety of *cues*, or information sources, in the image. There are generally considered to be at least five main cues in the retinal image:

1   shading: the varying level of brightness across the retinal image
2   texture: the small-scale repetitive elements across the retinal image
3   contour: the lines (straight or curved) in the retinal image
4   stereo: the differences between the retinal image in the left and right eyes
5   motion: a moving pattern of light across the retinal image

Furthermore, it is usually assumed that the perceptual system can recover environmental shape from an image that consists of only one of these cues. For example, it is assumed that a person can recover shape from purely shading information, because certain black-and-white photographs consist of only shading information, and yet the person is able to see such a photograph as representing a three-dimensional object. Such "existence proofs" lead to the conclusion that the visual system can carry out five independent computations. They are the recovery of:

shape-from-shading
shape-from-texture
shape-from-contour
shape-from-stereo
shape-from-motion

where, in each of these shape-from-x recovery procedures, "shape" means three-dimensional environmental shape and "x" is an information source in the two-dimensional retinal image.

11   Modularity

Recall now that, according to the image-formation methodology in contemporary computational vision, the answer to any research question is solved by starting with an analysis of the environment, or what Gibson called the *ecology*. Thus the question of why the perceptual system is capable of solving the above five shape-from-x recovery problems independently is answered by an examination of the structure of the environment.

The belief is that the ecology, itself, is divided into a number of independent domains – a condition that we will call *ecological modularity*. The independence of these domains allows the visual system to be divided correspondingly into independent rule systems – a condition we will call *computational modularity*. For example, because the ecological factors that determine what one can call "shading" in the image are independent of the ecological factors that determine what one can call "texture" in the image, the visual system has a set of rules specifically designed to compute shape-from-shading and a separate set of rules that are specifically designed to compute shape-from-texture. The researcher can therefore solve the shape-from-shading problem independently of the shape-from-texture problem. The belief that the researcher can solve the shape-from-x problems independently of each other will be called *research modularity*.

The reader should observe carefully that the three modularities – ecological, computational, and research modularity – are mutually supporting and dependent. Belief in these three forms is a belief against which we will be offering strong evidence in this essay. We shall argue that a single construct underlies all ecological domains, the construct of *causality*. This allows the computational system to possess a single restricted set of rules across all domains – rules by which causality, generally, can be recovered. Thus, to

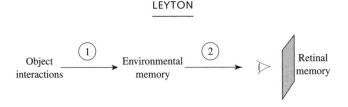

Figure 4.5

identify these rules, research must necessarily be research on all domains simultaneously.

Science, of course, attempts to find laws that maximally unify a field. Pylyshyn (1984) has shown that this principle can be used as a powerful tool to locate the appropriate *level* on which the cognitive system should be described. He says that "one is concerned to find the level at which the general principles . . . can be stated so as to maximize the domain's apparent systematicity" (p.93): or again, that one is concerned to find the "appropriate level on which the greatest regularity is to be found" (p. 108). This is our concern here. We argue that the three types of modularity to be found in contemporary computational vision exist because of an analysis of vision on the *wrong level*. When the analysis proceeds to the level that we define, the field becomes unified.

12   Causality and Computational Vision

Whereas the central recovered construct of contemporary computational vision is the *surface*, we argue that this construct should be replaced by that of *causality*. In our theoretical system, everything is *memory*, and something becomes memory when it is causally explained. In particular, the entire purpose of perception is to convert the retinal stimulus into memory.

We argue that perception structures this memory into two overall layers – layers that are phases of causal interactions. These phases are presented as the two arrows in figure 4.5. They are, respectively, as follows:

Phase 1: Object interactions → environmental memory   The first phase is indicated by the number 1 in figure 4.5. That is, the past consists of the interactions of environmental objects with each other – for example, rock hitting rock, foot kicking garbage can, hand crushing paper. (We exclude only those objects – photons – that constitute illumination.) These causal interactions leave environmental memory – for example, geological formations, dented garbage cans, crushed paper, etc. In fact, we will propose later that *everything* in the environment is perceptually defined as the memory of causal interactions.

Phase 2: Environmental memory → retinal memory   The second phase is indicated by the number 2 in figure 4.5. The objects that make up illumination – the photons – interact with environmental memory and proceed to interact with the retina, thus creating retinal memory.

The first phase will be called *environment formation*, the second, *image-formation*   It is important now to observe that contemporary computational vision is concerned with only phase 2, the phase called image formation, in which illumination projects the environmental structure onto the retina. In particular, the various recovery modules – shape-from-shading, shape-from-texture, shape-from-contour, etc. – are concerned purely with this phase.

13   What is the Present Environment?

The reason why researchers in current computational vision are concerned only with image formation is that they are concerned with how perception can reconstruct the *present* environment, the environment that sits immutably and unquestionably in front of the perceiver's eyes. These researchers are not interested in the reconstruction of the past. The past has no practical value to them. The past is no longer a reality and therefore need not be taken into account.

However, is the *present* environment actually in the present? Simple considerations reveal that what is called the present environment is actually in the *past*. That is, the projection process, by which light has traveled from the environment to the retina, has taken a *finite amount of time*. Therefore, the image that is created at the retina is of an environment that existed a finite amount of time previously, so an environment in the past.

One might object that the time traveled by light in moving from the environment to the retina is so short that it can effectively be ignored. But this is not true. We shall argue that it is fundamentally important to understand that the image-formation phase took a finite amount of time and that what is called the "present" environment is actually in the past. The reason is that *one cannot discover the regularities of the visual system if one assumes that the environment is in the present*. It is only by assuming the environment is in the past that the laws of perception become accessible. This is because the fundamental systematicities of the visual system are based on the fact that perception is a means of inferring the causal past: that is, perception is a form of memory.

We shall argue that there is, in addition, a serious problem with the view, in current computational vision, that perception is concerned *exclusively* with the image-formation phase. The problem is that one cannot obtain an understanding of the recovery of even this phase if one does not assume that perception attempts to recover the prior environment-formation phase. In particular, we

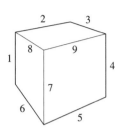

Figure 4.6

shall argue that perception cannot recover the image-formation phase without recovering the environment-formation phase.

To summarize, we will argue that there are two fundamental reasons why current computational vision is incorrect in assuming that perception is the recovery of the present environment:

1   Assuming that the environment is in the present prevents the researcher from identifying the regularities of the visual system.
2   Recovery of the image-formation phase is impossible without recovery of the previous environment-formation phase.

14   Three Layers of Asymmetry

The entire two-phase history described above involves three types of causal interactions which occur successively at the beginning, middle, and end of that history. Each introduces a new set of asymmetries into the history. Thus the image on the retina has three layers of asymmetry, as follows:

(1) Object asymmetries.   Environment-formation processes create the shapes of objects in the environment: for example, geological shapes, dented garbage cans, torn shirts, crushed newspapers, etc. By Leyton 1992, the shapes of these objects are a set of asymmetries, because any shape is a set of asymmetries.

(2) Illumination asymmetries.   Light interacting with an environmental object introduces a variation in brightness across the object. This brightness variation is an extra layer of asymmetry that is added to the surface of the object. That is, the surface is already asymmetric by virtue of its shape, as created by the environment-formation processes: but, in this new stage, the illumination asymmetries are then "painted" onto these surface asymmetries.

(3) Projective asymmetries.   Light, having left the environmental objects, projects onto the retina, creating an additional type of asymmetry: the *viewpoint asymmetries*. These asymmetries are illustrated in figure 4.6, which

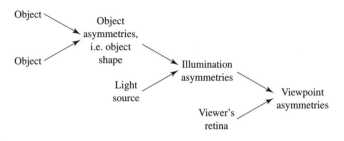

Figure 4.7

shows the retinal image of a cube. The nine visible edges were all equal in size in the environment, but projection has now made them all unequal in the image.

It is important to observe that, in accord with the Second System Principle (section 7), each of these layers of asymmetry is created by an interaction with an additional system. In (1), the object asymmetries are created by objects interacting with each other – for example, rock hitting rock, foot kicking garbage can, hands compressing paper. In (2), the illumination asymmetries are created by the interaction of the object shapes with a new system, the light rays. In (3), the viewpoint asymmetries are created when the light rays, reflected from the objects, interact with a new system, the viewer's retina. These successive interactions are diagrammed in figure 4.7. There are three successive pairs of converging arrows, from left to right, corresponding to the three stages. In each pair, the two arrows converge because they represent the fact that two systems are brought together in an interaction. The lower arrow in each pair introduces the new system in each case.

15   The Reinterpretation Thesis

In the last section we argued that there are three successive types of causal interactions in the history leading up to the retinal image, and that these interactions leave three layers of asymmetry on the image. We now propose that an image *is* a collection of asymmetries:

> IMAGE-IS-ASYMMETRY THESIS: *(1) The image is best characterized as a collection of asymmetries. (2) All perception should be regarded as the recovery of causal history from these asymmetries.*

It is in this way that the image is converted into memory.

In sections 16–22, we will attempt to corroborate this thesis first by examining it in relation to the image-formation phase and then by examining it in relation to the environment-formation phase.

The domain considered by current computational vision is the image-formation phase. Thus we will reinterpret the main principles and results of current computational vision within the framework we are developing here, showing that it is only by using this framework that one can discover that those principles and results are manifestations of much deeper regularities in the visual system.

Current computational vision, being concerned with the image-formation phase, takes as its main problem the recovery of surface structure – that is, the recovery of the *shape* of the environment. As we saw (section 10), current computational vision argues that environmental shape can be recovered from five major cues in the image: shading, texture, contour, stereo, motion. Correspondingly, researchers speak of five major recovery problems: shape-from-shading, shape-from-texture, shape-from-contour, shape-from-stereo, shape-from-motion. We shall argue the following:

> REINTERPRETATION THESIS: *(1) Each of the five major image cues of contemporary computational vision – shading, texture, contour, stereo, motion – is a type of* asymmetry. *(1) Each of the five major recovery procedures – shape-from-shading, shape-from-texture, shape-from-contour, shape-from-stereo, shape-from-motion – is the recovery of* history from an asymmetry – *that is, an instantiation of the* Asymmetry Principle.

The two parts of the Reinterpretation Thesis are instantiations of the two parts of the Image-is-Asymmetry Thesis (above). In sections 16–20, we shall validate this thesis by going through the five major shape-from-*x* problems in turn.

16 Shape-from-Shading

Shape-from-shading is the ability to recover the three-dimensional structure of the environment from an image consisting purely of shading. For example, given a black-and-white photograph, human beings can instantly recover from it the three-dimensional object that was photographed.

It is argued that the capacity to make this recovery is dependent on the following: Consider what happens when a flux of light rays coming from a distant light source hits a planar surface of some specific size. If the plane faces the light source directly, as shown in figure 4.8a, it will capture the maximum possible number of light rays. The more the plane is turned away from the source, the fewer light rays will hit the surface, as shown in figures 4.8b and 4.8c. With fewer light rays spread over the same area, the rays will be less dense, so the surface will appear darker. This is the reason why brightness is different on different parts of a mountain range: The different parts have different orientations with respect to the light.

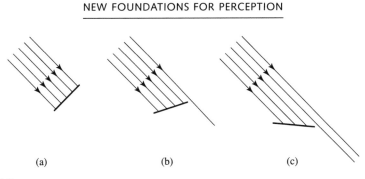

(a)   (b)   (c)

Figure 4.8

There is therefore a correspondence between *orientation* (with respect to the light source) and *brightness*, because there is a correspondence between the orientation and the density of rays illuminating the surface. Thus the visual system can use brightness to infer the orientation of different parts of a surface relative to the light source.

However, what is important to emphasize now is that this inference is actually a use of the Asymmetry Principle, as follows: First, in making the inference, the viewer assumes that before hitting the surface, the flux of rays was *uniform* – that is, symmetric under translations across the cross-section (figure 4.8a). This assumption is needed for the following reason. Let us consider the example of the mountain range in the sunlight. The density of light rays arriving at the retina from the mountain range varies across the retina. The viewer can attribute this varying density to the varying orientation on the mountain range only by assuming that the density was *uniform* prior to its hitting the mountain range; that is, the viewer must assume that the mountain range was responsible for the varying density hitting the eye. If the light could have had non-uniform density before hitting the mountain range, then the viewer would not be able to know which aspect of the varying density reaching the eye was due to the interaction of the light with the object and which aspect was due to the prior variation in density. Thus the viewer would not be able to make the correspondence between density on the retina and orientation on the mountain range.

The crucial point we wish to make now is this: While the uniformity assumption is standardly understood to be a tool that allows *specifically* the recovery of shape from shading, it is actually a *general* assumption in the inference of the *past* and *causality*: that is, the use of anything as *memory*. In fact, close examination reveals that it is an instantiation of the Asymmetry Principle, which states that an asymmetry in the present originated from a symmetry in the past. That is, the recovery of shape from shading is founded on the assumption that asymmetries in the light flux on the retina originated from symmetries in the light flux at some point in the past.

Observe that not only is the Asymmetry Principle fundamental to shape-from-shading, but so is the Second System Principle. According to the latter, the conversion of the past uniform flux into the present non-uniform flux

Figure 4.9

must have been due to a causal interaction with some second system that asymmetrized the flux. This second system is, of course, the environmental shape. Thus, according to our view, shape-from-shading is the recovery of the structure of the second system that can explain the asymmetrization of the flux density.

17   Shape-from-Texture

17.1   Projective asymmetrization

We have proposed that the theory of perception should be founded on the notion of *causality*. Recall that an image is formed on the retina because two causal interactions have taken place: Light has interacted with an object and has subsequently interacted with the retina. Close examination of the discussion in the previous section reveals that, in shape-from-shading, one considers the consequences only of the first of these causal interactions: the interaction of the light flux with the object and the resulting asymmetrization. We now consider the consequences of the second interaction: that occurring when the light is projected from the object onto the retina.

The process of projection adds an extra layer of asymmetry. This layer is crucial to the recovery of both shape-from-texture and shape-from-contour. Thus, we will examine this asymmetrization before examining, individually, these two recovery problems.

The layer of asymmetry added by the projection process has two separate components, which we will now discuss in turn.

17.2   Compression

Consider a plane consisting of a square grid, as shown in fig 4.9. Now let us imagine that this grid is slanted with respect to the viewer, and that we are looking at the grid and the viewer from the side, as shown in figure 4.10a. That is, the dots along the grid, on the right, show the positions of the horizontal grid lines. The plane on the left represents the image plane in the viewer.

Parallel rays

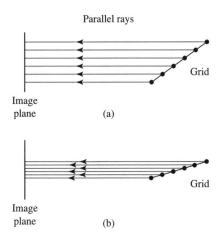

Grid

Image
plane   (a)

Grid

Image
plane   (b)

Figure 4.10

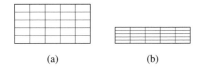

(a)   (b)

Figure 4.11

Now suppose that the grid lines are projected by parallel rays onto the image plane, as shown in figure 4.10a. We can see by comparing figure 4.10a with figure 4.10b that the greater the slant in the surface, the closer the parallel rays will be. Thus, greater slant causes the horizontal grid lines to be more compressed in the image. Figures 4.11a and 4.11b show how the grid appears in the image (to the viewer) in the two cases shown in figure 4.10. That is, figure 4.11a shows that the horizontal grid lines appear compressed due to the amount of slant in figure 4.10a, and figure 4.11b shows that the horizontal grid lines appear still more compressed when the slant is increased, as in figure 4.10b.

Observe, however, that the vertical grid lines are not compressed in either figure 4.11a or figure 4.11b. This is because there is no slant across these lines. We are therefore led to the following conclusion:

> *The slanting of a plane with respect to the retina causes the following* asymmetry *in the retinal image: Compression occurs in the direction of slant, and no compression occurs in the perpendicular direction.*

17.3   Scaling

Figures 4.10a and 4.10b show the process of projection as it occurs with parallel rays. In fact, in human perception, rays converge, because projection

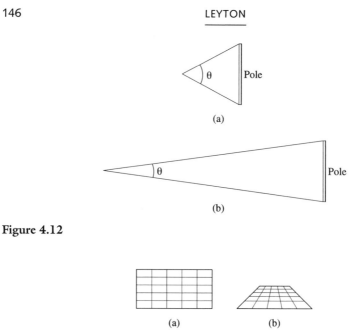

Figure 4.12

Figure 4.13

takes place via a lens. The compression effect described above still occurs: but an additional asymmetry is introduced due to the converging process.

Consider figure 4.12a. At the right of the figure is a pole sticking vertically out of the ground. The figure shows two rays, one from the top, the other from the bottom of the pole, travelling towards the left and converging there at the lens. The angle between the two rays is given by θ. Now take the pole and stick it in the ground further away from the viewer, as shown in figure 4.12b. The angle between the two rays will be much smaller. The consequence is that the pole will appear much smaller in the image on the retina. This size reduction is usually known as *scaling*. We are therefore led to the following conclusion:

> *The projection process adds a second asymmetry to the image: Objects of equal size in the environment become unequal in size in the image (in a manner that depends on their distance from the viewer).*

17.4   The total asymmetry

The asymmetry created by the projection process is the sum of the asymmetry that constitues the compression effect and the asymmetry that constitutes the scaling effect. Figure 4.13a shows the compression effect, and figure 4.13b adds the scaling effect, demonstrating the visual power of the combined asymmetries.

Having examined the asymmetries added by the projection process, let us now consider shape-from-texture, then shape-from-contour.

17.5   Texture and uniformity

Texture is generally understood to be the repeated occurrence of some visual primitive over some region. Thus, a texture consists of a two-level structure:

1   a primitive
2   a placement structure – that is, a structure that determines where the primitives are placed

Each of these levels has its own organization (Rosenfeld 1971, 1975; Rosenfeld and Lipkin 1970: Rosenfeld and Strong 1971; Rosenfeld and Milgram 1972; Haralick 1978). In projecting an environmental texture onto the retina, the texture becomes compressed and scaled in the manner described in sections 17.2 and 17.3. The recovery of shape-from-texture consists of removing the compression and scaling from the image and returning the texture to its uniform environmental state. Thus, suppose the image on the retina consists of the structure shown in figure 4.13b. A human being easily assumes that this structure corresponds to a square grid in the environment. Thus, human perception removes scaling and compression from the lines and shapes in figure 4.13b and produces the *uniform* structure of lines and shapes in a square grid. This applies not just to simple shapes, such as planes, but to complex shapes, such as the American flag waving in the wind. *In the retinal image*, the texture – that is, the stripes on the flag – are compressed and scaled at different points, because the flag has varying slant and distance across it. However, the viewer assumes that the stripes, on the flag *in the environment*, are uniform.

17.6   Shape-from-texture as the recovery of time

We shall now argue that these standard concepts from computational vision are, on a deeper level, examples of our theory of causal inference.

We have seen that the recovery of shape from texture works by the assumption, in the visual system, that compression and scaling of texture in the image correspond to a uniform texture in the environment. However, this correspondence has a *temporal* basis. The projection process *started* with a uniform texture in the environment and *finished* with a non-uniform one in the image. This means that the inference of the visual system, in going from the non-uniform image texture to the uniform environmental texture, is a process of going backward in time – that is, of recovering the *past*. Therefore, the assumption of a uniform texture in the environment is an instantiation of the Asymmetry Principle, which states that an asymmetry in the present is assumed to have arisen from a symmetry in the past.

Several different methods have been developed in the literature for recovering shape-from-texture. Examination of each of these methods, however, reveals that each is based on a uniformity assumption: an assumption that the texture was uniform prior to projection. Each method concentrates on a different structural aspect of the notion of texture and designates that aspect to be uniform prior to the projection process. Each method is therefore an example of the Asymmetry Principle, because each is an assumption that an asymmetry in the present arose from a symmetry in the past.

Below are listed the several different uniformity assumptions used in the several shape-from-texture methods.

1   *Uniform density* (Gibson 1950)   Non-uniform density of texture elements in the image is assumed to have arisen from uniform density of texture elements in the environment.
2   *Uniform boundary-lengths* (Aloimonos 1988)   Texture elements with non-uniform boundary lengths in the image are assumed to have arisen from texture elements with uniform boundary lengths in the environment.
3   *Uniform spatial-frequency* (Bajcsy and Lieberman 1976)   Non-uniform spatial frequency across the image is assumed to have arisen from uniform spatial frequency across the environmental surface.
4   *Uniform-sized texture elements* (Stevens 1981)   Texture elements of non-uniform size in the image are assumed to have arisen from texture elements of uniform size in the environment.
5   *Uniform spacing* (Kender 1979)   Texture elements with non-uniform spacing in the image are assumed to have arisen from texture elements of uniform spacing in the environment (in fact, a square grid).
6   *Uniform tangent direction* (Witkin 1981)   For irregular texture elements, such as blotches, the tangents to each boundary point on the element have an arbitrary direction – that is, there is uniform statistical probability across the range of possible directions. Non-uniform distribution of directions in the image is assumed to have arisen from uniform distribution in the environment.
7   *Symmetric texture elements* (Ikeuchi 1984)   Non-symmetric texture elements in the image are assumed to have arisen from symmetric ones in the environment.

In conclusion, we observe that, even though each of the above uniformity assumptions concerns a different structural factor, each is nevertheless an instantiation of the Asymmetry Principle; that is, each is the assumption that an asymmetry in the present originated from a symmetry in the past.

17.7 How many uniformity assumptions?

There has been much controversy in computational vision as to which uniformity assumption is correct. Each uniformity assumption is usually introduced by a researcher who also argues that some previous uniformity assumption cannot be valid (e.g., Witkin 1981).

However, we shall now see that, in fact, there are logically only two possible uniformity assumptions, and that the many uniformity assumptions in the literature are each examples of only these two. This, in turn, will allow us to understand more fully the fundamental role of the Asymmetry Principle in shape-from-texture. The two types of uniformity assumption follow from the two types of effects that the projection process has on texture: *compression* and *scaling*. Let us consider these again:

Compression As illustrated in figure 4.13a, compression causes squashing along one direction and leaves the perpendicular direction unchanged. Because compression alters the length-to-width ratio, it destroys any *rotational symmetry* in the original environmental surface (rotational symmetry means indistinguishability under rotations).

Scaling Scaling causes squashing in all directions, by the same amount. Thus its effects can be observed only if it occurs in different amounts at different positions across the image. For example, in the grid in figure 4.13b, scaling has occurred in greater amounts towards the top. Thus, to have evidence that scaling took place, one has to translate an element at some position in the image (e.g., at the bottom) to another position (e.g., the top) and see whether it is the same size as the element at the second position. If it is not, then a *translational symmetry* does not exist in the image (translational symmetry means indistinguishability under translations). Thus, to hypothesize that scaling actually took place in the image, one has to assume that *translational* symmetry existed prior to the projection process.

Each of the seven uniformity assumptions listed in the previous section is an example of one of these two assumptions: rotational symmetry or translational symmetry. In fact, the first five listed are examples of translational symmetry, and the last two are examples of rotational symmetry. Note that the last two are the statistical and deterministic versions, respectively, of the same assumption.

18 Shape-from-Contour

Because shape-from-contour concerns the same causal interation, projection, as shape-from-texture, a number of the shape-from-texture methods serve also as shape-from-contour methods. It is worthwhile, in particular, considering the method of Witkin (1981), mentioned above in the list of shape-from-texture methods. Witkin's method is appropriate for irregular shapes such as coastlines viewed obliquely from an airplane. He observes that an oblique image of an irregular coastline is not entirely irregular: the directions along the contour tend to be prejudiced towards the slant axis, due to the compression effect of slant. This means that all directions are not equally likely. Thus Witkin recovers the shape of the coastline in the *environment* by hypothesizing it to be one in which all directions are equally likely; that is, the environmental coastline is completely irregular. However, the equal likelihood condition, or maximal irregularity, is actually statistical *symmetry*. Thus, his method is a statistical instantiation of the Asymmetry Principle; that is, statistical asymmetry in the image coastline is assumed to have arisen from statistical symmetry in the environmental coastline.

Let us now consider a rather different type of method for the recovery of shape-from-contour, that due to Kanade (1981). Kanade proposes the following rule, called the Non-Accidentalness Rule:

> NON-ACCIDENTALNESS RULE: *Regularities observable in the image are not by accident, but are some projection of real regularities.*

Related proposals have been made by Lowe and Binford (1981); Lowe (1985); Witkin and Tenebaum (1983); and Rock (1983).

We shall soon see that by "regularities", Kanade means *symmetries*. Thus Kanade's rule states that a *symmetry* in the image arises from a *symmetry* in the environment.

Once again, close examination reveals that this rule must actually be a rule about time. It can be reformulated as saying that, *in going backwards in time*, a symmetry in the image arose from a symmetry in the environment. Thus Kanade's rule is actually an example of the Symmetry Principle which states that a symmetry is preserved backwards in time.

One example that Kanade gives of this rule is a rule for parallel lines (1981: 423):

> PARALLEL LINES RULE: *If two lines are parallel in the image, they depict parallel lines in the environment.*

Since parallelism is simply an example of a type of symmetry (indistinguishability under translation), this rule can easily be seen to be an example of the

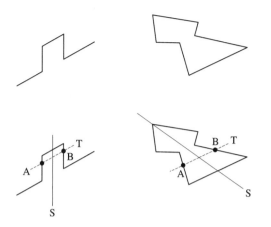

Figure 4.14

Symmetry Principle; that is, translational symmetry is preserved backwards in time.

A more complex rule that Kanade subsumes under the above Non-Accidentalness Rule is worth considering in detail.

Kanade develops a means for handling contours that have "skewed symmetries." Two examples are shown along the top in figure 4.14. Each has the following property: Points along the contour are equidistant, about some central axis, to points on the other side of the axis. The axis is labelled S in each of the figures, as shown along the bottom of the figure. The crucial aspect of skewed symmetry is that the line connecting symmetrical points is not at right angles to the axis; for example, in each figure, the line labeled T connects a pair of symmetrical (equidistant) points A and B on the contour. In a true reflectional symmetry, the transverse line T would be perpendicular to the symmetry axis S.

Kanade proposes the following heuristic concerning skewed symmetries in the image (1981:424):

> SKEWED SYMMETRY RULE: *A skewed symmetry depicts a real symmetry viewed from some (unknown) view direction.*

That is, in the *image*, a contour that contains a skewed symmetry (e.g., figure 4.14) corresponds to a contour in the *environment* that has a true reflectional symmetry.

We shall now see that this rule is a consequence of both the Symmetry Principle and the Asymmetry Principle, as follows.

Symmetry principle   Kanade's Skewed Symmetry Rule implies that a particular symmetry property of the image contour – namely, equidistance of points from a central axis – corresponds to the same property in the environmental contour – namely, equidistance of points from a central axis. This, of course,

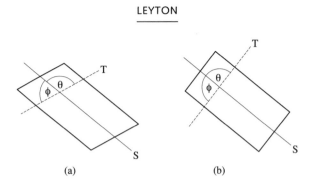

Figure 4.15

is an example of the Symmetry Principle, which states that a symmetry in the present is preserved backwards in time.

Asymmetry principle   Kanade's Skewed Symmetry Rule also implies that the *oblique* transverse line, T (figure 4.14), of a skewed symmetry in the image corresponds to a *perpendicular* transverse line in the environment. A crucial aspect of this correspondence is revealed by considering figure 4.15a. In the skewed symmetry in figure 4.15a, the transverse line T makes two different angles, θ and ϕ, to the symmetry axis S. However, in the case of a real symmetry, as shown in figure 4.15b, the transverse line, T, makes only one angle, 90°, to the symmetry axis. Thus, in going from a skewed symmetry to a real symmetry, the two *different* angles θ and ϕ become equal. That is, distinguishability is lost between the angles. However, observe now that, in going from the skewed symmetry in the image to the real symmetry in the environment, one is going backward in time. This means that, in going backwards in time, distinguishability between the angles θ and ϕ is lost. This accords with the Asymmetry Principle, which states that an asymmetry in the present originates from a symmetry in the past.

Thus Kanade's Skewed Symmetry Rule follows from our Symmetry Principle and Asymmetry Principle, in the following way. It accords with the Symmetry Principle in that the *symmetry content* (equidistance of points) of the skewed symmetry is preserved backwards in time. It accords with the Asymmetry Principle in that the *asymmetry content* (distinguishable angles θ and ϕ) becomes symmetrized backwards in time.

Let us now consider another method for recovering shape-from-contour, due to Brady and Yuille (1983). This method handles a larger number of situations than Kanade's, but again, as we shall see, conforms to our principles.

Observe first that in Kanade's Skewed Symmetry Rule an ellipse in the image would be interpreted as having the same shape in the environment, because an ellipse is a pure reflectional symmetry, not a skewed symmetry. However, people tend to interpret an ellipse in the image as a slanted circle in the environment. The more general method of Brady and Yuille handles both situations such as ellipses and skewed symmetries.

Brady and Yuille base their model on the observation, discussed earlier, that projection causes compression and thus converts a radially symmetric object, such as a circle, into a radially asymmetric object, such as an ellipse. This, of course, is an example of our proposal, in section 17.7, that the general effect of compression is the destruction of *rotational* symmetry – whether this be radial symmetry in a regular shape or statistical symmetry in the tangents of an irregular coastline.

Brady and Yuille propose using a standard measure of radial symmetry, $\frac{\text{Area}}{(\text{Perimeter})^2}$, to recover the environmental shape. The hypothesized environmental contour would be the contour that maximizes this measure. For example, on this measure, an ellipse in the image is explained by a circle in the environment, a parallelogram in the image is explained by a square in the environment, and a non-equal-sided triangle in the image is explained by an equal-sided triangle in the environment. Observe that, in each case, the resulting environmental shape is the radially symmetric version of the shape in the image. Again, because the rule of Brady and Uille converts a radially asymmetric shape in the image into a radially symmetric shape in the environment, it is an instantiation of the Asymmetry Principle and should be interpreted as a rule about the recovery of time – that is, as a rule for the construction of memory.

19 Stereo and Motion

In contrast to the above shape-from-x problems, only the briefest discussion is required to show that *stereo* and *motion* are examples of the Asymmetry Principle.

Consider, first, recovery from *stereo*. The two eyes each have a view of some object. We will consider, for the moment, the simplest possible object, a dot. Thus the image in the left eye is a single dot, and the image in the right eye is a single dot. The assumption made by the perceptual system is that these *two* dots, one in one eye and one in the other, arose from a *single* dot in the environment, as illustrated in figure 4.16. This means that a distinguishability, two dots, is converted into an indistinguishability, one dot.

Now since the removal of this distinguishability is actually the recovery of the *past* – that is, the two separate dots were once a single dot in the environment; thus the upward direction in figure 4.16 represents the reversal of time – stereo perception clearly conforms to the Asymmetry Principle, which states that a distinguishability in the present – the separate image dots – arose from an indistinguishability in the past – the single environmental dot.

Of course, the same argument applies not just to dots but to complex objects and whole scenes. For example, a scene is represented by two images, one in each eye. The distinguishability between the two image scenes is

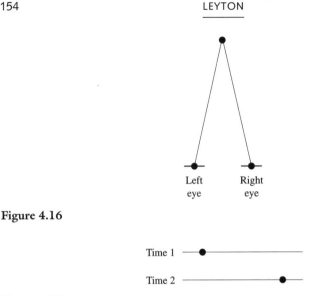

Left   Right
eye   eye

Figure 4.16

Time 1 ———●————————————————

Time 2 ————————————————————●———

Figure 4.17

removed backwards in time to create a single scene – in accord with the Asymmetry Principle.

Now let us consider the computation of *motion*. In this case one has different images occurring in the *same* eye over time. Figure 4.17 represents the fact that the images occur in a single eye by putting the images one below the other. The downward direction in figure 4.17 gives the successive images over time.

Again we consider the simplest possible object, a dot. It has some position at time 1, as shown in figure 4.17. If motion takes place, then a different image is produced at a later time, time 2, and the dot is in another position, as shown in figure 4.17. In the perception of motion, one assumes that the first dot *is* the second in a prior position. This inference conforms to the Asymmetry Principle: A distinguishability, the two dots, is explained as having arisen from an indistinguishability, the single dot.

Thus, stereo perception and motion perception are fundamentally similar: the distinguishability between two images is removed backwards in time, in accord with the Asymmetry Principle. For example, two dots are understood as having arisen from one dot.

It is important to observe that the difference between stereo and motion perception is exactly our distinction, given in section 8, between *external* and *internal* inference. To understand this, consider figure 4.16 again. As illustrated, stereo takes two images and infers a past that is *outside* the two images. In fact, the past is literally *out* in the environment. Since the inferred past is not within the images, stereo perception is an example of what we call *external* inference. In contrast, consider figure 4.17. As illustrated, motion perception takes two images and infers a past that is one of those images; that is, one of the dots is assumed to have been an earlier state of the other. This means that

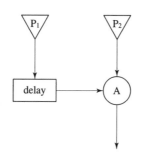

Figure 4.18

the past is *contained within* the set of images. Therefore, motion perception is an example of *internal* inference.

We conclude, therefore, that stereo and motion perception are, respectively, *external* and *internal* versions of the removal of distinguishability between two images.

Finally the reader might object that motion does not conform to our definition of the history-recovery problem – that is, the recovery of history from only the *present*. Motion seems to require observing also a previous moment. However, the past can never be observed. It is only the present that can ever be observed – an issue discussed in detail in Leyton 1992. Indeed, when one examines the structure of motion detectors, one finds that they are constructed in conformity with this constraint. Consider, for example, the mechanism that was proposed by Hassenstein and Reichardt (1956: Reichardt 1961) as a model for detectors in the visual system of the fly. This model is depicted in figure 4.18. At the top of the figure, two receptors are shown, one at position P_1 and the other at position P_2. The receptors are one unit distance apart. When a stimulus crosses a receptor, at the top of the figure, the receptor gives a response which is sent along the downward fiber from the receptor. Now consider a stimulus traveling from left to right across the two receptors, and suppose the stimulus is traveling at the speed of one unit distance per one unit time. The stimulus first passes P_1 which sends its response downward. However, this response is delayed, for one unit time, by the delay cell shown in the figure. Meanwhile, the moving stimulus continues along the top and passes over the second receptor P_2, which then sends its response down its own fiber. But because the response from the first receptor P_1 has been delayed by one unit time, the response from P_1 arrives at the cell labeled A at the same time as the response arrives from receptor P_2. The cell A fires in exactly this situation, when it receives a response *simultaneously* from both the delay cell and P_2. This means that the cell A possesses, with the *present* moment, the present response of receptor P_2 and the past response of receptor P_1 represented within the *present* by the delay cell. The cell A therefore observes a present, the delay cell and P_2, that has exactly the same structure as a scratch (recall our discussion of a scratch in section 8).

In conclusion, we can see that motion perception is made possible by giving the present a multi-state interpretation, in strict accordance with our definition of internal inference.

20   The Three-dimensional Problem in Motion

From the two-dimensional movement of light across the retina, the perceptual system must infer the structure of the three-dimensional object out in the environment that is creating the retinal movement.

When a three-dimensional object moves in the environment – for example, rotates – the two-dimensional image that it produces is often one of complex deformation. For example, when a sculpture rotates in the environment, its two-dimensional silhouette in the image deforms in such a way that different regions of the outline fluctuate in and out at different rates. It is remarkable that, from this flat deforming image, the perceptual system can recover a unique three-dimensional object.

To make this recovery, the perceptual system appears to use a rule proposed by researchers such as Wallach and O'Connell (1953) and Ullman (1979, 1984). The rule is that the hypothesized environmental object should be as *rigid* as possible. That is, although the distances between the points on the two-dimensional image might be changing to quite an extent, the distances between the corresponding points on the original three-dimensional shape are changing as little as possible. For example, the complex *deforming* image produced by a rotating sculpture is seen as the image of a three-dimensional sculpture having a *fixed* shape in the environment.

It is important to recognize that the maximizing rigidity constraint is an instantiation of the Asymmetry Principle in an interesting way. Up till now, we have seen that motion conforms to the Asymmetry Principle, in that different positions of an object are explained as having arisen temporally from a single position; that is, the different positions are understood as a *trace* starting from the initial position in the same way that the different points on a scratch are understood as a trace starting from one of the points. Thus, in motion, we have so far used the Asymmetry Principle to make *internal* inferences.

Now, the maximizing rigidity constraint also conforms to the Asymmetry Principle, but does so via *external* inference. The constraint states that changing distances in the image arise from fixed distances (rigidity) in the environment, and thus the constraint conforms to the Asymmetry Principle, because asymmetries in the image are being explained as having arisen from symmetries in the environment. However, the environment is outside the image; that is, the environmental configuration is not one of the states within the image. Thus inference of the environmental configuration is an example of external inference.

This means that in the recovery of environmental shape from motion in the

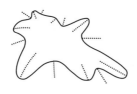

Figure 4.19

image the Asymmetry Principle is being used in two ways: *internally*, in structuring a set of positions as a trace across the image, and *externally*, in taking the image trace and removing distinguishability from the trace itself, by moving the trace backward in time until it becomes the trace of the object in the environment.

21   Environment Formation

Recall now that we have divided the entire history leading up to the image into two phases: (1) the image-formation phase and (2) the prior environment-formation phase. In sections 9–20, we examined the image-formation phase and showed that its perceptual recovery is based on a single restricted set of rules – rules based on the construct of *symmetry* and its violation *asymmetry*. In this and the next section, we turn to the environment-formation phase and show that its recovery is based on exactly the same set of rules. Subsequently, we will show that the recovery of environment formation is indeed carried out by the perceptual system and is essential for the recovery of image formation.

We shall consider how human beings extract history from complex natural shapes, such as embryos, tumors, clouds, etc. In Leyton 1988, 1989, we proposed that certain features of such shapes are particularly important for the extraction of history. These features are the *curvature extrema* – those points of extreme bend or extreme flatness in the outlines of such shapes. We proposed two rules by which the extraction of history takes place. The first is a theorem that was proved in Leyton 1987b.

SYMMETRY – CURVATURE DUALITY THEOREM: *Any section of curve that has only one curvature* extremum *has only one symmetry axis. This axis terminates at the* extremum.

The rule is illustrated in fig 4.19, where the shape has fourteen *extrema*, and therefore has fourteen axes associated with, and terminating at, those *extrema*. (The axes are the dotted lines shown.)

The second rule is a psychological principle that was proposed in Leyton 1984, 1986a, 1986c, 1987a, for which there is extensive supporting evidence in the areas of shape perception and motion perception.

INTERACTION PRINCIPLE: *Symmetry axes are the directions along which processes are hypothesized as most likely to have acted.*

When applied to figure 4.19, the principle implies that the boundary was deformed along the symmetry axes – for example, pushed out to create the protrusions and pushed in to create the indentations. In figure 4.20, we have taken the catalogue provided by Richards, Koenderink, and Hoffman (1987) for all shapes with up to eight extrema and have applied to these shapes the two rules. As the reader can see, the rules produce histories, the arrows shown, that strongly accord with intuition.

22   Reinterpretation of the Curvature-based Rules

When we presented the above two rules in Leyton 1988, 1989, we had not yet realized that underlying the use of these rules are the Asymmetry and Symmetry Principles presented here. We now show this to be the case.

First of all, close consideration of the second rule, the Interaction Principle, shows that it is an instantiation of the Symmetry Principle, which states that a symmetry in the present is assumed to be preserved backwards in time. In particular, to preserve symmetries, one must preserve symmetry axes, and this means that processes must travel along the axes, thus implying the second rule.

Again, it turns out that the first rule is used in the service of both the Asymmetry and the Symmetry Principles. We shall now clarify this in detail, in order to illustrate some of the real power of those principles.

It should be observed first that, because the Asymmetry and Symmetry Principles act respectively on the asymmetric and symmetric components of a shape, the principles *partition* the shape into its asymmetric and symmetric components. With respect to any individual shape in figure 4.20, these components are as follows:

1   Asymmetric component: The differences between the curvatures (amounts of bend) at the different points around the curve.
2   Symmetric component: The symmetry axes leading to the extrema.

Having partitioned the shape thus, the Asymmetry and Symmetry Principles then relate these components to *time* as follows: The curvature differences represent history, and the symmetry axes represent the absence of history. Thus, the Asymmetry Principle says that the curvature differences are removed backwards in time. By contrast, the Symmetry Principle *constrains* the way in which the Asymmetry Principle can be used to remove the curvature distinguishability backward in time. It says that this temporal change cannot affect the symmetry component; that is, the processes must move along the axes.

Level I

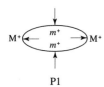

P1

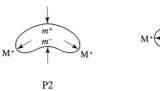

P2

P3

Level II

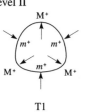

T1

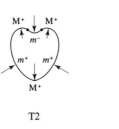

T2

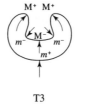

T3

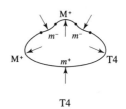

T4

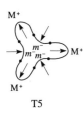

T5

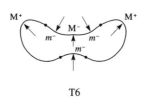

T6

Level III

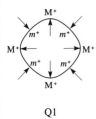

Q1

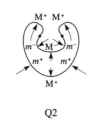

Q2

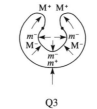

Q3

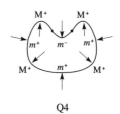

Q4

Q5

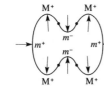

Q6

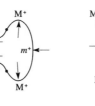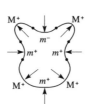

Q7

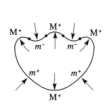

Q8

Q9

Q10

Q11

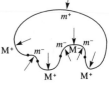

Q12

Figure 4.20

Note that, since the Asymmetry Principle requires the removal of curvature distinguishability backwards in time, the ultimate starting shape for smooth shapes such as those in figure 4.20 must be a *circle* – the only smooth shape in which curvature is the same at all points. In the case of a non-smooth shape – that is, one with corners – the ultimate starting shape must be a polygon with the same number of corners, because, in a polygon, curvature is again the same at any point along any side (see Leyton 1992 for details; see also Hayes and Leyton 1989 for process analysis of corners).

Let us now consider in detail the use of the Asymmetry Principle with regard to the shapes of figure 4.20. The derivation of the histories of these shapes rests crucially on our observation that the distinguishability in curvature is a form of asymmetry – that is, a form of symmetry violation. To understand this further, recall that, while symmetry is indistinguishability, one might often need to define this indistinguishability *relative to a transformation*. For example, a face is symmetric only relative to a reflection transformation that sends the left side of the face onto the right side.

Given this concept, we shall now see that curvature distinguishability can be regarded as existing relative in two kinds of transformation. That is, curvature distinguishability contains *two* forms of asymmetry, as follows.

Type 1 Asymmetry   In order to understand the first type of asymmetry inherent in curvature distinguishability, consider a smooth shape without any curvature distinguishability – that is, a circle. Imagine that the circle is a track around which one is driving a car. When one starts driving, one sets the steering wheel at a particular angle. However, because the track is circular, after one has set the initial angle of the wheel, one does not have to alter the wheel as one drives. This is a result of the fact that the curvature of the track is the same at every point – the curvature corresponds to the amount of turn made by the wheel. Thus, one's actions are indistinguishable – that is, symmetric – as one moves around the circle.

Suppose now that one is driving around a track that has distinguishability in curvature, as in figure 4.19. In this case, one continually has to readjust the wheel, because the curvature is continually altering. Therefore, in this case, one's actions are distinguishable – that is, asymmetric – as one moves around the track.

We have said that asymmetry is distinguishability relative to *transformations*. The transformations we have just considered are in fact *rotations*. Any direction (tangent) on the perfect circle is indistinguishable from any other direction with respect to rotation around the circle center: that is, the tangents can all be rotated onto each other. By contrast, the tangents on a complex curve cannot all be rotated onto each other using some common rotation center. Thus the first type of asymmetry embodied in curvature variation is rotational asymmetry.

Type 2 Asymmetry   A circle contains another type of symmetry that is violated when distinguishability is introduced into curvature. This symmetry is very

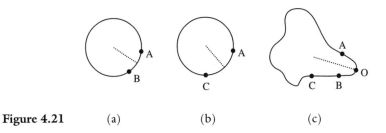

Figure 4.21 (a) (b) (c)

obvious, but it has non-obvious consequences in terms of the analysis of history, as we shall soon see. The symmetry is reflectional symmetry.

One first has to appreciate the enormity of the reflectional symmetry in a circle. Consider figure 4.21a. Point A is reflectionally symmetric to point B about the dotted axis. But, as shown in figure 4.21b, point A is reflectionally symmetric also to point C about the dotted axis shown in that figure. Indeed, point A is reflectionally symmetric to *every other point on the circle*.

Now consider a shape with distinguishability in curvature as shown in figure 4.21c. Consider an arbitrary point on the lower right protrusion – for example, point A. By the Symmetry–Curvature Duality Theorem, the protrusion has one and only one axis. Because there is only one axis, point A can be reflectionally symmetric to only one other point on the protrusion, the point B as shown in the figure. Thus, consider any other point C on the protrusion. Point A *was* reflectionally symmetric to C on the original circle from which the shape was derived, because A *was* reflectionally symmetric to any other point on the circle. However, pushing out the boundary into a protrusion has caused A to lose its symmetry with respect to C. Since there are an infinite number of points on the protrusion, all of which once had symmetry with A, the symmetry of A has jumped from infinity down to one.

Another aspect of the structure can be seen by considering, in figure 4.21c, the *extremum* O at which the axis of the protrusion ends. On the original circle, the point O would have been reflectionally symmetric to every other point. However, it is now symmetric only to itself. This means that we can now gain a deeper understanding of the *memory* inherent in the symmetry axis of the protrusion in figure 4.21c. In the original circle, the point O had an infinite number of symmetry axes associated with it; that is, the axes allowed reflectional symmetry with respect to *all* the other points on the circle. One of these axes was the axis about which O was self-symmetric. When the protrusion was created, each of the infinite number of axes was lost *except one*: the axis of self-symmetry. This became the axis of the protrusion. That is, the protrusion grew along the axis of self-symmetry of O. Furthermore, the self-symmetry axis of O became significant for many other points: For all the points such as A, which ended up on the same protrusion as O, the axis of O became the only axis about which they retained any symmetry.

Thus, one of the implications of the Symmetry–Curvature Duality Theorem, under the process analysis, is this: The theorem implies that a process destroys all symmetry axes except one, the self-symmetry axis of the *extremum*. By going backwards in time, one reinstates those lost axes.

This concludes our argument showing that the use of the rules presented in Leyton 1988, 1989 is motivated by the Asymmetry and Symmetry Principles.

23   Uniformity Assumptions

In the previous two sections, we have shown that the recovery of environment formation is based on the same fundamental rules as the recovery of image formation. Contemporary computational vision, however, is uninterested in the recovery of environment formation because it assumes perception to be the recovery of only the *present* environment. However, in section 14, we proposed that there are two fundamental reasons why current computational vision is incorrect in this viewpoint:

1   Assuming that the environment is in the present prevents the researcher from identifying the basic regularities of the visual system.
2   Recovery of the image-formation phase is impossible without recovery of the previous environment-formation phase.

So far, we have presented our argument supporting (1). We did this by showing that the visual system is revealed in its maximal regularity if we assume that it is composed of rules for the recovery of the past. Both the recovery of the image-formation phase and the recovery of the environment-formation phase are instantiations of such rules. Furthermore, both phases are instantiations of the same highly restricted set of rules. Thus the visual system is revealed at an extreme level of regularity.

Now, while we have demonstrated that the recovery of both the image-formation phase and the environment-formation phase can be achieved by the same rules, the contemporary researcher can reply that we have not yet demonstrated that the visual system actually does recover the environment-formation phase. The researcher can argue that, while it is demonstrably true that the visual system recovers the image-formation phase – otherwise one would not *see* the environment – it is not at all obvious that the recovery of environment formation takes place or, in particular, that it is part of perception.

It is here that we produce an argument that we believe is the most damaging to the theoretical structure of contemporary computational vision. In order to show that the mind does indeed recover the environment-formation phase, and that this is part of perception, we will show that it is impossible to carry out the recovery of the image-formation phase without the recovery of the environment-formation phase; that is, we will now demonstrate the validity of proposal (2) above. Thus we will show that even the limited program of contemporary computational vision cannot be carried out properly without the recovery of environment formation.

To do this, we will need to examine still further the contemporary use of uniformity assumptions in the analysis of the image-formation phase. We saw in sections 16–20 that, according to current computational vision, every shape-from-x module uses a uniformity assumption, and, indeed, every alternative solution to the same shape-from-x problem – for example, the seven alternative solutions listed for shape-from-texture – uses a uniformity assumption. No one can avoid a uniformity assumption. Why?

Given the analysis in sections 16–20, the answer is now obvious. A uniformity assumption is always of this form: Assume that some asymmetry in the image arose from some symmetry in the environment. That is, a uniformity assumption is always an instantiation of the Asymmetry Principle for the recovery of the past.

However, even though uniformity assumptions are always included in computational vision, they are viewed as peripheral adjuncts to the theory, mere extras brought in at the last minute to make the computation tractable. Recall, from section 10, that a computational analysis always proceeds by going through the following three-stage research program:

Stage 1: One first establishes a theory of the environment independent of the observer.

Stage 2: One then establishes a theory of how the environment is projected onto the observer's retina to create the image.

Stage 3: One establishes finally a theory of how the observer-independent environment can be recovered from the image.

Near the end of this program, one discovers that if one attempts to solve stage 3 by using only what has emerged at stages 1 and 2, then stage 3 is intractable. This is because the image, being only an impoverished representation of the environment, does not possess enough information to extract the environment. So one is forced to resort to a uniformity assumption. Then, suddenly, one's computation becomes tractable.

However, the analysis we have provided in sections 9–20 implies a very different view. Whereas, according to computational vision, research begins with a theory of the environment (stage 1) and progresses through the subsequent stages only to resort to a uniformity assumption at the last moment, on the analysis given here, the uniformity assumption *is* the theory of the environment. It *is* stage 1.

How could this be the case? Well, recall that, according to our analysis, each uniformity assumption is an instantiation of the Asymmetry Principle; that is, an asymmetry in the image is explained as having arisen from a symmetry in the environment. Thus, the uniformity assumption is a statement about the structure of the environment – that it is symmetrical in a certain way. Furthermore, since the uniformity assumption is a statement about how the environment was structured *prior* to its projection onto the retina, the uniformity assumption is about the *environment independent of the observer*. This means that the uniformity assumption is a crucial component of stage 1 of the research program, not an adjunct to stage 3. It is part of the foundation on which the subsequent research stages are built.

This issue must be fully understood because, as we shall see, when it is fully understood, it breaks the modularity that dominates computational vision today – a condition that, we shall argue, prevents computational vision arriving at genuine laws of perception.

In order to understand the role of uniformity assumptions, let us now involve another issue. In the literature it is usually supposed that one uniformity assumption will eventually prove itself to be better than the others. This view is challenged by the argument we have given here. To see this, let us return, for example, to Witkin's (1981) method for shape-from-texture. Recall that Witkin's method is based on the observation that an oblique image of an irregular coastline causes the coastline to gain a regularity: the directions in the coastline become aligned more with the direction of slant. Thus Witkin suggests that, when one is presented with the image, the appropriate inference rule is to hypothesize an environmental coastline in which the bias has been removed – that is, in which randomness is maximized.

Now, Witkin argues that this uniformity assumption is better than the uniformity assumption proposed by Gibson, which is that non-uniform *density* in the image arises from uniform density in the environment; for example, given an image of the American flag waving in the wind, the stripes, which have varying density across the image, arise from stripes of uniform density in the environment.

We argue that Witkin is incorrect in proposing that one of the uniformity assumptions is better than the other. They are of equal value. Witkin's uniformity assumption works for images of irregular coastlines, and Gibson's uniformity assumption works for images of American flags. They both *fail* when they are applied to the image handled by the other. For example, Witkin's fails when applied to the American flag because Witkin requires that bias in directionality be removed in recovering the environmental structure, and the American flag in the environment, being striped, represents the strongest possible directional bias.

Thus, we see that Witkin's uniformity assumption implies that one kind of environment is responsible for the image, while Gibson's implies that another kind of environment is responsible for the image. In fact, as we argued earlier, the uniformity assumption, in each case, *is* the specification of the type of environment that is involved.

Near the beginning of this chapter, we stated that we were going to attack the ecological modularity and consequent computational and research modularity that underlie contemporary computational vision – that is, attack the view that the ecology is divided into a set of independent domains and that, correspondingly, the computational system must be divided into a set of independent subsystems, as a result of which research can be carried out as a set of independent problems. However, we seem, in contradiction to our argument, to have arrived at a modularity position due to the uniformity assumptions. We have argued that each uniformity assumption is the specification of a different environment, one that excludes the existence of an alternative environment; for example, an environment that is like a coastline excludes an environment that is like an American flag. This mutual exclusion of environments thus seems to imply that research can be carried out in independent units.

However, this conclusion is not correct, and it is extremely important to examine why it is not correct, because such an examination leads to a much deeper understanding of the visual process.

Let us consider what would happen if one used Witkin's and Gibson's uniformity assumptions in each other's environmental situations. Thus consider first what would happen if one tried to use Witkin's uniformity assumption on an image of an American flag and tried to explain it as having arisen from an irregular coastline. One would, in particular, be trying to explain smooth lines in the image as having arisen from irregular lines in the environment. To do this, one would have to assume that the environmental lines were not only intrinsically irregular but that they had been drawn on an extremely irregular surface, and that the irregularities in the surface exactly fitted the irregularities in the lines, so that, when projected, the latter resulted in smooth lines in the image.

Now the reader might at first think that such a situation is excluded by the Non-Accidentalness Rule of Kanade, which states essentially that a regularity in the image should not be assumed to be the result of some unlikely accident of projection. However, even if one decides to use this rule, one would have to extend the non-accidentalness to exclude the unlikely and highly complicated process in which the creation of the surface irregularity had been exactly coordinated, point by point, with the creation of the line irregularity, so that the former exactly compensated for the latter. This means that one would have made reference to the history of the surface *prior* to the image-formation process. That is, considerations of image formation are not enough: one is forced to consider environment formation.

Non-accidentalness is not in fact the issue. To see this, consider the reverse situation – that in which one used the Gibson uniformity assumption on an image of an irregular coastline and tried to explain the coastline as the projection of part of an American flag. The Non-Accidentalness Rule would not be irrelevant, because one would be trying to explain irregularity in the image. Now, to explain the irregular image coastline as a projection, for example, of a pair of smooth parallel lines on the environmental flag, one would have to conjecture that the flag had been made very crumpled and then squeezed at the sides so that the two lines met at their ends and formed a closed coastline. That is, one would have to assume a complex environment-formation process.

Let us take stock: In both the use of the Witkin assumption on a Gibson-type image and the use of the Gibson assumption on a Witkin-type image one is forced to conjecture an immensely complicated environmental history prior to the image-formation phase. We propose therefore that the reason why one does not use these uniformity assumptions in the "wrong" situations is that one avoids conjecturing immensely complicated environment-formation histories.

The first important thing that this argument shows is that, in order to select the appropriate uniformity assumption, perception has to create a model of the environment-formation phase – that is, the history *prior* to image formation. That is, considerations of image formation are not enough.

The second important thing that this argument shows is that modularity is inappropriate in perception. To see this, observe first that a single rule excludes the inappropriate use of the Witkin and the Gibson uniformity assumptions. The rule is simply this: *Minimize the conjectured history.* We shall call the rule the History Minimization Principle. Observe that to decide whether to use the Witkin or the Gibson assumption in a situation, one need minimize only the environment-formation phase, because this phase is the only variable across the two cases; that is, the image-formation phase (projection) is the same in the two situations.

The History Minimization Principle, like the other principles presented here, is based on the concept of *symmetry*. It is the requirement that the conjectured history contain as little distinguishability as possible. More precisely, the conjectured history must be as translationally symmetric as possible, across time. Detailed structural aspects of the principle are discussed in Leyton 1992.

Now, the way in which the History Minimization Principle excludes the complex scenarios mentioned above is that it insures that the residual asymmetry that has not been explained in the image-formation phase – that is, the asymmetry left to be explained in the environment-formation phase – is as small as possible. This means that the History Minimization Principle has the following corollary:

MAXIMAL GAIN RULE: *Use the Asymmetry Principle in such a way that it gains maximal symmetry.*

In particular, one should use the Asymmetry Principle, in the image-formation phase, in such a way that it gains maximal symmetry for the use of the Asymmetry Principle in the environment-formation phase.

In fact, the single rule, the Maximal Gain Rule, replaces the large set of uniformity assumptions which contemporary computational vision believes to be part of the visual system. To see this, note first that the uniformity assumptions, being independent, are used in a modular form. Let us therefore contrast the use of our single rule with the current approach based on modularity and the associated use of many uniformity assumptions. A workable use of the modularity approach would be as follows: Different uniformity assumptions are needed for different ecological contexts. Therefore, extra computation is required, *prior* to the use of a uniformity assumption, in order to establish the ecological context and thus to select the appropriate uniformity assumption.

By contrast, the Maximal Gain Rule does not require establishing the ecological context. It requires merely that the Asymmetry Principle be used in such a way that causal history is minimized. On this view, there is no such thing as an appropriate ecological context. There is history that needs to be minimized. In that history, asymmetries are converted into symmetries backwards in time. The selection of the order in which these asymmetries are symmetrized is determined by the Maximal Gain Rule.

24   What is the Ecology?

The considerations of the previous section allow us now to understand what an "ecology" is. We have argued that perception is the use of four principles – the Asymmetry Principle, the Symmetry Principle, the Second System Principle, and the History Minimization Principle – that together determine a single process: the conversion of asymmetries to symmetries backward in time. According to this view, what could be called the "ecology" is the particular order chosen to convert the asymmetries back to symmetries – an order which, as we saw at the end of section 23, is determined by the History Minimization Principle. That is, the ecology is the minimal order in which image asymmetries can be changed back to symmetries; for example, this minimal order defines the environment to be either an American flag or a geographical outline.

It is worth understanding this more fully, and to do so we must clarify further the nature of the Second System Principle. This principle states that if a system undergoes a change from symmetry to asymmetry in the forward time direction, then a second system must have been involved. What we must be clear on now is that the sole explanatory role of the second system is that this system brings with it an extra set of asymmetries not contained in the first system alone. These asymmetries are, so to speak, passed on to the first system in the causal interaction. For example, consider the shape-from-shading problem. A non-uniform light flux reaching the retina is assumed to have been a uniform light flux at some time in the past. In accord with the Second System Principle, the change from symmetry to asymmetry in the light flux is explained by the introduction of a second system, a surface. The role of the surface is this: The surface has a collection of asymmetries – for example, it is undulating. In a causal interaction, these asymmetries are passed on to the light flux. (More fully, the new asymmetries introduced by the second system include those introduced by the *relationship* between the two systems.)

One can now explain, in a deep way, why Gibson and contemporary computation vision claim that *the* crucial aspect of the environment that the perceptual system attempts to recover is *surface structure* – what computational vision calls *shape*. The claim is usually justified by saying that shape is the primary aspect of the environment with which human beings interact on the level of scale on which they live. However, according to our argument, this is not correct. No matter what level of scale human beings were to live on, shape would always be what they would attempt to recover. The reason is this: As we argued in Leyton 1992, shape and asymmetry are literally the same thing. Thus, in accord with the Second System Principle, the recovery of environmental shape is the recovery of the asymmetry that, as a second system, introduced asymmetry into the stimulus energy.

This means that, whatever level of scale human beings were to live on, when presented with an asymmetric system – for example, a stimulus array – they would attempt to "undo" its asymmetry by postulating that it arose from a symmetrical past state in which it interacted with a second system that was asymmetrical. Furthermore, that second system would itself be explained as having arisen from a symmetrical past state in which it interacted with a third system that was asymmetrical, and so on. Each additional system would be what one would call "shape" because it would be a set of asymmetries.

Therefore, according to the rules presented here, at each stage backwards in time, perception recovers two things: a symmetrized version of a given system and an asymmetrical additional system. This argument defines the real meaning of the term *ecology*. An ecology is the set of symmetries and asymmetries that are pulled apart in the successive causal interactions inferred backwards in time by our four inference rules.

25   Gestalt Grouping

We have, in the previous section, shown how the construct "environmental shape", which is regarded as a fundamental construct in contemporary computational vision – that is, as having an ultimate explanatory role – is in fact derivable within a theory of memory. Let us now turn to the fundamental construct of the Gestalt tradition, grouping, and show that it too is derivable within a theory of memory.

According to the Gestalt tradition, the perceptual system applies criteria such as proximity and similarity to form groupings of retinal stimuli; that is, perception groups together those stimuli that are proximal and similar, etc. Examination of these criteria reveals that they are all examples of *symmetry* in the strict mathematical sense where symmetry means indistinguishability under a possible use of transformations. Criteria such as proximity and similarity mean indistinguishability under a possible use of transformations. Criteria such as proximity and similarity mean indistinguishability in spatial dimensions and non-spatial dimensions respectively. Criteria such as regularity mean indistinguishability under cyclic transformations. One can conclude, therefore, that grouping is generally aimed at identifying symmetries.

We can now explain the Gestalt construct as follows: Within the system elaborated here, the need to identify symmetries arises from an attempt *to construct memory*. According to the Symmetry Principle, a symmetry is memory of itself; that is, it is taken to have always existed. Thus Gestalt grouping is the attempt to establish those aspects of the stimulus set that have existed through all previous time.

Finally, let us observe that researchers in contemporary computational vision often speak of the symmetries of the image as those aspects that it is most profitable for the perceptual system to explain causally (e.g. Witkin and Tenenbaum 1983). This view is directly the opposite of ours. According to the principles developed here, it is asymmetries that require causal explanation and symmetries that do not. It is only by having things this way around that the image can be memory of the environment.

Acknowledgments

The writing of this paper was funded by a Presidential Young Investigator Award (NSF, IRI-8896110). Thanks go to Chuck Schmidt and Stacy Marsella for feedback on this paper.

References

Aloimonos, J. (1988) Shape from texture. *Biological Cybernetics* 58, 345–60.

Bajcsy, R. and Lieberman, L. (1976) Texture gradient as a depth cue. *Computer Graphics and Image Processing* 5, 52–67.

Barr, A. (1984) Global and local deformations of solid primitives. *Computer Graphics* 18, 21–30.

Brady, M. and Yuille, A. (1983) An extremum principle for shape from contour. AI-Memo No. 711, MIT.

Gibson, J. J. (1950) *The Perception of the Visual World*, Boston, MA: Houghton Mifflin.

Haralick, R. M. (1978) Stastical and structural approaches to texture. *Proceedings of the International Joint Conference on Pattern Recognition*, 45–60.

Hassenstein, B. and Reichardt, W. (1956) Systemtheoretische Analye der Zeit-Reihenfolgen und Vorzeichenauswertung bei der Bewgungs-perzeption der Russelkafers, *Chlorophanus. Z. Naturf* IIb, 513–24.

Hayes, P. J. and Leyton, M. (1989) Processes at discontinuities. *Proceedings of the International Conference of Artificial Intelligence*, Detroit, 1267–72.

Ikeuchi, K. (1984) Shape from regular patterns. *Artificial Intelligence* 22, 49–75.

Kanade, T. (1981) Recovery of the three-dimensional shape of an object from a single view. In J. M. Brady (ed.), *Computer Vision*, New York: North-Holland.

Kender, J. R. (1979) Shape from Texture. Ph.D. Thesis, Carnegie–Mellon University.

Leyton, M. (1984) Perceptual organization as nested control. *Biological Cybernetics* 51, 141–53.

—— (1986a) Principles of information structure common to six levels of the human cognitive system. *Information Sciences* 38, 1–120 (entire journal issue).

—— (1986b) A theory of information structure I: general principles. *Journal of Mathematical Psychology* 30, 103–160.

—— (1986c) A theory of information structure II: a theory of perceptual organization. *Journal of Mathematical Psychology* 30, 257–305.

—— (1987a) Nested structures of control: an intuitive view. *Computer Vision, Graphics, and Image Processing* 37, 20–53.

—— (1987b) Symmetry – curvature duality. *Computer Vision, Graphics, and Image Processing* 38, 327–41.

—— (1988) A process-grammar for shape. *Artificial Intelligence* 34, 213–47.

—— (1989) Inferring causal-history from shape. *Cognitive Science* 13, 357–87.

—— (1992) *Symmetry, Causality, Mind*, Cambridge, MA: MIT Press.

Lowe, D. (1985) *Perceptual Organization and Visual Recognition*, Holland: Kluwer.

Lowe, D. and Binford, T. O. (1981) The interpretation of three-dimensional structure from image curves. *Proceedings of the International Joint Conference of Artificial Intelligence*, Vancouver, 613–18.

Marr, D. (1982) *Vision: A Computational Investigation into the Human Representation and Processing of Visual Information*, San Francisco: W. H. Freeman.

Poggio, T., Torre, V. and Koch, C. (1985) Computational vision and regularization theory. *Nature* 317, 314–19.

Pylyshyn, Z. W. (1984) *Computation and Cognition: Toward a Foundation for Cognitive Science*, Cambridge, MA: MIT Press.

Reichardt, W. (1961) Autocorrelation, a principle for the evaluation of sensory information by the central nervous system. In W. A. Rosenblith (ed.) *Sensory Communication*, Cambridge, MA: MIT Press.

Richards, W., Koenderink, J. J. and Hoffman, D. D. (1987) Inferring three-dimensional shapes from two-dimensional silhouettes. *Journal of the Optical Society of America A* 4, 1168–75.

Rock, I. (1983) *The Logic of Perception*, Cambridge, MA: MIT Press.

Rosch, E. (1975) Cognitive reference points. *Cognitive Psychology* 7, 532–47.

—— (1978) Principles of categorization. In E. Rosch and B. B. Lloyd (eds), *Cognition and Categorization*, Hillsdale, NJ: Lawrence Erlbaum.

Rosenfeld, A. (1971) Isotonic grammars, parallel grammars, and picture grammars. In B. Meltzer and D. Michie (eds), *Machine Intelligence VI*, Edinburgh: Edinburgh University Press, 281–94.

—— (1975) A note on automatic detection of texture gradients. *IEEE Transactions on Computers.* C23, 988–91.

Rosenfeld, A. and Lipkin, B. S. (1970) Texture synthesis. In B. S. Lipkin and A. Rosenfeld (eds), *Picture Processing and Psychopictorics*, New York: Academic Press.

Rosenfeld, A. and Milgram, D. L. (1972) Web automata and web grammars. In B. Meltzer and D. Michie (eds), *Machine Intelligence VII*, Edinburgh: Edinburgh University Press, 307–24.

Rosenfeld, A. and Strong, J. P. (1971) A grammar for maps. In J. T. Tou (ed.), *Software Engineering*, vol. 2, New York: Academic Press.

Stevens, K. A. (1981) The information content of texture gradients. *Biological Cybernetics* 42, 95–105.

Ullman, S. (1979) *The Interpretation of Visual Motion*, Cambridge, MA: MIT Press.

—— (1984) Maximizing rigidity: the incremental recovery of 3-D structure from rigid and nonrigid motion. *Perception* 13, 255–74.

Wallach, H. and O'Connell, D. N. (1953) The kinetic depth effect. *Journal of Experimental Psychology* 45, 205–17.

Witkin, A. P. (1981) Recovering surface shape and orientation from texture. In J. M. Brady (ed.), *Computer Vision*, New York: North Holland.

Witkin, A. P. and Tenenbaum, J. M. (1983) On the role of structure in vision. In A. Rosenfeld and J. Beck (eds), *Human and Machine Vision*, Vol. 1, Hillsdale, NJ: Erlbaum.

5

Object Representation and Recognition

Sven J. Dickinson

1 Introduction

One of the primary functions of the human visual system is object recognition, an ability that allows us to relate the visual stimuli falling on our retinas to our knowledge of the world. For example, object recognition allows you to use knowledge of what an apple looks like to find apples in the supermarket, to use knowledge of what a shark looks like to swim in the other direction, and to use knowledge of the landmarks in your neighbourhood to find your way home. Recognition allows us to understand the content of images. Only by assigning a label to an image object can we ground the object in our own experience.

Human object recognition seems effortless. From prototypical or generic knowledge of an object, you can easily recognize novel instances of the object. For example, your internal model for how a dog appears is sufficient for you to recognize a new breed of dog (that you've never seen before) as a dog, regardless of whether it is standing, sitting, or running. And in cluttered scenes where an object is only partially visible (or occluded), recognition is still possible. Seeing only the front end of the car peeking out from behind the billboard is enough to allow you to recognize it as a police cruiser. These examples raise a number of important questions: How is visual knowledge of an object encoded? What information is recovered from an image in order to recognize an object? And how is this information compared to our stored knowledge in order to recognize the object?

Humans use many visual cues to recognize an object. For example, the pattern of black and white stripes on an animal may be a more powerful cue to identifying the animal as a zebra than the shape of its body. Or, back in the supermarket, although many of the fruits share the same spherical shape, the color orange draws you to the box of oranges. Clearly, the most powerful cue used to identify an object is its shape. Even while covering one eye, the human observer can quickly recognize the three-dimensional objects that appear as two-dimensional line drawings in a slide show. Coined "couch potato vision" by the psychologist Irving Biederman, the experiment shows that the shape information recovered from image contours is sufficient for object recognition; color, texture, shading, and stereo (the depth information gained by uncovering your other eye) are *not* essential to the task. Since shape plays such an important role in object recognition, this chapter will focus on the representation and recognition of objects based on their shape.

In this chapter, we will explore object recognition from the standpoint of computer vision. Building a computer vision system to perform a given visual recognition task requires careful attention to the entire process, including object representation, feature extraction, object database organization, and model indexing. Building computer vision systems allows us to prototype competing representations and algorithms, yielding powerful constraints and insight which can be used to postulate and evaluate theories of human object recognition. Conversely, to the extent that a computer vision system aspires to solve a recognition problem as well as a human does, the insight acquired by the human visual recognition community should be exploited when designing the system, and the human visual system should become the ultimate measuring stick by which the system is evaluated.

We begin by illustrating the recognition problem, using some well-known examples drawn from the computer vision community. Next, we discuss the problem of choosing an object representation given the recognition task, outlining a number of representational properties and their trade-offs. We then discuss the problem of matching recovered image features to object models, beginning with an illustrative case study drawn from the optical character recognition (OCR) domain and returning to our well-known examples from the computer vision community. One of the more powerful recognition paradigms to emerge, called "recognition by parts," is explored through two different approaches, one drawn from the human vision community and one from the computer vision community. The limitations of these two approaches will lead to a discussion of where the field of object recognition is heading and what the outstanding problems are.

2   Some Sample Problems

The input to an object-recognition system is a digital image, a two-dimensional array of numbers called pixels. Each pixel represents a measurement recorded by the sensor responsible for acquiring the image. For example, a typical black-and-white video camera will produce an image whose pixels represent how "bright" the picture is at that point; dark areas in the image have low-valued pixels, while light areas have high-valued pixels. Another popular sensor in the computer vision community is the *laser range-finder*, which produces an image whose pixels represent the distance to objects in the world. For example, objects in the field of view which are near the range-finder camera will have low-valued pixels, while objects far away will have high-valued pixels. Such *range images* are effectively three-dimensional, avoiding the ambiguity inherent in two-dimensional images.[1]

To illustrate the kinds of object-recognition problems facing computer vision systems, we show the actual images presented to a number of well-known object-recognition systems. Figure 5.1a shows a typical input image for the recognition system of Murase and Nayar (1995). The task is to identify the single, unoccluded object in the image from a database of 100 model objects. Figure 5.1b shows a typical input image for the recognition system of Huttenlocher and Ullman (1987). The task is to identify the polyhedral objects in the image from a small database of polyhedral object models. In this case, there may be multiple objects in the image, and the system is expected to not only identify objects that are partially visible, but determine their exact position and orientation in the world. This latter task is called *pose estimation*.

Figure 5.1c shows a typical input image for the recognition system of Lowe (1985). As in the previous example, multiple, occluded objects may be present in the image. However, in this case, the system is told what object (razor) is present, and the task is to compute the pose of any instance of that object (razor) found in the image. The final example, figure 5.1d, shows a typical input image for the recognition system of Brooks (1983). From aerial images of an airport, the task is not only to locate any jet aircraft, but to determine what kind of aircraft they are – for example, wide-bodied versus non-wide-bodied. The aircraft are assumed to be unoccluded, and the approximate viewpoint (both height and direction) is assumed to be known.

3   The Components of an Object Recognition System

The input to each of the recognition systems outlined above is a digital image, along with knowledge of one or more object models. The output is an object labeling and, in some cases, a specification of object pose. How, from a matrix of pixel values, is an object found? The typical framework for a recognition system is shown in figure 5.2. From the input digital image, an appropriate set of features are extracted; common features include edges (brightness discontinuities), corners (edge intersections), and regions (homogeneous image patches). The goal of the feature-extraction module is to take a large amount of image data and retain only that information necessary to identify or distinguish the object. Note that knowledge of what kinds of objects are present in the image may be used to govern the extraction of features. For

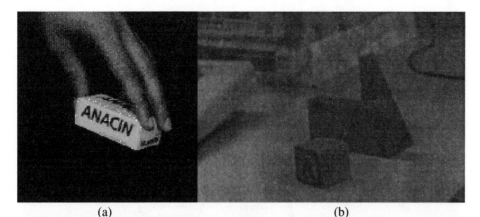

Figure 5.1. Sample object recognition tasks.
Reprinted with the permissions of: (a) Hiroshi Murase, NTT Basic Research Labs, Kanagawa, Japan; (b) Daniel Huttenlocher, Dept of Computer Science, Cornell University; (c) David Lowe, Dept of Computer Science, University of British Columbia; (d) Rodney Brooks, Artificial Intelligence Laboratory, MIT.

example, if we know we're looking at aerial images of airports (e.g., figure 5.1d), we may choose a feature-extraction operator that looks for long lines in the image (corresponding to runway boundaries).

Object recognition can be simply thought of as a database search problem, in which search keys are used to retrieve records from the database. In our case, the database contains object models, not records, while the search keys are collections of extracted features. Returning to figure 5.2, the extracted features must be grouped into meaningful collections, called *indexing primitives*. Examples of indexing primitives include collections of extracted edges or lines, collections of corner features, or even collections of homogeneous image regions. An indexing primitive represents a query to the object database of the form, "Get me all objects in the database that have this primitive as a

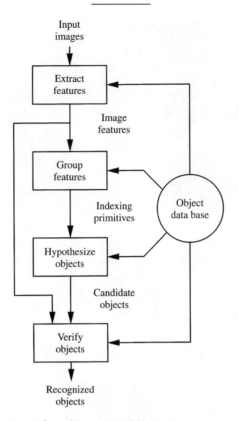

Input
images

Extract
features

Image
features

Group
features

Indexing
primitives

Object
data base

Hypothesize
objects

Candidate
objects

Verify
objects

Recognized
objects

Figure 5.2.   Components of an object recognition system.

component." As in the case of feature extraction, knowledge of the image domain may be used to affect the feature-grouping process.

   Once such a query has been posed, a matching algorithm compares the indexing primitive to the object models in the database, returning a set of *candidate objects*, all of which contain the indexing primitive. Unless the query returns only one candidate model, we're not yet finished, since we must decide which of the candidate objects we're looking at. Thus, the final component of the recognition algorithm evaluates, or *verifies*, each of the candidates in terms of how well it accounts for the image data. A score is typically assigned to each candidate, and the best-scoring candidate, or hypothesis, is chosen as the interpretation (or label) of the object. If there are other objects in the image, the entire process can be repeated until all the image features are accounted for.

4   A Two-dimensional Case Study

The backbone of any recognition system is its model object representation, for it governs what kinds of features are extracted, how features are grouped, and how features are matched to models. To illustrate the various components of an object-recognition system and how the choice of object representation affects the design of each component, we will examine the design of a system whose goal is to take an image containing an alphanumeric character and recognize the character. This problem, known as *optical character recognition*, or OCR, is a classic problem in object recognition.

For a few hundred dollars, you can purchase software to run on your PC which will recognize all the characters on a scanned page and automatically insert them in a file. Why would you want such a tool? If you want to enter a page of text (e.g., a magazine article, newspaper article, legal document, scientific article, etc.) into your computer, an OCR module frees you from manually typing the text. OCR systems have also been used in conjunction with speech synthesizers to provide reading machines for the visually impaired.

We will look at two solutions to the OCR problem. In the first case, we will assume that we know the font (including its point size) that will appear on the page, while in the second case, we assume no a priori knowledge of the font appearing on the page. We will call the first problem *single-font recognition* and the second problem *omni-font recognition*. The contrasting solutions to these two subproblems will help to illustrate a number of critical issues in choosing an object representation for a given recognition problem.

4.1   Single-font recognition

Given a digital image corresponding to an entire page of text, the first task is to *segment* the individual characters from the page image, resulting in a collection of character sub-images, each containing a single character. In general, identifying the parts of an image that correspond to a single object – that is, the segmentation problem – is a challenging problem. For our discussion, we will assume that some segmentation process has segmented the characters on the page. This reduces our problem to identifying single characters, each centered in its own small sub-image extracted from the entire page image.

Since we know the font and point size of the characters on the page, we will choose a model character representation that reflects our specific knowledge of the image objects. The simplest such representation for a character would be an image of the character itself, called a *template*. The model template might be acquired by, for example, scanning a page containing a single character repeated many times. The resulting sub-images could be "averaged" to yield a representative sub-image for that character. The identifier for that character would be stored with the model in the database. The process would then be repeated for each character in the font, resulting in a model database of character templates.

The matching of an image character with a model character is shown in figure 5.3. The model character image is effectively overlaid on the input character image. For each pixel that is "on" in both images, the score of the

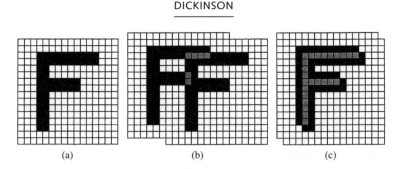

Figure 5.3. Template matching for OCR: (a) model character template; (b) overlaying (with offset) the model template on the character sub-image with shaded pixels contributing to the score; (c) better alignment of model with image, reflecting a higher score (shaded pixels).

match is incremented by one. To accommodate alignment error, the model character is overlaid in a number of different positions, with the best-scoring position chosen as the best match. Finally, the best score is compared to a threshold which must be met in order for the character to be recognized. For example, if the score exceeds 90 percent of the "on" pixels in the character template, then at least 90 percent of the model character has been found in the input image.

The advantages of the template-matching approach are clear. Looking back at our recognition framework in figure 5.2, we have essentially ignored both the feature-extraction step and the grouping step. Absolutely no abstraction or transformation of the input image is required in order to compare it with the model. Having such exact knowledge of the shape of the objects that can appear in the image means that the challenging problems of feature extraction and grouping can be avoided.

Until the mid-1980s, most commercial OCR systems worked on this principle, scanning and recognizing all the characters on a page in under 30 seconds. Template-matching systems performed exceptionally well on both original documents, where error rates better than 1 in 100,000 characters were reported, and photocopied documents, where error rates better than 1 in 50,000 were reported. If, due to poor reproduction, a number of pixels in the input character image were inverted or lost (i.e., set to zero), the score was relatively unaffected, regardless of where the pixels were lost. Furthermore, the template-matching algorithm could be easily implemented in hardware, resulting in recognition rates exceeding 50 characters per second.

The disadvantages of the template-matching approach are also clear. The system works for a single font and will not recognize characters from other fonts or of other point sizes.[2] Thus, character templates are not invariant with regard to scale, rotation, stroke thickness (due to boldface), slant (due to italics), or any shape deformation due to font change. Furthermore, the recognition complexity (or time required to recognize an input character) scales linearly with the number of fonts supported, resulting in slower recognition times as more fonts are added.

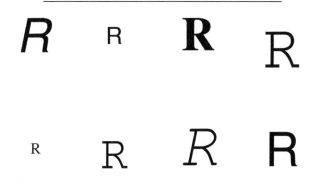

Figure 5.4. Different instances of the letter R.

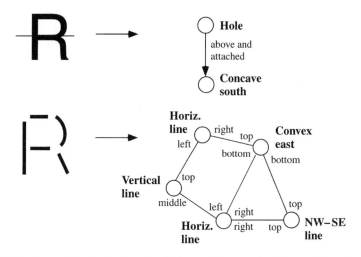

Figure 5.5. A possible description for the letter R: *top*, a simple, graph-based representation of the letter R which is ambiguous (the letter A yields the same graph); *bottom*, a more complex, graph-based representation of the letter R which is unambiguous.

4.2   Omni-font recognition

Each of the characters shown in figure 5.4 are the same, despite their differences in size, stroke thickness, slant, the presence of serifs (the small linear terminators on some lines), etc. What is it about each of these characters that gives them the same label? One possible description that is invariant with regard to size, slant, stroke thickness, etc. is shown in figure 5.5 (*top*). The letter R can be represented as a closed section above, attached to a concave section facing south or down. These two strokes, and the relation defined between them, can be represented as a graph; nodes represent (possibly overlapping) portions of the character, while arcs define relations between the nodes.

The simple representation for the letter *R* shown in figure 5.5 (*top*) is ambiguous in that both the letters *R* and *A* are described by the same graph; each has a closed contour above, attached to a concave contour facing downwards. In figure 5.5 (*bottom*), a more powerful representation is shown, in which nodes in the graph represent sections of contour that have been cut at places where the direction of the contour suddenly changes or where the shape of the contour changes – for example, from staight to curved, or vice versa.

Nodes in our new graph are labeled with a contour shape (e.g., line, convex curve, or concave curve) and a direction (e.g., horizontal, vertical, NW – SE, etc. for lines, and north, east, etc. for curves). The arcs, or relations, between nodes specify the attachments between the contour sections. For example, the horizontal line at the top of the *R* has a vertical line attached to its left end, while the vertical line has the horizontal line attached at its top. What we see here is that in order to make the representation of the *R* distinct from that of the *A*, we have had to add considerable complexity. The original *R* required two nodes and one arc, while the new *R* requires five nodes and six arcs. Storing the model for the enhanced *R* therefore requires more space or memory than storing the model for the original *R*.

Assuming that such a graph-based representation can be recovered from an image, it must be compared to the graph-based descriptions corresponding to the model characters. Just as we developed a method for comparing two template-based character descriptions, we now need a method for comparing two graph-based character descriptions. The method we will use to compare, or match, two graphs is known as interpretation-tree (IT) search, as proposed by Grimson and Lozano-Péez (1984). Although applied here to graphs representing characters, the method is quite general, supporting the matching of any description made up of features and constraints on the features. In fact, in some sense, the method can be seen as attempting to align two graphs just as we attempted to align two images in the template-matching approach.

The method is illustrated in figure 5.6. Assume that some preprocessing algorithm yields a graph of recovered image features, labeled I6 – I10. Shown below this graph is the graph describing the model character *R*, labeled M1 – M5. Of course, the character defined by the input character graph (top) is initially unknown and has to be compared to each of the model character graphs to find the best fit. For illustrative purposes, we show the process of comparing the input graph to the model graph corresponding to the letter *R*. Since the input character is, in fact, an *R*, we would expect the score of this comparison to be the maximum of all comparisons of the input character to a model character.

To begin the process of matching the two characters, we set up the interpretation tree whose number of levels (excluding the root of the tree) is equal to the number of nodes in the model character graph. The branching

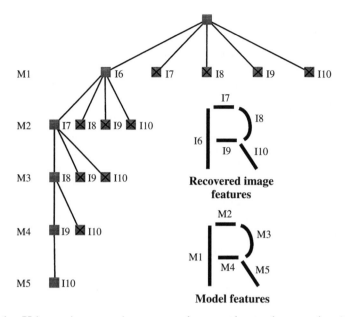

Figure 5.6.   Using an interpretation-tree search to match two character descriptions.

factor (number of children) of the tree's root is equal to the number of nodes in the input graph.[3] The first level of the tree represents the assignment of an input feature to the first model feature (M1). For example, the left-most branch defines the interpretation of input feature I6 as model feature M1.

M1 and I6 are features which have the same label; that is, they are both vertical lines. I7 and M1, on the other hand, have different labels: one is a vertical line, while the other is a horizontal line. Since these features are inconsistent, the interpretation of input feature I7 as model feature M1 is inconsistent, and the interpretation (node) is marked with an *x*. The interpretation tree will therefore not be expanded below I7 at the first level, since there is no interpretation of the input character as model character *R* with I7 corresponding to the vertical segment (M1) of the *R*. Similarly, I8 cannot be interpreted as M1, because I8 is a convex curve, and M1 is a vertical line. In fact, since there are no other vertical lines in the input graph, I6 is the only feature that can be interpreted as M1. The search below all the nodes in the tree other than I6 at the first level can therefore be terminated.

At the next level, we attempt to assign an input feature to M2. Since I6 is the only active tree node at the first level, we need only expand I6. Since I6 has already been interpreted as M1, I6 cannot also be interpreted as M2. Thus, we have one fewer children of I6, and therefore consider the interpretation of I7 – I10 as model feature M2. Examining the feature labels of I7 – I10, we see that both I7 and I9 are horizontal lines supporting their interpretation as M2. However, now that we have two nodes in our interpretation (I6 as M1 and, for example, I7 as M2), we need to make sure that the arcs between any assigned input nodes are consistent with the arcs defined over their matching model nodes. In this case, the arc between M1 and M2 is satisfied by the arc between I6 and I7, but not by the arc between I6 and I9 ("middle" connection instead of the correct "top" connection). In general, every time an input feature is added to the interpretation, any arcs between its corresponding model feature and other previously defined model features must be consistent with the arcs defined by their corresponding image features.

We can proceed in this fashion, using both model node labels and arc labels to prune the search below inconsistent interpretations. The "better" an input graph matches a given model graph, the deeper the search will continue. In our example, since the input and model graphs match exactly, the interpretation tree extends to its maximum depth, correctly assigning an input feature to each model feature. One possible method for assigning a score would be to determine the percentage of model nodes and arcs that were found in the input graph – very similar to the scoring method proposed in our single-font OCR solution.

The advantages of the above omni-font recognition scheme are clear. A vertical line is vertical regardless of its length and thickness, while a convex curve facing east is convex as long as its radius is finite and the center of its circular approximation lies approximately to its left. In general, the node and arc labels are *invariant* with respect to the size of the character (point size) and to minor deformations in the shape of the character. If we replaced absolute orientation with relative orientation in our model description, our description would be invariant with respect to rotation of the character. In this manner, our description should be able to handle any input R, provided that the graph belonging to the input R can be recovered reliably.

The reliable recovery of the input graph is, in fact, the major stumbling block of our omni-font method. It requires that we not only detect and extract the contours from our input character image, but that we correctly partition the contours into nodes and correctly label the relations (arcs) between the nodes. Errors in this challenging task can lead to graphs with more or less nodes (if too many or too few cuts are made), incorrect node labels (if orientations are miscalculated or borderline), or incorrect relations. These problems are compounded when there are gaps in the input character strokes. Although there are a number of clever extensions to the IT search method to handle partial matches of an input graph, the price of recovering invariant features is the difficulty and unreliability of their recovery.

4.3   Selecting a model for matching

We have presented two contrasting recognition approaches to comparing an input character image to a model character. Given an input character description, we have not yet discussed how model characters are chosen for comparison. Do we simply compare each model, in turn, to the input character, selecting the best-scoring model in the end to represent the interpretation of the character? Or, can we avoid this linear search by somehow ranking the model characters for comparison in decreasing order of likelihood?

The problem of selecting a model for comparison is called *indexing* and is a critical component of a recognition system. Ideally, you would like to extract some clues from the input character description that would allow you to suggest some likely candidate models to test. If no clues can be recovered, then a linear search of the model database is required – bad news indeed if the object model database is large. On the other hand, if you can recover some really distinguishing clues, you may have only one model to test, in which case you don't even need to test it!

The clues we're looking for are nothing but the grouped features that we saw in our recognition framework, shown in figure 5.2. The purpose of grouping features is to extract more discriminating meta-features that can serve as powerful indices in our database. We could, of course, simply use the features themselves as clues, without grouping them. It may, in fact, be the case that the features themselves are powerful enough to suggest a small number of candidate models. The best approach would be a dynamic indexing scheme in which the complexity of the indexing feature would be a function of its indexing power.

Let's consider an example. In our template-matching paradign, our original feature is really nothing more than a pixel value, and our grouping operation is nothing more than selecting all pixels. If we choose one pixel as our index whose value is on, we would choose for comparison all model templates whose pixel at that location (or perhaps at a nearby location to account for positional error) was also on. Such an index is practically useless for two reasons. First, there are probably many characters which, when overlaid on our input character, have many pixels in common. Second, due to noise, the input pixel may be incorrect (inverted or off), returning a set of candidate characters which don't occupy that position. In the end, you would most likely be testing most if not all the model characters!

Before we give up on our one-pixel index, let's consider how we might generate a set of candidates from this index. If the input image was not a binary image (pixel values of 0 or 1), but rather a one-byte image whose values fall between 0 and 255, we might compile a table which, for each possible pixel value, contained a list of those images which contained a pixel of that value and where those pixels were located. This table could be indexed by the pixel value in a random-access fashion; for example, if the pixel value is 55, then go to row 55 of the table and see what character images contain a pixel whose value is 55. More complicated mappings from feature values to our table locations are computed by *hash functions*.[4]

Given the weakness of our single-pixel index, we might decide to check a sub-image of our input character image. For example, we might choose a 10×10 sub-image near the center of the character. This sub-image, of size 100, is nothing more than a string of bits which could be interpreted as a single integer. This integer could be used to index to models which have that sub-image embedded in them. The table would be pre-computed off-line, so that it wouldn't cost any more to index with the sub-image than with a single pixel. However, the size of the table grows rapidly with the size of the sub-image.

Returning to our omni-font approach, we could build a table that contains all models having an eastward-facing convex curve or a vertical line. Or we could use feature groups as more powerful indices. For example, our table could store all models which have a vertical line with a horizontal line extending to the right from the top of the vertical line (top-left of R). If only a few characters have an eastward-facing convex curve, then it doesn't make much sense to spend time grouping additional contours with it to form a more powerful index. On the other hand, if many characters share a vertical line (which is, in fact, true), then it does make sense to add an additional line to the group to make the index more powerful.

What we have here is an important trade-off between the cost and reliability of grouping features into more powerful indices and the cost of testing or verifying more candidate models. As databases grow in size, the need for better indices (hence, better grouping) is clear. However, as discussed before, more complex features (or feature groups) are more prone to error, making effective indexing more difficult. This optimization can be computed on the fly: once a feature is extracted, index into the database to see how many models contain it. If there are too many, then go back and increase the scope of the indexing feature through further grouping, until a manageable number of candidate models is returned.

4.4   A final note on our two approaches

A very important trade-off is illustrated by our two character-recognition schemes. In the template-matching approach, the model is overconstrained, specifying the exact shape of the character down to where each pixel is. With such a strong model, little, if any, feature extraction is necessary. Our omni-font description, on the other hand, is a more abstract description of the character's shape, offering invariance with regard to scaling, orientation, and even some deformation. However, matching an abstract description to image data means recovering a comparable abstraction from the image. Recovering an abstract description from an image is the most important problem facing today's object-recognition systems.

Historically, OCR systems relied on the template-matching approach. However, as mentioned earlier, this approach gave way to the omni-font approach in the mid-1980s, when low-cost reliable feature-extraction approaches were developed. As computing power increased, more and more features could be extracted in the allowable time frame, leading to font-invariant software systems that can be run on a PC. As we will see in the next section, when we return to 3-D object recognition, the evolution from template-like approaches to more abstract, generic approaches is proceeding at a much slower pace. Since the mid-1980s, the computer vision community has been preoccupied with approaches that assume knowledge of the exact geometry or appearance of an object.

5 Adding the Third Dimension

Our case study in character recognition has revealed the issues in selecting an object representation for a recognition task. How many models are in the data base? How much is known about the shapes of the input objects? And how reliable are the extracted features and feature groupings? When moving to three dimensions, the issues are identical. In addition, we must consider the problem of occlusion, in which a nearer object obstructs the view of an object further from the camera. Accommodating occlusion means being able to both index and match using only partial information of the occluded object. It also means making sure that the indexing features come from the same object, which, in turn, means that the grouping module must not group features from different objects.

The real problem in recognizing a three-dimensional object is that although the object is three-dimensional, the image and its extracted features and feature groups are two-dimensional. As the viewpoint with respect to the object changes, so do the image features. For example, the front of a car looks different from the back, the top, or the side. In response to this phenomenon, two schools of 3-D recognition have emerged. In the *viewer-centered* approach, the 3-D object is modeled as a set of 2-D images, one for each different "appearance" of the object. In this way, 3-D recognition is reduced to 2-D recognition, except that a single 3-D object may consist of a large set of 2-D views. The complexity or size of the resulting object database is a serious concern and makes effective indexing even more important.[5]

In the *object-centered* approach, a single 3-D model is used to describe the object. Although providing a much more compact and efficient representation than the viewer-centered approach, we now have somehow to compare our 2-D extracted features to 3-D features making up the models. Since the model features look different in the image depending on where they are viewed from, we need to choose features whose appearance doesn't depend on viewpoint. If we could find such viewpoint-invariant features, they would give us a powerful means by which a 2-D image feature could be linked to a 3-D model feature.

What are these viewpoint-invariant features? For example, if two 3-D lines intersect in the world, then from almost all possible viewpoints, the two intersecting lines will appear as two intersecting lines in the image. Only when the camera lies in the plane defined by the two lines is the viewpoint-invariant feature (intersecting lines) lost; in this case, the two lines appear as a single line in the image. This allows us to hypothesize, with great confidence, that if we see two intersecting lines in the image, we're really looking at two 3-D lines intersecting in the world.

In fact, there are a suite of viewpoint-invariant features that have been used by computer vision researchers, most of which were proposed by the Gestalt psychologists (see, e.g., Wertheimer 1938). These viewpoint-invariant features include 3-D lines and curves (which project to 2-D lines and curves), parallel 3-D lines and curves (which project to parallel 2-D lines and curves), collinear 3-D lines (which project to 2-D collinear lines), and co-curvilinear 3-D lines (which project to co-curvilinear 2-D lines). An excellent discussion of these viewpoint-invariant features can be found in Lowe (1985). Other geometric invariants, such as the cross-ratio of any four points of an ellipse, have been used to index into databases of object models (Mundy and Zisserman 1992).

At this point, let's recap what we've discovered. We've seen that there is a trade-off between the power of complex indexing features to discriminate objects and the difficulty with which such features can be reliably recovered from an image. We've also seen that more abstract model representations can be used to describe more than one particular object exemplar – for example a single R chosen from a particular font. Finally, we've discussed two approaches to 3-D model representation, offering yet another trade-off: the potentially large number of views needed to reduce a 3-D model to a 2-D model versus the problem of inferring a compact 3-D model's features from 2-D image features. Armed with this insight, let's go back and see how the recognition problems in figure 5.1 were solved.

5.1   A viewer-centered approach using pixels

In the approach of Murase and Nayar (1995), each image is represented as a point in a high-dimensional space. Imagine laying all the rows of the image side by side until the entire image is a $1 \times n$ vector, where n is the number of pixels in the image. Murase and Mayar take the viewer-centred approach to object modeling that models a 3-D object as a set of views. Each of these views is an image of the object taken from a different viewpoint, as shown in figure 5.7, and each image becomes a vector, as described above. You may ask why we need a set of different views of the object and why one view won't suffice. The reason is that as you move the camera around the object, its appearance may change dramatically. If we're going to store an object as a collection of views, we need to make sure that we have one view for every possible appearance of the object.

Imagine now that we have a database of objects, with each object modeled as a collection of vectors (images). If we're presented with an arbitrary view of an unknown object and are asked to identify the object (and perhaps the viewpoint at which the image was acquired), our task is to find the "closest"

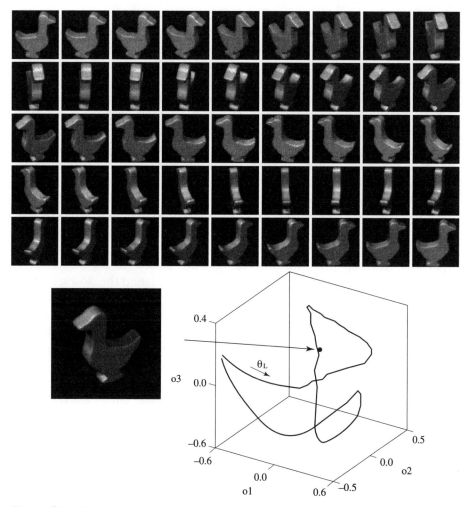

Figure 5.7. A view-based image representation: *top*, a dense set of views is acquired for each object; *bottom*, the views trace out a curve in a low-dimensional space, with each view lying on the curve.
Reprinted with the permission of Hiroshi Murase, NTT Basic Research Labs, Kanagawa, Japan.

image in our database. One simple approach would be to compute the vector distance between the input image vector and all the vectors in the database, choosing the closest database vector as the object's identity. However, this would be a very computationally expensive procedure, since each vector has n components, where n is the size of the image in pixels.

Murase and Nayar's approach is an extension of a very clever approach proposed by Turk and Pentland (1991). Consider an n-dimensional space, and let each image in the database be a point in that space. It turns out that for the resulting cloud of points, there is a more convenient coordinate system in which to represent the points. Although this coordinate system has the same number of dimensions as the original one, it has the property that the positions of the points can be approximated sufficiently by a small number of the coordinates (e.g., ≤ 20 instead of 16K for the images in figure 5.7). This new coordinate system is defined by the eigenvectors of the covariance matrix derived from the cloud of points. Furthermore, these eigenvectors can be prioritized according to their corresponding eigenvalues. The vectors that have high eigenvalues represent more definitive axes or coordinates in our new coordinate system.

Each view of a model object can now be represented in this new coordinate system using only a small number of coordinates. This is an inexpensive process called *projection*. As we move around the object, its different views trace out a curve in this new coordinate system. Since each object looks different, each object will have its own characteristic curve in this system. The database now becomes this new space (coordinate system), and the objects become curves passing through this space. Murase and Nayar therefore propose a two-step procedure for recognizing a view of an object. First, project the view into the new coordinate system. Next, find the closest (traced-out) object curve in the coordinate system, to determine the object's identity. Once the object's identity is known, we can move to a new coordinate system defined only by the views of that particular object. We again project the view on this object-specific coordinate system and find the nearest point on the curve to determine the object's pose (viewpoint), as shown in figure 5.7.

Murase and Nayar's system is very impressive and can recognize and estimate the pose of unoccluded objects in real time. Given a database of objects, some of which are shown in figure 5.8 (*top*), the result of the recognition approach applied to the image shown in figure 5.1a is shown in figure 5.8 (*bottom*). Some limitations of the approach should be noted, however. For example, if the object's shape changes slightly, or the texture or markings on the object change, or the lighting changes appreciably, or there are other objects in the scene, the approach is likely to fail. Although a number of researchers have extended the technique to provide limited invariance to these effects (e.g., Belhumeur and Kriegman 1995; Leonardis and Bischoff 1966; Schmid and Mohr 1996; Shokoufandeh et al. 1998), this technique draws its power from the fact that the object description is strictly local and therefore somewhat brittle. It is ideally suited to the recognition of object exemplars, not object categories or prototypes. The approach therefore resembles the template-matching approach we saw in our single-font OCR example.

5.2   An object-centered approach using corners

As seen in the previous subsection, Murase and Nayar took a viewer-centered approach to object modeling that reduced the recognition problem from 3-D to 2-D at the expense of requiring many views for each object. The alternative

Figure 5.8. Final recognition results (*bottom*) from an object database (*top*). Reprinted with the permission of Hiroshi Murase, NTT Basic Research Labs, Kanagawa, Japan.

approach to object modeling (and recognition) attempts to model a 3-D object using a 3-D object-centered model that is invariant with respect to viewpoint. Since the pioneering work of Roberts (1965), many researchers have taken this approach; we will illustrate one such approach – that of Huttenlocher and Ullman (1990).

In the object-centred approach to object recognition, we are faced with the problem that our input image is two-dimensional, while our object models are three-dimensional. Somehow, we must establish correspondence between 2-D features in the image and 3-D features on the model. If enough corresponding features can be found, it may lead us to believe that we've selected the right model. What are these features that will allow us to link 2-D image information with 3-D model information?

Let's back up a step and ask ourselves what desirable qualities we might look for in such features. First of all, a good feature on the object must not only be visible in the image, but easily and reliably recovered from the image. Second of all, a feature should be visible over a wide range of viewpoints. If you can see it only while looking from a particular viewpoint, the feature will rarely appear in the image and will therefore rarely serve to identify the object. The feature should also be sufficiently local, so that if you occlude part of the object, the feature will still be visible. If the feature is occluded, then we need enough features on the object to choose from so that the odds of not seeing any of the features are small.

The features that Huttenlocher and Ullman chose in their system are a popular choice that balances viewpoint invariance, locality, and ease of recovery. Given the input image in Figure 5.1b, they begin by extracting edges in the image, as shown in figure 5.9a. Edges are connected sets of points which correspond to positions in the image where brightness changes abruptly. The idea is that due to light reflecting in different directions off differently oriented surfaces of an object, the amount of light that each surface reflects towards the camera will be different. Depending on where the source of illumination is, the different surfaces will have different brightness.

Along the seams of these surfaces, there will be a brightness discontinuity where the pixel values jump significantly. Detecting these discontinuities allows us to infer that on the object we are looking at two different surfaces on either side of the line. This assumption, of course, is somewhat optimistic, for a painted line on the object will give rise to a line in the image which should not be interpreted as a surface discontinuity. Vision researchers will therefore often work with textureless objects or assume that enough of the lines in the image correspond to surface (i.e., shape) boundaries on the object.

Once the edges are extracted, we could, for example, try and match edges in the image with surface boundaries on the model. Moreover, we might try to match long edges in the image with long boundaries on the model. The problem is that the length of the surface boundary, as it appears in the image, changes depending on viewpoint. If the surface boundary is heavily foreshortened, its corresponding image edge will be very small. If the boundary is facing the camera, the edge will be maximally long. In choosing edges, we've reduced our image data considerably: we've chosen features that are abundant on an object (particularly a polyhedral object), and our features are somewhat local (if you cover up part of the object, some edges should survive). The problem is that the edges (i.e., their lengths) are not viewpoint-invariant.

Huttenlocher and Ullman rely on the fact that the place where two boundaries intersect *is* stable with respect to changes in viewpoint. Consider

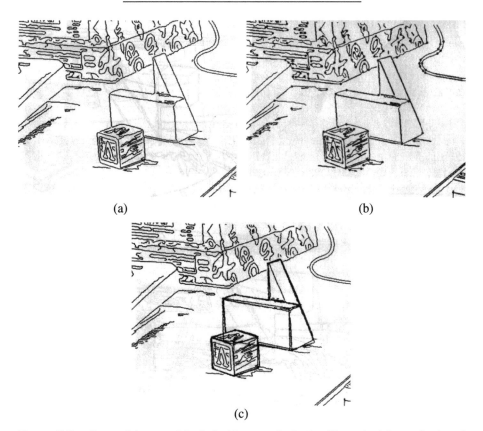

(a)   (b)

(c)

Figure 5.9. Recognizing a polyhedral object on the basis of hypothesizing point-based correspondences: (a) extracted edges; (b) extracted corners; (c) detected objects and their poses. Reprinted with the permission of Daniel Huttenlocher, Dept of Computer Science, Cornell University.

two 3-D lines that meet at a corner. As discussed earlier, with the exception of viewing the two lines in the plane defined by the two lines, the intersection of those two lines will appear as two intersecting edges in the image. Thus, from the extracted edge maps, Huttenlocher and Ullman look for edge corners – places where the edge changes direction significantly. The underlying assumption is that these corners in the image correspond to vertices on the model (places where three or more surfaces meet). In figure 5.9b, the detected corners have been marked with very small dark circles.

Now we're faced with the problem of deciding which corners in the image correspond to which vertices on the model. Since all the corners and vertices look pretty much the same, let's simply choose three of the image corners and three of the model corners and assume that the correspondence is correct. Huttenlocher and Ullman exploit the fact that for their particular projection model (scaled orthographic), there is a unique transformation (translation, rotation, and scaling) of the model that will bring those three model vertices into alignment with the three image corners. Consider, for example, an image with a circle in it. Someone tells you that you're looking at a pencil. In order to verify that this statement is true, you mentally rotate a pencil in space until you're looking along the length of it. You then say to yourself, "Yes, if I was looking along the end of the pencil, I would, in fact, see a circle!" However, the circle in the image is somewhat large. To resolve this, you figure that either the pencil is very large, or it's very close to your eye.

The problem here is that practically any three (mutually visible) vertices on the model can be aligned with practically any three corners in the image. How do we know when we have the correct correspondence? The final step in the procedure is known as hypothesis verification, where the transformed model is "overlaid" into the image. We know that the three vertices and corners will line up. But if the other vertices and surface boundaries in the model don't line up with their corresponding corners and edges in the image, our hypothesized correspondence must be wrong. What do we do in this case? We can keep the three image corners and pair them up with three new model vertices. Or we can keep the three model corners and pair them up with three new image corners. Eventually we'll find a correct assignment of three image corners to three model corners, as confirmed by our verification step. In figure 5.9c, the correctly transformed model has been aligned with the image.

The Huttenlocher and Ullman approach offers some powerful advantages over the Murase and Nayar approach, but suffers from some disadvantages as well. To begin with, the features are local, stable, and viewpoint-invariant. The approach can handle occlusion, changes in lighting, and changes in object scale (in the image). However, the features are not unique, which forces us to try all possible assignments of image features to model features. In fact, each polyhedral model in a data base is made up of the same features, so we may have to repeat the process using every object model. Since the Murase and Nayar approach is image-based, the objects can have rich markings on them, which would simply add extraneous corners to the current approach. The Huttenlocher and Ullman approach can be thought of as a slightly more abstracted recognition system than the Murase and Nayar approach. Although the Huttenlocher and Ullman approach offers more transformation invariance than does that of Murase and Nayar, it is still designed primarily for exemplar-based recognition. Relying on matching corners to vertices assumes that the object model is a geometrically exact duplicate of the object contained in the image. One could view the approach as a form of template matching, where, rather than storing each particular template, the template is generated on the fly from a 3-D model, using some viewpoint-invariant clues.

5.3   An object-centered approach using perceptual groups

One way of dealing with the computational complexity of the Huttenlocher and Ullman approach (i.e., the high number of corner–vertex triple correspondences that need to be verified) is to somehow make the features themselves more discriminating. What other features are local, viewpoint-invariant, and easy to recover, but carry more information so as to reduce the number of correspondences that have to be tried? We turn to a very important approach proposed by Lowe (1985), which took advantage of the powerful visual inferences identified by the Gestaltists.

Returning to the approach of Huttenlocher and Ullman, you recall that corner–vertex correspondences were chosen because, when seeing a corner in the image, you can infer, with very high confidence, that you're seeing a corner in the world. In an earlier section, we discussed many such powerful inferences that are made by the human visual system. For example, parallel edges in the image suggest parallel lines in the world; collinear edges in the image suggest collinear lines in the world; and close proximity of two edges' endpoints in the image suggests that the two lines in the world have endpoints in close proximity. The grouping of image features according to parallelism, symmetry, collinearity, and proximity is called *perceptual grouping* and is an active area of research in both human and computer vision.

Lowe exploited the notion of perceptual grouping in order to reduce the size of the search space. We can follow his approach applied to the image in figure 5.1c. In figure 5.10a, Lowe begins by extracting edges from the image. Next, as shown in figure 5.10b, he looks for pairs of edges that are parallel in the image. The idea here is that the number of parallel edge groups is likely to be much smaller than the number of, for example, corners. A given extracted pair of parallel edges is then paired with a set of parallel lines that bound a single surface on the model. A transformation and verification step similar to that used by Huttenlocher and Ullman is needed to finally recognize the object, as shown in figure 5.10c.

Grouping lower-level features, such as edges, into more complex groups, such as parallel edges, makes the resulting features more discriminating, leading to a more efficient search. It is important to draw a powerful distinction between a triple of image corners and a perceptual group – for example, a pair of parallel lines. If the scene is cluttered with many objects, then a given triple of corners will often contain corners arising from the vertices of different objects (although there are heuristics to reduce this effect). Such a triple is doomed, and the time expended to transform and verify the model is wasted. There is really no meaningful relationship among the edge corners, as they are purely local. The perceptual groups, on the other hand, are causally related, in that they are very likely to belong to the same surface or boundary (Witkin and Tenenbaum 1983).

Despite the increased power of Lowe's approach, it was still applied only to polyhedral objects, and it still relied on a one-to-one correspondence between image edge groups and model line groups. Like the other two approaches, it is suited to exemplar-based recognition and cannot, in its present form, be extended to more generic or prototypical object recognition. Like the Hutten-

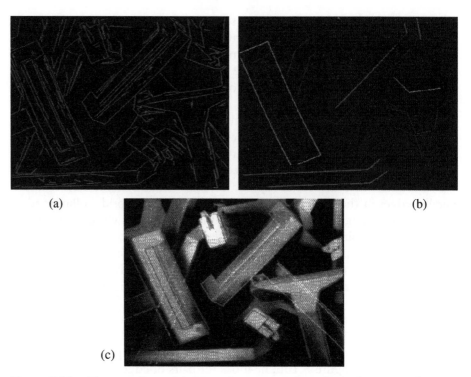

(a)

(b)

(c)

Figure 5.10. The use of perceptual grouping to prune hypothesized correspondences in 3-D object recognition: (a) extracted edges; (b) extracted perceptual groups; and (c) detected objects and their poses.
Reprinted with the permission of David Lowe, Dept of Computer Science, University of British Columbia.

locher approach, it can be viewed as a form of template matching where the template is generated at run-time from a 3-D model. It differs from the approach of Huttenlocher and Ullman in that it will arrive more efficiently at the correct template, at the cost of having to detect additional complex relations among features. Despite these limitations, the use of perceptual grouping to form meaningful feature groups and to improve search efficiency was an important contribution to the computer vision community.

5.4 An object-centered approach using volumes

The three approaches we've seen so far are very rigid in their insistence that the geometry (or appearance) of the model exactly mimic the geometry (or appearance) of the object being imaged. An example of a more flexible system is Brooks's (1983) ACRONYM system, which allows some degree of object parameterization. Rather than modeling objects using polyhedra, Brooks chose to model his objects using constructions of volumetric parts called

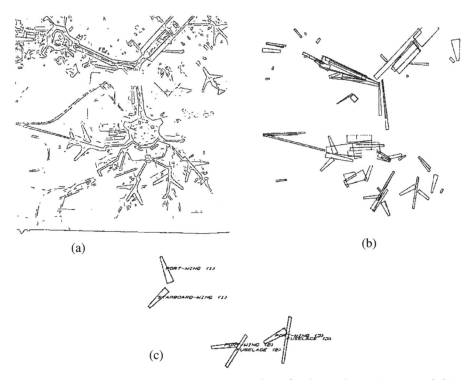

(a)   (b)

(c)

Figure 5.11.   Recognizing 3-D objects by searching for their volumetric parts and their part relations: (a) extracted edges; (b) extracted ribbons; and (c) recognized objects. Reprinted with the permission of Rodney Brooks, Artificial Intelligence Laboratory, MIT.

generalized cylinders (Binford 1971; Agin and Binford 1976; Nevatia and Binford 1977; Marr and Nishihara 1978). His modeling strategy allowed the user to parameterize the number of parts, the sizes and shapes of the parts, and the relative positions and orientations of the parts. This parameterization took the form of sets of constraints assigned to the parts of a model, allowing a single model to vary considerably within a class. Of the four systems we've seen so far, Brooks's system is the only one that can aspire to a single model that can describe all the coffee cups in your kitchen cupboard; the other systems would need separate appearance or geometric models for every differently shaped cup.

Brooks applied his system to the recognition of wide-bodied aircraft in airport scenes, as shown in figure 5.1d. As shown in figure 5.11a, Brooks began by extracting edges from the image. Like Lowe, Brooks decided that since he was looking for elongated parts belonging to an object, these parts would appear as "ribbons" in the image, or pairs of lines that correspond to the occluding boundaries of a volumetric part. Figure 5.11b shows the extracted ribbons from the edge image.

The constraints on the model's volumetric parts and their interrelations

were mapped, using a complex constraint-manipulation system, to corresponding constraints on the sizes, positions, and orientations of the ribbons
extracted from the image. The object database consisted of hierarchically
defined models whereby coarse, prototypical models near the top of the
hierarchy had weak constraints, while models further down had stronger
constraints, specifying exemplars. In Brooks's case, aircraft were broken into
wide-bodied and non-wide-bodied aircraft, which, in turn, were broken into
particular instances – for example, a Boeing 747. The results of labeling the
airport scene are shown in figure 5.11c.

Brooks's ACRONYM system is admirable in its aspiration to model and
recognize objects at different levels of abstraction. However, it has its limitations. For example, it was designed primarily as a target-recognition system
– for example, "Find the planes in the image" – rather than "What objects are
in the image?" The power of the approach was never fully explored, although
generalized cylinder modeling and recovery has survived (e.g., Ulupinar and
Nevatia 1993; Zerrong and Nevatia 1996). The generalized cylinders used
were heavily restricted, as was the viewpoint. Although the constraint-manipulation system was very powerful, it was somewhat cumbersome. Despite these
shortcomings, Brooks's system was a very important contribution to the area
of generic object recognition.

6   Indexing Primitive Trade-offs

In the previous section, we examined four approaches to object recognition,
based on successively more complex indexing features. We began with the
Murase and Nayar approach, which used an image's coordinates in a low-
dimensional eigenspace to index into a data base of model object views.
These features were based on an image's pixel values and required no feature
grouping or abstraction. Next, we saw how Huttenlocher and Ullman used
triples of viewpoint-invariant curvature discontinuities (corners) to solve for a
polyhedral model's pose with respect to the image. Lowe's approach went
one step further than Huttenlocher and Ullman's by exploiting causal
relationships among features using principles of perceptual grouping. Lowe's
perceptual groups were fewer in number and richer in description than the
corner triples used by Huttenlocher and Ullman. However, as they represent
more complex features, they are harder to recover reliably from an image.
Finally, we saw how Brooks attempted to model objects generically by para-
meterizing the geometries of their volumetric parts and the relations between
the parts. The ribbons recovered from an image (corresponding to projections of volumetric parts) were the most complex features recovered of the
four systems studied.

A comparison of object-recognition systems according to their indexing
primitives is given in figure 5.12. In the left column are various indexing

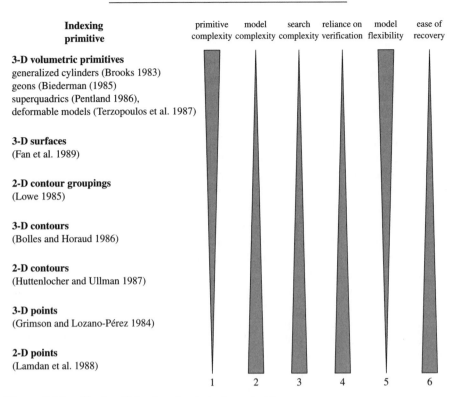

Indexing primitive	primitive complexity	model complexity	search complexity	reliance on verification	model flexibility	ease of recovery

3-D volumetric primitives
generalized cylinders (Brooks 1983)
geons (Biederman (1985)
superquadrics (Pentland 1986),
deformable models (Terzopoulos et al. 1987)

3-D surfaces
(Fan et al. 1989)

2-D contour groupings
(Lowe 1985)

3-D contours
(Bolles and Horaud 1986)

2-D contours
(Huttenlocher and Ullman 1987)

3-D points
(Grimson and Lozano-Pérez 1984)

2-D points
(Lamdan et al. 1988)

         1   2   3   4   5   6

Figure 5.12.   Trade-offs in choosing indexing primitives.

primitives, ranging in complexity from low (e.g., 2-D points) to high (e.g., 3-D volumes), as depicted by the width of the left-most bar (bar 1). Some of the indexing primitives are two-dimensional, while others are three-dimensional, often reflecting the type of input as intensity or range image data. Accompanying each indexing primitive is a reference to a system that employs that primitive. Note that this list of indexing primitives is not complete; it is meant only to exemplify the range in complexity of possible indexing primitives.

Working from left to right in figure 5.12, we see that as the complexity of indexing primitives increases, the number of features making up the object models decreases (bar 2), since an object can be described by a few complex parts or by many simple parts. This, in turn, implies that the search complexity – that is, the number of hypothesized matches between image and model primitives – decreases with increasing primitive complexity (bar 3). The high search complexity involving simple indexing primitives is compounded by large object data bases. As a result, most systems using simple indexing primitives – for example, Lowe 1985; Thompson and Mundy 1987; Lamdan et al. 1988; and Huttenlocher and Ullman 1990 – are applied to small data bases typically containing only a few objects.

Since the simple indexing primitives represent a more ambiguous interpretation of the image data (e.g., a few corners in the image may correspond to many corner triples on many objects), systems that employ simple primitives must rely heavily on a top-down verification step to disambiguate the data (bar 4). In this manner, the burden of recognition is shifted from the recovery of complex, discriminating indexing features to the model-based verification of simple indexing features. Since many different objects may be composed of the same simple features, these systems are faced with the difficult task of deciding which object to use in the verification step. However, there is a more fundamental problem with simple indexing features.

Relying on verification to group or interpret simple indexing primitives has two profound effects on the design of recognition systems. First, verifying the position or orientation of simple indexing features such as points or lines requires an accurate determination of the object's pose with respect to the image. If the pose is incorrect, searching a local vicinity of the image for some model feature may come up empty. Needless to say, accurately solving for the object's pose can be computationally complex, particularly when a perspective projection camera model is used.

Relying on verification also affects object modeling. Specifically, the resulting object models must specify the exact geometry of the object and are not invariant with respect to minor changes in the shape of the object (bar 5). Consider, for example, a polyhedral model of a chair. If we stretch the legs, broaden the seat, or raise the back, we would require a new model if our verification procedure were checking the position of points and lines in the image. Indexing with simple primitives restricts the object data base to models whose exact geometry is known. Excellent work has been done to extend these techniques to certain types of parameterized models – for example by Grimson (1987), Huttenlocher (1988), and Lowe (1991). However, by the nature of the indexing primitives, these models do not explicitly represent the gross structure of the object and therefore cannot easily accommodate certain types of shape changes.

Before leaving the issue of a model's sensitivity to shape changes, it is interesting to note that the same trade-offs arose in our OCR case study. In the template- or image-matching approach, no significant primitive extraction is performed. Instead, rigid models (image templates) are moved across the image until a match is found: if a model changes slightly, a new template is needed. In the feature-matching approach, more complex features are extracted from the image – for example, strokes and shape properties – and are compared to structural character models. Since the object models (characters) capture gross structure, they can be used to recognize characters from many different fonts and point sizes.

Bars 1–5 in figure 5.12 clearly indicate the advantages of using complex indexing features over simple ones. Why, then, do most 3-D from 2-D recognition systems use simple indexing primitives?[6] And why is the computer vision community moving away from more generic descriptions to more exact descriptions (the four 3-D systems presented in this chapter from less generic to more generic were, in fact, developed in reverse chronological order). First of all, simple indexing primitives have proven to be quite successful in certain domains; for example, in typical CAD-based recognition, in which the object data base is very small, object models are constructed from simple primitives, object shape is fixed, and exact pose determination is required. However, more importantly, the reliable recovery of more complex features, particularly from a single 2-D image, is a very difficult problem (bar 6), particularly in the presence of noise and occlusion. Clearly, the major obstacle in the path of any effort to build a recognition system based on complex indexing primitives will be the reliable recovery of those primitives.

7   Recognition by Parts: An Emerging Paradigm

In the previous section, we saw how increasing primitive complexity offered a number of recognition advantages at the expense of increased difficulty of recovery. At the upper end of the primitive complexity spectrum lie volumetric primitives, an example of which we saw in examining Brooks's ACRONYM system. Brooks chose generalized cylinders as his basic volumetric primitive – a representation specified by three arbitrary functions; cross-section, axis and sweep-rule. Since recovering a volumetric part from an image means recovering its defining parameters, a simpler part with fewer parameters is therefore easier to recover. To cope with the unbounded complexity of generalized cylinders (the three functions can be arbitrarily complex), Brooks assumed that his generalized cylinders had straight axes and rotationally symmetric cross-sections.

In the mid-1980s, two vision researchers, one from the human vision community, the other from the computer vision community, introduced to their respective communities two competing volumetric part representations. In the human vision community, Biederman (1985) introduced a volumetric shape vocabulary known as geons while in the computer vision community, Pentland (1986) introduced a shape representation known as superquadrics.[7] Both geons and superquadrics are restricted versions of Binford's generalized cylinders, which attempt to capture a rich variety of volumetric shapes with a much smaller number of parameters. In the following subsections, we will contrast these competing approaches, outlining both their strengths and their weaknesses.

7.1   Superquadrics

A superquadric can be thought of as a lump of clay subject to stretching, bending, twisting, and tapering deformations. The superquadric with length, width, and breadth α_1, α_2, and α_3 is described (adopting the notation $\cos \eta = C_\eta$, $\sin \omega = S_\omega$) by the following equation:

$$X(\eta, \omega) = \begin{pmatrix} a_1 C_\eta^{\varepsilon_1} C_\omega^{\varepsilon_2} \\ a_2 C_\eta^{\varepsilon_1} S_\omega^{\varepsilon_2} \\ a_3 S_\eta^{\varepsilon_1} \end{pmatrix}$$

where $X(\eta, \omega)$ is a three-dimensional vector that sweeps out a surface parameterized in latitude η and longitude ω, with the surface's shape controlled by the parameters ε_1 and ε_2. Additional parameters can be added to provide tapering, bending, twisting, pinching, etc. Even with these additional deformation parameters, the resulting deformable superquadric can be specified by some 10–20 parameters. Some examples of deformable superquadrics are shown in figure 5.13.

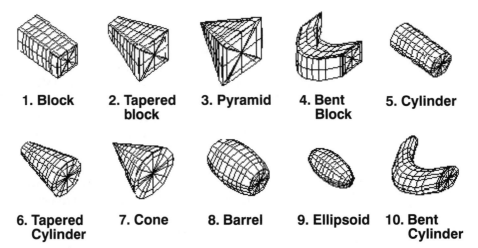

1. Block　　**2. Tapered block**　　**3. Pyramid**　　**4. Bent Block**　　**5. Cylinder**

6. Tapered Cylinder　　**7. Cone**　　**8. Barrel**　　**9. Ellipsoid**　　**10. Bent Cylinder**

Figure 5.13.　Some examples of deformable superquadric ellipsoids.

Superquadrics are appealing, in that they not only capture a rich diversity of shape with a small number of parameters, but also capture a human's intuitive notion of shape and deformation. As mentioned above, the parameters of a superquadric can be thought of as a set of intuitive deformations on a lump of clay. For example, the parameters define dimensional stretching of the clay, bending and tapering of the clay, and shaping of the clay to be smooth or faceted. Pentland argued that these parameters would be ideal for modeling the volumetric parts that make up many classes of objects in our environment. His introduction of superquadrics to the computer vision community spawned a great deal of subsequent work, particularly in the recovery of superquadrics from laser range-finder (3-D) data (e.g. Gupta 1991; Terzopoulas and Metaxas 1991; Raja and Jain 1992; Ferrie et al. 1993; Metaxas and Terzopoulas 1993; Dickinson and Metaxas 1994; Leonardis et al. 1994; Wu and Levine 1994; Dickinson et al. 1997.)

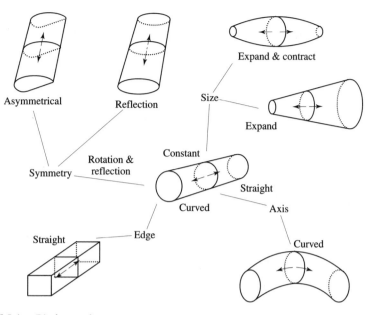

Figure 5.14. Biederman's geons.
Reprinted with the permission of Irving Biederman, Dept of Psychology, University of Southern California.

7.2 Geons

Biederman took a different approach to reducing the complexity of generalized cylinders. Adhering to the three functions defining a generalized cylinder, he proposed heavily restricting the three functions and adding a fourth. The cross-section function would be specified as a binary-valued function that could take on the value of either straight-edged or curved-edged. Similarly, the axis function would be specified as a binary-valued function that could take on the value of either straight or curved. The cross-section sweep function would have three possible values: constant, expanding, or expanding followed by contracting. Biederman added a fourth function describing the symmetry of the cross-section. The cross-section function takes on one of three values: rotationally symmetric, reflectively symmetric, or asymmetric. By permuting the values of these properties, Biederman arrived at his vocabulary of 36 geons, as shown in figure 5.14.

Biederman argued that the four definitive properties could be easily and quickly recovered from viewpoint-invariant properties of image contours. Geons offer a qualitative abstraction of shape whose 36 categories are invariant under minor deformations of shape. For example, the fact that a cylinder is bent is critical, whereas the degree to which it is bent is not. Biederman's introduction of geons to the computer vision community motivated many researchers to build computer vision systems based on Biederman's geons, (e.g., Hummel et al. 1988; Dickinson et al. 1990, 1992a, 1992b, 1997a; Fairwood 1991; Bergevin and Levine 1992a, 1992b, 1993; Biederman et al. 1992; Jacot-Descombes and Pun 1992; Raja and Jain 1992, 1994; Wu and Levine 1994; Du and Munck-Fairwood 1995).

7.3   What's missing?

Both superquadrics and geons represent a restricted form of generalized cylinders. Although not as powerful as generalized cylinders, they nevertheless offer a rich vocabulary with which to construct objects. The challenge has been in their recovery from image data. Superquadric recovery has been mainly restricted to laser range-finder data, where the number of 3-D image data points greatly exceeds the number of parameters that must be recovered, overconstraining the shape-fitting problem. For 2-D images, the data points to which the superquadric can be fitted lie only along the gradient discontinuities or edges. These points are too poorly distributed along the surface of the superquadric to guarantee a unique solution for the recovered shape parameters. Hence, superquadric recovery from image data has met with very little success.

Even if superquadrics could be reliably recovered from image date, they still provide no shape categorization, as required for recognition. Somehow, the parameter space of the superquadric must be carved up into hypervolumes that correspond to some set of shape classes – for example, Wu and Levine 1994. Once these classes are known, a part label can be assigned to a recovered superquadric, and this label, along with the labels of adjacent parts, can be used as an index into the object data base. The part labels, or classes, can be used as a coarse-level index, while the sizes and relative orientations of the parts can be used to prune candidates having the same coarse part structure.

Although geons provide a qualitative shape description, they capture no metric shape information. A description of two geons does not specify their absolute or relative orientation, their absolute or relative size, or, for example, how curved or tapered they are (assuming that they are curved or tapered). Granted, Biederman's goal was a qualitative representation for distinguishing between different classes of objects; however, such information is essential for interacting with the object and for distinguishing between subclasses of an object.

Geons also represent a somewhat arbitrary choice of qualitative shape properties and their dichotomous and trichotomous properties. Why four properties, not three or five? Why tapering, not twisting? Why curved versus straight cross-section shape, and not some combination of both? Although Biederman's choice of shape properties and their values are well motivated, the computer vision community has been reluctant to embrace them. Part of the problem has been the computer vision community's inability to recover geons from real images of real objects (see Dickinson et al. 1997a).

8   The Road Ahead: Generic Object Recognition

The key problem facing object recognition is shape abstraction. Although a particular image feature – for example, a line, curve, or region – may be salient in the *image*, it may not be salient in the *world*. For example, the edges separating the stripes on a coffee cup may have very high contrast and may yield the "best" edges in the image. However, in terms of a generic coffee cup model (e.g., a handle attached to the side of a cylinder), such edges play absolutely no role. Any object-recognition paradigm that assumes that such edges have corresponding edges on the model cannot recognize objects based on their prototypical shape. In such a paradigm, object models must mimic the exact structure of the objects appearing in the image. If three different coffee cups appear in an image, each with different oriented stripes, a separate model will be required for each cup.

Deriving generic shape representations that capture the coarse, prototypical shape of an object is well within our grasp. Both superquadrics and geons, for example, are quite suitable for this task, with each capturing the definitive part structure of an object. However, to index into object models with such parts requires that such parts be recovered from the image. Complex objects with textured surfaces give rise to a plethora of edges or regions in the image. Somehow, these edges or regions must not only be grouped into larger structures, they must be abstracted to form "meta-regions" which correspond to the projected abstract surfaces on the object. This daunting task is seldom addressed in the computer vision community.

This chapter has sought to shed some light on the problem of representing and recognizing objects. To the designers of computer vision systems and to those modeling the human visual system, the issues are the same. What are the relevant image features? How are they grouped or abstracted? How are model objects represented, and how is indexing performed? Is recognition more bottom-up, more top-down, or a combination of both? We have explored some of these issues through some illustrative examples; many references are provided for further study. Object recognition is a fascinating, multidisciplinary topic, offering many exciting avenues for further research.

Notes

1   There is no way of telling whether a disk in a video image is a small disk positioned close to the camera or a large disk positioned further away. On the other hand, a range image containing the same disk will specify the actual distance from the sensor to the disk.

2   Some template-matching systems in the mid-1980s were able to accommodate as many as 12 different fonts by storing 12 sets of templates.

3   Conversely, we could have set the depth equal to the size of the input graph and the branching factor equal to the size of the model graph.

4   For a discussion on how the topology of a 2-D silhouette can be compactly encoded for use as an index, see Siddiqi et al. 1998.

5   Plantinga and Dyer (1990) have shown that a polyhedral object with n faces has an aspect graph (structured collection of views) whose number of views is $O(n^9)$, implying an explosive growth in the number of 2-D models in the data base. Articulated objects only compound the problem.

6   Many of the more complex indexing primitives – e.g., 3-D surface patches, deformable models, and superquadrics – are typically recovered from range data images.

7   Superquadrics, or more formally, superquadric ellipsoids, were originally conceived by the Danish architect Hein (see Gardiner 1965), brought to the computer graphics community by Barr (1981), and brought to the computer vision community by Pentland (1986) and Solina and Bajcsy (1990).

References

Agin, G. and Binford, T. (1976) Computer description of curved objects. *IEEE Transactions on Computers* C-25(4), 439–49.

Barr, A. (1981) Superquadrics and angle-preserving transformations. *IEEE Computer Graphics and Applications* 1, 11–23.

Belhumeur, P. and Kriegman, D. (1995) What is the set of images of an object under all possible lighting conditions. In *IEEE Conference on Computer Vision and Pattern Recognition*, San Francisco, CA. June 1996, 270–7.

Bergevin, R. and Levine, M. D. (1992a) Extraction of line drawing features for object recognition. *Pattern Recognition* 25(3), 319–34.

—— (1992b) Part decomposition of objects from single view line drawings. *CVGIP: Image Understanding* 55(1), 73–83.

—— (1993) Generic object recognition: building and matching coarse 3d descriptions from line drawings. *IEEE Transactions on Pattern Analysis and Machine Intelligence* 15, 19–36.

Biederman, I. (1985) Human image understanding: recent research and a theory. *Computer Vision, Graphics, and Image Processing* 32, 29–73.

Biederman, I., Hummel, J., Gerhardstein, P. and Cooper, E. (1992) From images edges to geons to viewpoint invariant object models: a neural net implementation. In *Proceedings, SPIE Applications of Artifical Intelligence X: Machine Vision and Robotics*, Orlando, FL, 570–8.

Binford, T. (1971) Visual perception by computer. In *Proceedings, IEEE Conference on Systems and Control*, Miami, FL.

Bolles, R. and Horand, P. (1986) 3DPO: a three-dimensional part orientation system. *International Journal of Robotics Research* 5(3), 3–26.

Brooks, R. (1983) Model-based 3-D interpretations of 2-D images. *IEEE Transactions on Pattern Analysis and Machine Intelligence* 5(2), 140–50.

Dickinson, S. and Metaxas D. (1994) Integrating qualitative and quantitative shape recovery. *International Journal of Computer Vision* 13(3), 1–20.

Dickinson, S., Pentland, A. and Rosenfeld, A. (1990) A representation for qualitative 3-D object recognition integrating object-centered and viewer-centered models. In K. Leibovic (ed.), *Vision: A Convergence of Disciplines*, New York, Springer Verlag, 398–421.

—— (1992a) From volumes to views: an approach to 3-D object recognition. *CVGIP: Image Understanding* 55(2), 130–54.

—— (1992b) 3-D shape recovery using distributed aspect matching. *IEEE Transactions on Pattern Analysis and Machine Intelligence* 14(2), 174–98.

Dickinson, S., Metaxas, D. and Pentland, A. (1997b) The role of model-based segmentation in the recovery of volumetric parts from range data. *IEEE Transactions on Pattern Analysis and Machine Intelligence* 19(3), 259–67.

Dickinson, S., Bergevin, R., Biederman, I., Eklundh, J.-O., Jain, A., Munck-Fairwood, R. and Pentland, A. (1997a) Panel report: the potential of geons for generic 3-D object recognition. *Image and Vision Computing* 15(4), 277–92.

Du, L. and Munck-Fairwood, R. (1995) Geon recognition through robust feature grouping. In *Proceedings, 9th Scandinavian Conference on Image Analysis*, Uppsala, Sweden, June 1995, 715–22.

Fairwood, R. (1991) Recognition of generic components using logic – program relations of image contours. *Image and Vision Computing* 9(2), 113–22.

Fan. T., Medioni, G. and Nevatia, R. (1989) Recognizing 3-D objects using surface descriptions. *IEEE Transactions on Pattern Analysis and Machine Intelligence* 11(11), 1140–57.

Ferrie. F., Lagarde, J. and Whaite, P. (1993) Darboux frames, snakes, and super-quadrics: geometry from the bottom up. *IEEE Transactions on Pattern Analysis and Machine Intelligence* 15(8), 771–84.

Gardiner, M. (1965) The superellipse: a curve that lies between the ellipse and the rectangle. *Scientific American* 213, 222–34.

Grimson, W. and Lozano-Pérez, T. (1984) Model-based recognition and localization from sparse range or tactile data. *International Journal of Robotics Research* 3(3), 3–35.

Gupta, A. (1991) Surface and volumetric segmentation of 3D objects using parametric shape models. Technical Report MS-CIS-91-45, GRASP LAB 128, University of Pennsylvania, Philadelphia, PA.

Hummel, J., Biederman. I., Gerhardstein, P. and Hilton, H. (1988) from edges to geons; a connectionist approach. In *Proceedings, Connectionist Summer School*, Carnegie Mellon University, June 1988, 462–71.

Huttenlocher, D. (1988) Three-dimensional recognition of solid objects from a two-dimensional image. Technical Report 1045. Artificial Intelligence Laboratory, MIT, Cambridge, MA.

Huttenlocher, D. and Ullman, S. (1987) Object recognition using alignment. In *Proceedings, First International Conference on Computer Vision*, London, 102–11.

—— (1990) Recognizing solid objects by alignment with an image. *International Journal of Computer Vision* 5(2), 195–212.

Jacot-Descombes, A. and Pun, T. (1992) A probabilistic approach to 3-D inference of geons from a 2-D view. In *Proceedings, SPIE Applications of Artificial Intelligence X: Machine Vision and Robotics*. Orlando, FL, 579–88.

Lamdan, Y., Schwartz, J. and Wolfson, H. (1988) On recognition of 3-D objects from

2-D images. In *Proceedings, IEEE International Conference on Robotics and Automation*, Philadelphia, PA, 1407–13.

Leonardis, A. and Bischoff, H. (1996) Dealing with occlusions in the eigenspace approach. In *Proceedings, IEEE Conference on Computer Vision and Pattern Recognition*, San Francisco, CA, June 1996, 453–8.

Leonardis, A., Solina, F. and Macerl, A. (1994) A direct recovery of superquadric models in range images using recover-and-select paradigm. In *Proceedings, Third European Conference on Computer Vision (Lecture Notes in Computer Science*, Vol. 800), Stockholm: Springer-Verlag, 309–18.

Lowe, D. (1985) *Perceptual Organization and Visual Recognition* Norwell, MA: Kluwer Academic Publishers.

—— (1991) Fitting parameterized three-dimensional models to images. *IEEE Transactions on Pattern Analysis and Machine Intelligence* 13(5), 441–50.

Marr, D. and Nishihara, H. (1978) Representation and recognition of the spatial organization of three-dimensional shapes. *Royal Society of London* B200, 269–94.

Metaxas, D. and Terzopoulos, D. (1993) Shape and nonrigid motion estimation through physics-based synthesis. *IEEE Transactions on Pattern Analysis and Machine Intelligence* 15(6), 580–91.

Mundy, J. and Zisserman, A. (ed.) (1992) *Geometric Invariance in Computer Vision*, Cambridge, MA: MIT Press.

Murase, H. and Nayar, S. (1995) Visual learning and recognition of 3-D objects from appearance. *International Journal of Computer Vision* 14, 5–24.

Nevatia, R. and Binford, T. (1977) Description and recognition of curved objects. *Artificial Intelligence* 8, 77–98.

Pentland, A. (1986) Perceptual organization and the representation of natural form. *Artificial Intelligence* 28, 293–331.

Plantinga, H. and Dyer, C. (1990) Visibility, occlusion, and the aspect graph. *International Journal of Computer Vision* 5(2), 137–60.

Raja, N. and Jain, A. (1992) Recognizing geons from superquadrics fitted to range data. *Image and Vision Computing* 10(3), 179–90.

—— (1994) Obtaining generic parts from range images using a multi-view representation. *CVGIP: Image Understanding* 60(1), 44–64.

Roberts, L. (1965) Machine perception of three-dimensional solids. In J. Tippett et al. (eds), *Optical and Electro-Optical Information Processing*, Cambridge, MA: MIT Press, 159–97.

Schmid, C. and Mohr R. (1996) Combining greyvalue invariants with local constraints for object recognition. In *Proceedings, IEEE Conference on Computer Vision and Pattern Recognition*, San Francisco, CA, June 1996, 872–7.

Shokoufandeh, A., Marsic, I. and Dickinson, S. (1998) View-based object matching. In *Proceedings, IEEE International Conference on Computer Vision*, Bombay, January 1998, 588–95.

Siddiqi, K., Shokoufandeh, A., Dickinson, S. and Zucker, S. (1998) Shock graphs and shape matching. In *Proceedings, IEEE International Conference on Computer Vision*, Bombay, January 1998, 222–9.

Solina, F. and Bajcsy, R. (1990) Recovery of parametric models from range images: the case for superquadrics with global deformations. *IEEE Transactions on Pattern Analysis and Machine Intelligence* 12(2), 131–46.

Terzopoulos, D. and Metaxas, D. (1991) Dynamic 3D models with local and global deformations: deformable superquadrics. *IEEE Transactions on Pattern Analysis and Machine Intelligence* 13(7), 703–14.

Terzopoulos, D., Witkin. A. and Kass, M. (1987) Symmetry-seeking models and 3D object recovery. *International Journal of Computer Vision* 1, 211–21.

Thompson, D. and Mundy, J. (1987) Model-directed object recognition on the connection machine. In *Proceedings, DARPA Image Understanding Workshop,* Los Angeles, CA, 93–106.

Turk, M. and Pentland, A. (1991) Eigenfaces for recognition. *Journal of Cognitive Neuroscience* 3(1), 71–86.

Ulupinar, F. and Nevatia, R. (1993) Perception of 3-D surfaces from 2-D contours. *IEEE Transactions on Pattern Analysis and Machine Intelligence* 15, 3–18.

Wertheimer, M. (1938) Laws of organization in perceptual forms. In W. Ellis (ed.), *Source Book of Gestalt Psychology,* New York: Harcourt, Brace.

Witkin, A. and Tenenbaum, J. (1983) On the role of structure in vision. In J. Beck, B. Hope, and A. Rosenfeld (eds.) *Human and Machine Vision,* New York: Academic Press, 481–548.

Wu, K. and Levine, M. (1994) Recovering parametric geons from multiview range data. In *Proceedings, IEEE Conference on Computer Vision and Pattern Recognition,* Seattle, WA, June 1994, 159–66.

Zerroug, M. and Nevatia, R. (1996) Volumetric descriptions from a single intensity image. *International Journal of Computer Vision* 20(1/2), 11–42.

6

Does Vision Work?
Towards a Semantics of Perception

Jacob Feldman

1   Seeing is Believing

As the old saying goes, seeing is believing. To the average person – a naive perceiver – the perceptual experience is so compelling as to leave no room for doubt. What you see is – precisely, unambiguously, and quite literally – what is out there in the world. After all, our very lives depend on the reliability of vision. Every time we cross the street, step into a forest, or put a piece of food in our mouths, we are counting on vision to accurately report the state of the world – no car, no tiger, no hemlock.

But what justifies our faith in vision? To the naive perceiver, perceptual beliefs are justified simply because they are *true* – or, in the terminology of vision science, "veridical." How can one doubt what is before one's eyes? But there are a few simple facts about perception that ought to send a shudder of epistemological doubt through our hearts.

Vision is fallible. First of all, the visual system is vulnerable to being tricked by certain types of images and scenes, usually called *optical illusions*. (Figure 6.1 shows two famous examples.) Really, "perceptual illusions" would be a more appropriate term, because usually the explanation has nothing to do with optics, but, rather, with the way perceptual inference works. These displays have been carefully constructed in order to take advantage of the tricks the visual system exploits all the time (but which usually don't lead to errors).

Traditionally, textbooks emphasize the sometimes subtle way in which optical illusions reveal the internal operation of the visual system. But the more basic lesson of these illusions is simply that vision is capable of providing

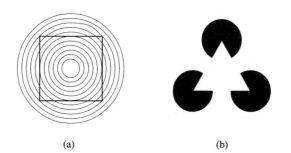

(a)   (b)

Figure 6.1. Two famous perceptual illusions. In (a) the square appears "squished," but isn't. In (b) (due to Gaetano Kanizsa) most people see a triangle in front of three circles (rather than simply three "pac-men." In addition, most people report that the triangle is a brighter white than the background, with a noticeable boundary between them. Actually there is no brightness difference, as can be confirmed simply by blocking out two pac-men with your fingers.

you with a completely compelling but *false* belief. This can hardly help but make one wonder about the justification for all the *other* beliefs provided by vision – the ones on whose reliability we daily pledge our lives. How do we know that those don't have an equally shaky foundation? Indeed, how would one go about showing that ordinary, garden-variety beliefs generated by the visual system are well-founded? Indeed, what does it mean for a perceptual belief to be well-founded? Philosophers have pointed out that, for a belief to be justified, it has to be more than simply *true* – after all, that could simply be a fortunate accident, like a broken watch being correct twice a day. To be justified, a perceptual belief must be true in virtue of some reliable causal connection to the world around us. But what is the nature of this connection? This is one of the questions considered in this chapter.

Vision is ambiguous. A closely related point is that, as vision scientists never tire of repeating, the visual stimulus is inherently ambiguous. The visual image that falls on the retina contains only a limited amount of information, which is perfectly consistent with a multitude of different states of the world. In the lingo, the *proximal stimulus* – the pattern of stimulation on the retina, the light-sensitive surface of the eye – is consistent with many distinct interpretations of the *distal stimulus* – the thing "out there" that you are actually trying to perceive.

The most notorious example is depth. The world is three-dimensional, the retinal image two-dimensional; the third dimension, depth, is lost when the world is projected onto our retinas. Figure 6.2 gives an example showing how even a simple picture is consistent with any number of totally different 3-D interpretations, some of them quite bizarre. The reconstruction is unconscious and automatic – you're not aware of having to work at it – but it is nonetheless complex and, in a certain way, intelligent.

We take it for granted that the interpretation we pick – for example, (a) in the figure – is objectively the correct one. But given that all the wrong

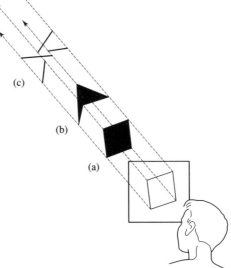

Figure 6.2. Ambiguity of three-dimensional structure. The image is consistent with a rectangular object (a), which is what we see. But it is also *equally* consistent with an irregularly-shaped object (b), or even with the disconnected collection of line segments (c).

interpretations are just as consistent with what we see, what makes us so sure that the one we see is the right one?

2 A Semantics for Perception

These questions of justification and epistemology in vision bear on what we might call the *semantics* of perception. This is a somewhat fuzzy term, used in different ways by philosophers, linguists, and computer scientists, and hardly used at all by psychologists, ever eager to affirm their empiricist *bona fides*. The common threads through all the uses are the twin ideas of *meaning* and *truth conditions*. In philosophy the term usually refers to attempts to clarify the meaning, and thus the content, of ordinary concepts – and hence to spell out what transforms an ordinary belief (an idea held by an agent) into a piece of knowledge (a *justified, true* belief). Philosophical semantics is thus about adding content and substance to otherwise dry syntactic (i.e., formal) constructs.

In this sense, vision seems like a ripe domain for inquiries about semantics, because the visual system is nothing other than a system for mechanically (i.e., computationally) producing beliefs – peculiarly compelling ones, in fact. Yet the philosopher Jerry Fodor (1980) has argued that psychological theories – for example, of perception – cannot have a semantic component, because such theories properly concern only internal mechanisms and representations, while the truth of the resulting beliefs depends on the state of the world outside. The result is that computational theories of perception concern the production of *belief*, but not of *knowledge*. That is, nothing in the perceptual theory directly explains whether perceptual conclusions are true or justified, only how they are produced.

Yet it is commonplace for vision researchers to give casual, informal justifications for particular perceptual rules and algorithms, explaining why they perform with reasonable success in practice. And indeed, such explanations must depend on characterizations of the way the world typically behaves, and hence take the theorist "outside the head." Such additional theoretical comments may be strictly extraneous to what psychologists usually call a "process model" (a theory of what mechanisms actually occur inside the system). But they certainly seem like part of a full account of the system – explaining for example why the system works, and why it might have evolved the way it did. In the case of vision, this means explaining why the visual system tends to produce true beliefs.

Vision researchers have hardly ever touched on semantics in an explicit way. Notable exceptions are Bennett, Hoffman, and Prakash (1989), who have proposed a single, unified mathematical framework for all canonical acts of perceptual inference. In this framework it is possible to express truth conditions for a perceptual hypothesis in a consistent and general way, in much the same spirit as the ideas presented here (although with a very different mathematical flavor).

In computer science and mathematical logic, semantics has a similar goal, but superficially a very different form. Here the idea is to construct explicit truth conditions for the complex syntactic forms that are the main substance of formal theory. Typically the enterprise is to specify formal conditions that would make a logical formula – a purely syntactic object – true or false. An example is the construction of truth tables, which exhaustively enumerate the truth of a propositional formula as a function of the truth of its atomic propositions. In first- and second-order logic, semantic theory gets more complicated and subtle, often centering around attempts to prove that a certain abstract syntactic theory actually has a "model", a concrete object that obeys all the theory's formal characteristics. To non-logicians, such proofs often have a somewhat anticlimatic air, as the "concrete objects" actually turn out to themselves be symbolic objects (e.g., the so-called Herbrand universe). This can leave the newcomer grasping for some link to the real world. Still, the results can lend a satisfying completeness to syntactic theories, justifying in a completely rigorous way that the theory does what it was intended to do, and under what assumptions. Spelling out those assumptions is especially critical. Tacit assumptions sometimes pop up unexpectedly, and different sets of assumptions tend to produce different conceptions of what is going on.

The aim of this chapter is to try to point the way to a semantics of perception, in a sense combining the conceptual goal of philosophical semantics (explaining why perceptual beliefs tend to be true) with the methodology of computational semantics (using formal methods). Although the goal is a formal theory, the treatment here will be mostly informal and tutorial.

3   Tricks and Cheats

Let's start by trying to characterize the canonical logical form of an act of perceptual inference. As discussed above, vision is inherently a problem in which not enough information is given to choose the right answer – as vision scientists say, the image "underdetermines" the interpretation. Another way of putting it is that vision is *inductive* – many conclusions are consistent with the bare facts of visual stimulation. All of vision in one way or another deals with inferring from limited information something that is hidden or not directly perceivable.

A very general way of stating the problem is that there are *observable variables* and *hidden variables*. The visual system has access to the value of the former but not the latter. But unfortunately, it is usually the latter that are of interest. A canonic example is the dilemma facing our favourite caveman, Ugg, when he picks a piece of fruit. For a piece of fruit x, he would like to know whether the fruit is edible

$$\texttt{edible}(x)$$

or poisonous

$$\neg\texttt{edible}(x)$$

These Boolean predicates, which I will write in a typewriter font, are logical properties that are true or false of their argument x. Unfortunately for Ugg, the value of the predicate $\texttt{edible}$ is not in any way *directly* perceivable – he doesn't, for example, have "edibility" sensors on his retina. All he knows is whether the fruit is $\texttt{blue}$

$$\texttt{blue}(x)$$

or yellow

$$\neg\texttt{blue}(x)$$

(I'll assume throughout that fruits are always either blue or yellow, and that a fruit is edible if and only if it is not poisonous.) How can he infer edibility from color? Clearly, there is no *necessary* relationship between these two variables. But does this mean that there is no usable relationship at all? Indeed it does not.

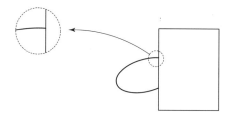

Figure 6.3. A T-junction. The heuristic rule used is: interpret a T-junction so that the top of the T is the contour of a nearer object, and the stem of the T is the contour of a more distant object. Note that in the setting shown, which is typical, this interpretation is correct.

Let's say that Ugg (or maybe Ugg's ancestors) has some experience with fruit. Specifically, he (or his ancestors) has learned the following "fruit rule":

All blue fruit are poisonous

because, say, in the valley where Ugg lives there exist only blue, poisonous hemlock and yellow, edible bananas. (In fact, I realize that hemlock isn't a fruit, and as far as I know it isn't blue, but let's pretend.)

We can write this rule in logical notation using the operator $\Rightarrow$, usually read as "implies," and the so-called universal quantifier $\forall$, usually read as "for all":

$$\forall x\, \texttt{blue}(x) \Rightarrow \neg\texttt{edible}(x)$$

The predicate `blue`, unlike the predicate `edible`, is observable, in that inspection of (or some prior inference about) the proximal stimulus can uncover its value. This difference in the epistemological status of the two predicates is crucial.

I admit that this may seem like an odd example, because it seems doubtful that knowledge of the relationship between color and edibility would be hard-wired into the visual system – and indeed, the example is completely artificial in that sense. But the point is that there is a crucial relationship between a rule that Ugg uses and a putative fact about the world Ugg lives in.

Such a rule is called a *heuristic*, a loose term meaning more or less that the rule usually tends to work in practice, although there is no definite logical or a priori reason why it should work. Such rules are pervasive in the visual system, as indeed in any successful inductive inference system. Indeed, the entire operation of the visual system can be thought of as an attempt to "cheat" by picking up *indirectly* information that is not available directly.

One example of a visual heuristic is the way the perceptual system treats a T-junction, a point in the image where one contour abuts against the middle of another (figure 6.3). The default interpretation here is that the top of the T is the edge of a nearer object, while the stem of the T is the edge of a more

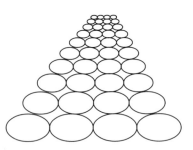

Figure 6.4.   Another heuristic rule: a repetitive texture with a gradually changing scale is interpreted as a uniform texture slanted in depth.

distant object. It is entirely possible for this interpretation to be false. For example, the T could be a wire frame, with neither part actually an occluding edge of any object. However, as the picture suggests, this interpretation is usually right under ordinary circumstances.

Another example of a heuristic rule is illustrated by figure 6.4. Here a repetitive pattern of ellipses, growing smaller as one moves up the page, is interpreted as a uniform pattern on a surface that is slanted back in depth. (The technical term for such a uniform pattern is *isotropic*, meaning the "same in every direction.") Again, this interpretation may well be wrong. But it is compelling, nonetheless, and one suspects that it is right most of the time.

The list of specific heuristic tricks proposed by vision researchers over the years is very large and varied, and, it sometimes seems, not very systematically organized. Even within a seemingly limited domain, such as that of line drawings, it has been proposed that people assume that lines are parallel, that vertices tend to form right angles, that lines tend to align with gravity, that surfaces formed tend to be convex, that our viewing direction tends not to align with surfaces, and on and on for dozens more. And this is not to even mention the myriad tricks outside line drawings, involving shading, stereopsis, motion, color, texture, and so forth. This has sometimes led to the idea that vision is nothing more than a "bag of tricks" – a collection of unrelated heuristics with no underlying theory connecting them. Actually, though, many of the rules have a certain underlying formal similarity (see chapter 4 above). Even beyond that, though, I will argue that the seeming chaos in the inventory of visual inference mechanisms is illusory. To see the argument, we must first ask what makes these heuristic rules tick.

The "fuzzy" nature of heuristic rules tends to make people casual about justifying why they usually work. But of course such rules are far from arbitrary. A crucial insight is that if the world had a completely random structure – so that distinct properties were in no way causally related to one another – then we would not expect any heuristic rules to work. Rather, the success of these rules follows from the way in which they depend on things being orderly and well-structured. The rules are parasitic on regularity in the world. This point has been made in a number of thought-provoking articles by Horace Barlow, a pioneer in the modern study of vision (Barlow 1974, 1990, 1991, 1994). Barlow argued that vision depends on what he called "suspicious coincidences" or "significant associations" among what otherwise might be unrelated properties in the visual world. Roger Shepard (1989), a pioneer in the study of learning, called these coincidences "regularities" and argued that the ability of the visual system to accurately recover the structure of the world depends on its being sensitive to such regularities in the right kind of way. Richards and Bobick (1988) have termed this general idea the "Principle of natural modes." In a similar vein, Richards, Rubin, and Hoffman (1982) have taken an important step towards a formal characterization of the validity of perceptual inferences, by stating express mathematical conditions for the existence, uniqueness, and correctness of the solutions to perceptual problems.

The overarching idea in all this work is that behind every perceptual rule is some reliable relationship between some hidden property (e.g., the poisonousness of the fruit, the structure of the surface containing the texture) and some observable property (e.g., the color of the fruit, the texture on the surface). The fact that you can infer something about the one from the other depends on the fact that the relationship between them tends to be well-behaved.

4   Constraints

But what does it mean for a rule to be "based on" a fact about the world? Take the isotropic texture rule above as an example. The heuristic rule can be stated more or less as:

> *Isotropic texture heuristic:* If a repetitive texture changes scale, then interpret the scale change as a depth change.

As such, the rule is of the form: if a certain proximate situation obtains, infer a certain distal situation. But note that this rule is *entailed* by (though not equivalent to) a certain hypothesis about the world, namely:

> *Isotropic texture constraint:* All repetitive textures are isotropic.

If this is true in the world, then when one encounters a repetitive texture that does *not* appear isotropic, one can only conclude that it is really uniform but is slanted back in depth – so the heuristic rule holds water. In fact, if textures in the world are *always* isotropic, without exception, then the rule becomes deductively valid; its heuristic nature stems only from the fact that the world occasionally contains a non-isotropic texture. Hence there is a close relationship between the two ideas, but they are not ontologically equivalent.

The one is a rule about what to think when a certain image appears, whereas the other is a statement about the structure of the world.

The latter type is what David Marr (1982) one of the founders of computer vision, called a *constraint*. A constraint is an assertion that the world is well-behaved – more well-behaved than it absolutely has to be – in some particular way that a perceiver can benefit from. If textures in the world are random and idiosyncratic, then a perceiver cannot infer much about the world by analyzing any particular texture. But if textures tend to be isotropic, then the perceiver gets some foothold onto distal structure. Hence a constraint really has two claims: (1) *if* the world behaves a certain way, then a certain kind of inference will be possible, and (2) the world really *does* behave that way, at least most of the time. Hence the success of the rule is directly dependent on the truth of the second claim.

One can see intuitively (without spelling it out completely formally) that the texture constraint entails the validity of the texture heuristic, but not vice versa. The heuristic is consistent with many different models of the world, only *one* of which precisely embodies the constraint – an important point, to which we shall return later.

Like the fruit rule, one can easily express the constraint as some sort of quantified logical statement about the world – for example:

$$\forall x \, \text{texture}(x) \Rightarrow \text{isotropic}(x)$$

This type of logical formalism is very useful, because it makes it feasible to express, and even prove, statements about the relationship between specific inference rules used by a perceiver and the abstract universe in which the perceiver is embedded – just what we need for semantics. Hence mathematical logic is a convenient language for getting at the semantics of perception, a suggestion first made by Raymond Reiter and Alan Mackworth (Mackworth 1988; Reiter and Mackworth 1989).

In this connection, the switch in the isotropy rule's ontological status – from a heuristic rule to a constraint – may seem subtle, but is important. Unlike the heuristic rule formulation, a constraint formulation such as the above is a (small part of a) *theory of the world*. Thus we have a chance to make an explicit connection between the rules that we use to see and the theories that we (tacitly, unconsciously) hold about the world.

In this light, it begins to seem that there really isn't all that much of a distinction between the "bag of tricks" idea and the idea that perceptual inference is systematically organized. Each trick is entailed by a constraint on the world. Put all those constraints together, and you have (a part of) a theory of the world. The bag of tricks may seem heterogeneous, but that's only because the underlying theory of the world is heterogeneous – because in fact the *world* is heterogeneous, and the theory is more or less faithful to the world it describes. As for justification, if the theory of the world is right, each of the rules entailed by one of its parts is right; hence perceptual interpretations based on these rules are justified.

But what does it mean for the perceiver's underlying "theory of the world" to be right?

5 Having the Right Theory of the World

A common intuition about the justification of visual rules is that the system makes the right inferences when it has *the right theory of the world*. But what does it mean to have the right theory? First we must ask, "What is a theory of the world?"

In mathematical logic, a sentence is a (possibly quantified) statement such as

$$\exists x \, \text{duck}(x)$$

(the existential quantifier $\exists$ is usually read "there exists," hence "there exist ducks") and

$$\forall x \, \text{duck}(x) \Rightarrow \text{quack}(x)$$

(all ducks quack) and

$$\text{duck (Ernest)}$$

(Ernest is a duck.) A *theory* is a set of sentences that is *closed under logical entailment*, meaning that it includes all sentences implied by sentences within it (see Genesereth and Nilsson 1987 for an introduction). For example, the above set of sentences is not a theory, but would become one by including the additional sentence

$$\text{quack (Ernest)},$$

which is entailed by the previous three. A theory describes an artificial universe, and in a certain sense *creates* a universe by describing all of its properties. (Note that a set of sentences that is not closed under entailment describes some, but not all, of the properties of its universe.)

One can imagine a theory, in this technical sense, that describes the *actual* universe – the one we live in. Call this theory τ_0 – "God's own theory of the world." Such a *universal theory* contains all scientific facts and laws and also contains a myriad of trivial but true facts about what is where and so forth in the world as it stands. By hypothesis, a statement is empirically true if it is contained in τ_0. Such a theory is more or less what was envisioned by Logical Positivism, a school of thought about the epistemology of science that many feel more or less describes the attitude of the typical working scientist today. (Strictly speaking, what we usually think of as "science" is really a small subset of T_0, containing only the most general and sweeping laws and omitting many details.) It may be difficult to accept that such a theory can exist in practice, and indeed even in principle there are well-known inductive obstacles to completely discovering such a theory. But at least the idea has some foundation in conventional philosophy of science.

Now, imagine that we have some hypothetical perceptual inference rule, of the general form

$$A \Rightarrow \alpha,$$

where A is some observable property or variable, and α is some hidden variable. (In general, I'll use Latin characters for observable properties and Greek characters for hidden properties.) Here I'm taking the implies operator $\Rightarrow$ to mean more or less that from the antecedent one should infer the consequent.

Clearly, in order for this rule to be justified by reality, it must be the case that

$$T_0 \Rightarrow \left[A \Rightarrow \alpha \right],$$

the universal theory, entails the rule; or, equivalently,

$$T_0 \wedge A \Rightarrow \alpha,$$

($\wedge$ is the usual logical operator *and*). That is, if the theory of the world holds true, and the observable variable holds true, then the implied hidden variable also holds true – very intuitive. However, this formulation is far too weak, suggesting that the justification of a single little perceptual rule requires the support of an entire theory of the universe. This means that the only perceptual rules that are justified are the ones that are valid throughout the whole universe under all circumstances – certainly sufficient, but hardly necessary. We can do better.

What we need instead is a way of reflecting "local" conditions that, while not true in the universe in general, are true in the limited universe of the perceiver. The relationship between color and edibility in Ugg's valley is an example; there is no *general* relationship between color and edibility that holds universally, but there is a *contingent* relationship that holds in Ugg's environment and can support valid inferences within its limited scope.

To build up a formal expression of specialized conditions, notice first that some theories imply others. We can denote this using the ordinary implication operator, as, for example.

$$T_1 \Rightarrow T_2,$$

meaning that if theory T_1 holds, then so must T_2. As we have defined it, this is equivalent to

$$T_2 \subseteq T_1,$$

because everything entailed by a theory is contained in it ($\subseteq$ is the set operator *subset of*). Now consider augmenting a theory T by some additional knowledge, encoded in a set of sentences S. Denote by $\langle S \rangle$ the transitive closure of a set S of sentences. When we add S to some theory T and then transitively close their union, we get a new theory

$$\langle T \cup S \rangle.$$

($\cup$ is the ordinary set operator *union*.) The additional set of sentences S is called a *refinement to T*, and the new theory $\langle T \cup S \rangle$ is called the *refined theory*.

A famous example drawn from the history of science is the relationship between Newtonian and Einsteinian mechanics. In classical physics, momentum (p) is the product of mass and velocity,

$$p = mv.$$

In everyday physical situations, this expression is so nearly perfectly empirically correct that nineteenth-century physicists could hardly be blamed for taking it as gospel. However, using the Lorentz transformations, Einstein showed that momentum could more correctly be expressed by the more complex expression

$$p = \frac{mv}{\sqrt{1 - \frac{v^2}{c^2}}},$$

where c is the speed of light. At first, this expression looks very different; how could Newton have been so wrong? But a closer examination reveals that the two expressions are not so different under ordinary conditions – namely, when velocity is much less than the speed of light. In everyday life, and in all the physical experiments on which classical mechanics was based, $v \ll c$. This means that the "Lorentz correction" approaches unity,

$$\sqrt{1 - \frac{v^2}{c^2}} \approx 1,$$

which means that Einstein's expression reduces to Newton's. Putting this in our terms (though speaking loosely, of course), when the refinement $v \ll c$ is added to Einstein's theory, you get Newton's:

$$\langle T_{\text{Einstein}} \cup [v \ll c] \rangle \approx T_{\text{Newton}}$$

This example is not as far from perception as it might seem. Certain aspects of motion perception, for example, make assumptions about the momentum of moving objects in the field of view. Clearly, the Newtonian expression is adequate in theories of motion perception, simply because in the environment in which the visual system operates, this expression is almost perfectly true. In other words, the refined theory assumed by the visual system tacitly – but quite reasonably – assumes that objects don't move at near the speed of light.

For a more perceptual example, consider our caveman Ugg and his poisonous hemlock. Say that in the universe in general there is no relationship between color and edibility, but that in Ugg's valley (the Boolean predicate in_valley set to true) blue fruits are poisonous and yellow fruits edible, while outside the valley the reverse is true. Hence, by hypothesis, the universal theory T_0 contains the following set of sentences:

$$\texttt{fruit}(x) \wedge \texttt{blue}(x) \wedge \texttt{in\_valley} \Rightarrow \neg\texttt{edible}(x),$$
$$\texttt{fruit}(x) \wedge \neg\texttt{blue}(x) \wedge \texttt{in\_valley} \Rightarrow \texttt{edible}(x).$$
$$\texttt{fruit}(x) \wedge \texttt{blue}(x) \wedge \neg\texttt{in\_valley} \Rightarrow \texttt{edible}(x),$$
$$\texttt{fruit}(x) \wedge \neg\texttt{blue}(x) \wedge \neg\texttt{in\_valley} \Rightarrow \neg\texttt{edible}(x).$$

Now, Ugg lives in the valley, so for him the predicate in_valley is true. Hence, although the universal theory T_0 does *not* entail the rule "blue fruit are poisonous,"

$$T_0 \not\Rightarrow [\texttt{blue}(x) \wedge \texttt{fruit}(x) \Rightarrow \neg\texttt{edible}(x)],$$

Ugg's refined theory $T_{\text{Ugg}} = \langle T_0 \cup \texttt{in\_valley}\rangle$ *does* entail this rule:

$$\langle T_0 \cup \texttt{in\_valley}\rangle \Rightarrow [\texttt{blue}(x) \wedge \texttt{fruit}(x) \Rightarrow \neg\texttt{edible}(x)].$$

That is, the refinement to Ugg's own environment justifies Ugg's inference rule.

Now we need to abstract a bit and see how multiple theories relate. When there exists some refinement S that allows one theory T_1 to entail another theory T_2, we write

$$T_1 \rightsquigarrow_S T_2,$$

sometimes dropping the subscript when the refinement used is obvious. Clearly, the relation $\rightsquigarrow$ is transitive; that is:

$$(T_1 \rightsquigarrow T_2) \wedge (T_2 \rightsquigarrow T_3) \Rightarrow (T_1 \rightsquigarrow T_3).$$

In fact, one can collect refinements along the chain, using union:

$$(T_1 \rightsquigarrow_A T_2) \wedge (T_2 \rightsquigarrow_B T_3) \Rightarrow (T_1 \rightsquigarrow_{A \cup B} T_3).$$

That is, refining a very broad theory to a much more specific one in many little steps is equivalent to refining it all the way in one big step, which is the union of all the little steps. Figure 6.5 illustrates the general situation, as well as Ugg's situation.

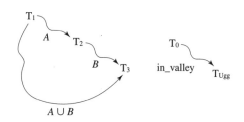

Figure 6.5. Schematic illustrating refinement: on the left, the general situation, showing how broad theories are refined into specific ones; on the right, Ugg's situation, showing how the universal theory T_0, when augmented by the true predicate in valley, leads to Ugg's refined theory, which justifies his rule *blue implies poisonous*.

The important thing about this is that the refinement represents the additional, local knowledge – above and beyond universal laws – that is required to justify Ugg's perceptual rules. Exactly how general versus how specific this knowledge must be – or is, in practice – is not captured by the formalism; nor does it need to be. It might concern the environment only in the perceiver's own backyard, as in the Ugg example; but it might just as well encode some physical fact which has been stable on Earth as long as the human cognitive system has been evolving. For the moment, we are concerned only with the logical role this knowledge plays in justifying the perceiver's inferences, not its substance.

When is a perceptual belief justified? Having laid out the language of theories, we are at last in a position to state a justification – a truth condition – for an arbitrary perceptual rule. A perceptual rule R of the form $A \Rightarrow \alpha$ is justified for a perceiver P if, for some theory T and refinement S,

Justification condition:
    (i) $T_0 \rightsquigarrow_s T$
    (ii) S holds for perceiver P
    (iii) $T \Rightarrow R$.

In this case, the refined theory of the world held by the perceiver is true, and this theory supports the rule in question; hence the rule is justified. The isotropic texture rule discussed earlier is justified for observers (such as ourselves, approximately) who live in a world with isotropic textures. Ugg's fruit is justified because he lives in a valley with poisonous hemlock. When he moves outside the valley – and the predicate in_valley becomes false – the rule is no longer justified. Again, notwithstanding the formalism, this is all in accordance with common sense.

It is obvious that perceivers don't hold the full theory of the world T_0 in their heads. Quite to the contrary, the mechanism in the head may consist entirely of a very impoverished implementation of the heuristic rules that the person uses. Nevertheless, the full theory T_0 does play a causal role in establishing the *truth* of the perceiver's beliefs – and hence plays a central role in the semantics of those beliefs.

6 Minimal Theories

We've seen how holding a certain theory justifies using a corresponding set of perceptual rules, supplying the "truth conditions" one wants as part of a semantics. But what about "meaning"? Given a perceptual rule, which, let us assume, is a purely syntactic or formal construct, what is the meaning behind the rule?

This question is essentially the reverse of the first question. Above, we used a theory to justify a rule. Now we will see how a rule implies the assumption of a certain theory behind it. In a sense, the implied theory gives *meaning* to the rule – in the fairly literal sense of providing a pointer to the kind of world that would justify it. That is, the implied theory supplies the semantics behind the inference.

But *which* theory is implied by a given set of perceptual rules? It seems pretty clear that *many* theories would be consistent with any rules one might pick. For example, consider again Ugg's rule for fruit:

$$\forall x\, \texttt{blue}(x) \Rrightarrow \neg\texttt{edible}(x),$$

"if it is blue, then it is poisonous." What type of world would support such a rule? Clearly, one such world is one in which there exist poisonous blue hemlock and edible yellow bananas and nothing else. Such a universe might be defined by the axiom set A_1:

$A_1 = \{$
    $\exists x\, \texttt{hemlock}(x)$
    $\forall x\, \texttt{hemlock}(x) \Rrightarrow \texttt{blue}(x)$
    $\forall x\, \texttt{hemlock}(x) \Rrightarrow \neg\texttt{edible}(x)$
    $\}$

(in part: for brevity, I'll omit the part about bananas). This miniature universe is what logicians would call a *model* of the heuristic rule: a concrete object that satisfies it. Notice that simply postulating the existence of poisonous hemlock is not enough to justify Ugg's rule, since there might well be other types of blue plants that were *not* poisonous. In addition, we need some version of what computational logic people call the *Closed World Assumption* (Reiter 1978; see Feldman 1997b for applications to perception). For our purposes, this is simply the assumption that there are no entities in our theory other than those explicitly assumed – for example, no other kinds of fruit besides hemlock and bananas. With this general assumption and the above axioms, it follows that all blue things are not edible, justifying Ugg's inferences.

But A_1 is by no means the only set of axioms that justifies the rule. For example, consider the following universe A_2:

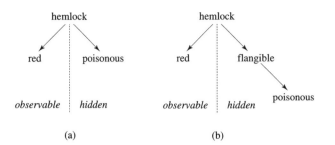

Figure 6.6. (a) A minimal theory of Ugg's edibility rules (b) a non-minimal theory.

$A_2 = \{$
    $\exists x\, \texttt{hemlock}(x)$
    $\forall x\, \texttt{hemlock}(x) \Rrightarrow \texttt{blue}(x)$
    $\forall x\, \texttt{hemlock}(x) \Rrightarrow \texttt{flangible}(x)$
    $\forall x\, \texttt{flangible}(x) \Rrightarrow \neg\texttt{edible}(x)$
    $\}$

This theory invents a new (hidden) predicate, flangible, which intervenes between hemlock and ¬edible. Figure 6.6 illustrates the situation.

The problem is that the second theory has additional structure over and above the first theory which adds little – an additional property with no new information. Clearly, by Occam's razor, it makes sense to prefer the simpler theory.

However, there is a subtlety here. A_1 is clearly simpler than A_2, because it is a proper subset of it. But there is no way to prove that A_1 is *absolutely* minimal, because there may well be other universes, perhaps involving other types of terms or statements, that are neither subsets nor supersets of A_1. For example, it seems natural to postulate the existence of particular tangible entities that bear the properties that you observe, as is done in these two theories. But there may well be other, quite different ways of describing universes.

One solution is to restrict the language in which universes may be described. Unfortunately, there is no absolutely optimal way of doing this. Different choices about what kinds of universe underlie the observations simply lead to different conceptions of the "meaning" of those observations. I will refer to each such choice – each axiomatic description language for universes – as a *semantic language*. This allows us to state the minimality condition explicitly.

Minimality condition:
    Given a semantic language Σ, and a perceptual rule R, for all theories such that $\mathcal{T} \Rrightarrow R$, use the one that is minimal under Σ.

Some examples are given in the next section.

7   The Entities–Properties Semantics

A semantic language makes axiomatic assumptions about the structure and organization of the "real world" that underlie the observations a perceiver makes. For example, the two theories A_1 and A_2 given above stipulate certain types of entities and their associated properties, and nothing else. Simple and spare as this is, it seems like a good starting place for a semantics.

> Entities–properties semantics:
> Theories are constructed from the following two types of sentences:
> (i) *Existential statements* of the form
> $$\exists x \, \lambda(x)$$
> (ii) *Property statements* of the form
> $$\forall x \, \lambda(x) \Rightarrow A(x) \text{ [observable properties]}$$
> $$\forall x \, \lambda(x) \Rightarrow \alpha(x) \text{ [hidden properties]}$$

To understand this conception of semantics, consider again the fruit rule: "if it is blue, then it is poisonous." Such a rule is purely *syntactic;* it expresses a relationship between one property and another. It does not actually say anything at all about the world *per se*. From a purely logical point of view, in fact, such a rule is valid in a world without *any* entities (since it is vacuously satisfied). Nevertheless, it is very hard to think about this rule without in some sense inferring or assuming that there are blue, poisonous fruit lurking behind it. I propose that this conception is, in effect, the *meaning* behind the rule. But it is important to understand that this apparently implied reality is *not directly entailed* by the rule by itself. Once coupled with a semantic language *and* the minimality condition, however, the blue poisonous fruit are an immediate consequence. This, then, is the main idea: the "meaning" of a perceptual rule is the minimal theory that entails it, modulo a fixed conception of semantics.

In fact, we can state the relationship between a perceptual rule and its minimal theory in a stronger way. Because the theory entails the rule, and (assuming a fixed semantics *and* assuming minimality) the rule entails the theory, from a logical point of view the rule and the theory are *equivalent*. This is a surprisingly strong conclusion. An observer may only have certain reflexive reasoning rules explicitly encoded, but these rules may be logically equivalent to a substantive theory of the environment. This renders moot much discussion about whether the organism "really knows" about this or that aspect of the physical world; such knowledge may be equivalent to the inferential strategies which the organism demonstrably uses. This is especially interesting when, as is the case with much of the visual system, the inferential system is thought to be largely hard-wired. Our hard-wired computational system is in essence equivalent to a particular theory of the world, so we can in effect think of this theory as itself hard-wired.

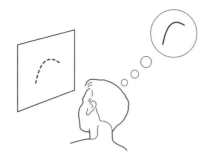

Figure 6.7. A series of collinear elements is interpreted as a distal curve or contour in the world.

Let's take a more perceptual example. Consider the perception of *collinearity* (Figure 6.7). It has long been known that the visual system pays special attention to elements of images that are collinear with another – that is, that appear to fall along a line or curve. Much research has been devoted to the process whereby such patterns are processed (e.g., see Glass 1969; Foster 1979; Smits and Vos 1987; Pizlo et al. 1997; Feldman 1997a). Normally such rules are purely syntactic: they indicate that when the geometry of the image elements has certain properties, the elements should be grouped together. Now tacitly, we assume that such rules make sense, because elements with that sort of geometry are likely to indicate a particular kind of entity out there in the world: namely, an object contour or some other kind of coherent curvilinear object. In fact, in computer vision, where researchers are more oriented toward real-world situations that require the use of perceptual grouping, this inference is sometimes spelled out explicitly (e.g., see Parent and Zucker 1989). But in psychological research the distal curve usually plays no formal role in grouping rules, although it is often conspicuous in *in*formal elucidations and justifications for various candidate rules. The goal of semantics is to bring this informal role out in the open.

The entities–properties semantics captures the essence of the inference in a canonical act of perceptual grouping. Loosely, the rule "group collinear items" entails (again, on this semantics and assuming minimality) a universe that contains curvilinear objects, elements of which will be nearly collinear with each other when observed in the image. This is the mental model underlying the grouping rule, and I suggest that this is the "meaning" of the raw perceptual agglomeration, Moreover, as argued above, in a certain sense the perceptual rule can be thought of as equivalent to the belief that there exist contours in the environment. The perception of collinearity is very basic in our visual system, because the existence of contours is a very stable aspect of the physical world around us.

Again, though, it must be kept in mind that this relationship is strictly dependent on the choice of semantics and the assumption of minimality.

Without minimality, or with a different semantic language, the same perceptual rules might entail a different theory of the environment.

Causal semantics   It is important to understand that the entities–properties semantics is a very limited conception of the universe; at best, it's a starting place. There is no dynamism, no relationship between different entities, no teleology – all things that one might conceive of applying to the world around us. One alternative is to center the semantics on the concept of *causality*, as has been advocated by Michael Leyton (see Leyton 1992 and ch. 4 above), as well as myself (Feldman 1997c).

In a causal semantics, special status is given to the historical sequence of transformations that brought the observed properties into existence. The assumption is that the world began in some initial state and was then transformed by some operations into its current state, leading to the observed values of variables. Rather than just inferring a static world with certain properties, here the perceiver infers the relevant history of the world, thus placing additional meaning on observations in light of how they (apparently) came to achieve their current structure. The same perceptual rule implies a different universe when the world is conceived causally. Of course, other semantics are possible.

8   Does Perception Need Semantics?

So what does all this mean for our naive perceiver? She might be surprised at the complexity of the machinery required simply to assure her that she can believe her eyes. But after all, if one wants to establish that perceptual beliefs are well-founded, one must at some point make a connection between the state of the world and the content of those beliefs. The problem with doing this is that the world is made of stuff and things, but beliefs are made of representations and symbols – a type mismatch. To say in a rigorous way that a certain perceptual belief is true or false, we must relate it to the stuff "out there," but we can't, at least not directly. Instead, what I've proposed in this chapter is to replace the world with an abstract theory of the world – something we *can* relate a propositional belief to explicitly. The circuit is closed entirely within the logical realm. The real world is only relevant to the extent that it is well-described by the theory.

But do we really need to establish that perceptual beliefs are well-founded? That is, do we need semantics? As I've suggested, vision researchers routinely include semantic characterizations in their discussions, not usually as an explicit part of their models, but rather, in a casual manner, in order to suggest why a particular perceptual rule might be useful to the perceiver. Yet it is clear that such characterizations are part of the complete story, if we want a theory of perception which has explanatory as well as descriptive value. Certainly, if one is interested in the adaptive value of perceptual mechanisms, one needs to show how those mechanisms benefit the organism. Since, presumably, the benefit of perception is in yielding true beliefs, one cannot fully explain perception without showing why the beliefs it produces tend in fact to be true – no more than one would try to explain the digestive system without mentioning nutrition. And one cannot do this without bringing the world into the equation in a thorough, systematic fashion.

The truth-conditional part of this chapter, culminating in the justification condition, represents what is really a fairly straightforward attempt to do this. First I proposed a canonical logical form for perceptual rules; then I attempted to formalize the notion that a given rule is justified in a given universe if the validity of that rule is entailed by a theory that describes that universe. Carrying all this out in a formal, rather than an *ad hoc* manner may seem difficult, but it adds clarity. In the past, casual, inexplicit intuitions about what assumptions are actually required to justify particular perceptual inferences have occasionally led to frank errors, such as the fallacy of non-accidentalness (see Jepson and Richards 1992 for a discussion).

The other part of this chapter, concerning meaning and minimal theories, was somewhat more subtle. Here the goal was not simply to establish that the content of perceptual inferences tends to be true, but rather to *identify* that content. The key was simply to recognize that there are many underlying theories of the world that might lead one to use a given perceptual rule or mechanism. The minimum rule suggested here picks out one of these theories and gives it special status. I have argued that this minimal model is in effect the meaning of the rule, because it names the world that is pointed to by the rule – the reality behind the curtain, so to speak. The position I have implicitly taken here is that defining perceptual content is essentially a technical question, rather than a purely philosophical one: the content or meaning of a particular perceptual inference is a *model* of that inference in the logical sense – that is, a well-defined mathematical object. This mathematical object seems to have a certain *prima facie* role in the formation of perceptual belief. Whether it has any deeper psychological validity remains a question to be explored.

Acknowledgment

I am grateful to Ernie Lepore, Zenon Pylyshyn, Whitman Richards, and Chuck Schmidt for many interesting discussions.

References

Barlow, H. B. (1974) Inductive inference, coding, perception, and language. *Perception* 3, 123–34.

—— (1990) Conditions for versatile learning, Helmholtz's unconscious inference, and the task of perception. *Vision Research* 30(11), 1561–71.

—— (1991) Vision tells you more than "what is where." In A. Gorea (ed.), *Representations of Vision: Trends and Tacit Assumptions in Vision Research,* Cambridge: Cambridge University Press.

—— (1994) What is the computational goal of the neocortex? In C. Koch and J. L. Davis (eds), *Large-scale Neuronal Theories of the Brain,* Cambridge, MA: MIT Press, 1–22.

Bennett, B. M., Hoffman, D. D. and Prakash, C. (1989) *Observer Mechanics: A Formal Theory of Perception,* London: Academic Press.

Feldman, J. (1997a) Curvilinearity, covariance, and regularity in perceptual groups. *Vision Research* 37 (20), 2835–48.

—— (1997b) Regularity-based perceptual grouping. *Computational Intelligence* 13 (4), 582–623.

—— (1997c) The structure of perceptual categories. *Journal of Mathematical Psychology* 41, 145–70.

Fodor, J. (1980) Methodological solipsism considered as a research strategy in cognitive psychology. *Behavioral and Brain Sciences* 3, 63–73. Reprinted in J. Fodor, (1981), *Representations: Philosophical Essays on the Foundations of Cognitive Science,* Cambridge, MA: MIT Press, 1981, 225–53.

Foster, D. H. (1979) Discrete internal pattern representations and visual detection of small changes in pattern shape. *Perception and Psychophysics* 26(6), 459–68.

Genesereth, M. R. and Nilsson, N. J. (1987) *Logical Foundations of Artificial Intelligence,* Palo Alto, CA: Morgan Kauffman.

Glass, L. (1969) Moiré effects from random dots. *Nature* 223, 578–80.

Jepson, A. and Richards W. A. (1992) What makes a good feature? In L. Harris and M. Jenkin (eds), *Spatial Vision in Humans and Robots,* Cambridge: Cambridge University Press.

Leyton, M. (1992) *Symmetry, Causality, Mind,* Cambridge, MA: MIT Press.

Mackworth, A. K. (1988) Adequacy criteria for visual knowledge representation. In Z. Pylyshyn (ed.), *Computational Processes in Human Vision: An Interdisciplinary Perspective,* Norwood, NJ: Ablex, 462–74.

Marr, D. (1982) *Vision: A Computational Investigation into the Human Representation and Processing of Visual Information,* San Francisco: W. H. Freeman.

Parent, P. and Zucker, S. W. (1989) Trace inference, curvature consistency, and curve detection. *IEEE Transactions on Pattern Analysis and Machine Intelligence* 11(8), 823–39.

Pizlo, Z., Salach-Golyska, M. and Rosenfeld, A. (1997) Curve detection in a noisy image. *Vision Research* 37(9), 1217–41.

Reiter, R. (1978) On closed world data bases. In H. Gallaire and J. Minker (eds), *Logic and Data Bases,* New York: Plenum Press.

Reiter, R. and Mackworth, A. K. (1989) A logical framework for depiction and image interpretation. *Artificial Intelligence* 41 125–55.

Richards, W. A. and Bobick, A. (1988) Playing twenty questions with nature. In Z. Pylyshyn (ed.), *Computational Processes in Human Vision: An Interdisciplinary Perspective*, Norwood, NJ: Ablex, 3–26.

Richards, W. A., Rubin, J. M. and Hoffman D. D. (1982) Equation counting and the interpretation of sensory data. *Perception* 11, 557–76.

Shepard, R. N. (1989) Internal representation of universal regularities: a challenge for connectionism. In L. Nadel, L. A. Cooper, P. Culicover, and R. M. Harnish (eds), *Neural Connections, Mental Computation*, Cambridge, MA: MIT Press, 104–34.

Smits, J. T. and Vos, P. G. (1987) The perception of continuous curves in dot stimuli. *Perception* 16(1), 121–31.

7

The Brain as a
Hypothesis-constructing-and-testing Agent

Thomas V. Papathomas

1   Introduction

This chapter deals with the question of how the brain arrives at stable percepts that best represent the environment, based on the input it receives from the sensory organs. Perhaps it is best to introduce and motivate the material in this chapter with an analogy from logic. The analogy involves the ancient Greek "liar's paradox," attributed to Epimenides (Gardner 1982), a legendary philosopher who was born in Crete and moved to Athens as an old man, ca. 500 BC. The paradox is composed of two sentences:

> Epimenides, the Cretan, said:
> 'All Cretans are liars.'

For the paradox to work, you need the assumptions that liars always lie, and that truth-tellers – let's call them *knaves*, following Smullyan's (1987) notation – always tell the truth. When we are first exposed to the sentence pair, we quickly come to the realization that there is an endless loop of alternating *states*, or *hypotheses*, or *schemata*, under these assumptions. The first state is that we accept the statement, "All Cretans are liars" as true. But then Epimenides must also be a liar, since he is a Cretan. However, if he is a liar, then his statement is a lie, that is, all Cretans must be knaves, which is the second state. Well, if this is so, Epimenides must also be a knave as a Cretan. As such, he must have spoken the truth when he said "All Cretan are liars." We are now back to the first state, where we started, accepting Epimenides' statement as true. Ultimately, we are led to a logical vicious circle, alternating between accepting either the statement itself ("All Cretans are liars") or its opposite ("All Cretans are knaves").

There are numerous such "puzzles" that result in multiple semistable states in logic (Dodds 1951; Gardner 1982; Hofstadter 1980; Smullyan 1978, 1987). Typically, puzzles are given as a set of propositions. When faced with such input, people attempt to make sense of it and to arrive at a solution. One common approach is to make a hypothesis and proceed to test it against the available evidence from the propositions at hand. With ordinary puzzles, there is a unique solution: that is, a stable hypothesis that satisfies all the propositions. However, *multistable puzzles* result in competing semistable solutions that refute each other *ad infinitum*, as illustrated above. At first glance, such puzzles may appear as contrived oddities to the average person, who may think that they have very little to do with reality. After all, logical systems have well-defined rules and axiomatic formulations that lead to a self-consistent structure. However, it turns out that such puzzles are quite important: the liar's paradox can be related to Gödel's famous theorem, which showed that any consistent axiomatic mathematic system includes undecidable propositions (just like the liar's paradox); in other words, such systems can never be proved to be consistent. In fact, Hofstadter (1980: 17) makes the point that "Gödel's discovery involves the translation of an ancient paradox in philosophy into mathematical terms. The paradox is the so-called Epimenides paradox." So, after all, it may not sound so strange that the philosopher Chrysippus (280–206 BC) wrote no fewer than six treatises on the liar's paradox or that the poet Philetas (fourth century BC) is said to have worried to an early grave over it (Gardner 1982).

The point of this chapter is that multistable stimuli, as well as related classes of stimuli, reveal a wealth of information on the *perceptual* process, just like multistable puzzles reveal a lot about *logical* systems. Rather than regarding them as oddities, we can look at them as useful tools in studying how the brain arrives at a stable percept based on the available sensory input. This chapter reviews evidence indicating that the sensory/perceptual component of the brain adopts an approach similar to that of the logical component of the brain:[1] it arrives at a stable percept by constructing and testing alternative competing *hypotheses*, based on the input it receives from the sensory organs (Rock 1983). Gregory (1968, 1970, 1980, 1997) must be credited with formulating best this view of perceptions as hypotheses and the brain as the agent for generating and testing them. This chapter serves as one of two reports, in conjunction with chapter 9 by Papathomas, Kovács, Fehér, and Julesz, casting binocular rivalry as a special case of dealing with multistable stimuli.

The material is organized as follows: section 2 presents the view of the brain as an agent that constantly makes and tests alternative hypotheses and deals with the conflicting requirements for stability and plasticity in the brain. Section 3 presents evidence that supports this view from visual stimulation with multistable, "concealed," and "impossible" figures. Theoretical and computational models that deal with the interaction of data-driven and concept-driven processes are briefly discussed in section 4. Finally, additional evidence and concluding remarks are given in section 5.

2   Theories of Perception as an Interactive Process

The brain's main sensory/perceptual function is to enable organisms to interact with their environment on a moment-to-moment basis for survival. Visual input plays a significant role in this function. However, the very nature of this input forces the visual system to work always with partial information in assessing the state of the environment. This is only partly due to occlusions, either of far objects by near objects or of rear surfaces by front surfaces of the same object (self-occlusions). Even under optimal circumstances, without occlusions, the input that is extracted by the visual system is but a small subset of the information that is available in the environment in the form of Adelson and Bergen's (1991) plenoptic function. This is due to limitations in the viewing angle and eye geometry and the limited sampling frequency of sensors that sample the input along the dimensions of space and wavelength.

Thus we only have the illusion of working with a complete input. One must conclude that the brain *must* go beyond the sensory data in providing us with an accurate representation of the environment. One view of how this is accomplished holds that the brain *constantly* constructs hypotheses based on the input it receives from the sensory organs; it then tests these alternative competing hypotheses, rejecting the weak ones and adopting the strongest one to arrive at a stable state. Gregory (1970) makes the point that the brain constructs hypotheses that go beyond available data, to formulate *object hypotheses*. Indeed, the point can be made that perception always involves the subject's *perceptual set*, in addition to the sensory input (Schiffman 1996: 187). The first modern account of this idea was given by Bruner (1957), who argued that the final percept is influenced by the perceiver's beliefs and state of mind.

The reason for emphasizing the word "constantly" in the previous paragraph is that there is evidence from multistable stimuli suggesting that this hypothesis-constructing-and-testing process does not stop after arriving at a stable state. The sensory input is continuously used to explore alternative hypotheses, in an endless quest to assess the state of the external world. Another way of putting it is that the brain goes continually through a "reality check," as the term so aptly suggests. In natural circumstances, when there is plenty of redundant sensory information, "reality" appears to be stable, and we are not aware of this continuous hypothesis-testing process. In these cases, the brain arrives at a dominant perceptual state and never departs from it, since there are only weak competing alternatives, if there are any at all.

However, there are circumstances, even in everyday life, when this influence of concept-driven processes becomes obvious. This happens, for instance, when some unexpected coincidences create a stimulus that results in the adoption of a wrong hypothesis that lasts for several seconds. In such cases the observer has to invoke top-down processes to construct a cognitively correct hypothesis that is finally verified and adopted. An example is given in Sekuler and Blake (1994: 82): one of the authors woke up and mistook the pattern of light on his wife's hair, formed by a narrow beam of light through the window, for a sudden discoloration of her hair.

There are more extreme manifestations of the role of concept-driven processes, in which they almost override the input from the data-driven sensory organs. An example of this extreme is provided by Johnston and Hawley (1994: 69): one of the authors "saw" his cat on a couch for a moment, before realizing that he was looking at a stack of papers. I myself have also had examples of such extreme percepts: during the first night in a hotel room, I was woken by a thunderstorm, went to the window, and mistook the patterns formed by the tree-tops for puddles on the parking lot. I was immediately "transported" mentally to the ground floor, although I knew I had checked into a room on the third floor. My perceptual set influenced my mind-set. The combination of my sleepy state, the unfamiliar environment, and the stimulus's mild ambiguity contributed to the wrong hypothesis. Most of my similar extreme perceptual errors were obtained in hypnagogic or hypnopompic states, which are the states of drowsiness immediately preceding sleep and just before full awakening, respectively (notice that this was also the case in the example of Sekuler and Blake (1994: 82) in the previous paragraph). This can be taken as evidence that we need a "fully awake" concept-driven mechanism in the brain to arrive at accurate percepts of the environment, and it argues for the view of the brain as a hypothesis-constructing-and-testing agent.

It is reasonable to argue that the brain needs two conflicting characteristics in its effort to provide organisms with very accurate representations of the environment. Grossberg (1987) termed this conflict "the stability/plasticity dilemma": the brain needs stability to maintain continuity across time for expected, predictable inputs; at the same time, the brain must have plasticity and agility to deal with sudden changes and unexpected inputs. In a recent paper, Johnston and Hawley (1994) review evidence from their experiments which indicates the following: (1) Observers localize objects more easily in displays with exclusively familiar objects than in those with exclusively novel objects. They argue that this baseline effect is a manifestation of the brain's preference for stable, expected inputs. (2) Familiar objects are easier to localize in displays with exclusively familiar objects than in ones with one novel object among familiar ones, which they termed *"familiar sink-in"*. (3) By contrast, novel objects are easier to localize when they are the only novel item in the display than when all objects are novel, the so-called *novel-pop-out* effect. The last two effects seem to argue that the brain is more attuned to novel, unexpected input, which is contrary to the tendency displayed by the baseline effect.

It appears that *the brain is simultaneously biased toward familiar and unfamiliar inputs.* Johnston and Hawley review evidence from a wide variety of sources, which provides additional support both for the perceptual inhibition of expected inputs and for the perceptual facilitation of novel inputs. They proposed the *mismatch theory* (Johnston and Hawley 1994), which explains these biases by postulating the following: The bias toward expected inputs is due to concept-driven[2] processes which suppress data-driven processing of expected stimuli. The bias toward novel inputs is a consequence of this same suppression, which frees up data-driven mechanisms to deal with unexpected stimuli. Their neural model implementing some aspects of the mismatch theory is dealt with in section 4.

Johnston and Hawley's mismatch theory is only one of many models that attempt to explain these characteristics; some of these models will be discussed in section 4. Similar paradigms regarding perception as a continuous interaction of data-driven units that provide the raw input and concept-driven processes that provide the hypotheses to be tested against the data were proposed a long time ago (e.g., Sokolov 1963; Gregory 1970). Sokolov (1963) formulated the *dishabituation theory*, based mainly on evidence from the orienting response, which is the spontaneous reaction of subjects to orient themselves toward novel or unexpected stimuli. One of the main tenets of his theory, shared with the mismatch theory, as well as Grossberg's (1976) adaptive resonance theory (ART), discussed in section 4, is that the output of data-driven processes is enhanced for unexpected inputs and inhibited for predictable ones. On the other hand, there is another group of theories, exemplified by McClelland and Rumelhart's (1981) *interactive-activation model* of perception. There is a substantial difference between the two groups of theories: the latter propose that data-driven processing is suppressed for unexpected inputs and enhanced for expected ones. Despite their differences, all these theories involve the formation of perceptual hypotheses, or schemata, based on environmental input from data-driven mechanisms and continuous interaction of the schema-driven and data-driven mechanisms for the formation of the final percept.

3 Evidence for Interaction of Data-driven and Concept-driven Processes

As mentioned above, the interaction of data-driven and concept-driven processes is not evident in everyday life; instead, most of us have the illusion of immediate, stable percepts all the time. In the previous section, examples were presented of cases in which this interaction is manifested in everyday life. Additional examples are provided in the next three subsections for three special classes of visually ambiguous stimuli: multistable, concealed, and impossible figures.

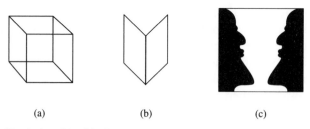

(a)   (b)   (c)

Figure 7.1.   Classical multistable figures: (a) Necker's cube; (b) Mach's book; (c) Rubin's vase/faces.

3.1   Multistable figures

In multistable figures, the physical stimulus is fixed, but it can give rise to a multiplicity of almost equi-probably stable percepts. Stadler and Kruse (1995) have compiled a list of categories of multistable figures that include (i) fluctuations of complex patterns, (ii) figure – ground reversals (see fig. 7.1c), (iii) figures with multiple symmetry axes, (iv) two-dimensional figures that give rise to multiple three-dimensional interpretations (see figures 7.1a and b), (v) actual three-dimensional objects that allow multiple interpretations, (vi) moving stimuli with multistable direction percepts, and (vii) drawings with multiple meanings (see figure 7.4). Examples of multistable percepts from fixed stimuli also exist in audition (Deutsch 1975).

Some early examples of multistable visual stimuli that have been established as classics are shown in figure 7.1: figure 7.1a shows the Necker cube (Necker 1832), which can be perceived in two stable 3-D states; figure 7.1b is the two-dimensional version of "Mach's book" (cited in Stadler and Kruse 1995), which can be viewed as a book with its spine toward or away from the viewer; figure 7.1c is Rubin's (1921) "vase/faces" reversing figure–ground image, in which the alternating percepts are the center vase and the two faces. A stimulus which has characteristics of both types (i) and (ii) above appears in Papathomas (1995). Factors that influence which parts of an image are most likely to be considered as figure and which parts as ground are reviewed by Kanizsa and Luccio (1995).

When presented with multistable stimuli for long intervals, observers experience spontaneous reversals among the stable percepts: one percept is adopted for a while, suppressing the alternative interpretation(s), then is supplanted by another competing percept, and the random alternation continues forever. It is as if the brain is simultaneously accepting a hypothesis and also getting ready to reject it as soon as contrary evidence warrants it, reminiscent of the seemingly conflicting simultaneous biases of the brain toward expected and unexpected inputs (Johnston and Hawley 1994). The theory that views the brain as a hypothesis-constructing-and-testing agent is one possible explanation of this continuous alternation: namely, that this alternation occurs, even though there is one fixed stimulus, because the brain keeps constructing and adopting different hypotheses that are consistent with the visual input. Some researchers have suggested that this alternation could be explained by selective adaptation and fatiguing mechanisms. This view holds that different mechanisms are responsible for different stable percepts, and they become fatigued when their preferred percept dominates for some interval; at that point an antagonistic mechanism takes over, and the process continues *ad infinitum* (von Grünau et al. 1984; Long et al. 1992). The advantage of well-designed multistable figures is that they allow the researcher to conduct experiments in which the time course of the putative adoption of alternative perceptual hypotheses, or schemata, can be observed and measured.

Mach's book of figure 7.1b exhibits bi-stability even in its 3-D implementation (category (v) of Stadler and Kruse 1995), which is obtained by folding a rectangular piece of cardboard in half along its long dimension, as suggested in the figure, and setting it upright on a flat surface such as a desk. Suppose that the "book" is set with its "spine" away from you. If you now close one eye, so as to suppress stereoscopic vision, and stare at the object, your percept will eventually change spontaneously from the veridical one to a "false" stable state with the spine toward you. The fact that this perceptual change is accompanied by changes in apparent brightness of surfaces prompted Gregory (1997) to suggest a top-down signal modifying primary processing and to introduce the idea of "sideways" rules, as distinguished from schema-generating knowledge. According to Gregory (personal communication, 5 Feb. 1998) both "sideways" rules and knowledge are top-down and cognitive, but they are different, rather like syntax and semantics. The two states of the Mach book will continue to alternate as long as you view the object. What is remarkable is that, if you move your head left and right while you perceive the false state, the object will appear to move, as if suspended in the air, as long as you maintain the false state; the moment you obtain the veridical percept the object will appear stationary, as indeed it is. Explanations of this latter phenomenon have been provided by Gregory (1970: 128) and Wallach (1976).

Another example of an actual 3-D multistable figure, also belonging to a category (v) of Stadler and Kruse (1995), is obtained by viewing the inside of a hollow mask of a human face, painted on the inside (concave) surface with natural human features. The hollow mask is seen as a natural convex face (the *false* state), even when viewed with both eyes, as long as the viewing distance is reasonably large, say two meters or so. It appears in its false state even more easily, and from shorter distances (one meter or less), when viewed with only one eye. What is remarkable in this case is that, as a rule, people cannot perceive the hollow mask unless they come very close to it, and even after they perceive it as a hollow mask, once they move far enough away, a stable percept of a regular face is restored again. This is a clear case of a top-down process (experience, knowledge) overcoming bottom-up signals to form the percept. The reason why the false state is more difficult to perceive with binocular than

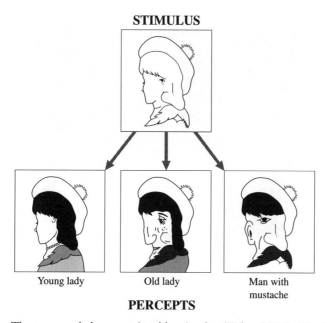

Figure 7.2. The top panel shows a tri-stable stimulus (Fisher 1968). The bottom three panels sketch the three possible interpretations.

with monocular vision is most likely that stereopsis provides an additional bottom-down signal to be overcome by knowledge. As with Mach's book, when the viewer moves while maintaining the false perceptual state, the "face" appears to turn toward the observer (Gregory 1970: 128).

An interesting tri-stable ambiguous figure (Fisher 1968), together with sketches of its possible interpretations, is shown in figure 7.2. This is one of the figures used by Stark and Ellis (1981) to test the role of fixational eye movements in the perception of ambiguous stimuli. While observers viewed the top figure, the experimenters recorded their eye movements, as well as the observers' reports about which of the three percepts of the bottom panel they were experiencing. By analyzing the data, Stark and Ellis (1981) concluded that the fixational pattern of the observers during the time of any given percept was well correlated to the corresponding perceptual hypothesis. They obtained similar results with Necker-cube stimuli. Gale and Findlay (1983) conducted a similar study with the so-called "daughter/mother" bi-stable figure that was introduced to the psychology literature by Boring (1930). They observed that the most important factor in the perception of multistable figures is selective visual attention, and that eye movements are important because they play a significant role in the deployment of attention. They also report that the eye fixational location pattern correlated closely with the dominant percept, but that percept alternation does not necessarily occur right after a major change in fixation location. The overall conclusion of Gale and Findlay (1983) is that saccadic eye movements are not exclusively determined

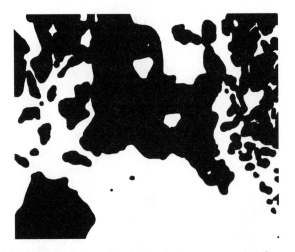

Figure 7.3. This is a typical example of an ambiguous concealed figure. The identity of the figure is not given in this caption, to give the reader the opportunity to appreciate the process of arriving at a meaningful percept. See the text for the "solution."

by the perceptual hypothesis, or by the stimulus characteristics, but by the interaction of the two factors.

It should be mentioned that the reversals of perceptual states cannot be attributed solely to the effect of eye movements, because such reversals occur even with paralyzed eye muscles (see Zinchenko and Vergiles 1972). However, one may argue that the image appears to move when a viewer whose eye muscles have been temporarily paralyzed attempts an eye movement. It turns out that the reversals still occur when retinal after-images are employed (Magnussen 1970). Since this method produces stabilized retinal images by construction, it rules out eye movements as the exclusive source of the alternation of percepts. Finally, we note that the cyclopean versions of these ambiguous figures also result in reversals of percepts (Julesz 1971: 40). This is to be expected, because the "cyclopean retina" (Julesz 1971) is very early in the visual pathway (Poggio 1995), well before the high-level site(s) of the brain where perceptual hypotheses are putatively generated.

3.2 Ambiguous concealed figures

Typical well-known examples of such figures are the "concealed Dalmatian dog" (Sekuler and Blake 1994: 137) and the "concealed cow" (Dallenback 1951; also in Schiffman 1996: 190–2 and in Sekuler and Blake 1994: 15–16). Some of these figures are inherently ambiguous by coincidences in the natural world. Others are obtained by degrading originally unambiguous images; this can be done by adding visual noise, or by "thresholding" (assigning black or white to all pixels below or above a certain intensity, respectively), or by fragmenting their parts, etc. Figure 7.3 is meant to illustrate how extremely difficult these figures are to identify/recognize. The semantic content of figure 7.3 is revealed in the next paragraph, to give the reader who sees it for the first time the opportunity to appreciate the process of arriving at a meaningful percept. Upon first seeing this figure, you catch yourself making cognitive/perceptual hypotheses (Is it a landscape? Is it a face? Is it an animal?) and testing them against the visual input. The time required for recognition varies widely across individuals. In anecdotal tests, the author has found some people who identified the figure in a matter of a few seconds and others who gave up after repeated attempts, each lasting several minutes. People in the latter group achieved recognition only after shown a visual sketch of the actual concealed figure.

Stark and Ellis (1981) used figure 7.3 to study saccadic eye movements before and after identification of the concealed figure. Observers viewed the figure, and were asked to signal the moment they achieved recognition. By the way, this figure shows a man with a mustache, beard, and long hair; he is shown from the chest up, centered in the picture, with half of his forehead clipped off at the top border of the picture (Porter 1954). The results obtained by Stark and Ellis (1981) show a significant change in eye movements after recognition. They start as a nearly random pattern of eye movements during the 75 seconds preceding identification, and they change to a well-recognized scanpath that visits the salient features of the face during the 75 seconds following identification. Stark and Ellis (1981) interpret these results as evidence that cognitive, schema-driven models direct eye movements. Figure 7.4 is another example that has elements of both bi-stable and concealed figures. It has an obvious stable percept of an apple core seen against a background composed of tree branches and a blue sky. The concealed figures are easier to find if the viewer knows the title of the painting. Again, in the interest of allowing the viewer time to appreciate the perceptual process, the title is given in the caption of figure 7.5.

It's worth mentioning that similar effects are also obtained in audition; for example, Deutsch (1972) has shown that a familiar tune is not recognized if each note in the sequence is selected randomly from one of three adjacent octaves. However, when observers are primed about the tune, they find it much easier to recognize it.

3.3 Impossible figures

Another class of figures with which one can "catch" the brain in the hypothesis-constructing-and-testing mode is the class of impossible figures (Simon 1967). These are images of "objects" that cannot physically exist, because they violate global constraints of physical objects, even though they are locally coherent. Two classical examples are shown in figure 7.5: Figure 7.5a displays the so-called devil's fork (Ernst 1992); and the impossible triangle of Penrose and Penrose (1958) is shown in figure 7.5b. A remarkably rich collection of

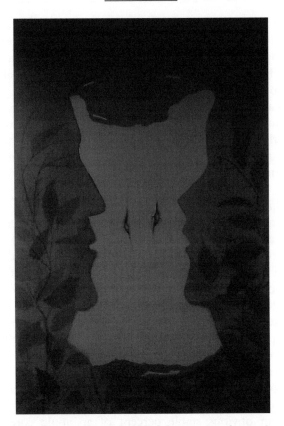

Figure 7.4. An image that contains concealed figures. See the caption of figure 7.5 for the title of the painting, which gives a hint about the concealed figures.

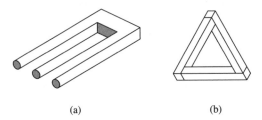

(a)   (b)

Figure 7.5. Typical examples of impossible figures: (a) the "devil's fork"; (b) an impossible triangle. By the way, the title of the painting in figure 7.4 is "Adam and Eve," a watercolour by artist Emily Holmes, in the author's collection.

impossible figures was compiled by Ernst (1992, 1996). The work of M. C. Escher (1967; see also Ernst 1976) contains numerous examples of ingeniously designed impossible figures. When one stares at impossible objects, one is aware of being in an endless loop of constantly constructing hypotheses based on local features, in an attempt to resolve global inconsistencies and arrive at a percept of a physically realizable object; however, one constantly finds her/himself rejecting each global hypothesis, to give way to alternative hypotheses that are also rejected in turn.

In addition to phenomenological differences, there is a fundamental difference between ambiguous figures of the types discussed in sections 3.1 and 3.2 on the one hand, and impossible figures, on the other. The former cause perceptual alternations by virtue of the image features that the viewer attends to, but the ensuing percept accounts for the entire image, with parts of the scene perceived possibly as background. By contrast, the perception of impossible figures depends critically on the focal point. For example, when you look at the right part of figure 7.5a, you see a coherent solid object bounded by planar surfaces, and two poles of square cross sections extending to the left; at the same time, the left part of the figure, seen in the periphery, appears indistinct. As soon as you stare at the left of the picture, you perceive three cylindrical rods extending to the right. What is a material object for the three rods is empty space for the two poles. and vice versa. The impossibility arrives when one tries to integrate the two contradictory percepts. The conflict is obvious even in the above verbal description. You cannot "bind" *two square-cross-section* poles with *three cylindrical* rods.

4   Neural models

In addition to occupying vision researchers, the perception of ambiguous multistable figures has attracted the attention of theoreticians and physicists who deal with multistable phenomena in physics (Haken 1977) or chemistry (Plath and Stadler 1994). A computational model based on synergetic systems was developed by Ditzinger and Haken (1989) to account for the temporal aspects of the alternation with multistable figures. It obtains respectable fits to empirical data by mimicking the effect of saturation of attention. Johnston and Hawley (1994) also developed a simple neural model to implement some basic characteristics of their mismatch theory. The neural model assumes just two layers of nodes: a data-driven layer of iconic nodes, which are activated by excitatory bottom-up connections but inhibit each other through lateral connections. The next layer contains two classes of nodes: location and identity nodes, which are activated by the outputs of the iconic nodes and in turn send inhibitory signals to the iconic nodes via a feedback pathway. Additional excitatory and inhibitory connections are assumed by the model, and the simulations are in close agreement with the experimental results.

Grossbeg's (1976) adaptive resonance theory (ART) was generalized by Carpenter, Grossberg and Rosen (1991) using fuzzy set theory to handle analog, in addition to binary, input patterns. The model is based on the premise that the input received from early data-driven sensory organs, appropriately coded, triggers top-down processes, which in turn constantly construct *hypotheses*, or *schemata*; an interaction ensues between top-down and bottom-

Table 7.1   Coding scheme for presence or absence of features

	ON channel	OFF channel
Feature present	1	0
Feature missing in image	0	1
Feature not extracted yet	0	0

up processes, to test these alternative competing hypotheses, rejecting the weak ones and adopting the strongest one to arrive at a stable state. Accordingly, in *Fuzzy ART*, as the authors call the new model, the sensory input I generates an activity pattern and transmits it to a first-layer (mostly data-driven) mechanism F_1, which in turn transforms it and provides input T to the top-layer (concept-driven) mechanism F_2; activation of F_2 may be viewed as "making a hypothesis" about the input. In turn, F_2 generates its own top-down signal U, based on T, which it transmits back to F_1; this can be viewed as "testing the hypothesis." This two-way interaction between F_1 and F_2 continues until the signal received by F_1 and F_2 (expected input, according to the hypothesis of F_2) matches the actual input I, in which case the input is classified as per the previous training of the network. If a match cannot be found, it means that this is a novel input schema, and it must therefore be added to the repertoire of the available hypotheses.

Fuzzy ART was further extended by Aguilar and Ross's (1994) *Incremental ART* model, which incorporates ideas for efficient classification of input patterns based on partial feature information. The algorithm proceeds in three basic steps: (1) A partial set of features is extracted from the image, and supplied as input to the F_1 layer. (2) The interaction of F_1 and F_2, as outlined in the paragraph above for ART, tries to classify the image on the basis of the partial input; if it succeeds in converging, the process is over when a match is found. (3) If no convergence is possible, Incremental ART determines which feature to extract next from the image and repeats the process. The classification of features is accomplished by representing each feature by an ON channel, which is active (1) when the feature is present, and an OFF channel, which is active (1) when the feature is entirely absent from the image. In Fuzzy ART, all features are extracted first, and the absence of a feature from the input stimulus is coded as 0 in the ON channel and as a 1 in the OFF channel. However, Incremental ART can work with a partial list of features, which means that a feature can be absent because it has not *yet* been extracted from the image; in this case the states of both the ON and OFF channels are 0. Table 7.1 summarizes the three possibilities.

The major advantage of Incremental ART over Fuzzy ART is computational efficiency. Convergence may be reached with a partial feature vector, which means that the time required for extraction of the rest of the features has been saved. After all, humans also often achieve recognition based on partial input, giving this model biological relevance, as well. In addition, the decision on which features to extract next, when the image cannot be classified on the basis of the presently available feature vector, offers the possibility of modeling saccadic scanning patterns. It is this last property of the model that allows it to mimic alternations between perceptual states in multistable figures, including the role of fixational eye movements in influencing this alternation process (Aguilar and Ross 1997).

5   Discussion and Conclusions

This chapter has reviewed evidence that demonstrates the plausibility of complex interactions between concept-driven and data-driven processes in the perceptual act. In particular, the brain's property of simultaneously showing a preference for both expected and unexpected stimuli can be explained by concept-driven processes exerting an inhibitory effect on the processing of expected inputs. We also reviewed studies with three main classes of visual stimuli, which support the theory that concept-driven components in the brain constantly construct perceptual hypotheses which are tested against the outputs of data-driven early mechanisms. Finally, we discussed computational models that attempt to emulate the view of the brain as a perceptual hypothesis-testing agent, with results that are in adequately close agreement with empirical data.

Another area that can offer support for this theory of the brain as a "hypothesis-constructing-and-testing engine" is what happens in dreams. During sleep, the brain has no sensory visual stimulation to drive its construction of hypotheses. Thus, it can roam free in an open-loop mode and can construct its own "reality" which is devoid of the real-world visual feedback, constrained by physical laws, that would be provided by the eyes in a fully awake state. This may well explain the fantastic quality of most dreams. But how about the other senses that can still provide physical stimulation even in sleep? For example, how about auditory input? It turns out that there are cases where, in accordance with the hypothesis-constructing-and-testing theory, dreams are "molded" to account for sounds experienced during sleep. As a striking example, I once dreamt about being in a street where a worker was operating a loud pneumatic drill, only to wake up and realize that a woodpecker was pecking on my home's wooden shingles. Apparently, the brain constructed a "reality" that incorporated the physical sound, driven by the auditory input. Parenthetically, a view has been proposed that such dreams are designed to protect us from waking up when we are disturbed by strong stimuli during sleep (Horne 1988).

The theme of top-down assumptions and expectations influencing early mechanisms is common. For example, Pinker (1997: 213) attributes visual illusions to conditions that violate the visual system's assumptions. He also suggests that the visual system may compare the probabilities of different hypotheses/percepts that are consistent with the raw data (ibid., 243). Adelson (1997) has identified some top-down processes that affect the apparent lightness of surfaces. These processes are not necessarily driven by schemas or hypotheses, but originate instead at some intermediate level, by computing gray-level statistics over some local area. He found evidence that these mechanisms compute their statistics over areas that are consistent with natural "atmospheric" boundaries, as signaled by T-, X-, and psi-junctions, and use this input to estimate the illumination level, haze, and properties of interposed filters (Adelson 1997).

Finally, we note that stimulation by binocularly rivalrous stimuli has several important similarities to stimulation by ambiguous multistable figures, but the difference is that, in rivalry, the two eyes are presented with different visual inputs. Chapter 9 below, by Papathomas, Kovács, Fehér, and Julesz, deals with how the brain reacts when stimulated by binocularly rivalrous visual inputs. It offers a view of binocular rivalry which is compatible with the theory that the brain uses high-order processes to construct and test possible interpretations of the available stimulus in an attempt to arrive at meaningful percepts.

It should be noted that the issue of whether concept-driven processes can affect data-driven mechanisms in vision is still under debate. This chapter has presented a partial review of the literature that interprets the evidence in favor of an affirmative answer. The other view has been argued forcefully through the years; an excellent review that offers strong arguments for the opposite view was given recently by Pylyshyn (1999), who concludes that visual perception is cognitively impenetrable (see also Fodor 1983). At this point in time, it seems that the evidence is equivocal, and the debate is far from over. Additional work is needed to investigate this important issue in perception/cognition.

Acknowledgments

I am truly indebted to Mario Aguilar for enriching this chapter with invaluable references on a wide range of research in multistable figures and for introducing me to his computational model. I was fortunate that Richard Gregory and Diana Deutsch were kind enough to read an early draft and to provide me with expert advice. I wish to thank Bela Julesz, Ilona Kovács, and Akos Fehér for useful discussions and ideas. My good friend Charalambos (Harry) Constantinides, who appreciates the classics more than anyone I know and has quite a broad knowledge of the classic literature, provided me with valuable references on the liar's paradox. Tiffany Conway helped me to clarify many points in the chapter. Many thanks to the McDonnell Foundation for supporting the research at the Laboratory of Vision Research through grant 95–60.

Notes

1   The sophisticated reader is asked to excuse the oversimplification in partitioning the brain into sensory, perceptual, and logical "components."

2   The notation of Johnston and Hawley (1994) will be used here. The terms *data-driven* and *concept-driven* will refer to the origin of the information; the former will indicate early sensory mechanisms that receive input from the external world, the latter, mechanisms that are provided input by higher-order cognitive processes. The terms *bottom-up* and *top-down* will be used to signify the direction of the information flow, the former going from early, low-level units to later stages, the latter in the opposite direction.

References

Adelson E. H. (1997) Atmospheric boundaries in lightness perception. *Perception* 26 suppl., 5.

Adelson, E. H. and Bergen, J. R. (1991) The plenoptic function and the elements of early vision. In M. S. Landy and J. A. Movshon (eds), *Computational Models of Visual Processing*, Cambridge, MA, MIT Press, 3–20.

Aguilar, J. M. and Ross, W. D. (1994) Incremental ART: a neural network system for recognition and incremental feature extraction. In *Proceedings of 1994 International Neural Network Society Annual Meeting*, San Diego, CA, vol. 1, 1593–8.

—— (1997) Multistable perception and selective attention. *Investigative Ophthalmology and Visual Science* 38(4), S1006.

Boring, E. G. (1930) A new ambiguous figure. *American Journal of Psychology* 42, 444.

Bruner, J. S. (1957) On perceptual readiness. *Psychological Review* 64, 123–52.

Carpenter, G. A., Grossberg, S. and Rosen, D. B. (1991) Fuzzy ART: fast stable learning and categorization of analog patterns by an adaptive resonance system *Neural Networks* 4, 759–71.

Dallenbach, K. M. (1951) A puzzle-picture with a new principle of concealment. *American Journal of Psychology* 64, 431–3.

Deutsch, D. (1972) Octave generalization and tune recognition. *Perception and Psychophysics* 11(6), 411–12.

—— (1975) Musical illusions. *Scientific American* 233(4), 92–104.

Ditzinger, T. and Haken, H. (1989) Oscillations in the perception of ambiguous patterns: a model based on synergetics. *Biological Cybernetics* 61, 279–87.

Dodds, E. R. (1951) *The Greeks and the Irrational*, Sather Classical Lectures, 25, Berkeley: University of California Press.

Ernst, B. (1976) *The Magic Mirror of M. C. Escher*, New York: Ballantine.

—— (1992) *Optical Illusions*, trans. K. Williams. Originally published as Het Begoochelde Oog. Cologne: Taschen Verlag.

—— (1996) *Adventures with Impossible Objects*, trans. K. Williams and H. Warden, New York: Taschen America. Originally published as *Avinturen met Onmogelijke Figuren*. Cologne: Taschen Verlag.

Escher, M. C. (1967) *The Graphic Work of M. C. Escher*, trans. J. E. Brigham. New York: Ballantine.

Fisher, G. H. (1968) "Mother, father and daughter": a three-aspect ambiguous figure. *American Journal of Psychology* 81, 274–7.

Fodor, J. A. (1983) *The Modularity of Mind: An Essay on Faculty Psychology*, Cambridge, MA: MIT Press.

Gale, A. G. and Findlay, J. M. (1983) Eye movement patterns in viewing ambiguous figures. In R. Groner, C. Menz, D. F. Fisher and R. A. Monty (eds) *Eye Movements and Psychological Functions: International Views*, Hillsdale, NJ Lawrence Erlbaum Associates; 145–68.

Gardner, M. (1982) *Aha! Gotcha: Paradoxes to Puzzle and Delight*. San Francisco: W. H. Freeman.

Gregory, R. L. (1968) Perceptual illusions and brain models. *Proceedings of the Royal Society of London B* 171, 279–96.

—— (1970) *The Intelligent Eye*, London: Weidenfeld & Nicolson.

—— (1980) Perceptions as hypotheses. *Philosophical Transactions of the Royal Society of London B* 290, 181–97.

—— (1997) Knowledge in perception and illusion. *Philosophical Translations of the Royal Society of London B* 352, 1121–8.

Grossberg, S. (1976) Adaptive pattern classification and universal recoding, II: Feedback, expectation, olfaction, and illusions. *Biological Cybernetics* 23, 187–202.

—— (1987) Competitive learning: from interactive activation to adaptive resonance. *Cognitive Science* 11, 23–63.

Haken, H. (1977) *Synergetics – An Introduction*, Berlin: Springer Verlag.

Hofstadter, D. R. (1980) *Gödel, Escher, Bach: An Eternal Golden Braid*, New York: Basic Books.

Horne, J. (1988) *Why We Sleep*, Oxford: Oxford University Press.

Johnston, W. A. and Hawley, K. J. (1994) Perceptual inhibition of expected inputs: the key that opens closed minds. *Psychonomic Bulletin & Review* 1(1), 56–72.

Julesz, B. (1971) *Foundations of Cyclopean Perception*, Chicago: University of Chicago Press.

Kanizsa, G. and Luccio, R. (1995) Multistability as a research tool in experimental phenomenology. In P. Kruse and M. Stadler (eds), *Ambiguity in Mind and Nature: Multistable Cognitive Phenomena*, Berlin: Springer Verlag, 47–68.

Long, G. M., Toppino, T. C. and Mondin, G. W. (1992) Prime time: fatigue and set effects in the perception of reversible figures. *Perception and Psychophysics* 52, 609–16.

Magnussen, S. (1970) Reversibilityof perspective in normal and stabilized viewing. *Scandinavian Journal of Psychology* 11, 153–6.

McClelland, J. J. and Rumelhart, D. E. (1981) An interactive activation model of context effects in letter perception: part I. An account of basic findings. *Psychological Review* 88, 375–407.

Necker, L. A. (1832) Observations on some remarkable phenomenon which occurs on viewing a figure of a crystal or geometrical solid. *London and Edinburgh Philosophical Magazine and Journal of Science* 3, 329–37.

Papathomas, T. V. (1995) Bistable ambiguous tiling patterns with converging/diverging arrows. In C. Pickover (ed.), *The Pattern Book: Fractals, Art, and Nature*, London: World Scientific Publishing, 317–18.

Penrose, L. S. and Penrose, R. (1958) Impossible objects: a special type of illusion. *British Journal of Psychology* 49, 31.

Pinker, S. (1997) *How the Mind Works*, New York: W. W. Norton.

Plath, P. and Stadler, C. (1994) Multistability in molecules and reactions. In P. Kruse and M. Stadler (eds), *Ambiguity in Mind and Nature: Multistable Cognitive Phenomena*, Berlin: Springer Verlag, 441–61.

Poggio, G. F. (1995) Stereoscopic processing in monkey visual cortex: a review. In T. V. Papathomas, C. Chubb, A. Gorea and E. Kowler (eds), *Early Vision and Beyond*, Cambridge, MA: MIT Press, 43–53.

Porter, P. B. (1954) Another picture puzzle. *American Journal of Psychology* 67, 550–1.

Pylyshyn, Z. (1999) Is vision continuous with cognition? The case for cognitive impenetrability of visual perception. *Behavioural and Brain Sciences*, in press.

Rock, I. (1983) *The Logic of Perception*, Cambridge, MA: MIT Press.

Rubin, E. (1921) *Visuel wahrgenommene Figuren*, Copenhagen: Gyldenalske Boghandel.

Schiffman, H. R. (1996) *Sensation and Perception: An Integrated Approach*, 4th edn, New York: Wiley.

Sekuler, R. and Blake, R. (1994) *Perception*, 3rd edn, New York: McGraw-Hill.

Simon, H. A. (1967) An information-processing explanation of some perceptual phenomena. *British Journal of Psychology* 58, 1–12.

Smullyan, R. (1978) *What is the Name of This Book?* Englewood Cliffs, NJ: Prentice-Hall.

—— (1987) *Forever Undecided: A Puzzle Guide to Gödel*, New York: Knopf.

Sokolov, E. N. (1963) Higher nervous functions: the orienting reflex. *Annual Review of Psychology* 25, 545–80.

Stadler, M. and Kruse, P. (1995) The function of meaning in cognitive order formation. In P. Kruse and M. Stadler (eds), *Ambiguity in Mind and Nature: Multistable Cognitive Phenomena*, Berlin, Springer Verlag, 5–21.

Stark, L. and Ellis, S. R. (1981) Scanpaths revisited: cognitive models direct active looking. In D. Fisher, R. Monty and J. Senders (eds) *Eye Movements: Cognition and Visual Perception*, Hillsdale, NJ: Lawrence Erlbaum Associates, 193–226.

von Grünau, M. W., Wiggins, S. and Reed, M. (1984) The local character of perspective organization. *Perception and Psychophysics* 35, 319–24.

Wallach, H. (1976) The apparent rotation of pictorial scenes. In M. Henle (ed.), *Vision and Artifact*, New York: Springer, 65–9.

Zinchenko, V. P. and Vergiles, N. Y. (1972) *Formation of Visual Images. Studies of Stabilized Retinal Images*, trans. B. Haigh. New York: New York Consultants Bureau.

8

What Movements of the Eye Tell us about the Mind

Eileen Kowler

People take oculomotor skills and capacities for granted. We may be searching a drawer for lost keys, or keeping our eyes fixed on the car in front of us as we drive on a rainy night, or reading through the text in this book. Eye movements are crucial for all these activities and, in fact, are crucial for virtually anything we do involving the apprehension of any sort of visual scene. Yet we typically give no thought at all to their planning or control. How is it possible for us to use eye movements so effectively to look at the target we choose while at the same time paying hardly any attention at all to what the eye is doing?

One way of achieving accurate eye movements with relatively little effort is to allow them to function more or less reflexively, with the line of sight drawn to one or another target on the basis of its physical characteristics, such as contrast or retinal eccentricity. In fact, attempts to study relationships between eye movements and low-level sensory characteristics of the visual stimulus form a very prominent tradition in eye movement research (for general reviews see Hallett 1986; Carpenter 1988; Kowler 1990). The problem with relying exclusively on control by low-level sensory characteristics, however, is that high accuracy is achieved at the cost of losing the option of moving the eye wherever and whenever you wish. On the other hand, exclusive reliance on voluntary, deliberate planning requires a substantial commitment of attentional resources that may be better devoted to thinking about the visual scene or the task at hand.

The central thesis of this chapter is that accurate control of eye movements can be achieved with minimal effort by an effective division of labor between

Supported by AFOSR F49620-96-1-0081

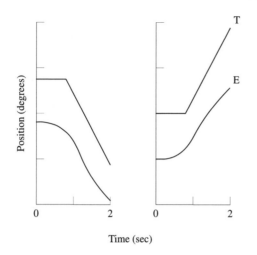

Figure 8.1. Horizontal eye positions (bottom traces) as a function of time during smooth pursuit of a single point (top traces) moving to the left or to the right at a constant velocity of 130 minutes of arc per second. (From Kowler 1989: 1050.)

cognitive and sensory factors. To illustrate the interplay between such very different, potentially opposing influences, I will describe some examples of oculomotor phenomena where cognitive and sensory control have proved to be important.

Anticipatory Smooth Eye Movements

Figure 8.1 illustrates a type of eye movement known as *smooth pursuit*. The top traces in each graph depict the horizontal trajectory of motion of a single small target. The target is stationary for ¾ of a second and then begins moving to the left or to the right at about 1.5 degrees per second. The smooth eye movements, shown in the bottom traces, do a reasonable job of keeping up with the motion of the target. This is typical performance. As a result of the effective smooth pursuit eye movements, the target stays relatively stationary on the retina, which allows its smallest details to be perceived clearly (for reviews see Steinman and Levinson 1990; Hallett 1986; Carpenter 1988; Kowler 1990). In natural situations, outside the oculomotor laboratory, we might use smooth eye movements to track the motion of a running rabbit or a flying bird, or the motion of our own fingers as we sew a button on a shirt. More importantly, we need smooth eye movements to keep the line of sight on stationary objects, perhaps a tree or a sign along the side of our path, as we move about the world.

Smooth eye movements are under the control of the stimulus in the sense that people cannot willfully create the oculomotor trajectory shown in the figure; there has to be a moving target in the field of view. Moreover, if the moving target is the only thing visible, it is not possible to prevent the eye from following along (although you can slow eye velocity to as much as half that of the target by exerting some effort: Steinman et al. 1969). It isn't all stimulus control, however. If the visual field contains *both* stationary and moving objects at the same time, smooth eye movements will track the attended object, with little influence of the unattended background (Kowler et al. 1984; Khurana and Kowler 1987). (There will be more discussion of attention later in the chapter.)

Because of their involuntary nature – that is, once you choose which target to track, the eye will move along smoothly on its own in pursuit of the target – smooth eye movements are usually treated as a sensorimotor reflex. The idea is that visual motion signals are detected and coded by specialized neurons in the cortex and are later transformed into the appropriate oculomotor command. "Error signals" (differences between the current eye velocity and the velocity of the target) are used to adjust eye velocity to keep retinal motion within tolerance limits. Neural areas involved in various stages of this process have been identified, but the nature of the neural transformations that occur along the way have yet to be worked out (Keller and Heinen 1991).

Despite the appeal of such classical reflexive approaches to smooth eye movements, they don't explain the behavior. The reason why can be seen in the lower traces of figure 8.1. The eye starts to move smoothly in the direction of target motion *before* the target motion begins. These are anticipatory smooth eye movements, noticed originally by Raymond Dodge in 1931 and studied by others since in a variety of different experimental contexts (see, e.g., Kowler 1990; Pavel 1990; Heinen and Liu 1997). Moreover, anticipatory effects do not disappear once the target starts moving: eye velocity shortly after onset of target motion is faster when the subject has been led to expect faster motion (Kowler 1990). Pursuit never even gets off the ground unless subjects expect the target to continue moving for several hundred milliseconds at least (Kowler and McKee 1987).

How can smooth pursuit, which cannot be initiated without a moving target, nevertheless be influenced by expectations? There must be an internal signal controlling the eye movements, but what sort of signal? How is it generated? And why is the oculomotor system, which we assume has the job of keeping the eye on target, apparently happy to create visual error, moving the eye away from the target for some period of time?

The anticipatory smooth eye movements could be generated by the neural correlate of a cognitive expectation: a signal representing the target motion extrapolated several hundred milliseconds into the future. Alternatively, some lower-level process might be at work, with anticipatory smooth eye movements representing a habit, learned as a result of having tracked the same motion repeatedly over a sequence of trials.

These two possibilities – expectations and habits – were distinguished by using the stimulus shown in figure 8.2. A small disc was moved smoothly

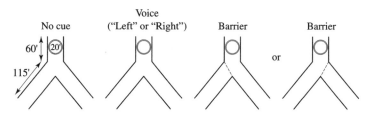

Figure 8.2.   The stimulus display in an experiment comparing habits to cognitive expectations. It consisted of a stationary inverted Y-shaped tube and an annulus which served as the moving target. The target moved down the tube and continued at the same velocity (130'/sec) down either the right-hand or left-hand oblique branch of the Y (the horizontal component of velocity when the target was in either branch of the Y was 92'/sec). The target was equally likely to travel down either branch. The branch in which the target moved was either undisclosed before each trial (no cue), disclosed by a voice cue, or disclosed by a visible barrier cue blocking access to either the lefthand or the righthand branch. (From Kowler 1989:1050.)

down the outline drawing of a tube towards the choice point, where it took either the left- or right-hand path (probability = 0.5). In some cases ("no cue") there was no advance warning about the path to be taken. In other cases (voice cue or visible barrier) the path was disclosed at the onset of a trial.

Horizontal eye velocities in the "no cue" condition are shown in figure 8.3. Time zero on the abscissa represents the time when the disc entered the left- or right-hand path, so any motion of the eye before then is the anticipatory portion. These are separate traces in the figure for trials in which the target moved to the left or to the right. There are also separate traces for trials in which the motion on the prior trial was to the left or to the right. Figure 8.3 shows that in the absence of a cue there were, nevertheless, anticipatory eye movements, which can be seen as an increase in horizontal smooth eye velocity occurring shortly before time zero. The direction of the anticipatory smooth eye movements depended on the direction of the target motion seen on the prior trial. Thus, there is an influence of the immediate past. Figure 8.4 shows performance when one of the symbolic cues, the visible barrier (performance was similar with the voice cue), disclosed the direction of future motion of the target. It is clear that the cue easily overrode the effect of the past and produced relatively fast anticipatory smooth eye movements in the direction of the target's future motion. There was only a small residual effect of the prior trial. The result means that cognitive expectations, not habits, determined the direction of the anticipatory pursuit.

This is a remarkably efficient arrangement. If our smooth pursuit system were dependent solely on sensory signals, it would inevitably fall behind the target and generate large tracking errors, reminiscent of the frustrated bat trying to catch a moth flying in a random, evasive path. In fact, human beings cannot pursue complex, random motions with any reasonable degree of accuracy, another testament to the importance of expectations in controlling pursuit. By having a system that allows expectations to give us a head start, we

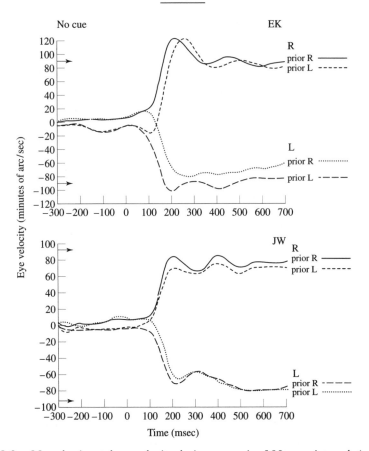

Figure 8.3. Mean horizontal eye velocity during successive 100 msec intervals (onsets 10 msec apart) as a function of the midpoint of the interval when no cue about the direction of future horizontal target motion was given. Top graphs, EK; bottom graphs, naive subject JW. Time 0 is the start of horizontal target motion (the first entry of the moving target into the oblique branch of the Y-shaped tube). Arrows on the ordinate show horizontal target velocity; negative values denote leftward motion. The top pair of functions in each graph show eye velocity when the eye moved down the left-hand branch. One function in each pair shows eye velocity when the target motion in the prior trial was to the right, the other when motion in the prior trial was to the left. Each mean is based on 80–100 observations. (From Kowler 1989: 1052.)

create small momentary tracking errors, but, more importantly, we avoid the larger tracking errors caused by processing delays, errors that would otherwise occur once the target motion is under way. The smooth pursuit system appears to have arrived at an elegant solution to minimizing the tracking error. It uses both the sensory signals generated by the current target motion across the retina as well as the knowledge, already coded somewhere in the brain, of the future target path. It might even be argued that the primary purpose of having a cognitive system that understands symbols and cues sufficiently to make rapid, accurate predictions of the future is to enable the motor system

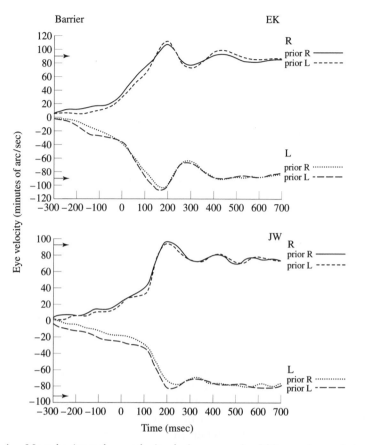

Figure 8.4. Mean horizontal eye velocity during successive 100 msec intervals (onsets 10 msec apart) as a function of the midpoint of the interval when a visible barrier cue disclosing the direction of future horizontal target motion was given. Top graphs, EK; bottom graphs, naive subject JW. Time 0 is the start of horizontal target motion (the first entry of the moving target into the oblique branch of the Y-shaped tube). Arrows on the ordinate show horizontal target velocity; negative values denote leftward motion. The top pair of functions in each graph show eye velocity when the eye moved down the left-hand branch. One function in each pair shows eye velocity when the target motion in the prior trial was to the right; the other when motion in the prior trial was to the left. Each mean is based on 80–100 observations. (From Kowler 1989: 1052.)

to do its critical planning far enough in advance so that it is possible to keep up with a changing (yet predictable) signal. The anticipatory smooth eye movements shown in figure 8.4 provide evidence that such cognitive predictions are indeed readily and efficiently incorporated into the motor command.

It would not be surprising to find that tracking movements of the limbs anticipate future motion of the target, because we can control limb movements and willfully plan ahead. But anticipatory pursuit can be neither initiated nor suppressed voluntarily. The pursuit system has no option; the cognitive signal is as compelling as the sensory one. The two signals might not even be separate if it were to turn out that expectancies are built into the coding of cortical motion signals. (And if so, would they influence perceived motion as well?) A significant open question is how and where an accurate neural representation of expected motion is generated. The answer would shed light not only on mechanisms of sensory-motor integration, but also, potentially, on the cortical control of higher processes involved in interpreting, remembering, and thinking about symbolic cues in the visual environment.

Saccadic Eye Movements in Natural Visual Scenes

Smooth eye movements, described above, constitute one major class of eye movements. The second major class is saccades. Saccades are voluntary jumps of the eye made to look around stationary scenes. Saccades are voluntary in the sense that you can look in any direction at almost any time, the one major restriction being that saccade rates are limited to no more than about three per second.

Given the obvious tendency of people to want to look at areas they find of interest, there have been long-standing attempts to use saccadic patterns as overt indicators of otherwise hidden decisions. A famous example is Yarbus's (1967) recordings of eye movements made while examining various paintings, in which he showed large, systematic differences in the scanning patterns, depending on the sort of question the viewer was asked to answer (e.g., viewers looked at different places when they were trying to guess the ages of the people in the painting than when they were trying to guess their economic status). This result was important, because it showed that cognitive decisions, not sensory or perceptual aspects of the paintings, determined where one looked.

Despite the compelling logic of using saccadic patterns to infer sequences of decisions, the validity of such inferences has been subject to substantial criticism. One of the most effective critiques was offered by Viviani (1990). He pointed out, among other things, that the serial, episodic nature of saccades was a feature of the motor system and should not constrain or necessarily reveal the continuous flow of thoughts and decisions proceeding in the background. Attempts to devise cognitive models solely from the eye movement sequences themselves were given little chance of succeeding. The only thing that might work, Viviani argued, was a strategy of formulating a specific cognitive theory independently of the eye movements, which made particular predictions about saccadic patterns (see Suppes 1990 for a similar argument). Several laboratories have recently begun to take up this challenge, attempting to weave eye movements into broader theories of memory (Ballard et al. 1995; Epelboim et al. 1995), problem solving (Epelboim and Suppes 1996), skilled task performance (Land and Furneaux 1997), and language processing (Tanenhaus et al. 1995). Others have been concerned with the question of how we manage to integrate material across successive glances so that we continue to perceive a stable, unchanging world, despite the continual and abrupt changes in the retinal image (O'Regan 1992).

The ability to produce an effective saccadic pattern while scanning a natural scene is not just a matter of voluntary choice. Saccades in natural scenes are made to objects of some spatial extent, yet the saccade must land at a single point within the object. We're not aware of deliberately choosing the precise landing position. How can landing position be determined without requiring too much effort or attention on the part of the observer? Once again, as in the case of smooth eye movements, the solution will involve a combination of cognitive and sensory events, as will be discussed below.

Saccadic localization of objects

Saccades made to small targets (single points of light, for example) are extremely accurate and precise. Landing positions are distributed around the target with a standard deviation (SD) of only about 7 per cent of the target's eccentricity. Differences between average landing position and the target's location can be quite small (1 per cent of eccentricity) (Kowler and Blaser 1995).

The precision of landing positions is not impaired by large increases in target size. This was shown by asking subjects to make a single saccade to look at a target object as a whole, without aiming for any particular place within it (the sort of thing we do when we look around any ordinary natural scene). Surprisingly, landing position remains precise (SDs < 10 per cent of eccentricity), even for targets whose diameter is as large as their eccentricity. Precise landing positions have been found for outline drawings of simple shapes (He and Kowler 1991; Kowler and Blaser 1995), and clusters of random dots (McGowan et al. 1998). With such targets, the average landing position is quite close to the center of gravity of the target.

Finding such good performance with large targets suggests that the visual or motor system makes use of some kind of spatial pooling process to compute saccadic landing position. One plausible scheme would be to have individual detectors positioned over different regions of the target. Each detector represents a different position (i.e., each has its own "local sign"). Landing position is then computed as the average local sign, with the contribution of each detector weighted according to the number and intensity of the elements falling in its "receptive field" (McGowan et al. 1998). This scheme is quite similar to models proposed earlier for both the perceptual localization of large random dot targets (Morgan et al. 1990) and the aiming of arm movements (Georgopolous et al. 1993).

The localization model described above predicts that saccades rely on a very primitive representation of the target, in which the local density and intensity of component elements are important, but global shape is not (i.e., elements

Figure 8.5. Examples of four different saccadic targets with the same shape but differing according to the density of dots making up the boundary and the presence of dots inside the boundary. When subjects start from a fixation point 4 degrees away from any of these targets and aim a saccade to the target as a whole, the saccade lands near the center of the area of the shape for all four of the shapes shown.

along the boundary are as important as elements within the boundary). This is quite different from object perception, where boundaries, but not local elements, are crucial for recognition. It might seem reasonable that localization should proceed by such different rules, given the current popularity of the view that motor and perceptual localization systems are distinct from systems handling form perception and shape recognition (see Goodale 1995).

We recently subjected this element-based localization model to a stricter test by asking subjects to make a single saccade to an eccentric target shape in which both the density of elements along the boundary and the presence and location of elements within the boundary were varied (Melcher and Kowler 1999). We found that, contrary to the simple localization model described above, variation in element spacing and the addition of internal elements made no difference whatsoever. In figure 8.5, for example, all the shapes have different component elements, but all produced the same average landing position. Saccades landed at the center of the shape: it didn't matter how the shape was created or what its internal structure was.

The failure of either element spacing or internal elements to affect landing position was not due to the failure of these characteristics to be detected; it's easy to distinguish the patterns in figure 8.5, yet all were equivalent as far as saccades were concerned. The results show that saccades tap into the visual system at a point after representations of shape are constructed.

How can we explain the complete insensitivity to elements? In fact, this is precisely the kind of outcome one would expect if attention played an important role in saccadic targeting. By "attention" I mean any process that selectively increases the processing capacity assigned to a local region or to an object (see Sperling and Weichselgartner 1995; Liu and Dosher 1998) at the expense of processing capacity available in the surround (Bahcall and Kowler 1999). If we spread an "attentional field" over the spatial extent of the object and assume that the neurons involved are insensitive to visual content (Schall et al. 1995), then the average local sign of these neurons could determine a landing position of the saccade. According to this view, the elements making up the object are important for defining its shape (e.g., Kovács and Julesz 1994; Field et al. 1993; Feldman 1997; Pizlo et al. 1997), and shape is important for the targeting of attention. Once the attended region is defined, the command to launch the saccade takes it to the center of that region. These speculations are made more plausible by experiments, described below, that demonstrate links between attentional allocation and oculomotor control.

Eye movements and attention

The prior section emphasized the role of stimulus factors, in particular, shape-coding, in saccadic control. Once the decision was made to look at the object as a whole, the saccadic system, using visually-coded shape, computed a very precise landing position by pooling information across the shape. In natural scenes, however, the chosen visual target is surrounded by all kinds of objects in the background, objects that ideally should not divert the saccade from the selected goal. This is where attention comes into play, not in guiding the eye movements directly, but rather in defining the effective target that is used to compute the motor command.

Before considering the role of attention in saccadic control, it is useful to discuss the effect of attention on smooth eye movements, since attention plays analogous roles for both types of movements. Attention is important for allowing smooth eye movements to maintain the line of sight on a chosen target in the face of all kinds of competing stationary or moving objects in the background, an ability originally noted and appreciated by Ernst Mach (1906/1959). By comparison, smooth eye movements of the rabbit apparently cannot select, but instead respond on the basis of retinal location and physical characteristics of the moving stimulus (Collewijn 1981). Human beings excel at using attention to choose the effective target for smooth eye movements. We can even do this for patterns of dense, superimposed fields of moving random dots, where the overlap of retinal locations of target and background means that effective selection must be based on attending to the object and not the place (Kowler et al. 1984). By combining the oculomotor task of tracking a target in the presence of a background with a perceptual task of identifying features of both target and background, it can be shown that perceptual attention is indeed weighted toward the selected target (Khurana and Kowler 1987).

A link between attentional allocation and saccadic control was demonstrated in an experiment that measured the trade-offs between perceptual and saccadic performance when subjects had to look at one target and identify another. Figure 8.6 shows the stimulus, a 4 degree-diameter array of eight letters. Subjects were told before the trial that they would have to do two things: aim the saccade in the direction of the arrow (down, in this example) and also identify the target in a different location (e.g., on the right of the array of letters, at 3 o'clock). Arrays were on briefly (130 msec) and were followed by masks, so that perceptual performance could be measured while saccadic programming was in progress, before the occurrence of the saccade itself changed the retinal eccentricities of the letters. We used instructions that

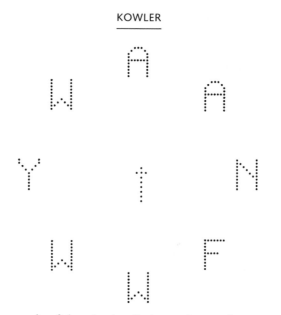

Figure 8.6. An example of the stimulus display used to study concurrent saccadic and perceptual performance. The eight randomly chosen letters were located along the boundary of an imaginary circle, of diameter 2 degrees. The subject fixated the central cross hair, and a cue (the line pointing downward in this case) indicated where the saccade was to be directed. The cue was shown either before or concurrent with the onset of this stimulus display, and the onset of the display was the cue to make the saccade. Display duration was 130 msec. Subjects had to look in the direction of the line cue and at the same time identify a letter in a different position. To minimize the information the subject had to keep track of, the position to be identified remained the same during each experimental session. (From Kowler et al. 1995: 1901.)

allowed us to measure performance trade-offs (see Sperling and Dosher 1986). In some sessions subjects were told to do as well as they could on the perceptual task and to delay the saccade if necessary in order to improve perceptual performance. In other sessions they were told to make the saccade as promptly as possible, even if that strategy resulted in more perceptual errors.

The results are shown by the attentional operating characteristics (AOCs) in figure 8.7, which plots saccadic latencies against percent correct perceptual identifications for two different subjects. There is a clear trade-off – achieving best perceptual performance requires a delay of the saccade – indicating that programming an accurate saccade is achieved at some attentional cost – that is, the saccadic system does not have its own exclusive selective attentional filter. Surprisingly, the attentional cost of the saccade was modest. Latency increases of only 20 per cent or so were enough to produce perceptual performance matching that observed in trials when no saccades had to be made. Perhaps this result means that attentional allocation is important for saccadic control during only a small portion of the latency interval. The rest might be "free time", allowing observers to distribute attention over the display to recognize objects or identify potential new saccadic targets. Similar

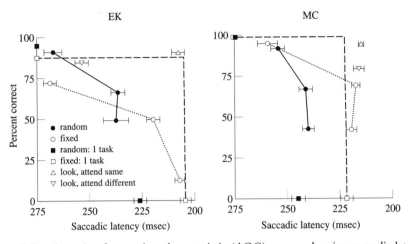

Figure 8.7. Attentional operating characteristic (AOC) curves, showing saccadic latency (abscissa) and proportion of correctly identified letters (ordinate). The location of the letter to be reported remained the same throughout an experimental session. The saccadic target was either selected at random (filled symbols) or remained fixed throughout the session (open symbols). The three circles in each function show performance under instructions to give priority to the saccadic task (lower circles), to the perceptual task (upper circles), or to adopt an intermediate priority (middle circles). Squares, plotted on the axes, show performance when doing only one task, either the saccadic or the letter identification task. The intersection of the dashed lines emanating from the open squares represents the independence point – that is, the point at which there would be no interference in the performance of the two concurrent tasks. The triangles represent attempts to reach the independence point by trying to minimize latency and maximize letter identification simultaneously. Saccadic and perceptual targets were either at the same (upright triangle) or different (inverted triangle) locations. Each datum point was based on approximately 100 observations. Error bars represent +/− 1 SE. (From Kowler et al. 1995: 1910.)

modest attentional demands apply to smooth pursuit eye movements as well (Khurana and Kowler 1987). (See Hoffman 1997; Hoffman and Subramaniam 1995; Kustov and Robinson 1997; Rizzolatti et al. 1987; Andersen and Gnadt 1989; and Colby and Duhamel 1996 for other research showing links between saccadic programming and attentional allocation.)

The links between eye movements and attention help show why using saccades appears to be so effortless. No special separate decision needs to be made to select the target for the saccade. The saccadic system taps into the same mechanism that assigns perceptual attention to one or another object based on its properties or on the overall strategies of performing the task. All the saccadic system needs to do is issue the "go" signal to trigger the movement once attention has shifted to the chosen target (see Munoz and Wurtz 1993 for discussion of the possible neural bases of the trigger signal). The attentional requirements of saccades are apparently so modest that plenty of processing resources are available for thinking and making decisions about the contents of the display.

*

The research summarized in this chapter shows that the effective control of eye movements depends on a combination of sensory and cognitive influences. Each plays a separate and distinct role. For example, attention selects the target for both smooth eye movements and saccades, while lower-level sensorimotor mechanisms compute the precise trajectory of the eye movements. Trajectory computation is influenced by a combination of immediate visual cues about target position, shape or motion on the retina, combined with cognitive signals, specifically, expectations about future target motion.

Cognitive influences are important because they allow the eye to be directed to interesting or important locations without relying on deliberate planning of the movements. The control of eye movements is thus seamlessly woven into the performance of the task at hand – be it reading, search, sewing, or surgery – becoming an effective tool, rather than an additional task burden. Given that cognitive influences on eye movements are so fundamental, so lawful, and so readily assessed quantitatively, the goal of eventually finding and understanding the neural basis for the relevant cognitive contributions to eye movements seems within reach. The oculomotor phenomena described here present a promising way to study the neural correlates of expectations and attention, because tasks involving eye movements can be adopted to closely simulate real-world visuomotor activities, and because the relevant cognitive phenomena can be specified precisely in time by using the eye movements as the temporal landmarks.

References

Andersen, R. A. and Gnadt, J. W. (1989) Posterior parietal cortex. In R. H. Wurtz and M. I. Goldberg (eds), *Reviews of Oculomotor Research*, Vol. 3: *The Neurobiology of Saccadic Eye Movements*, Amsterdam: Elsevier, 315–36.

Bahcall, D. O. and Kowler, E. (1999) Attentional interference at close spatial separations. *Vision Research* 39, 71–86.

Ballard, D. H., Hayhoe, M. M. and Pelz, J. B. (1995) Memory representation in natural tasks. *Journal of Cognitive Neuroscience* 7, 66–80.

Carpenter, R. (1988) *Movements of the Eyes*, London: Pion Limited.

Colby, C. L. and Duhamel, J. R. (1996) Spatial representations for action in parietal cortex. *Cognitive Brain Research* 5, 105–15.

Collewijn, H. (19981) *The Oculomotor System of the Rabbit and its Adaptive Plasticity*, Berlin: Springer Verlag.

Dodge, R. (1931) *Conditions and Consequences of Human Variability*, New Haven: Yale University Press.

Epelboim, J., Steinman, R. M., Kowler, E., Edwards, M., Pizlo, Z., Erkelens, C. J. and Collewijn, H. (1995) The function of visual search and memory in sequential looking tasks. *Vision Research* 35, 3401–22.

Epelboim, J. and Suppes, P. (1996). Window on the mind? What eye movements reveal about geometrical reasoning. *Proceedings of the Cognitive Science Society* 18, 59.

Feldman, J. (1997) Curvilinearity, covariance and regularity in perceptual groups. *Vision Research* 37, 2835–48.

Field D. J., Hayes, A. and Hess, R. F. (1993) Contour integration by the human visual system: evidence for a local "association field." *Vision Research* 33, 173–93.

Georgopoulos, A. P., Taira, M. and Lukashin A. (1993) Cognitive neurophysiology of the motor cortex. *Science* 260, 47–52.

Goodale, M. (1995) The cortical organization of visual perception and visuomotor control. In S. Kosslyn (ed.), *Invitation to Cognitive Science*, Cambridge, MA: MIT Press, 167–214.

Hallett, P. (1986) Eye movement. In K. R. Boff, L. Kaufman, and J. P. Thomas (eds), *Handbook of Perception and Human Performance*, New York: Wiley, ch. 10.

He, P. and Kowler E. (1991) Saccadic localization of eccentric forms. *Journal of the Optical Society of America A* 8, 440–9.

Heinen, S. J. and Liu, M. (1997) Single neuron activity in the dorsomedial frontal cortex during smooth pursuit eye movements to predictable target motion. *Visual Neuroscience* 14, 853–65.

Hoffman, J. E. (1997) Visual attention and eye movements. In H. Pashler (ed), *Attention*, London: University College London Press, 119–53.

Hoffman, J. and Subramaniam, B. (1995) Saccadic eye movements and visual selective attention. *Perception and Psychophysics* 57, 7787–95.

Keller, E. L. and Heinen, S. J. (1991) Generation of smooth-pursuit eye movements: neuronal mechanisms and pathways. *Neuroscience Research* 11, 79–107.

Khurana, B. and Kowler, E. (1987) Shared attentional control of smooth eye movements and perception. *Vision Research* 27, 1603–18.

Kovács, I. and Julesz, B. (1994) A closed curve is much more than an incomplete one. *Proceedings of the National Academy of Sciences* 90, 7495–7.

Kowler, E. (1989) Cognitive expectations, not habits, control anticipatory smooth oculomotor pursuit. *Vision Research* 29, 1049–57.

—— (1990) The role of visual and cognitive processes in the control of eye movement. In E. Kowler (ed) *Reviews of Oculomotor Research*. Vol. 4: *Eye Movements and their Role in Visual and Cognitive Processes*, Amsterdam: Elsevier, 1–70.

—— (1995) Eye movement. In S. Kosslyn (ed) *Invitation to Cognitive Science*, vol. 2, Cambridge, MA: MIT Press, 215–65.

Kowler, E., Anderson, E., Dosher, B. and Blaser, E. (1995) The role of attention in the programming of saccades. *Vision Research* 35, 1897–1916.

Kowler, E. and Blaser, E. (1995) The accuracy and precision of saccades to small and large targets. *Vision Research* 35, 1741–54.

Kowler, E. and McKee, S. P. (1987) Sensitivity of smooth eye movements to small differences in target velocity. *Vision Research* 27, 993–1015.

Kustov, A. A. and Robinson, D. L. (1997) Shared neural control of attentional shifts and eye movements. *Nature* 384, 74–7.

Kowler, E., van der Steen, J., Collewijn, H. and Tamminga, E. P. (1984) Voluntary selection of the target for smooth eye movement in the presence of superimposed full-field stationary and moving stimuli. *Vision Research* 24, 1789–98.

Land, M. F. and Furneaux, S. (1997) The knowledge base of the oculomotor system. *Philosophical Transactions of the Royal Society of London*. B352, 1231–9.

Liu, Z. L. and Dosher, B. A. (1998) External noise distinguishes attention mechanisms. *Vision Research* 38, 1183–98.

Mach, E. (1906/1959) *Analysis of Sensation*, New York: Dover.

McGowan, J., Kowler, E., Sharma, A. and Chubb, C. F. (1998) Saccadic localization of random dot targets. *Vision Research* 38, 895–909.

Melcher, D. and Kowler, E. (1999) Shape, surfaces and saccades. *Vision Research*, in press.

Morgan, M. J., Hole, G. J. and Glennester, A. (1990) Biases and sensitivities in geometrical illusions. *Vision Research* 30, 1793–1810.

Munoz, D. and Wurtz. R. H. (1993) Fixation cells in monkey superior colliculus. I. Characteristics of cell discharge. *Journal of Neurophysiology* 70, 559–75.

O'Regan, J. K. (1990) Eye movements and reading. In E. Kowler (ed) *Reviews of Oculomotor Research*, Vol. 4: *Eye Movements and their Role in Visual and Cognitive Processes*, Amsterdam: Elsevier, 395–453.

—— (1992) Solving the "real" mysteries of visual perception: the world as an outside memory. *Canadian Journal of Psychology* 46, 461–88.

Pavel, M. (1990) Predictive eye movement. In E. Kowler (ed) *Reviews of Oculomotor Research*, Vol. 4: *Eye Movements and their Role in Visual and Cognitive Processes*, Amsterdam: Elsevier.

Pizlo, Z., Salach-Golyska, M. and Rosenfeld, A. (1997) Curve detection in a noisy image. *Vision Research* 37, 1217–41.

Rizzolatti, G., Riggio, L., Dascola, I. and Umita, C. (1987) Reorienting attention across the horizontal and vertical meridians: evidence in favor of a premotor theory of attention. *Neuropsychologia* 25, 31–40.

Schall, J. D., Hanes, D. P., Thompson, K. G. and King, D. J. (1995) Saccade target selection in frontal eye field of macaque. I. Visual and premovement activation. *Journal of Neuroscience* 15, 6905–18.

Sperling, G. and Dosher, B. (1986) Strategy and optimization in human information processing. In K. R. Boff, L. Kaufman, and J. P. Thomas (eds), *Handbook of Perception and Human Performance*, New York: Wiley, ch. 2.

Sperling, G. and Weichselgartner E. (1995) Episodic theory of the dynamics of spatial attention. *Psychological Review* 102, 503–32.

Steinman, R. M. and Levinson, J. Z. (1990) The role of eye movement in the detection of contrast and spatial detail. In E. Kowler (ed), *Reviews of Oculomotor Research*, Vol. 4: *Eye Movements and their Role in Visual and Cognitive Processes*, Amsterdam: Elsevier, 115–212.

Steinman, R. M., Haddad, G. M., Skavenski, A. A. and Wyman, D. (1973) Miniature eye movement. *Science* 181, 810–19.

Steinman, R. M., Skavenski, A. A. and Sansbury, R. V. (1969) Voluntary control of smooth pursuit velocity. *Vision Research* 9, 1167–71.

Suppes, P. (1990) Eye movement models for arithmetic and reading performance. In E. Kowler (ed), *Reviews of Oculomotor Research*, Vol. 4: *Eye Movements and their Role in Visual and Cognitive Processes*, Amsterdam: Elsevier, 455–77.

Tanenhaus, M. K., Spivey-Knowlton, M. J., Eberhard, K. M. and Sedivy, J. C. (1995) Integration of visual and linguistic information in spoken language comprehension. *Science* 268, 1632–4.

Viviani, P. (1990) Eye movements in visual search: cognitive, perceptual and motor control aspects. In E. Kowler (ed), *Reviews of Oculomotor Research*, Vol. 4: *Eye Movements and their Role in Visual and Cognitive Processes*, Amsterdam: Elsevier, 353–93.

Yarbus, A. L. (1967) *Eye Movements and Vision*, New York: Plenum Press.

9

Visual Dilemmas: Competition between Eyes and between Percepts in Binocular Rivalry

Thomas V. Papathomas, Ilona Kovács,
Akos Fehér, and Bela Julesz

1 Introduction

The brain receives many signals from the sensory organs simultaneously. One mild form of rivalry occurs constantly as events vie to grab the limited attention resources of the brain and compete to register for awareness. For example, a car driver's attention can be captured by the weather report on the radio, by the conversation of his or her passengers, or by visual input that alerts him or her to initiate a difficult maneuver. Even after a stable stimulus enjoys the full attention for a long time interval, the brain is constantly attempting to arrive at a meaningful percept by testing competing hypotheses that are consistent with the sensory signals that the stimulus gives rise to (see chapter 7 above).

If the brain is to perform a task without noticeable degradation in performance, then it must focus on only that task, because of limited attentional resources (e.g., Neisser and Becklen 1975). In everyday life, the sensory signals associated with a particular object or event have a high degree of correlation across sense modalities. For example, visual, auditory and olfactory signals can provide consistent cues for the location and movement of an object in space. This consistency enables the brain to process these signals, arrive at stable percepts within each modality, integrate them across modalities, and obtain an accurate representation of the environment. Ultimately, this kind of signal processing, coupled with haptic feedback, enables organisms to interact effectively with their environment.

An extreme form of rivalry ensues when the usual consistency between the signals carried by the two eyes is disrupted. This is done by providing each eye with a substantially different stimulus from that of its partner for long periods of time. Under such conditions, observers perceive a never-ending spontaneous alternation of percepts over time, termed *binocular rivalry*. This chapter provides a brief review of binocular rivalry and concentrates on whether rivalry is due to competition between the eyes at the level of monocular neurons, or to competition between percepts at higher levels, or to a combination of these factors. We present evidence from new experiments that challenges current models of binocular rivalry that favor eye competition. Most previous studies used conventional stimuli with coherent patterns within each eye's image; thus eye competition and stimulus competition are confounded. We have recently developed a "patchwork stimuli" technique which separates these two factors (Kovács et al. 1996). The experimental results indicate that the alternations in binocular rivalry cannot be accounted for by eye suppression alone, but that stimulus coherence plays some role as well. One of the possibilities is that, when faced with binocular rivalrous stimuli, the visual system continually constructs and tests likely stimulus interpretations, or hypotheses, in an attempt to arrive at a meaningful percept.

This hypothesis-construct-and-test function of the brain has been suggested before (Gregory 1970). It seems to us that the most parsimonious solution to the problem of arriving at a stable percept is to use the same strategies across all cases that involve competing percepts; there is no a priori reason for the brain to adopt a different strategy in the special case of binocular rivalry. In this scenario, it is not only the eyes, but also the percepts, that compete for awareness; if necessary, the brain will integrate information across the two eyes, if neither eye's input is coherent. Monocular suppression does not necessarily contradict the putative process of constructing and testing interpretations. In fact, it seems quite plausible for the brain to block temporarily one eye's view altogether and try to arrive at a meaningful percept from the other eye's stimulus.

This chapter is organized as follows. In section 2 we present arguments on why rivalry is a worthwhile research endeavor. Some temporal and spatial characteristics of binocular rivalry that are within the scope of this chapter are presented in section 3. A brief review of the role of bottom-up and top-down processes in rivalry is found in section 4. Section 5 presents the two sides of the controversy on whether rivalry is due to competition between the eyes or competition between percepts; models for eye competition theories are presented in section 5.1, and evidence for percept competition in section 5.2. Section 6 presents our experiments with the patchwork-rivalry stimuli, and section 7 consists of discussion and conclusions.

2   Why Study Binocular Rivalry?

We briefly discussed earlier the consistency among the sensory signals that define an object or an event. In vision (or audition), the two eyes (or ears) receive very consistent signals from the environment under most circumstances. In such cases, the brain can easily combine the two signals to arrive at a stable percept. In fact, the relatively small differences in the two signals between the two eyes (or ears) are processed by the brain to estimate distances between the observer and objects in the environment.

In the special case of vision, the two eyes receive slightly disparate images by virtue of their horizontal separation and vergence movements. As a result, the *disparities* are mostly along the horizontal dimension. The visual system is able to combine the two monocular images into a stable binocular (cyclopean) percept, utilizing any disparities to extract depth relationships in the environment. However, when the signals coming from the two eyes differ substantially, by stimulating corresponding areas of the two retinas with radically different patterns, such a combination is no longer possible. Instead, the two signals compete for awareness, and the percept alternates randomly across time in a tug-of-war. There are periods of the order of a few seconds during which one percept dominates and suppresses the competing percept, only to give way to its rival after a random interval, in an endless alternation of competing states. The word "dilemma," Greek for "two lemmas"[1] or "two premises" (Pirsig 1974: 229), is very appropriate here. It is usually reserved for intellectual vacillations between two equally balanced alternatives, but it can be applied metaphorically to perceptual vacillations during binocular rivalry.

Parenthetically, similar phenomena happen in audition, when the two ears are provided with drastically different signals under dichotic stimulation, giving rise to binaural rivalry (Treisman 1964; Deutsch 1975, 1982; Egeth 1992). However, Treisman questions how close the parallels are between binocular rivalry and binaural rivalry: "In particular, we seem to have much more voluntary control over choosing which ear to listen to. Also, synchrony may be a stronger cue to fusion in the auditory than in the visual modality, at least for speech" (personal communication, 19 July 1997).

Rivalry can be considered as one of the three components of binocular vision, along with fusion and stereopsis. *Fusion* occurs when the images of the two eyes are nearly identical, and it results in the percept of a single surface. *Stereopsis* requires stimulating the eyes with images that contain moderate values of binocular disparities, and their combination results in the percept of surfaces in depth. Julesz and Miller (1975) have demonstrated that stereopsis and rivalry can coexist, providing evidence for the possibility of separate pathways for the two components (Wolfe 1986). On the other hand, de Weert and Wade (1988) used binocularly correlated (hence fusible) and uncorrelated (hence unfusible) microstructures that coexisted with rivaling macrostructures. One of their main results was that the macrostructure rivalry was diminished when the microstructures were fusible rather than unfusible. This indicates some interacting, rather than separate, pathways for fusion and rivalry. Finally, O'Shea, Sims and Govan (1997) conclude that all three binocular components (rivalry, fusion and stereopsis) seem to share a common mechanism; details of their paradigm are presented in section 3 below. The issue of whether the three components are processed by separate or common pathways is still undecided.

Skeptics and novices may raise some questions, which look legitimate at a first glance: Why study such a contrived condition, which rarely occurs in everyday life? Can the study of binocular rivalry help in understanding binocular vision? What benefits to cognitive science in general and to vision research in particular can be derived by investigating the response to rivalrous visual stimulation? We elaborate below on some propositions and arguments, selected from a wide variety of sources, to address these questions.

(1) For purposes of clarity in introducing binocular rivalry, it has been presented so far in this chapter as an artificially induced stimulation. However, one cannot ignore a theory of binocular vision in which rivalry plays a central role in perception. According to this *suppression theory* of binocular vision, rivalry occurs under all stimulus conditions, even if both eyes receive very similar images. There are several variants of the theory, but the common theme among its proponents' models is that, even after the two eyes' images are fused, only one eye's stimulus is perceived at any given moment from any given region of the visual field (Verhoeff 1935; Asher 1953; Hochberg 1964; Kaufman 1974; Wolfe 1986). Blake, among others, has presented experimental evidence against this theory (Blake and Boothroyd 1985) and has offered an alternative neural theory (Blake 1989), according to which binocular rivalry occurs only when fusion fails to establish correspondence. The issue has not been decided yet. In fact, a broad unsolved problem in vision research is the formulation of a general theory of binocular vision that encompasses stereopsis, fusion, and rivalry (Fox 1991). Thus binocular rivalry, far from being an oddity, is relevant to normal binocular vision.

(2) Binocular rivalry is one of those rare conditions in which a stable suprathreshold stimulus is completely blocked from visual awareness for long intervals at a time. As such, it touches on the concept of awareness, and thus it may offer an experimental tool toward studying consciousness (Myerson et al. 1981; Crick and Koch 1992; Crick 1996).

(3) Binocular rivalry can be viewed as a simple example of more complex bi-stable phenomena, in which a stable unchanging stimulus gives rise to a spontaneous alternation among multiple percepts (see chapter 7 above by Papathomas). Viewed from this angle, it is a rare, if not the only, such bi-stable percept for which neurophysiologists have established the presence or absence of a correlation between perceptual performance and neural activity (Logothetis and Schall 1989; Leopold and Logothetis 1996; Logothetis et al. 1996; Lehky and Maunsell 1996). This must be coupled with strong evidence from studies with alert animals, starting with the pioneering study of Myerson,

Miezin and Allman (1981), that macaque monkeys and humans exhibit almost identical responses when subjected to binocularly rivalrous stimuli. Thus, binocular rivalry offers a fertile area for collaboration among psychophysicists and neurophysiologists to study the structure and information flow in the neural pathways as a result of complex stimulation.

(4) Binocular rivalry has potential clinical relevance, because it exhibits some similarities to chronic suppression of one eye's input in people with dysfunctional binocular vision (Burian and von Noorden 1974). As an example, one eye's input may be permanently inhibited in individuals with strabismus (deviation, or misalignment, of one eye) to avoid diplopia ("double vision"), even though the suppressed eye is kept open whenever the dominant eye is open. The similarities and differences between temporary rivalry perception in "normal" observers and chronic suppression in people with binocular disorders have been studied to some extent (e.g., Fahle 1983; Holopigian 1987), but more systematic investigation is needed to establish any connections at a deep level. A deep understanding of such connections will enable better treatment techniques for binocular pathologies.

(5) With regard to relevance in cognitive science, binocular rivalry offers a prime opportunity to study influences of top-down processes on bottom-up mechanisms. Can knowledge or attention or active engagement affect the putative spontaneous alternation of percepts during binocular rivalry? There is equivocal evidence for the affirmative (e.g., Lack 1978) and the negative (e.g., Blake 1988) answers to the above question. However, experiments with more objective criteria are necessary to settle the dispute, and we will return to this issue in section 4.

(6) Even if the suppression theory of binocular vision proves to be wrong (see (1) above), binocular rivalry may occur locally under normal stereoscopic conditions. Even after successful stereoscopic fusion, there are areas of the visual field that are occluded for one eye but visible for the other eye. These *monocular occlusions* may define spatially extended regions of potential binocular rivalry, in the sense that very different stimulations may exist for the two eyes. How does the visual system resolve these rivalries? This problem has not attracted the attention it deserves, excepting some recent efforts to address it (Nakayama and Shimojo 1990; Anderson 1994; Anderson and Nakayama 1994).

(7) Finally, binocular rivalry has some practical significance in the ergonomic design of optical equipment that forces the operator to view very different monocular fields separately (Kama 1988; Kimchi et al. 1993).

3   Characteristics of Binocular Rivalry

In this section we present a review of binocular rivalry, examined from a narrow point of view. Specifically, we concentrate on some characteristics that are relevant to the material presented in sections 5 and 6, having to do with the role of eye competition and percept competition. A comprehensive review of most aspects of binocular rivalry is offered by Fox (1991). In addition, papers by Wolf (1986) and Blake (1989) provide extensive reviews in support of the neural models that they propose in their papers. The present summary updates these reviews with important recent developments. Finally, the interested reader is referred to an on-line bibliography on binocular rivalry featured on the World-Wide Web (O'Shea 1999).

We start with the temporal characteristics of binocular rivalry. It has been established that when the two eyes are stimulated with rivalrous images, binocular fusion is experienced in the first 150 ms or so, before rivalry sets in. This pre-rivalrous state has been termed *false* (or *abnormal*) *fusion* (Hering 1920/1964; Goldstein 1970; Wolfe 1983; O'Shea and Crassini 1984). It seems that the brain, accustomed to receiving consistent signals from the two eyes, fuses the two stimuli as a first step[2], in an attempt to start the process of constructing and testing hypotheses. At about the same time, upon recognizing the incompatibility of the stimuli, the brain signals the oculomotor system to change the vergence angle in an attempt to bring the stimuli into registration, if possible. This process is repeated continuously, and it explains the apparent sliding of the two monocular images past one another, as the rivalry finds no resolution (Blake 1989).

According to most models of binocular rivalry (e.g., Blake 1989), the spontaneous temporal alternations among multistable percepts in rivalry commence after all attempts at fusion fail (but be reminded that, according to the suppression theories of binocular vision, these alternations continue even after fusion has been achieved). The fact remains that, under artificial rivalry-inducing conditions with radically different stimuli, these temporal alternations are adequately discernible to be monitored and recorded by observers. Such recordings have shown that the histograms of the dominance time intervals are well fitted by the Gamma distribution, which is characterized by two parameters λ and r:

$$f(x) = [\lambda^r / \Gamma(r)] \, x^{r-1} \exp(-\lambda x), \qquad \text{with } \Gamma(r) = (r-1)! \qquad (1)$$

For humans, early experiments of this kind (Levelt 1965; Fox and Herrmann 1967) were used to characterize the alternations with various types of rivaling stimuli (Wade 1975; Walker 1975; Logothetis et al. 1996; Leopold and Logothetis 1996; Kovács et al. 1996). Similar experiments have also been tried with animals (Myerson et al. 1981; Logothetis and Schall 1990; Leopold and Logothetis 1996). It is mainly the remarkable similarity of the parameters of the Gamma distribution in human and non-human observers that provides strong evidence that the two classes of observers experience very similar phenomena during rivalry. Parenthetically, the issue of the neural substrate of binocular rivalry, investigated in recent neurophysiological experiments, will be taken up in section 5.2.2.

We next turn briefly to the spatial properties of binocular rivalry. Based on subjective reports from human observers, it is generally believed that, when the affected retinal areas are small, of the order of 1 square degree[3], the entire patterns of the two eyes alternate in time with each competing percept exhibiting *exclusive visibility* at the expense of its rival percept. When larger areas are involved, the alternating percepts are composed of mosaics of the two eyes' patterns that change dynamically over time, a mode commonly referred to as *piecemeal rivalry*. Recently, however, O'Shea, Sims, and Govan (1997) have studied systematically how exclusive visibility varies as a function of spatial frequency and field size, using stimuli in which there exists orientation rivalry between gratings of identical frequencies. Their results indicate that threshold field sizes for producing exlusive visibility were inversely proportional to the spatial frequency contained inside them, and that these field sizes could become much larger than 1 square degree. O'Shea, Sims, and Govan (1997) compare their rivalry results to similar results obtained for static stereopsis (Schor et al. 1984a, 1984b), dynamic stereopsis (Schor et al. 1984b), binocular fusion (Schor et al. 1984a), and binocular rivalry (Liu and Schor 1994). O'Shea, Sims, and Govan (1997) note that the similarity among all these results indicates that all three binocular phenomena (fusion, stereopsis, and rivalry) seem to share a common mechanism.

Finally, we mention briefly the phenomenon of *monocular rivalry* (Campbell and Howell 1972; Atkinson et al. 1973). A typical instance involves a set of red vertical lines coexisting with another set of green horizontal lines that, together, form a plaid against a neutral yellow background that is chromatically equidistant from both the red and the green hues of each line (*unique* yellow). When staring at such a stimulus for long periods of time, in excess of ten seconds, there are spontaneously alternating intervals of dominance, during which the set of red vertical (or green horizontal) lines seems to be perceived exclusively, blocking the rivalrous set from visual awareness. The temporal distributions of these intervals are very close to those observed in binocular rivalry. The relevance of monocular rivalry to our presentation is discussed in section 7.

4   Role of Bottom-up and Top-down Processes in Rivalry

The key question in this section is: Can binocular rivalry phenomena be explained purely by the activity of preconscious bottom-up mechanisms, or do top-down processes, such as attention and conscious effort, play a role as well?

When the brain is confronted with competing percepts under binocular rivalry, one may distinguish two extreme types of functions. *Bottom-up* mechanisms may process elementary attributes, such as color, orientation, local contours, local motion, etc. *Top-down* processes may take advantage of global coherence characteristics to construct a meaningful percept. It is possible that such processes and characteristics include previous knowledge, assumptions about illuminants, global contour continuity, shading, global motion attributes (including occlusion and disocclusion), object recognition, semantic content, etc.

There is a long-standing controversy about the role of top-down processes in binocular rivalry that can be illustrated through two key reports. Blake (1988) found that attention was not effective in rivalrous reading tasks, whereas Lack (1978) reported that observers could exert some control over alternation rates. However, Lack's data can accept the alternative interpretation that they were due to a change in the observers' criterion, as argued by Fox (1991), who suggests that more objective criteria are necessary to settle the dispute. A comprehensive, albeit dated, review of the controversy is in Walker 1978.

The issue is further complicated by the lack of an effective dialogue among the diverse fields of research in binocular rivalry, ranging from eye movements (Sabrin and Kertesz 1983) to social psychology (Reitz and Jackson 1964), and the related fact that reports are scattered across the literature. As an example, cognitive vision researchers often cite Neisser and Becklen's (1975) finding that observers can attend selectively to a coherent episode when it is presented monocularly, simultaneously with a rival episode, superimposed on the same part of the visual field. However, the companion study with *binocularly rivaling* episodes, presented in the *same* paper, in which Neisser and Becklen report that attention plays a major role in binocular rivalry, is almost never cited in recent papers. One reason may be that there were methodological problems in their experiments, but one could easily point them out. Unfortunately, there has not been much research recently on the influence of top-down processes in binocular rivalry.

5   Eye Competition or Percept Competition: Messengers or Messages?

As a rule, visual signals arriving from two small corresponding retinal areas are interpreted by the brain as coming from the same location in 3-D space (monocular occlusions are an exception to this rule). Binocular rivalry is based on a natural contraint: two things cannot occupy the same space at the same time in the observed world. Thus, one pattern dominates temporarily by suppressing the competing pattern, only to be suppressed spontaneously at a later time, and so on *ad infinitum*. At what level, and how, is this constraint implemented in the brain? What strategies does the brain use?

At one extreme, various *eye-suppression* hypotheses state that, since the eyes receive conflicting stimulation, the visual system's strategy is to alternately suppress one eye's input. At the other extreme are alternative hypotheses based on the view of the sensory/perceptual brain as a hypothesis-constructing-and-testing agent (see chapter 7 above, by Papathomas). An extreme version of such a *percept-suppression* theory could posit that the brain tries to arrive at meaningful percepts based solely on the coherence of the stimuli, *regardless of the eye-of-origin*. Essentially, eye-suppression hypotheses favor competition between the *messengers* (eyes), whereas stimulus-suppression hypotheses favor competition between the *messages* (stimuli). Naturally, these theories represent two extreme positions. In reality, the brain may use a combination of the two strategies, or an assortment of these and other strategies, according to the task at hand, akin to Ramachandran's (1985) "bag of tricks" idea.

5.1   Eye-suppression hypotheses

The common idea among eye-suppression hypotheses is that binocular rivalry is the result of mutual inhibition between monocular mechanisms (Sugie 1982; Matsuoka 1984; Grossberg 1987; Lehky 1988; Blake 1989), or combinations of monocular and OR-binocular units (Wolfe 1986). What differs among the proposals of these researchers is the neural model that each suggests to implement the main idea of interocular inhibition. These models were developed to account for empirical results from psychophysical experiments and were based on known properties of neuronal mechanisms in the visual system. Within these constraints, each model makes conjectures about plausible neural units and connections that could predict known properties of binocular rivalry.

As a first example, Blake's (1989) model starts with the well-established variability of ocular dominance in cortical neurons (Hubel and Wiesel 1962) and proposes the existence of inhibitory interneurons that receive synaptic excitatory signals from the homologous eye and non-recurrent inhibitory signals from the other eye. He theorizes that these interneurons occur at or just above the level of cortical hypercolumns. His model predicts adequately a variety of phenomena, including the correlation between ocular dominance histograms and psychophysical performance in normal, non-amblyopic suppressors, and deep amblyopic observers (Blake 1989).

Wolfe's (1986) model is different enough from the others to provide the second example. For one thing, Wolfe argues for the inevitability of rivalry, even in the presence of identical stimuli in the two eyes, thus joining the camp of suppression theorists of binocular vision. The fundamental proposition of his theory is that rivalry and stereopsis involve separate independent pathways. In the first stage of processing, he assumes the existence of three classes of neurons: *purely monocular*, that are excited by one eye exclusively; *OR-*

binocular, that respond to stimulation in either eye; and *AND-binocular*, that respond only when both eyes receive matching stimuli. Rivalry involves the competition between left-eye and right-eye monocular neurons, each gated by OR-binocular neurons. The stereopsis pathway involves mainly AND-binocular neurons.

Grossberg's (1987) model is too complex to be done justice in a brief review. In any case, binocular rivalry is just a small aspect of it, and it is based on inhibitory interactions among orientation-tuned units. The three other models of monocular suppression (Sugie 1982; Matsuoka 1984; Lehky 1988) deal with the temporal characteristics of rivalry. What is common in all the eye-competition theories considered here is that they do not incorporate any top-down processes in their models of binocular rivalry[4]. In addition to direct psychophysical evidence that supports specific implementation models of such eye-suppression hypotheses (such references are cited in the corresponding papers), indirect evidence is offered by the fact that strabismic ("cross-eyed") infants develop an extreme form of permanent binocular rivalry. Since their eyes do not register the same visual scene, the visual system's solution is to suppress the input from one eye permanently, presumably through inhibition of monocular mechanisms.

However, most of the experiments that provide supporting evidence for eye-suppression hypotheses use conventional stimuli that confound the effects of eye competition and stimulus competition. Figure 9.1 provides an example of such a conventional stimulus. Both images of the rivalrous pair are coherent patterns. As a result, when one eye's stimulus dominates during binocular rivalry, one could argue that it is the coherence of that eye's stimulus that suppresses the other eye's stimulus, and not one eye that suppresses the other eye. In other words, does the ape image of figure 9.1 dominate temporarily because all the details arrive from a dominant eye, or because it is a perfectly consistent image with coherent characteristics? What are the contributions of eye competition and stimulus competition in "recovering" the coherent percept? A class of stimuli that can decouple the two influences on binocular rivalry is presented in section 6.

5.2   Evidence for percept suppression

There is documented evidence challenging the theory that mere eye competition can account for all phenomena in binocular rivalry. Some of the evidence has been around for some time, but the most compelling experimental evidence is rather recent. We present such evidence from psychophysical and neurophysiological studies separately in the following two subsections.

Figure 9.1. This binocular pair, together with that of figure 9.3, offers a critical test for investigating the role of eye competition and pattern coherence in binocular rivalry. Throughout this chapter, we will assume that the left and right images of a rivalrous pair of stimuli are presented to the left and right eye, respectively. This figure depicts a conventional "coherent-image within-eye" rivalrous pair of stimuli, in which each eye's image is coherent; thus eye of origin and pattern coherence are confounded. When one image dominates temporarily during binocular rivalry, there can be at least two explanations: (1) the corresponding eye suppresses the other eye (eye-suppression theory), or (2) one image, because of its coherence, suppresses the other image. Reprinted from Kovács, Papathomas, Yang, and Fehér 1996, with the permission of *Proceedings of the National Academy of Sciences, USA.*

5.2.1 Psychophysical evidence for percept suppression

Stirling's effect (Stirling 1901; Creed 1935) involves the fusion of a color from one eye's image and a contour from the other eye's rivaling image. Both eyes' images are coherent, yet the brain forms an unusual conjunction of attributes across the two eyes. This effect argues against the concept of non-selective monocular suppression, according to which suppression operates non-selectively on the whole set of monocular neurons, not only on a subset of those that are specific to a particular attribute (Blake 1989). Stirling's effect also offers evidence against suppression theories of binocular vision, because the unusual binocular conjunction is stable and lasts for long intervals at a time.

There are early reports of experiments in which stimulus coherence and eye of origin were decorrelated by the use of appropriate stimuli that are usually not coherent within either eye (Crain 1961; Treisman 1972; Whittle et al. 1968; Wade 1973; Kulikowski 1992; Kulikowski and Walsh 1995). The common theme in these experiments was that some rivaling percepts during binocular rivalry were formed by combining attributes across the two eyes. As an example, the structure of a weak-contrast moving monocular image might be suppressed, but its motion field overcame suppression and was grafted on

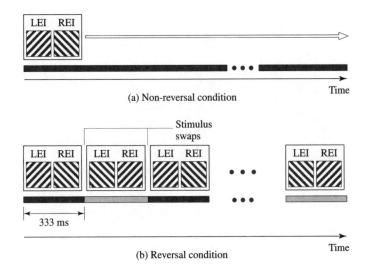

Figure 9.2. A schematic of the stimuli employed by Logothetis, Leopold, and Sheinberg (1996). LEI and REI stand for left-eye image and right-eye image, respectively. (a) Non-reversal condition; (b) reversal condition in which swappings are performed every 333 ms. Despite the frequent swapping of images in condition (b), the average dominance time was over 2,300 ms, almost identical to that in (a). Thus, the percept was held fixed for long intervals, over which the causative stimulus shifted several times across the eyes. Adapted from figure 1 in Logothetis et al. (1996), *Nature*, 380, pp. 621–4. Reprinted with permission of the authors and *Nature*; copyright © 1996 Macmillan Magazines Limited.

to the dominant stationary pattern of the contralateral eye (Reventlow 1961), in a manner similar to Stirling's effect. However, there has been no systematic study of this issue (Fox 1991).

Logothetis, Leopold and Sheinberg (1996) presented psychophysical evidence for the competition of percepts independently of the eye of origin. They used two stimulus conditions, each involving rivaling gratings of orthogonal orientations in the two eyes. One, the *non-reversal* condition, was a conventional one, in which the grating of one orientation (+45°) was shown to one eye, and the other one (−45°) was shown to the other eye for the entire duration of the trial. In the *reversal* condition, the gratings were swapped between the eyes every 333 ms, as shown schematically in figure 9.2. We refer to this mode as a *time-multiplexed* rivalrous stimulation.

Given that the dominance phases in the non-reversal condition lasted in excess of 2.3 seconds, this swapping changed the eye's stimulus an average of seven times per dominance interval. The distribution of the dominance intervals in the reversal condition was statistically the same as in the non-reversal condition. Thus, one grating's orientation percept dominated through several swappings; it is the percept, then, and not the eye of origin that seems to determine the alternation rate. This implies that the brain is trying to make sense of both eyes' images together, not simply suppressing the input from one eye. However, an alternative explanation, albeit less likely, is that the dominance periods are initiated by interocular suppression, and hysteresis (or inertia) keeps them from quickly ceasing. Section 6 presents a *space-multiplexed* mode of rivalrous stimulation, which we also call *patchwork rivalry* stimulation, that bypasses this potential problem of the time-multiplexed stimuli.

5.2.2 *Neurophysiological evidence for percept suppression*

Due to the classical view of eye suppression, there was a long delay in finding sites where neural activity correlates with behavioural response during rivalry. The putative monocular suppression hypothesized by most models of rivalry is assumed to take place prior to binocular combination, either at a very early stage, at the level of monocular input to the lateral geniculate nucleus (LGN), or at a later stage, at the level of the primary (striate) visual cortex. Lehky and Maunsell (1996) state that the LGN could provide the first locus for binocular rivalry, as suggested earlier (Blakemore et al. 1972; Singer 1977; Lehky 1988; Blake 1989; Lehky and Blake 1991) for two reasons: (1) Separate ocular LGN laminae could allow for inhibitory interactions. (2) The LGN receives feedback from striate cortex, and one feedback component could indicate whether the binocular inputs are fused or rivalrous. However, when Lehky and Maunsell (1996) recorded from LGN neurons of alert macaque monkeys under rivalrous and non-rivalrous excitation, they found no neural correlate of rivalry. This negative finding pushes the site of binocular rivalry beyond the LGN. However, it does not exclude the possibility that some populations of monocular neurons in striate cortex are exclusively responsible for rivalry.

Recently, however, evidence that eye-suppression theories need to be revised was provided by several neurophysiological laboratories. Among others, Logothetis and his colleagues, as well as Sengpiel, Blakemore and their colleagues, provided such experimental evidence for monkeys and cats, respectively. The first group recorded from neurons in monkeys while the animals were indicating their perceptual states (Logothetis and Schall 1989; Leopold and Logothetis 1996; Sheinberg and Logothetis 1997). They found a continuum of types of binocular neurons in post-striate areas V4, STS, IT, and MT: some correlated with the reported state, but, more importantly, others were not affected by the reported rivalry; thus input to these binocular neurons was provided from both eyes' units independently of the perceptual rivalry state, contrary to the prediction of eye-suppression theories. Crick (1996) singles out these two papers (Logothetis and Schall 1989; Leopold and Logothetis 1996) as "among the opening salvoes of a concerted attack on the baffling problem of consciousness." Similar evidence was found in the cat by the second group (Sengpiel and Blakemore 1994; Sengpiel et al. 1995; Sengpiel 1997).

Unfortunately, it may be premature to infer the structure of the pathways from the results of the above studies in enough detail to trace neural connections. Although the results of the above studies point to a need to revise monocular suppression models (e.g., Blake 1989), it may be difficult to use the same results toward validating or rejecting Wolfe's (1986) model of binocular rivalry. With respect to more recent models of rivalry, Dayan (1996) was motivated by neurophysiological (Logothetis and Schall 1989; Leopold and Logothetis 1996) and psychophysical results (Logothetis et al. 1996) to build a hierarchical model that uses top-down connections to account for the new developments.

6 A New Look at Rivalry: Interocular Grouping with Patchwork Rivalry Stimuli

Binocular rivalry shares at least four important similarities with stimulation by ambiguous multistable figures (see chapter 7). In both cases: (1) the physical stimuli are stable; (2) phenomenally, there are spontaneous random alternations of percepts over time; (3) when one percept dominates, the other(s) are blocked from awareness – that is, no two competing percepts can coexist; (4) observers have the impression that they can influence somewhat the percept alternation by exerting effort, although the evidence is equivocal about whether or not this is possible. The main difference is that, in binocular rivalry, there are two channels with different visual inputs. Nevertheless, despite this difference, the brain's perceptual task remains to make sense of the rivalrous visual inputs. In this endeavor, the brain might continuously construct and test alternative percepts (or assertions or hypotheses), based on the stimuli. In this section we present evidence that percept competiton, in addition to eye competition, plays a role in binocular rivalry (Kovács et al. 1996; Papathomas et al. 1997; Fehér et al. 1997). The common theme of these experiments is that the visual system is able to integrate, or group, a coherent percept across the two eyes, even though neither eye contains such a coherent percept.

6.1 Interocular grouping with patchwork rivalry of natural images

In figure 9.1, there is a confounding effect of eye of origin and stimulus coherence that makes it difficult to separate their roles in binocular rivalry. This is because each eye is presented with a separate coherent image; thus, when the image of one eye temporarily dominates over the other, it is not clear whether it is that eye that dominates or the eye's image.

Since conventional rivalrous stimuli, as in figure 9.1, confound the effects of eye competition and stimulus competition, there is a clear need for stimuli that will allow the experimenter to isolate the two effects. To this end, we have developed a paradigm of *patchwork-rivalrous*, or *space-multiplexed*, stimuli, in which eye of origin and pattern of coherence are decorrelated to a large degree (Kovács et al. 1996). In our class of stimuli, we replace conventional images by complementary patchworks of intermingled rivalrous images. Figure 9.3 illustrates such a "patchwork rivalry" stimulus for the same two images that

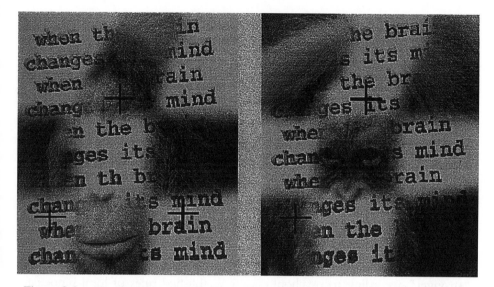

Figure 9.3. "Patchwork-rivalrous" version of the stimuli in figure 9.1. Unlike figure 9.1, where each eye's image is coherent, eye of origin and pattern coherence are uncorrelated in this figure. These images can be called "incoherent-image within-eye," or "coherent-image across-eyes" stimuli. When observers view these dichoptically, most can still experience alternations between the ape and the text, which cannot be explained by eye-competition theories of rivalry. Reprinted from Kovács, Papathomas, Yang, and Fehér 1996, with the permission of *Proceedings of the National Academy of Sciences, USA.*

were used in figure 9.1. We start with two coherent images P and Q (in figure 9.1, P = ape, and Q = text). Subsequently, the left eye's stimulus is formed by "patching" intermingled blocks from P and Q; the right eye's stimulus contains the complementary blocks, such that corresponding areas of the two retinae receive different images, resulting in binocular rivalry (see figure 9.3).

These stimuli are designed to obtain clear evidence for testing the two competing theories of eye supresion and stimulus suppression by answering the following key question: Can we unscramble the pieces of figure 9.3 across the eyes, to recover the original coherent images P and Q? In fact, the two theories predict radically different experimental outcomes with the patchwork stimuli. Obviously, eye suppression would predict either alternation between the two monocular images (for small images) or percepts that are random mosaics of the two monocular patchwork images in figure 9.3 (for larger images). However, if the two original stimuli P and Q that make up the composite eye images (P = ape, and Q = text in figure 9.3) can drive the visual system to *integrate interocularly* the coherent patterns in them, then one can perceive the ape face and the text in figure 9.3.

It turns out that most observers, after some practice with long viewing of patchwork rivalry natural stimuli of the type shown in figure 9.3, can group the two incoherent images across the two eyes into a coherent percept.[5] This indicates that the two coherent stimuli compete for awareness, independently of the eye of origin. Furthermore, this outcome offers evidence that the visual system is equipped with the ability to take advantage of the coherence of the competing percepts to construct a meaningful stable, albeit temporary, percept. It seems that this ability involves some top-down processes, but it is too early to speculate about the neural sites of such mechanisms. During intervals in which the ape face comes together as a whole, or the text dominates throughout the picture in figure 9.3, the principle of eye competition is valid only locally; more importantly, there is a parallel global process that allows the visual system to integrate a coherent stimulus across the two eyes.

This phenomenon of interocular grouping also defies local competition rules of binocular rivalry related to stimulus strength (e.g., Levelt 1965; Fox 1991). In other words, when a single coherent percept is obtained with the stimulus of figure 9.3, the global stimulus structure seems to determine the suppression fate of each local patch. Thus, *all* local patches of the temporarily dominant coherent percept prevail *simultaneously* over their rival patches, despite the fact that some of the temporarily suppressed patches may be "stronger" according to psychophysically established rules of local binocular dominance (Levelt 1965).

Another property of binocular rivalry that seems to be violated by the phenomenon of interocular grouping is the tendency of large rivalrous regions (larger than about $1° \times 1°$) to break into piecemeal rivalry (see section 3). The patterns of figure 9.3 that are able to be grouped interocularly to produce a coherent pattern are typically larger than $4° \times 4°$. Thus the fact that the visual system is able to integrate the coherent percept across the two eyes over such large regions is all the more remarkable, given that even within-eye coherent images break out into piecemeal rivalry. In this regard, interocular grouping seems to be the opposite of piecemeal rivalry.

At first glance, these patchwork rivalry images appear to be quite artificial. After all, there doesn't seem to be any natural situation where the visual system is faced with stimuli of this type. What is there to learn about binocular vision with such contrived stimuli? We hope that the following analogy will clarify the utility of the patchwork rivalry paradigm. One can easily imagine someone asking similar questions about the utility of random-dot stereograms (RDS) (Julesz 1960, 1971: 75–6), when first presented with such stimuli: "What everyday stimuli look like RDS? What is there to learn about stereopsis with such contrived stimuli?" Well, there are instances of camouflage, albeit rare, in which natural stimuli resemble RDS, whereas one would be hard-pressed to come up with natural stimuli that come close to patchwork rivalry. Nevertheless, the analogy is a good one and can be driven further: (1) RDS isolate disparity from confounding depth cues. Patchwork rivalry stimuli isolate image coherence from eye-of-origin factors. (2) The visual system has the capability to utilize disparity by itself for reconstructing depth. Thus, the initial "mystery" that RDS create vivid depth was studied and explained (significantly, physiologists have identified disparity-tuned neurons (for a review, see Poggio 1995)). The visual system is also built to utilize the coherence of natural images to reconstruct "reality"; thus, the initial "mystery" that patch-work rivalry images result in interocular grouping could be studied and explained (additional neurophysiological research is needed to identify the grouping mechanisms).

The meaning of stimulus coherence is only intuitive at present. The next step is to characterize it by studying what constitutes coherence in an image. Figure 9.3 demonstrates that complex natural images that are defined by several stimulus dimensions can induce consistent, interocularly grouped percepts. Pattern coherence in these complex images might include contour continuity, color appearance, and texture similarity at the lower ends of the cortical processing hierarchy, but also expectation, familiarity, and semantic interpretation at the higher ends. The patchwork rivalry stimuli offer a convenient tool for an operational definition of coherence. An image is coherent if, when presented in patchwork rivalry, it can be reconstructed and perceived in alternation with competing percepts, of course; the easier it is to obtain the percept, the more coherent the image. Thus, one way to compare two images for coherence is to see which is easier to integrate across the two eyes in a patchwork rivalry setting.

6.2   Interocular grouping of low-level attributes

In this section we examine the role played by early bottom-up processes in pattern coherence and interocular grouping. In order to isolate one low-level attribute X (such as color, contrast, spatial frequency, etc.), we can simplify the patchwork stimuli to induce rivalry by virtue of the single attribute X under study; the other attributes are matched in the two eyes, as much as possible. Thus, we can compare performances with two extreme conditions to assess the ability of the visual system to integrate X across the two eyes: (1) conventional "coherent-X within-eye" stimuli, where one eye contains elements characterized by one value, X_1 of X, and the other eye contains elements characterized by another value, X_2, of X, such that X_1 and X_2 elicit rivalry; (2) patchwork ("incoherent-X within-eye") stimuli, where the left eye contains both types of elements, X_1 and X_2, and the right eye contains elements in exact positional correspondence with the left eye, but of the opposite value. First, we report on experimental data that we have obtained on the role of color in this process, which we have examined in some detail.

6.2.1   *Interocular grouping of color*

Figure 9.4 illustrates how the effect of a low-level attribute, in this case color, can be isolated from among other attributes such as orientation, texture, motion, etc. Figure 9.4a is a conventional rivalry-inducing stimulus, with a coherent color pattern within each eye's image ("coherent-color within-eye"); figure 9.4b is a patchwork rivalry stimulus, with mixed colors within each eye

(a)

(b)

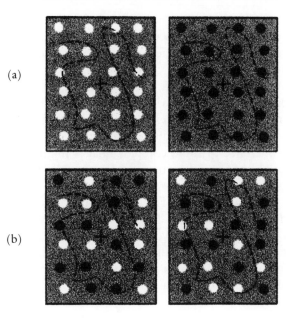

Figure 9.4. (a) Top panel: "Conventional" color-rivalrous pair of stimuli, in which each eye's image contains only one colour ("coherent-color within-eye"). Eye of origin and pattern coherence are confounded. (b) Bottom panel: "Patchwork-rivalrous" pair of stimuli, derived from the top panel by mixing colors in each eye ("incoherent-color within-eye"). Eye of origin and pattern coherence are decorrelated. Eye competition would predict mixed percepts only with the patchwork stimuli; however, all-red and all-green percepts are also obtained. Light (dark) dots stand for red (green) dots.

("incoherent-color within-eye"). The right-eye image contained elements in exact positional correspondence with the left eye, but of the opposite color, designed to produce binocular rivalry. Elements were equi-luminant to the background, to remove all cues other than color and eye of origin; these two are pitted against each other in the patchwork stimulus of figure 9.4b. The fundamental question is whether the visual system can "construct" a percept of uniform-color elements from the incoherent-color within-eye stimuli of figure 9.4b. Elements were low-pass filtered spatially with a circular Guassian envelope, so that they gradually blended with the background at their edges.

Three observers with normal stereopsis participated in the experiments. Four possible stable percepts were identified, as shown in figure 9.5: (1) "all-red" and (2) "all-green" percepts, in which all the elements appeared to be of only one color; (3) a "mixed-color" percept, in which some elements appeared as red, the rest as green; (4) an "all-yellow" percept, in which only the yellow background and fixation marks were perceived, and the elements disappeared.

In the main experiments, observers viewed the stimuli for at least 24 trials for each of the two stimulus configurations: coherent-color within-eye (figure

STIMULUS

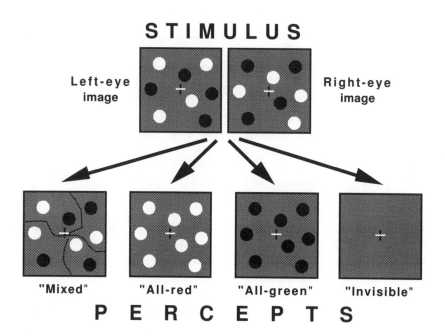

P E R C E P T S

Figure 9.5. Top row: patchwork-rivalrous stimuli in which each eye contains targets of both colors. Bottom row: possible percepts. In both rows, red and green targets are shown by light and dark regions, respectively. The most likely percept, as expected from current theories of binocular rivalry is the "mixed" percept; the thin lines are used to demarkate ocular dominance zones and, of course, they are not visible. The "all-red" and "all-green" percepts are less likely, according to current theories. The "invisible" percept was also obtained in our experiments. Light (dark) dots stand for red (green) dots.

9.4a) and incoherent-color within-eye (figure 9.4b). Observers were instructed to report changes in the percept as soon as they occurred, by pressing one of four buttons. These actions were recorded by the computer, together with the time of their occurrence, and were analyzed off-line to yield data on the time course of the perceptual changes. In every trial, we measured the length of each dominance interval for each of the four alternating percepts, as recorded by the observer's pressing of the buttons.

The most important question in this group of experiments was whether the visual system can integrate a given color (either red or green) across the two eyes in the patchwork condition. Of course, the single most telling measure of this ability is the percentage of time that observers spent in the "all-red" or "all-green" percepts – that is, the frequencies of occurrence. Thus, it was important to analyze the data to obtain these frequencies in both conditions. The cumulative duration of all intervals reporting a given percept was obtained for each of the four percepts across observers, and then divided by the total

Table 9.1 Frequencies of the four possible percepts for the two types of stimuli of figures 4a and 4b

| | STIMULUS | |
PERCEPT	Conventional (figure 4a)	Patchwork (figure 4b)
Uniform color (all-red)	0.251	0.185
Uniform color (all-green)	0.353	0.285
Uniform color (total)	0.604	0.470
Mixed color	0.366	0.496
All-yellow (disappearing elements)	0.030	0.034

duration of all trials to yield the desired frequency. These frequencies are shown in table 9.1 separately for the two conditions.

Some important points can be made about the pattern of results: (1) The most striking figure is the significant frequency (0.470) of the uniform-color percept in the patchwork condition. This by itself provides clear evidence that the visual system can use the chromatic coherence to "construct" all-red and all-green percepts through interocular grouping. (2) The fact that observers obtain the mixed-color percept with the conventional stimuli (frequency = 0.366) indicates that there are periods of piecemeal rivalry (see section 3); this is expected, given the large size ($6° \times 6°$) of the stimuli (Blake et al. 1992). This makes the achievement of the uniform-color percepts under the patchwork rivalry conditions even more remarkable. (3) The fact that the uniform-color frequency with the conventional stimuli is higher than with the patchwork stimuli (0.604 as compared to 0.470) can be taken to mean that eye of origin also plays a role in binocular rivalry, as previously theorized (Blake 1989). To expand on statement (3): If stimulus competition was the only process driving binocular rivalry alternations, the expected frequencies in the two conditions (conventional and patchwork) would be identical. This is because, if the eye of origin did not play a role, the two conditions would be indistinguishable to higher stages. The fact that the conventional condition produces higher frequencies than the patchwork condition indicates that eye competition also plays a role, in addition to stimulus competition.

We mention parenthetically that we validated further our methodology and results by analyzing the data to check if the dominance intervals obey the Gamma distribution (see eq. (1), section 3). We found that the data fit well with Gamma distributions. In addition, the parameters λ and r of the distributions were not significantly different in the conventional and patchwork conditions. This indicates that the temporal dynamics of a uniform percept are very similar in the two conditions. This would not be expected if only eye of origin played a role in generating uniform percepts. Overall, the results indicate that chromaticity is indeed a strong organizing force in itself, but may not be completely independent of eye of origin; this is in agreement with observations on interactions among parallel processing streams in the visual system (De Yoe and Van Essen 1988).

At this point, one may think that color is unique in its ability to group interocularly. After all, color plays an important role in textural grouping (Papathomas and Gorea 1990; Gorea and Papathomas 1991; Papathomas 1996), texture segregation (Callaghan 1989; Gorea and Papathomas 1993; Papathomas et al. 1997a) and spatial linking (Kingdom et al. 1992). Thus, it may not be surprising that color groups interocularly to yield a coherent single-color percept, even in patchwork rivalry conditions (figure 9.4b). How do other attributes compare with respect to this ability to group interocularly?

6.2.2 *Interocular grouping of other attributes*

In this subsection, we report on some preliminary experiments, in which we repeated the procedure of the previous subsection with the attributes of spatial frequency (F), orientation (O), and motion (M), in addition to color (C), but we used only the patchwork rivalry condition. These attributes were used to drive rivalry by themselves, as well as in combinations among them. Targets were eight Gabor patches that blended smoothly into the uniform yellow background. Figure 9.6a shows the patchwork rivalry stimuli in which spatial frequency alone (condition "F") induces rivalry, because all the other attributes are common in the two eyes. Figure 6b illustrates the "FO" condition in which the combination of spatial frequency and orientation induces rivalry. In each case there were two types of targets, A and B. In the F condition, A had $F = F_1$ (low spatial frequency), and B had $F = F_2$ (high spatial frequency). In the FO case, A had $F = F_1$ and $O = O_1$ ($-45°$), and B had $F = F_2$ and $O = O_2$ ($+45°$). The contrast of the low-frequency patches was adjusted to produce balanced dominance intervals between the two frequencies. The direction of motion was orthogonal to the grating's orientation and was perceived as such, because the Gaussian apertures were circular. When all four attributes were combined in case "FOMC," elements of type A had $F = F_1$, $O = O_1$, C = red, with the M vector in the southwest direction, whereas elements of type B had $F = F_2$, $O = O_2$, C = green, with the M vector in the northwest direction.

Stimuli were shown for abitrarily long intervals, and were terminated one minute after the observer started responding by pressing the first button. Observers were instructed to view the display and press no buttons until rivalry set in. *Uniform* (interocularly grouped) percepts were taken to be cases where at least seven targets appeared to be of type A (or type B). Any other percept was classified as *mixed*. For each condition, observers were instructed to press one button for the uniform condition where targets appeared to be of type A, another button when at least seven targets appeared to be of type B, and a third button for the "mixed-types" condition. The results are shown in table 9.2 below for observers TVP and IK (IK did not run any color conditions). We show the sum of the frequencies of the two uniform percepts. For example, in the case of orientation, we calculated the frequencies with which the

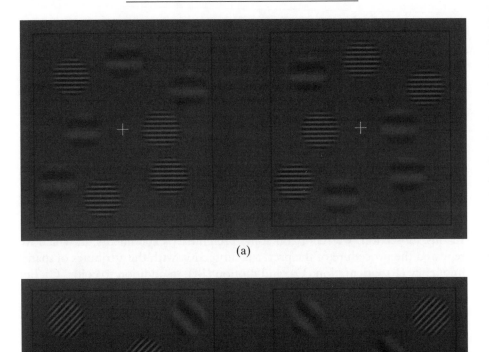

(a)

(b)

Figure 9.6. 'Patchwork-rivalrous' stimuli for attributes and their combinations. The structure of these rivalrous stimuli is the same as that of figure 9.4b; instead of using patches that are rivals with respect to colour, as is the case in figure 9.4.b, these stimuli use patches that are rivals with respect to other attributes: (a) The rivalrous attribute is spatial frequency (condition "F", top panel); (b) rivalry is elicited by the combination of spatial frequncy and orientation (condition "FO", bottom panel).

uniform +45° and uniform −45° percepts were obtained, and we added the two to get the combined frequency of occurrence. This is a measure of the ability of the corresponding attribute (or combination of attributes) to drive interocular grouping.

The results indicate that color is the most potent attribute in achieving interocular rivalry. Among the rest, spatial frequency is much more powerful than either motion or orientation, with orientation being the weakest of all. At first glance, the pattern of results is similar across the two observers.

Table 9.2 Sum of frequencies for the uniform percepts obtained with individual attributes and their combination

OBSERVER	C color	F spatial frequency	O orientation	M motion	FO	FM	OM	FOM	FOC	FOMC
				CONDITION						
TVP	0.444	0.353	0.072	0.126	0.364	0.334	0.154	0.293	0.424	0.248
IK	–	0.375	0.095	0.124	0.544	0.476	0.274	0.605	–	–

However, the results differ when one compares how combinations of attributes fare in eliciting interocular grouping. For TVP the strongest attribute in the combination seems to dominate the effect. In other words, the uniform-percept frequency for the combination of attributes X and Y is practically the same as that of the strongest attribute. An obvious exception is case FOMC, in which performance is much worse than C alone. For IK there seems to be some probability summation; that is, the frequency for the combination of X and Y is higher than that of either attribute. Additional experiments are needed to examine the interaction of attributes in this paradigm.

6.3   Interocular grouping of contours

In this section we ask whether contour continuity in itself can drive interocular grouping during binocular rivalry. We used an earlier finding by two of us (Kovács and Julesz 1993, 1995; Kovács 1996) that closed contours composed of aligned Gabor patches are easily detected when displayed amidst substantial visual noise. To examine whether such contours can be grouped interocularly, we "distributed" the contour elements between the two eyes, using the patchwork rivalry technique, such that neither eye alone could detect the closed contour. The key question is whether the visual system can "reconstruct" the contour by grouping the elements across the two eyes.

Contours consist of a closed circular chain of aligned Gabor patches; the orientation of each element is tangential to the contour that is outlined by the ensemble of these elements. A background of randomly oriented and positioned Gabor patches constitutes the noise. The method of constructing the stimuli is illustrated in figure 9.7a. Rivalry is induced by showing orthogonal patches on corresponding locations of the eyes. Interocular grouping is enabled by showing every other element of the contour in one eye; these tangentially oriented elements are highlighted in figure 9.7a by higher luminances. The rest of the elements in that same eye are replaced by a patch that is orthogonal (radially oriented) to that of the other eye; these are highlighted in the figure by circumscribing them by thin black ellipses. The other eye

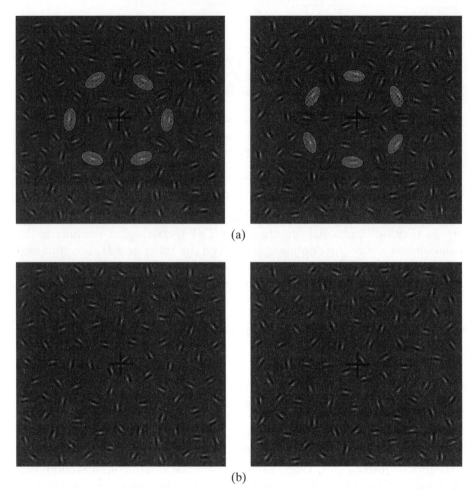

(a)

(b)

Figure 9.7. "Patchwork-rivalous" stimuli for closed contours. (a) top panel: illustration of the method of constructing the stimuli. Higher luminance is used to highlight the elements that constitute the collinear contour. The orientiation of each element is tangential to the circle that is outlined by the ensemble of these elements. The rivaling orthogonal elements are highlighted by circumscribing them by thin black elipses. Notice that the entire circular contour, outlined by tangential elements, exists only across the two eyes. (b) bottom panel: the actual stimuli, after removing the highlighting features. It is very difficult to see the circle in either eye's image.

contains the complementary orthogonal patches. As a result, neither eye alone contains the tangentially defined closed contour. The circular contour, in its entirety, exists only across the two eyes. The actual stimuli are shown in figure 9.7b.

The following stimuli conditions were used in the contour experiments: (1) a non-rivalrous contour, formed exclusively by tangentially oriented elements and both eyes presented with the identical image – this is the classical condition of Kovács and Julesz (1993); (2) the rivalrous "interocularly grouped" contour of figure 9.7b; (3) another non-rivalrous condition, in which both eyes viewed the left-eye image of condition 2 above – that is, the left image of figure 9.7b and the contour was formed by the spatial alternation of tangential and radial elements; (4) a last non-rivalrous control condition, formed by replacing every element of condition 1 above by a "Gabor plaid," formed by superimposing the original element and its orthogonal mate – thus the observers were asked whether a closed contour was present or not in each trial. Half of the trials, chosen at random, contained a contour.

The only test is provided by condition 2 above (figure 9.7b). The rest are control conditions. Condition 1 establishes an optimal standard. Indeed, observers achieved very good contour-detection performances in condition 1. Condition 3 was selected to examine whether the contour can be detected in either eye in test condition 2. The good performances which observers obtained in condition 2, coupled with near chance-level performances in condition 3, provide evidence that the visual system can integrate the contour across the two eyes, even though neither eye alone can detect the contour (Fehér et al. 1997). Finally, control condition 4 was used to investigate the possibility that the detection of the contour in the patchwork condition may be due to "abnormal fusion" (see section 3). Abnormal fusion combines the rivalrous stimuli and would produce the percept of condition 4 when the eyes are presented with condition 2. Since performance in condition 4 was significantly worse than that in condition 2 with the patchwork stimuli, the detection in the patchwork case seems to be based on interocular grouping, not on abnormal fusion.

Discussion and Conclusions

Similar effects of interocular grouping during binocular rivalry have been reported in the literature (Le Grand 1967; Whittle et al. 1968), including local chromatic effects (Treisman 1962; Kulikowski 1992; Kulikowski and Walsh 1995). In particular, the role of contours in influencing the apparent luminance of rivalrous shapes was studied extensively by Levelt (1965), who also observed binocular interactions of Gestalts (ibid., 59–60). The effect of motion on interocular percepts has also been reported (Duensing and Miller 1979; Grindley and Townsend 1965). Our stimuli extend their results by demonstrating that interocular grouping of color, as well as other low-level attributes, can be achieved with rather large visual fields. Beusmans's (1966) "Chimera" effect is similar in spirit to ours. We have observed that interocular grouping is greatly facilitated by displays lacking sharp edges. This is true for both isolated targets, which work best when their edges blend smoothly into the background (figure 9.4 and 9.6), and for tessellated interocular assemblies of natural images, where the best border is a smooth transition from one image to the other (figure 9.3). Perhaps sharp edges impede the integration process of a coherent image across the two eyes because they are perceived by the visual system as physical edges that somehow need to be interpreted and incorporated in a percept, in the never-ending search for a stable percept.

When it comes to the color case (subsection 6.2.1), the "all-yellow" percept obtained with figures 9.4a and 9.4b is probably attributable to Troxler's effect, which involves the fading of targets under extremely stable fixation conditions (Levelt 1965). It is particularly pronounced with blurred, low-contrast targets viewed outside the fovea. Blake and Ahlstrom (personal communication, 29 July 1997) have tried a condition where one eye receives the left panel of figure 9.4b and the other eye receives just the yellow background. The all-green and all-red percepts are still experienced, and one interpretation is that Troxler's effect is color-selective (ibid.). This can also be seen as an extreme case of monocular rivalry (see section 3). It is quite puzzling how, when the two eyes are stimulated with the patchwork rivalry images of figure 9.4b, the same color dominates simultaneously in both eyes. In any case, to discount an explanation of interocular grouping based exclusively on some variant of Troxler's effect, we followed the suggestion of Blake and Ahlstrom who created a version of the color patchwork rival display of figure 9.4b in which each spot is flashed off and on, to discourage fading due to Troxler's effect. Observers in both laboratories still experienced the all-red and all-green percepts, indicating that other processes, in addition to Troxler's effect, are at play in interocular grouping.

Where and how is stimulus coherence "extracted" and taken advantage of in order to form meaningful percepts? One possibility is that this happens at an intermediate level that integrates the outputs of early stages, such as color mechanisms, disparity detectors, edge extraction, motion analysis, texture processing, etc. It is possible that, in addition, top-down cognitive influences, driven by stimulus coherence in both space and time, play a major role in binocular rivalry. The starting point is that binocular rivalry can be considered as another case where multistable perceptual states arise from a fixed ambiguous stimulus. The visual system's task is to arrive at a stable percept, consistent with the two eyes' stimuli, that provides an accurate representation of the outside world. After all, the visual system evolved to allow organisms to interact with their environment. To accomplish this task, the brain might constantly construct and test perceptual hypotheses based on the sensory input. In this view, the percepts of figure 9.5 are possible hypotheses that the brain visits, based on the rivalrous stimulus. Note the parallelism to ambiguous stimuli by comparing figure 9.5 to figure 7.2 in chapter 7 above, by Papathomas.

The variants of the eye-suppression theory have a lot of evidence and merit, and they represent a reasonable strategy, which is not necessarily contrary to the hypothesis-construct-and-test scenario.[6] The brain has evolved to expect correlated stimulation from the two eyes, and this is an experiential constraint that one needs to take into account. Along the same lines, false fusion (see section 3) can also be considered as a natural strategy to fuse instinctively the two eyes' images, based on the overwhelming evidence of prior experience with correlated binocular images, before breaking into rivalry. This may account for the delayed onset of rivalry. Once the system recognizes that the binocular input is rivalrous, it tries to resolve the ambiguity. The brain may first attempt to construct and test percepts coming exclusively from one eye, before trying to group interocularly; this could be tested in the laboratory. Thus, ocular suppression theories do not contradict the hypothesis-construct-and-test theory. As a final note on this issue, suppression can be viewed from a positive perspective: it allows the visual system to examine alternative hypotheses. In interocular grouping, it allows the brain to construct meaningful coherent percepts by selectively suppressing regions from both eyes. Suppression is definitely an efficient solution in pathological cases of binocular vision to avoid diplopia.

In summary, our results show that color, spatial frequency, and collinearity play an important role in enabling the visual system to integrate pieces from the original images, scattered across the two eyes, to reconstruct the original coherent images. Orientation and direction of motion are much less potent for interocular grouping. Little information is presently available regarding temporal and spatial aspects of stimulus coherence in rivalry. Systematic characterization of the role of low-level attributes is required prior to testing natural stimuli that invoke explicitly high-level processes. Our findings concur with similar neurophysiological (Sengpiel and Blakemore 1994; Sengpiel et al. 1995; Logothetis and Schall 1989; Leopold and Logothetis 1996) and psychophysical (Logothetis et al. 1996) results, providing evidence that binocular rivalry goes beyond eye suppression and follows more complex rules of perceptual organization. Thus the eye-competition view must be revised to form an "eye-and-percept-competition" hypothesis that accounts, in addition to the ocular competition, for the role that high-order processes play in taking advantage of the coherence of the stimulus.

Acknowledgments

We acknowledge the contributions of Ming Yang in the color experiments of section 6.2.1. We thank Zsófia Bán and Katalin Orbán for useful discussions, and Nikos Logothetis for informative exchanges. Anne Treisman and Diana Deutsch provided us with valuable information and references on dichotic listening. Janos Szatmary developed the programs to generate the stimuli, provide the interface, and collect the data for the experiments of section 6.2.2. Jim McGowan helped us with statistical analyses of the data. Tiffany Conway administered some of the experiments; we appreciate her feedback, as well as Richard Gregory's expert advice, on an earlier draft of this essay. We thank Randy Blake for providing us with invaluable encouragement and advice. Finally, and equally importantly, we are grateful to the McDonnell Foundation for grant 95–60 to T. V. Papathomas and I. Kovács and to the US National Science Foundation and the Hungarian Science Foundation for the US–Hungarian Joint Fund JF–360 to I. Kovács.

Notes

1 The use of the word *dilemma* for rivalry becomes even more appropriate when one realizes that the word *lemma* derives from the verb *lambanein* which means "to receive." Thus, a free translation of "lemma" is "input" or "stimulus" in the case of sensory organs.

2 Liu, Tyler and Schor (1992) report a phenomenon that could, but should not, be confused with false fusion. They noticed that, when the eyes were presented with orthogonal rival gratings of low contrast, observers obtained fusion. They experienced a stable compound plaid over a range of low contrasts for periods of several seconds, and this long duration is the main difference between this phenomenon and false fusion.

3 As a reminder, the width of one's thumb at arm's length subtends about one degree of visual angle.

4 Blake (1989) mentions that his theory could be modified to introduce top-down influences, to account for any effect of cognitive processes on predominance.

5 If we use the abbreviated term "coherent-image within-eye" for the stimulus of figure 9.1, then appropriate terms for figure 9.3 would be "incoherent-image within-eye" or "coherent-image across-eyes" or, better, "incoherent-image within-eye/coherent-image across-eyes."

6 In fact, eye-suppression theories do not state that the input from an entire eye gets suppressed; this would be contrary to the observed phenomenon of piecemeal rivalry. Instead, they argue that small regions of an eye (so-called suppression zones) are blocked. As Blake and Ahlstrom (personal communication, 29 July 1997) put it, interocular grouping demonstrates that these zones are not independent; rather, the brain seeks coherence by bringing to dominance those left- and right-eye patches that cohere.

References

Anderson, B. L. (1994) The role of partial occlusion in stereopsis. *Nature* 367, 365–8.

Anderson, B. L. and Nakayama, K. (1994) Toward a general theory of stereopsis: binocular matching, occluding contours, and fusion. *Psychological Review* 101, 414–5.

Asher, H. (1953) Suppression theory of binocular vision. *British Journal of Ophthalmology* 37, 37–49.

Atkinson, J., Campbell, F. W., Fiorentini, A. and Maffei, L (1973) The dependence of monocular rivalry on spatial frequency. *Perception* 2, 127–33.

Beusmans, J. (1996) Evidence for striate cortex site for binocular rivalry. *Society for Neuroscience* 22, 887.

Blake, R. (1988) Dichoptic reading: the role of meaning in binocular rivalry. *Perception and Psychophysics* 44, 133–41.

—— (1989) A neural theory of binocular rivalry. *Psychological Review* 96, 145–67.

Blake, R. and Boothroyd, K. (1985) The precedence of binocular fusion over binocular rivalry. *Perception and Psychophysics* 37, 114–24.

Blake, R., O'Shea, R. P. and Mueller, T. J. (1992) Spatial zones of binocular rivalry in central and peripheral vision. *Visual Neuroscience* 8, 469–78.

Blakemore, C., Iversen, S. and Zangwill, O. (1972) Brain functions. *Annual Review of Psychology* 23, 413–50.

Burian, H. M. and von Noorden, G. (1974) *Binocular Vision and Ocular Motility*, St Louis, MO: C. V. Mosby.

Callaghan, T. C. (1989) Interference and dominance in texture segregation: hue, geometric form, and line orientation. *Perception and Psychophysics* 46, 299–311.

Campbell, F. W. and Howell, E. R. (1972) Monocular alternation: a method for the investigation of pattern vision. *Journal of Physiology* 225, 19–21P.

Crain, K. (1961) Binocular rivalry: its relation to intelligence, and a general theory of its nature and physiological correlates. *Journal of General Psychology* 64, 259–83.

Creed, R. S. (1935) Observations on binocular fusion and rivalry. *Journal of Physiology* 84, 381–92.

Crick, F. (1996) Visual perception: rivalry and consciousness. *Nature* 379, 485–86.

Crick, F. and Koch, C. (1992) The problem of consciousness. *Scientific American* 267, 152–9.

Dayan, P. (1996) A hierarchical model of visual rivalry. Internal report, Department of Brain and Cognitive Sciences, MIT, Cambridge, MA, 9 June 1996.

de Weert C. M. M. and Wade, N. J. (1988) Compound binocular rivalry. *Vision Research* 28, 1031–40.

Deutsch, D. (1975) Two-channel listening to musical scales. *Journal of the Acoustical Society of America* 57 (5), 1156–60.

—— (1982) Dichotic listening to melodic patterns, and its relationship to hemispheric specialization of function. *Music Perception* 3, 1–28.

DeYoe, E. A. and Van Essen, D. C. (1988) Concurrent processing streams in monkey visual cortex. *Trends in Neuroscience* 11, 219–26.

Duensing, S. and Miller, B. (1979) The Cheshire cat effect. *Perception* 8, 269–73.

Egeth, H. E. (1992) Dichotic listening: long-lived echoes of Broadbent's early studies. *Journal of Experimental Psychology: General* 121, 124–5.

Fahle, M. (1983) Non-fusable stimuli and the role of binocular inhibition in normal and pathologic vision, especially strabismus. *Documenta Ophthalmologica* 55, 323–40.

Fehér, A., Kovács, I. and Papathomas, T. V. (1997) Contour continuity can drive interocular grouping during binocular rivalry. *Investigative Ophthalmology and Visual Science* 38(4), S642.

Fox, R. (1991) Binocular rivalry, in D. Regan (ed.) *Binocular Vision: Vision and Visual Dysfunction*, vol. 9, Boca Raton, FL: CRC Press, 93–110.

Fox, R. and Herrmann, J. (1967) Stochastic properties of binocular rivalry alterations. *Perception and Psychophysics* 2, 432–6.

Goldstein, A. G. (1970) Binocular fusion and contour suppression. *Perception and Psychophysics* 7, 28–32.

Gorea, A. and Papathomas, T. V. (1991) Texture segregation by chromatic and achromatic visual pathways: an analogy with motion processing. *Journal of the Optical Society of America A.* 8(2), 386–93.

—— (1993) Double-opponency as a generalized concept in texture segregation illustrated with color, luminance and orientation defined stimuli. *Journal of the Optical Society of America A* 10(7), 1451–62.

Gregory, R. L. (1970) *The Intelligent Eye*, London: Weidenfeld & Nicolson.

Grindley, G. C. and Townsend, V. (1965) Binocular masking induced by a moving object. *Quarterly Journal of Experimental Psychology* 17(2), 97–109.

Grossberg, S. (1987) Cortical dynamics of three-dimensional form, color, and brightness perception: 2. Binocular theory. *Perception and Psychophysics* 41, 117–58.

Hering, E. (1920/1964) *Outlines of a Theory of the Light Sense*, trans. L. Hurwich and D. Jameson. Cambridge, MA: Harvard University Press.

Hochberg, J. (1964) Depth perception loss with local monocular suppression: a problem in the explanation of stereopsis. *Science* 145, 1334–5.

Holopigian, K. (1987) Psychophysical comparison of clinical suppression and binocular rivalry suppression. Ph.D. Thesis, Northwestern University.

Hubel, D. and Wiesel, T. N. (1962) Receptive fields, binocular interaction and functional architecture in the cat's visual cortex. *Journal of Physiology* 160, 106–54.

Julesz, B. (1960) Binocular depth perception of computer-generated patterns. *Bell System Technical Journal* 38, 1001–20.

—— (1971) *Foundations of Cyclopean Perception*, Chicago: University of Chicago Press.

Julesz, B. and Miller, J. E. (1975) Independent spatial-frequency-tuned channels in binocular fusion and rivalry. *Perception* 4, 125–43.

Kama, W. N. (1988) The effect of binocular rivalry on the performance of a simple target detection/recognition task. AAMRI–TR–88–156.

Kaufman, L. (1974) *Sight and Mind*, New York: Oxford University Press.

Kimchi, R., Gopher, D., Rubin Y. and Raij, D. (1993) Performance under dichoptic versus binocular viewing conditions: effects of attention and task requirements. *Human Factors* 35, 35–55.

Kingdom, F., Moulden, B. and Collyer, S. (1992) A comparison between colour and luminance contrast in a spatial linking task. *Vision Research* 32, 709–17.

Kovács, I. (1996) Gestalten of today: early processing of visual contours and surfaces. *Behavioural Brain Research* 82, 1–11.

Kovács, I. and Julesz, B. (1993) A closed curve is much more than an incomplete one: effect of closure on figure–ground segmentation. *Proceedings of the National Academy of Sciences USA* 90, 7495–7.

—— (1995) Long-range spatial interactions of early vision. In B. Julesz and I. Kovács (eds), *Maturational Windows and Adult Cortical Plasticity*, SFI Studies in the Sciences of Complexity. 23, Reading, MA: Addison-Wesley, 127–36.

Kovács, I., Papathomas, T. V., Yang, M. and Fehér, A. (1996) When the brain changes its mind: interocular grouping during binocular rivalry. *Proceedings of the National Academy of Sciences USA* 93, 15508–11.

Kulikowski, J. J. (1992) Binocular chromatic rivalry and single vision. *Ophthalmic and Physiological Optics* 12, 168–70.

Kulikowski, J. J. and Walsh, V. (1995) Demonstration of binocular fusion of color and texture. In T. V. Papathomas, C. Chubb, A. Gorea, and E. Kowler (eds) *Early Vision and Beyond*, Cambridge, MA: MIT Press, 27–32.

Lack, L. C. (1978) *Selective Attention and the Control of Binocular Rivalry* (The Hague: Mouton.)

Le Grand, Y. (1967) *Form and Shape Vision*, Bloomington, IN: Indiana University Press.

Lehky, S. R. (1988) An astable multivibrator model of binocular rivalry. *Perception* 17, 215–88.

Lehky, S. R. and Blake, R. (1991) Organization of binocular pathways: modeling and data related to rivalry. *Neural Computation* 3, 44–53.

Lehky, S. R. and Maunsell, J. H. R. (1996) No binocular rivalry in the LGN of alert macaque monkeys. *Vision Research* 36, 1225–34.

Leopold, D. A. and Logothetis, N. K. (1996) Activity changes in early visual cortex reflects monkeys' percepts during binocular rivalry. *Nature* 379, 549–53.

Levelt, W. J. M. (1965) *On Binocular Rivalry*, Assen: Royal Van Gorcum.

Liu, L. and Schor, C. M. (1994) The spatial properties of binocular suppression zone. *Vision Research* 34, 937–47.

Liu, L., Tyler, C. W. and Schor, C. M. (1992) Failure of rivalry at low contrast: evidence of a suprathreshold binocular summation process. *Vision Research* 32, 1471–9.

Logothetis, N. K., Leopold, D. A. and Sheinberg, D. L. (1996) What is rivalling during binocular rivalry? *Nature* 380, 621–4.

Logothetis, N. K. and Schall, J. D. (1989) Neuronal correlates of subjective visual perception. *Science* 245, 761–3.

—— (1990) Binocular motion rivalry in macaque monkeys: eye dominance and tracking eye movements. *Vision Research* 30(10), 1409–19.

Matsuoka, K. (1984) The dynamic model of binocular rivalry. *Biological Cybernetics* 49, 201–8.

Myerson, J., Miezin, F. and Allman, J. (1981) Binocular rivalry in macaque monkeys and humans: a comparative study in perception. *Behaviour Analysis Letters* 1, 149–59.

Nakayama, K. and Shimojo, S. (1990) Da Vinci stereopsis: depth and subjective occluding contours from unpaired image points. *Vision Research* 30, 1811–25.

Neisser, U. and Becklen, R. (1975) Selective looking: attending to visually specified events. *Cognitive Psychology* 7, 480–94.

O'Shea, R. P. (1999) Bibliography on binocular rivalry. *World-Wide Web* http://psy.otago.ac.nz/r_oshea/br_bibliography.html.

O'Shea, R. P. and Crassini, B. (1984) Binocular rivalry occurs without simultaneous presentation of rival stimuli. *Perception and Psychophysics* 36, 266–76.

O'Shea, R. P., Sims, A. J. H. and Govan, D. G. (1997) The effect of spatial frequency and field size on the spread of exclusive visibility in binocular rivalry. *Vision Research* 37(2), 175–83.

Papathomas, T. V. (1996) The contribution of color and contrast in vision: psychophysics, modelling, and image processing. *Proceedings of IEEE/IS&T Image and Multidimensional Signal Processing Workshop* held in Belize, March 1996, 5–10.

Papathomas, T. V. and Gorea, A. (1990) The role of visual attributes in texture perception. In B. E. Rogowitz and J. P. Allebach (eds). *Human Vision and Electronic Imaging: Models, Methods, and Applications*, SPIE 1249, 395–403.

Papathomas, T. V., Kashi, R. S. and Gorea, A. (1997a) A human vision based computational model for chromatic texture segregation. *IEEE Transactions On Systems, Man and Cybernetics – Part B: Cybernetics* 27(3), 428–40.

Papathomas, T. V., Szatmary, J., Fehér, A. and Kovács, I. (1997b) Interaction of attributes in interocular grouping during binocular rivalry. *Investigative Ophthalmology and Visual Science* 38(4), S642.

Pirsig, R. M. (1974) *Zen and the Art of Motorcycle Maintenance*, New York: Morrow.

Poggio, G. F. (1995) Stereoscopic processing of monkey visual cortex: a review. In T. V. Papathomas, C. Chubb, A. Gorea, and E. Kowler (eds). *Early Vision and Beyond*, Cambridge, MA: MIT Press, 43–53.

Ramachandran, V. S. (1985) The neurobiology of perception – guest editorial. *Perception* 14, 97–103.

Reitz, W. E. and Jackson, D. N. (1964) Affect and stereoscopic resolution. *Journal of Abnormal and Social Psychology* 69, 212–15.

Reventlow, I. (1961) Note on movement and binocular fusion. *Scandinavian Journal of Psychology* 2, 139–41.

Sabrin, H. and Kertesz, A. (1983) The effect of imposed fixational eye movements on binocular rivalry. *Perception and Psychophysics* 34, 155–7.

Schor, C. M., Wood, I. C. and Ogawa, J. (1984a) Binocular sensory fusion is limited by spatial resolution. *Vision Research* 24, 661–5.

—— (1984b) Spatial tuning of static and dynamic local stereopsis. *Vision Research* 24, 573–8.

Sengpiel, F. (1997) Binocular rivalry: ambiguities resolved. *Current Biology* 7, R447–50.

Sengpiel, F. and Blakemore, C. (1994) Interocular control of neuronal responsiveness in cat visual cortex. *Nature* 368, 847–50.

Sengepiel, F., Blakemore, C. and Harrad, R. (1995) Interocular suppression in the primary visual cortex: a possible neural basis of binocular rivalry. *Vision Research* 35, 179–95.

Sheinberg, D. L. and Logothetis, N. K. (1997) The role of cortical temporal areas in perceptual organization. *Proceedings of the National Academy of Sciences USA* 94, 3408–13.

Singer, W. (1977) Control of thalamic transmission by corticofugal and ascending reticular pathways in the visual system. *Physiological Review* 57, 386–420.

Stirling, W. (1901) An experiment on binocular colour vision with half-penny postage-stamps. *Journal of Physiology, London* 27, 1901–2.

Sugie, N. (1982) Neural models of brightness perception and retinal rivalry in binocular vision. *Biological Cybernetics* 43, 12–21.

Treisman, A. (1962) Binocular rivalry and stereoscopic depth perception. *Quarterly Journal of Experimental Psychology* 14, 23–37.

—— (1964) Monitoring and storage of irrelevant messages in selective attention. *Journal of Verbal Learning and Verbal Behaviour* 3, 449–59.

Verhoeff, F. H. (1935) A new theory of binocular vision. *Archives of Ophthalmology* 13, 152–75.

Wade, N. J. (1973) Contour synchrony in binocular rivalry. *Perception and Psychophysics* 13, 423–5.

—— (1975) Binocular rivalry between single lines viewed as real images and after-images. *Perception and Psychophysics* 17, 571–7.

Walker, P. (1975) Stochastic properties of binocular rivalry alternations. *Perception and Psychophysics* 18, 467–73.

—— (1978) Binocular rivalry: central or peripheral selective processes? *Psychology Bulletin* 85, 376–89.

Whittle, P., Bloor, D. C. and Pocock, S. (1968) Some experiments on figural aftereffects in binocular rivalry. *Perception and Psychophysics* 4, 183–8.

Wolfe, J. M. (1983) Influence of spatial frequency, luminance, and duration on binocular rivalry, and abnormal fusion of briefly presented dichoptic stimuli. *Perception* 12, 447–56.

—— (1986) Stereopsis and binocular rivalry. *Psychological Review* 93, 269–82.

10

Linguistic and Cognitive Explanation
in Optimality Theory

Bruce Tesar, Jane Grimshaw, and Alan Prince

Generative linguistics aims to provide an analysis of the grammar-forming capacity that individuals bring to the task of learning their native language (Chomsky 1965, 1981, 1991, 1995). Pursuing this goal amounts to developing a linguistic theory that achieves maximum universality and generality in its premises, while at the same time offering explicit, limited means for representing possible interlinguistic variation. The term "Universal Grammar" is used to refer to the system of principles defining what the grammar of a human language can be.

Optimal Theory (Prince and Smolensky 1993) asserts that Universal Grammar provides a set of general, universal constraints which evaluate possible structural descriptions of linguistic objects. These constraints are assumed to be strongly universal, in the sense that they are present in every grammar; they must be simple and general if they are to have any hope of universality. The structural description that is *grammatical* for a linguistic object in a given language is the one, among all possible structures assignable to that object, which is *optimal*, in the sense that it best satisfies the universal constraints, given the defining characteristics of that object. The theory builds from a notion of "best satisfaction" – optimality rather than perfection – because constraints are often in conflict over the well-formedness of a given candidate analysis, so that satisfying one constraint entails violating others to varying degrees. Indeed, an optimal structural description will typically violate some (or many) of the constraints, because no possible description satisfies all of them.

Differences between languages then emerge as the different ways allowed by the theory for resolving the conflicts that are inherent in the universal constraint set. The theory is therefore one of constraint *interaction*: the effects of any constraint are determined both by its intrinsic demands and by its relation to the other constraints; fixing the relations between the universal constraints defines the grammar of a particular language. Interactionism is the heart and soul of the theory: it places a heavy empirical burden on the positing of constraints, since all interactions must yield possible grammars; it leads to a pattern of explanation in which many universally observed properties of language follow not from hypothesized special principles designed to encode them directly, but from nothing more than the interaction of more general constraints which are not specifically concerned with those particular properties; it opens the way to tremendous simplification of the constraints themselves, since they need not contain codicils and complications that emerge from interaction; and, at the methodological level, it enforces the research ethic that posited constraints *must not* contain such codicils and complications, thereby guiding the search for a general understanding of the nature of the constraints active in human language.

This essay presents an overview of selected work making use of Optimality Theory, with the goal of illuminating these general ideas. Section 1 presents and illustrates the central principles of Optimality Theory. Section 2 gives an example of syntax within the theory. Section 3 examines possible implications of Optimality Theory for studies of language processing, discussing work on the computability of Optimality-theoretic grammars, as well as some conceptual similarities between Optimality Theory and work in connectionism and dynamical systems. Section 4 discusses work on language learnability and acquisition within Optimality Theory.

A useful resource is the Rutgers Optimality Archive (ROA). This is an electronic repository of papers on Optimality Theory and is accessible on the Internet. The World-Wide Web URL is http://ruccs.rutgers.edu/roa.html.

1   The Principles of the Theory

A *grammar* is a formal specification of the structure of a language; cognitively construed, it characterizes a speaker's internalized unconscious grasp of the language. In generative grammar, the structure of a linguistic object such as a sentence is given as a set of representations that explicate meaning, sound, and syntactic form. The grammar defines how such representations can go together to form a legitimate linguistic entity. Grammars are typically organized so as to map from one representation to another, from an "input" to an "output": from the lexical representation of a word (input) to its pronunciation (output), from an argument structure (input) to a syntactic structure embodying it (output), and so on. Different linguistic theories within generative grammar put forth different assumptions about what the relevant representations are, and how the mapping between them is accomplished.

A grammar, then, specifies a *function* which assigns to each type of linguistic input an output structural description (or, possibly, a set of such). The grammar itself does not provide an *algorithm* for effectively computing this function. The distinction between function and algorithm is worth emphasizing, because of the ambiguous role of computational procedures in some linguistic theories. For example, early generative phonology defines grammars in terms of serial derivation – a sequence of procedural steps, each a "phonological rule"; similarly, many theories of syntax have followed this model. Is the derivation only a means for defining the grammatical function, or is it additionally a theory of how language processing is actually conducted in the mind of a language user? Different authors have taken different positions, as have the same authors at different times. Optimality Theory forces the issue by giving an explicitly non-procedural definition of the grammar. How the functions defined by Optimality-theoretic grammars might be explicitly computed is discussed in section 4.

1.1   Constraints and their violation

To see how grammars are organized to represent linguistic generalizations, let us consider the case of syllabification. In every language, when words are pronounced, they divide into syllables, which group consonants and vowels together. Syllable structure typically has important further consequences for pronunciation, determining numerous features of articulation, including tone and stress placement. In this domain of linguistic patterning, there are two basic facts to explain. First, syllabification is predictable, given the grammar of the language and knowledge of the sounds of which a word is composed: in English, for example, "Memphis" is pronounced *mem.phis*, not *me.mphis* or *memph.is*. (Periods indicate syllable divisions; the notation *X indicates that the form X is ill-formed.) Second, languages place various limits on what syllables are admissable. English is fairly free in this regard, though there are languages that are freer (for example, *Mtsensk* is a legitimate single-syllable word in Russian, though not in English, even though all the individual sounds are shared by the two languages; and "Mom" is a monosyllable in English, but not in Japanese, though Japanese has all the requisite sounds). Thus, the syllabic grammar of a given language must not only predict how the various sounds of a word are grouped into syllables, it must also tell us that some groupings are simply not allowed.

Since syllable structure is predictable in each language, we can assume that the input represents only consonants and vowels ('segments') not syllables. The mapping from input to output supplies the syllables, predicting their composition. Suppose the grammar faces an input like /apot/. There are many possible outputs that it could give rise to: some which simply parse the input differently, others that more aggressively insert or delete material, perhaps to facilitate the creation of syllables. Table 10.1 lists a few alternatives. It is the job of a language's grammar to determine which candidate output

Table 10.1 A few candidate analyses of the input /apot/

Analyses of /apot/		Remarks
a	.a.pot.	*bisyllabic*: first syllable open
b	.ap.ot.	*bisyllabic*: first syllable closed
c	.a.po.	*bisyllabic*: with deletion of *t*
d	.pot.	*monosyllabic*: via deletion of *a*
e	.po.	*monosyllabic*: via deletion of both *a* and *t*
f	.ʔa.pot.	*bisyllabic*: with insertion of *ʔ*
g	.a.po.ti	*trisyllabic*: with the insertion of *i*
h	.ʔa.po.ti.	*trisyllabic*: with the insertion of both *ʔ* and *i*
…	…	… *and many, many others* …

Table 10.2 A few syntactic candidates

Candidate analyses		Remarks
a	John will eat what	Question operator in canonical object position
a	John will eat what	Question operator in canonical object position
b	*will* John eat what	Auxiliary placed in fronted position
c	*what* John will eat	Q-operated fronted
d	*what will* John eat	Aux and Q-operator fronted, Q first
e	*what do* John will eat	Q-operator fronted, supporting aux inserted
…	…	… *many, many others* …

analysis is the actual one, for a given language. Analysis (a) would be chosen in a language like English, analysis (f) in a language like German or Arabic; Japanese would choose an analysis something like (h), though with a different inserted vowel. Although option (b) simply exploits locally permissible structures, it is not found – a fact that will be explained below.

The same considerations arise in the theory of syntactic structure. Consider the analysis of a question like "What will John eat?" The input must specify the presence of the words, with their semantic and syntactic properties: the verb *eat* is a two-place predicate; *John* is a noun, *will* an auxiliary, *what* a pronoun and an operator. (It is, of course, the categories that are important, not the particular words, for languages share categories, rather than words.) For concreteness and simplicity, we will present the structures as word-strings here; below, we expand on the relevant structural analyses. Even limiting ourselves to those candidate outputs that observe the basic patterns of English phrase structure, quite a number of alternatives present themselves, as shown in Table 10.2. All of these reflect real structural possibilities, whose components at least are directly observed in many natural languages. English chooses (d); many languages choose (c), and indeed English uses this when the question is syntactically subordinated ('I know *what John will eat*'). Option (a) is also common; structural options (b) and (e), though composed of independently observable substructures, are universally impossible: a fact to be explained.

We assume that every language has the ability to choose from the entire collection of possible candidate analyses. Universal Grammar – the set of principles defining the way grammars can be constructed – must be organized to support this choice by making all the alternatives available to particular grammars. We therefore have our first principle of grammatical organization:

> Principle 1: *Universal Grammar provides a function, Gen, which maps each input to its set of candidate structural descriptions.*

A linguistic input α thus universally gives rise to the same set of candidate outputs, Gen (α), in every language. The domain of the function Gen defines the set of possible inputs; its range is the set of possible outputs. In table 10.1 we have listed a fragment of Gen (*apot*); in table 10.2, some of the members of Gen ($\langle V(x, y); x = DP, y = wh, aux = will \rangle$), to anticipate the notation of section 3. Specification of the function Gen involves detailing the set of formal primitives of linguistic structure and their basic, ineluctable modes of combination: linguistic representations are constructed by virtue of these, as both inputs and outputs. Principle 1 asserts that the description assigned by the grammar of any particular language must be drawn from the set of candidates provided by Gen.

How, then, is the choice among the candidates to be accomplished? Optimality Theory claims that this is done by a set of constraints on structural configurations and on the fidelity of input to output: these constraints are also posited as universal.

> Principle 2: *Universal Grammar provides Con, a set of universal constraints assessing the well-formedness of structural descriptions.*

The constraints of Con assess the well-formedness of all candidate descriptions for a given input. Such evaluation works *in parallel*: that is, the constraints evaluate each candidate independently, so that the assessment of one candidate does not depend upon the assessment of another candidate.

Table 10.3 shows a set of constraints relevant to the assignment of syllable structure. There is a fundamental formal division among constraints: ONSET and NOCODA examine only the character of the output: they are *structural constraints*; the others compare input with output and in each case require that the output preserve some feature of the input: these are *faithfulness constraints*.

Given an input and a candidate description of it, we can determine the extent to which each of the constraints is violated. Table 10.4 records this information for the candidates from Gen (*apot*) cited above. Each violation is

Table 10.3 Some basic universal constraints relevant to syllable theory

Name	Content
ONSET	A syllable must begin with a consonant: must have an *onset*.
NoCODA	A syllable must not end on a consonant: must lack a *coda*.
NoDEL	Input segments must appear in the output: must not be *deleted*.
NoInsV	The output must not contain an *inserted* vowel: one not present in the input.
NoInsC	The output must not contain an *inserted* consonant: one not present in the input.

Table 10.4 Evaluation of the candidate set

	/apot/	ONSET	NoCODA	NoDEL	NoInsV	NoInsC
a	.a.pot.	*	*			
b	.ap.ot.	**	*			
c	.a.po.	*		*		
d	.pot.		*	*		
e	.po.			**		
f	.ʔa.pot.	*				*
g	.a.po.ti	*			*	
h	.ʔa.po.ti.				*	*

notated with an asterisk; lack of violation is not indicated. Multiple violations are recorded as multiple asterisks.

Observe that the fully faithful parse (a) *.a.pot.* does quite poorly on the structural constraints ONSET and NoCODA, violating both of them. Complete success on the structural constraints can be achieved, as in (e) *.po.* and in (h) *.ʔa.po.ti.*, but the cost is failure, even multiple failure, on one or both of the faithfulness constraints. A range of intermediate successes and failures can be found in the rest of the table.

We can already see why candidate (b) *.ap.ot.* is essentially doomed. Although it is locally composed of licit syllables, it fares the same as or worse than candidate (a) on *every* constraint. It is hard to imagine an evaluation system that would rate it as the winner over (a) in these circumstances.

Relations between the other competitors are not so straightforward: there is outright conflict on the question of which member of various pairs of candidates should be judged more successful. Is (a) *.a.pot.* better than (h) *.ʔa.po.ti.*? Candidate (a) is structurally inferior to (h), but (h) is less faithful to the input. Other similar forms of conflict are rife throughout the table. Is it better to lack an onset (*ONSET) or to have an inserted consonant (*NoInsC)? Is it better to insert a vowel (*NoInsV) or to delete a consonant (*NoDEL)? To insert a vowel or to have a coda? The answers to such questions will determine what the grammar generates.

Table 10.5 Evaluation of syntactic candidates

$\langle V = (x, y); x = John, y = what, aux = will \rangle$	OPSPEC	OBHD	NOINS/LEX	NOMVT
a John will eat what	*			
b *will* John eat what	*			*
c *what* John will eat		*		*
d *what will* John eat				**
e *what do* John will eat			*	*

Exactly the same situation arises in syntax. Table 10.5 shows how the candidates of table 10.2 fare with respect to a set of syntactic constraints. The meaning of the syntactic constraints will be discussed in section 3 below; what is significant here is the clear formal parallel with constraint evaluation in phonology. We can immediately see why any candidate formed like (b) will never surface in any language: it fares the same as or worse than (a) on every constraint. Relations elsewhere are more complicated. Is it better to have an operator out of position, as in (a), or is it better to have a defective ('headless') syntactic constituent, as in (c)? Is it better to insert the dummy element *do*, violating NOINS as in (e), or to displace the auxiliary *will* from its canonical position, violating NOMVT as in (d)? A grammar must be able to decide these issues.

1.2 Optimality and harmonic ordering

The constraints of Con provide the basis for selecting the correct output from among the candidate set of alternative analyses. Yet, if the constraints are to be simple and universal, they must be violable, and there is sure to be conflict among them, as we have seen. We must therefore seek to define what it means to "best satisfy" the constraint set, presupposing that there will be much constraint violation in grammatical forms.

To fulfill the goal of articulating a Universal Grammar that allows only the licit grammars of human languages, we seek a scheme of conflict resolution that is as restrictive as possible, allowing just the variation between languages that is empirically observed. Merely summing up violations across the entire constraint set cannot work: as the above examples show, it cannot select a single winning candidate, given the kind of constraints proposed there; worse, it cannot allow the expression of interlinguistic variation while maintaining the universality of the constraint set Con: there could be only one grammar. At the opposite pole of descriptive richness, allowing free numerical weighting opens up a Pandora's box of logical possibilities, with little hope for significant restrictions on the grammars that are generable.

Optimality Theory therefore posits a single, symbolically based mechanism of conflict resolution: prioritization. In case of conflict between two con-

Table 10.6   ONSET >> NOINSC

	/aopu/	ONSET	NOINSC
a	.a.o.pu.	**	
b	.ʔa.o.pu.	*	*
c	.a.ʔo.pu.	*	*
☞ d	.ʔa.ʔo.pu.		**

Table 10.7   NODEL >> NOINSC

	/aopu/	ONSET	NODEL	NOINSC
☞ d	.ʔa.ʔo.pu.			**
e	.pu.		**	

straints, one is specified as taking absolute priority over the other: the one constraint "strictly dominates" the other. In case of conflict, the interests of the dominant constraint must be served, at the cost of as much violation of the subordinate constraint as is necessary.

> Principle 3: *A grammar is a total ranking of the constraints of Con into a strict domination hierarchy.*

A form which best satisfies the strict domination hierarchy is the *output* for a given *input*; it is said to be *optimal*. What does this mean for the choice among competing candidates?

Suppose ONSET strictly dominates NOINSC, which we notate as ONSET >> NOINSC. Then the requirement that syllables begin with consonants takes unqualified precedence over the prohibition against inserted consonants. Therefore, any number of consonants can be inserted to ensure that the output's syllables all have onsets.

Consider an input /aopu/. Let us assume that other dominant constraints limit the insertable consonant to the glottal stop [ʔ] and limit syllables to containing just one vowel, forcing a tri-syllabic parse. Then we have the competition shown in table 10.6 between the faithful parse and various alternatives with insertion. Notation: a table of this sort, with the constraints arrayed in domination order, is called a *tableau*: the optimal form is marked with the sign ☞.

Candidate (d) does best on the dominant constraint ONSET; anything that does worse is eliminated. In order to achieve success on ONSET, the winner tolerates more violations of NOINSC than any other candidate in this set.

To complete the selection of (d), a wider candidate set must be examined. In particular, success on ONSET can also be achieved by deletion, leading to conflict among faithfulness constraints, as shown in table 10.7. These argu-

Table 10.8 A typical competition

/apot/	ONSET	NOCODA	NODEL	NOINSC
☞ f .ʔa.pot.		*		*
d .pot.		*	*!	

ments show that if the C-insertion solution to the onset problem is to be taken in a grammar, it must conform to two distinct ranking conditions:

ONSET >> NOINSC
NODEL >> NOINSC

Any total ranking of the constraint set that meets these conditions will suffice.

Permuting the crucial ranking relations leads directly to the selection of a different winner. If we invert the ranking of the two faithfulness constraints, so that ONSET >> NODEL, the deletion-derived candidate (e) becomes optimal. If we subordinate ONSET to *both* faithfulness constraints, then neither deletion nor insertion is allowed to modify the input, and we must live with *.a.o.pu.* as the optimal output, despite its two onsetless syllables.

The calculation of optimality rests, at bottom, on competitions between pairs of candidates. Imagine two competitors α and β. Any given constraint C may either distinguish them in terms of degree of violation of C or evaluate them as equivalent, if they both violate C exactly the same number of times. Faced with a constraint hierarchy H, we say that form α is *better* than, or "more harmonic than" form β, if α fares better than β *on the highest-ranked constraint that distinguishes them*. Table 10.8 illustrates a typical competition. Assume that the order of constraints across the top of the table reflects a strict domination ranking. Candidate (f) is more harmonic than candidate (d), because it fares better on NODEL, the first constraint distinguishing them: the crucial violation is marked with an exclamation point. Although (f) violates NOCODA, this is of no consequence to the comparison, because (d) is just as bad on that constraint. Observe that (f) involves insertion and is therefore *worse* than (d) on NOINSC; but this does not affect the calculation either, since the competition is concluded at the level of NODEL in the ranking, above the ranking level where NOINSC has its effect.

An *optimal form* ω stands at the top of the competitive heap: it never loses any of these pairwise comparisons. If there is only one optimal form, then it is better than all other candidates: it wins against every other candidate.

This discussion has proceeded from the following observation:

> A grammar's constraint hierarchy induces a harmonic ordering of all the candidate descriptions for an input.

Table 10.9   Constraint table for /apot/ with ranking (1)

	/apot/	ONSET	NOINSV	NODEL	NOINSC	NOCODA
a	.a.pot.	*				*
b	.ap.ot.	**				*
c	.a.po.	*		*		
d	.pot.			*		*
e	.po.			**		
☞ f	.ʔa.pot.				*	*
g	.a.po.ti	*	*			
h	.ʔa.po.ti.		*		*	

The harmonic ordering, essentially a lexicographic order on the candidate set, determines the relative "harmony" of every pair of candidates. An optimal form is a maximal element in this order.

1.3   Constraint ranking and linguistic typology

> Principle 4: *Cross-linguistic variation is explained by variation in the ranking of the universal constraints.*

Analysis of the optimal descriptions arising from all possible rankings of the constraints provided by Universal Grammar gives the typology of possible human languages. This can be illustrated by considering a different constraint ranking for the constraints of Basic CV Syllable Theory. Table 10.9 gives the tableau for input /apot/ using the ranking in (1).

(i) ONSET >> NOINSV >> NO DEL >> NOINSC >> NOCODA

In this language, codas are possible: they are permitted when necessary to avoid violation of the faithfulness constraints, NOINSV, NODEL, NOINSC, as with input /apot/. Note that codas are not required, however. Consider the input /po/: the candidate description .po. does not have a coda but is the optimal description. In fact, candidate .po. violates none of the constraints, and therefore is the optimal candidate for /po/ under any ranking. Therefore, this subsystem predicts this input-output relation in all languages, modulo other constraints.

Analysis of all possible rankings of the Basic CV Syllable Theory constraints reveals that the resulting typology of basic CV syllable structures instantiates and indeed goes beyond Jakobson's fundamental cross-linguistic generalizations on patterns of syllabification (Jakobson 1962; Clements and Keyser 1983; see Prince and Smolensky 1993: ch. 6 for full discussion). In this typology, a language may require onsets or may merely allow them; independently, a language may forbid codas or allow them. No grammar produced by ranking these constraints can *ban* onsets or *require* codas; this is guaranteed by the optimality of the mapping /*po*/→.*po*. under all rankings. This result provides us with an example of how significant generalizations about linguistic structure, like Jakobson's, can emerge from the range of permissible interactions in a constraint set. The theory allows every ranking – a natural null hypothesis – yet it is far from true that every *outcome* is thereby allowed; and the patterns of permitted outcomes predict the structure of linguistic variation.

To support a claim that a particular grammar does not permit some particular type of structure, it must be demonstrated that for any possible input, the optimal description assigned by the grammar does not include the structure in question. This is due to a principle known as richness of the base.

> Principle 5: *Richness of the base: the set of possible inputs is the same for all languages.*

The inventory of a grammar is defined as the types of structures that appear in the set of descriptions arising from all possible inputs. The lexicon of a language is a sample from the inventory of possible inputs.

> Principle 6: *The universal constraints include faithfulness constraints, which are violated by discrepancies between the surface form of a description and the input.*

Faithfulness is an essential part of Optimality Theory. For example, NODEL is violated by "underparsing" when elements from the input fail to appear in the output; and the NOINSC constraints are violated by "overparsing", when material that is not precedented in the input makes its appearance in the output. The presence of faithfulness constraints means that disparities between the input and the output form (both being essential components in a structural description) will only be tolerated in order to satisfy other, higher-ranked constraints. This is why the same grammar assigns different grammatical descriptions to different inputs.

1.4   Linguistic markedness

The concept of linguistic markedness, or inherent complexity of structures, has played a significant role in linguistic thought in the twentieth century, though more often as an unformalized perspective or side issue within generative grammar. Optimality Theory rests directly on a theory of linguistic markedness: "marked", or linguistically complex, structures are literally marked as such by the constraints they violate. This can be illustrated by the effects of low-ranked constraints. Consider the language described above. The constraints NoInsC and NoCoda are the lowest-ranked constraints. This does not mean, however, that they play no role in the language. For the input /apot/, the optimal candidate, .ʔa.pot., violates only NoInsC and NoCoda and has one coda. Another candidate for the same input, .ʔap.ʔot., has two codas. It also only incurs violation of NoInsC and NoCoda, but to a greater extent (an additional violation of each), rendering it suboptimal. Codas are still avoided when possible. The presence of NoCoda in Con entails the presence of NoCoda in the rankings for all languages. Even in languages that permit codas, they are permitted *only when necessary*. Optimality Theory provides a precise definition of "when necessary": structures marked by a constraint are permitted only when all candidates avoiding that structure contain other structures marked by higher-ranked constraints.

This also illustrates a key conceptual difference between constraint rankings in Optimality Theory and parameter settings in the Principles and Parameters framework (Chomsky 1981). One could imagine a simple parameter set giving rise to the basic inventories of the Jakobson typology. One parameter, OnsetP, would have two settings: an unmarked setting requiring syllables to have onsets and a marked setting allowing syllables with and without onsets. Another parameter, CodaP, would have an unmarked setting forbidding codas and a marked setting allowing syllables with and without codas. What the parameter CodaP fails to capture is any sense that codas are marked structures even within languages that permit them. Once it is set to the marked setting, CodaP is mute concerning where and when codas will actually appear. By contrast, an Optimality-theoretic constraint still has the potential to play a crucial role in analyses when low-ranked. Placing both Onset and NoCoda at the bottom of the ranking will not stop /poto/ from being assigned the description .po.to. (as opposed to, say, .pot.o.). The same constraints explaining the cross-linguistic markedness of structures also explain the markedness of structures within languages permitting those marked structures.

The basic notion of a marked structure is directly built into the theory: a marked structure is one receiving a violation mark by a constraint in Con. The distribution across environments of marked structures in a language is not directly built into the theory, but follows as a consequence of the constraint ranking for that language. Implications regarding the cross-linguistic distribution of marked and unmarked structures (of the form "If a language allows structures marked along a certain dimension, it allows structures less marked along that dimension") are likewise not built into the theory, but follow from the properties of the entire set of possible constraint rankings.

1.5 Work in phonology

Work in phonology in Optimality Theory is too extensive to quote without raising the specter of tendentiousness. Interested readers should consult the Rutgers Optimality Archive (http://ruccs.rutgers.edu/roa.html), which contains many works voluntarily posted and freely available to the research community, as well as an extensive bibliography (current only to June 1996, however). Here we cite some works whose authorship overlaps with that of this paper. Prince and Smolensky 1993 is the foundational work, laying out the theory and exploring it in the context of empirical issues in phonology, including those just discussed. McCarthy and Prince 1993b develops an approach to prosodic morphology based on Optimality Theory and introduces ideas about correspondence of representations which are developed into a general formal reconstrual of faithfulness in McCarthy and Prince 1995. McCarthy and Prince pursue a variety of issues in prosodic morphology in such papers (McCarthy and Prince 1993b, 1994, 1995) including accounts of reduplicative phenomena, where the base of reduplication actually changes to be more like the reduplicant, defying standard derivational copying accounts. Work on generalized alignment (McCarthy and Prince 1993a) discusses an important type of constraint, the alignment constraint, which plays a role in defining structural relations throughout phonology, morphology, and syntax.

2   A Syntax Example: English Interrogative Inversion and *Do* Support

The essential properties of English interrogatives and *do* support are derived from the interactions of constraints on structure and faithfulness. The two properties we will focus on here are these: that "inversion" of an auxiliary verb and the subject occurs in interrogatives but not in declaratives (see 2a, b), and that in the absence of another auxiliary verb *do* appears, except when it is the subject that is being questioned (unless the *do* is stressed, a case we set aside) (see 3a, b).

2a   **He will** read this book. *__Will he__ read this book?
 b   Which book **will he** read? *Which book **he will** read?
3a   Which book **did he** read? * Which book **he read**?
 b   **Which boy read** the book? * **Which boy did** read the book?

The account presented here is a simplified version of the analysis in Grimshaw 1997b, which we have modified slightly to accentuate the fundamental similarities between the phonological theory of syllable structure and the syntactic theory of phrase structure. (Related accounts of interrogatives and similar phenomena can be found in Ackema and Neeleman 1998 to appear; Legendre et al. 1995, 1998; Muller 1997; Pesetsky 1998; Sells et al. 1994.)

An input consists of a lexical verb (V) along with its argument structure, the verb's arguments (such as *the boy, which book*), and the tense and meaningful auxiliary verbs which encode future tense and aspect. Thus the lexical items in the input are like segments in the phonological input. The

Table 10.10   Basic universal syntactic constraints relevant for inversion theory

Name	Content
OBHD	A projection must have head
OPSPEC	An operator must be in a specifier position
NOMVT	The output must not contain a chain
NOMVT/LEX	The output must not contain a chain with a lexical head
NOINS/LEX	The output must not contain an *inserted* lexical item

candidate analyses are the various possible ways of organizing these lexical items into a phrase-structure tree. As the phonological constraints determine the organization of segments into syllables, so the syntactic constraints force certain structural representations of the inputs.

Constraints not discussed here give us some background assumptions: we consider only candidates which are consistent with the basic theory of phrase structure as instantiated in English syntax and only candidates in which the subject of the verb is in a specifier position, preceding the head auxiliary or main verb when one is present. (See Samek-Lodovici 1996; Grimshaw and Samek-Lodovici 1995, 1998; for an analysis of subjects within OT assumptions.) Every "projection" or subpiece structure has this basic form, where any of the specifier (always a phrase), head (always a single word), and complement may be missing in a given case:

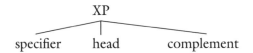

The constraints are given in table 10.10. These constraints are of two types, exactly as for the phonological constraints discussed above. One kind of constraint (the upper group) bans certain types of marked structures: projections without heads, operators outside specifier positions, chains, and chains with lexical heads.[1] The second kind of constraint enforces faithfulness to the input, in particular NOINS/LEX prohibits the insertion of lexical items not in the input.

Thus we see the same fundamental division into structural and faithfulness constraints that appears in the phonological constraints in table 10.3. The ranking of the constraints for English is given in (4). A *wh* word is a syntactic operator and is thus required by OPSPEC to be in a specifier position, where it can take scope. This pressure to move *wh* words into specifier position is the primary cause of activity in this analysis, and the phenomena of inversion and *do* support are explained by the interaction between OPSPEC and the other constraints.

Table 10.11 English declaratives

$\langle V(x, y); x = DP, y = DP, aux = \text{will}\rangle$		OPSPEC	OBHD	NOINS/LEX	NOMVT
☞ a	$[_{IP} \text{ DP } will [_{VP} \text{ V DP}]]$				
b	$[_{CP} [_{IP} \text{ DP } will [_{VP} \text{ V DP}]]]$		*!		
c	$[_{CP} will_1 [_{IP} \text{ DP } t_1 [_{VP} \text{ V DP}]]]$				*!
d	$[_{CP} do [_{IP} \text{ DP } will [_{VP} \text{ V DP}]]]$			*!	

(4) The constraint hierarchy for English (*simplified: other rankings are motivated within the full system*)

OPSPEC, NOMVT/LEX, OBHD >> NOINS/LEX >> NOMVT

When there is no operator in the input, as in a declarative, the optimal candidate violates none of these constraints. Table 10.11 shows a few of the candidates for a declarative sentence having a main verb, an auxiliary verb, and subject and object DPs, such as (2a) above. The auxiliary *will* is included in the input, marking future tense. (NOMVT/LEX is not relevant to the evaluation of these candidates and is omitted from the tableau.)

The key point in table 10.11 is that the optimal candidate, (a) has minimal structure. The representation which includes just two projections can satisfy all constraints: OPSPEC is satisfied vacuously, and no chains are formed to violate either of the NOMVT constraints. Every projection has a head, and no material is inserted. It is clear that all other structural arrangements of the material can only add violations, with no benefit, since the optimal candidate is already as good as it could be.

The relevant modifications of the analysis in (a) involve adding an extra projection, or indeed multiple extra projections, although this is not illustrated. Regardless of how the additional projection is constructed, one of the structural or faithfulness constraints is necessarily violated. (b) fatally violates the structural OBHD. There are two strategies available for avoiding the OBHD violation: namely, forming a chain to fill the empty head as in (c) and inserting *do* as in (d). The chain option violates NOMVT, and the insertion option violates NOINS/LEX. We can conclude that functional projections will occur only in optimal candidates in response to constraints.

This provides the answer to part of the question posed above: why there is no inversion in declaratives. In fact, with just these constraints, the theory predicts that no language could have inversion in a declarative, since the inversion candidate is harmonically bound by the optimal one. However, additional constraints are at work in linguistic systems, with the result that verb-subject order is cross-linguistically possible.

The true richness of the system becomes apparent when we consider a more challenging input. When the input contains a *wh* word (such as *which*, a syntactic operator), OPSPEC becomes relevant, exerting pressure to move *wh* words into specifier position. If a *wh* word fills an argument role normally

Table 10.12 English interrogatives with an auxiliary

$\langle V\,(x,\,y);\ x = DP,\ y = wh,\ aux = \text{will}\rangle$		OpSpec	ObHd	NoIns/Lex	NoMvt
a	$[_{\text{IP}}\ \text{DP } \textit{will } [_{\text{VP}}\ \text{V } \textit{wh}]]$	*!			
b	$[_{\text{CP}}\ \textit{will}_1\ [_{\text{IP}}\ \text{DP } t_1\ [_{\text{VP}}\ \text{V } \textit{wh}]]]$	*!			*
c	$[_{\text{CP}}\ \textit{wh}_j\ [_{\text{IP}}\ \text{DP } \textit{will } [_{\text{VP}}\ \text{V } t_j]]]$		*!		*
☞ d	$[_{\text{CP}}\ \textit{wh}_j\ \textit{will}_1\ [_{\text{IP}}\ \text{DP } t_t\ [_{\text{VP}}\ \text{V } t_j]]]$				**
e	$[_{\text{CP}}\ \textit{wh}_j\ \textit{do } [_{\text{IP}}\ \text{DP } \textit{will } [_{\text{VP}}\ \text{V } t_j]]]$			*!	*

realized in complement position, then the *wh* word may "move" to a specifier position only by forming a chain with a co-indexed trace in the argument role position. Such a chain violates NoMvt: thus OpSpec and NoMvt conflict. The fact that the *wh* phrase appears in specifier position in the optimal candidate, (d) in table 10.12, establishes the ranking OpSpec >> NoMvt. The candidates in table 10.12, (a) and (b), which leave the *wh* phrase in the object position, are thus eliminated.

Now, however, it is clear that the situation is quite different from that faced in declaratives. In an interrogative the optimal candidate *must* contain an extra projection, in order to provide the specifier position to house the operator. As noted in the context of the declarative, an extra projection poses a grammatical challenge: what to do with the head position. ObHd conflicts with both NoMvt and NoIns/Lex. Forming a chain can redeem a violation of ObHd, but at the cost of a NoMvt violation. NoIns/Lex bars filling a head position with inserted material and hence conflicts with ObHd. Thus the three choices for the head position – leaving it empty, filling it with inserted material, and having it be part of a chain – each violate a constraint. The grammar must decide which of the constraints will be violated in this configuration.

Since the optimal candidate, (d), has the auxiliary verb heading a chain in violation of NoMvt but satisfying ObHd, we conclude that ObHd >> NoMvt. Why doesn't the language choose to avoid violating ObHd with the other strategy, namely insertion? This is because NoIns/Lex dominates NoMvt, so the ban against chains has lower priority than the ban against inserting material that is not in the input.

We have just seen that English prefers the marked structure involving a chain to the even more marked structure involving epenthesis of a verb. This does not mean, however, that the insertion of a verb is never possible in the language. In fact it is the solution of choice for a different input. Table 10.13 shows candidates for the same input, except that the tense is past instead of future, hence there is no auxiliary verb in the input. All the candidates shown satisfy OpSpec. The problem to be solved here is this: the "extra" projection is required, and ObHd mandates that its head be filled. The options for filling the head position for this input, however, are not quite the same as before. In particular, there is no auxiliary verb in the input which can be moved into the empty position. The only verb available is the main verb, but a main verb is

Table 10.13   English interrogatives with *do*

$\langle V(x, y); x = DP, y = wh, tense = past \rangle$		OPSPEC	NOMVT/LEX	OBHD	NOINS/LEX	NOMVT
a	$[_{\text{IP}} \, wh_j \, [_{\text{VP}} \, V \, t_j]]$			*!		*
b	$[_{\text{CP}} \, wh_j \, V_j \, [_{\text{VP}} \, t_i \, t_j]]]$		*!			**
☞ c	$[_{\text{CP}} \, wh_j \, do_i \, [_{\text{IP}} \, DP \, t_i \, [_{\text{VP}} \, V \, t_j]]]$				*	**
d	$[_{\text{CP}} \, wh_j \,_{[\text{IP}} \, DP \, do \, [_{\text{VP}} \, V \, t_j]]]$			*!	*	*

Table 10.14   English interrogatives with a *wh* subject

$\langle V(x, y); x = wh, y = DP, tense = past \rangle$		OPSPEC	NOMVT/LEX	OBHD	NOINS/LEX	NOMVT
☞ a	$[_{\text{VP}} \, wh \, V \, DP]]$					
b	$[_{\text{IP}} \, wh_j \, [_{\text{VP}} \, t_i \, V \, DP]]]$			*!		*
c	$[_{\text{IP}} \, wh_j \, do \, [_{\text{VP}} \, V \, t_j]]]$				*!	*

lexical, and if this verb inverts the constraint, NOINS/LEX is violated. This constraint makes chains with lexical heads (a main verb in this case) more marked than chains headed by non-lexical material (such as an auxiliary verb). Any movement violates NOMVT; lexical movement additionally violates NOMVT/LEX.

It is in this circumstance that insertion is the best strategy and *do* surfaces, as in (3a) above. Candidate (c) in table 10.13 has *do* inserted as an auxiliary, which forms a chain filling both the head of CP and the head of IP. This is the optimal candidate: it violates NOMVT/LEX once and NOMVT twice, but satisfies the other three (higher-ranked) constraints. The inversion of *do* is required; without the inversion, the insertion of *do* is simply a gratuitous violation of NOINS/LEX, as shown by (d). It is the fact that NOMVT/LEX dominates NOINS/LEX that determines the outcome here: the opposite ranking gives a language with no "*do* support", one in which a main verb can raise to fill an empty head. French exemplifies such a system.

The verb *do* is admitted into interrogatives of the kind just discussed because it solves a problem: it fills an empty head position. We have already seen that when there is a better solution to the problem: namely, when an auxiliary verb from the input is available, *do* is impossible. It is also impossible when the problem doesn't arise: in configurations with no empty head. This is the explanation for the case illustrated above in (3b), where *do* does not occur in an interrogative, despite the lack of any other auxiliary. This happens where the *wh* operator is the subject, shown in table 10.14. Because, for independent reasons, the subject is in a specifier position, OPSPEC is satisfied with no movement. Thus, as in the declaratives, there is no motivation for inversion or *do* support, as demonstrated by the suboptimality of (b) and (c) in the table.

Thus, with a combination of constraints which ban marked structures and

constraints which enforce faithfulness to the input, we can derive the fundamental properties of the English interrogative inversion system. The constraints evaluate all the alternative organizations of the input into a syntactic
structure and select the optimal one under a given ranking.

This analysis illustrates how the Optimality Theory framework naturally
captures the intuitive notion of economy that has received much attention
recently (e.g., Chomsky 1991, 1995). Chains are not prohibited absolutely,
but are tolerated only to the extent necessary; the most economical option is
selected, relative to other constraints. The universal constraint NoMvt is
active in all languages, prohibiting unmotivated chains. This is quite apparent
even in English, where NoMvt is the lowest-ranked constraint of those
discussed. Resources like functional projections, chains, and insertion are used
only when necessary, and only as much as necessary. Optimality Theory gives
a precise characterization of "only when necessary"; violation is permitted only
when all alternatives either violate a higher-ranked constraint or incur greater
violation of the same constraint.

The many recent studies carried out under Optimality-theoretic assumptions
cover a much wider range of empirical issues than can be even touched on
here. Interesting examples include aspects of pronominal systems (Grimshaw
1997a and Bresnan, to appear), discourse-related constraints (Choi 1996 and
Samek-Lodovici 1998), and null pronouns (Speas 1997). Further work on the
syntactic constraint system promises to elucidate further the similarities
between phonological and syntactic representations under OT.

3 Language Processing

Central to language processing is the assigning of structural descriptions to
linguistic material via algorithms. Within the Optimality Theory framework,
the most obvious such mapping is the assigning of a structural description to
a linguistic input. This mapping is naturally understood as mapping from an
underlying form to a description including the surface phonetic form, and
thus as corresponding to language production. Language comprehension
corresponds to a mapping from a surface form to a complete description
which includes the underlying form. The exact relationship between these
defining input/output mappings and the performance processes of comprehension and production remains an open issue.

The computability of these mappings was a matter of concern to some
people early in the development of the theory. Because a grammar is described
in terms of the simultaneous generation, evaluation, and comparison of an
infinite number of candidates, a literal, mechanical interpretation of this
description would suggest that to compute the optimal description of an
input, an algorithm would need to generate and evaluate an infinite number
of candidate descriptions. Fortunately, work on the computation of optimal

descriptions has shown that it is not necessary to generate and evaluate an infinite number of candidates in order to compute the optimal description. Probably correct algorithms have been developed which efficiently compute the optimal description for several classes of grammars.

Section 3.1 presents an illustration of an algorithm for efficiently computing optimal descriptions for a grammar employing an infinite candidate set. Section 3.2 discusses some philosophical affinities between Optimality Theory and contemporary work on cognitive modeling in connectionism and dynamical systems theory.

3.1 Computing optimal structural descriptions

The infinite size of the candidate set results from the possibility of candidates containing material not found in the corresponding input; epenthesis (insertion) in the CV Syllable Theory is an example. Once the possibility of such insertions is granted (a rather uncontroversial position), there isn't any principled basis for placing any absolute limit on the number of insertions a candidate description may contain. Fortunately, no such limit is necessary, because the faithfulness constraints, specifically NODEL, are violated by such deviations from the input and thus occur in grammatical descriptions only to the extent necessary to satisfy other high-ranked constraints. Thus the independently motivated faithfulness constraints provide the means to ensure that grammatical descriptions have only a finite number of insertions.

The faithfulness constraints themselves say nothing about how to compute optimal descriptions. However, an approach to computing optimal descriptions has been developed by Tesar (1995a, 1995b, 1996). This approach is based upon the computational technique of dynamic programming. This section provides a brief sketch of the approach.

The key to the dynamic programming approach is to build up to the optimal description piece by piece, rather than generating and considering lots of complete candidates. The algorithm uses a table to record the pieces, called *partial descriptions*, as they are built, and uses the pieces already recorded to build bigger pieces, until a small number of full descriptions are built, one of which is guaranteed to be optimal. Table 10.15 shows the table built by the algorithm when computing the optimal description for input /ap/. The ranking in use is that shown in (5).

(5)   ONSET >> NOCODA >> NOINSV >> NODEL >> NOINSC

The table has four rows. The rows labeled for each of the possible syllabic positions (Onset, Nucleus, Coda) contain partial descriptions with the final (right-most) position corresponding to the row label: the Onset row only contains partial descriptions ending with an onset position, and so forth. The None row contains partial descriptions with no syllabic positions; this limits

Table 10.15 Dynamic programming table for the input /ap/ in L_1; each cell contains a partial description, along with the description's constraint violations. Epenthesized segments are shown in italics

	Begin	i_1 = a	i_2 = p
None		NoDel *	NoDel **
Onset	.ʔ NoInsC *	.ʔa.ʔ NoInsC **	.ʔa.p NoInsC *
Nucleus	.ʔi. NoInsC * NoInsV *	.ʔa. NoInsC *	.ʔa. NoInsC * NoDel *
Coda	.ʔiʔ. NoInsC ** NoInsV * NoCoda *	.ʔaʔ. NoInsC ** NoCoda *	.ʔap. NoInsC * NoCoda *

the row to partial descriptions containing only deleted input segments. There is a column for each input segment (in order), plus a Begin column containing partial descriptions with none of the input segments. The interpretation of the cell in row Nucleus and column i_1 [Nucleus, i_1], is that it contains the most harmonic partial description containing the input segments up to i_1 and having a nucleus as the right-most position. The algorithm fills the columns in succession, left to right. A cell is filled by considering ways of adding structure to the partial descriptions already contained in the table. Out of all the partial descriptions considered for a cell, the one that is most harmonic with respect to the constraint ranking actually fills the cell. The Begin column is filled first. It is relatively easy to fill; because this column is prior to the consideration of the first input segment, each cell is filled with the structure containing the minimum number of insertions necessary to reach the syllable position indicated by the row.

Consider the ways to fill cell [Nucleus, i_1], assuming that the Begin column has already been filled. The structure in [Nucleus, Begin], .ʔi., could be used with i_1 deleted, incurring a NoDel violation, with the result having violations {NoInsC NoInsV NoDel}. The structure in [Onset, Begin] could be used with i_1 parsed into a nucleus position, giving .ʔa., which has violations { NoInsC}. The structure in [Onset, i_1] could have an inserted nucleus position added, giving .ʔa. ʔi., which has violations {NoInsC NoInsC NoInsV}. When the limit set of possibilities for filling the cell are compared, the most harmonic, .ʔa., is placed in the cell. When processing of the column i_1 is complete, the cell entries are used as building blocks for filling the cells of the next column.

This is how the algorithm keeps the large number of combinations forming different candidates under control: as each input segment is considered, the different ways of adding that segment are winnowed down to four (one for each row), and only those partial descriptions are used when considering how to add the next input segment.

Actions filling the cells of a column must be coordinated. This is because insertion actions can add onto an entry in one cell to fill another cell of the same column, and these dependencies are cyclical. The solution is to first consider only candidates that delete or parse the new input segment, because those actions only add onto partial descriptions in the previous column. Then partial descriptions with one insertion at the right edge are considered. If any of them replace the previous entry in a cell, then partial descriptions with two insertions at the right edge are considered. Soon the accumulated faithfulness violations (each insertion is a separate violation of either NoInsC or NoInsV) will prevent any further changes in the cell contents; at that point the column may be declared finished, and the algorithm proceeds to the next column. In this way, the algorithm uses the constraints to tell it how many insertions need to be considered.

Once all the cells have been filled, the optimal description may be selected from the final column. In the example in table 10.15, the optimal description is .ʔa., in cell [Nucleus, i_2].

3.2 Relation to connectionism and dynamical systems

Although it is perhaps not immediately apparent, Optimality Theory shares some principles with connectionism and dynamical systems theory. In fact, Optimality Theory traces its origin to an effort by Prince and Smolensky to combine generative grammar and optimization ideas operative in certain forms of connectionism (Prince and Smolensky 1991, 1997). As emphasized in section 1, Optimality Theory's strong commitments are about grammatical functions, not algorithms. The connection, then, is between Optimality theory and connectionist theory, the mathematical characterizations of connectionist network behavior.

Perhaps the single most influential concept in connectionist theory is the understanding of networks in terms of optimization (Hopfield 1982). The weighted connections of the network define a function, often labeled energy or harmony (Smolensky 1986), over the space of possible activation states. Different inputs determine different spaces of possible activation states. For a given input, the network searches for the available activation state which optimizes the harmony function defined over those activation states. Issues in connectionist algorithms concern when connectionist algorithms do or do not converge on the network configuration optimizing the harmony function. Issues in connectionist theory concern the nature of the function which maps the network inputs to their globally optimal configurations as determined by the weighted connections of the network (independent of any particular algorithm).

The connections of the network determine the harmony function and can be understood as constraints on the activations of the units they connect, and thus as constraints evaluating network activation states. However, the common situation is that the connections (constraints) conflict: there exists no configuration satisfying all the connections (constraints) (McClelland and Rumelhart 1981). Thus, connectionist networks can be understood in terms of optimization over violable, or "soft" constraints. But that is how Optimality Theory is defined: optimization of violable constraints over a space of candidate representations.

The most significant difference between Optimality Theory and connectionist theory is the nature of the harmony function. Connectionist theory uses numerical optimization: the constraints are assigned numeric weights, so the relative strength of different constraints is determined by the relative magnitudes of their respective numeric weights. Optimality Theory uses strict domination optimization (Principles 3 and 4). The possible relationships between connectionist numeric optimization and Optimality-theoretic strict domination optimization is a wide open topic, the subject of much future research.

3.3   Other work

Ellison (1994) has developed a way of representing the candidate set for an input as a finite state automaton, along with an algorithm for identifying the optimal candidate by searching for the least-weight (highest-harmony) path through the automaton. The least-weight path algorithm, based upon dynamic programming, is not itself a finite-state algorithm. Work in a similar spirit has been done by Eisner (1997). Frank and Satta (1998) have investigated actual finite-state algorithms for computing optimal forms, demonstrating that faithfulness as normally conceived is strictly beyond the computational capacity of finite-state automata, but can be approximated. Hammond (1997) has computationally modeled the comprehension of syllable structure.

Several computational tools related to Optimality Theory have been made available on the Internet. Tools for simulating OT generation include those created by Andrews (1994), Walther (1996), and Hammond (1997). Raymond and Hogan 1993 is a tool for aiding in the study of factorial typologies, and the software suite of Hayes (1998) facilitates both factorial typology and the study of particular systems. The Rutgers Optimality Archive "Utilities" page provides links to these programs.

4   Language Learnability and Acquisition

Cross-linguistic variation is explained in Optimality Theory through the rankings of the universal constraints. Therefore, an important part of language learning in Optimality Theory is learning the correct ranking of the universal constraints for a given language, from positive data. One challenging aspect of this problem in Optimality Theory is imposed by the use of violable constraints. Given a grammatical description, a learner might observe that it violates some of the universal constraints. But if grammatical descriptions are allowed to violate constraints, how can anything be learned from those observations? There is also a combinatorial concern.[2] The number of distinct total rankings is a factorial function of the number of constraints: 10 constraints have 10! = 3,628,800 rankings, and 20 constraints have 20! = 2,432,902,008,176,640,000 rankings. If the amount of data required to learn the correct ranking scales as the number of possible rankings, then a grammar with many constraints could require a prohibitively large amount of data to be learned successfully.

Fortunately, the problem of finding a ranking consistent with a set of grammatical descriptions turns out to be quite tractable. In fact, the optimizing structure of Optimality Theory can be a significant asset with respect to language learnability. Section 4.1 describes an approach to language learning which makes use of the formal structure of Optimality Theory. Section 4.2 describes recent work using Optimality Theory grammars to account for child language acquisition data.

4.1   Learnability

The learning of constraint rankings is illustrated here using a simplified Optimality-theoretic analysis of metrical stress (more general systems, along with corresponding learning results, can be found in Tesar 1997, 1998b). In this system, languages assign stress to a word by first grouping two of the word's syllables into a foot and then assigning main word stress to one of the syllables in the foot. The foot is assigned at one edge of the word, and languages vary as to which edge (left or right) the foot is assigned. Another form of variation is the form of the foot. A trochaic foot assigns stress to the first of the two syllables of the foot, while an iambic foot assigns stress to the second syllable of the foot. A word is here delimited by square brackets, with parentheses indicating the foot grouping. Each numeral represents the stress level of a syllable, with 1 denoting primary stress, 2 denoting secondary stress, and 0 denoting an unstressed syllable. The word [(1 0) 0 0 0] has five syllables, with the first two grouped into a trochaic foot; the result is that the main stress falls on the first syllable.

The Optimality-theoretic analysis presented here uses four constraints, as

Table 10.16 Constraints for metrical stress theory

Name	Content
ALLFTL	A foot must be at the left edge of the word.
ALLFTR	A foot must be at the right edge of the word.
TROCH	A foot must stress its first syllable.
IAMB	A foot must stress its last syllable.

Table 10.17 The disjunction problem

		ALLFTL	ALLFTR	IAMB	TROCH
winner	[0 (0 1)]	*			*
loser	[(1 0) 0]		*	*	

shown in table 10.16. The constraint ALLFTL is violated once for each syllable intervening between a foot and the left edge of the word.

The challenge of learning constraint rankings is illustrated in table 10.17. The winner is the grammatical description. The goal of learning is to find a constraint ranking that makes the winner more harmonic than all competitors, such as the loser in table 10.17. For the winner to be more harmonic than the loser, at least one of the constraints violated by the loser must dominate all of the constraints violated by the winner. The precise information contained in this loser/winner pair is given in (6).

(6) (ALLFTR **or** IAMB) >> (ALLFTL **and** TROCH)

The tricky part is the disjunction (the logical *or*) of the constraints violated by the loser: we know one of them must dominate the constraints violated by the winner, but we don't know which (if not both). In systems with a larger number of constraints, it may be possible for a single loser/winner pair to have quite a few constraints in the disjunction, and attempting to maintain and reconcile such information across many examples could be difficult.

A solution to this problem is the Error-Driven Constraint Demotion algorithm of Tesar and Smolensky (1995, 1998). At any given time this algorithm has a hypothesis ranking. The algorithm identifies the highest-ranked constraint violated more by the loser. Every constraint which (a) is violated by the winner and (b) is not currently dominated in the hierarchy by the highest-ranked loser constraint is demoted to immediately below the highest-ranked loser constraint. This ensures that the resulting ranking will hold the winner more harmonic than the loser. This is illustrated in table 10.18 for the loser/winner pair in table 10.17, assuming that the starting hypothesis ranking is the ranking in (7).

Table 10.18 Constraint demotion: ALLFTL is demoted to below ALLFTR, into a tie with
IAMB

		Before		After		
		ALLFTL	ALLFTR	ALLFTL	IAMB	TROCH
winner	[0 (0 1)]	(*)		*		*
loser	[(1 0) 0]		*		*	

(7)   ALLFTL >> ALLFTR >> IAMB >> TROCH

The highest-ranked constraint violated by the loser is ALLFTR. One constraint
violated by the winner, TROCH, is already dominated by ALLFTR and so is left
alone. The other constraint violated by the winner, ALLFTL, is not so
dominated. Thus, constraint demotion demotes ALLFTL to the stratum
immediately below ALLFTR (effectively creating a tie between ALLFTL and
IAMB). With respect to the resulting constraint hierarchy, the winner is more
harmonic than the loser.

The hypothesis rankings used by the algorithm are of a particular form,
called a *stratified hierarchy*. A stratified hierarchy consists of ranked strata,
where each stratum contains one or more of the constraints. The hierarchy
resulting from the constraint demotion in table 10.18, is an example: ALLFTL
and IAMB are in the same stratum, neither dominating the other. This freedom
to have hypotheses that aren't totally ranked is important to the success of the
algorithm. However, the algorithm will always converge to a hierarchy consistent with at least one total ranking.

The algorithm is error-driven in the way that it selects loser/winner pairs to
be used for demotion (Tesar 1995a, 1998a). When presented with a grammatical description, the algorithm computes the description for the same input
that is optimal with respect to the current hypothesis hierarchy. If it is not the
same as the grammatical description, then an error has occurred, and the
grammatical description is made the winner, and the description currently
optimal is made the loser. If the currently optimal description matches the
given grammatical one, no error has occurred, so no learning takes place.

The error-driven structure of the algorithm makes it convenient to measure
data complexity in terms of the number of errors (mismatches that result in
constraint demotions) that can occur prior to convergence on a hierarchy
generating the correct language. There is a mathematically provable bound on
the worst-case number of errors that can occur prior to convergence: $N(N-1)$
errors, where N is the number of constraints. In practice, this worst case is a
large overestimate, and the algorithm reaches the correct ranking far more
quickly. This demonstrates that the amount of data required to learn a ranking
does not scale anything like the number of total rankings (see table 10.19).

Constraint demotion is guaranteed to find a correct ranking, given the
correct full structural descriptions of grammatical utterances. But that is only

Table 10.19 Data complexity of constraint demotion

No. of constraints	No. of total rankings	Maximum no. of errors
5	5! = 20	5(5 − 1) = 20
10	10! = 3,628,800	10(10 − 1) = 90
20	20! = 2,432,902,008,176,640,000	20(20 − 1) = 380

part of the learning story. One of the challenging aspects of language learning is that the learner does not have direct access to full structural descriptions. The learner has direct access only to the audible, overt information in the phonetic stream, referred to here as an *overt* form. The problem is made challenging by the fact that overt forms are often ambiguous: they are consistent with more than one distinct full structural description. Figuring out the correct descriptions of the overt forms is part of the learner's task. An example is the overt form [0 1 0] – that is, a three-syllable word with stress on the middle syllable. This overt form is ambiguous between the interpretations of a left-aligned iambic foot, [(0 1) 0], and a right-aligned trochaic foot, [0 (1 0))]. The "hidden structure" not present in the overt form is the foot structure.

   Recent work on learnability has investigated a learning strategy for overcoming ambiguity by capitalizing on Optimality Theory's optimizing structure (Tesar and Smolensky 1996; Tesar 1997, 1998b). The strategy, inspired by work in statistical learning theory (Baum 1972; Dempster et al. 1977), is to give the learner a starting hypothesized constraint ranking, and then compute the structural description for an overt form that is most consistent with the hypothesized constraint ranking. Such a computation is dubbed *robust interpretive parsing*; it is in essence the same mapping as that suggested earlier for language comprehension. The advantage provided by Optimality Theory is that the interpretive mapping is defined even for overt forms which are not consistent with a learner's hypothesis grammar (constraint ranking), hence the label *robust*. Robust interpretive parsing, when given an overt form and the learner's current ranking, selects, from among those structural descriptions with an overt portion matching the overt form, the description most harmonic with respect to the learner's current ranking, even if the ranking selects as optimal a different structural description (one with a different overt portion). When presented with an overt form inconsistent with their current grammar, the learner makes its best attempt to interpret the utterance.

   The iterative strategy is for the learner to use this best-guess interpretation for learning, on the (quite possibly mistaken) assumption that it is correct. The interpretation is used for learning by treating it as a winner and applying constraint demotion as described above. The intuition behind the strategy is that even if the interpretation arrived at by the learner is incorrect, it will still contain useful information because it has been constrained to match the overt

Table 10.20 Before the first demotion

		ALLFTL	*ALLFTR*	*IAMB*	*TROCH*
winner	[0 0 (0 1) 0]	**	*		*
loser	[(0 1) 0 0 0]		***		*

form (the information the learner is attempting to learn from). This approach results in an iterative procedure: use a hypothesized constraint ranking to construct hypothesized full structural descriptions of available overt forms, then use the hypothesized structural descriptions to construct a new hypothesized constraint ranking (via constraint demotion). This may then be repeated, back and forth, using the new hypothesized ranking to determine new hypothesized structural descriptions of the overt forms. Learning is successful when the process converges on the correct ranking and the correct structural descriptions. This strategy has been investigated with Optimality-theoretic systems for metrical stress with quite promising results (Tesar 1997, 1998b).

As an illustration, suppose that the learner is attempting to learn a language which places the main stress foot on the right of the word and uses a trochaic foot. However, the learner here starts with the constraint ranking shown in (8), generating a very different language.

(8)   ALLFTL >> ALLFTR >> IAMB >> TROCH

Suppose the learner is confronted with the overt form [0 0 0 1 0], a five-syllable word with main stress on the fourth syllable. The learner will apply interpretive parsing to this form, using its current ranking, the result being as shown in the winner row of table 10.20. The learner will also use its ranking to determine the optimal description of a five-syllable word in its current grammar, which is an iambic foot on the left side of the word, and shown in the loser row of the table.

The winner matches the overt form; it has main stress on the fourth syllable. Notice, however, that the winner contains an incorrect analysis; it assigns an iambic foot grouping the third and fourth syllables, while the language being learned in fact requires a trochaic foot grouping the last two syllables. The learner, however, has no way of knowing this in advance and proceeds (temporarily) on the assumption that their analysis of the overt form is correct. The learner proceeds by applying constraint demotion, which demotes ALLFTL to below ALLFTR and into a tie with IAMB.

(9)   ALLFTR >> {IAMB ALLFTL} >> TROCH

The learner has now modified its ranking, but it is not done yet. Now that it has modified its ranking, it reinterprets the overt form using the new constraint ranking. Table 10.21 shows the new interpretation on the winner row; the

Table 10.21 Before the second demotion

		AllFtL	AllFtR	Iamb	Troch
winner	[0 0 0 (1 0)]	***		*	
loser	[0 0 0 (0 1)]	***			*

Table 10.22 After the second demotion, the learner has reached the correct ranking

		AllFtR	AllFtL	Troch	Iamb
winner	[0 0 0 (1 0)]		***		*
loser	[0 0 0 (1 0)]		***		*

loser row shows the optimal stress assignment for a five-syllable word under the new ranking.

The interpretation of the overt form has now changed, and for the better: the learner now has the correct interpretation of the overt form. The learner now applies constraint demotion again, demoting Iamb to below Troch; the result is shown in table 10.22.

What is important is that even though the learner initially misanalyzed the overt form, due to an incorrect ranking, the learner was able to make progress using its own analysis. The overt information was enough to get the learner moving in the right direction, ultimately arriving at both the correct analysis and the correct constraint ranking.

4.2 Acquisition

Several recent papers on child language acquisition have accounted for observed patterns in child language development in terms of changes in constraint rankings (Levelt 1994, to appear; Demuth 1995; Gnanadesikan 1995). There is a theme that has emerged in much of this work, one that has been explicitly articulated by Smolensky (1996): children start with the faithfulness constraints ranked below structural constraints. This results in early child language production exhibiting only the most unmarked forms. The claim here is that children have underlying forms closely matching the surface forms they hear from adults, but that the low ranking of faithfulness results in outputs which modify the structure to contain less marked forms than appear in the underlying form (or appear in the surface forms they hear). Over time, children demote some structural constraints to below some faithfulness constraints, permitting marked structures to appear in optimal descriptions and thus in their language production.

4.3   Other work

Turkel (1994) has investigated the learning of Optimality Theory rankings using genetic algorithms. Broihier (1995) has investigated issues in the learning of OT grammars which make use of non-vacuous ties among constraints.

Optimality Theory explains linguistic phenomena in terms of optimization over violable constraints. In so doing, it formalizes notions of linguistic markedness and economy and makes them central to the explanations. Linguistic markedness is captured by the use of constraints which can be violated, but are nevertheless present and active in all languages. Economy is reflected (and generalized) in the use of optimization to choose among several ways of describing an input: the grammar always selects the best way possible. Optimality theory shares several underlying principles with certain forms of connectionism, and those shared principles are apparent in work on language processing within Optimality Theory. By defining grammaticality in terms of optimization over violable constraints, and by differentiating the strength of constraints via strict domination, Optimality Theory makes possible new directions in language learning, with some significant results already obtained both in formal language learnability and in empirical language acquisition studies. Current and future work within Optimality Theory promises to provide further interesting results and directions for research on fundamental issues of linguistic theory.

Notes

All the analyses presented in this paper are simplified from the originals for reasons of space and clarity. The authors alone are responsible for any and all errors and misrepresentations.

1   A chain is a set of positions in a clause, such that one element, the head, effectively fills them all. It is the representational characterization corresponding to the notion of "movement".

2   This combinatorial concern is similar to that faced by the Principles and parameters framework (Chomsky 1981). A system with 10 binary parameters has $2^{10} = 1,024$ distinct parameter settings, a system with 20 binary parameters has $2^{20} = 1,048,576$. While these exponential functions grow fast enough to make brute-force enumeration impractical, the factorial functions of possible rankings grow faster yet.

References

Ackema, P. and Neeleman, A. (1998) WHOT? In Barbosa et al. 15–33.

Andrews, A. (1994). OT for Windows 1.1 (prolog/C++ program). ROA–91.

Barbosa, P., Fox, D., Hagstrom, P., McGinnis, M. and Pesetsky, D. (eds) (1998) *Is the Best Good Enough?* Cambridge, MA: MIT Press and MIT Working Papers in Linguistics.

Baum, L. (1972). An inequality and associated maximization technique in statistical estimation for probabilistic functions of Markov processes. *Inequalities* 3, 1–8.

Beckman, J., Dickey, L. W. and Urbanczyk, S. (eds.) (1995), *Papers on Optimality Theory*, GLSA, University of Massachusetts, Amherst, MA. University of Massachusetts Occasional Papers, 18.

Bresnan, J. (forthcoming). The emergence of the unmarked pronoun: Chichewa pronominals in Optimality theory. In *Proceedings of the Berkeley Linguistics Society* 23.

Broihier, K. (1995) Optimality Theoretic rankings with tied constraints: Slavic relatives, resumptive pronouns and learnability. MS, Department of Linguistics, MIT. ROA–46.

Choi, H. W. (1996) Optimizing structure in context: scrambling and information structure. Ph.D. Thesis, Stanford University.

Chomsky, N. (1965) *Aspects of the Theory of Syntax*, Cambridge, MA: MIT Press.

—— (1981) *Lectures on Government and Binding*, Dordrecht: Foris Publications.

—— (1991). Some notes on economy of derivation and representation. In R. Freidin (ed.) *Principles and Parameters in Comparative Grammar*, Cambridge, MA: MIT Press, 417–53.

—— (1995) *A Minimalist Program for Linguistic Theory*, Cambridge, MA: MIT Press.

Clements, G. and Keyser, S. (1983) *CV Phonology*, Cambridge, MA: MIT Press.

Dempster, A., Laird, N. and Rubin, D. (1977) Maximum likelihood from incomplete data via the *EM* algorithm. *Journal of the Royal Statistical Society B* 39, 1–38.

Demuth, K. (1995) Markedness and the development of prosodic structure. In *Proceedings of NELS 25*, GLSA, University of Massachusetts, Amherst.

Eisner, J. (1997) Efficient generation in primitive Optimality theory. MS. ROA–206.

Ellison, T. N. (1994) Phonological derivation in Optimality Theory. In *Proceedings of the Fifteenth International Conference on Computational Linguistics*, 1007–13. ROA–75.

Frank, R. and Satta, G. (1998) Optimality Theory and the generative complexity of constraint violability. *Computational Linguistics* 24(2), 307–15.

Gnanadesikan, A. (1995) Markedness and faithfulness constraints in child phonology. MS, Department of Linguistics, University of Massachusets, Amherst.

Grimshaw, J. (1977a) The best clitic: constraint interaction in morphosyntax. In L. Haegeman (ed.), *Elements of Grammar: Handbook of Generative Syntax*, Kluwer, 169–96.

—— (1997b) Projection heads and optimality. *Linguistic Inquiry* 28, 373–422.

—— (forthcoming). Constraints on constraints in optimality theoretic syntax. In Mark Baltin and Chris Collins (eds.), *The Handbook of Temporary Syntactic Theory*, Oxford: Blackwell.

Grimshaw, J. and Samek-Lodovici, V. (1995) Optimal subjects. In Beckman et al., 589–605.

—— (1998). Optimal subjects and subject universals. In Barbosa et al., 193–219.

Hammond, M. (1997) Parsing syllables: modeling OT computationally (prolog program). MS, Department of Linguistics, University of Arizona. ROA–222.

Hayes, B. P. (1998) Optimality theory software. UCLA: Department of Linguistics website. Http://www.humnet.ucla.edu/humnet/linguistics/people/hayes/otsoft/otsoft.htm.

Hopfield, J. J. (1982) Neural networks and physical systems with emergent collective computational abilities. In *Proceedings of the National Acadamy of Sciences* 18, 2554–8.

Jakobson, R. (1962) *Selected Writings 1: Phonological Studies*, The Hague: Mouton.

Legendre, G., Smolensky, P. and Wilson, C. (1998) When is less more? Faithfulness and minimal links in *wh*-chains. In Barbosa et al. 249–89.

Legendre, G., Wilson, C., Smolensky, P., Homer, K. and Raymond, W. (1995) Optimality and *wh*-extraction. In Beckman et al., 607–36.

Levelt, C. (1994) *On the Acquisition of Place*. Holland Institute of Generative Linguistics Dissertations in Linguistics, 8. The Hague: Holland Academic Graphics.

—— (forthcoming) The segmental structure of early words: articulatory frames or phonological constraints? In E. Clark (ed.), *Proceedings of the 27th Child Language Research Forum*, Stanford University, Stanford, CA: CSLI Publications.

McCarthy, J. and Prince, A. (1993a) Generalized alignment. In G. Booij and J. van Marle (eds.), *Yearbook of Morphology*, Dordrecht: Kluwer, 79–154.

—— (1993b) Prosodic morphology I: constraint interaction and satisfaction. Technical report, TR–3, Rutgers University Center for Cognitive Science. To appear in the Linguistic Inquiry Monograph Series, Cambridge, MA: MIT Press.

—— (1994) The emergence of the unmarked: optimality in prosodic morphology. In Mercè Gonzàlez (ed.), *Proceedings of the North-East Linguistics Society* 24, Amherst, MA, GLSA, University of Massachusetts, 333–79. ROA–13.

—— (1995) Faithfulness and reduplicative identity. In Beckman et al., 249–384.

McClelland, J. and Rumelhart D.(1981) An interactive activation model of context effects in letter perception: part 1. An account of basic findings. *Psychological Review* 88, 375–407.

Müller, G. (1997) Partial wh-movement and Optimality theory. *Linguistic Review* 14, 249–306.

Pesetsky, D. (1998) Some optimality principles of sentence pronunciation. In Barbosa et al., 337–83.

Prince, A. and Smolensky, P. (1991) Notes on connectionism and harmony theory in linguistics. Technical report CU-CS-533-91, Department of Computer Science, University of Colorado, Boulder.

—— (1993) Optimality Theory: constraint interaction in generative grammar. Technical report, TR–2, Rutgers University Center for Cognitive Science, and CU-CS-696-93, Department of Computer Science, University of Colorado, Boulder. To appear in the Linguistic Inquiry Monograph Series, MIT Press.

—— (1997) Optimality: from neural networks to universal grammar. *Science* 275, 1604–10.

Raymond, W. and Hogan, A. (1993) The optimality interpreter, and a user's guide to the optimality interpreter (C program). ROA–130.

Samek-Lodovici, V. (1996) Constraints on subjects: an optimality theoretic analysis. Ph.D. thesis, Rutgers University.

—— (1998) Opposite constraints: left and right focus-alignment in Kanakuru. *Lingua* 104.

Sells, P., Rickford, J. and Wasow, T. (1994) An Optimality-Theoretic approach to variation in negative inversion in AAVE. MS, Stanford University. ROA–53.

Smolensky, P. (1986) Information processing in dynamical systems: foundations of harmony theory. In D. Rumlhart and J. McClelland (eds.), *Parallel Distributed Processing: Explorations in the Microstructure of Cognition*, Col. 1: *Foundations*, Cambridge, MA: MIT Press/Bradford Books, 194–281

—— (1996) On the comprehension/production dilemma in child language. *Linguistic Inquiry* 27, 720–31. ROA–118.

Speas, M. (1997) Optimality Theory and syntax: null pronouns and control. In D. Archangeli and D. T. Langendoen (eds.), *Optimality Theory: An Overview*, Oxford: Blackwell, 171–99.

Tesar, B. (1995a) Computational Optimality Theory. Ph.D. Thesis, Department of Computer Science, University of Colorado, Boulder. ROA–90.

—— (1995b) Computing optimal descriptions for Optimality Theory: basic syllabification. Technical Report CU-CS-763-95, Department of Computer Science, University of Colorado, Boulder. ROA–52.

—— (1996) Computing optimal descriptions for Optimality Theory grammars with context-free position structures. In *Proceedings of the 34th Annual Meeting of the Association for Computational Linguistics*, 101–7.

—— (1997) An iterative strategy for learning metrical stress in Optimality theory. In E. Hughes, M. Hughes and A. Greenhill (eds.), *The Proceedings of the 21st Annual Boston University Conference on Language Development*, Somerville, MA, Cascadilla Press, 615–26. ROA–177.

—— (1998a) Error driven learning in Optimality Theory via the efficient computation of optimal forms. In Barbosa et al., 421–35.

—— (1998b) An iterative strategy for language learning. *Lingua* 104, 131–45.

Tesar, B. and Smolensky, P. (1995) The learnability of Optimality Theory. In *Proceedings of the Thirteenth West Coast Conference on Formal Linguistics*, Stanford, CA: CSLI Publications, 122–37.

—— (1996) Learnability in Optimality Theory (long version). Technical Report JHU-CogSci-96-4, Department of Cognitive Science, The Johns Hopkins University. ROA–156.

—— (1998) Learnability in Optimality Theory. *Linguistic Inquiry* 29(2), 229–68.

Turkel, W. (1994) The acquisition of Optimality Theoretic systems. MS, Department of Linguistics. University of British Columbia. ROA–11.

Walther, M. (1996) OT SIMPLE – a construction kit approach to Optimality Theory implementation. ROA–152.

11

Impossible Words?

Jerry Fodor and Ernest Lepore

The idea that quotidian, middle-level concepts typically have internal structure – definitional, statistical, or whatever – plays a central role in practically every current approach to cognition. Correspondingly, the idea that words that express quotidian, middle-level concepts have complex representations "at the semantic level" is recurrent in linguistics; it's the defining thesis of what is often called *lexical semantics*, and it unites the generative and interpretive traditions of grammatical analysis. We're not going to survey that whole issue here; but recently, Hale and Keyser[1] have endorsed a version of lexical decomposition according to which "denominal" verbs are typically derived from phrases containing the corresponding nouns: "sing$_{vtr}$" is supposed to come from something like DO A SONG; "saddle$_{vtr}$" is supposed to come from something like PUT A SADDLE ON; "shelve$_{vtr}$" is supposed to come from something like PUT ON A SHELF, and so forth.[2] Their case for these claims revives a form of argument, the "impossible word" argument, which has been for some time in eclipse. The present essay will claim that, whatever the right story about lexical decomposition eventually turns out to be, impossible word arguments are infirm and should be discounted. We will use the Hale and Keyser article as a text for this critique.

HK's arguments for the derivational analysis of denominal verbs are all variations on the same general theme. The derivational account predicts/explains the intuitive impossibility of certain verbs by showing that the syntactic processes that would be required to derive them are prohibited by independently well-confirmed grammatical constraints. We think there are principled objections to this form of argument. So, rather than squabble, we're prepared to take HK's word as to what grammatical constraints are independently well-confirmed; if they say that a derivation is blocked, we'll assume that indeed it is. (We remark in passing, however, that a number of our linguistic friends have cautioned us against conceding (e.g.) that structures like (11) (below) violate the Empty Category Principle (ECP). No comment.)

Since we think that their logic – hence their limitations – has not been made clear in the literature, we start by trying to be explicit about how "impossible word" arguments are supposed to run. Three points about them will be assumed throughout our discussion.

(1) The *conclusion* of an impossible word argument is that there is plausible evidence for a grammatical rule/operation of *lexicalization*. (For exposition, we assume that lexicalization is a transformation.) The defining property of lexicalization is that it derives a surface lexical item from an underlying semantic representation. In the cases of interest:

(1.1) the presumed underlying representation has internal constituent structure (in effect, it's a phrase), and

(1.2) the surface item is more or less synonymous[3] with the semantic representation that it's derived from.

(2) The basic form of argument for lexicalization is that it satisfies independently motivated constraints on syntactic rules. Since it does, a grammar that fails to recognize lexicalization thereby misses a certain generalization: namely, that the formation rules for lexical items are a species of the formation rules for overtly complex linguistic structures like phrases.

(3) The evidence for (2) is that lexicalizations that violate such independently motivated grammatical constraints produce intuitively "impossible words." Impossible words correspond not to *de facto* gaps in the lexicon, but to expressions that couldn't occur in a language modulo the grammatical universals.[4] In fact, all HK's examples are of the following form (see HK, 60–4): We're given a sentence that contains a neologistic verb, together with a paraphrase; and what is explained by appeal to the putative independently motivated grammatical constraints is why the former couldn't be derived from the latter. (More precisely, why the former couldn't be derived from the representation that directly underlies the latter.) HK says that the existence of constraints which block these derivations explains why "English simply does not have verbs . . . [that] . . . have meanings corresponding more or less to the . . . paraphrases given here" (HK, 59–60).

We especially wish to emphasize how this sort of argument fits into the discussion about lexical decomposition (i.e., about whether surface lexical items sometimes have complex semantic representations underlying them). From that perspective, the interest is not in whether there are impossible words; it is not even in how to explain why impossible words are impossible. The question of interest is: *Does the putative explanation of why they are impossible offer an argument for lexicalization*; that is, does it offer an argument that some surface lexical items are derived from underlying phrasal representations. We'll argue that it doesn't and couldn't.

Prima facie, there are two kinds of ways in which constraints on possible lexical items might be predicted from general properties of grammatical derivations. Roughly, it might turn out that the derivation of a lexical item is blocked because it would violate some independently motivated constraint on the *kinds of grammatical rules* there can be, or because it violates some independently motivated constraint on the *kinds of structures* that grammatical rules are allowed to generate.[5] (Though they don't discuss this difference, HK actually offer examples of both kinds.) It will be convenient for our exposition to consider these two kinds of blocked derivations separately, since reasons why neither can provide evidence for lexicalization are slightly different. But it's well to keep the bottom line in mind: We claim that neither of these kinds of impossible word argument can work. And since, as far as we can tell, these two are all the kinds of impossible word arguments that there could be, we also claim that impossible word arguments are infirm in principle: *no "impossible word" argument could be evidence for lexicalization.*

> Case 1: The derivation is blocked because a rule (a movement rule in all the examples that HK give) that the derivation depends on is impossible.

For example, HK claims that there couldn't be a verb "to cow" such that (1) is well-formed and means a *cow had a calf.*

(1) *It cowed a calf.

Here's their explanation of why this is so: Since, by assumption, lexical items typically derive from the structures that underlie their phrasal synonyms, sentence (1) would presumably come from the same structure as underlies sentence (2).

(2) A cow had a calf.

The structure of (2) is presumably (3), and the derivation would crucially depend on a transformation of subject lowering (followed by insertion of dummy "it" in the surface subject position).

(3)

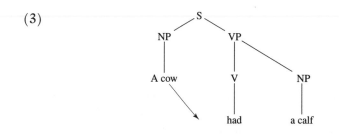

But, as HK remarks: "It is well known that a subject . . . cannot incorporate into the verb that heads its predicate." Since *subject lowering* is an illicit operation, the putative derivation (3) is impossible – hence the intuition that (1) too is impossible.

Preliminary comment: We think that this account isn't plausible even independently of the general issues about lexical decomposition. In effect, HK traces the non-existence of (1) to a (presumably universal) prohibition against transformations that lower subjects into predicates. Notice, however, that (4) is also impossible on the reading (1). However, the derivation of (4) requires, not lowering the subject NP, but raising the predicate (followed by insertion of dummy "do" in the surface verb position). Since (4) is impossible, the derivation (5) presumably has to be blocked.

(4) *A cow did a calf

(5)

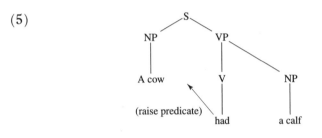

But, presumably (4) can't be blocked by a prohibition against raising predicates, since doing so is required to derive (e.g.) causative transitives from their intransitive counterparts, as in (6). (6) is, in fact, a kind of derivation of which HK approves (see HK, 79).

(6)

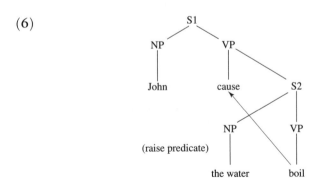

The symmetry between (1) and (4) suggests that the right explanation of the impossibility of the former isn't that subject lowering is illegal. Rather, it's that deriving either (1) or (3) from (4) would involve lexicalizing an expression that isn't itself a well-formed constituent, namely a "cow did". That lexicalizing a non-constituent is illegal would presumably follow just from the assumption that lexicalization is a transformation; in any case, it is widely taken for granted in the generative semantics literature that only constituents can be lexicalized.

But we don't insist on this analysis. We are about to present an argument that *neither* examples where derivations block because *the rules that they employ* are illegal *nor* derivations that block because *the structures that they generate* are illegal can provide evidence for lexicalization. Here is our complaint about the first disjunct.

There *must* be something wrong with the HK account of cases like (1) since, even if it did explain why there couldn't be a *derived* verb "to cow" with the paraphrase (2), it doesn't explain why there couldn't be a *primitive*, underived verb "to cow" with the paraphrase (2). As far as we can tell, this sort of point applies to any attempt to explain why a word is impossible by reference to the impossibility of a certain transformation. By definition, "impossible word" arguments purport to explain intuitions of the form "there couldn't be a word *w* that means *e*" by showing that $\ulcorner e \urcorner$ couldn't be a derivational source for *w*. But, on the face of it, this doesn't show that there couldn't be a word that means *e*; the most it could show is that if there *is* a word that means *e*, then it must be primitive.[6] We assume, along with HK, that the intuition about (1) is that it is *impossible* – not just that *if* it's possible, then it's derived. (We don't suppose that anybody, except maybe some linguists, *has* intuitions of the latter kind.) So we claim, contrary to the advertising, that HK haven't explained the intuition that "to cow" is impossible.

We repeat that this sort of complaint holds in any case where a derivation is said to be blocked by the lack of transformations that would construct an appropriate domain for lexicalization; as, for example, the lack of a subject-lowering transformation is supposed to explain why there is no "the cow had" to provide a domain for the introduction of "cowed". Assuming that *a cow had* is a well-formed meaning, HK's sort of account provides no explanation of why there couldn't be a primitive lexical item "cowed" that means *a cow had*. Likewise in the general case: *assuming that* e *is a well-formed meaning*, the assumption that the derivation of the corresponding expression $\ulcorner e \urcorner$ is blocked doesn't explain why *e* can't be the meaning of a primitive lexical item, *whether or not* $\ulcorner e \urcorner$ is syntactically derivable.

It may be well explicitly to distinguish the two kinds of theories mentioned in note 2. Presumably $\ulcorner e \urcorner$ is underivable either because *the grammar of English* lacks the relevant rules or because *no grammar of a natural language* could have the relevant rules. In the first case, the most that would follow is that, if *w* is a lexical primitive, it can't be defined *in English* (i.e., there is no phrase in English that is synonymous with *w*). In the second case, the most that would follow is that if *w* is a lexical primitive, then it can't be defined in *any* natural language. It would then require further argument to show that if the meaning of *w* can't be defined in a natural language, *w* is *ipso facto* an impossible word.

(It's not obvious that such arguments would be forthcoming, given the empirical plausability of the claim that the majority of lexically primitive expressions in every natural language are not definable).

It's important to bear in mind, at this point, what in our view impossible word arguments are forever forgetting: What is supposed to make a word impossible is that there is something defective *about its meaning*; that is, that what makes it impossible that *w* should mean *e* is that *e isn't a possible meaning*. (Patently, if *e* isn't a possible meaning, then you don't need an explanation of why no word can mean it.) But how could any conclusion of that sort follow from a demonstration that ⌜*e*⌝ isn't derivable from the grammar of a (or any) natural language? Maybe it's derivable in Fortran. We suspect that impossible word arguments are up to their ears in a use/mention confusion; in particular, in the confusion of "the expression ⌜*e*⌝ isn't possible" (which is what instances of the argument actually show when they are successful) with "the meaning *e* isn't possible" (which is what using impossible word arguments to defend lexicalization would actually require). There may be sound arguments the conclusion of which take the form *e is not a possible meaning*, but we don't know what they would look like; and we're pretty sure that we've never seen one. (Notice that even *round square* is a possible meaning; in fact, it's what "round square" means in English.)

> Case 2: The derivation is blocked because the structure it generates is impossible. (The constraint is on the product rather than the process.)

HK doesn't always assume that what blocks derivations in their examples is a prohibition against moving a certain constituent to (or from) a certain position (e.g., the putative principle that there can't be a transformation that lowers a subject into a predicate). Sometimes the constraint is, rather, on the form of the tree that a derivation *would* produce if it were legal. Here is HK's explanation of why there can't be a verb "shelve . . . on" such that (9) is grammatical and means (10).[7]

> (*9) He shelved the books on.
> (10) He put the books on a shelf.

> Each of these hypothetical items, *shelve (books) on* . . . is derived by incorporation of the noun that heads the complement of the preposition, as shown in [11]. The trace of incorporation is thus "too far" from its antecedent and is therefore not properly governed, violating ECP. Although the trace is co-indexed with the verb to which its antecedent is adjoined (as indicated by the asterisk notation), this verb does not govern the trace. The preposition is a "closer governor," defining PP as the minimal governing domain for the trace . . . By Minimality, therefore, PP is a barrier to government from the more distant verb. (HK, 61)

(11)

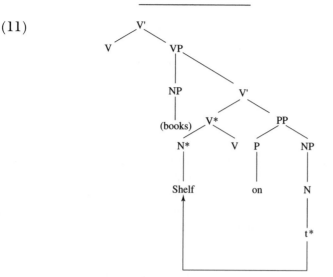

The long and the short of it is that (10) can't come from (9) because (9) is illegal; and that (9) is illegal because (11) violates a constraint on variable binding that well-formed formulas are *ipso facto* required to comply with. Notice, crucially, that this explanation would account for why (9) is ungrammatical *whether or not the putative verb "shelve . . . on" is supposed to be derived; a fortiori* whether or not (9) is supposed to be derived from (10). In particular, *ECP would block (9) even if "shelve . . . on" is primitive and is base-generated.* So, in this sort of case, HK's explanation of the "impossible" form really does explain why it is *impossible.* Compare case 1 where the fact that the derivation of (1) was blocked showed only that if "to cow" is possible, then it must be primitive. So HK's account of case 2 has the virtue that their account of case 1 crucially lacked.

However, it also has the defects that go with this virtue. Remember that the whole point of running an impossible word argument *is to provide evidence for lexicalization*: that is, to provide evidence for inferring that there is a grammatical process that derives surface lexical items from complex, phrasal underlying structures. So, the assumption that lexicalization respects independent constraints on derivations was supposed to explain why intuitively impossible words *are* impossible; and the fact that, *if lexicalization obeys independent constraints on derivations, it explains why impossible words are impossible*, was supposed to be the evidence that there is such a process.

But how would this pattern of inference go in the present case? If (9) is ill-formed for the reason that HK alleges – that is, because there is a mandatory constraint that the structure (11) fails to meet – then, patently, (9) is ill-formed *whether or not* there is a lexicalization transformation. Indeed, on the present assumption, the ill-formedness of (9) depends entirely on features of its geometry; it's, as it were, intrinsic and hence independent of *any* assumption about how (9) was derived. But if (9) would be ill-formed *whether or not* there is a grammatical process of lexicalization, how could the fact that it *is* ill-formed be evidence for such a process? We assume it's a general principle, not in dispute, that *if Q whether or not P, then P isn't evidence for Q.*

Conclusion

"Generative semanticists" and "interpretive semanticists" both hold that some surface lexical items are represented by phrases at (some of) the level(s) of grammatical representation at which semantic interpretations are assigned. The difference is that generative semanticists also think that such surface lexical items are *derived from* the corresponding underlying phrases. The strategy of "impossible word" arguments is to provide evidence for the stronger claim by showing that the derivations of certain lexical items would be blocked by independently motivated grammatical constraints, and that, when they are, the corresponding lexical items are intuitively impossible.

We claim, however, that all such arguments are either too weak or too strong to support the thesis that the derivation of words from phrases is a *bona fide* grammatical process. In one kind of case, it is left open that *underivable* works might not be *impossible* (i.e., because it's left open that they might be primitive); in the other kind of case, precisely because the blocked structures are ungrammatical in virtue of their geometry rather than their derivational histories, their being ill-formed provides no evidence for or against there being such a process as lexicalization.

Anyhow, quite aside from the relatively mechanical questions that have primarily concerned us, there is a *prima facie* reason to think that "impossible word" arguments must be deeply crazy. In effect, such arguments infer conclusions of the form "*e* isn't a possible word meaning" from premises of the form "$\ulcorner e \urcorner$ isn't derivable in a certain grammar." Now it's true that, once upon a time, philosophers dreamt of a "logically perfect" language in which all and only the *meaningful (verifiable?) (truth-evaluable?)* sentences would be *syntactically* well-formed (see, e.g., Wittgenstein in the *Tractatus*). But even philosophers never thought that you could formalize English in such a language; the most they hoped for was to formalize mathematics or physics. In any case, these days everybody thinks that both projects are hopeless. Our point is that the inference from "$\ulcorner e \urcorner$ is underivable" to "*e* isn't a possible meaning" would be sound *only on the assumption that $\ulcorner e \urcorner$ is an expression in such a language.* So cognitive scientists who buy into the impossible word arguments are thereby committed to a kind of linguistic utopianism that even philosophers are unable to believe.

Barring blatant confusions of use with mention, such facts as that there is no rule of subject raising, or that ECP controls variable binding, say *nothing at all about what words are possible.* All they tell us is exactly what they seem to: namely, why sentences like (1) and (9) aren't grammatical.[8]

Notes

1 Hale, K. and Keysor, S., "On argument structure and the lexical expression of syntactic relations," in K. Hale and S. Keyser (eds), *The View from Building 20* (Cambridge, MA: MIT Press) 53–109; hereafter HK.

2 We use capital letters for canonical names of semantic representations and italics for canonical names of meanings. (So, according to the decompositional view of causatives, "kill" derives from CAUSE TO DIE and means *cause to die*.) However, for convenience, we will sometimes not distinguish between a semantic representation and the corresponding surface phrase; e.g., we'll say that "kill" is derived from "cause to die" to abbreviate the view that "kill" and "cause to die" are both derived from CAUSE TO DIE. Corner quotes (⌜ ⌝) enclose variables that range over quoted formulas.

3 There is considerable unclarity in the lexical semantics literature about just what meaning relations are required to hold between a lexical item and the semantic representation from which it is derived. Some claim, for example, that such derivations capture only the core or paradigmatic meaning(s) of surface lexical items. We will be neutral on this issue. We're concerned with the evidential status of the claim that surface lexical items ever derive from underlying phrases, whatever semantic relations such derivations are supposed to preserve.

4 We are assuming that the constraints in question are universal. A weaker view might relativize the impossibility of lexical items to particular languages; (e.g., *w* is impossible *in English* if its derivation would require rules or structures that English grammar happens not to acknowledge. As we understand them, impossible word arguments generally have the stronger notion of constraint in mind. But the considerations we will raise don't depend on the distinction.

5 This corresponds to the familiar distinction between derivations that block because they don't terminate and derivations that block because they generate structures that are subsequently filtered.

6 We put it this way because, strictly speaking a demonstration that ⌜*e*⌝ isn't well-formed could only show that if *w* is possible and derived, it can't be derived from ⌜*e*⌝. Notice that this would leave open not just that *w* is derived, but that it is derived *and means e*: The derivational source of *w* might be some *phrasal synonym* of ⌜*e*⌝.

7 Notice that (10) expresses a possible meaning (in fact, it expresses the meaning that "He put the books on the shelf" actually has). This seems to be a clear case where the question "What expressions are syntactically derivable?" has been confused with the question "What lexical items are (semantically) possible?" However, the discussion that follows does not rely on this criticism. (It adds to the confusion that expressions like "phone up" may well be complex words – i.e., lexical items with internal constituent structure. This is *not*, however, the sort of analysis HK is imagining for "shelve . . . on" in (9). In particular, the structure HK is considering is one where "the shelf" is the object of the preposition "on", not one where it's the object of a complex verb "shelve on".)

8 A slightly different version of this chapter was first published in *Linguistic Inquiry* 30(3), 1999.

12

Bridging the Symbolic–Connectionist Gap in Language Comprehension

Suzanne Stevenson

1 Symbolic and Connectionist Paradigms

Over the past two decades, a significant debate has been waged within the field of cognitive science over the appropriate computational paradigm within which models of human knowledge and intelligent behavior should be cast. The traditional symbolic approach views information processing in the mind as discrete, rule-governed computation, applied to hierarchical structures with explicit symbolic content (Fodor 1975; Newell 1990). Within this paradigm, the complexity of human behavior is reflected in the complexity of both mental representations and the cognitive processes that operate on them. The conectionist approach, by contrast, conceives mental computation as the parallel operation of "soft" (continuously valued) constraints. On this view, the individual components of the cognitive system are quite restricted in power, and complex behavior is the result of a large number of simple numeric processors working in concert (Feldman and Ballard 1982; Rumelhart et al. 1986; Smolensky 1988). The consequences of these divergent computational positions are not limited to "implementational details" of a cognitive model – rather, the underlying information-processing paradigm that is assumed can determine to a large degree the nature of a cognitive theory and the behavior that it can explain. These two approaches thus represent fundamentally opposing positions on what constitutes human intelligence.

The central issues of the symbolic-connectionist debate are currently in the forefront of the study of language comprehension. Modern linguistics has been dominated by the search for a set of hierarchical structures and rules that can represent our abstract linguistic knowledge (e.g. Chomsky 1957; Bresnan

1982; Chomsky 1986; among numerous others). Traditional theories of how that knowledge is used in language comprehension have assumed that the structures and rules that are postulated in the linguistic theory are directly encoded within the human language processor (Kimball 1973; Frazier 1978; Bresnan 1982; Pritchett 1988). Following the focus on syntax in generative grammar, the dominant theoretical approach has emphasized the role of syntactic structure in shaping interpretation, and structure-based rules have long been the definitive component of language comprehension models (Kimball 1973; Frazier 1978; Frazier and Rayner 1982; Clifton and De Vincenzi 1990; Ferreira and Henderson 1991). However, connectionist researchers have questioned the ability of a discrete, symbolic, structure-based approach to capture the flexibility and adaptation to experience that are crucial in human language processing (McClelland and Kawamoto 1986; St John and McClelland 1990). Recently, a connectionist-inspired paradigm known as the lexicalist constraint-based approach has gained prominence within the field of language comprehension (McDonald et al. 1994; Trueswell and Tanenhaus 1994).[1] This approach de-emphasizes the role of global structural operations, instead largely attributing crucial behaviors in language processing to the combined effect of individual sub-properties of words and their frequency of usage and association (e.g., among many others, Juliano and Tanenhaus 1994; MacDonald 1994; Spivey-Knowlton and Sedivy 1995; Trueswell 1996).

The tension between these two theoretical positions on language comprehension has triggered considerable progress in the field by inspiring novel experimental and computational investigations, but it has also led to a polarization of theories of the human language processor. The view espoused here is that neither approach alone can explain the range of empirical evidence that has accumulated over the last several decades of experimental research in language comprehension. The traditional, structure-based approaches are very rigid and have difficulty in consistently accommodating continuous behavioral effects in their theories. On the other hand, the lexicalist constraint-based approaches are very unconstrained and fail to explain sharp contrasts in behavior. This chapter describes an alternative information-processing paradigm that addresses these complementary shortcomings by integrating critical aspects of both approaches, in an attempt to reconcile the disparate views underlying the debate.

2 Ambiguity in Language Comprehension

The specific goal of language comprehension research is to discover the mental representations used to encode linguistic structures, and to determine the cognitive operations that create and interpret them. As in many areas of scientific endeavor, the mechanism that we are trying to understand is concealed: we observe only the output behavior of the language-processing system and must hypothesize a model that would produce that behavior. Specifically, the output behaviors we are interested in are ones that reveal the interpretation, or meaning, assigned by the human language processor to some sentence. Part of the meaning is dictated by the grammar of the language, which we assume is a component of the knowledge of the human language processor. But the grammar of the language seldom determines uniquely the interpretation of a sentence, because of the prevalence of ambiguity at all levels of linguistic knowledge. If there are two or more possible interpretations for a sentence, our grammatical knowledge will dictate the appropriate representation for each, but will say nothing about which is the *best* interpretation. People, however, tend to focus on a single meaning for a sentence and in fact show consistent preferences in how they interpret ambiguous sentences. The assumption is that if knowledge of grammar allows multiple valid interpretations of an ambiguous input, then it must be computational properties of the human language processor – its representational abilities and cognitive operations – that are responsible for the observed preferences in interpretation. Thus, by determining which interpretation of an ambiguity people generally prefer at critical points in processing, we can infer hidden computational properties of the language comprehension mechanism.

This chapter will discuss how different information-processing assumptions yield different views of the processing of ambiguity in human language comprehension. The focus will be on the processing of syntactic, or structural, ambiguities, which most clearly highlight the debate between the structure-based and constraint-based approaches. Syntactic ambiguities arise when a sequence of words can be assigned different structures by the grammar. For example, in sentence (1a), the prepositional phrase *with the telescope* can be structured together with the noun *child*, as in (1b), or with the verb *saw*, as in (1c):

(1a)   Jane saw the child with the telescope.
(1b)   Jane saw [the child [with the telescope]].
(1c)   Jane [saw [the child] [with the telescope]].

It is important to observe that the structure assigned to the sentence contributes to its interpretation. The structure of (1b) entails that *with the telescope* modifies *the child*, indicating that the child has the telescope. The structure of (1c) entails that *with the telescope* modifies the action of seeing, indicating that Jane has the telescope (and is looking through it). This clearly illustrates that syntactic structure is one important determinant of the meaning of a sentence, and, furthermore, that focusing on syntactic structure does not indicate a disregard for meaning in language comprehension – it simply means attending to one well-understood aspect of meaning.

Typically, investigations of the human language processor look at *temporary* ambiguities – ambiguities that arise during the incremental processing of a sentence over time, and are resolved (or disambiguated) by the end of the sentence. Temporary ambiguities are an important source of information, because they allow us to investigate two facets of language comprehension: what the initially preferred interpretation of an ambiguity is, and how the language processor responds to additional input over time that may change that interpretation. For example, consider our intuitive reaction over the course of a sentence like (2) (adapted from Charniak 1983):

(2)   The astronomer gazed at the star, dreaming of marrying him.

We observe that, in the context of *astronomer*, the word *star* is initially interpreted as meaning "celestial body"; later, in the context of *marrying*, its interpretation is revised to something like "famous actor." This example involves an ambiguity at the word level (due to *star* having two meanings), but temporary ambiguities may also be syntactic (involving the structuring of a group of words). As words are heard or read, the language processor attempts to structure them immediately according to syntactic knowledge, which, as noted above, often allows multiple alternatives. For example, in a sentence such as (3a) below, the noun phrase *the president* may be the direct object of the verb *know*, as in (3b), or may instead be the subject of a subordinate clause that is the direct object, as in (3c).

(3a)   Mary knows the president . . .
(3b)   Mary knows the president very well.
(3c)   Mary knows the president will win.

When presented with syntactically ambiguous input, people quickly focus on a single interpretation and are typically not even aware that there are other possible meanings. One method of investigation is to observe, through appropriate experiments, the interpretation that people initially fix on when processing a temporary ambiguity. From a set of experimental results, we can then infer the properties of the comprehension mechanism that lead to the observed choices.

As in the word-level ambiguity of sentence (2), we can also examine how the initial resolution of a syntactic ambiguity is affected by additional input over time. For an input such as (3a), either continuation of the ambiguous initial string is easily understood. Sometimes, however, a temporary ambiguity must be assigned a strongly dispreferred structure, leading to difficulties of interpretation and even processing breakdown. For example, sentence (4a) is generally found to be uninterpretable (Pritchett 1988), yet it *is* grammatical, as indicated by the syntactically equivalent and unambiguous sentence in (4b).

(4a)   Jo gave the child the dog bit a hug. (≡ *Jo gave the child that the dog bit a hug.*)
(4b)   Jo gave the child she knew a hug.

In (4a), people overwhelmingly prefer to interpret the ambiguous initial input (*Jo gave the child the dog*) as a complete sentence, and appear to not even consider the alternative structure, in which *the dog* is the subject of a relative clause modifying *the child* (i.e., *the child* (that) *the dog* . . .). In contrast to the example in (3c), here the language processor experiences great difficulty when the continuation of the input requires the initially dispreferred analysis. Difficulty in processing a dispreferred continuation of a temporary ambiguity can provide additional clues about the language processor. In particular, it can reveal the computational limitations on the comprehension mechanism that restrict its ability to incrementally extend and revise interpretations.

The processing of temporary structural ambiguities has been a rich source of experimental data relevant to the investigation of the computational properties of the human language processor. The remainder of this chapter discusses the consequences of different information-processing assumptions for the interpretation of this data.

3   Structure-based versus Constraint-based Theories

The incremental processing of temporary ambiguities raises a number of issues that are critical in formulating a theory of the human language processor. Here the focus will be on the following questions and their relation to the different information-processing assumptions:

- Preference factors: Given a structurally ambiguous input, how does the processor decide which of the possible alternative structures yields the preferred interpretation?
- Degree of parallelism: Does the processor create and maintain all possible structures, or does it immediately restrict itself to a single alternative?
- Processing breakdown: If the initially preferred alternative turns out to be incompatible with the remainder of the sentence, how easily can the processor revise its preference?

Each of these seemingly simple questions relates to critical properties of a theory of the human language processor, and all remain the object of intense investigation and debate in the study of language comprehension. Table 12.1 briefly summarizes the answers given by the structure-based and constraint-based approaches, highlighting the fundamental difference in view that their underlying assumptions give rise to. Note that the classifications do not refer to a single proposal, but rather to the predominant characteristics of the traditional and connectionist *class* of theories. The computational characteristics of each type of approach are discussed below, in the context of behavioral evidence supporting each property. This summary is not intended to be a comprehensive survey of experimental work supporting the two positions.

Table 12.1 Comparison of structure-based and constraint-based models

Property	Structure-based	Constraint-based
Preference factors	structure-based rules	soft constraints
Degree of parallelism	serial	parallel
Processing breakdown	discrete	gradual

Rather, the aim is to illustrate how each class of theory answers these critical questions and to give examples of the types of evidence used to support these divergent views.

The primary characteristic of traditional, structure-based approaches is that the preferred interpretation of an ambiguity is determined by rules that refer to the syntactic properties of the alternatives. This assumption accords with numerous experiments supporting the role of structure in initial comprehension (e.g. Frazier and Rayner 1982; Ferriera and Clifton 1986). It is also generally assumed that the processor is a serial mechanism, maintaining only this single preferred interpretation. Evidence for a strict serial approach includes the consistent, strong preferences for a single reading in the incremental interpretation of syntactically ambiguous input, as well as increased difficulties in processing the less preferred continuation of an ambiguity (Ferreira and Henderson 1993; Frazier and Rayner 1982). If the preferred interpretation is incompatible with subsequent input, then the processor is also guided by structure-based rules in the attempt to adapt its single interpretation. A successful application of the rules leads to a revisable analysis, and an unsuccessful attempt to apply the rules leads to processing breakdown (Frazier and Clifton 1998). Evidence for this kind of discrete cut-off occurs in the contrast between less preferred continuations of an ambiguity which cause no conscious awareness, as in (3c), and those which appear impossible under normal processing, as in (4a).

The lexicalist constraint-based paradigm answers each of the above questions very differently, beginning with the assumption that the processor initially activates all possible interpretations of an input in parallel (MacDonald et al. 1994). Relative preferences among the interpretations are indicated by levels of activation, as in a connectionist network – the higher the activation of some processing unit, the stronger the commitment to the analysis in which it participates. Soft (continuously valued) constraints, such as frequency information, are assumed to play a critical role in determining levels of activation, reflecting the influence of prior linguistic experience.[2] Multiple interpretations are thus maintained in parallel, with levels of activation indicating relative preference. Strong evidence exists for such parallel activation: signs of competition among alternative interpretations (MacDonald 1994), the anticipation of the less preferred continuation (Gorrell 1987; Juliano and Tanenhaus 1994; Trueswell et al. 1993), and the lack of conscious awareness of there even

being an ambiguity in a sentence such as (3c). Ease of revising an interpretation is predicted to lie along a continuous scale, largely determined by the
strength (derived from frequency and salience) with which the input supports
the new interpretation. Frequency and salience effects have been demonstrated
experimentally in both initial and revised interpretations (MacDonald et al.
1994; Trueswell et al. 1993; Trueswell 1996).

Note that the experimental data concerning each computational aspect of
language comprehension in table 12.1 appears contradictory, or at best
inconclusive. There are indications that both structure and numerical constraints have the primary effect in determining preferences, signs of both
serialism and parallelism in maintaining alternatives, and evidence in the
revision of preferences for both a gradual increase in difficulty as well as a
sharp breakdown in processing. One conclusion might be that the data, or
some large subset of it, is suspect. An alternative hypothesis, adopted here, is
that the overall experimental data convey an accurate picture of the human
language processor, and that the problem resides instead within the basic
assumptions of the theoretical positions. The suggestion is that the sharp
division into the traditional (structure-based) versus connectionist (constraint-
based) camps prevents either side from providing an account of the full range
of the data. While each of these two types of approaches appears compatible
with certain aspects of human behavior in language comprehension, each also
has its limitations due to founding principles of the underlying information-
processing paradigm. The chapter turns next to a description of a third
information-processing paradigm that integrates symbolic and connectionist
principles in an effective way.

4   Integration of the Approaches

In computer science, the goal of an information-processing paradigm is to
provide the computational primitives – a representational formalism and
processing operations – that can serve as the appropriate building blocks for a
class of systems. To be successful, an information-processing paradigm must
support the modeling of a domain at a level of abstraction that allows the
system designer to capture the relevant properties of the represented knowledge and achieve the appropriate behavioral characteristics of the domain in
question. Likewise, in cognitive science, an information-processing paradigm
must provide the primitives with which to model human cognitive processing
at an appropriate level of abstraction. For language processing, the representation and operations must accommodate both the rich linguistic knowledge
posited by linguistic theory, and the fine-grained, on-line behaviors that we
observe experimentally. The problem with the predominant paradigms for
language comprehension is that neither one provides the right level of
abstraction for both these aspects of our linguistic capacity. The traditional

Symbolic theories

Abstract formal system: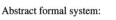

Cognitive processing:

Neural processing: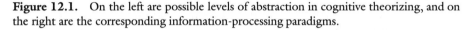

Connectionist theories

Figure 12.1.   On the left are possible levels of abstraction in cognitive theorizing, and on the right are the corresponding information-processing paradigms.

symbolic approach – the foundation of the structure-based models – successfully encodes our abstract grammatical knowledge and its discrete consequences, but maintains too high a level of abstraction to adequately model finer-grained effects in the use of that knowledge. On the other hand, the connectionist paradigm – the inspiration for the constraint-based proposals – successfully captures fine-grained experiential effects on processing behavior, but operates at too low a level of abstraction, the basic metaphor of neuron-like processing being far removed from our formalisms for complex symbolic knowledge. Figure 12.1 illustrates these different information-processing approaches and the gap between them with respect to the possible levels of abstraction of cognitive theory.

Smolensky (1990) addresses the discrepancy between symbolic formalisms and neural processing by developing a connectionist technique for encoding symbolic structural relations through the composition of numeric vector operations. This method essentially maps from the level of abstract linguistic knowledge directly to the neurally-inspired substrate (skipping the "?" in figure 12.1). The approach allows the expression of symbolic relations within a pure connectionist network, capturing the desirable characteristics of connectionist processing (such as distributed representations and graceful degradation). However, the mapping from the linguisic theory and parsing operations to their implementation is quite indirect. An alternative approach is to introduce an information-processing paradigm at an intermediate level of abstraction of "cognitive processing" (indicated by the "?" in the figure), which can effectively interface with abstract grammatical theories, but can also support the encoding of continuous effects on behavior. Adding this cognitive processing level may sacrifice some of the advantages of a pure connectionist approach, but in exchange could enable a transparent expression of linguistic knowledge and parsing operations.

We have developed a novel computational framework, called the competitive attachment model, that takes a step toward the development of such an information-processing paradigm for language comprehension, in an attempt to bridge the gap between abstract linguistic knowledge and brain-like processing mechanisms (Stevenson 1993a, 1993b, 1994a; Stevenson and Merlo 1997). Our approach, like the proposal in Smolensky (1990), attempts to achieve symbolic computation within a connectionist framework. However, instead of encoding symbolic knowledge with numeric functions, we take an alternative tack: the representations for symbolic and numeric information are distinct, but allow similar processing algorithms within a single network architecture. Our approach is motivated by the observation that, over the recent history of linguistic theory, formalisms for grammatical knowledge have progressed from elaborate sets of complicated rules to systems of simple, declarative constraints (Chomsky 1981; Rizzi 1990; Prince and Smolensky 1993; Grimshaw 1997; Bresnan 1998). The progression of linguistic theory towards a symbolic constraint-based formulation enables a more uniform treatment of symbolic and numeric constraint processing in the competitive attachment approach, with the potential to support a convergence between the structure-based and constraint-based views of language processing. While some approaches to modeling language comprehension have used symbolic constraint-based linguistic knowledge, it has not previously been explored within a computational approach that can exploit the similarities of symbolic and numeric constraints (e.g., Abney 1989; Fong 1991; Lin 1993; Merlo 1996).[3]

The competitive attachment framework falls within the class of hybrid connectionist approaches, in which symbolic and connectionist techniques are incorporated within a single computational model (Sun and Alexandre 1996). Hybrid connectionism is motivated by the desire to exploit the complementary strengths of symbolic and connectionist processing, but typically assumes that explicit symbolic processing and distributed numeric processing are incompatible. In particular, hybrid connectionist approaches to language processing have taken a modular approach, in which subsystems of a larger mechanism are separately formulated as either a traditional symbolic system or a connectionist network, depending on the sub-task performed (Waltz and Pollack 1985; Hendler 1987; Wermter and Lehnert 1989; Kwasny and Faisal 1992). The competitive attachment framework contrasts with these approaches that segregate symbolic and connectionist parsing algorithms; instead we inject simple symbolic processing abilities into a connectionist model. The competitive attachment theory has been implemented within a computational system to demonstrate the feasibility of this approach, and the results reported here are based on the actual performance of that system. (For more detail, see Stevenson 1994b.)

In the model, pieces of syntactic structures are explicitly represented by processing nodes and their pattern of connectivity within a connectionist network, as shown in figure 12.2. The network is created incrementally in response to a sequence of words comprising a sentence, and potential structural relations among syntactic phrases are activated in parallel. As in a pure

(a)   (b)

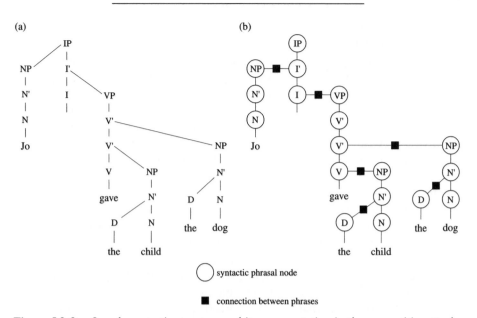

Figure 12.2.   Sample syntactic structure and its representation in the competitive attachment model. (a) The syntactic structure for *Jo gave the child the dog.* NP is noun phrase, VP is verb phrase, IP is inflection phrase (a sentence), D is determiner (or article). (b) The network representation of the sentence. The nodes in the syntactic tree in (a) are in a one-to-one correspondence with the processing nodes representing syntactic phrases in the network (the round nodes in (b)). Syntactic connections (attachments) between different phrases – the diagonal links in (a) – are also in a one-to-one relation with processing nodes in the network, themselves also being represented explicitly by processing nodes (the square nodes in (b)).

connectionist model, the interpretation of an input is determined solely through the local computations among the processing nodes, which focus activation onto a preferred structure. Unlike a pure connectionist system, the local computations operate on simple symbolic features as well as numeric activation values. A novel mechanism uses grammatical knowledge to control the local communication of symbolic features through the network, achieving a distributed formulation of a constraint-based linguistic theory (Government–Binding Theory) (Chomsky 1981; Rizzi 1990). Symbolic processing enforces grammatical constraints on potential structures in the network representation, while numeric processing enforces soft constraints, such as frequency. The model treats symbolic and numeric information uniformly as simple values to be propagated and combined by the individual nodes, thus establishing a new computational paradigm that tightly integrates the symbolic and connectionist frameworks.

The explicit symbolic content in the model places no constraints on the creation of structure aside from those enforced by the grammar – that is, the model has no explicit rules that guide the processing of ambiguity, as in traditional structure-based theories of comprehension. However, the unique formulation of the numeric functions within the approach entails that numeric processing does have significant consequences for the representation of potential structures. The goal of the numeric functions is to focus activation onto the preferred syntactic structure. Focusing of activation is typically achieved in a connectionist model through the use of inhibitory links, which explicitly dampen activation. In cognitive modeling, however, there is often little justification for explicit inhibitory relationships. (For discussion of this point, see Reggia et al. 1988.) Since the goal of this approach is to support computational modeling at the cognitive level (providing appropriate primitives for cognitive theorizing), the use of inhibitory links is prohibited within the framework. Activation is instead focused through a method known as *competition-based spreading activation*, in which processing nodes with a common neighbor compete for the output from that neighbor (Reggia et al. 1991). In contrast to the use of inhibitory links, this method cannot on its own prevent all potential incompatible syntactic structures in the network. To avoid the activation of invalid syntactic trees, an additional restriction must be imposed on the possible connections among the syntactic processing nodes. The simple restriction is that, as new syntactic phrases are allocated during the incremental processing of a sentence, they can be grouped only with earlier phrases that occur along the right edge of the existing syntactic structure represented by the network, as shown in figure 12.3. Maintaining this restriction further requires that only one syntactic structure for an input can be activated within the network at any given time.

Numeric processing in the framework thus not only directly encodes numeric influences; it also indirectly imposes stringent limitations on the number and type of structures representable within the network. Specifically, cognitively motivated restrictions on the (continuous) numeric functions lead to substantive discrete structural restrictions in the theory. This property places the model in sharp contrast with both constraint-based and structure-based approaches. In constraint-based approaches, all interpretations are in principle available, and only more or less activated. In structure-based approaches, interpretations are explicitly restricted by a set of symbolic rules, whose relation to underlying computational principles is often not clear. Here the set of potential interpretations is highly constrained, and the restrictions arise from independent properties of the computational architecture.

5   Behavior of the Hybrid Model

The consequences of the above properties can now be seen by examining the behavior of the competitive attachment model with respect to the computational properties listed in table 12.1. Recall that these properties relate to the fuller questions in section 3: (1) How are structural preferences determined? (2) Does the processor operate in serial or in parallel? (3) What factors affect

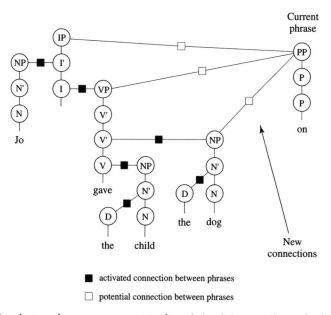

Figure 12.3. A new phrase can connect to the existing interpretation only along the right edge of the network representation in the model. The figure shows the connections established when the sentence *Jo gave the child the dog* is continued with the word *on*. The network of figure 12.2 must be extended along the right edge. The prepositional phrase (PP) for *on* cannot be grouped with *the child*, and thus can only modify the sentence, the verb phrase, or the noun phrase *the dog*, as shown.

the revision of preferred structures? The discussion of the model's answer to these questions will focus on a few simple examples to illustrate the general features of the framework in processing syntactic ambiguities.

In answer to the first question, both structural and numeric factors in the model play an important role in the determination of preferred interpretations. Consider the model at the point of processing the noun phrase *the president* in the sentence beginning *Mary knows the president* (as in example (3)). Activation in the network settles within a configuration in which *the president* is interpreted as the direct object of the verb *knows*, as shown in figure 12.4. Structural influences are responsible for this initial interpretation. Because the model activates the network incrementally, and there is no direct evidence of a subordinate clause at the time the noun phrase *the president* is processed, the direct object structure is the only alternative available to the model at that point. Similar structural factors entail that the model initially interprets the input *Jo gave the child the dog* as a simple main clause, having a direct and indirect object (see figure 12.2b above). Here again, there simply is no evidence from the input of a more complex structure (incorporating *the dog* into a modifying clause of *the child*, as in the less preferred alternative in example (4a)). The model thus exhibits general structural preferences as in the structure-based approach, but without the need for explicit structure-based

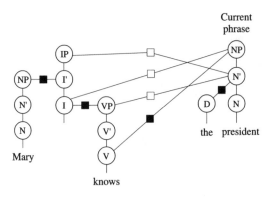

17 cycles of network processing

Figure 12.4. The network at the point of processing *the president* in the input beginning *Mary knows the president*. The noun phrase *the president* can only be structured as the direct object of *knows*, represented by the connection node between the V and NP nodes.

rules (as are needed in, e.g., Kimball 1973; Frazier 1978; Frazier and Rayner 1982; Frazier and Clifton 1998).

However, preference behavior is also immediately affected by numeric influences as well – for example, frequency or salience – as in a constraint-based approach. Given the input *Mary knows the president*, the frequency with which the main verb occurs with a noun phrase or sentential object determines the precise time required for activation to settle on the preferred interpretation. Even with no competing analyses, a higher or lower frequency value for a given interpretation will shorten or lengthen, respectively, the time for the structure to accrue sufficient activation to be considered a stable interpretation, as in experimental findings (Juliano and Tanenhaus 1994; Trueswell et al. 1993). The model also exhibits well-attested recency effects, due to the decay of activation of nodes over time. For example, given a choice between two or more interpretations, each of which complies with structural preferences, activation in the model will settle on the structure which involves the nodes that have been activated most recently, conforming to observed human behavior (Kimball 1973; Frazier 1978; Ferreira and Henderson 1991).

The second computational property of interest is that of serialism versus parallelism in maintaining interpretations of an ambiguity, and again in this model we see aspects of both. In the example beginning *Mary knows the president*, the pressure in the network to structure phrases together and to focus activation onto a single interpretation leads to a strong initial preference for *president* as the direct object, as in a serial model. However, as in a parallel approach, the model exhibits ease of incorporating the less preferred input if the sentence continues with the words *will win*. Figure 12.5 shows that the new subordinate clause structure becomes the new direct object of *knows*, and the noun phrase *the president* is successfully restructured as the subject of this sentential direct object. But the complexity of the new structure increases the

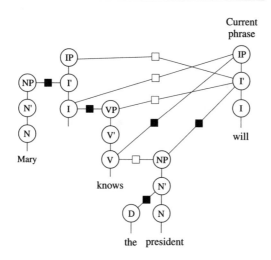

Current
phrase

Mary

knows

the   president

24 cycles of network processing

Figure 12.5.   The network at the point of processing *will* in the sentence *Mary knows the president will win*. When *will* is processed, the network is able to successfully revise its initial interpretation (as in figure 12.4), because the necessary restructuring involves nodes along the right edge of the network. The connection between *knows* and *the president* becomes deactivated; the new sentential phrase (IP) becomes the direct object of *knows*, and *the president* becomes its subject. Note that the restructuring here requires more cycles of network processing than the initial structuring in figure 12.4.

time required for activation in the network to stabilize, accounting for the longer reading times that have been claimed to support the serial approach (Frazier and Rayner 1982). Thus, the model exhibits the attested mix of serial and parallel behaviors.

The third question concerns the factors that contribute to the ease or difficulty of revising initially preferred interpretations. In the competitive attachment model, the same symbolic and numeric influences that affect initial structuring decisions are at work in their revision. As noted above, the model can easily process the dispreferred continuation in *Mary knows the president will win*, with only a small increase in processing time. Numeric influences entail that the model exhibits a gradual increase in the time needed to revise an earlier interpretation, proportional to a decrease in the recency of the nodes involved or in their frequency values (compare the evidence in Frazier and Rayner 1982; Ferreira and Henderson 1993; Trueswell et al. 1993). For example, if we lengthen the ambiguous region, as in *Mary knows the president of the club she joined will win*, or use a main verb that occurs less frequently with a sentential direct object, the network processing time at the subordinate verb *will* increases; an example is shown in figure 12.6.

In addition to these continuous numeric effects, we also observe the consequences of discrete structural factors. In particular, not all initial analyses are capable of being revised when needed. The restriction on network

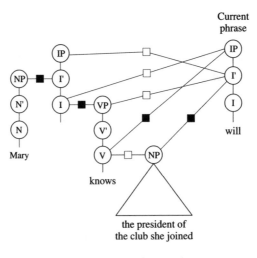

31 cycles of network processing

Figure 12.6. Lengthening the ambiguous region of a sentence increases the time for the network to settle on a new interpretation; compare the number of cycles here to the structurally equivalent situation in figure 12.5.

configurations that limits incremental growth to the right edge of the network determines a precise structural definition of possible revisions of interpretations. Consider sentence (4a), repeated here, which is extremely difficult to process.

> (4a) Jo gave the child the dog bit a hug. (≡ *Jo gave the child that the dog bit a hug.*)

As mentioned earlier, after processing the noun phrase *the dog*, the network has settled on a structure of the input conforming with human preferences, in which *the child* is the indirect object and *the dog* the direct object of the verb *gave*, as in figure 12.2b. A grammatical analysis incorporating the next word, *bit*, requires *the dog bit* to be structured together as a relative clause modifying the noun phrase *the child* (i.e., *the child* (that) *the dog bit*). As figure 12.7 illustrates, the necessary syntactic relationships are not representable within the network, because the noun phrase *the child* is not along the right edge of the network structure, so is not available for restructuring. (Figure 12.7 shows that there are no processing nodes in the network which relate the phrases for *the child* and *bit*, as would be required for a grammatical analysis of the sentence.) Thus, like constraint-based approaches, the competitive attachment model exhibits a gradual decrease in ease of revising interpretations, but, like traditional theories, can also experience a discrete breakdown determined by structural configurations.

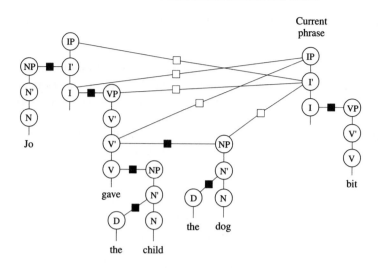

No new connections are formed

Figure 12.7.   The breakdown in processing on the difficult sentence *Jo gave the child the dog bit a hug*. The sentential phrase activated in response to *bit* needs to modify *the child* (as a relative clause) to form a grammatical interpretation of the input, but there are no potential connections between *the child* and the new sentence, since *the child* is no longer on the right edge of the network.

6   Consequences of the New Computational Framework

In summary, the unique hybrid connectionist approach of the competitive attachment model leads to interesting new answers to the computational questions raised earlier.

- Preference factors: Both structural restrictions and numeric information have an immediate influence on the time course of processing ambiguities and on the resulting preferences. Furthermore, the structural restrictions actually result from restrictive properties of the numeric functions, yielding a unique interaction of structural and numeric effects in a model of language comprehension.
- Degree of parallelism: A constrained set of structures is activated in parallel, but a competitive process focuses activation quickly onto a single preferred interpretation. Because the parallel competition includes both new attachments and old attachments, initial attachments and revision of prior attachments are determined uniformly.
- Processing breakdown: The exact same factors that play a role in initial preferences – both structural and numeric influences – affect the ease of revising incremental interpretations. Structural restrictions can even pre-

vent certain necessary restructuring operations, leading to processing breakdown.

The set of behaviors arises from fundamental properties of the model and conforms with a range of experimental data that appears inconsistent when viewed from the perspective of either the structure-based or the constraint-based approaches. The competitive attachment model, by unifying structural and numeric processing within a massively parallel network architecture, enables us to reconcile data previously interpreted as incompatible and to explain human behavior as a result of a particular pattern of interaction between structural and numeric influences.

Not surprisingly, the framework advocated here leads to "hybrid" answers to more general questions about the representations and operations used in language comprehension. Mental representations are conceived as structures with explicit symbolic content, but whose level of strength or preference is encoded by numeric activation. Cognitive operations consist of both construction (as in traditional approaches) and activation (as in connectionist approaches) of linguistic interpretations, which are crucially restricted by both structural and numeric properties. These properties result from a particular instantiation of a class of hybrid connectionism in which symbolic and numeric processing are truly integrated. The integrated hybrid information-processing paradigm is constrained "from above" by the symbolic and structural properties of formal linguistic theories and "from below" by the numeric properties of neural-inspired connectionist models (cf. figure 12.1), and appears to be a promising framework within which to model processes at the cognitive level, such as human language comprehension.

Notes

Thanks to Paola Merlo, Paul Smolensky, and Sven Dickinson for detailed comments on this manuscript. The research reported here is supported by the National Science Foundation, through NSF grant no. 9702331.

1   There is an unfortunate terminological confusion resulting from the overuse of the term "constraint-based". In linguistic theory, it typically refers to a statement of grammatical knowledge as a set of very general, declarative (symbolic) well-formedness conditions on a representation. In language processing, it typically refers to the evaluation of linguistic forms in terms of a large number of numerically weighted factors. In this chapter, it will of necessity (to be consistent with accepted usage) be used with both meanings: it is hoped that context will make clear which type of theory is being referred to.

2   Constraint-based approaches suggest that a number of features of the input are brought to bear as soft constraints on determining preferred interpretations. The focus here is on numeric constraints such as frequency, to illustrate clearly the contrast with the assumptions of the traditional models.

3   Other approaches are more similar to the framework here in attempting to unify the structural and numeric influences on language processing, but the uniformity in these approaches does not extend to the algorithms for creating linguistic structure (McRoy and Hirst 1990; Gibson 1991).

References

Abney, S. (1989) A computational model of human parsing, *Journal of Psycholinguistic Research* 18(1), 129–44.

Bresnan, J. (ed.) (1982) *The Mental Representation of Grammatical Relations*, Cambridge, MA: MIT Press.

Bresnan, J. (1998) Explaining morphosyntactic competition. In M. Baltin and C. Collins (eds), *Handbook of Contemporary Syntactic Theory*, Oxford: Blackwell, to appear.

Charniak, E. (1983) Passing markers: a theory of contextual influence in language comprehension. *Cognitive Science* 7, 171–90.

Chomsky, N. (1957) *Syntactic Structures*, The Hague: Mouton.

—— (1981) *Lectures on Government and Binding: The Pisa Lectures*, Dordrecht: Foris Publications.

—— (1986) *Knowledge of Language: Its Nature, Origin, and Use*. New York: Praeger.

Clifton, C. and De Vincenzi, M. (1990) Comprehending sentences with empty elements. In D. Balota, G. Flores d'Arcais and K. Rayner (eds), *Comprehension Processes in Reading*, Hillsdale, NJ: Lawrence Erlbaum, 265–83.

Feldman, J. and Ballard, D. (1982) Connectionist models and their properties. *Cognitive Science* 6, 205–54.

Ferreira, F. and Clifton, C. (1986) The independence of syntactic processing. *Journal of Memory and Language* 25, 348–68.

Ferreira, F. and Henderson, J. M. (1991) Recovery from misanalyses of garden-path sentences. *Journal of Memory and Language* 30, 725–45.

—— (1993) Reading processes during syntactic analysis and reanalysis. *Canadian Journal of Experimental Psychology* 47, 247–75.

Fodor, J. (1975) *The Language of Thought*, New York: Crowell.

Fong, S. (1991) Computational Properties of Principle-Based Grammatical Theories. Ph.D. thesis, MIT.

Frazier, L. (1978) On Comprehending Sentences: Syntactic Parsing Strategies. Ph.D. thesis, University of Connecticut. Available through the Indiana University Linguistics Club, Bloomington, IN.

Frazier, L. and Clifton, C. (1998) Sentence reanalysis, and visibility. In J. D. Fodor and F. Ferreira (eds), *Reanalysis in Sentence Processing*, Boston: Kluwer Academic, 143–75.

Frazier, L. and Rayner, K. (1982) Making and correcting errors during sentence comprehension: eye movements in the analysis of structurally ambiguous sentences. *Cognitive Psychology* 14, 178–210.

Gibson, E. (1991) A Computational Theory of Human Linguistic Processing: Memory Limitations and Processing Breakdown. Ph.D. thesis, Carnegie–Mellon University.

Gorrell, P. (1987) Studies of Human Syntactic Processing: Ranked-Parallel versus Serial Models. Ph.D. thesis, University of Connecticut.

Grimshaw, J. (1997) Projection, heads and optimality. *Linguistic Inquiry* 28(3), 373–422.

Hendler, J. (1987) Marker-passing and microfeatures. In *Proceedings of the Tenth International Joint Conferences on Artificial Intelligence*, San Francisco: Morgan Kaufmann, 151–4.

Juliano, C. and Tanenhaus, M. (1994) A constraint-based lexicalist account of the subject/object attachment preference. *Journal of Psycholinguistic Research* 23(6), 459–71.

Kimball, J. (1973) Seven principles of surface structure parsing in natural language. *Cognition* 2, 15–47.

Kwasny, S. and Faisal, K. (1992) Connectionism and determinism in a syntactic parser. In N. Sharkey (ed), *Connectionist Natural Language Processing: Readings from Connection Science*, Dordrecht: Kluwer.

Lin, D. (1993) Principle-based parsing without overgeneration. In *Proceedings of the 31st Annual Meeting of the Association for Computational Linguistics*, San Francisco: Morgan Kaufmann, 112–20.

MacDonald, M. C. (1994) Probabilistic constraints and syntactic ambiguity resolution. *Language and Cognitive Processes* 9(2), 157–201.

MacDonald, M., Pearlmutter, N. and Seidenberg M. (1994) Lexical nature of syntactic ambiguity resolution. *Psychological Review* 101(4), 676–703.

McClelland, J. and Kawamoto, A. (1986) Mechanisms of sentence processing: assigning roles to constituents. In J. McClelland, D. Rumelhart, and the PDP Research Group (eds), *Parallel Distributed Processing: Explorations in the Microstructure of Cognition*, vol. 2, Cambridge, MA MIT Press, 272–325.

McRoy, S. W. and Hirst, G. (1990) Race-based parsing and syntactic disambiguation. *Cognitive Science* 14, 313–53.

Merlo, P. (1996) *Parsing with Principles and Classes of Information*, Dordrecht: Kluwer Academic.

Newell, A. (1990) *Unified Theories of Cognition*, Cambridge, MA: Harvard University Press.

Prince, A. and Smolensky, P. (1993) *Optimality Theory: constraint interaction in generative grammar*. Technical Report TR-2, Rutgers Center for Cognitive Science, Rutgers University.

Pritchett, B. (1988) Garden path phenomena and the grammatical basis of language processing. *Language* 64(3), 539–76.

Reggia, J., Marsland, P. and Berndt, R. (1988) Competitive dynamics in a dual-route connectionist model of print-to-sound transformation. *Complex Systems* 2.

Reggia, J., Peng, Y. and Bourret, P. (1991) Recent applications of competitive activation mechanisms. In E. Gelenbe (ed.), *Neural Networks: Advances and Applications*, Elsevier Science Publishers, 33–61.

Rizzi, L. (1990) *Relativized Minimality*, Cambridge, MA: MIT Press.

Rumelhart, D., McClelland, J. and the PDP Research Group (1986) *Parallel Distributed Processing: Explorations in the Microstructure of Cognition*, vol. 1. Cambridge, MA: MIT Press.

Smolensky, P. (1988) On the proper treatment of connectionism. *Behavioral and Brain Sciences* 11(1), 1–23.

—— (1990) Tensor product variable binding and the representation of symbolic structures in connectionist systems. *Artificial Intelligence* 46, 159–216.

Spivey-Knowlton, M. and Sedivy, J. C. (1995) Resolving attachment ambiguity with multiple constraints. *Cognition* 55(3), 227–67.

St John, M. and McClelland, J. (1990) Learning and applying contextual constraints in sentence comprehension. *Artificial Intelligence* 46, 217–57.

Stevenson, S. (1993a) A competition-based explanation of syntactic attachment preferences and garden path phenomena. In *Proceedings of the 31st Annual Meeting of the Association for Computational Linguistics.* San Francisco: Morgan Kaufmann, 266–73.

—— (1993b) Establishing long-distance dependencies in a hybrid network model of human parsing. In *Proceedings of the 15th Annual Conference of the Cognitive Science Society*, Hillsdale, NJ: Lawrence Erlbaum, 982–7.

—— (1994a) Competition and recency in a hybrid network model of syntactic disambiguation. *Journal of Psycholinguistic Research* 23(4), 295–322.

—— (1994b) A Competitive Attachment Model for Resolving Syntactic Ambiguities in Natural Language Parsing. Ph.D. thesis, Department of Computer Science, University of Maryland, College Park. Available as technical report TR-18 from Rutgers Center for Cognitive Science, Rutgers University.

Stevenson, S. and Merlo, P. (1997) Lexical structure and parsing complexity. *Language and Cognitive Processes* 12(2/3), 349–99.

Sun, R. and Alexandre, F. (eds) (1996) *Connectionist–Symbolic Integration: From Unified to Hybrid Approaches.* Hillsdale, NJ: Lawrence Erlbaum. (See also the *Working Notes of the IJCAI Workshop on Connectionist–Symbolic Integration*, 1995).

Trueswell, J. C. (1996) The role of lexical frequency in syntactic ambiguity resolution. *Journal of Memory and Language* 35, 566–85.

Trueswell, J. and Tanenhaus, M. J. (1994) Toward a lexicalist framework for constraint-based syntactic ambiguity resolution. In C. Clifton, L. Frazier and K. Rayner (eds), *Perspectives on Sentence Processing*, Hillsdale, NJ: Lawrence Erlbaum, 155–79.

Trueswell, J. C., Tanenhaus, M. K. and Kello, C. (1993) Semantic influences on parsing: use of thematic role information in syntactic ambiguity resolution. *Journal of Experimental Psychology: Learning, Memory, and Cognition* 19(3), 528–53.

Waltz, D. and Pollack, J. (1985) Massively parallel parsing: a strongly interactive model of natural language interpretation. *Cognitive Science* 9, 51–74.

Wermter, S. and Lehnert, W. (1989) A hybrid symbolic/connectionist model for noun phrase understanding. *Connection Science* 1(3), 255–72.

13

Cognitive and Neural Aspects of Language Acquisition

Karin Stromswold

Overview

Because the ability to learn a language is a uniquely human ability, language acquisition is an important topic in cognitive science. Perhaps the most fundamental question about language and language acquisition is the extent to which the ability to learn language is the result of innate mechanisms or predispositions (henceforth referred to as "innate abilities"). Innate abilities often share certain characteristics. If an ability is innate, it is usually present in all normal individuals. Its acquisition tends to be uniform and automatic, with all normal individuals going through the same stages at the same ages, without specific instruction being required. There may be a critical period for successful acquisition. The ability is likely to be functionally and anatomically autonomous or modular from other abilities, and the trait may be heritable.

Although these characteristics are by no means definitive, they can be used to evaluate traits which may be innate. For example, the ability to walk is presumably innate and exhibits most of the hallmarks of innate abilities, whereas the ability to knit is presumably not innate and exhibits few of these hallmarks. If children's brains are innately predisposed to learn language, then, given adequate exposure to language, all children with normal brains should, without instruction, learn language in a relatively uniform way, just as normal vision develops, given adequate exposure to visual stimuli (Hubel and Wiesel 1970). If the ability to learn language is not innate, then instruction may be necessary to learn language, the course of acquisition may vary greatly from person to person (perhaps as a function of the quality of instruction), and it is possible that there will be no critical period for acquisition.

Even if the ability to learn language is the result of innate mechanisms and predispositions, the question still remains as to whether these mechanisms are specific to language and language acquisition (e.g., Chomsky 1981, 1986; Pinker 1994), or whether they are also involved in tasks and abilities which are not linguistic (e.g., Karmiloff-Smith, 1991; Elman et al. 1996). If the ability to acquire language is the result of innate mechanisms which are used solely for language and language acquisition, language may be functionally and anatomically autonomous or modular from other abilities, and developmental and acquired lesions may specifically impair or spare the ability to learn language. Conversely, if general-purpose mechanisms are involved in language acquisition, we would not expect to find evidence of the functional or anatomical modularity of language or language acquisition.

2 Language Development

2.1 Linguistics and the universal features of language

Superficially, learning to talk differs from learning to walk in that children are capable of learning many different languages, but only one basic walk. If children really are predisposed to be able to learn all human languages, then all languages must be fundamentally the same. In fact, linguists have discovered that, although some languages seem, superficially, to be radically different from other languages (e.g., Turkish from English), in essential ways all human languages are remarkably similar to one another (Chomsky 1981, 1986; Croft 1990). For example, within principles-and-parameters (P&P) theory (Chomsky 1981, 1986), all languages are said to share a common set of grammatical principles. Differences among languages result from the different parametric values chosen for those principles.

Generative linguists usually assume that language involves rules and operations that have no counterparts in nonlinguistic domains and that the ability to use and acquire language is part of our innate endowment. According to P&P theory, at some level, children are born knowing the principles that are universal to all languages (Universal Grammar), and all they must do to learn a particular language is learn the vocabulary and parametric settings of that language. Similarly, within another generative linguistic theory, Optimality Theory (OT), the same universal constraints operate in all languages, and languages differ merely in the ranking of these constraints (Prince and Smolensky 1993). Because, according to OT, children are born "knowing" the universal constraints, what all children must do to learn a particular language is learn the vocabulary and ranking of constraints for that language (Tesar and Smolensky 1996). Linguists working within the functionalist tradition (e.g., Foley and Van Valin 1984) are more likely to assume that language shares properties with nonlinguistic abilities, and that operations used in the acquisition of language are used in other nonlinguistic domain (e.g., Bates and MacWhinney 1982; Budwig 1995; Van Valin 1991).

2.2   Uniformity in language acquisition

Within a given language, the course of language acquisition is remarkably uniform (Brown 1973).[1] Most children say their first referential words at around 9–15 months of age (Morley 1965; Benedict 1979; Fenson et al. 1994; Huttenlocher and Smiley 1987), and for the next 6–8 months, children typically acquire single words in a fairly slow fashion until they have acquired approximately 50 words. For most children acquiring English, the majority of their first 50 words are labels for objects such as *cookie, mother, father,* and *bottle,* with a few action verbs such as *eat, come,* and *go,* social terms such as *good-bye* and *hello,* and prepositions such as *up* and *down* rounding out the list (Nelson 1973; Bates et al. 1994; Benedict 1979). Once children have acquired 50 words, their vocabularies often increase in size rapidly (e.g., Reznick and Goldfield 1992; Benedict 1979; Mervis and Bertrand 1995), with children acquiring between 22 and 37 words per month (Benedict 1979; Goldfield and Reznick 1990).

At around 18–24 months of age, children learning morphologically impoverished languages such as English begin to combine words and form two-word utterances such as *want cookie, play checkers,* and *big drum* (Brown 1973). During the two-word utterance stage, the vast majority of children's utterances are legitimate portions of sentences in the language they are learning. Thus, in a language such as English that has restricted word order, children will say *want cookie* but not *cookie want* (Brown 1973), and *he big* but not *big he* (Bloom 1990). Children acquiring morphologically impoverished languages gradually begin to use sentences longer than two words, but for several months their speech often lacks phonetically unstressed functional category morphemes such as determiners, auxiliary verbs, and verbal and nominal inflectional endings (Brown 1973; Mills 1985; Schieffelin 1985). Representative utterances during this period include *Sarah want cookie, Where Humpty Dumpty go?,* and *Adam write pencil.* Because children's speech during this stage is similar to the way adults speak when words are at a premium (e.g., when they send a telegraph), children's early speech is often described as telegraphic (Brown 1973). Gradually, omissions become rarer, until by the time children are between three and four years old, the vast majority of English-speaking children's utterances are completely grammatical (Stromswold 1990a, 1990b, 1994c). Children who are acquiring languages such as Turkish which have rich, regular, perceptually salient morphological systems generally begin to use functional category morphemes at a younger age than children acquiring morphologically impoverished languages (Aksu-Koç and Slobin 1985; Berman 1986; Peters 1995). For example, in striking contrast to the telegraphic speech of English-speaking children, Turkish-speaking children often begin to produce morphologically complex words before they begin to use multi-word utterances (Aksu-Koç and Slobin 1985).[2]

Within a given language, children master the syntax (grammar) of their language in a surprisingly similar manner (Brown 1973). For example, children acquire the 14 grammatical morphemes of English in essentially the same order (Brown 1973; de Villiers and de Villiers 1973). Similarly, all 15 of the children I studied acquired the 20-odd English auxiliary verbs in essentially the same order (Stromswold 1990b). The order in which these 15 children acquired complex constructions such as questions, negative constructions, passives, datives, exceptional case-marking constructions, embedded sentences, preposition-stranding constructions, causative constructions, small clause constructions, verb-particle constructions, and relative clause constructions was also extremely regular (Stromswold 1988, 1989a, 1989b, 1990a, 1990b, 1992, 1994c, 1995; Stromswold and Snyder 1995; Snyder and Stromswold 1997). Lastly, to a remarkable degree, within and across languages, children make certain types of mistakes and not others (see section 2.5).

2.3   The acquisition of syntactic categories

In order to acquire their language, children must not only learn the meanings of words like *cat* and *eat*; they must also learn that words like *cat* are nouns and words like *eat* are verbs. Learning the categorical membership of words (i.e., which words are nouns, which words are verbs, etc.) is critical, because whether a syntactic or morphological rule applies to a particular word depends on the categorical membership of that word, not on the meaning of the word. This can easily be demonstrated with an example. Upon hearing the sentence *Linus cratomizes Lucy*, any speaker of English automatically knows that *Linus* is the grammatical subject of the sentence (because within an intonational clause, it is in preverbal position), *Lucy* is the grammatical object of the sentence (because it is in postverbal position), and that the nonsense word *cratomize* is a lexical verb. Even without knowing what *cratomize* means, an English-speaker automatically knows, for example, that its progressive form is *cratomizing* and its past tense form is *cratomized*; that *do*-support is required to ask a standard matrix question (e.g., *Did Linus cratomize Lucy?*, not *Cratomized Linus Lucy?*[3] or *Linus cratomized Lucy?*) or negate an utterance (e.g., *Linus didn't cratomize Lucy*, not *Linus cratomized not Lucy*, *Linus not cratomized Lucy*, etc.); and that the grammatical subject precedes rather than follows *cratomize* in simple declarative utterances (e.g., *Linus cratomizes Lucy*, not *Cratomizes Linus Lucy*). The fact that English-speakers know the syntactic and morphological behavior of *cratomize* without having the slightest idea what *cratomize* means demonstrates that categorical membership, not meaning, determines syntactic and morphological behavior. A central question in the field of language acquisition is how children learn the categorical membership of words. For adults, the answer is simple. Even from the single sentence

Linus cratomizes Lucy, to an adult, *cratomize* is clearly a verb because it appears after the grammatical subject (*Linus*) and before the object (*Lucy*), has the third-person verbal inflection *-s,* and exhibits other verb-like properties. The answer is much trickier for children.

How do children learn which words are verbs if they do not know what properties are typical of verbs, and how can they learn the properties of verbs if they do not know which words are verbs? One simple possibility is that every verb in every human language shares some readily accessible property and children are innately predisposed to look for this property. Unfortunately, there doesn't seem to be any such property. Instead, infants must probably rely on a combination of prosodic cues, semantic cues, and correlational cues to learn which words are nouns and which words are verbs in their language (Pinker 1987). Infants may use prosodic cues such as changes in fundamental frequency and lengthening to help determine where major clausal and phrasal boundaries are, and this plus knowledge of universal properties of clauses and phrases (e.g., that verbs are contained within verb phrases and sentential clauses contain noun phrases and verb phrases) could help children learn which words are verbs (Jusczyk et al. 1992; Jusczyk and Kemler Nelson 1996; Morgan and Demuth 1996). Infants might also set up an enormous correlation matrix in which they record all the behaviors associated with words, and categories are the result of children noticing that certain behaviors tend to be correlated. For example, the verb category would result from children noticing that there is a class of words that often end in *-ing, -ed,* or *-s,* frequently occur in the middle of sentences and rarely appear in the beginning of a sentence (see Maratsos and Chalkley 1981). The problem with a simple, unconstrained, unbiased correlational learner is that there are an infinite number of correlations that children must consider, most of which will never appear in any language (Pinker 1984, 1987). If infants are born "knowing" that in all languages, objects are expressed by nouns, physical actions by verbs, and attributes by adjectives, infants could infer that words referring to physical objects are nouns, words referring to actions are verbs, and words referring to attributes are adjectives. They could learn the properties of nouns and verbs from these semantically prototypical cases, a process often referred to as a semantic bootstrapping (see Pinker 1984, 1987).

2.4   The acquisition of auxiliary and lexical verbs

In a sense, the paradox of syntax acquisition is that unless children basically know what they have to learn before they begin, they cannot succeed in learning the grammar of their language. One might argue that, although it has been demonstrated that children must have innate mechanisms which allow them to learn the categorical membership of words, it is possible that these innate mechanisms are not specifically linguistic (for one such proposal, see Ellman et al. 1996). The acquisition of auxiliary verbs and lexical verbs can be used to determine whether children have specifically linguistic innate mechanisms that allow them to acquire language.

The acquisition of English auxiliary and lexical verbs is a particularly good test case, because the two types of verbs are so semantically, syntactically, and lexically similar to one another that a learner who has no knowledge about auxiliary and lexical verbs (i.e., a simple, unbiased, correlational learner) is almost certain to confuse the two types of verbs. For example, for many auxiliaries there is a lexical verb counterpart with an extremely similar meaning (e.g., the pairs *can* and *is able to*, *will* and *is going to*, *must* and *have to*). Auxiliary and lexical verbs are syntactically similar, in that both often take verbal endings, follow subject noun phrases, and lack all of the grammatical properties of nouns, adjectives, and other syntactic categories. Lastly, auxiliary and lexical verbs are typically identical forms (e.g., copula and auxiliary forms of *be*, possessive and auxiliary forms of *have*, lexical verb and auxiliary forms of *do*). The remarkable degree of similarity can be appreciated by comparing pairs of sentences such as *He is sleepy* and *He is sleeping*, *He has cookies* and *He has eaten cookies* and *He does windows* and *He does not do windows*.

The syntactic and morphological behavior of auxiliaries is extremely complex, and there are no obvious non-linguistic correlates for this behavior to aid in learning (Stromswold 1990b). Without innate, specifically linguistic mechanisms, it is unclear how children would be able to correctly identify the 99 unique strings of auxiliaries that are acceptable in English from among the over 23! (2.59 × 10²²) unique strings of English auxiliaries.[4] Descriptively, the basic restrictions on auxiliaries can be summarized as follows:

AUX → (Modal) (*have -en*) (progressive *be -ing*) (passive *be -en*).

Any or all of the auxiliaries are optional; but if they are present, they must occur in the above order. In addition, each auxiliary requires that the verb that follows it be of a certain form. Modal auxiliaries (e.g., *can, will*, and *might*) require that the verb that follows be an infinitival form (e.g., *eat*), perfect *have* requires that the verb that follows be a perfect participle (e.g., *eaten*), progressive *be* requires that the verb that follows be a progressive participle (e.g., *eating*), and passive *be* requires that the main verb be a passive participle (e.g., *eaten*). In addition, the first verbal element must be tensed in a matrix clause. Lastly, matrix questions and negative statements are formed by inverting or negating the first auxiliary. If no auxiliary is present, *do*-support is required (see Stromswold 1990b, 1992, for additional restrictions and complications). Lexical and auxiliary verbs pose a serious learnability question (Baker 1981; Pinker 1984; Stromswold 1989a, 1990b, 1992): How can children distinguish between auxiliary and lexical verbs before they learn the behavior of the two types of verbs, and how do children learn the two types of verbs' behaviors before they can distinguish between them?

If children don't distinguish between auxiliary and lexical verbs, they will generalize what they learn about one type of verb to the other type of verb.

This will result in rapid learning. It will also lead children to make errors that can only be set right by negative evidence (explicit information that a particular construction is ungrammatical). Unfortunately, parents don't seem to provide usable negative evidence (Brown and Hanlon 1970; Marcus 1993). Thus, if children do not distinguish between auxiliaries and lexical verbs, they are destined to make certain types of inflectional errors (e.g., *I aming go, *I musts eat) and combination errors involving multiple lexical verbs (e.g., *I hope go Disneyland), negated lexical verbs (e.g., *I eat not cookies), lone auxiliaries (e.g., *I must coffee), and unacceptable combinations of auxiliaries (e.g., *I may should go). They will also make word-order errors, scrambling the order of lexical verbs and auxiliaries (e.g., *I go must), scrambling the order of auxiliaries (e.g., *He have must gone), and incorrectly inverting lexical verbs (e.g., Eats he meat?). If, on the other hand, children have innate predispositions that allow them to distinguish between auxiliary and lexical verbs, they will not make these errors.

In order to test whether English-speaking children distinguish between auxiliary and lexical verbs, I searched the transcripts of 14 children's speech, examining by hand the more than 66,000 utterances of these children that contained auxiliaries (Stromswold 1989a, 1990b). I found that the children acquired the auxiliary system with remarkable speed and accuracy. In fact, I found no clear examples of the types of inflectional errors, combination errors, or word-order errors that would result from confusing auxiliary and lexical verbs. Thus, children seem to have innate, specifically linguistic mechanisms that allow them to distinguish between auxiliary and lexical verbs.

2.5   Errors, instruction, and the automaticity of language acquisition

One of the hallmarks of innate abilities is that they can be acquired without explicit instruction. This seems to be true for language. Although parents do correct their children when they make errors that affect the meaning of utterances, parents do not seem to correct children's grammatical errors reliably (Brown and Hanlon 1970; Marcus 1993). Furthermore, even when parents do try to correct grammatical errors, their efforts are often in vain (McNeill 1966). Lastly, correction is not necessary for lexical and syntactic acquisition, because some children who are unable to speak (and therefore cannot be corrected by their parents) have normal receptive language (Stromswold 1994a). If teaching and correction are necessary for language development, it should not be possible for children to have impaired production but intact comprehension. Recently, I have been studying the language acquisition of a young boy who is unable to speak. Despite the fact that he has essentially no expressive language (he can say only a handful of phonemes), his receptive language is completely intact. For example, at age 4 he was able to distinguish between reversible active and passive sentences (correctly distinguishing the meanings conveyed by sentences such as The dog bit the cat, The cat bit the *dog, The dog was bitten by the cat,* and *The cat was bitten by the dog*) and to make grammaticality judgments (e.g., correctly recognizing that *What can Cookie Monster eat?* is grammatical, whereas * *What Cookie Monster can eat?* is not) (see Stromswold 1994a).

Children learn language quickly, never making certain types of errors that seem very reasonable to make (e.g., certain types of auxiliary errors). But as Pinker (1989) points out, children are not perfect: they *do* make certain types of errors. They overregularize inflectional endings, saying *eated* for *ate* and *mouses* for *mice* (Pinker 1989). They make lexical errors, such as sometimes passivizing verbs such as *die* that do not passivize (e.g., *he get died* (from Pinker 1989). They also make certain types of syntactic error, such as using *do*support when it is not required (e.g., *Does it be around it?* and *This doesn't be straight* (Stromswold 1990a, 1992) and failing to use *do*-support when it is required (e.g., *What she eats?* (Stromswold 1990b, 1994c). What do these errors tell us? First, they confirm that children use language productively and are not merely repeating back what they hear their parents say, because parents do not use these unacceptable forms (Pinker 1989). These errors may also provide an insight into the peculiarities of languages. For example, children's difficulty with *do*-support suggests that *do*-support is not part of Universal Grammar, but rather is a peculiar property of English (Stromswold 1990a, 1990b, 1994c).

Lastly, these errors may provide insight into the types of linguistic categories that children are predisposed to acquire. Consider, for example, the finding that children overregularize lexical *be, do,* and *have* but never overregularize auxiliary *be, do,* and *have* (Stromswold 1989a, 1990b, forthcoming a). The fact that children say sentences like * *She beed happy* but not sentences like * *She beed smiling* indicates that children not only can distinguish between auxiliary verbs and lexical verbs (see section 2.4), but they treat the two types of verbs differently. What kind of innate learning mechanism could result in children overregularizing lexical verbs but not the homophonous auxiliaries? One possibility is that children have innate learning mechanisms that specifically cause them to treat auxiliaries differently from lexical verbs. Unfortunately, there are problems with this explanation. Although many languages contain words that are semantically and syntactically similar to English auxiliaries (Steele 1981), and all languages are capable of making the semantic and syntactic distinctions that in English are made by auxiliaries, some languages appear either not to have auxiliaries (instead making use of inflectional affixes) or not to distinguish between auxiliaries and lexical verbs. Given that not all languages contain auxiliary verbs that can easily be confused with lexical verbs, it seems unlikely that there are innate mechanisms which permit children to distinguish specifically between auxiliary verbs and lexical verbs. In addition, hypothesizing specific innate mechanisms that allow children to distinguish between auxiliaries and lexical verbs has little explanatory power, because it explains nothing beyond the phenomena that led us to propose its existence in the first place.

Alternatively, children's ability to distinguish between auxiliary and lexical verbs might reflect a more general ability to distinguish between functional categories (determiners, auxiliaries, nominal and verbal inflections, pronouns, etc.) and lexical categories (nouns, verbs, adjectives, etc.). Lexical categories are fairly promiscuous: they freely admit new members (e.g., *fax, modem, email*, etc.), and the grammatical behavior of one member of a lexical category can fairly safely be generalized to another member of the same lexical category. Functional categories are conservative: new members are not welcome, and generalizations even within a functional category are very dangerous (see Stromswold 1990b, 1994b). Innate mechanisms that specifically predispose children to distinguish between lexical and functional categories have a number of advantages over similar mechanisms for auxiliary and lexical verbs. Unlike the auxiliary/lexical verb distinction, the lexical/functional category distinction is found in all human languages, and thus mechanisms that predispose children to distinguish between lexical categories and functional categories are better candidates a priori for being innate. In addition, research on speech errors (e.g., Garrett 1976), neologisms (Stromswold 1994b), parsing (e.g., Morgan and Newport 1981), linguistic typology (e.g., Croft 1990), aphasia (e.g., Goodglass 1976), developmental language disorders (e.g. Guilfoyle et al. 1991), event-related potentials (Neville 1991; Holcomb et al. 1992; Neville et al. 1992, 1993; Neville 1995) and functional magnetic resonance imaging (Neville et al. 1994a) all point to the importance of the lexical/functional distinction.

If children have innate mechanisms that predispose them to distinguish between lexical and functional categories, this would help them to distinguish not only between auxiliary and lexical verbs, but also between pronouns and nouns, determiners and adjectives, verbal stems and verbal inflections, and other pairs of lexical and functional categories that are hard to distinguish using nonlinguistic knowledge. If children have innate mechanisms that specifically predispose them to distinguish between syntactic categories that allow for free generalization (lexical categories) and those that do not (functional categories), this would explain why children overregularize lexical *be, do*, and *have*, but not auxiliary *be, do*, and *have*. It would also help explain why children are able to learn language so rapidly and with so few errors, because such a learning mechanism would permit children to generalize only where it is safe to do so (i.e., within a lexical category). Computationally, the difference between lexical and functional categories might be expressed as the difference between rule-based and list-based generalizations or, within a connectionist framework, between network architectures that have different degrees and configurations of connectivity (see Stromswold 1994b).

The Role of Linguistic Input and Critical Periods
in Language Acquisition

3.1   Pidgins

The uniformity of language development under normal conditions described in section 2 could be due to biological or environmental processes. One way to investigate the relative roles of biological and environmental factors is to investigate the linguistic abilities of children whose early language environments are suboptimal. Studies of creolization provide compelling evidence that human children are innately endowed with the ability to develop a very specific kind of language even with minimal input. Creolization may occur when migrant workers who speak a variety of languages are brought together to work and their only common language is a simplified pidgin of the dominant language. Pidgins typically consist of fixed phrases and pantomimes and are only able to express basic needs and ideas. Bickerton (1981, 1984) has studied the language of second-generation pidgin-speakers (i.e., children whose parents spoke pidgin) and has found that they use a creolized language which is much richer than their parents' pidgin. For example, the creolized language of second-generation pidgin-speakers includes embedded and relative clauses, aspectual distinctions, and consistent word order, despite the absence of such features in the input (pidgin) language (Bickerton 1981, 1984). Thus, second-generation pidgin-speakers "invent" a language that is more complex than the pidgin language they are exposed to.

3.2   Homesign: gestural systems of deaf isolates

How minimal can the input be? Although children who hear only pidgin languages have impoverished input, there are even more extreme situations of language deprivation. Deaf children born to hearing parents who do not use or expose their infants to sign language receive normal care from their parents (i.e., they are not abused or neglected). However, they receive essentially no linguistic input. These deaf isolates provide a fascinating picture of the limits of the innate endowment to create language and, hence, a glimpse at the early unfolding of language in all infants. As infants and toddlers, deaf isolates seem to achieve the same early language milestones as hearing children. Right on schedule at around 6–8 months of age, deaf isolates begin to make hand motions analogous to the spoken babbling of hearing babies. They invent their first signs at about the same age that hearing children produce their first words. They even begin to form short phrases with these signs, also on a comparable schedule to hearing children (Goldin-Meadow and Mylander 1984, 1998; Morford 1996). Thus, these early linguistic milestones are apparently able to unfold despite no linguistic input. Preliminary research on older deaf isolates indicates that their gestural communication systems are more sophisticated than those used by young deaf isolates, although even their systems do not exhibit the complexity of natural sign languages (Coppola et al. 1998).

Although the ability to learn languages appears to be the result of innate processes, exposure to language during childhood is necessary for normal language development, just as the ability to see is innate, yet visual stimulation is necessary for normal visual development (Hubel and Wiesel 1970). The hypothesis that exposure to language must occur by a certain age in order for language to be acquired normally is called the "critical period hypothesis." The critical period for language acquisition is generally believed to coincide with the period of great neural plasticity and is often though to end at or sometime before the onset of puberty (see Lenneberg 1967).

3.3   Wild children

Skuse (1984a, 1984b) reviewed nine well-documented cases of children raised in conditions of extreme social and linguistic deprivation for 2.5–12 years. All these cases involved grossly impoverished environments and, frequently, malnourishment and physical abuse. At the time of discovery, the children ranged in age from 2.5 years to 13.5 years, had essentially no receptive or expressive language, and were globally retarded in non-linguistic domains. The six children who eventually acquired normal or near-normal language function were all discovered by age 7 and had no signs of brain damage. Of the three children who remained language-impaired, one was discovered at age 5 but had clear evidence of brain damage (Davis 1940, 1947) and one was discovered at age 3.5 but had organic abnormalities not attributable to extreme deprivation (Skuse 1984a). Genie, the third child with persistent linguistic impairments, is remarkable both for having the most prolonged period of deprivation (12 years) and, at almost 14 years of age, for being the oldest when discovered (Curtiss 1977). Neuropsychological testing suggested that Genie did not have the expected left-hemisphere lateralization for language. Although it is tempting to conclude that Genie's failure to acquire normal language and her anomalous lateralization of language function are both the result of her failure to be exposed to language prior to the onset of puberty, it is possible that cortical anomalies in the left hemisphere are the cause of her anomalous lateralization and her failure to acquire language (Curtiss 1977).

3.4   Deaf isolates

As Curtiss (1977, 1989) points out, it is impossible to be certain that the linguistic impairment observed in children such as Genie is the result of linguistic isolation and not the result of social and physical deprivation and abuse. Curtiss (1989) has described the case of Chelsea, a hearing-impaired woman who had essentially no exposure to language until age 32. Unlike children such as Genie, Chelsea did not experience any social or physical deprivation. Chelsea's ability to use language (particularly syntax) was at least as impaired as Genie's, an observation consistent with the critical period hypothesis (Curtiss 1989). To test whether there is a critical period for first language acquisition, Newport and colleagues have studied the signing abilities for deaf people whose first exposure to American Sign Language (ASL) was at birth (native signers), before age 6 (early signers), or after age 12 (late signers). Consistent with the critical period hypothesis, even after 30 years of using ASL, on tests of morphology and complex syntax, native signers outperform early signers, who in turn outperform late signers (Newport 1990).

3.5 Second language acquisition

To test whether there is a critical period for second language acquisition, Johnson and Newport (1989) studied the English abilities of native speakers of Korean and Chinese who first became immersed in English between the ages of 3 and 39. For subjects who began to learn English before puberty, age of English immersion correlated extremely highly with proficiency with English syntax and morphology, whereas no significant correlation was found for subjects who began to learn English after puberty (Johnson and Newport 1989).

Evidence from studies of children such as Genie, deaf isolates, and people who acquire a second language suggests that the ability to acquire language diminishes with age. Consistent with research that shows that (essentially) complete language recovery rarely occurs if a left-hemisphere lesion occurs after age 5 and substantial recovery rarely occurs if a lesion is acquired after the onset of puberty (see section 4.4), subtle tests of linguistic abilities reveal that native fluency in a language is rarely attained if one's first exposure to that language occurs after early childhood, and competence in a language is rarely attained if first exposure occurs after the onset of puberty. This is consistent with Hubel and Wiesel's (1970) finding that normal visual development requires visual stimuli during a critical period of neural development and suggests that neural fine-tuning is a critical to normal language acquisition and that this fine-tuning can occur only with exposure to language during a certain time period.

4   Language Acquisition and Brain Development

In section 2, results of research on normal language acquisition were used to argue that the ability to learn language is the result of innate, language-specific learning mechanisms. Section 3 investigated the extent to which normal language development depends on receiving appropriate linguistic input during a critical window of cognitive (and presumably neuronal) development. Section 4 will review neurobiological evidence for language being the result of innate, language-specific learning mechanisms.

4.1   The development of language regions of the brain

Contrary to claims by Lenneberg (1967), the language areas of the human brain appear to be anatomically and functionally asymmetrical at or before birth. Anatomically, analysis of fetal brains reveals that the temporal plane is larger in the left hemisphere than in the right hemisphere (Wada et al. 1975).[5] Development of the cortical regions that subserve language in the left hemisphere consistently lags behind the development of the homologous regions in the right hemisphere. The right temporal plane appears during the thirtieth gestational week, whereas the left temporal plane first appears approximately 7–10 days later (Chi et al. 1977). Even in infancy, dendritic development in the region around Broca's area on the left lags behind that found in the homologous region on the right (Scheibel 1984). Even-related potential (ERP) and dichotic listening experiments suggest that the left hemisphere is differentially sensitive for speech from birth (for a review, see Mehler and Christophe 1995).

Relatively few researchers have investigated the neural bases of lexical or syntactic abilities in neurologically intact children. For example, Molfese and his colleagues (Molfese 1990; Molfese et al. 1990) have taught infants as young as 14 months labels for novel objects and have then compared the children's ERPs when the novel objects were paired with correct verbal labels and with incorrect verbal labels. A late-occurring response was recorded in the left hemisphere electrode sites when the correct label was given, but not when an incorrect label was given. Similarly, an early-occurring response was recorded bilaterally in the frontal electrodes when the correct label was given, but not when an incorrect label was given. In recent work, Mills, Coffey-Corina, and Neville (1997) recorded the ERPs when children between 13 and 20 months of age listened to words for which the children knew the meanings, words for which they did not know the meanings, and backwards words. They found that the ERPs differed as a function of meaning within 200 msec of the onset of the word. Between 13 and 17 months, the ERP differences for known versus unknown words were bilateral and widely distributed over anterior and posterior regions. By 20 months, the differences were limited to left temporal and parietal regions.

In another ERP study, Holcomb, Coffey, and Neville (1992) found no clear evidence prior to age 13 of the normal adult pattern of greater negativity in the left hemisphere than the right hemisphere for semantically plausible sentences (e.g., *We baked cookies in the oven*) and greater negativity in the right hemisphere than left hemisphere for semantically anomalous sentences (e.g., *Mother wears a ring on her school*). In addition, the negative peak associated with semantic anomalies (the N400) was later and longer in duration for younger subjects than older subjects. Holcomb, Coffey, and Neville (1992) also found evidence that the normal adult pattern of a left anterior N280 wave form associated with functional category words and a bilateral posterior N350 waveform associated with lexical category words (Neville et al. 1992) does not develop until around puberty. Four-year-old children typically have N350 response to both lexical and functional words. By 11 years of age, the N350 is greatly reduced or absent for functional category words. It isn't until approximately 15 years of age that functional category words result in a clear N280 response with adult-like distribution (Holcomb et al. 1992). In summary, although simple linguistic stimuli (e.g., lexical words) appear to evoke similar types of electrical activity in young children's brains as those recorded in adult brains, for some types of linguistic stimuli, children's ERPs may not become indistinguishable from adult ERPs until around puberty. That the critical period for language acquisition (especially syntax) ends at approximately the same age that children develop adult-like ERPs for grammatical aspects of language is intriguing and raises the possibility that once adult-like pathways and operations are acquired, neural plasticity is reduced so greatly that the ability to acquire all but the most rudimentary aspects of syntax is lost.

4.2   The modularity of language acquisition

With exceptions such as those mentioned above, most of what is known about the relationship between brain development and lexical and syntactic development has come from studying language acquisition by children who have developmental disorders, syndromes or brain lesions. If, as was argued earlier, language acquisition involves the development of specialized structures and operations that have no counterparts in non-linguistic domains, then it should be possible for a child to be cognitively intact and linguistically impaired or to be linguistically intact and cognitively impaired. If, on the other hand, language acquisition involves the development of the same general symbolic structures and operations used in other cognitive domains, then dissociation of language from general cognitive development should not be possible. Recent studies suggest that language development is selectively impaired in some children with specific language impairment (SLI) and selectively spared in children who suffer from disorders such as Williams Syndrome.

Specific language impairment

The term "specific language impairment" is often used to refer to developmental disorders that are characterized by severe deficits in the production and/or comprehension of language that cannot be explained by hearing loss, mental retardation, motor deficits, neurological or psychiatric disorders, or lack of exposure to language. Because SLI is a diagnosis of exclusion, SLI children are a very heterogeneous group. This heterogeneity can and does affect the outcome of behavioral and neurological studies, with different studies of SLI children frequently reporting different results, depending on how SLI subjects were chosen. The exact nature of the etiology of SLI remains uncertain (for a review, see Leonard 1998; Stromswold 1997), with suggestions ranging from impoverished or deviant linguistic input (Cramblit and Siegel 1977; Lasky and Klopp 1982), transient, fluctuating hearing loss (Bishop and Edmundson 1986; Gordon 1988; Gravel and Wallace 1992; Teele et al. 1990), impairment in short-term auditory memory (Graham 1968, 1974; Rapin and Wilson 1978), impairment in auditory sequencing (Efron 1963; Monsee 1961), impairment in rapid auditory processing (Tallal and Piercy 1973a, 1973b, 1974), general impairment in sequencing (Poppen et al. 1969), general impairment in rapid sensory processing (Tallal 1990), general impairment in representational or symbolic reasoning (Johnston and Weismer 1983; Kahmi 1981; Morehead and Ingram 1973), general impairment in hierarchical planning (Cromer 1983), impairments in language perception or processing (e.g., the inability to acquire aspects of language that are not phonologically salient (Leonard 1989, 1994; Leonard et al. 1992)), impairments in underlying grammar such as the lack of linguistic features such as tense and number (Crago and Gopnik 1994; Gopnik 1990a, 1990b; Gopnik and Crago 1991), the inability to use government to analyze certain types of syntactic relations (van der Lely 1994), the inability to form certain types of agreement relations (Clahsen 1989, 1991; Rice 1994), or some combination of the above. Some researchers have even suggested that SLI is not a distinct clinical entity, and that SLI children just represent the low end of the normal continuum in linguistic ability (Johnston 1991; Leonard 1991).

At the neural level, the cause of SLI is also uncertain. Initially, it was theorized that children with SLI had bilateral damage to the perisylvian cortical regions that subserve language in adults (Bishop 1987). Because SLI is not a fatal disorder and people with SLI have normal life spans, to date, only one brain of a possible SLI child has come to autopsy. Post-mortem examination of this brain revealed atypical symmetry of the temporal planes and a dysplastic micro-gyrus on the interior surface of the left frontal cortex along the inferior surface of the sylvian fissure (Cohen et al. 1989), findings similar to those reported in dyslexic brains by Geschwind and Galaburda

(1987). Although it is tempting to use the results of this autopsy to argue – as Geschwind and Galaburda (1987) have done for dyslexia – that SLI is the result of subtle anomalies in the left perisylvian cortex, the child whose brain was autopsied had a performance IQ of only 74 (verbal IQ 70); hence the anomalies noted on autopsy may be related to the child's general cognitive impairment rather than to her language impairment.

Computed tomography (CT) and magnetic resonance imaging (MRI) scans of SLI children have failed to reveal the types of gross perisylvian lesions typically found in patients with acquired aphasia (Jernigan et al. 1991; Plante et al. 1991). CT and MRI scans have revealed, however, that the brains of SLI children often do not have the normal pattern of the left temporal plane being larger than the right temporal plane (Jernigan et al. 1991; Plante 1991; Plante et al. 1989, 1991). Examination of MRI scans has revealed that dyslexics are more likely to have an additional gyrus between the postcentral sulcus and the supramarginal gyrus than are normal readers (Leonard et al. 1993). Jackson and Plante (1997) recently performed the same type of gyral morphology analyses on MRI scans of 10 SLI children, their parents, 10 siblings, and 20 adult controls.[6] For the control group, 23 per cent of the hemispheres showed an intermediate gyrus, whereas 41 per cent of the hemispheres for SLI family members (probands and their siblings and parents combined) showed an intermediate gyrus. However, affected family members did not appear to be more likely to have an intermediate gyrus than unaffected members. Clark and Plante (1995) compared the morphology of Broca's area in parents of SLI children and adult controls. Overall, parents of SLI children were no more likely to have an extra sulcus in the vicinity of Broca's area. However, parents with documented language impairments were more likely to have an extra sulcus than unaffected parents.

A number of researchers have studied the functional characteristics of SLI children's brains. Data from dichotic listening experiments (e.g., Arnold and Schwartz 1983; Bolick et al. 1988; Cohen et al. 1991) and ERP experiments (e.g., Dawson et al. 1989) suggest that at least some SLI children have aberrant functional lateralization for language, with language present either bilaterally or predominantly in the right hemisphere. Single photon emission computed tomography (SPECT) studies of normal and language-impaired children have revealed hypoperfusion in the inferior frontal convolution of the left hemisphere (including Broca's area) in two children with isolated expressive language impairment (Denays et al. 1989), hypoperfusion of the left temporoparietal region and the upper and middle regions of the right frontal lobe in 9 of 12 children with expressive and receptive language impairment (Denays et al. 1989), and hypoperfusion in the left temporofrontal region of language-impaired children's brains (Lou et al. 1990).

Courchesne and colleagues (1989) did not find any differences in ERP amplitude or latency between SLI adolescents and adults and age-matched controls. However, in a subsequent study of school-age SLI children, Lincoln, Courchesne, Harms and Allen (1995) found that the normal pattern of larger amplitude N100s for more intense auditory stimuli intensity was seen for normal age-matched controls but not for SLI subjects, suggesting that there may be some abnormality of the auditory cortex in SLI children. Neville and colleagues (1993) compared SLI children's and normal age-matched controls' ERPs for three tasks. In the first task, subjects pressed a button when they detected 1,000 Hz tones among a series of 2,000 Hz tones. In the second task, subjects were asked to detect small white rectangles among a series of large red squares. In the third task, children read sentences one word at a time and judged whether or not the sentences were semantically plausible (half of the sentences ended with a semantically appropriate word, and half ended with a semantically inappropriate word). Overall, for the auditory monitoring task, the SLI children's ERPs did not differ from the control children's ERPs. However, when the SLI children were divided into groups according to their performance on Tallal and Piercy's (1973a, 1973b) auditory processing task, children who performed poorly on Tallal and Piercy's task were found to have reduced amplitude ERP waves over the anterior portion of the right hemisphere, and the latency for the N140 component was greater. In general, the SLI children had abnormally large N400s on the sentence task. As is typically seen with adults, the normal children's N400s for closed-class words were larger over the anterior left hemisphere than the anterior right hemisphere. However, the SLI children with the greatest morphosyntactic deficits did not exhibit this asymmetry.[7]

Unfortunately, despite decades of intensive and productive research on SLI, a number of fundamental questions remain unanswered. Researchers disagree about the etiology of SLI at a neural or cognitive level and offer proposals ranging from a specific impairment in a circumscribed aspect of abstract linguistics to general cognitive/processing impairments to environmental causes. Even among researchers who believe that SLI specifically affects linguistic competence, there is disagreement about what aspects of the underlying grammar is impaired. Furthermore, numerous studies have revealed that many (if not most) children with SLI exhibit non-linguistic deficits, although some researchers argue that these non-linguistic deficits are secondary to SLI children's primary linguistic impairments (for a review, see Leonard 1998). A first step in seeking answers to these questions is to study more homogeneous subgroups of children diagnosed with SLI.[8] In summary, although generally consistent with there being a specific module for language and language acquisition, the picture of SLI that is emerging is not as "clean" as modularists might hope: SLI children are a heterogeneous group, and it is not the case that all SLI children are perfectly intact but for a damaged language module.

Williams Syndrome

Although mental retardation generally results in depression of language function (Rondal 1980), researchers have reported that some mentally retarded children have remarkably intact language. This condition has been reported in some children with hydrocephalus (Swisher and Pinsker 1971), Turner's syndrome (Yamada and Curtiss 1981), infantile hypercalcemia or Williams Syndrome (Bellugi et al. 1992), and mental retardation of unknown etiology (Yamada 1990).

Williams Syndrome (WS) is a rare (1 in 25,000) genetic disorder involving deletion of portions of chromosome 7 around and including the elastin gene (Ewart et al. 1993a, 1993b). People with WS often have particularly extreme dissociation of language and cognitive functions (Bellugi et al. 1992). Hallmarks of WS include microcephaly with a "pixie-like" facial appearance, general mental retardation with IQs typically in the 40s–50s range, delayed onset of expressive language, and "an unusual command of language combined with an unexpectedly polite, open and gentle manner" by early adolescence (Von Armin and Engel 1964). A recent study which used the MacArthur Communicative Development Inventory (a parental report measure) to assess the earliest stages of language development for children with WS and children with Down's Syndrome (DS) revealed that WS and DS children were equally delayed in the acquisition of words, with an average delay of two years for both groups (Singer Harris et al. 1997). WS and DS children who had begun to combine words (mean age = 46 months) did not differ significantly in language age (mean ages 23.7 months and 21.0 months, respectively). However, compared to the DS children, these older WS children had significantly higher scores on grammatical complexity measures and on mean length of utterance for their longest three sentences (Singer Harris et al. 1997). The gap in linguistic abilities of WS and DS children increases with age (Bellugi et al. 1994). By adolescence, although people with WS use language which is often deviant for their chronological age and do poorly on many standardized language tests, they have larger vocabularies and speak in sentences that are more syntactically and morphologically complex and well-formed than do children of equivalent mental ages. In addition, WS adolescents and adults demonstrate good metalinguistic skills, such as the ability to recognize an utterance as ungrammatical and to respond in a contextually appropriate manner (Bellugi et al. 1992).

Volumetric analyses of MRI scans indicate that, compared to normal brains, cerebral volume and cerebral grey matter of WS brains are significantly reduced in size, and the neocerebellar vermal lobules are increased in size, with paleocerebellar vermal regions of low-normal size (Jernigan and Bellugi 1994; Jernigan et al. 1993; Wang et al. 1992). To date, only one WS brain has come to autopsy (Galaburda et al. 1994). This brain had extensive cytoarchitectural abnormalities, including exaggeration of horizontal abnormalities within layers, most striking in area 17 of the occipital lobe, increased cell density throughout the brain, and abnormally clustered and oriented neurons. In addition, although the frontal lobes and most of the temporal lobes were relatively normal in size, the posterior forebrain was much smaller than normal. Galaburda and colleagues interpreted these findings as evidence of developmental arrest between the end of the second trimester and the second year of life. They further suggested that these findings may be related to hypercalcemia found in WS. Alternatively, elastin may have a direct neurodevelopmental function which has yet to be discovered, and the macroscopic and microscopic abnormalities may be associated with the decreased levels of elastin in WS.

Early studies revealed that, although auditory ERPs for WS adolescents have similar morphology, distribution, sequence, and latency as those found in age-matched controls, WS adolescents display large-amplitude responses even at short inter-stimulus intervals, suggesting hyperexcitability of auditory mechanisms at the cortical level with shorter refractory periods (Neville et al. 1989, 1994b). When WS subjects listened to spoken words, their ERPs had grossly abnormal morphology not seen in normal children at any age. In contrast, the morphology of their ERPs for visually presented words was normal. Compared with normal subjects, WS subjects had larger priming effects for auditorily presented words, but priming effects for visually presented words were normal or smaller than those observed for normal subjects (Neville et al. 1994b). These results suggest that WS subjects' relative sparing of language function is related to hypersensitivity to auditorily presented linguistic material. To date, no PET or SPECT studies of WS children have been reported. It will be interesting to learn from such studies whether the classically defined language areas in general or just primary auditory cortex in WS brains become hyper-perfused in response to auditory linguistic stimuli. In summary, although generally consistent with there being a specific module for language and language acquisition, the picture of WS that is emerging is not as "clean" as modularists might hope: although WS adolescents and adults have better linguistic abilities than others with comparable IQs, their language is far from perfect and the mechanisms they use for language acquisition may not be the same as those used by normal children (see, e.g., Karmiloff-Smith et al. 1997, in press; Stevens and Karmiloff-Smith, 1997).

4.3   The genetic basis of language

If the acquisition of language is the result of specialized structures in the brain and these linguistically specific structures are coded for by information contained in the genetic code, then one might expect to find evidence for the hereditability of language (see Pinker and Bloom 1990; Ganger and Stromswold 1998). If, on the other hand, language acquisition is essentially the result of instruction and involves no specifically linguistic structures, there should be no evidence of genetic transmission of language.

Familial aggregation studies

A comprehensive review of family aggregation studies, sex ratio studies, pedigree studies, commingling studies, and segregation studies of spoken language disorders reveals that spoken language disorders have a strong tendency to aggregate in families (Stromswold 1998). I reviewed 18 family aggregation studies of spoken language impairment (Stromswold 1998); (see table 13.1). The incidence of positive family history was significantly greater for probands than controls in all seven studies that collected data for both probands and controls.[9] In these studies, the reported incidence of positive family history for probands ranged from 24 per cent (Bishop and Edmundson 1986) to 78 per cent (van der Lely and Stollwerck 1996), with a mean incidence of 46 per cent and a median incidence of 35 per cent.[10] For controls, positive family history rates ranged from 3 per cent (Bishop and Edmundson 1986) to 46 per cent (Tallal et al. 1989a), with a mean incidence of 18 per cent and a median incidence of 11 per cent.

Of the studies I reviewed, 11 reported the percentage of probands' relatives who were impaired. For probands, the percentage of family members who were impaired ranged from 20 per cent (Neils and Aram 1986) to 42 per cent (Tallal et al. 1989a), with a mean impairment rate of 28 per cent and a median impairment rate of 26 per cent. For controls, the percentage of family members who were impaired ranged from 3 per cent (Neils and Aram 1986) to 19 per cent (Tallal et al. 1989a), with a mean impairment rate of 9 per cent and a median impairment rate of 7 per cent. The incidence of impairment was significantly higher among proband relatives than control relatives in seven of the eight studies that made such a comparison.

Although data on familial aggregation of language disorders suggest that some developmental language disorders have a genetic component, it is possible that children with language-impaired parents or siblings are more likely to be linguistically impaired themselves because they are exposed to deviant language (the Deviant Linguistic Environment Hypothesis, or DLEH). Some studies have reported that mothers are more likely to use directive speech and less likely to use responsive speech when talking to their language-impaired children than are mothers speaking to normal children (e.g., Conti-Ramsden and Friel-Patti 1983; Conti-Ramsden and Dykins 1991). However, children's language impairments may cause mothers to use simplified speech, rather than vice versa. For example, mothers of language-impaired children may use directive speech because they cannot understand their impaired children and their impaired children do not understand them if they use more complicated language. Furthermore, although within a fairly wide range, linguistic environment may have little or no effect on language acquisition by normal children (e.g., Heath 1983), there could be a synergistic effect between genetics and environment, and children who are genetically at risk for developing language disorders may be particularly sensitive to subtly impoverished linguistic environments.

Contrary to the DLEH prediction that the most severely impaired children should come from families with the highest incidence of language impairments, Byrne, Willerman and Ashmore (1974) found that children with profound language impairments were less likely to have positive family histories of language impairment than were children who were moderately language-

Table 13.1 Family aggregation studies of spoken language disorders

Study	Sample size	Other family diagnoses	Positive family history	Frequency of impairment among relatives (proband vs control)
Ingram 1959	75 probands	none	24% parental history 32% sibling history	N/A
Luchsinger 1970	127 probands	none	36% probands	N/A
Byrne et al. 1974	18 severely impaired, 20 moderately impaired	none	17% "Severe" probands 55% "Moderate" probands**	N/A
Neils and Aram 1986	74 probands, 36 controls	dyslexia, stuttering, articulation	46% 1st-degree proband 8% 1st-degree controls****	20% vs 3% all relatives***
Bishop and Edmundson 1987	34 probands, 131 controls	none (for strict criteria)	24% 1st-degree proband 3% 1st-degree control****	N/A
Lewis et al 1989	20 probands, 20 controls	dyslexia, stuttering, LD	N/A	any: 12% vs 2% all relatives**** 26% vs 5% 1st-degree relatives*** SLI: 9% vs 1% all relatives****
Tallal et al 1989a	62 probands, 50 controls	dyslexia, LD, school problems	77% 1st-degree proband 46% 1st-degree control**	42% vs 19% 1st-degree relatives***
Tomblin 1989	51 probands, 136 controls	stuttering, articulation	53% 1st-degree probands controls: N/A	23% vs 3% 1st-degree relatives****
Haynes and Naido 1991	156 probands	none	54% all probands 41% 1st-degree probands	29% proband parents 18% proband sibs
Tomblin et al. 1991	55 probands, 607 controls	none	35% probands 17% controls***	N/A

Study	Sample	Conditions assessed	Rate	Detailed results
Whitehurst et al. 1991	62 probands, 55 controls	speech, late talker, school problems	N/A	any: 24% vs 16% 1st-degree relatives; speech: 12% vs 8% 1st-degree relatives; late talker: 12% vs 7% 1st-degree relatives; school: 7% vs 5% 1st-degree relatives
Beitchman et al. 1992	136 probands, 138 controls	dyslexia, LD, articulation	47% vs 28% all relatives***; 34% vs 11% 1st-degree****	Multiple affected relatives: 19% vs 9%*
Lewis 1992	87 probands, 79 controls	dyslexia, LD, stuttering, hearing loss	N/A	LI: 15% vs 2% all relatives****, 32% vs 5% 1st-degree relatives****; dyslexia: 3% vs 1% all relatives****, 6% vs 3% 1st-degree relatives; LD: 3% vs 1% all relatives****, 6% vs 1% 1st-degree relatives*
Tomblin and Buckwalter 1994	26 probands	none	42% 1st-degree	overall: 21%, mother: 15%, father: 40%, sister: 6%, brother: 24%
Lahey and Edwards 1995	53 probands	learning problems	60% 1st-degree	overall: 26%, mother: 26%, father: 22%, siblings: 29%
Rice et al. 1998	31 probands, 67 controls	reading, spelling, learning	N/A	any: 18% vs 9% all relatives***, 26% vs 13% 1st-degree relatives**; LI: 15% vs 6% all relatives***, 22% vs 7% 1st-degree relatives***; other: 7% vs 5% all relatives 12% vs 9% 1st-degree relatives
Tomblin 1996	534 probands, 6684 controls		29% probands, 11% controls****	
van der Lely and Stollwerck 1996	9 probands, 49 controls	reading or writing	78% 1st-degree probands, 29% 1st-degree controls**	Overall: 39% vs 9%*****, Mothers: 33% vs 2%****; Fathers: 38% vs 8%*, Sisters: 40% vs 8%*; Brothers: 44% vs 19%

Significance tests are one-tailed test: *p < 0.05; ** p < 0.01; *** p < 0.001, **** p < 0.0001

SLI = specific language impairment, LI = speech or language impairment; LD = learning disability

Source: Adapted from Stromswold 1998

impaired, and Tallal et al. (1991) found no differences in the language abilities of children who did and did not have a positive family history of language disorders. According to the DLEH, the deficits exhibited by language-impaired children are the result of the children "copying" the ungrammatical language of their parents. Thus, the DLEH predicts that language-impaired children should have the same type of impairment as their relatives. Contrary to this prediction, Neils and Aram (1986) found that 38 per cent of parents with a history of a speech and language disorder said that the disorder they had was different from their children's disorder. According to the DLEH, parents with a history of spoken language impairment who are no longer impaired should be no more likely to have language-impaired children than parents with no such history. Contrary to this prediction, Neils and Aram (1986) found that a third of the probands' parents who had a history of a spoken language disorder no longer suffered from the disorder as an adult. Contrary to the DLEH prediction that all children with SLI should have at least one close relative with a language impairment, in the studies reviewed, an average of 58 per cent of the language-impaired children had no first-degree relatives with impairments. If the DLEH is correct, birth order might affect how likely a child is to exhibit a language disorder. But, contrary to this prediction, birth order does not affect the severity or likelihood of developing language disorders (e.g., Tomblin et al. 1991). In our society, mothers typically have the primary responsibility for child-rearing. Thus, the DLEH predicts that the correlation of language status should be greatest between mother and child. Contrary to this prediction, Tomblin (1989) found that among the family relations he studied (e.g., mother–child, father–child, male sibling–child, female sibling–child), the relationship was weakest between mother and child. In addition, Tomblin and Buckwalter (1994) found that the ratio of impaired fathers to impaired mothers was 2.7:1; Neils and Aram (1986) found the ratio was 1.4:1; and Tallal et al. (1989a), Whitehurst et al. (1991), and Lewis (1992) all found the ratio was approximately 1:1.

Twin studies

The influences of environmental and genetic factors on language disorders can be teased apart by comparing the concordance rates for language impairment in monozygotic (MZ) and dizygotic (DZ) twins. Because MZ and DZ twins share the same pre- and postnatal environment, if the concordance rate for a particular trait is greater for MZ than DZ twins, this can be taken to reflect the fact that MZ twins share 100 per cent of their genetic material, whereas, on average, DZ twins share only 50 per cent of their genetic material (for a review, see Eldridge 1983). I reviewed five studies which examined the concordance rates for written language disorders and four studies which examined the concordance rates for spoken language disorders (Stromswold 1996, forthcoming b; see tables 13.2 and 13.3). In all nine studies, the concordance rates were greater for MZ than DZ twin pairs, with the differences being significant

Table 13.2 Concordance rates for twins with written language disorders

Study	Twin pairs	Diagnosis	Proband concordance
Zerbin-Rubin 1967	17 MZ 33 DZ	word blindness	100% MZ vs 50% DZ***
Bakwin 1973	31 MZ 31 DZ	dyslexia	overall: 91% MZ vs 45% DZ*** Male: 91% MZ vs 59% DZ* Female: 91% MZ vs 15% DZ****
Matheny et al 1976	17 MZ 10 DZ	dyslexia or academic problems	86% MZ vs 33% DZ
Stevenson et al. 1987	18 MZ† 30 DZ†	reading and spelling retardation (Neale and Schonell tests)	Neale reading: 33% MZ vs 29% DZ Schon'ell reading: 35% MZ vs 31% DZ spelling: 50% MZ vs 33% DZ
DeFries and Gillis 1991	133 MZ 98 DZ	dyslexia (PIAT scores)	66% MZ vs 43% DZ***
Overall††	212 MZ, 199 DZ		74.9% MZ vs 42.7% DZ****

Significance tests are one-tailed tests: $* \ p < 0.05; ** \ p < 0.01; *** \ p < 0.001; **** \ p < 0.0001$

† Number of pairs of twins varied according to diagnosis.

†† Overall rates include data for Stevenson et al.'s "Schonell reading retarded" group.

Tests: PIAT = Peabody Individual Achievement Test Word Recognition Reading (Dunn and Markwardt 1970); Schonell Reading & Spelling Tests (Schonell and Schonell 1960), Neale Reading Test (Neale 1967).

Source: Adapted from Stromswold, forthcoming b

Table 13.3 Concordance rates for twins with spoken language disorders

Study	Twin pairs	Diagnosis	Proband concordance
Lewis and Thompson 1992	32 MZ† 25 DZ†	received speech or language therapy	any disorder: 86% MZ vs 48% DZ** articulation: 98% MZ vs 36% DZ**** LD: 70% MZ vs 50% DZ delayed speech: 83% MZ vs 0% DZ*
Tomblin and Buckwalter 1994	56 MZ 26 DZ	SLI (questionnaire to speech pathologists)	89% MZ vs 55% DZ**
Bishop et al. 1995	63 MZ 27 DZ	SLI (by test scores)	strict criteria: 70% MZ vs 46% DZ* broad criteria: 94% vs 62% DZ**
Tomblin and Buckwalter 1995	37 MZ 16 DZ	SLI (composite score > 1 SD below mean)	96% MZ vs 61% DZ**
Overall†	188 MZ, 94 DZ		84.3% MZ vs 52.0% DZ****

Significance tests are one-tailed tests: * $p < 0.015$; ** $p < 0.01$; *** $p < 0.001$; **** $p < 0.0001$

LD = Learning disorder

† Overall rates include data for Lewis and Thompson's (1992) "any diagnosis" group and Bishop et al.'s (1995) strict criteria group.

Source: Adapted from Stromswold, forthcoming, b

in all the studies except Stevenson et al. 1987. In these studies concordance rates ranged from 100 per cent (Zerbin-Rudin 1967) to 33 per cent (Stevenson et al. 1987) for MZ twins and from 61 per cent (Tomblin and Buckwalter 1995) to 29 per cent (Stevenson et al. 1987) for DZ twins.[11]

The studies I reviewed (Stromswold 1996 and forthcoming, b) included 212 MZ and 199 DZ twin pairs in which at least one member of the twin pair had a written language disorder, for concordance rates of 74.9 per cent for MZ twins and 42.7 per cent for DZ twins ($z = 6.53$, $p > 0.00000005$). The studies included 188 MZ and 94 DZ twin pairs in which at least one member of the twin pair had a spoken language disorder, for concordance rates of 84.3 per cent for MZ twins and 52.0 per cent for DZ twins ($z = 5.14$, $p > 0.00000025$). Overall, the studies included 400 MZ twin pairs and 293 DZ twin pairs, for concordance rates of 79.5 per cent for MZ twins and 45.8 per cent for DZ twins ($z = 8.77$, $p > 0.00000005$).

The finding that concordance rates were significantly greater for MZ twins than DZ twins indicates that genetic factors play a significant role in the development of language disorders. The overall concordance rates for written and spoken language disorders are reasonably similar, with concordance rates for spoken language disorders being approximately 10 percentage points higher than the rates for written language disorders. However, the fact that the difference between MZ and DZ concordance rates was very similar for written and spoken language disorders is consistent with genetic factors playing an equal role in both types of impairments.

Modes of transmission

In a recent review of behavioral genetic studies of spoken language disorders, I concluded (Stromswold 1998) that most familial language disorders are the product of complex interactions between genes and the environment. In rare cases, however, language disorders may have a single major locus. For example, researchers have reported a number of kindreds with extremely large numbers of severely affected family members (e.g., Arnold 1961; Gopnik 1990a; Hurst et al. 1990; Lewis 1990) in which transmission seems to be autosomal dominant, with variable rates of expressivity and penetrance. Samples and Lane (1985) performed a similar analysis on a family in which all six of six siblings had a severe developmental language disorder and concluded that the mode of transmission in that family was a single autosomal recessive gene. If there are multiple modes of transmission for SLI, as the above results seem to indicate, this suggests that SLI is genetically heterogeneous, just as dyslexia appears to be genetically heterogeneous (see below).

The final – and most definitive – method for determining whether there is a genetic basis for familial language disorders is to determine which gene (or genes) is responsible for the language disorders found in these families. The typical way this is done is to use linkage analysis techniques to compare the genetic material of language-impaired and normal family members and to determine how the genetic material of affected family members differs from that of unaffected family members. Linkage analyses of dyslexic families suggest that written language disorders are genetically heterogenous (Bisgaard et al. 1987; Smith et al. 1986), with different studies revealing involvement of chromosome 15 (Smith et al. 1983; Pennington and Smith 1988), the HLA region of chromosome 6 (Rabin et al. 1993), and the Rh region of chromosome 1 (Rabin et al. 1993). Froster et al. (1993) have reported a case of familial speech retardation and dyslexia that appears to be caused by a balanced translocation of the short arm of chromosome 1 and the long arm of chromosome 2. Recently, Fisher and colleagues (1998) conducted the first linkage analyses for spoken language disorders, performing genome-wide analyses of the genetic material of the three-generation family studied by Gopnik (1990a) and Hurst et al. (1990). They determined that the orofacial dyspraxia and speech and language disorders exhibited by members of this family are linked to a small region on the long arm of chromosome 7, confirming autosomal dominant transmission with near 100 per cent penetrance. However, it is important to note that in addition to the grammatical deficits described by Gopnik (1990a), affected members of this family also suffer from orofacial dyspraxia and associated speech disorders (see Hurst et al. 1990; Fisher et al. 1998). Hence, we should not conclude that the identified region of chromosome 7 necessarily contains gene(s) which are specific to language. Clearly, linkage studies must be performed on other families whose deficits are more circumscribed.

At least three distinct relationships could obtain between genotypes and behavioral phenotypes. It is possible (although unlikely) that there is a one-to-one relationship between genotypes and phenotypes, with each genotype causing a distinct type of language disorder. Alternatively, there might be a one-to-many mapping between genotypes and phenotypes, with a single genetic disorder resulting in many behaviorally distinct types of language disorders. For example, one MZ twin with a genetically encoded articulation disorder might respond by refusing to talk at all, whereas his co-twin with the same genotype might speak and make many articulation errors. Lastly, there may be a many-to-one mapping between genotypes and phenotypes, with many distinctive genetic disorders resulting in the same type of linguistic disorder. For example, SLI children who frequently omit grammatical morphemes (see Leonard 1998; Stromswold 1997) might do so because they suffer from an articulation disorder such as dyspraxia which caused them to omit grammatical morphemes that are pronounced rapidly, because they have difficulty processing rapid auditory input such as unstressed, short-duration grammatical morphemes, or because they have a syntactic deficit.

Although it is possible for a single genotype to result in different linguistic profiles and, conversely, for different genotypes to result in very similar profiles, researchers should attempt to limit behavior heterogeneity among their subjects. Doing so will increase the likelihood of identifying whether specific genotypes are associated with specific types of linguistic disorders, and hence will help answer the question of whether the ability to learn language is the result of genetically encoded, linguistically specific operations.

4.4   Recovery from acquired brain damage

Lesions acquired during infancy typically result in relatively transient, minor linguistic deficits, whereas similar lesions acquired during adulthood typically result in permanent, devastating language impairments (see, e.g., Guttmann 1942; Lenneberg 1967; but see Dennis 1997 for a critique).[12] The generally more optimistic prognosis for injuries acquired during early childhood may reflect the fact that less neuronal pruning has occurred in young brains (Cowan et al. 1984), and that the creation of new synapses and the reactivation of latent synapses is more likely in younger brains (Huttenlocher 1979). Language acquisition after childhood brain injuries has typically been attributed either to recruitment of brain regions that are adjacent to the damaged perisylvian language regions in the left hemisphere or to recruitment of the topographically homologous regions in the undamaged right hemisphere. According to Lenneberg (1967), prior to puberty, the right hemisphere can completely take over the language functions of the left hemisphere. The observation that infants and toddlers who undergo complete removal of the left hemisphere acquire or recover near-normal language suggests that the right hemisphere can take over *most* of the language functions of the left hemisphere if the transfer of function happens at an early enough age (Byrne and Gates 1987; Dennis 1980; Dennis and Kohn 1975; Dennis and Whitaker 1976; Rankin et al. 1981; but see Bishop 1983 for a critique). Because few studies have examined the linguistic abilities of children who undergo left hemispherectomy during middle childhood, the upper age limit for hemispheric transfer of language is unclear. Right-handed adults who undergo left hemispherectomy typically become globally aphasic with essentially no recovery of language (e.g., Crockett and Estridge 1951; Smith 1966; Zollinger 1935). The observation that a right-handed 10-year-old child (Gardner et al. 1955) and a right-handed 14-year-old child (Hillier 1954) who underwent left hemispherectomy reportedly suffered from global aphasia with modest recovery of language function suggests that hemispheric transfer of language function is greatly reduced but perhaps not completely eliminated by puberty.

Studies which reveal that left-hemisphere lesions are more often associated with (subtle) syntactic deficits than are right-hemisphere lesions (Aram et al. 1985, 1986; Byrne and Gates 1987; Dennis 1980; Dennis and Kohn 1975; Dennis and Whitaker 1976; Kiessling et al. 1983; Rankin et al. 1981; Thal et al. 1991; Woods and Carey 1979) call into question the complete equipotentiality of the right and left hemispheres for language and suggest that regions in the left hemisphere may be uniquely suited to acquire syntax. It should be noted, however, that some studies have not found greater syntactic deficits with left- than right-hemisphere lesions (e.g., Basser 1962; Feldman et al.

1992; Levy et al. 1992). These studies may have included children whose lesions were smaller (Feldman et al. 1992) or in different locations from those in studies that have found a hemispheric difference for syntax. Bates and colleagues have examined early language acquisition in children who suffered unilateral brain injuries prior to 6 months of age (Bates et al. 1997). Parents of 26 children (16 with left-hemisphere lesions, 10 with right-hemisphere lesions) between the ages of 10 and 17 months completed the MacArthur Communicative Development Inventory. According to parental report, over-all, children with brain injuries had smaller vocabularies than normal children.[13] Consistent with Neville et al.'s (1997) ERP findings that the right hemisphere is particularly crucial in the perception of unknown words by children between 13 and 20 months of age, children with right-hemisphere lesions had *smaller* expressive vocabularies and used fewer communicative gestures than children with left-hemisphere lesions (Bates et al. 1997). Parental report for 29 children (17 with left-hemisphere lesions and 12 with right-hemisphere lesions) between 19 and 31 months of age generally revealed that children with left-hemisphere lesions had more limited grammatical abilities than children with right-hemisphere lesions (Bates et al. 1997). This was particularly true for children with left temporal lesions. Bates and colleagues (1997) also compared the mean length of utterance (MLU) in free speech samples for 30 children (24 with left-hemisphere lesions and 6 with right-hemisphere lesions) between the ages of 20 and 44 months. Consistent with the parental report results, children with left-hemisphere lesions had lower MLUs than children with right-hemisphere lesions. MLUs for children with left temporal lesions were especially depressed compared to children without left temporal injuries.

In children who suffer from partial left-hemisphere lesions rather than complete left hemispherectomies, language functions could be assumed by adjacent undamaged tissues within the left hemisphere or by homotopic structures in the intact right hemisphere. Results of Wada tests (in which lateralization of language is determined by testing language function when each hemisphere is temporarily anesthetized) indicate that children with partial left-hemisphere lesions often have language represented bilaterally or in the right hemisphere (Mateer and Dodrill 1983; Rasmussen and Milner 1977). However, one ERP study suggests that children with partial left-hemisphere lesions are more likely to have language localized in the left hemisphere than the right hemisphere (Papanicolaou et al. 1990). There are a number of possible reasons for this discrepancy, including differences in the types of linguistic tasks used in the ERP and Wada studies and possible differences in sizes and sites of left-hemisphere lesions in the children studied. In addition, it is possible that the discrepancy is due to the fact that most of the children in the ERP study acquired their lesions after age 4, and, furthermore, it is unclear the extent to which any of the children in the ERP study ever exhibited signs of language impairment.

Although there is disagreement about the details of language recovery after postnatally acquired left-hemisphere lesions, the following generalizations can be made (but see Dennis 1997). Behaviorally, the prognosis for recovery of language is generally better for lesions that are acquired at a young age, and syntactic deficits are among the most common persistent deficits. If a lesion is so large that there is little or no undamaged tissue adjacent to the language regions of the left hemisphere, regions of the right hemisphere (presumably homotopic to the left-hemisphere language areas) can be recruited for language. The essentially intact linguistic abilities of children with extensive left-hemisphere lesions are particularly remarkable when contrasted with the markedly impaired linguistic abilities of SLI children who have minimal evidence of neuropathology on CT or MRI scans. Perhaps the reason for this curious finding is that, although SLI children's brains are not deviant on a macroscopic level, SLI brains may have pervasive, bilateral microscopic anomalies such that there is no normal tissue that can be recruited for language function (see the section on SLI). One piece of evidence that supports this hypothesis is the result of an autopsy performed on a boy who suffered a severe cyanotic episode at 10 days of age and subsequently suffered from pronounced deficits in language comprehension and expression until his death (from mumps and congenital heart disease) at age 10. Autopsy revealed that the boy had bilateral loss of cortical substance starting at the inferior and posterior margin of the central sulci and extending backwards along the course of the insula and sylvian fissures for 8 cm on the left side and 6 cm on the right side (Landau et al. 1960). Perhaps the reason why this child did not "outgrow" his language disorder is that, because he had extensive bilateral lesions, there were no appropriate regions that could be recruited for language.

5 Summary

Evidence from normal and abnormal language acquisition suggests that innate mechanisms allow children to acquire language. Just as in the case with vision, given adequate, early exposure to language, children's language develops rapidly and with few errors, despite little or no instruction. The brain regions that permit this to occur seem to be functionally and anatomically distinct at birth and may correspond to what linguists refer to as Universal Grammar. It is possible that the reason why exposure to a particular language must occur during infancy and early childhood in order for that language to be mastered is that the type of neural fine-tuning that is associated with learning the parameters of a particular language must occur while there is a high degree of neural plasticity. There is some evidence to suggest that the structures and operations that are involved in language are at least partially anatomically and functionally modular and apparently do not have non-linguistic counterparts. One possibility is that children have innate mechanisms that predispose them to perceive categorically linguistic stimuli such as phonemes, words, syntactic categories, and phrases, and that exposure to these types of linguistic stimuli facilitates the neural fine-tuning necessary for normal language acquisition. For example, children might have innate mechanisms that predispose them to assume that certain types of meanings and distinctions are likely to be conveyed by morphemes. They might also have innate mechanisms that specifically predispose them to distinguish between syntactic categories that allow for free generalization (lexical categories) and those that do not (functional categories). These innate mechanisms may allow children's brains to solve the otherwise intractable induction problems that permeate language acquisition.

In the future, fine-grained linguistic analyses of the speech of language-impaired children may be used to distinguish between different types of SLI. Linkage studies of SLI may tell us which genes code for the brain structures that are necessary for language acquisition. MRI's exquisite sensitivity to white matter/gray matter distinctions means that MRI could be used to look for more subtle defects that may be associated with developmental language disorders, such as subtle disorders of neuronal migration or dysmyelinization (Barkovich and Kjos 1992; Edelman and Warach 1993). Furthermore, the correlation between myelinization and development of function (Smith 1981) means that serial MRIs of normal children, SLI children, and WS children could potentially shed light on the relationship between brain maturation and normal and abnormal language development. Lastly, functional neuroimaging techniques such as ERP, PET, and functional MRI will undoubtedly help answer questions about the neural processes that underlie language and language acquisition in normal children, SLI children, WS children, children with left-hemisphere lesions, and children who are exposed to language after the critical period.

Notes

Preparation of this chapter was supported by a Merck Foundation Fellowship in the Biology of Developmental Disabilities and a Johnson and Johnson Discovery Award. I am grateful to Willem Levelt for his support during the writing of this chapter and to Anne Christophe, Steve Pinker, and Myrna Schwartz for their comments on earlier versions.

1   Children differ dramatically in the rate of acquisition. For example, Brown (1973) and Cazden (1968) investigated when three children mastered the use of 14 grammatical morphemes. Although all three children eventually obtained competence in the use of the third-singular verbal inflection -s (as in he sings), and all three children reached this point after they achieved adult-like performance on plurals and possessives, one of the children reached competence at 2;3 (two years and three months), one at 3;6, and one at 3;8. Similar findings concerning individual differences have been found in rate of acquisition of questions (Stromswold 1988, 1995), auxiliaries (Stromswold 1990b), datives, verb particles and

related constructions (Snyder and Stromswold 1997; Stromswold 1989b). A number of studies have also reported that children's vocabulary development can vary greatly in both rate and style (e.g., Nelson 1973; Goldfield and Reznick 1990).

2   Although the observation that the pattern of acquisition varies depending on the structure of the language is consistent with functionalist accounts of language acquisition (e.g., MacWhinney 1987), such observations can be accounted for within generative theories if one makes the assumption that children must receive a certain amount of positive data from the input in order to set parameters (for P&P) or rank constraints (for OT).

3   Throughout the chapter, ungrammatical sentences are indicated with an asterisk (*).

4   There are 23! logically possible unique orders of all 23 auxiliaries. The total number of orders including sets with fewer than 23 auxiliaries is considerably bigger. Because the 23 term is the largest term in the summation, it serves as a lower bound for the number of unique orders and suffices as an estimation of the number of orders.

5   The mere existence of cerebral asymmetries does not prove that there is an innate basis for language, as other mammals exhibit such asymmetries.

6   Fifteen of the 20 parents and 4 of the 10 siblings had language deficits. The controls had no history or family history of language impairment or delay.

7   These were not, however, the same children who did poorly on Tallal and Piercy's (1973a, 1973b) auditory processing task.

8   Although clinicians and researchers generally agree that considerable diversity exists in the behavioral profiles and manifestations of children diagnosed with SLI and that it is important to distinguish between various subtypes of SLI, no system for classifying subtypes of SLI is generally accepted (Stromswold 1997).

9   The term "proband" is the term used to refer to an affected individual through whom a family is first brought to the attention of an investigator.

10 The variance is due in large part to what was counted as evidence of language impairment in families. As indicated in table 13.1, some studies considered family members to be affected only if they suffered from a spoken language disorder, whereas other studies counted as affected family members with a history of dyslexia, non-language learning disabilities, or school problems.

11 In this chapter, all concordance rates are proband-wise concordance rates. Proband-wise concordance rates are calculated by taking the number of affected individuals in concordant twin pairs (i.e., twin pairs where both twins are affected) and dividing this number by the total number of affected individuals.

12 In a recent review of research on children whose brain injuries occurred after the onset of language acquisition, Dennis (1997) argues that the prognosis is no better for children than adults once the etiology of the brain injury is taken into account.

13 Bates and colleagues (1997) report large variance in language abilities among their lesioned subjects, with some of the children's language being at the high end of the normal range and other children suffering from profound impairments. This probably reflects, at least in part, variations in the size and sites of the lesions among their subjects.

References

Aksu-Koç, A. A. and Slobin, D. I. (1985) The acquisition of Turkish. In Slobin 839–80.

Aram, D. M., Ekelman, B. L., Rose, D. F. and Whitaker, H. A. (1985) Verbal and cognitive sequelae of unilateral lesions acquired in early childhood. *Journal of Clinical and Experimental Neuropsychology* 7, 55–78.

Aram, D. M., Ekelman, B. L. and Whitaker, H. A. (1986) Spoken syntax in children with acquired unilateral hemisphere lesions. *Brain and Language* 27, 75–100.

Arnold, G. E. (1961) The genetic background of developmental language disorders. *Folia Phoniatrica* 13, 246–54.

Arnold, G. and Schwartz S. (1983) Hemispheric lateralization of language in autistic and aphasic children. *Journal of Autism and Developmental Disorders* 13, 129–39.

Baker, C. L. (1981) Learnability and the English auxiliary system. In C. L. Baker and J. J. McCarthy (eds) *The Logical Problem of Language Acquisition*, Cambridge, Mass., MIT Press, 297–323.

Bakwin, H. (1973) Reading disabilities in twins. *Developmental Medicine and Child Neurology* 15, 184–7.

Barkovich, A. J. and Kjos, B. O. (1992) Grey matter heterotopias: MR characteristics and correlation with developmental and neurological manifestations. *Radiology* 182, 493–9.

Basser, L. S. (1962) Hemiplegia of early onset and faculty of speech, with special reference to the effects of hemispherectomy. *Brain* 85, 427–60.

Bates, E. and MacWhinney, B. (1982) Functionalist approaches to grammar. In L. Gleitman and E. Wanner (eds), *Language Acquisition: The State of the Art*, Cambridge: Cambridge University Press, 173–218.

Beitchman, J. H., Hood, J. and Inglis, A. (1992) Familial transmission of speech and language impairment: a preliminary investigation. *Canadian Journal of Psychiatry* 37(3), 151–6.

Bellugi, U., Birhle, A., Neville, H., Jernigan, T. L. and Doherty, S. (1992). Language, cognition, and brain organization in a neurodevelopmental disorder. In M. Gunnar and C. Nelson (eds), *Developmental Behavioral Neuroscience*, Hillsdale, NJ; Erlbaum Press, 201–32.

Bellugi, U., Wang, P. P. and Jernigan, T. L. (1994) Williams Syndrome: an unusual neuropsychological profile. In S. H. Bronman and J. Grafman (eds), *Atypical Cognitive Deficits in Developmental Disorders: Implications for Brain Function*, Hillsdale, NJ: Lawrence Erlbaum, 23–56.

Benedict, H. (1979) Early lexical development: comprehension and production. *Journal of Child Language* 6, 183–200.

Berman, R. A. (1986) A crosslinguistic perspective: morphology and syntax. In P. Fletcher and M. Garman (eds), *Language Acquisition* 2nd edn, Cambridge: Cambridge University Press, 429–47.

Bickerton, D. (1981) *Roots of Language*, Ann Arbor, MI: Karoma.

—— (1984) The language bioprogram hypothesis. *Behavioral and Brain Sciences* 7, 173–221.

Bisgaard, M., Eiberg, H., Moller, N., Niebuhr, E. and Mohr J. (1987) Dyslexia and chromosome 15 heteromorphism: negative lod score in a Danish material. *Clinical Genetics* 32, 118–19.

Bishop, D. V. M. (1983) Linguistic impairment after left hemidecortication for infantile hemiplegia: a reappraisal. *Quarterly Journal of Experimental Psychology* 35A, 199–207.

—— (1987) The causes of specific developmental language disorder ('developmental dysphasia'). *Journal of Child Psychology and Psychiatry* 28, 1–8.

Bishop, D. V. M. and Edmundson, A. (1986) Is *otitis media* a major cause of specific developmental language disorders? *British Journal of Disorders of Communication* 21, 321–38.

Bishop, D. V. M., North, T. and Donlan, C. (1995) Genetic basis of specific language impairment: evidence from a twin study. *Developmental Medicine and Child Neurology* 37, 56–71.

Bloom, P. (1990) Syntactic distinctions in child language. *Journal of Child Language* 17, 343–55.

Boliek, C. A., Bryden, M. P. and Obrzut, J. E. (1988). Focused attention and the perception of voicing and place of articulation contrasts with control and learning-disabled children. Paper presented at the 16th Annual Meeting of the International Neuropsychological Society, January.

Brown, R. (1973) *A First Language: The Early Stages*, Cambridge, MA: Harvard University Press.

Brown, R. and Hanlon, C. (1970). Derivational complexity and order of acquisition in child speech. In J. R. Hayes (ed), *Cognition and the Development of Language*, New York: Wiley, 11–53.

Budwig, N. (1995) *A Developmental-Functionalist Approach to Language*, Mahwah, NJ; Lawrence Erlbaum Associates.

Byrne, J. M. and Gates, R. D. (1987) Single-case study of left cerebral hemispherectomy: development in the first five years of life. *Journal of Clinical and Experimental Neuropsychology* 9, 423–34.

Byrne, J. M., Willerman, L. and Ashmore, L. L. (1974) Severe and moderate language impairment: evidence for distinctive etiologies. *Behavioral Genetics* 4, 331–45.

Cazden, C. (1968) The acquisition of noun and verb inflections. *Child Development* 39, 433–48.

Chi, J. G., Dooling, E. C. and Gilles, F. H. (1977) Left-right asymmetries of the temporal speech areas of the human brain. *Archives of Neurology* 34, 346–8.

Chomsky, N. (1981) *Lectures on Government and Binding*, Dordrecht: Foris.

—— (1986) *Knowledge of Language: Its Nature, Origin and Use*, New York: Praeger.

Clahsen, H. (1989) The grammatical characterization of developmental dysphasia. *Linguistics* 27(5), 897–920.

—— (1991) *Child Language and Developmental Dysphasia: Linguistic Studies of the Acquisition of German*, Philadelphia: J. Benjamins Publishing Company.

Clark, M. and Plante, E. (1995) Morphology in the inferior frontal gyrus in developmentally language-disordered adults. Paper presented at the Conference on Cognitive Neuroscience, San Francisco.

Cohen, M., Campbell, R. and Yaghmai, F. (1989) Neuropathological abnormalities in developmental dysphasia. *Annals of Neurology* 25, 567–70.

Cohen, H., Gelinas, C., Lassonde, M. and Geoffroy, G. (1991) Auditory lateralization for speech in language-impaired children. *Brain and Language* 41, 395–401.

Conti-Ramsden, G. and Dykins, J. (1991) Mother–child interactions with language-impaired children and their siblings. *British Journal of Disorders of Communication* 26, 337–54.

Conti-Ramsden, G. and Friel-Patti, S. (1983) Mothers' discourse adjustments with language-impaired and non-language-impaired children. *Journal of Speech and Hearing Disorders* 48, 360–7.

Coppola, M., Senghas, A., Newport, E. L. and Supalla T. (1998) The emergence of grammar: evidence from family-based gesture systems in Nicaragua. Unpublished manuscript, University of Rochester.

Courchesne, E., Lincoln, A., Yeung-Courchesne, R., Elmasian, R. and Grillon, C. (1989) Pathophysiological finding in nonretarded autism and receptive developmental language disorder. *Journal of Autism and Developmental Disorders* 19, 1–17.

Cowan, W. M., Fawcett, J. W., O'Leary, D. D. and Stanfield, B. B. (1984) Regressive events in neurogenesis. *Science* 225, 1258–65.

Crago, M. B. and Gopnik, M. (1994) From families to phenotypes: theoretical and clinical implications of research into the genetic basis of specific language impairment. In R. V. Watkins and M. L. Rice (eds), *Specific Language Impairments in Children*, Baltimore: Paul H. Brookes Publishing Co., 35–52.

Cramblit, N. and Siegel, G. (1977) The verbal environment of a language-impaired child. *Journal of Speech and Hearing Disorders* 42, 474–82.

Crockett, H. G. and Estridge, N. M. (1951) Cerebral hemispherectomy. *Bulletin of the Los Angeles Neurology Society* 16, 71–87.

Croft, W. (1990) *Typology and Universals*, New York: Cambridge University Press.

Cromer, R. (1983) Hierarchical planning disability in the drawings and constructions of a special group of severely aphasic children. *Brain and Cognition* 2, 144–64.

Curtiss, S. (1977) *Genie: A Psycholinguistic Study of a Modern Day "Wild Child"*, New York: Academic Press.

—— (1989) The independence and task-specificity of language. In A. Bornstein and J. Bruner (eds), *Interaction in Human Development*, Hillsdale, NJ: Erlbaum, 105–37.

Davis, K. (1940) Extreme social isolation of a child. *American Journal of Sociology* 45, 554–65.

—— (1947) Final note on a case of extreme isolation. *American Journal of Sociology* 52, 432–7.

Dawson, G., Finley, C., Phillips, S. and Lewy, A. (1989) A comparison of hemispheric asymmetries in speech-related brain potentials of autistic and dysphasic children. *Brain and Language* 37, 26–41.

DeFries, J. C. and Gillis, J. J. (1993) Genetics of reading disability. In R. Plomin and G. E. McClearn (eds), *Nature, Nurture, and Psychology*, Washington, DC: American Psychological Association, 121–45.

Denays, R., Tondeur, M., Foulon, M., Verstraeten, F., Ham, H., Piepsz, A. and Noel, P. (1989) Regional brain blood flow in congenital dysphasia studies with technetium-99M HM-PAO SPECT. *Journal of Nuclear Medicine* 30, 1825–9.

Dennis, M. (1980) Capacity and strategy for syntactic comprehension after left or right hemidecortication. *Brain and Language* 10, 287–317.

—— (1997) Acquired disorders of language in children. In T. E. Feinberg and M. J. Farah (eds), *Behavioral Neurology and Neuropsychology*, New York: McGraw-Hill, 737–54.

Dennis, M. and Kohn, B. (1975) Comprehension of syntax in infantile hemiplegics after cerebral hemidecortication: left hemisphere superiority. *Brain and Language* 2, 475–86.

Dennis, M. and Whitaker, H. A. (1976) Language acquisition following hemidecortication: linguistic superiority of the left over the right hemisphere. *Brain and Language* 3, 404–33.

de Villiers, J. and de Villiers, P. (1973) A cross-sectional study of the acquisition of grammatical morphemes in child speech. *Journal of Psycholinguistic Research* 2, 267–78.

Dunn, L. M. and Markwardt, F. C. (1970) *Peabody Individual Achievement Test Manual*. Circle Pines, MN: American Guidance Service.

Edelman, R. R. and Warach, S. (1993) Magnetic Resonance Imaging (Part 1). *New England Journal of Medicine* 328, 708–16.

Efron, R. (1963) Temporal perception, aphasia, and déjà vu. *Brain* 86, 403–24.

Eldridge, R. (1983) Twin studies and the etiology of complex neurological disorders. In C. L. Ludlow and J. A. Cooper (eds), *Genetic Aspects of Speech and Language Disorders*, New York: Academic Press, 109–21.

Elman, J., Bates, E., Johnson, M., Karmiloff-Smith, A., Parisi, D. and Plunkett, K. (1996) *Rethinking Innateness: A Connectionist Perspective on Development*, Cambridge, MA: MIT Press.

Ewart, A. K., Morris, C. A., Atkinson, D., Wieshan, J., Sternes, K., Spallone, P., Stock, A. D., Leppert, M. and Keating, M. T. (1993a) Hemizygosity at the elastin locus in a developmental disorder: Williams syndrome. *Nature Genetics* 5, 11–16.

Ewart, A. K., Morris, C. A., Ensing, G. J., Loker, J., Moore, C., Leppert, M. and Keating, M. (1993b) A human vascular disorder, supravalvular aortic stenosis, maps to chromosome 7. *Proceedings of the National Academy of Science* 90(8), 3226–30.

Feldman, H., Holland, A. L., Kemp, S. S. and Janosky, J. E. (1992) Language development after unilateral brain injury. *Brain and Language* 42, 89–102.

Fenson, L., Dale, P. S., Reznick, J. S., Bates, E., Thal, D. J. and Pethick, S. J. (1994) Variability in early communicative development. *Monographs of the Society for Research in Child Development* 59, (serial No. 242).

Fisher, S. E., Vargha-Khadem, F., Watkins, K. E., Monaco, A. P. and Pembrey, M. E. (1998) Localization of a gene implicated in a severe speech and language disorder. *Nature Genetics* 18, 168–70.

Foley, W. and Van Valin, R. (1984) *Functional Syntax and Universal Grammar*, Cambridge: Cambridge University Press.

Froster, H., Schulte-Korne, G., Hebebrand, J. and Remschnoidt, H. (1993) Cosegregation of balanced translocation (1; 2) with retarded speech development and dyslexia. *Lancet* 342, 178–90.

Galaburda, A. M., Wang, P. R., Bellugi, U. and Rossen, M. (1994) Cytoarchitectonic anomalies in a genetically based disorder: Williams Syndrome. *Neuroreport* 5, 753–7.

Ganger, J. and Stromswold, K. (1998) The innateness, evolution and genetics of language. *Human Biology* 70, 199–213.

Gardner, W. J., Karnosh, L. J., McClure, C. C. and Gardner, A. K. (1955) Residual function following hemispherectomy for tumour and for infantile hemiplegia. *Brain* 78, 487–502.

Garrett, M. (1976) Syntactic processes in sentence production. In R. Wales and E. Walker (eds) *New Approaches to Language Mechanisms*, Amsterdam: North-Holland, 231–56.

Geschwind, N. and Galaburda, A. (1987) *Cerebral Lateralization: Biological Mechanisms, Associations, and Pathology*, Cambridge, MA: MIT Press.

Goldfield, B. A. and Reznick, J. S. (1990) Early lexical acquisition: rate, content and vocabulary spurt. *Journal of Child Language* 17, 171–84.

Goldin-Meadow, S. and Mylander, C. (1984) Gestural communication in deaf children: the effects and non-effects of parental input on early language development. *Monographs of the Society for Research in Child Development* 49, 1–121.

—— (1998) Spontaneous sign systems created by deaf children in two cultures. *Nature* 391, 279–81.

Goodglass, H. (1976) Agrammatism. In H. Whitaker and H. Whitaker (eds) *Perspectives in Neurolinguistics and Psycholinguistics*, New York: Academic Press.

Gopnik, M. (1990a) Feature-blind grammar and dysphasia. *Nature* 344–715.

—— (1990b) Feature blindness: a case study. *Language Acquisition* 1, 139–64.

Gopnik, M. and Crago, M. B. (1991) Familial aggregation of a developmental language disorder. *Cognition* 39, 1–50.

Gordon, A. G. (1988) Some comments on Bishop's annotation "Developmental dysphasia and otitis media." *Journal of Child Psychology and Psychiatry* 29, 361–3.

Graham, N. C. (1968) Short term memory and syntactic structure in educationally subnormal children. *Language and Speech* 11, 209–19.

—— (1974) Response strategies in the partial comprehension of sentences. *Language and Speech* 17, 205–21.

Gravel, J. S. and Wallace, I. F. (1992) Listening and language at 4 years of age: effects of early otitis media. *Journal of Speech and Hearing Research* 35, 588–95.

Guilfoyle, E., Allen, S. and Moss, S. (1991) Specific language impairment and the maturation of functional categories. Paper presented at the 16th Annual Boston University Conference on Language Development, 19 October.

Guttman, E. (1942) Aphasia in children. *Brain* 65, 205–19

Haynes, C. and Naido, S. (1991) *Children with Specific Speech and Language Impairment*, London: MacKeith Press.

Heath, S. B. (1983) *Ways with Words: Language, Life and Work in Communities and Classrooms*, New York: Cambridge University Press.

Hillier, W. F. (1954) Total left cerebral hemispherectomy for malignant glioma. *Neurology* 4, 718–21.

Holcomb, P. J., Coffey, S. A. and Neville, H. J. (1992) Visual and auditory sentence processing: a developmental analysis using event-related brain-potentials. *Developmental Neuropsychology* 8, 203–41.

Hubel, D. and Wiesel, T. (1970) The period of susceptibility to the physiological effects of unilateral eye closure in kittens. *Journal of Physiology* 206, 419–36.

Hurst, J. A., Baraitser, M., Auger, E., Graham, F. and Norell, S. (1990) An extended family with a dominantly inherited speech disorder. *Developmental Medicine and Child Neurology* 32, 347–55.

Huttenlocher, J. and Smiley, P. (1987) Early word meanings: the case of object names. *Cognitive Psychology* 19, 63–89.

Huttenlocher, P. R. (1979) Synaptic density in human frontal cortex – Developmental changes and effects of aging. *Brain Research* 163, 195–205.

Ingram, T. T. S. (1959) Specific developmental disorders of speech in childhood. *Brain* 82, 450–67.

Jackson, T. and Plante, E. (1997) Gyral morphology in the posterior sylvian regions in families affected by developmental language disorders. *Neuropsychology Review* 6, 81–94.

Jernigan, T. L. and Bellugi, U. (1994) Neuroanatomical distinctions between Williams and Down Syndrome. In S. H. Bronman and J. Grafman (eds), *Atypical Cognitive Deficits in Developmental Disorders: Implications for Brain Function*, Hillsdale, NJ: Lawrence Erlbaum, 57–66.

Jernigan, T. L., Bellugi, U., Sowell, E., Doherty, S. and Hesselink, J. (1993) Cerebral morphological distinctions between Williams and Down Syndromes. *Archives of Neurology* 50, 186–91.

Jernigan, T. L., Hesselink, J. R., Sowell, E. and Tallal, P. A. (1991) Cerebral structure on Magnetic Resonance Imaging in language-impaired and learning-impaired children. *Archives of Neurology* 48, 539–45.

Johnston, J. R. (1991) The continuing relevance of cause: a reply to Leonard's "Specific language impairment as a clinical category." *Language, Speech and Hearing Services in Schools* 22, 75–9.

Johnson, J. R. and Newport, E. (1989) Critical period effects in second language learning: the influence of maturational state on the acquisition of English as a second language. *Cognitive Psychology* 21, 60–99.

Johnston, J. R. and Weismer, S. (1983) Mental rotation abilities in language-disordered children. *Journal of Speech and Hearing Research* 26, 397–403.

Jusczyk, P. W. and Kemler Nelson, D. G. (1996) Syntactic units, prosody, and psychological reality in infancy. In Morgan and Demuth, 389–408.

Jusczyk, P. W., Hirsch-Pasek, K., Kemler Nelson, D. and Kennedy, L. J. (1992). Perception of acoustic correlates of major phrasal units by young infants. *Cognitive Psychology* 24, 252–93.

Kahmi, A. (1981) Nonlinguistic symbolic and conceptual abilities in language-impaired and normally developing children. *Journal of Speech and Hearing Research* 24, 446–53.

Karmiloff-Smith, A. (1991) *Beyond Modularity*, Cambridge, MA: MIT Press.

Karmiloff-Smith, A., Grant, J., Berthoud, I., Davies, M., Howlin, P. and Udwin, O. (1997) Language and Williams syndrome: how intact is "intact"? *Child Development* 68(2), 246–62.

Karmiloff-Smith, A., Tyler, L. K., Voice, K., Sims, K., Udwin, O., Howlin, P. and Davies, M. (1998) Linguistic dissociations in Williams syndrome: evaluating receptive syntax in on-line and off-line tasks. *Neuropsychologia* 36, 343–51.

Kiessling, L. S., Denckla, M. B. V. and Carlton, M. (1983) Evidence for differential hemispheric function in children with hemiplegic cerebral palsy. *Developmental Medicine and Child Neurology* 25, 727–34.

Lahey, M. and Edwards, J. (1995) Specific language impairment: preliminary investigation of factors associated with family history and with patterns of language performance. *Journal of Speech and Hearing Research* 38, 643–57.

Landau, W. M., Goldstein, R. and Kleffner, F. R. (1960) Congenital aphasia: a clinicopathological study. *Neurology* 10, 915—21.

Lasky, E. and Klopp, K. (1982) Parent–child interactions in normal and language-disordered children. *Journal of Speech and Hearing Disorders* 47, 7–18.

Lenneberg, E. H. (1967) *Biological Foundations of Language*, New York: John Wiley & Sons.

Leonard, C. M., Voeller, K., Lombardino, L., Morris, M., Hynd, G., Alexander, A.,

Anderson, H., Garofalakis, M., Honeyman, J., Mao, J., Agee, O. and Staab, E. (1993) Anomalous cerebral structure in dyslexia revealed with magnetic resonance imaging. *Archives of Neurology* 50, 461–9.

Leonard, L. B. (1989) Language learnability and specific language impairment in children. *Applied Psycholinguistics* 10, 179–202.

—— (1991) Specific language impairment as a clinical category. *Language, Speech and Hearing Services in Schools* 22, 66–8.

—— (1994) Some problems facing accounts of morphological deficits in children with specific language impairments. In R. V. Watkins and M. L. Rice (eds), *Specific Language Impairments in Children*, Baltimore: Paul H. Brookes Publishing Co., 91–106.

—— (1998) *Children with Specific Language Impairment*, Cambridge, MA: MIT Press.

Leonard, L. B., McGregor, K. K. and Allen, G. D. (1992) Grammatical morphology and speech perception in children with specific language impairment. *Journal of Speech and Hearing Research* 35, 1076–85.

Levy, Y., Amir, N. and Shalev, R. (1992) Linguistic development of a child with congenital localised L.H. lesion. *Cognitive Neuropsychology* 9, 1–32.

Lewis, B. A. (1990) Familial phonological disorders: four pedigrees. *Journal of Speech and Hearing Disorders* 55, 160–70.

—— (1992) Pedigree analysis of children with phonology disorders. *Journal of Learning Disabilities* 25(9), 586–97.

Lewis, B. A. and Thompson, L. A. (1992) A study of developmental speech and language disorders in twins. *Journal of Speech and Hearing Research* 35, 1086–94.

Lewis, B. A., Ekelman, B. L. and Aram, D. M. (1989) A familial study of severe phonological disorders. *Journal of Speech and Hearing Research* 32, 713–24.

Lincoln, A., Courchesne, E., Harms, L. and Allen, M. (1995) Sensory modulation of auditory stimuli in children with autism and receptive developmental language disorder: event-related brain potential evidence. *Journal of Autism and Developmental Disorders* 25, 521–39.

Lou, H. D., Henriksen, L. and Bruhn, P. (1990) Focal cerebral dysfunction in developmental learning disabilities. *Lancet* 335, 8–11.

Luchsinger, R. (1970) Inheritance of speech deficits. *Folia Phoniatrica* 22, 216–30.

MacWhinney, B. (1987) The competition model. In B. MacWhinney (ed.), *Mechanisms in Language Acquisition*, Hillsdale, NJ: Lawrence Erlbaum Associates, 249–308.

Maratsos, M. and Chalkley, M. (1981) The internal language of children's syntax: the ontogenesis and representation of syntactic categories. In K. Nelson (ed.), *Children's Language*, vol. 2, New York: Gardner Press, 127–214.

Marcus, G. F. (1993) Negative evidence in language acquisition. *Cognition* 46(1), 53–85.

Martin, J. A. (1981) *Voice, Speech and Language in the Child: Development and Disorder*. New York: Springer.

Mateer, C. A. and Dodrill, C. B. (1983) Neuropsychological and linguistic correlates of atypical language lateralization: evidence from sodium amytal studies. *Human Neurobiology* 2, 135–42.

Matheny, A. P., Dolan, A. B. and Wilson, R. S. (1976) Twins with academic learning problems: antecedent characteristics. *American Journal of Orthopsychiatry* 46(3), 464–9.

McNeill, D. (1966) Developmental psycholinguistics. In F. Smith and G. Miller (eds), *The Genesis of Language*, Cambridge, MA: MIT Press, 15–84.

Mehler, J. and Christophe, A. (1995) Maturation and learning of language in the first year of life. In M. S. Gazzaniga (ed.) *The Cognitive Neurosciences*, Cambridge, MA: MIT Press, 943–54.

Mervis, C. B. and Bertrand, J. (1995) Early lexical acquisition and the vocabulary spurt: a response to Goldfield and Reznick. *Journal of Child Language* 22, 461–8.

Mills, A. (1985) The acquisition of German. In Slobin, 141–254.

Mills, D. L., Coffey-Corina, S. and Neville, H. J. (1997) Language comprehension and cerebral specialization from 13 to 20 months. *Developmental Neuropsychology* 13(3), 397–445.

Molfese, D. L. (1990) Auditory evoked responses recorded from 16-month old human infants to words they did and did not know. *Brain and Language* 36, 345–63.

Molfese, D. L., Morse, P. A. and Peters, C. J. (1990) Auditory evoked responses to names for different objects: cross-modal processing as a basis for infant language acquisition. *Developmental Psychology*, 26(5), 780–95.

Monsee, E. K. (1961) Aphasia in children. *Journal of Speech and Hearing Disorders* 26, 83–6.

Morehead, D. and Ingram, D. (1973) The development of base syntax in normal and linguistically deviant children. *Journal of Speech and Hearing Research* 16, 330–53.

Morford, J. P. (1996) Insights to language from the study of gesture: a review of research on the gestural communication of non-signing deaf people. *Language and Communication* 16(2), 165–78.

Morgan, J. L. and Demuth, K. (eds) (1996) *Signal to Syntax: Bootstrapping from Speech to Grammar in Early Acquisition*, Hillsdale, NJ: Lawrence Erlbaum Associates.

Morgan, J. and Newport, E. (1981) The role of constituent structure in the induction of an artificial language. *Journal of Verbal Learning and Verbal Behavior* 20, 67–85.

Morley, M. (1965) *The Development and Disorders of Speech in Children*, Edinburgh: E. & S. Livingstone.

Neale, M. D. (1967) *Neale Analysis of Reading Ability*, London: Macmillan.

Neils, J. and Aram, D. M. (1986) Family history of children with developmental language disorders. *Perceptual and Motor Skills* 63, 655–8.

Nelson, K. (1973) Structure and strategy in learning to talk. *Monographs of the Society for Research in Child Development* 38.

Neville, H. J. (1991) Neurobiology of cognitive and language processing: effects of early experience. In K. Gibson and A. Petersen (eds), *Brain Maturation and Cognitive Development*, New York: Aldine de Gruyter, 355–80.

—— (1995) Developmental specificity in neurocognitive development in humans. In M. S. Gazzaniga (ed.), *The Cognitive Neurosciences*, Cambridge, MA: MIT Press, 219–31.

Neville, H. J., Coffey, S., Holcomb, P. and Tallal, P. (1993) The neurobiology of sensory and language processing in language-impaired children. *Journal of Cognitive Neuroscience* 5, 235–53.

Neville, H. J., Corina, D., Bavalier, D. et al. (1994a) Biological constraints and effects of experience on cortical organization for language: an fMRI study of sentence processing in English and American Sign Language (ASL) by deaf and hearing subjects. *Society for Neuroscience Abstracts* 20.

Neville, H. J., Holcomb, P. J. and Mills, D. M. (1989) Auditory sensory and language processing in Williams Syndrome: an ERP study. Paper presented at the International Neuropsychological Society, January.

Neville, H. J., Mills, D. L. and Bellugi, U. (1994b) Effects of altered auditory sensitivity and age of language acquisition on the development of language-relevant neural systems: preliminary studies of Williams Syndrome. In S. H. Bronman and J. Grafman (eds), *Atypical Cognitive Deficits in Developmental Disorders: Implications for Brain Function*, Hillsdale, NJ: Lawrence Erlbaum, 67–83.

Neville, H. J., Mills, D. L. and Lawson, D. S. (1992) Fractionating language: different neural subsystems with different sensitive periods. *Cerebral Cortex* 2(3), 244–58.

Newport, E. (1990) Maturational constraints on language learning. *Cognitive Science* 14, 11–28.

Papanicolaou, A. C., DiScenna, A., Gillespie, L. and Aram, D. (1990) Probe-evoked potential finding following unilateral left-hemisphere lesions in children. *Archives of Neurology* 47, 562–66.

Pennington, B. and Smith, S. (1988) Genetic influences on learning disabilities: an update. *Journal of Consulting and Clinical Psychology* 56, 817–23.

Peters, A. M. (1995) Strategies in the acquisition of syntax. In P. Fletcher and B. MacWhinney (eds), *The Handbook of Child Language*, Oxford: Basil Blackwell, 462–83.

Pinker, S. (1984) *Language Learnability and Language Development*, Cambridge, MA: Harvard University Press.

—— (1987) The bootstrapping problem in language acquisition. In B. MacWhinney (ed.), *Mechanisms of Language Acquisition*, Hillsdale, NJ: Lawrence Erlbaum, 399–441.

—— (1989) *Learnability and Cognition: The Acquisition of Argument Structure*, Cambridge, MA: MIT Press.

—— (1994) *The Language Instinct: How the Mind Creates Language*, New York: William Morrow.

Pinker, S. and Bloom, P. (1990) Natural language and natural selection. *Behavioral and Brain Sciences* 13, 707–84.

Plante, E. (1991) MRI findings in the parents and siblings of specifically language-impaired boys. *Brain and Language* 41, 67–80.

Plante, E., Swisher, L. and Vance, R. (1989) Anatomical correlates of normal and impaired language in a set of dizygotic twins. *Brain and Language* 37, 643–55.

Plante, E., Swisher, L., Vance, R. and Rapsak, S. (1991) MRI findings in boys with specifically language impairment. *Brain and Language* 41, 52–66.

Poppen, R., Stark, J., Eisenson, J., Forrest, T. and Werthheim, G. (1969) Visual sequencing performance of aphasic children. *Journal of Speech and Hearing Research* 12, 288–300.

Prince, A. and Smolensky, P. (1993) Optimality theory. Cognitive Science Technical Report, Rutgers University and University of Colorado.

Rabin, M., Wen, X. L., Hepburn, M., Lubs, H. A., Feldman, E. and Duara, R. (1993) Suggestive linkage of developmental dyslexia to chromosome 1p34–p36. *Lancet* 342, 178.

Rankin, J. M., Aram, D. M. and Horwitz, S. J. (1981) Language ability in right and left hemiplegic children. *Brain and Language* 14, 292–306.

Rapin, I. and Wilson, B. C. (1978) Children with developmental language disability: neuropsychological aspects and assessment. In M. A. Wyke (ed.), *Developmental Dysphasia*, London: Academic Press, 13–41.

Rasmussen, T. and Milner, B. (1977) The role of early left-brain injury in determining lateralization of cerebral speech functions. *Annals of the New York Academy of Science* 299, 335–69.

Reznick, J. S. and Goldfield, B. A. (1992) Rapid change in lexical development in comprehension and production. *Developmental Psychology* 28, 406–13.

Rice, M. L. (1994) Grammatical categories of children with specific language impairments. In R. V. Watkins and M. L. Rice (eds), *Specific Language Impairments in Children*, Baltimore: Paul H. Brookes Publishing Co., 69–90.

Rice, M. L., Haney, K. R. and Wexler, K. (1998) Family histories of children with SLI who show extended optional infinitives. *Journal of Speech and Hearing Research* 41, 419–32.

Rondal, J. (1980) Language delay and language difference in moderately and severely retarded children. *Special Education in Canada* 54, 27–32.

Samples, J. and Lane, V. (1985) Genetic possibilities in six siblings with specific language learning disorders. *Asha* 27, 27–32.

Scheibel, A. B. (1984) A dendritic correlate of human speech. In N. Geschwind and A. M. Galaburda (eds), *Cerebral Dominance: The Biological Foundations*, Cambridge, MA: Harvard University Press.

Schieffelin, B. B. (1985) The acquisition of Kaluli. In Slobin, 525–94.

Singer Harris, N. G., Bellugi, U., Bates, E., Jones, W. and Rossen, M. (1997) Contrasting profiles of language development in children with Williams and Downs Syndromes. *Developmental Neuropsychology* 13(3), 345–70.

Skuse, D. H. (1984a) Extreme deprivation in early childhood – I: diverse outcomes for 3 siblings from an extraordinary family. *Journal of Child Psychology and Psychiatry* 25, 523–41.

—— (1984b) Extreme deprivation in early childhood – II: theoretical issues and a comparative review. *Journal of Child Psychology and Psychiatry* 25, 543–72.

Slobin, D. I. (ed.) (1985) *The Crosslinguistic Study of Language Acquisition*. Vol. 1: *The Data*, Hillsdale, NJ: Lawrence Erlbaum.

Schonell, F. J. and Schonell, P. E. (1960) *Diagnostic and Attainment Testing*, Edinburgh: Oliver & Boyd.

Smith, A. (1966) Speech and other functions after left dominant hemispherectomy. *Journal of Neurology, Neurosurgery and Psychiatry* 29, 467–71.

Smith, J. F. (1981) Central nervous system. In C. L. Berry (ed.), *Paediatric pathology*, Berlin: Springer Verlag, 147–8.

Smith, S., Pennington, B., Fain, P., Kimberling, W. and Lubs, H. (1983) Specific reading disability: identification of an inherited form through linkage analysis. *Science* 219, 1345–7.

Smith, S., Pennington, B., Kimberling, W., Fain, P., Ing, P. and Lubs, H. (1986) Genetic heterogeneity in specific reading disability (Abstract 500). *American Journal of Clinical Genetics* 39, A169.

Snyder, W. and Stromswold, K. (1977) The structure and acquisition of English dative constructions. *Linguistic Inquiry* 28, 281–317.

Steele, S. (1981) *An Encyclopedia of AUX: A Study in Cross-Linguistic Equivalence*, Cambridge, MA: MIT Press.

Stevens, T. and Karmiloff-Smith, A. (1997) Word learning in a special population: do individuals with Williams syndrome obey lexical constraints? *Journal of Child Language* 24, 737–65.

Stevenson, J., Graham, P., Fredman, G. and McLoughlin, V. (1987) A twin study of genetic influences on reading and spelling ability and disability. *Journal of Child Psychology and Psychiatry* 28, 229–47.

Stromswold, K. (1988) Linguistic representations of children's *wh*-questions. *Papers and Reports on Child Language* 27, 107–14.

—— (1989a) How conservative are children? *Papers and Reports on Child Language* 28, 148–55.

—— 1989b) Using naturalistic data: methodological and theoretical issues (or How to lie with naturalistic data). Paper presented at the 14th Annual Boston University Child Language Conference, 13–15 October.

—— (1990a) The acquisition of language-universal and language-specific aspects of Tense. Paper presented at the 15th Boston University Child Language Conference, 19–21 October.

—— (1990b) Learnability and the acquisition of auxiliaries. Unpublished Ph.D. dissertation, available through MIT's Working Papers in Linguistics.

—— (1992) Learnability and the acquisition of auxiliary and copula *be*. In *ESCOL '91*, Columbus, OH: Ohio State University.

—— (1994a) Language comprehension without language production: implications for theories of language acquisition. Paper presented at the 18th Boston University Conference on Language Development, January.

—— (1994b) Lexical and functional categories in language and language acquisition. Unpublished MS, Rutgers University.

—— (1994c) The nature of children's early grammar: evidence from inversion errors. Paper presented at the 1994 Linguistic Society of America Conference, Boston, Massachusetts, January.

—— (1995) The acquisition of subject and object *wh*-questions. *Language Acquisition* 4, 5–48.

—— (1996) The genetic basis of language acquisition. In *Proceedings of the 20th Annual Boston University Conference on Language Development*, Somerville, MA: Cascadilla Press, ii., 736–47.

—— (1997) Specific language impairments. In T. E. Feinberg and M. J. Farah (eds), *Behavioral Neurology and Neuropsychology*, New York: McGraw-Hill, 755–72.

—— (1998) The genetics of spoken language disorders. *Human Biology* 70, 297–324.

—— (forthcoming, a) Formal categories in language: evidence from regularization errors in acquisition. *Language and Cognitive Processes*.

—— (forthcoming, b) The heritability of language: a review of twin and adoption studies. *Language*.

Stromswold, K. and Snyder, W. (1995) Acquisition of datives, particles, and related constructions: evidence for a parametric account. In *Proceedings of the 19th Annual Boston University Conference on Language Development*, ii. 621–8.

Swisher, L. P. and Pinsker, E. J. (1971) The language characteristics of hyperverbal hydrocephalic children. *Developmental and Child Neurology* 13, 746–55.

Tallal, P. (1990) Fine-grained discrimination deficits in language-learning impaired children are specific neither to the auditory modality not to speech perception. *Journal of Speech and Hearing Research* 33, 616–21.

Tallal, P. and Piercy, M. (1973a) Defects of non-verbal auditory perception in children with developmental dysphasia. *Nature* 241, 468–9.

—— (1973b) Developmental aphasia: impaired rate of non-verbal processing as a function of sensory modality. *Neuropsychologia* 11, 389–98.

—— (1974) Developmental aphasia: rate of auditory processing as a selective impairment of consonant perception. *Neuropsychologia* 12, 83–93.

Tallal, P., Ross, R. and Curtiss S. (1989a) Familial aggregation in specific language impairment. *Journal of Speech and Hearing Disorders* 54, 167–73.

Tallal, P., Townsend, J., Curtiss, S. and Wulfeck, B. (1991) Phenotypic profiles of language-impaired children based on genetic/family history. *Brain and Language* 41, 81–95.

Teele, D. W., Klein, J. O., Chase, C., Menyuk, P. and Rosner, B. A. (1990) Otitis media in infancy and intellectual ability, school achievement, speech, and language at age 7 years. *Journal of Infectious Diseases* 162, 685–94.

Tesar, B. and Smolensky, P. (1996) Learnability in optimality theory. Technical report JHU-CogSci 96-2, Johns Hopkins University.

Thal, D. J., Marchman, V., Stiles, J., Aram, D., Trauner, D., Nass, R. and Bates, E. (1991) Early lexical development in children with focal brain injury. *Brain and Language* 40, 491–527.

Tomblin, J. B. (1989) Familial concentrations of developmental language impairment. *Journal of Speech and Hearing Disorders* 54, 287–95.

—— (1996) The big picture of SLI: results of an epidemiologic study of SLI among kindergarten children. Paper read at Symposium on Research in Child Language Disorders, Madison, Wisconsin.

Tomblin, J. B. and Buckwalter, P. R. (1994) Studies of genetics of specific language impairment. In R. V. Watkins and M. L. Rice (eds), *Specific Language Impairments in Children*, Baltimore: Paul H. Brookes Publishing Co., 17–34.

—— (1995) The heritability of developmental language impairment among twins. Unpublished manuscript, University of Iowa.

Tomblin, J. B., Hardy, J. C. and Hein, H. A. (1991) Predicting poor-communication status in preschool children using risk factors present at birth. *Journal of Speech and Hearing Research* 34, 1096–1105.

van der Lely, H. K. J. (1994) Canonical linking rules: forward versus reverse linking in normally developing and specifically language-impaired children. *Cognition* 51(1), 29–72.

van der Lely, H. and Stollwerck, K. (1996) A grammatical specific language impairment in children: an autosomal dominant inheritance? *Brain and Language* 52, 484–504.

Van Valin Jr., R. (1991) Functionalist linguistic theory and language acquisition. *First Language* 11, 7–40.

Von Armian, G. and Engel, P. (1964) Mental retardation related to hypercalcaemia. *Developmental Medicine and Child Neurology* 6, 366–77.

Wada, J. A., Clarke, R. and Hamm, A. (1975) Cerebral hemispheric asymmetry in humans. *Archives of Neurology* 32, 239–46.

Wang, P. P., Hesselink, J. R., Jernigan, T. L., Doherty, S. and Bellugi, U. (1992) The

specific neurobehavioral profile of Williams Syndrome is associated with neocerebellar hemispheric preservation. *Neurology* 42, 1999–2002.

Whitehurst, G. J., Arnold, D. S., Smith, M., Fischel, J. E., Lonigan, C. J. and Valdez-
Menchacha, M. C. (1991) Family history in developmental expressive language
delay. *Journal of Speech and Hearing Research* 34, 1150–7.

Woods, B. T. and Carey, S. (1979) Language deficits after apparent clinical recovery
from childhood aphasia. *Annals of Neurology* 6, 405–9.

Yamada, J. (1990) *Laura: A Case for the Modularity of Language*, Cambridge, MA:
MIT Press.

Yamada, J. and Curtiss, S. (1981) The relationship between language and cognition
in a case of Turner's Syndrome. *UCLA Working Papers in Cognitive Linguistics* 3,
93–115.

Zerbin-Rudin, E. (1967) Congenital word blindness. *Bulletin of the Orton Society* 17,
47–54.

Zollinger, R. (1935) Removal of left cerebral hemisphere: report of a case. *Archives of
Neurology and Psychiatry* 34, 1055–64.

14

Connectionist Neuroscience: Representational and Learning Issues for Neuroscience

Stephen José Hanson

These have been revolutionary times for cognitive and behavioral scientists. There have been many recent advances in both method and concept, which have revived the neural or connectionist modeling research area in the last decade. A central question is: How do these computational and mathematical insights from the fields of neural computation and connectionism intersect in the fields of cognitive neuroscience and neuroscience more generally? These connectionist paradigms have always been logical competitors with other artificial intelligence and cognitive science paradigms (in particular, "rule-based" or "symbolist" approaches). The huge research activity and the increasing community of researchers currently working in this area signal a potential paradigm shift in cognitive science. Within psychology many areas of research have found new, viable lines of communication, while researchers in neuroscience, computer science, physics, and psychology have found a common ground for attacking what has been the formidable frontier of the human brain. Many philosophers tout this approach as a new theory of "mind," one that has long-term implications for the philosophy and methodology of the "science of mental life." And the technology arising from these and related fields of neural networks has become standard methodology according to the official engineering standards committees (e.g., IEEE) that have found a use for the techniques in enduring and difficult problems in signal processing and adaptive control. Nonetheless, the neural computational fields have had much less impact on the related fields in neuroscience. Although "tolerated" as a viable area of research, there has been little mainstream acknowledgment of the tremendous advances in the mathematics and computational methods that have arisen in the past decade in the field of neural computation. There are, I think, three reasons for this:

Note: figures 14.5–14.13 have been adapted from C. R. Olson and S. J. Hanson, "Spatial Representation of the Body" in Hanson and Olson (eds), *Connectionist Modeling and Brain Function* (Cambridge, MA: MIT Press, 1990).

1   Neuroscience, for nearly 100 years, has been an exclusively empirical
    enterprise, one that has not readily embraced common abstract principles
    underlying common behavioral/physiological observations.
2   System neuroscience, which should have the greatest impact on computa-
    tional approaches, is in general the most difficult level on which to obtain
    requisite data to constrain network models or provide common principles,
    due to the potential underlying complexity of the multiple n <*euron*>
    body problem.
3   Most problematic is the level of analysis that most neuroscientists continue
    to cling to: the cellular level. This focus is despite the lack of any
    fundamental identification of this anatomically distinct structure as also a
    distinct unit of computation. Worse, it has been demonstrated that com-
    putational regularity at the behavioral level does not necessarily entail
    unique neural implementations.

In this chapter, I will first outline some of the basics of the neural computation and discuss some of the important features and results as they relate
to learning and representational issues in this field over the last decade. I
will then focus on these three problems that underlie the interface between
neural computational approaches and related fields of neuroscience. In order
to better understand the context of neural computation (neural networks,
connectionism, etc.,) it is worth returning to the beginning for some
background.

1   Neural Networks and Neuroscience: What Happened?

Neural networks of the 1950s had serious problems. More to the point,
Minksy and Papert have taken the blame for far too long. The life and times
of "neural networks" and their subsequent revival in the recent past would
make a fascinating case study in the history and philosophy of science. What
such a study would show, I think, is that the blame for the neural network
demise in the late 1950s and early 1960s lies not in Minsky and Papert's
(1969) concise, lucid, and even perhaps well-intentioned little book concerning certain aspects of computational geometry, but in the foundations of the
enterprise itself. This problem was not just in terms of what neural networks
could or could not in principle compute, but rather, in terms of what they
were good for. And, more critically, what were the principles that related them
to representation and learning in real biological brains?

   About seven years before Minsky and Papert's book appeared, a research
program was introduced under the rubric "perceptron" by Frank Rosenblatt
(1962). Rosenblatt was a perception psychologist who was interested in
"ecological," particularly "Brunswickian," accounts of sensory experience.
Egon Brunswick was the forerunner of other ecologically minded psycholo-

gists, such as J. J. Gibson. The "perceptron" was a computational framework for exploring certain principles of perception, especially in the domain of visual perception. But, more than that, the perceptron was meant to be a basic unit of "neural" perception – a fundamental unit or construct for psychological theorizing. Unfortunately, Rosenblatt was attempting to navigate many streams at once. Even before his book was published in 1962 things were turning sour. He tries to clarify the "problems" in the preface:

> There seem to have been at least three main reasons for negative reactions to the program. First, was the admitted lack of mathematical rigor in preliminary reports. Second, was the handling of the first public announcement of the program in 1958 by the popular press, which fell to the task with all of the exuberance and sense of discretion of a pack of happy bloodhounds. Such headlines as "Frankenstein Monster Designed by Navy Robot That Thinks" were hardly designed to inspire scientific confidence. Third and perhaps most significant, there has been a failure to comprehend the difference in motivation between the perceptron program and the various engineering projects concerned with automatic pattern recognition, "artificial intelligence," and advanced computers. (Rosenblatt 1962: preface)

Rosenblatt was convinced that he had discovered an important principle of perception and its underlying neural medium. The "perceptron" was truly a breakthrough, but one that would be lost for three decades, due to some deep misunderstandings about the relationship between learning and the representations that support it. However, Rosenblatt made several missteps in developing his idea further. For example, (1) it took him several more years (1958–60) to get the mathematics correct. (2) He focused on contrasting and defending intellectual territory from the emerging Artificial Intelligence explosion. Many workshops (e.g., the "Self-Organizing Systems Workshop of 1958") were the backdrop for long, unsatisfying debates between Minsky and Rosenblatt concerning the proper way to build learning machines. These arguments set the stage for the perceptron book seven years later. Finally, (3) Rosenblatt made vague references to neural substrate in the form of units, weights, and learning rules, without attempting to clarify the basic relationship between the formalism and actual neural tissue.

Although connectionism has deep roots in computer science and psychology, roots that have been running in parallel for some time, they have recently collided in cognitive science, particularly in cognitive neuroscience. It is worth reviewing some of this historical context in more detail.

1.1 Psychological and computational foundations: explaining the brain

In psychology, the 1890s and the early twentieth century gave rise to the concept of associationism, and in the next decade to what was coined as "connectionism." E. L. Thorndike first used the term "connectionism" to identify his particular form of associationism. The early connectionists in psychology were closely tied to associationists and adopted many of their basic assumptions. Where they deviated from the canons of associationism was in pursuing concepts that brought them closer to what was known about implementation details in the brain. Hence, learning became seen as the connections between one brain area representing sensory elements and other brain areas that supported relevant motor responses. This kind of characterization predates Hebbian learning (Hebb 1949), which is purely associationist and, in the form of simple vector dot products, takes on the presumption of neuronal activations and synaptic potentials.

By the 1920s, computer science was emerging as a distinct field, due to various mathematicians, including Von Neumann and Wiener and of course Alan Turing. Interestingly, early computer science, as defined by these researchers, was preoccupied with the definition and creation of "learning machines" and "intelligent systems." Von Neumann made it clear that the goal of his studies was nothing other than brain function. Turing was obsessed with a machine that would demonstrate learning proclivities and incrementally approach some sort of human intelligence. Ironically, the architectures which these early computer scientists came up with, although serviceable for computing, provided no clues regarding how the brain learned or computed simple pattern-recognition functions.

By the 1940s, concepts of the brain as a very specialized computing device began to emerge. Versions of this idea were first put forth by McCulloch and Pitts (1943). McCulloch in particular was instrumental in bringing about biophysics, mathematical biology, and neural networks; these areas quickly diverged in the next 40 years and have been brought back together only in the last decade or so. McCulloch and Pitts developed a general characterization of the brain as made up of discrete units of computation that could excite, inhibit, and send binary signals through passive and active (recurrent) networks. They, in fact, proved that such networks had the power of a predicate calculus – unfortunately still far from the goal of what a brain might specifically compute.

As mentioned earlier, by the 1950s a perception psychologist, Frank Rosenblatt, introduced an important new type of computational architecture which in effect could "learn." This foray into learning machines by researchers who supported their representations with neural units and synaptic weights (analog) began to put computer scientists, engineers, and psychologists on common ground. Rosenblatt's type of neural network was dubbed "PERCEPTRON," and a set of proofs and demonstrations were given in his book *Principles of Neuro-Dynamics*. The most critical theorem proved in the volume was labeled the "perceptron convergence theorem." This theorem postulated that, given general types of categorization problems, the network would be guaranteed to learn from some small finite set of examples it was shown. This remarkable little result ushered in a tremendous flurry of activity in engineering and computer science which attempted to learn complex functions in pattern recognition, as in handwriting or speech. Basically, these problems proved much too difficult for the perceptron, and it wasn't until 30 years later that such problems were taken up again with some modicum of success. This research prompted several other neural network learning models and frameworks, including LMS or ADALINE, due to Widrow and Hoff (1960). These kinds of methods proved to be very effective for certain classes of linear problems; they are part of linear filter tools and were the basis of adaptive noise suppression in modems, for example.

In the 1960s and 1970s such general formalisms for learning and intelligence were challenged by another approach to creating and representing intelligent systems, one that basically eschewed the original goal of "explaining the brain," and rather assumed that it was throwing out the bath water but keeping the baby. This approach dubbed itself "Artificial Intelligence" (AI), presumably to contrast itself with notions of "Natural Intelligence" or, in particular, perceptrons, neural networks and anything remotely connected to brain-like computation. In fact, this approach seemed categorically to ignore any representational constraints from brain physiology or anatomy. Moreover, part of its approach was philosophically incompatible with the numeric, analog, nature of neural networks.

As mentioned above, during this decade two ardent AI researchers, M. Minsky and S. Papert, began a series of attacks at workshops and conferences on Rosenblatt and his colleagues. The perceptron book was really the logical culmination of all these attacks, however. And although Minsky has said that the point of the book was only to "elucidate the properties and computational nature of perceptrons," it proved to be more of a summary of the limitations of such machines and the context of extremely critical, sometimes hysterical attacks (see, e.g., the 1958 "Self-Organizing Systems Workshop" floor discussions between Minsky and Rosenblatt cited in Minsky, 1961), over a ten-year period had the force of an ideological suppression of learning research, especially as it was related to brain-like implementations. This early separation of learning and representational issues was to haunt the relationship of AI and neural computation for many decades, and its effects are still present today in one form or another.

AI flourished through the 1970s and 1980s. The community swelled to well over 10,000 active researchers. This field's popularity affected psychology in a number of ways. The first way was in the form that cognitive science took as it was reconstituted both by large funding initiatives and by an attempt to produce a more rational psychology. The second way was in the form that cognitive psychology took in its escape from behaviorism, which created yet another source of suppression of studies involving learning, especially as they relate to general or domain-independent principles.

By the mid-1980s a revolution was afoot. In the areas of AI, cognitive science, and neuroscience there was a possible integration that could cause the fields to collide. In 1984, two simple learning algorithms appeared, one which shoved the fields together in an abrupt fashion and helped to redefine the normal science of each area. AI had made too many unkept promises, and many psychologists were becoming disillusioned with the possibility of any reasonable theories arising from the GOFAI ("good old-fashioned AI") approach. In 1986, the PDP book and PDP research program were set out while a single chapter in the book captured an enormous volume of researchers from cognitive science, AI and cognitive psychology. The physics community also joined the fray in the mid-80s due to J. Hopfield. Hopfield (1982), although he had not focused on learning, was dedicated to analog computation and various forms of associative memory. This started a friendly competition between the psychologists from the PDP (Rumelhart and McClelland 1986) style group and the physicists from the Hopfield group. In spite of many promising algorithms and applications arising from both kinds of endeavors, the simple learning algorithm called "backpropagation" proved too flexible, too easy to use, and too accessible (also very productive for learning methods; cf. Hinton 1987). Within one year of the first general international conference on neural networks (NIPS), discussion and paper submissions related to Hopfield nets virtually disappeared! However, once again since Rosenblatt first introduced the concept of a perceptron, psychologists, engineers, computer scientists, and even physicists had common ground for exploring and attempting to find some consensus for explaining the brain. Unfortunately, this growing convergence between different fields seemed to make the connections between neuroscience and neural networks more confusing. Different research strategies, different levels of analysis and different research goals seemed to collide in the yeasty field called "neural networks" (cf. Hanson and Burr 1990).

2   Principles of Model Neurons and their Relationship to Real Neurons

Neurons are complex. It is easy to show that, given any number of assumptions you can make about neurons, you will end up underestimating the complexity of their structure, physiology and underlying functional nature. Nonetheless, the basics of what neurons do are straightforward, both chemically and electrically, and are fairly well known.

In effect, cells appear to mimic threshold devices by integrating local input and, once above an endemic threshold, produce a fixed electrical discharge. Biochemically, the story can also be told very compactly, although the underlying details, as shown in figure 14.1, indicate part of the underlying complexity. While the threshold story told before about neurons is basically correct, closer examination of the electrical properties of single cells reveals that the underlying structure of voltage changes depends on a complex interplay of ion channels. Analysis of these channels leads to the now famous Hodgkin–Huxley (H&H) equations shown below.

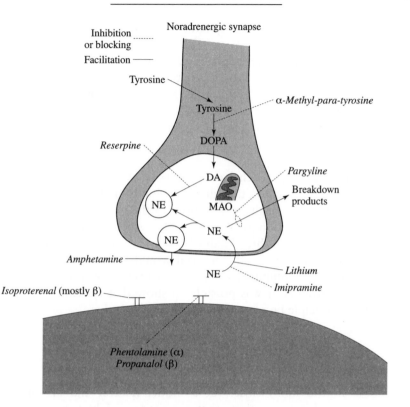

Figure 14.1. The biochemistry of the synaptic processes of a neuron.

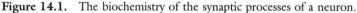

$$I = Cm\frac{dV}{dt} + g_k n^4 (V - V_k) + g_{Na} m^3 h (V - V_{Na}) + g_l (V - V_l)$$

where

$$\frac{dn}{dt} = \alpha_n (1 - n) - \beta_n n, \frac{dm}{dt} \alpha_m (1 - m) - \beta_m m, \frac{dh}{dt} = \alpha_h (1 - h) - \beta_h h$$

These first-order differential equations describe total membrane current (I) as a function of time (t) and voltage (V) in a single neuron with impressive accuracy. Hodgkin and Huxley (1952) won the Nobel Prize for showing how their equations agreed with actual measures of current in real neurons. Hence, it would seem that this level of description is the correct one and should inform further modeling efforts. There are two reasons why this strategy fails, however:

1 Even connecting 3 H&H cells together and asking what they compute would entertain a very large super-computer for some time. Moreover, the

underlying dynamics of these systems would be extremely hard to analyze, if not control.

2   More fundamental is the question of what level of analysis is the correct one. If we must use the H&H equations, then so be it. We should grit our collective teeth and get a large, high-performance parallel appliance and have at it. But if this isn't the basic level or unit of computation in the system, we have wasted a lot of cycles and obscured many system-level questions.

A more conservative approach has been taken by most connectionists. This involves a level of abstraction that allows exploration of system-level questions and minimizes the complexity assumptions of the neuron model. Historically, the first level of abstraction involved simplifying neurons to binary outcomes. McCulloch and Pitts had three kinds of constraints: inputs would be coded as binary signals, either on or off; each cell would have a fixed threshold, and each could be either inhibitory (negative) or excitatory (positive). With only these three constraints, it was possible to show that systems of such simple cells could in principle be equivalent to a logical calculus.

2.1   Anatomy of a model neuron

Let's look a little more closely at a model neuron and at some of the implications of the assumptions that are made and how they relate more generally to neuroscience. At the heart of any net is a simple function that integrates information and transmits it from one set of units to another. Each unit has a distinct "fan-in," or set of input connections, which defines the input to that unit, plus a "fan-out," or set of output connections, which defines the output of the unit. In a net with recurrence, the input and output lines may be thought of as shared; accordingly, it makes sense to think of a logical fan-in and fan-out to any such unit.

Figure 14.2 shows a typical unit, with distinct fan-in and fan-out lines and associated functions (e.g., the fan-in is integrated by a summation function). The inset shows a fan-out that is associated with a decision function: a threshold step (Heaviside) function. Note that, irrespective of whether the output is discrete or continuous over the activation range (as in the case of the popular sigmoidal, logistic, or tanh functions), a non-linearity must be present.

The Heaviside function includes a term which orients the fan-in function in feature space. Omitting threshold functions can seriously reduce the computational power of the net. What remains, however, is the sum of a large number of smooth continuous functions; this is known to be able to yield a powerful function approximator (as in Fourier analysis). It is possible to have non-linear fan-in functions of the input that would allow the formation of complex partitions of feature space called "decision boundaries." One general

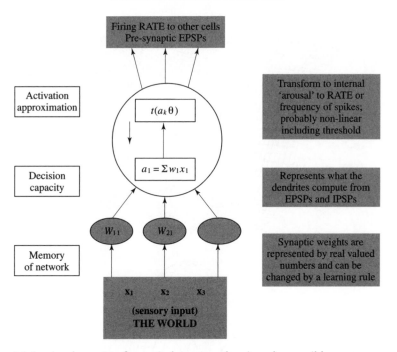

Figure 14.2 A schematic of a typical neuron showing the possible components of a neuron and their potential function in terms of physiology and computation.

form for such units is a polynomial of abritrary order which creates arbitrary boundaries (see figure 14.3, for example).

There are generalizations of fan-in functions which deviate from the usual dot-product function (linear in the decision boundary). One might think of these as analogous to complex "synaptic–dendritic" interactions within or between units (cf. Shepherd and Brayton 1987). In figure 14.4, for example, we show five general cases of fan-in functions. The first is linear, this is in a sense the most constrained function, in that there are no interactions with other units. The second, quadratic case weakens this constraint by allowing units to have more than one "axonal projection" (or connection) to a "dendrite." This allows interactions within the unit such that "synaptic" connections from the same unit can modulate each other. This sort of within-unit interaction is sufficient to produce quadratic boundaries or volumes like spheres (the third case). The fourth case, polynomial units, allows further interactions between units on the same dendrite. These are the general, arbitrary-degree polynomials, including the sigma–pi case (Williams 1986; Durbin and Rumelhart 1989) and all possible decision conics, including hyperspheres (Cooper 1962), hyperellipsoids and hyper-hyperboloids (Specht 1967). The last and most general kind of fan-in function is an arbitrary decision volume based on still more general fan-in function.

(a)

(b)

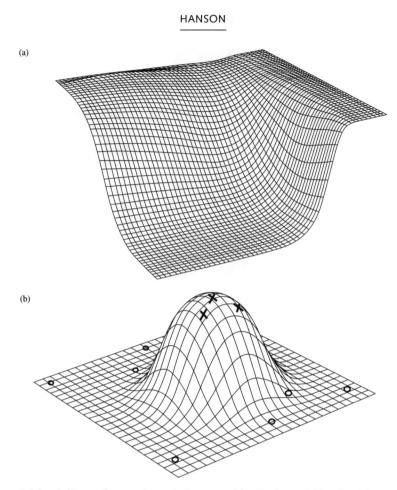

Figure 14.3 Arbitrary features boundaries created by "polynomial" units: (a) a quadratic surface separating background and foreground; (b) a "spherical" unit separating center from surround.

    As these fan-in functions become more complex, increasingly complex interactions are required at the neuronal level, with a corresponding need for more "neural" hardware to support them. Also, as the fan-in function of the individual unit is made more complex, fewer system properties are required to make the computation more general. In other words, individual units become more powerful at the expense of the interactive properties of the system as a whole. Obviously, positing greater hardware complexity doesn't obviate the need to analyze it. Moreover, this may be undesirable when one is modeling learning. For example, it is unclear how the degrees of freedom inherent in the shape of decision boundaries trade off with the complexity of learning such boundaries. A learning problem may be made worse as local node complexity is increased. This trade-off is analogous to the relationship between linear and non-linear regression, where the non-linearity increases the degrees of freedom in the model, allowing more flexibility in the accom-

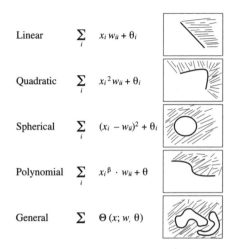

Linear	$\sum\limits_{i} x_i w_{ii} + \theta_i$	
Quadratic	$\sum\limits_{i} x_i{}^2 w_{ii} + \theta_i$	
Spherical	$\sum\limits_{i} (x_i - w_{ii})^2 + \theta_i$	
Polynomial	$\sum\limits_{i} x_i{}^\beta \cdot w_{ii} + \theta$	
General	$\sum \Theta (x; w, \theta)$	

Figure 14.4. Possible fan-in functions that would support increasing complex surfaces in the feature space of a cell, also characterized as the "receptive field" properties of neurons. Such decision surfaces interact with the network complexity.

modation of data, while making the parameter search problem harder and the fit of the model to the data potentially more arbitrary.

The fan-out function of a unit can also be varied, but with much less effect. What seems to be most important is the smoothness of the individual unit response. The output rate of real presynaptic neurons suggests a rationale for the existence and nature of fan-out functions. Neurons apparently produce spikes at a rate that is a function of their stimulation. Their spike rate would be stochastic and might well be fitted as a *Poisson* process (Tomko and Crapper 1974), implying a stochastic independence between cells. The latency between spikes (or the average interspike interval obtained by integrating over time) provides rate information that could be used by postsynaptic units. The specific sort of rate function one gets from such integration is a *Gamma* distribution function, which is smooth and sigmoidal.

The logistic or hyperbolic tangent functions have been used in the fan-out of units in models like ART (adaptive resonance theory, Grossberg 1987), brain-state-in-box (Anderson et al. 1977), Boltzmann machines (Ackley et al. 1985), CMAC (Albus 1975), and back-propagation (Rumelhart et al. 1986). The specific properties of either the gamma or the logistic as spike rate functions seem to be less important than the smoothness – although this has never been tested – of the generalization surface as composed by such units. Equally important is the rate at which the surface falls off from some maximal point in the feature space. Many possible fan-out functions can be considered for various problems. For example, combining spherical regions with periodic decay can produce lateral inhibition effects and so-called center-surround or Marr–Hildreth units (Marr 1982). Such variations may have very specific applications to vision, audition, or motor control. Different fan-out functions may be useful for different kinds of function approximation. Whether or not particular function approximation classes are suited to particular problem domains is unclear and in general would seem to be unnecessary, since such function-approximation theorems are very general.

Although monotone increasing activation functions are suggested by analogy with the firing rate information received by postsynaptic units, a stronger reason for using such fan-out functions is that they can be shown to be used for composing real valued functions (cf. Williams 1986; Hornik et al. 1988; Cybenko 1989). Another critical aspect of the fan-out function is its role in categorization. The contours and smoothness of the output space will determine the relationship among stimuli – the clusters they may form and their distribution within each category. Fan-out functions can also be interpreted probabilistically, which can lead to deeper connections between neural modeling, multivariate statistics, and inductive inference (Golden 1988). Finally, the parameters of rate functions could also be varied to explore search strategies during learning (cf. Hanson 1990).

Given this plethora of neuron properties, what does this have to do with the ability of humans to store, process, and represent information in the world?

2.2   Model neurons and representational issues in cognitive science

The usual reasons for complaining about the simple representational properties of neurons discussed previously is the focus on whether or not some new view of knowledge representation results from assuming that sensory information is somehow encoded by neuron properties. This has lead to many unsatisfying debates by connectionists and symbolists regarding whether distributed representations are special (Fodor and Pylyshyn 1988). It should be clear that local encodings are symbolist encodings. If the brain stores the world cell by cell and these cells have some productive combinatorics that does not lead to exponential explosion, then symbolists and connectionists have nothing to disagree about. Apparently the brain prefers distributed representations; whether one considers multiple cell recordings or PET or EEG or fMRI, there is little doubt that the sensory and cognitive information is encoded and activated by many cells distributed homogeneously over relatively large portions of cortex.

Earlier in the twentieth century Hubel and Wiesel discovered cells in the visual cortex that seemed to provide the basis for local functionality of brain mechanism. In effect, it appeared that there were cells whose only function was edge information of a stimulus while other cells seemed to prefer more complex stimuli up to and including faces. This one cell–one concept discovery seems to indicate that the brain constructs more complex objects that are neither edges nor faces from some hierarchical compilation of lower-level features. Hence, although the groundwork for a vocabulary of canonical features seems to exist, it does not at the same time suggest how the combination of lower-level cell function would be transformed into higher-level recognition structure.

On the other hand, it has been pointed out by linguists and philosophers that the apparent inability of a distributed code to deal with the systematic aspects of sentences like "Mary loves John" versus "John loves Mary" leaves open the question of how a distributed system could in principle keep track of the relevant binding and directionality of the agent and recipient in the requisite case grammar. Regardless of the nature of the distributed representation, it is clear that operators of some sort are required for the reconstitution, manipulation, and binding of input that are distributed through memory and required to be systematic with other inputs that are encoded in a similar way.

3 Anti-Occam

Simple does not also Guarantee Correct.

D. O. Hebb (1949) had posited one of the simplest sorts of associative rules that could govern neurons:

> When an axon of cell A is near enough to excite a cell B and repeatedly or persistently takes part in firing it, some growth process or metabolic change takes place in one or both cells such that A's efficiency as one of the cells firing B, is increased.

In effect, Hebb is claiming that cells which contingently fire with other cells, presumably in some tonic background of cell firings, construct some causal relationship between themselves. This is the most basic type of associationist principle at the cellular level that could be invented. Hebbian cells have been purportedly identified in the brain (Kelso et al. 1986); on the other hand, there seems to be little or no computational evidence for Hebbian cells being useful for more complex cognitive functioning. The evidence for the presence of Hebbian-like cells in the brain doesn't also imply that such a basic correlation function wouldn't be useful for implementation of more interesting learning functions, like back-propagation. It is well known that the combination of Hebbian and "anti-Hebbian" cells could, in principle, be used to construct the Delta Rule (Gluck and Thompson 1987), which is an essential step in creating error-correcting rules, ones that could potentially implement more interesting cognitive phenomena.

Below I review some of the many problems with Hebb's law for simple behavioral phenomena and for more complex cognitive functions.

Hebb's law is simple, but it is just plain wrong!

There are nine specific areas where Hebb's law as a behavioral learning rule is false:

1   Order specificity. Although classical conditioning is known to have to be sequentially sensitive, without some modification, Hebb's law predicts that forward pairing of a UCS and a CS (CS(UCS)) should be as effective as backward pairing (UCS(CS)). This is false. In fact, backward pairing may produce inhibitory connections, albeit ones that would satisfy a sort of Hebb's law; however, in many other documented cases backward pairings of the CS and the UCS (UCS(CS)) are ineffective in producing any change in behavior.

2   Temporal specificity. Classical conditioning depends on a fairly precise time delay between the CS and the UCS. This delay seems to be most efficacious for learning around 100ms between the offset of the CS and the onset of the UCS. Hebb's law predicts that delay specificity is irrelevant.

3   Positive changes only to Delta W. Classical conditioning depends on synaptic change that is modulated by both inhibitory and excitory inputs. Hebb's rule specifies only positive changes to the synaptic efficacy.

4   Runaway instability. Cells saturate and have finite activation limits. Hebb's law requires an ever increasing level of activation as more input is stored in the network. Without some normalization or choice of network limits, Hebb's law leads to instabilities.

5   Input patterns must be orthogonal. In order to prevent memory interference, input patterns must somehow be constructed to be orthogonal. If not, memory patterns will not be reconstructed veridically but will produce blends based on the original correlation of the patterns prior to storage.

6   Small capacity. For M patterns one typically needs M^2 units. A typical estimate of the vocabulary of undergraduates is nearly 100,000 words by the time they finish college. Assuming that each word can be stored on average with the same sensory encoding, it would require the brain to allocate 10 billion neurons, assuming the words were stored with a Hebb-style law. Although the brain is big, there wouldn't be much room left to do anything with all these words, not to mention anything else we might want to do with pictures, sounds, movements, etc.

7   Architectural variations are trivial. Since these are linear models, one level of weights is as good as 1,000 levels. Nothing is gained by making the architecture more complex, notwithstanding the fact that cortex has at least six distinct architectural layers.

8   Recurrence is not relevant. Since Hebb's law is fundamentally linear, feedback from various layers is just further matrix multiplication, which is tantamount to scalar products.

9   Can only do recognition, not recall. Given the nature of the Hebb's rule, that an input is required for input storage and for subsequent retrieval, no form of free recall is possible. No general categorical cue or just time itself can produce recall based on prior storage.

Despite these difficulties, many different kinds of memory models (hippocampal models, but see Gluck and Myers 1993) invoke the simplest sorts of Hebb's law, presumably on the assumption that it should be possible to modify it to accomplish more complex behavior or cognition. In fact, such modifications bring the models out of the realm of Hebb's law and into the realm of non-linear, error-correcting rules that are more commensurate with aspects of human memory and learning. Unfortunately for neuroscience, there seems to be less, or really no strong, evidence for such complex rules. Notwithstanding, the simplest and most neuroscientifically accepted rule has no computational relevance to cognition! This dichotomy is common in neuroscience, because many of the principles seem to derive from possible cellular implementations, without consideration of more complex top-down formulations.

4   Neuroscience Implementations are not Unique!

Unfortunately, this is not where the confusion between bottom-up observations and top-down regularities stops. For example, it is possible for a neuroscientist to discover a circuit that implements classical conditioning and to assume that the preparation was fundamental enough to reveal something essential about the associative learning process itself. Consider, though, that there is a multitude of ways in which a given logical function might be implemented at a lower level of analysis. Does this imply that all of the particular cellular details are necessary for the implementation of the function that is seen at the behavioral or cognitive level? Not really. What follows are two cases in point: one based on a disagreement between two laboratories about physiological nature of classical conditioning, the second on a series of simulations of forward kinematics and spatial representation that indicates there is more than one way to "skin a cat" and, more to the point, to make an arm movement.

4.1   Learning rules for "hors d'oeuvres"

Alkon (1983) and his colleagues have reported that a classical conditioning preparation in the mollusk *Hermmisenda* occurred by the sensitization of a particular sensory neuron ("b") that was central to the conditioning outcome. In particular, no synaptic change whatever appeared to be required for classical conditioning to occur. At the same time Kandell and his colleagues (Hawkins et al. 1986) reported on a similar preparation of classical conditioning with the mollusk *Aplysia*. In this preparation, definite synaptic changes appeared to be necessary for classical conditioning to occur. In this case the synaptic changes were clearly central to the classical conditioning mechanism. This produced a dispute in the literature concerning neural details and the kind of circuitry that would be required to implement basic functions of associative learning in primitive species. The exact nature of the neural circuits, given the simple organisms involved, might have been expected to be basic and fundamental as regards classical conditioning. Given the apparently minor differences in preparation and level of complexity of the species involved, it is surprising that the same sort of neural mechanisms would not have been involved. Several interpretations are possible:

1   One lab is wrong.
2   One mollusk is undergoing a different form of classical conditioning heretofore unobserved.

or, most likely:

3   Evolution has provided for many types of classical conditioning implementation since the associative function is so useful for the success of a given organism, but has been insensitive to the physiological details of how the asociative mechanism is implemented.

Hence, one bit of bad news for neuroscience would be that neural implementations are opportunistic with respect to a given behavioral or cognitive function. Hence, it would follow that little could be gleaned from precise details of a given implementation at the system level. The next example provides more support for this particular conclusion.

4.2   Spatial representation: it depends on where you start

Carl Olson and I (Olson and Hanson 1990) studied the postural capabilities of multilayered networks. We trained them on spatial problems involving an arm–neck–eye system possessing altogether 13 degrees of rotational freedom (figure 14.5). The simulated system had two degrees of freedom at the wrist, two at the elbow, three at the shoulder, three at the neck, and three at the eye. The shoulder was treated as a fixed ball-and-socket joint incapable of motions such as shrugging that result from scapular translation. This was one of the most complex articulated systems to have been modeled at that time with a connectionist network.

The networks we used for these simulations was a garden variety two-layered (sets of weights) network trained by backpropagation. The network

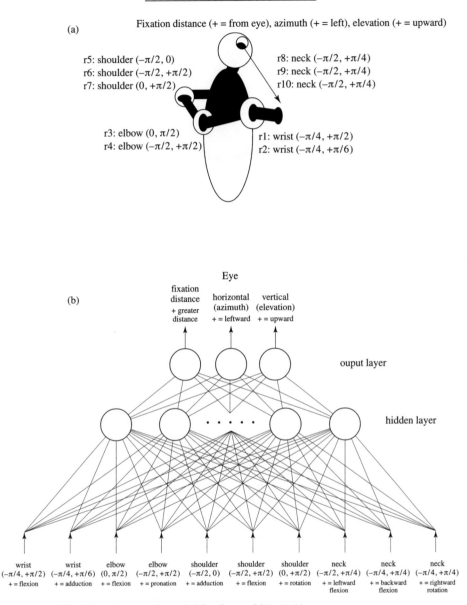

(a)

Fixation distance (+ = from eye), azimuth (+ = left), elevation (+ = upward)

r5: shoulder (−π/2, 0)
r6: shoulder (−π/2, +π/2)
r7: shoulder (0, +π/2)

r8: neck (−π/2, +π/4)
r9: neck (−π/2, +π/4)
r10: neck (−π/2, +π/4)

r3: elbow (0, π/2)
r4: elbow (−π/2, +π/2)

r1: wrist (−π/4, +π/2)
r2: wrist (−π/4, +π/6)

(b)

Eye

fixation
distance
+ greater
distance

horizontal
(azimuth)
+ = leftward

vertical
(elevation)
+ = upward

ouput layer

hidden layer

wrist	wrist	elbow	elbow	shoulder	shoulder	shoulder	neck	neck	neck
(−π/4, +π/2)	(−π/4, +π/6)	(0, π/2)	(−π/2, +π/2)	(−π/2, 0)	(−π/2, +π/2)	(0, +π/2)	(−π/2, +π/4)	(−π/4, +π/4)	(−π/4, +π/4)
+ = flexion	+ = adduction	+ = flexion	+ = pronation	+ = adduction	+ = flexion	+ = rotation	+ = leftward flexion	+ = backward flexion	+ = rightward rotation

Figure 14.5. Neural network model for forward kinematics.

was trained on two kinds of problems. The first involved the 13 degrees of freedom, with 10 inputs from wrist, arm, and shoulder and 3 outputs controlling horizontal angle, vertical angle, and fixation distance of the eye(s). Although the network worked well in this configuration, we then chose a simpler configuration in order to view the solutions in three sets of three dimensions each. This simpler system (with five degrees of freedom), like the more complex one, required the network to learn to direct the eye to the

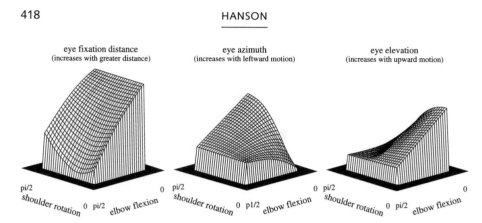

Figure 14.6   Target surfaces for the eye – hand kinematics problem.

fingertip on being given, in the simple case, two inputs, or in the complex case, ten inputs. In the simpler case the two inputs were the rotational angle of the shoulder (from thumb up to thumb left over a range of 90 degrees) and the flexional angle of the elbow (from extension to flexion over a range of 90 degrees). The other arm and neck angles were fixed throughout train- ing and testing: the head points straight ahead on the shoulder and the hand is colinear with the forearm. The eye is controlled by three output lines encoding fixation distance, horizontal gaze angle, and vertical gaze angle, respectively.

Training was carried out by repeatedly exposing the network to a set of 1,000 input-target pairs generated by randomly stipulating the arm angles and then computing the eye angles required to bring the fixation point to the fingertip. The set was presented 100 times, for a total of 100,000 trials. As a general measure of performance, we used the mean distance of the fixation point from the finger tip expressed as a percent of the total length of the arm (from shoulder to fingertip). Performance improved rapidly over the first few thousand trials, and then gradually approached an asymptote. The asymptotic level of performance was around 2 percent of the length of the arm for 20 networks with 10 hidden units each. Networks with fewer than 10 hidden units performed much more poorly, but networks with more than 10 hidden units were only slightly better. The training set covered the state space of the system sufficiently densely that the network was forced to learn a generalized input–output function, rather than storing special cases of the input or forming localized approximations regions.

How do the networks represent this problem? Consider figure 14.6, which shows the three required target surfaces for the task. Each surface represents the desired output (fixation distance, horizontal gaze angle, and vertical gaze angle) as a function of the two input variables (elbow flexional angle and shoulder rotational angle). The input–output functions of trained networks can be represented as surfaces and compared directly to the target surfaces. In a linear network each output surface is a plane giving the best least-

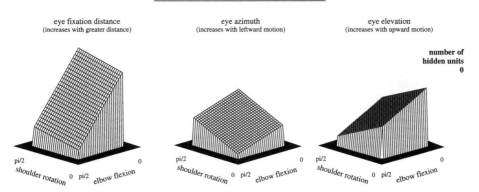

Figure 14.7. Response of linear network to target surfaces.

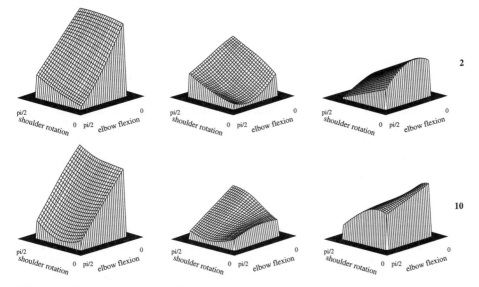

Figure 14.8. Response of non-linear units to target surfaces.

squares to fit to the corresponding target surface (figure 14.7, top row). In a non-linear network, each output surface has possible curvature.

As the number of hidden units increases (figure 14.8, second and third rows), so does the subtlety with which the output surface captures the inflections of the target surface. Surfaces that are weighted sums of sigmoids differ from just sigmoids in the crucial respect that they can be non-monotonic. Non-monotonicity is required for the solution of some problems.

For example, in the two-inputs problem, with the shoulder in a state of full lateral rotation, the eye must move to the right as the elbow flexes (bringing the hand up toward the ear), whereas, with the shoulder in a state of full medial rotation, the eye must move to the left as the elbow flexes

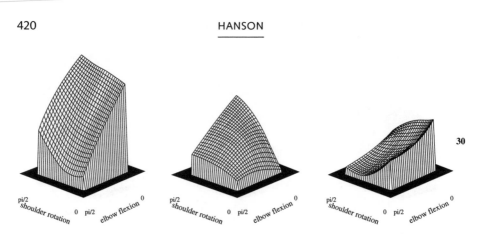

Figure 14.9.   Best non-linear surfaces fit to target surfaces using 30 hidden units for the 2-input problem.

(bringing the hand in towards the chest). This requirement is reflected in the local changes of slope of the horizontal gaze target surface (figure 14.9).

The transition from linear input-unit activation surfaces through sigmoidal hidden-unit activation surfaces to sum of sigmoidal output-unit activation surfaces can be seen in the representative network of figure 14.10.

It would be of considerable theoretical interest to know whether networks trained on the same problem contain similar kinds of hidden units. The claim that this is so has been made on subjective grounds (Lehky and Sejnowski 1988; Zipser and Anderson 1988), but supporting it objectively has proved difficult. Two reservations should be noted at the outset:

1   To expect that networks trained on the same problem will necessarily contain incidental hidden units is unrealistic, because any given input–output function can be embodied in different networks. A network functionally equivalent to a trained network can be produced simply by inverting the sign of every input and ouput synapse on an arbitrary set of hidden units. The resulting "anti-hidden units" produce the same effect at the output layer as the hidden units they have replaced, but their dependence on the input variables is exactly reversed.
2   To expect that a trained network will contain multiple examples of a given "type" of hidden units is unrealistic, because duplication is incompatible with an efficient solution to the problem. Any effect produced by two hidden units with identical activation surfaces can also be produced by only one. Consequently, the efficient use of the second hidden unit would be to capture distinct inflection of the target function.

With these qualifications in mind, we now consider how to determine whether networks trained on the same problem contain reidentifiable units – hidden units that have been reinvented by a number of networks for the same task. To assume that they would be reinvented without some method-

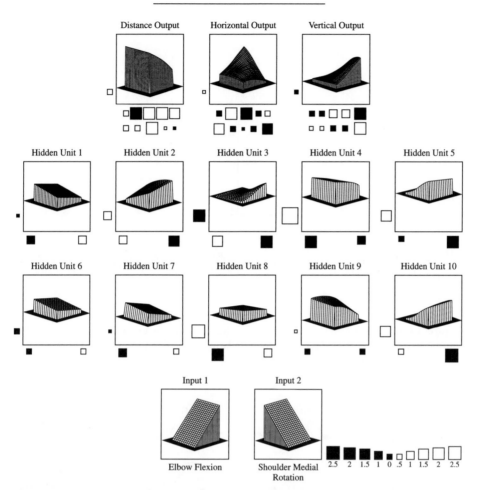

Figure 14.10. A complete representation of a typical solution to the 2-input problem showing the surfaces, weight connections, thresholds, and hence complete composition of the input to output in a visual array.

ology for testing this assumption is naive and turns out to be a possible fallacy in past work. To test the reidentifiability hypothesis requires devising a measure of similarity between hidden units. The measure that we have used is the absolute value of the correlation coefficient of the two activation surfaces. This index indicates just how closely two hidden units could be brought, by an appropriate adjustment of the weight to their output synapses, to producing an identical effect on an output unit. We tested the reidentifiability hypothesis by analyzing a population of 200 hidden units drawn from 20 hidden units networks trained on the same problem. The hidden units were represented as points in a multidimensional space, with the interpoint distance set equal to the additive inverse of the pairwise similarity index. Complete linkage clustering procedures were then applied. The results of the clustering analysis are illustrated in figure 14.11.

Figure 14.11. Clustering dendrogram for the 200 hidden units from 20/ten hidden unit networks receptive fields. Notice the regularity of the dendrogram and the clear four-cluster subpopulation.

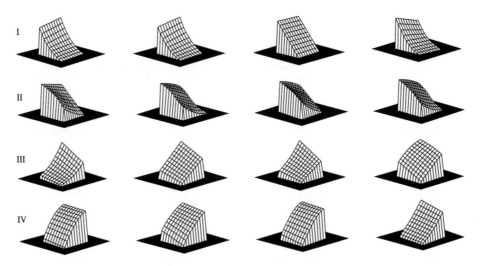

Figure 14.12. The activation surfaces subsampled from the dendrogram-identified clusters in figure 14.11. Four examples are chosen from each subpopulation and shown corresponding to each cluster group (I, II, III, IV).

Passing down the dendogram (see Everitt 1975) from top to bottom is equivalent to cutting the population of hidden units into progressively finer clusters. The activation surfaces in figure 14.12 belong to representative hidden units drawn from the four subpopulations formed when the cut is made at the level of four clusters.

On the basis of reidentifiability hypothesis, one would predict that when a cut is made at around ten clusters, there should be a tendency for the cluster to be of uniform size and for hidden units from the same network to be dispersed amongst the clusters. Both tendencies were present and highly significant.

Changing the input encoding: does the implementation stay the same?

In the case that Olson and I considered, the angle of each joint was represented by the level of activation of one input unit. However, it would be more realistic to have input codes that were represented by a population of units. This type of code is available in the joints of biological systems and is sometimes referred to as a *recruitment code*. In a recruitment code each angle is represented by activity in a population of input units with different thresholds. Two questions arise:

1 Can the network solve the two-input problem with an apparently much more complex input encoding?
2 Will the hidden unit receptive field properties be similar to the solution found with the single, thermometer-style input encoding?

Networks presented with recruitment-coded joint angle do solve the two-input problem and actually perform marginally better at asymptote than networks with an activation-coded input (mean error around 1 versus 2 percent). However, the hidden unit representation by means of which they solve the problem is significantly different (see figure 14.13). Generally, these hidden unit receptive fields contain many units with sharply inflected and non-monotonic activation surfaces. Apparently the dependence of the network's representation on the characteristics of the task is rather weak. Different sensory encodings can lead to very different but functionally equivalent representations.

Several conclusions follow:

1 Different sensory encodings can lead to very different, but functionally equivalent, representations.
2 Implementation details at the neuronal level are irrelevant at a behavioral or cognitive level of analysis; evolution has found many ways for implementing useful survival mechanisms.
3 Measuring single cells in order to infer system-level function is a *doomed* strategy.

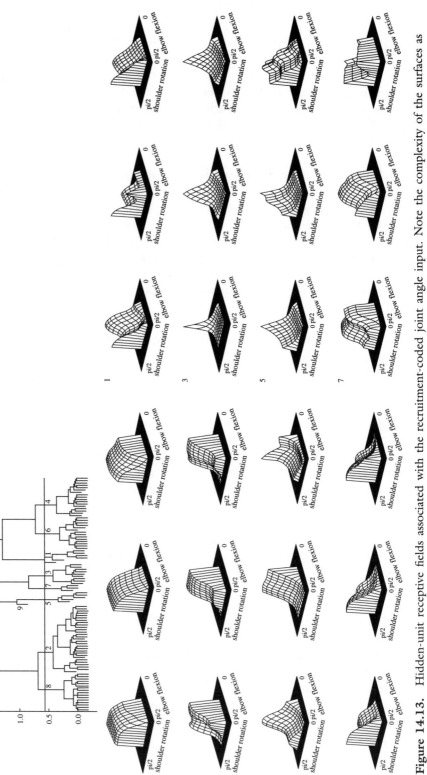

Figure 14.13. Hidden-unit receptive fields associated with the recruitment-coded joint angle input. Note the complexity of the surfaces as compared to figure 14.12. Also note the irregularity of the dendrogram indicating the higher variance of the solutions that were found.

5 Conclusions

Connectionist models have been fundamentally about system-level brain accounts. Without appreciating that commitment, it is hard to understand how a simplified neuron model and synaptic connectivity could be informative for actual brain function. To the contrary, without a commitment to elucidating basic system-level phenomena, neuroscience will be unable to concentrate any of its vast data base on principles that govern more than two cells at time. It is a common experience in the neurosciences to discover cells that behave in some orderly way without at the same time understanding what their larger purpose might be in terms of system-level function, which in turn requires a deep understanding of the way cells interact and what emergent properties might arise when millions of cells that code for spatial, temporal, or structural properties of the world begin to compute something (somehow this reminds me of early behaviorism at the cellular level). This problem doesn't go away

1 by measuring more cells
2 by measuring more cells more precisely
3 by measuring hundreds or thousands or even millions of cells independently
4 by measuring molecular properties of cells.

In fact, the problem can only be addressed by a systems-level theory that takes into account some simplified assumptions about systems of cells and simplified self-organizing principles such as learning. In this way testable hypotheses and principles can result from simulations and models that have some common infrastructure and targets. This agenda is most likely to result in long-term understanding of the basic functions of systems of cells that compute relevant behavioral and cognitive function, requiring both the voluminous data from the neurosciences and increasing complexity of computations that actually account for behavioral or cognitive functions. Coincidentally, this has been the research agenda of connectionists for the past decade.

References

Ackley, D., Hinton, G. E. and Sejnowski, T. J. (1985) A learning algorithm for Boltzmann machines. *Cognitive Science* 9(1), 147–69.
Albus, J. S. (1975) A new approach to manipulator control: the cerebellar model articulation controller (CMAC). *American Society of Engineers, Transactions G (Journal of Dynamic Systems, Measurement and Control)* 97(3), 220–7.

Alkon, D. L. (1983) Learning in a marine snail. *Scientific American* 249, 70–84

Anderson, J. A., Silverstein, J. W., Ritz, S. R. and Jones, R. S. (1977) Distinctive features, categorical perception, and probability learning: some applications of a neural mode. *Psychological Review* 84, 413–51.

Cooper, R. (1962) The hypersphere in pattern recognition. *Information and Control* 5, 324–46.

Cybenko, (1989) Approximation by superposition of a sigmoidal function. *Mathematical Control Systems Signals* 2, 303–14.

Durbin, R. and Rumelhart, D. E. (1989) Product units: a computationally powerful and biologically plausible extension to backpropagation networks. *Neural Computation* 1, 133–42.

Everitt, B. (1975) *Cluster Analysis*, London: Heinemann Educational Books.

Fodor, J. and Pylyshyn, Z. (1988) Connectionism and cognitive architecture: a critical analysis. *Cognition* 28, 3–71.

Gluck, M. A. and Myers, C. (1993) Hippocampal mediation of stimulus representation: a computational theory. *Hippocampus* 3(4), 491–516.

Gluck, M. A. and Thompson, R. F. (1987) Modeling the neural substrates of associative learning and memory: a computational approach. *Psychological Review* 94(2), 176–91.

Goelet, P., Castellucci, V., Schacher, S. and Kandel, E. R. (1986) The long and short of long-term memory. *Nature* 322, 419–22.

Golden, R. M. (1988) A unified framework for connectionist systems. *Biological Cybernetics* 59, 109–20.

Grossberg, S. (1987) Competitive learning: from interactive activation to adaptive resonance. *Cognitive Science* 11(1), 23–64.

Hanson, S. J. (1990) The stochastic delta rule. *Physica D* 42, 265–72.

Hanson, S. J. and Burr, D. J. (1990) What connectionist models learn: learning and representation in connectionist models. *Behavioral and Brain Sciences* 13(3) 47.

Hanson, S. J. and Olson, C. R. (1988) A connectionist network that computes limb position in a head centered coordinate frame. *Society for Neuroscience Abstracts*, 2376.

Hawkins, R. D., Carew, T. J. and Kandel, E. R. (1986) Effects of interstimulus interval and contingency on classical conditioning in Aplysia. *Journal of Neuroscience* 6, 695–701.

Hebb, D. O. (1949) *Organization of Behavior: a Neuropyschological Theory*, New York: Wiley.

Hinton, G. E. (1986) Learning distributed representations of concepts. Paper read at Cognitive Science Meeting, Amherst, MA.

—— (1987) Learning procedures for connectionist models. Technical report, CMU.

Hodgkin, A. L. and Huxley, A. F. (1952) A quantitative description of membrane current and its application to conduction and excitation in nerve. *Journal of Physiology* (London) 117, 500–44.

Hopfield, J. J. (1982) Neural networks and physical systems with emergent collective computational abilities. *Proceedings of the National Academy of Sciences* USA 79, 2554–8.

Hornik, K., Stinchcombe, M. and White, H. (1988) Multi-layer feedforward are universal approximators. Unpublished MS.

Kelso, S. R., Ganong, A. H. and Brown, T. H. (1986) Hebbian synapses in hippocampus. *Proceedings of the National Academy of Sciences* USA 83, 5326–30.

Lehky, S. R. and Sejnowski, T. J. (1988) Network model of shape-from-shading: neural function arises from both receptive and projective fields. *Nature* 333, 452–4.

Marr, D. (1982) *Vision*, New York: Freeman.

McCulloch, W. S. and Pitts, W. (1943) A logical calculus of the ideas imminent in nervous activity. *Bulletin of Mathematical Biophysics* 5, 115–33.

Minsky, M. (1961) Steps towards artificial intelligence. *Proceedings of the Institute of Radio Engineers* 49, 8–30.

Minsky, M. and Papert, S. (1969) *The Perceptron: Principles of Computational Geometry*, Cambridge, MA: MIT Press.

Olson, C. R. and Hanson, S. J. (1990) Spatial representation in the body. In S. J. Hanson and C. R. Olson (eds), *Connectionist Models and Brain Function*, Cambridge, MA: MIT Press, 193–254.

Rosenblatt, F. (1962) *Principles of Neuro-Dynamics*. Washington, DC: Spartan.

Rumelhart, D. E. and McClelland, J. J. (eds) (1986) *Parallel Distributed Processing: Explorations in the Microstructure of Cognition*, vol. 1: *Foundations*, Cambridge, MA. Bradford Books/MIT Press.

Rumelhart, D. E., Hinton, G. E. and Williams, R. (1986) Learning internal representations by error propagation. *Nature* 323, 553–6.

Sejnowski, T. and Rosenberg, C. (1986) NET talk: a parallel network that learns to read aloud. EE and CS Technical Report, Johns Hopkins University, January.

Shepherd, G. M. and Brayton, R. K. (1987) Logic operations are properties of computer-simulated interactions between excitable dendritic spines. *Neuroscience* 21, 151–66.

Specht, D. F. (1967) Generation of polynomial discriminant functions for pattern recognition. *IEEE Transactions Electronic Computers*, EC 16(3), 308–19.

Tomko, G. J. and Crapper, D. R. (1974) Neural variability: non-stationary response to identical visual stimuli. *Brain Research* 79, 405–18.

Widrow, B. and Hoff, M. E. (1960) Adaptive switching circuits. In WESCON Convention Record, Part IV, 96–104.

Williams, R. J. (1986) The logic of activation functions. In Rumelhart and McClelland, 545–80.

Zipser, D. and Anderson, R. (1988) Back-propagation learning simulates response properties of a subset of posterior parietal neurons. *Nature* 332, 679–84.

Index

1ᗡ88

8841